D0444420

Bulgaria

Richard Watkins
Christopher Deliso

JUN 1 8 2008

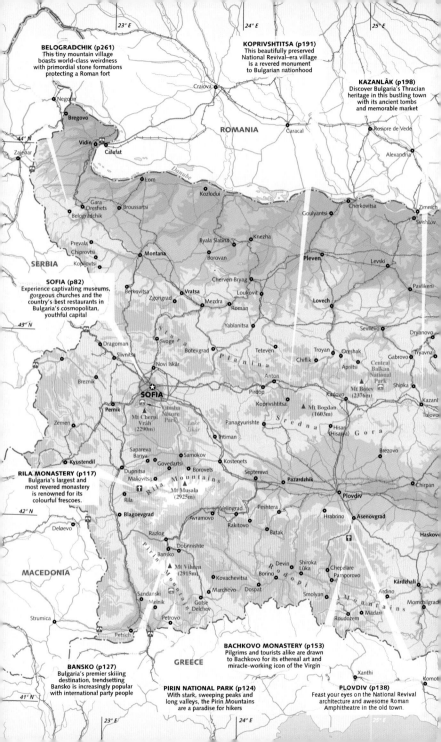

BELOGRADCHIK (p261)
This tiny mountain village boasts world-class weirdness with primordial stone formations protecting a Roman fort

KOPRIVSHTITSA (p191)
This beautifully preserved National Revival–era village is a revered monument to Bulgarian nationhood

KAZANLÃK (p198)
Discover Bulgaria's Thracian heritage in this bustling town with its ancient tombs and memorable market

SOFIA (p82)
Experience captivating museums, gorgeous churches and the country's best restaurants in Bulgaria's cosmopolitan, youthful capital

RILA MONASTERY (p117)
Bulgaria's largest and most revered monastery is renowned for its colourful frescoes.

BACHKOVO MONASTERY (p153)
Pilgrims and tourists alike are drawn to Bachkovo for its ethereal art and miracle-working icon of the Virgin

BANSKO (p127)
Bulgaria's premier skiing destination, trendsetting Bansko is increasingly popular with international party people

PIRIN NATIONAL PARK (p124)
With stark, sweeping peaks and long valleys, the Pirin Mountains are a paradise for hikers

PLOVDIV (p138)
Feast your eyes on the National Revival architecture and awesome Roman Amphitheatre in the old town.

ROMANIA

SERBIA

MACEDONIA

GREECE

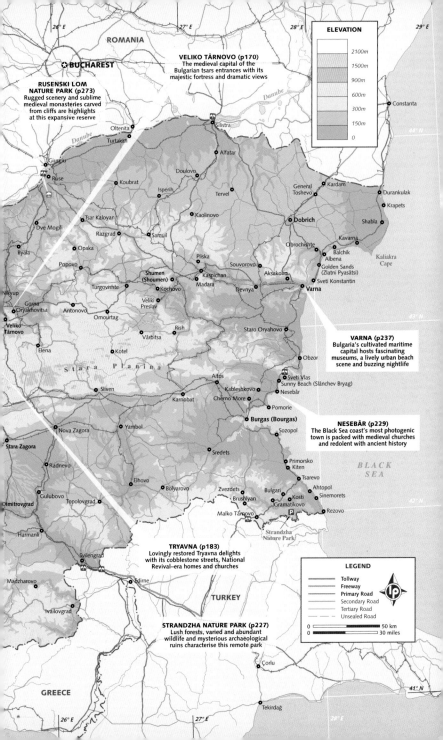

ELEVATION

2100m
1500m
900m
600m
300m
150m
0

ROMANIA

✧ BUCHAREST

VELIKO TÂRNOVO (p170)
The medieval capital of the
Bulgarian tsars entrances with its
majestic fortress and dramatic views

**RUSENSKI LOM
NATURE PARK (p273)**
Rugged scenery and sublime
medieval monasteries carved
from cliffs are highlights
at this expansive reserve

Danube

Oltenita
Turtakan
Silistra
Alfatar
Giurgiu
Ruse
Doulovo
Koubrat
Isperih
Tervel
Tsar Kaloyan
Razgrad
Samuil
Dve Mogili
Byala
Opaka
Popovo
Pliska
Shumen
(Shoumen)
Kaspichan
Madara
Devnya
Turgovishte
Kochovo
Veliki
Preslav
Rish
Staro Oryahovo
Nikyup
Gorna
Oryakhovitsa
Antonovo
Omourtag
Veliko
Târnovo
Elena
Kotel
Vârbitsa
S t a r a   P l a n i n a
Sliven
Aitos
Kableshkovo
Karnobat
Chérno More
Pomorie
Nova Zagora
Yambol
Burgas (Bourgas)
Sozopol
Stara Zagora
Rádnevo
Sredets
Gulubovo
Topolovgrad
Primorsko
Kiten
Dimitrovgrad
Elhovo
Bolyarovo
Zvezdets
Tsarevo
Harmanli
Brushlyan
Bulgari
Ahtopol
Sinemorets
Malko Târnovo
Kosti
Gramatikovo
Rezovo
*Strandzha
Nature Park*
Svilengrad
Madzharovo
Edirne
Ivailovgrad

TURKEY

Constanta
Durankulak
Krapets
Kardam
General
Toshevo
Dobrich
Shabla
Obrochishte
Kavarna
Balchik
Albena
Golden Sands
(Zlatni Pyasâtsi)
Sveti Konstantin
Varna
Souvorovo
Aksakovo
Kaliakra
Cape

Obzor
Sveti Vlas
Sunny Beach (Slánchev Bryag)
Nesebâr

VARNA (p237)
Bulgaria's cultivated maritime
capital hosts fascinating
museums, a lively urban beach
scene and buzzing nightlife

NESEBÂR (p229)
The Black Sea coast's most photogenic
town is packed with medieval churches
and redolent with ancient history

**BLACK
SEA**

TRYAVNA (p183)
Lovingly restored Tryavna delights
with its cobblestone streets, National
Revival–era homes and churches

STRANDZHA NATURE PARK (p227)
Lush forests, varied and abundant
wildlife and mysterious archaeological
ruins characterise this remote park

Çorlu

GREECE

Tekirdağ

LEGEND

Tollway
Freeway
Primary Road
Secondary Road
Tertiary Road
Unsealed Road

0 ——————— 50 km
0 ——————— 30 miles

On The Road

RICHARD WATKINS Coordinating Author

I studied ancient history at university, so I'm always drawn to brooding archaeological sites like the impressive Roman Thermae (p240) at Varna. I've been there a few times now, but it's still a great place to explore, even on a baking hot day. There were only a couple of other visitors ambling around when I was there, and I managed to get myself locked in after the caretaker decided to knock off early – but luckily there's a back way out, over some pointy railings. I'm taking a break on some recumbent entablature here (who wouldn't?), possibly in the *frigidarium* (cold-water pool) area. If only it was still there.

CHRISTOPHER DELISO

After marvelling at the sublime frescoes at the Basarbovo and Ivanovo cliff monasteries, we drove through the heat to Cherven (p274), a dusty, untroubled village that's home to a key medieval fortress. A cheery old couple foisted large bunches of homegrown white grapes upon us. They were especially delicious after the arduous climb up to the fortress, where ancient rulers surveyed their dominions; from here we could see Cherven's red roofs extending beneath us to one side, and the bleak, beautiful expanse of Rusenski Lom Nature Park outstretched to the other, as far as the eye could see.

See full author bios page 319

Bulgarian Highlights

Whether you're looking forward to exploring ancient Roman ruins, hiking the Pirin mountains, relaxing along the Black Sea coast, drinking with the locals after wandering through timeless cobblestoned streets or marvelling at stunning church frescoes, Bulgaria won't disappoint. There's nothing quite like a personal recommendation from someone who's been there to get you started, so we asked travellers, Lonely Planet authors and staff for their highlights from Bulgaria. This is what they told us.

ILIAN TRAVEL / ALAMY

① BELOGRADCHIK ROCKS

There is a little town in the northwest called Belogradchik (p261) where they have some beautiful old forts and rock formations.

ratsnrop (Thorn Tree name), traveller, Australia

HIKING AROUND BANSKO

Use Bansko (p127) as a base and do some hiking out of there. You can get to ski lifts that will take you higher and from there do some nice hikes. There is also a narrow-gauge railroad that travels to Bansko – it's quite slow, but the scenery is very impressive.

daveelmstrom (Thorn Tree name), traveller, US

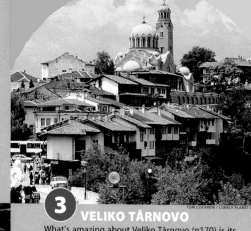

PHILIP GAME / LONELY PLANET IMAGES

2

3 TOM COCKREM / LONELY PLANET IMA

VELIKO TÂRNOVO

What's amazing about Veliko Târnovo (p170) is its amazing geographic location.

pupesh (Thorn Tree name), traveller, Belgium

ILJAN TRAVEL / AL

4 TRYAVNA

Tryavna (p183) is worth visiting to see the traditional woodcarvings, cobblestone streets and good architecture.

mcparkinson (Thorn Tree name), traveller

HIKING THE LAKES

I would recommend the Seven Lakes area (p115). There is a great network of huts (called *hizhas*) which you can hike between so you don't have to bring camping or cooking equipment.

zellturtle (Thorn Tree name), traveller, US

⑤

RICHARD NEBESKY / LONELY PLANET IMAGES

TRADITIONAL TAVERNS

⑥

Imbibe traditional Bulgarian hospitality at one of the many sociable *mehanas* (taverns) found all over the country. Decked out in colourful folksy style, and often providing live traditional music, they're great places to tuck into hearty rustic cuisine, rounded off with some excellent local wines and beers. *Nazdrave!*

Richard Watkins, Lonely Planet author, UK

BULGARIA / ALNUMICS / ALAMY

7 THE KINDNESS OF STRANGERS

I had a little bit of a scare in a train bathroom, because I couldn't manage to open the door from the inside. So I banged and banged on the door until the guy who was standing outside – with his cartons full of live chickens – came to my rescue. Not that we really could communicate, but I finally managed to open the door. A little bit before I had warned the guy that his chickens were crawling out of the boxes and were flying around the back of the train, so after my 100 *mercis* he and I were best buddies.

NomadWorld (Thorn Tree name), traveller, US

GREGORY WRONA / ALA

8 MELNIK

Visit the wine town of Melnik (p134), where houses and wine cellars are dug into the hillsides and where weird, eroded sandstone spires stick up from the valley floor. The food served at the taverns is as good as it gets, and to shake off the extra weight, there's a lovely walk up the valley to the Rozhen Monastery (p137), overlooking the mountains.

Jeroen van Marle, travel writer, Netherlands

9

RICHARD WATKINS

NESEBÂR

Nesebâr (p229) has tons of history and ancient ruins. You can explore several Roman ruins as well as a couple of centuries-old traditional houses and churches. Nesebâr has nice beaches nearby if you go to the new town, south of the causeway that leads into old Nesebâr… There are plenty of nice sandy beaches there.

**guenovnd
(Thorn Tree name),
traveller**

HELENE ROGERS / ALAMY

NIKREATES / ALA

10 KYUSTENDIL & BOYANA CHURCH

The elegant spa town of Kyustendil (p111), near the border with Macedonia, is a great place to relax, have a bath or walk in the forests. On the way to or from Sofia, stop off at Boyana to visit the ancient, frescoed church (p108).

Jeroen van Marle, travel writer, Netherlands

3 1833 05247 5834

RICHARD WATE

11 VARNA

Varna (p237) is lively and fun even (or maybe especially) during the summer months. You will find a lot of Bulgarian tourists here and can still go to one of the beaches for the day… I enjoyed the hot spring that runs across the beach and into the sea very much.

Dakini73 (Thorn Tree name), traveller

KOPRIVSHTITSA, NATIONAL REVIVAL VILLAGE

12

Koprivshtitsa (p191) is a charming old village with some lovely places to stay in the old Bulgarian revival style.

mcparkinson (Thorn Tree name), traveller

RICHARD NEBESKY / LONELY PLANET IMAGES

GREGORY WRONA / ALAMY

PLOVDIV

The old town (p138) is wonderful, and you might want to visit one of the many house-museums as well as the Roman amphitheatre. That will keep you busy for a day or two. If you have the time, there are at least two worthwhile side trips: the Bachkovo Monastery (p153) is the second-largest in Bulgaria, and is in a beautiful setting in the hills south of Plovdiv; similarly, the Tsarevets Fortress (p171) is an old encampment of buildings and churches in the hills south of town.

daveelmstrom (Thorn Tree name), traveller, US

BRENDAN HOFFMAN / ALAMY

13

TROYAN

Troyan (p189) is good for traditional pottery and the journey through the pass southwards is stunning.

mcparkinson (Thorn Tree name), traveller

14

DOUG MCKINLAY / LONELY PLANET IMA...

KAZANLÂK MARKET

15

Where to repair your umbrella is usually something you don't think about until it's too late. At the market of Kazanlâk (p201), however, the voluble vendors are on it. They're proactive enough, in fact, to urge you to purchase things you may not need even if it rains – items like live chickens, saddles and whips. Nevertheless, the tomatoes are ruddy and ripe and the pure, thick mountain honey is certainly worth a couple of *leva*.

Christopher Deliso,
Lonely Planet author, Macedonia

Тук
се приемат
ЗА РЕМОНТ
всички видове
ЧАДЪРИ

CHRISTOPHER DELISO

Contents

Regional Map Contents

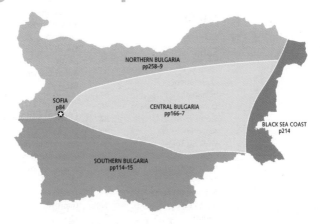

NORTHERN BULGARIA
pp258–9

SOFIA
p84

CENTRAL BULGARIA
pp166–7

BLACK SEA COAST
p214

SOUTHERN BULGARIA
pp114–15

Destination Bulgaria

Five centuries subjugated to Ottoman rule and, more recently, four decades locked very firmly behind the Iron Curtain turned Bulgaria into a distant, enigmatic country in the eyes of much of the rest of the world. Images of cheap wine downed at student house parties, budget ski holidays and umbrella-wielding Cold War assassins were once among the popular stereotypes, but Bulgaria today is a vastly different country from what it was even 10 years ago.

A fully paid-up member of NATO and (since 2007) the EU, Bulgaria has the feel of a nation at a very important crossroads. Massive foreign investment has created a construction boom, not just around the larger beach and mountain tourist resorts, but in the cities, too. More tourists than ever are discovering this country and an ever-rising number of foreigners are investing in property here. At the same time, the Bulgarian population is declining faster than almost anywhere else in Europe, wages are amongst the lowest on the continent – prompting increasingly long and bitter strikes – and the old problems of bureaucratic incompetence and organised crime bubble away in the background. The environmental damage caused by overdevelopment has been a particular cause for public alarm over recent years, and there are several national and international organisations campaigning to bring some of these issues to wider world attention (see p72). However much they complain, though, Bulgarians are a patriotic, if modest, bunch – when they ask you, as they often will, if you like their country, they genuinely care that you leave with good impressions.

For most foreign holidaymakers, Bulgaria's main lure is its long, sandy coastline – which still boasts swaths of stunning beaches and picturesque bays despite the expansive construction work – but there is so much more to this country, and so much of it remains largely untouched and unvisited by overseas tourists. Networks of well-maintained hiking trails and horse-riding routes allow you to discover Bulgaria's lush mountainous and forested landscapes, inhabited by bears, lynx, rare birds and other kinds of wildlife now becoming scarce elsewhere in Europe.

Getting around the country is easy, with cheap and efficient public transport to ferry you between the cities and into the remoter, rural corners, where the traditional, slow pace of life continues much as it has done for centuries. Here you'll come across multicoloured monasteries, filled with fabulous icons and watched over by bushy-bearded priests, and impossibly pretty timber-framed villages with smoke curling lazily over the stone-tiled roofs and donkeys complaining in the distance, where headscarfed old ladies and their curious grandchildren still stare in wonderment at the arrival of outsiders. The cities, too, are often overlooked highlights, from dynamic, cosmopolitan Sofia with its lovely parks, sociable alfresco bars and fascinating museums, to the National Revival architectural treasures and Roman remains of Plovdiv, and the youthful maritime cockiness of Varna.

Prices have certainly risen since Bulgaria became a member of the EU, but compared with countries in Western Europe, travellers will find it by and large a pleasingly cheap destination, and an easy and enjoyable one to travel round once you've mastered the Cyrillic alphabet and enough Bulgarian to buy a bus ticket. Bring your own transport and the whole country is yours to explore.

FAST FACTS

Population: 7.33 million

Area: 110,910 sq km

GDP per capita: US$10,700

Inflation: 7.3%

Unemployment rate: 9.6%

Average life expectancy: 69 (m), 76 (f)

Literacy rate: 98.2%

Highest point: Mt Musala (2925m)

Export: Bulgaria produces 10% of the world's rose oil

Body language: Bulgarians shake their heads for 'yes' and nod for 'no'

Getting Started

Travelling independently in Bulgaria is cheap, relatively hassle-free and immensely rewarding. Public transport is generally reliable and inexpensive, and will get you around most of the country, although if you're looking to explore the place in any great depth, you'll certainly require your own wheels, especially for the more remote, rural areas. The accommodation options are vast, ranging from private rooms and budget guesthouses, where nobody is likely to speak foreign languages, up to international five-star hotels that can be booked online.

Remember that Bulgarians use the Cyrillic alphabet, and it's essential that you get acquainted with this before you travel. English is widely understood in the big cities and tourist centres, and German is the more common second language in the coastal resorts, but in the countryside, knowledge of foreign languages is rare. Older, better-educated Bulgarians often have a smattering of French. Don't rely on staff at bus and train stations anywhere, even in Sofia, speaking anything but Bulgarian, but learning a few basic phrases will certainly ease your passage and make your trip much more enjoyable. The new tourist offices in the main cities will be very happy to help with any queries and staff at backpacker hostels and upscale hotels, which are more used to dealing with international guests, almost always speak English and will have plenty of information to hand.

Most foreign tourists still come to Bulgaria on all-inclusive package deals, either for sunbathing on the coast or skiing in the mountains, which can work out to be quite cost-effective as they also include airfares. If you're based at a beach or ski resort, it's easy to visit nearby attractions by public bus, hire car or on day trips organised by local tour companies. Some agencies based in Sofia (see p86) run a huge range of day trips and multiday activity and special-interest tours, so if you're keen on archaeology, bird-watching, botany, caving or climbing (to name just a few), these are a good way to see the best that the country has to offer.

WHEN TO GO

See Climate Charts (p285) for more information.

Bulgaria has a temperate climate with cold, damp winters and hot, dry summers. The Rodopi Mountains form a barrier to the moderating Mediterranean influence of the Aegean, while the Danube Plain is open to the extremes of central Europe. Sofia's generally favourable climate is one of its main attributes, with average daytime highs of 28°C in July and August and 3°C from December to February. The Black Sea moderates temperatures in the east of the country. Rainfall is highest in the mountains, and in winter life throughout Bulgaria is sometimes disrupted by heavy snowfalls.

Spring (particularly April to mid-June) is an excellent time to visit. The weather is good, the theatres and other cultural venues are in full swing and low-season rates still generally apply. Summer (mid-June to early September) is ideal for hiking and festivals, but it's also the peak holiday season, especially on the Black Sea coast. Temperatures can be very high during this period too. September is perhaps one of the best months to see Bulgaria. The autumn trees are glorious, fruit and vegetables are plentiful, the tourist hordes have returned home, and you can still sunbathe and swim in the Black Sea.

By mid-October, almost all Black Sea resorts have closed down. As the weather gets colder over the next two months, a gloom about the

DON'T LEAVE HOME WITHOUT...

- Valid travel insurance (see p288)
- Sturdy boots and a day-pack if you intend to do any hiking
- Toilet paper
- A towel if staying at budget accommodation
- Sunscreen and a sun-hat if travelling in summer
- An adaptor plug
- A water bottle for filling at public fountains
- Mosquito repellent
- A travel insurance policy (www.lonelyplanet.com/bookings) covering mountaineering, rock climbing, diving and skiing
- Checking out the Thorn Tree forum (www.lonelyplanet.com/thorntree) for more great tips, travel news and views

impending winter (December to March) permeates Bulgaria. Then, as soon as the first snows fall in around mid-December, Bulgarians start to perk up and flock to the ski resorts, which sometimes stay operating until mid-April.

The high season along the Black Sea coast is mid-July to late August; at the ski resorts, it's Christmas/New Year and February to mid-March. If you avoid these places at these times, you may be astounded at how few tourists there are in Bulgaria.

COSTS & MONEY

Since Bulgaria joined the EU in 2007, the dual-pricing system that used to be in force – whereby foreigners were often charged considerably more for hotel rooms and museum admission fees than locals – has been abolished. Inevitably, prices have risen, but travelling around the country remains relatively cheap. All food, drink and forms of transport are surprisingly inexpensive compared with Western European countries, but imported luxury goods, such as international-brand fashion and cosmetics, cost much the same as anywhere else.

A camping site costs about 10 lv per person and a room in a private home can cost anywhere between 12 lv and 30 lv, depending on the location. In a budget hotel (outside Sofia) a single room costs from 20 lv, 40 lv for a double. In a mid-range hotel a single room is roughly 40 lv, a double 60 lv. You can get a simple meal at a cheap café from as little as 3 lv, and you're unlikely to spend more than about 15 lv for a main course, even in more upmarket restaurants.

Many museums and galleries offer free entry on one day of the week, a bonus if you're travelling with a family. These details are noted where relevant in reviews throughout the book. Also, if you fancy staying at a top-class hotel but don't fancy paying the top-class tariff, remember that most offer discounted weekend rates (which usually means Friday to Sunday night). Some top-end hotels in Sofia offer discounts during August, when most tourists have gone to the coast.

If you stay at budget hotels or in private rooms, eat cheap Bulgarian food and catch public buses and 2nd-class trains, allow at least 50 lv per person per day. If you want to stay in midrange hotels, eat at higher-quality restaurants, charter occasional taxis, take 1st-class trains and buy souvenirs, allow about 80 lv per person per day. If you're staying in Sofia, you can basically double this cost.

HOW MUCH?

Coffee at street kiosk: 0.60 lv

Bus/tram ticket: 0.70 lv

Kebabche (grilled spicy meat sausages) and chips: 4 lv

Bottle of decent Bulgarian wine: 5 lv

CD of Bulgarian music: 15 lv

TOP PICKS

BULGARIA'S MOST PICTURESQUE VILLAGES

The heart of Bulgaria can be found in its small, rural communities, and the country has numerous little timber-framed villages where the style and pace of life seem to belong to another time. The following villages are worth visiting for their architecture, ambience and surrounding landscapes.

- Koprivshtitsa – National Revival architecture at its best (p191)
- Melnik – famous for its excellent wine (p134)
- Arbanasi – known for its wonderful religious murals (p179)
- Shiroka Lûka – famous for its humpbacked bridges and pretty cobbled lanes (p160)
- Bulgari – best known for its annual fire-dancing festival (p227)
- Kotel – renowned for its handmade carpets (p209)
- Shipka – the heartland of the Thracians (p202)

BULGARIA'S BEST RELIGIOUS ART

Bulgaria is well known for its beautiful religious icons, a rich tradition going back many centuries into the Byzantine and Slavic past. Churches and monasteries across the country are a blaze of colour, with wonderful frescoes, murals and icons on show, while many ancient and precious examples of this art can now be seen in museums. Listed below are the best places to see Bulgaria's most important and most exquisite religious art.

- Museum of Icons (Aleksander Nevski Crypt), Sofia (p91)
- Boyana Church, Sofia (p108)
- Rila Monastery (p117)
- Bachkovo Monastery (p153)
- Sveti Stefan Church, Nesebâr (p232)
- Nativity Church, Arbanasi (p180)
- Troyan Monastery (p190)

To read more lists of recommended travel experiences, and for the chance to create your own, visit www.lonelyplanet.com/bluelist.

Midrange and top-end hotels, as well as car hire firms and tour agencies often quote prices in euros, and it's possible to pay in this currency, or in leva. Bulgaria is unlikely to formally join the single European currency for some years yet.

TRAVELLING RESPONSIBLY

Since our inception in 1973, Lonely Planet has encouraged our readers to tread lightly, travel responsibly and enjoy the magic independent travel affords. International travel is growing at a jaw-dropping rate, and we still firmly believe in the benefits it can bring – but, as always, we encourage you to consider the impact your visit will have on the global environment and the local economies, cultures and ecosystems.

The rapid development of tourism in Bulgaria in recent years may have given a boost to the economy, but many Bulgarians are beginning to wonder at what cost. Hotel and holiday-home developments all along the Black Sea have been particularly controversial, with some stretches of coastline resembling colossal building sites as developers try to cash in on the property boom. There has even been illegal construction in supposedly protected nature reserves. The other main areas of development have been the mountain ski resorts, especially Bansko, and a massive new project based around Borovets has just been given the green light.

However, 'green' tourism is also on the up in Bulgaria, and several operators offer nature tours, activity trips and so on, with the emphasis on sustainable tourism. With a healthy sense of adventure you can experience the very best the country has to offer by going off the beaten track and staying in small, family-run hotels in rural villages. The best company to contact for a wide range of tours is Odysseia-In in Sofia (p86). Before you travel, it's also worth checking out the Bulgarian Association for Alternative Tourism (baatbg.org).

For more information on the environmental challenges being faced in Bulgaria, see the Environment chapter on p69.

> Bulgaria is the fourth largest exporter of medicinal herbs in the world; some 170 species thrive in the countryside.

Getting There & Away

If you are worried about the environmental impact of air travel, and don't want to fly to Bulgaria, you can also reach the country by bus from many other European countries, although the sheer distances involved from Western Europe may put off all but the hardy few. You can also buy an InterRail ticket, hop on a train and make Bulgaria your final port of call on a European odyssey. For information on train travel in Bulgaria and elsewhere in Europe, visit www.seat61.com.

Most towns in Bulgaria are well served by cheap public transport, and you'll probably find buses the quickest and most convenient way of getting around the country; trains tend to be slower, although the major cross-country lines do offer the faster 'express' trains. Unfortunately, city buses are often old and cause a good deal of pollution, though inter-city buses tend to be newer and more energy-efficient. Sofia also has trams and a metro system. Bicycles are not recommended for urban areas, but are a great mode of transport for exploring the open countryside in rural regions.

DID YOU KNOW?

Bulgaria boasts over 500 mineral springs dotted around the country. Sapareva Banya (102°C), in the Rila Mountains, is said to be the hottest spring in Europe.

Accommodation & Food

As a foreign tourist your leva can make a real difference to the local economy. Instead of staying at international chain hotels, which all take money out of the country, consider staying in private rooms; pensioners, who often have to survive on tiny incomes, advertise spare rooms in their homes outside bus and train stations, and if you take them up on the offer you'll know the money is going straight into their pockets. You can also book these rooms through agencies, who will take a small commission from the homeowners. There are plenty of small, family-run hotels and guesthouses all over the country, and staying at these often ecologically-aware places, especially in the poorer, more remote locations will inject much-needed cash into the locality. We've made sure to include some of these in this book, while the excellent *Bed & Breakfasts Guidebook* (see p280) is a good source of information, with contact details and reviews of numerous small, rural, family-run hotels all over the country.

You won't find many restaurants advertising organic ingredients but much Bulgarian food, especially that grown on small family farms or in people's gardens, is organic, and a lot of this ends up being sold in street markets. These are often the best places to find good, fresh food, and, again, purchasing goods directly from small producers rather than supermarkets means you'll be helping the local economy.

Responsible Travel Schemes

There are a number of organisations and programmes promoting sustainable tourism and supporting small-scale, ecologically friendly businesses in Bulgaria. These include:

Authentic Bulgaria (www.authenticbulgaria.org)
Bulgarian Association for Alternative Tourism (www.baatbg.org)
Bulgarian Biodiversity Foundation (www.bbf.biodiversity.bg)
Ecotourism Bulgaria (www.ecotourism.bulgariatravel.org)
Neophron (www.neophron.com)
Odysseia-In (www.odysseia-in.com)
World Wide Workers on Organic Farms (www.wwoofbulgaria.org)

TRAVEL LITERATURE

There are relatively few books by foreign writers devoted solely to Bulgaria; most include the country as part of a journey around Eastern Europe and/or the Balkans.

DID YOU KNOW?

The Gerak Family (1911) by Elin Pelin tells the nostalgic story of a traditional rural community in transition, and has twice been made into a film.

Under The Yoke by Ivan Vazov is Bulgaria's best loved novel, and a new English translation has been published recently after being out of print for decades. The book tells the patriotic story of the iconic April Uprising of 1876 and Bulgaria's struggle for independence from the Ottoman Empire.

The Black Sea: The Birthplace of Civilization and Barbarism by Neal Acherson is a fascinating overview of the turbulent history of the peoples living around the Black Sea, from earliest times onwards.

Liberation of Bulgaria: War Notes of 1877 by Wentworth Huyshe offers a first-hand account of the hard-fought Russo-Turkish War by a British journalist.

Turkish Gambit by Boris Akunin offers a lighter, fictional view of the Russo-Turkish War, as seen through the eyes of the popular novelist's Russian detective.

Bury Me Standing by Isabel Fonseca is a thoughtful insight into the customs, myths and troubled history of the Romany people across Eastern Europe.

INTERNET RESOURCES

There's no better place to start your web explorations than the Lonely Planet website (www.lonelyplanet.com). Here you will find succinct summaries on travelling to most places on earth, postcards from other travellers and the Thorn Tree bulletin board, where you can ask questions before you go or dispense advice when you get back.

Other useful websites (all in English) to access before you travel:

Beach Bulgaria (www.beachbulgaria.com) Information on the Black Sea resorts, plus details of many hotels on the coast.
Bulgarian Insider (www.the-bulgarian-insider.com) Interesting range of information on the country, including history, culture and practical details.
Bulgarian Ministry of Foreign Affairs (www.mfa.government.bg) Good for current affairs and links to all government departments.
HotelsCentral.com (www.hotelsbulgaria.com) Offers attractive discounts for hotel rooms (if booked for three or more nights).
Lonely Planet (www.lonelyplanet.com) Get quick Bulgaria info and inspiration with our travel stories, podcasts and hotel and hostel reviews. Ask other travellers on the Thorn Tree forum.
Novinite (www.novinite.com) The latest Bulgarian news and views from the Sofia-based news agency.
Pictures of Bulgaria (www.picturesofbulgaria.com) Comprehensive site with information on tourist sights and hotels and links to other sights.

Sofia Echo (www.sofiaecho.com) Up-to-the-minute news about Bulgaria as well as restaurant and entertainment reviews for the capital.
Travel Bulgaria (www.travel-bulgaria.com) Excellent site for travel information, including links.
Vagabond (www.vagabond-bg.com) Bulgaria's only English-language lifestyle magazine, with features on current talking-points.
Visit to Bulgaria (www.visittobulgaria.com) Excellent portal with information on a wide range of topics.

Events Calendar

Bulgaria hosts a bewildering number of religious, folkloric, music and wine festivals. Most have traditions dating back hundreds of years, while others are established mainly to attract tourists. There's at least one major festival every summer weekend somewhere in the country.

JANUARY

ST VASIL'S DAYFOLK CONCERT 1 Jan
(Sandanski) Traditionally, New Year's Day is marked by young boys, known as *sourvakari*, tapping people with decorated twigs to wish them luck. The day ends with traditional festive music and partying.

KUKERI 1 Jan
(Bansko) Traditional pagan mummer performance with men dressed in hideous masks and shaggy costumes, ringing bells to scare away bad spirits. Also occurs in the countryside around Pernik in mid-January.

IORDANOVDEN 6 Jan
(Koprivshtitsa) Religious event dedicated to the healing powers of water. A priest throws a crucifix into the river and local youths dive in to retrieve it.

FEBRUARY

TRIFON ZAREZAN FESTIVAL 1 Feb
(Melnik) To celebrate the patron saint of wine-making, the vines are pruned, sprinkled with wine and blessed by a priest. Then the music and drinking begins.

MARCH

BABA MARTA 1 Mar
(Nationwide) 'Granny March' signifies the beginning of spring, and Bulgarians present each other with red and white woollen tassels, known as *martinitsi,* as good luck tokens.

KUKERI 1st Sun in Mar
(Shiroka Lûka) Locals parade in elaborate goatskin costumes and startling masks in this ancient fertility rite.

**SOFIA INTERNATIONAL
FILM FESTIVAL** early Mar
(Sofia) Bulgaria's main movie event, showcasing the latest Bulgarian feature films and documentaries, plus independent films from overseas.

**PANCHO VLADIGEROV
MUSICAL DAYS** mid-Mar
(Shumen) The life and works of the local classical composer are musically celebrated at the city's Museum Complex of Pancho Vladigerov.

**MARCH DAYS OF MUSIC
FESTIVAL** last two weeks of Mar
(Ruse) One of the oldest classical music festivals in Bulgaria, held since 1961, with concerts around town.

TODOROVDEN 1st Sat of Lent
(Koprivshtitsa) St Theodore's Day is marked with horse racing and music in a meadow at the edge of town.

APRIL

FOLKLORIC FESTIVAL 1 Apr
(Melnik) Fun day out with traditional music concerts and wine on tap.

MUSIC FESTIVAL one week in mid-Apr
(Shiroka Lûka) Traditional Bulgarian music and dancing at its best, with participants from the town's music academy and the region.

MAY

FLORA FLOWER EXHIBITION all month
(Burgas) The city comes alive with colourful blooms for the annual celebration of all things floral and botanical.

**RE-ENACTMENT OF
THE APRIL UPRISING** 1 & 2 May
(Koprivshtitsa) The momentous events of 1876 are remembered by patriotic locals in period costumes.

INTERNATIONAL FESTIVAL
OF HUMOUR & SATIRE   biannual
(Gabrovo) The city revels in its reputation for mockery with a street carnival and international competitions for humorous artwork. Entries remain on show till September.

VARNA SUMMER
INTERNATIONAL FESTIVAL   May–Oct
(Varna) One of the oldest and biggest festivals in Bulgaria, comprising music, theatre and numerous other cultural events.

INTERNATIONAL
PLOVDIV FAIR   one week in mid-May
(Plovdiv) Going since 1892, this is the pre-eminent commercial trade fair in the Balkans, with varying business and industry exhibitions.

DAYS OF SHUMEN
CULTURAL FESTIVAL   mid-May
(Shumen) Hearty celebration of civic culture, with concerts, theatre performances and art exhibitions.

CELEBRATION OF
BANSKO TRADITIONS   17-24 May
(Bansko) Locals take to the streets to celebrate regional folklore with dancing, live music and a craft fair.

CULTURAL MONTH
FESTIVAL   late May–mid-Jul
(Plovdiv) Major cultural celebration with music performances, dancing and opera, and exhibitions on Bulgarian art and literature.

JUNE

FIRE DANCING FESTIVAL   early Jun
(Bulgari, Strandzha Nature Park) Held in the first few days of June in the tiny village of Bulgari, this is a magical occasion, dedicated to Sts Konstantin and Elena, with fire-walking, music, wine and communal merriment.

FESTIVAL OF
ROSES   1st weekend in Jun
(Kazanlâk, Karlovo and Shipka) Cheery community festival honouring the local flower crop, with street parades, dancing, concerts and the crowning of the Rose Queen.

VERDI FESTIVAL   two weeks in early Jun
(Plovdiv) Highly regarded annual event celebrating the music of the great Italian composer, with concerts arranged around town.

MADARA HORSEMAN INTERNATIONAL
MUSIC DAYS FESTIVAL   mid-Jun–mid-Jul
(Madara) Held in the Unesco-listed archaeological reserve, with an impressive programme of orchestral performances.

INTERNATIONAL FESTIVAL
OF RELIGIOUS MUSIC   mid-Jun
(Veliko Târnovo) A feast of ecclesiastical choral music in the dramatic setting of the city's medieval fortress.

INTERNATIONAL FOLKLORE
FESTIVAL   three weeks in late Jun–mid-Jul
(Veliko Târnovo) A colourful event regularly attracting hundreds of performers from across the country, with shows of traditional dance and music.

JULY

BALKANFOLK   last two weeks of Jul
(Bankya, near Sofia) Major international gathering for everyone interested in Balkan traditions, with music, dance and language classes and workshops for the very keen.

AUGUST

INTERNATIONAL
FOLK FESTIVAL   every five years
(Koprivshtitsa) One of the biggest festivals of its kind in Bulgaria, attracting thousands of dancers, musicians and folk ensembles. Next staged in 2010.

INTERNATIONAL JAZZ FESTIVAL   7-15 Aug
(Bansko) Jazz musicians from all across Europe play in free concerts staged in the main square.

THRACIA SUMMER
MUSIC FESTIVAL   early–mid-Aug
(Plovdiv and other towns in Bulgarian Thrace) Traditional tunes played in venues in the old town, with concerts also staged in Stara Zagora and Chirpan.

FOLKLORE DAYS FESTIVAL   mid-Aug
(Koprivshtitsa) Another of Bulgaria's many lively and sociable festivals dedicated to traditional music and dancing.

PIRIN SINGS FOLK FESTIVAL   mid-Aug
(Bansko) Annual event bringing together thousands of traditional musicians, choirs and dancers from the Pirin region, with a larger gathering every four years (the next is in 2009).

WATERMELON FESTIVAL   mid-Aug
(Salmanovo, Shumen region) A celebration of rural life in this village outside Shumen, featuring music, dancing, watermelon carving and watermelon seed spitting contests.

MILK FESTIVAL   last weekend in Aug
(Smilyan) Near Smolyan. Local bovines compete for the coveted title of 'Miss Cow' in this celebration of all things dairy.

**INTERNATIONAL
FOLKLORE FESTIVAL**   late Aug
(Burgas) Festive street parades, craft workshops, music concerts and dance performances bring international colour to the seaside.

**ANNUAL INTERNATIONAL
FILM FESTIVAL**   one week, late Aug-early Sep
(Varna) Art house and independent films from across the world get a rare screening.

SEPTEMBER

CITY HOLIDAY   6 Sep
(Plovdiv) A civic celebration of the day back in 1885 when Plovdiv, along with the province of Eastern Rumelia, was finally reunited with the rest of Bulgaria.

PIRIN FOLK NATIONAL FESTIVAL   early Sep
(Sandanski) Yet another high-spirited, regional celebration of traditional musical and Terpsichorean talent.

PLOVDIV JAZZ NIGHTS   early Sep
(Plovdiv) Highly regarded international gathering of jazz masters, with performances and jam sessions around the city.

APOLLONIA ARTS FESTIVAL   1st half of Sep
(Sozopol) A huge festival of music, drama and dance that attracts big names and national TV coverage.

**SCENE AT THE CROSSROADS THEATRE
FESTIVAL**   13 days in mid-Sep
(Plovdiv) Yearly drama gala featuring theatrical groups from Bulgaria and abroad.

**INTERNATIONAL SHORT
FILM FESTIVAL**   one week in late Sep
(Balchik) A filmic fest offering a rare chance to view screenings of low-budget independent movies.

**INTERNATIONAL
PLOVDIV FAIR**   one week in late Sep
(Plovdiv) The city welcomes another round of trade, craft and industry fairs.

**INTERNATIONAL PUPPET
THEATRE FESTIVAL**   late Sep
(Stara Zagora) The city's State Puppet Theatre hosts performances, workshops, exhibitions, seminars, and street art with professional puppeteers from around the world.

OCTOBER

DAYS OF RUSE   early Oct
(Ruse) Yearly cultural festival focusing on music, dancing and drama performances.

FAIR DAY   14 Oct
(Etâr) Held in the Ethnographic Museum, featuring demonstrations of regional music and dancing.

FEAST OF ST JOHN OF RILA   19 Oct
(Rila Monastery) Ivan Rilski, the monastery's revered patron saint, is honoured with religious services and sacred music.

CARNIVAL OF FERTILITY   biannual
(Shumen) Local folk traditions are celebrated with a masked carnival, flower and vegetable shows and a craft fair.

NOVEMBER

**CINEMANIA FILM
FESTIVAL**   all month
(Sofia) The National Palace of Culture (NDK) hosts a well-attended movie gala, with screenings of new independent films from around the world.

DECEMBER

**YOUNG RED WINE
FESTIVAL**   early Dec
(Sandanski) The vine harvest is celebrated with numerous events including music concerts and wine tastings.

Itineraries
CLASSIC ROUTES

CITIES, CULTURE & SEASIDE
Two to Three Weeks

Start off in the capital, **Sofia** (p82), with its excellent museums and galleries, expansive parks and Bulgaria's best restaurant and nightlife scene. For a complete contrast, take the train to the beautifully restored village of **Koprivshtitsa** (p191), a stunning spot filled with gorgeous National Revival-era house-museums. It's a peaceful spot to stay for a day or two.

From here, take a bus to busy **Plovdiv** (p138), where you can easily pass a couple of days browsing through the art galleries, exploring the Roman remains or just taking it easy at one of the many street cafés.

From Plovdiv, make for the Black Sea coast and stop overnight in the bustling city of **Burgas** (p213) before heading up to **Nesebâr** (p229), famed for its beautiful medieval churches. Spend a few days here, maybe taking a day trip to **Sunny Beach** (Slânchev Bryag; p235) for a spot of sunbathing, then continue up the coast towards **Varna** (p237). This city's superb Archaeological Museum and Roman Thermae are definitely worth a visit, while the beachfront promenade has some of the best bars and clubs on the coast.

Start back westwards, stopping at historic **Veliko Târnovo** (p170) on the way; its ancient fortress is unmissable and the views fantastic. Spend at least one night here before returning to Sofia.

Two weeks is not a lot of time to see all that Bulgaria has to offer, but it's enough to give you a taster, and maybe help you decide where you'd like to return to at a later date.

MONASTERIES & MOUNTAINS   One Week

From Sofia, head out to **Dragalevtsi** (p109) in **Vitosha Nature Park** (p109), just on the outskirts of the city. Take a peek at the much-revered Dragalevtsi Monastery, and then take the chairlift up to Goli Vrâh. Depending on the season you can then go walking or skiing in the Mt Vitosha range, which affords some spectacular views back over Sofia, weather permitting.

The following day, take a minibus from Sofia for the short journey to **Samokov** (p119), looking over its History Museum and mosque, then catch another minibus to Bulgaria's burgeoning ski mega-resort at **Borovets** (p120). Again, depending on the time of year, you can either slip on your skis and take to the slopes or, in summer, go hiking in the beautiful **Rila National Park** (p115), south of town.

After whiling away a few days in Borovets, return to Samokov for a connecting minibus to Dupnitsa, where you can get another bus to the village of **Rila** (p116). Here you can either stay overnight in the village's sole hotel, or else at one of the places near **Rila Monastery** (p117), just a short bus ride away. This spectacular monastery is the holiest pilgrimage site in Bulgaria, and is one of the country's most visited attractions. Try to ignore the inevitable tour buses and snap-happy crowds and just admire the stunning wall frescoes and beautiful architecture of the place.

From Rila village, you can catch a bus back to Sofia.

This quick trip will give you a good idea of the attractions around the capital and the conveniently close hiking and skiing areas, and take you to Bulgaria's holiest pilgrimage destination, Rila Monastery.

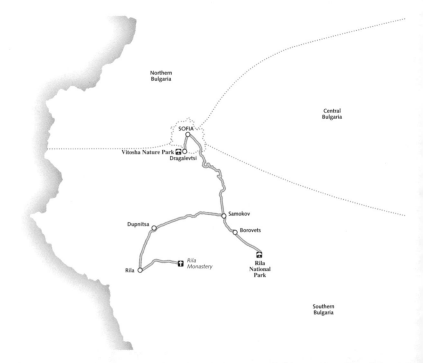

ROADS LESS TRAVELLED

THE NORTHERN LINE   Two Weeks

Starting at Sofia, head north by train to **Vidin** (p257), where you can stay overnight, see the Danube and visit the **Baba Vida Museum-Fortress** (p257). From here, travel south to gorgeous **Belogradchik** (p261), where you can explore the even more interesting fortress and see the fantastic Belogradchik rocks.

The next day, continue by train to **Vratsa** (p265) and spend a day walking in the nearby mountains before moving on to **Lovech** (p188). The old town is a great place to explore and you can make an excursion to nearby **Troyan Monastery** (p190) to see some of Bulgaria's best fresco painting.

Next, travel to **Veliko Târnovo** (p170), where, instead of staying in the town, you could enjoy a relaxing few days in nearby **Arbanasi** (p179). Take time to visit the **Etâr complex** (p187) and other local attractions, such as **Tryavna** (p183) or the **Dryanovo Monastery** (p182), before heading on to **Shumen** (p165). Here you'll find the most intricately decorated mosque in Bulgaria as well as another great fortress. You could also take an interesting excursion from here to **Kotel** (p209).

Carry on to **Dobrich** (p277), which has an excellent open-air ethnological museum. Finally, head to the Black Sea and the off-the-beaten-track destination of **Balchik** (p251). This lovely place makes for a total contrast to the resorts further down the coast, and while there isn't a great beach, the swimming is still good and there's the superb botanical gardens and Queen Marie's palace to visit.

This trip takes you across the often neglected northern region of Bulgaria, beginning in the far northwest at Vidin on the Danube and ending up at charming Balchik on the Black Sea.

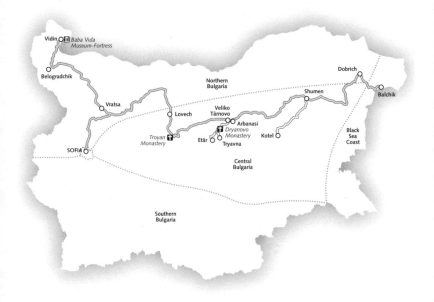

SOUTHERN SPLENDOUR   Two Weeks

Start off in Sofia, and take the bus down to **Blagoevgrad** (p124), which, though it might not be brimming over with sights, is a lively provincial town and a convenient overnight stop. From here, travel on to **Sandanski** (p131), birthplace of Spartacus and a popular and sunny spa town. The town makes an ideal base for a day trip to nearby **Melnik** (p134), famous for its wine and its bizarre sand pyramids, and you could also, perhaps, carry on to **Rozhen Monastery** (p137).

From Sandanski you can catch a bus to the charming mountain town of **Bansko** (p127): outside the tourist high seasons in winter and midsummer, it's a quiet, laid-back place to rest up. The more energetic can take advantage of the excellent hiking country nearby.

Continue by bus to **Plovdiv** (p138). Bulgaria's second city is worth a few days' stopover, with one of the country's best preserved old towns and a host of art galleries to visit. The lovely **Bachkovo Monastery** (p153) is also an easy day trip from Plovdiv.

Following this route, you'll get away from the main tourist centres and see southern Bulgaria at its best.

Head south to **Smolyan** (p158), Bulgaria's highest (and longest) town. The climate here is often cool and refreshing, and the town has an excellent historical museum. Take a day trip to nearby **Shiroka Lŭka** (p160), a typically charming Rodopian village famed for its *kukeri* festival and humpbacked bridges. Carry on to the spa town of **Devin** (p160), where you can indulge in some hydrotherapy or a massage. This peaceful little town makes a great base for visiting the spectacular caves at **Trigrad** (p162) and **Yagodina** (p163). You can then head back to Sofia either directly or via Plovdiv.

TAILORED TRIPS

DOWN THE COAST

As well as the huge beach resorts, this trip will take you to small coastal villages, ancient peninsula towns and charming Varna.

Head first to **Varna** (p237), and spend a few days here to take advantage of the city's many charms, including the excellent Archaeological Museum, lively beachfront and the attractive Primorski Park. Take a day trip north to **Balchik** (p251) for a snoop round the summer palace and botanical gardens, and from Varna head south to scenic, if over-commercialised, **Nesebâr** (p229). Stay either in the old town or in the nearby package-tour resort of **Sunny Beach** (Slânchev Bryag; p235), where you'll also find a great beach and plenty of water sports.

From here, go south to **Burgas** (p213) to soak in its laid-back, Mediterranean atmosphere, then carry on to **Sozopol** (p220) by bus. Spend a couple of days here exploring the old town and enjoying the town's two beaches. Further south, head to **Primorsko** (p225) or **Kiten** (p226), both of which have long, sandy beaches ideal for families, or go a little further to **Tsarevo** (p226) for quieter, uncommercial beach life. If time permits, head to **Sinemorets** (p228) with its access to the **Strandzha Nature Park** (p227) and its two beaches, some of the quietest on the entire Bulgarian coast.

THE UNESCO HERITAGE TOUR

This tour takes you to nearly all of Bulgaria's Unesco World Heritage sites. Some are awkward to reach by public transport; see relevant sections for details. From Sofia, take a day trip to the suburb of Boyana, and the delightful **Boyana Church** (p108) with its 13th-century murals. Going south, call by the splendid **Rila Monastery** (p117) on a (long) day trip from Sofia, or from Blagoevgrad. It's the country's largest monastery, and a true highlight. The **Pirin National Park** (p124), best explored via Bansko, offers numerous walking trails and remarkable scenery.

Travelling east to Kazanlâk, you'll come upon the **Thracian Tomb of Kazanlâk** (p200). The tomb, dating from the 4th century BC, is open to the public.

Going northwards, the impressive **Ivanovo Rock Monastery** (p274) is inside the Rusenski Lom Nature Park, near Ruse, and the **Srebârna Nature Reserve** (p274) is best reached from Silistra. Get a bus down to Shumen, from where it's possible to visit the **Madara Horseman** (p169), an 8th-century cliff carving.

Finally, head to Varna, then down the coast to picturesque **Nesebâr** (p229), the last stop on the Unesco trail.

OUTDOOR ACTIVITIES

This tour takes in most of Bulgaria's best outdoor activities. From Sofia, head south to the Rila Mountains, where you can hike to the magical **Seven Rila Lakes** (p123), sleeping in mountain huts along the way in summer; in winter, ski the venerable resort of **Borovets** (p120) nearby. Further south, the Pirin Mountains also boast great skiing at **Bansko** (p127) and vast acres of untamed wilderness for hikers.

From here continue east to Plovdiv, and drop down into the Rodopi Mountains for more hiking and some therapeutic dips in the mineral hot baths of **Devin** (p160); Devin's also a good base for visiting Bulgaria's best caves, at **Yagodina** and **Trigrad** (p162). Returning to Plovdiv, continue north to Veliko Târnovo, where you can arrange horse riding through rolling meadows and forests in nearby **Arbanasi** (p179).

Continuing north, stop off at swinging Ruse on the Danube to explore the **Rusenski Lom Nature Park** (p273), home to both rare bird species and unique cliff monasteries. Head further east along the river to reach **Lake Srebârna** (p274), Bulgaria's best spot for blissful bird-watching, or try your hand at fly-fishing at nearby **Vetren** (p274).

In summer, it's obligatory to end up on the Black Sea coast, for swimming and sailing at **Albena** (p249) or the quieter beach at **Kavarna** (p254).

WINE ROUTES

This tour takes you through Bulgaria's most famous wine-producing regions, and to wineries where you can sample some of the country's best vino. Start in Varna, at the sumptuous **Chateau Euxinograde** (p66). Here, at the former Bulgarian royal palace, you can marvel at its century-old wine cellar while sampling a delicate white from the Black Sea coastal plain. From here, head west along the Danube to atmospheric **Ruse** (p267), where you can try a glass or two of northern Bulgaria's signature red, Gamza, along with dinner in one of the excellent local restaurants.

Next, head south to the lively city of Plovdiv; in Brestovitsa, 15km further south, seek out **Todoroff Wine Cellars** (p67), makers of some of the country's best Mavrud (a classic Bulgarian red). Returning to Plovdiv, continue west towards Pazardzhik, turning off at Ognyanovo village, home of the sophisticated, foreign-owned **Bessa Valley Vineyards winery** (p67). Terrific tasting tours here include the winery's award-winning Merlot and Cabernet Sauvignon blends.

The final part of the tour takes you to Bulgaria's southwestern corner, and the likeable village of **Melnik** (p134), nestled between cliffs and bursting with medieval ruins. The village's 600-year-old tradition of producing the full-bodied Shiroka Melnishka Loza red is celebrated with tastings held in cave cellars, wine museums and sunny garden restaurants. For further information on Bulgarian wine, see p63.

History

The land that gave birth to the legendary Orpheus and Spartacus, Bulgaria is a country with a long, tumultuous and fascinating history. It has been invaded, conquered and settled by Greeks, Scythians, Romans, Byzantines and Turks, all of whom left their indelible marks on the landscape. Bulgaria's medieval 'Golden Age', when the Bulgar Khans ruled over one of the largest empires in Europe, was bright but brief, while 500 years of subsequent, brutal Turkish domination isolated the country from the rest of Europe. More recently, Bulgaria spent four decades as a totalitarian Soviet satellite, again leaving this small Balkan nation in the shadows as far as the Western world was concerned. It's no wonder, then, that Bulgarians are so passionate about preserving their history and their culture, which has survived so often against the odds. In the last years of the 20th century Bulgaria began opening up, and is one of the newest members of the EU.

The Shortest History of Bulgaria by Nikolay Ovcharov runs quickly through the highpoints of Bulgaria's past, cramming a lot of interesting facts into just 70 brightly illustrated pages.

BEGINNINGS

Excavations of caves near Pleven (in the Danubian plains in northern Bulgaria) and in the Balkan Mountains have indicated human habitation as far back as the Upper Palaeolithic Period around 40,000 BC. However, archaeologists now believe that the earliest permanent settlers, arriving around 6000 BC, were Neolithic people who lived in caves, such as at Yagodina in the southern Rodopi Mountains (p162) and later, between about 5500 BC and 4500 BC, in round mud huts. The best preserved examples are on show in Stara Zagora (see p204). Burnt grain found here indicates these people were farmers. Chalcolithic (copper-using) cultures developed during the fourth millennium BC, and a superb collection of artefacts from this period, including possibly the earliest worked gold jewellery ever discovered, is on show at Varna Archaeological Museum (p240).

A Concise History of Bulgaria by RJ Crampton is a scholarly and comprehensive overview of the country's history from prehistoric times up to the present day.

TRIBAL TIMES

The Greek historian Herodotus tells us that the population of Thrace was 'greater than that of any country in the world except India', and that if the various tribes ever united under a single leader, then they would be the most powerful nation on earth; history, of course, tells us that they never did get their act together. Several tribes, who collectively came to be known as the Thracians, settled in modern-day Bulgaria, and in the early stages built settlements based around cave systems and near springs, which they considered sacred. As time went by, they built larger, more permanent villages around rudimentary fortresses, placed on elevated sites for defence.

TIMELINE

6000–5000 BC	4000–1000 BC	611 BC
Bulgaria's earliest permanent inhabitants establish settlements in and around caves during the Neolithic period. By around 5000 BC, the caves have been abandoned in favour of mud huts, and farming develops.	The warlike and disparate Thracian tribes dominate the region covered by modern-day Bulgaria, creating settlements such as Mesembria on the Black Sea coast around 3000 BC and expanding into Greece and Anatolia by 2000 BC.	Greek settlers from the city-state of Miletus establish Apollonia Pontica (Sozopol) on the Black Sea coast. It is the first classically democratic state on Bulgarian territory, with all males over the age of 18 eligible to vote for the governing assembly.

HERITAGE OF THE THRACIANS

The ancient Thracians, who once ruled over modern-day Bulgaria, are, in many ways, a mysterious and misunderstood people. Magnificent treasures such as the Varna necropolis treasure, on show in Varna's Archaeological Museum (p240) and the Panagyurishte Treasure (p108) in Sofia's National Museum of History suggest that this was a rich and sophisticated society, while major recent discoveries have cast new light on these tribes, surprising historians both in Bulgaria and overseas and forcing a rethink on their murky civilisation. In 2004, archaeologists unearthed two Thracian gravesites, both around 2400 years old, near Shipka and Kazanlâk, an area which has become known as the Valley of the Thracian Kings due to the concentration of rich royal burials found there. One tomb yielded a solid gold mask, thought to represent the Thracian ruler Teres, and resembling the mask of Agamemnon from Mycenae, and a superb bronze portrait head, possibly of King Sevt III – a masterpiece of Hellenistic art – was discovered in the other. Both are now on display in Sofia's Archaeological Museum (p91).

Excavations, headed by the respected archaeologist Dr Georgi Kitov, have continued apace and several new tombs, and more fabulous artefacts, have been brought to light around the country, most recently around Sliven in 2007, where another regal golden mask was found. Perhaps even more intriguingly, archaeologists now claim to have identified the ruins of the famed Oracle of Dionysus at Perperikon, near Kârdzhali, where Alexander the Great was informed that he would become master of Asia, and the tomb of Orpheus, at Tatul near the Turkish border. Unfortunately, the archaeologists have to work fast to contend with looters once sites are discovered, but it is hoped that this amazing Thracian heritage will become a big tourist draw in years to come. See www.ancient-bulgaria.com for more information on Bulgaria's Thracian treasures.

Among the more powerful tribes were the Serdi, who settled around modern Sofia; the Getae, who lived along the Danube in northeastern Bulgaria; and the Odrysai, from the eastern Rodopi region. Despite their constant quarrels, the Thracian tribes shared much in common, and were feared and respected by outsiders as great warriors and horsemen: the fierce Thracian weaponry displayed at archaeological museums around the country will give you an inkling of what potential invaders were up against. The Greek historian Polybius wrote in the 2nd century BC of the 'insoluble state of war' between the Thracians and the Greeks of the city-state of Byzantium. It was impossible, he says, to gain a decisive victory over these 'barbarians', or to end the fighting, due to their sheer numbers: 'If the Byzantines overcome one chieftain, three others still more formidable invade his territory'.

They worshipped many gods, but were particularly devoted to Dionysus, whom they celebrated in orgiastic rites, and believed an afterlife. Greek chroniclers regarded the Thracians' customs with disdain, though were not averse to reporting the racier aspects of their lives. We are told that they practised polygamy and that their young women were encouraged to be sexually promiscuous before marriage, while the historian Strabo comments on one

335 BC	AD 46	293
Macedonian king Alexander the Great extends the Thracian holdings of his father Philip II by marching to the Danube River, securing it as the northernmost border of his massive empire.	Thrace falls under the sway of the Roman Empire and is carved up into the administrative provinces of Thrace (in the south) and Moesia (in the north), with Ulpia Serdica (modern-day Sofia) becoming capital of Inner Dacia.	Roman Emperor Diocletian establishes the 'Tetrarchy' (rule of four), radically reorganising Imperial administration. Regional 'capitals' are established, including Serdica (Sofia), which flourishes as a centre of government and trade.

tribe's use of inhaled intoxicants (probably burning hemp seeds). Tales of their lurid tattoos also wrinkled many an Athenian nose.

Far from being the bloodthirsty savages portrayed by classical authors, though, the Thracians were accomplished artists and farmers, and grew wealthy from trading jewellery, copper and gold. Recent archaeological excavations around Shipka in central Bulgaria have unearthed some astounding works of art, including the gold mask and bronze head of a Thracian king, now on show at Sofia's Archaeological Museum (p91).

The Thracians significantly influenced the religion, architecture and culture of the subsequent Roman and Greek rulers. Some geographical names used today, such as 'rila' (for Rila Monastery) and 'yantra' (the name of the river through Veliko Târnovo) probably originate from Thracian words.

Thracian Reminders

Remains of Thracian settlements can be found along the Black Sea coast near Burgas and at the town of Mesembria (Nesebâr), while other remnants can be found on Nebet Tepe in Plovdiv, where the Thracians built the fortress of Eumolpias in about 5000 BC (see p141). Other Thracian settlements grew into the modern-day towns of Stara Zagora, Sandanski, Melnik, Bansko, Smolyan, Shumen and Madara.

By the first millennium BC the Thracians had spread as far north as Cherven, near the Danube, and as far west as Sofia. One tribe known as the Serdi created Sardonopolis, which was later renamed Serdica, and subsequently became Sofia, today's capital city.

The most famous Thracian remains are the tombs dating from about 4000 BC, which are displayed in the excellent Archaeological Museum in Varna (see p240) and the tomb at Kazanlâk built in the 4th century BC (see p200). Close by, the area around Shipka has been termed the Valley of the Thracian Kings due to its high concentration of Thracian burial mounds. Other Thracian artefacts can be seen in museums in Haskovo, Smolyan, Sofia and Sliven.

Legend tells that Orpheus, the semimythical musician and underworld explorer, was born in Thrace, near the modern-day village of Gela (see the boxed text, p34), while Spartacus, his famous fellow Thracian who led a slave revolt against the Romans in Sicily, came from the vicinity of modern Sandanski.

ARRIVAL OF THE GREEKS...

From the 7th century BC onwards, enterprising Greeks sailed up the Black Sea coast of Bulgaria seeking out good harbours and trade opportunities, and founded settlements including Apollonia Pontica (modern-day Sozopol), Odessos (Varna), Mesembria (Nesebâr), Krounoi (Balchik) and Pirgos (Burgas). They established large ports for exporting wheat, fish and salt, and traded Greek pottery for Thracian metalwork and jewellery.

DID YOU KNOW?
The Thracian Getae tribe would send 'messengers' to their god, Salmoxis, by hurling them onto a row of upturned spears.

Bulgarians: Civilisers of the Slavs by Bojidar Dimitrov is a small and readable, but somewhat biased, telling of the country's religious and cultural history. It's also available in French and German.

The Valley of the Thracian Rulers by Georgi Kitov is an up-to-date account of the fascinating archaeological discoveries made in central Bulgaria in recent years, with some beautiful colour photographs.

443–47	681	855
Attila the Hun and his army cross the Danube, sweeping into Roman territory and sacking the cities of Serdica (Sofia) and Philipopolis (Plovdiv) before being paid off with gold by the emperor.	The First Bulgarian Empire is founded by Khan Asparuh, with its capital at Pliska. Expanded under Khan Tervel (701–18), it reaches its largest extent under the rule of Tsar Simeon (893–927) before settling into a slow decline.	Saints Kiril and Metodii create the Glagolic alphabet to help promote Christianity through the Bulgarian lands and beyond. It subsequently develops into the Cyrillic script.

ORPHEUS IN THRACE

The legend of Orpheus, the semidivine lyre-player and singer, was one of the most popular and enduring in antiquity, even spawning a 'mystery cult' in Greece and elsewhere in the Hellenistic world, but it is thought that the original Orpheus was a real person, born somewhere in the neighbourhood of Gela, north of Shiroka Lûka. His story is well known: his music soothed men, beasts and even trees, he travelled with Jason and the Argonauts in search of the Golden Fleece, when his lyre-plucking helpfully drowned out the alluring wails of the Sirens, and, of course, he descended into the underworld to rescue his dead wife, Eurydice, from the clutches of Hades. Having lost her again at the last moment, Orpheus spent the rest of his days wandering around the Rodopi Mountains, until his mournful singing drove the Bacchantes (ecstatic female devotees of Dionysus) to tear him into pieces and dump his dismembered remains in the river. Harsh critics indeed. It is said that his blood splattered, and permanently stained, the endemic Rodopian flower, the *silivriak* (see p71).

The Greeks avoided most of southern and central Bulgaria because the belligerent Thracians had settled there in large numbers; estimates suggest that during the first millennium BC the Thracians outnumbered the Greeks by four to one between the Danube and the Aegean.

Only a few towns away from the Black Sea show any evidence of Greek settlement. These include Pautalia (Kyustendil), southwest of Sofia, and Silistra on the Danube in northern Bulgaria.

The Rose of the Balkans – A Short History of Bulgaria by Ivan Ilchev offers an up-to-date, detailed survey of the country's colourful history, with a selection of photographs.

However, the Greeks did have a profound influence on religion, arts and culture throughout the Balkans for over 900 years. The Greek language was used extensively by non-Greeks for business, administration and education. The Bulgarian language still has many words of Greek origin, and the patriarch of the Bulgarian Orthodox Church was based in Athens for centuries. Towns such as Sozopol, Melnik and Sandanski still had large Greek populations at the beginning of the 20th century.

In the middle of the 4th century BC, the Macedonians, under the leadership of Philip II, and later his son, Alexander the Great, conquered all of Thrace. Philip made his capital at Philipopolis (Plovdiv), which developed into an important military outpost, while Odessos (Varna) and modern-day Sofia were also occupied. Macedonian rule was to be brief, though, and they soon had the might of Rome to contend with.

…AND THE ROMANS

The Romans defeated the Macedonian Empire in 168 BC, but it wasn't until the middle of the 1st century AD that they began making inroads into the territory of the Thracians, occupying major Greek ports such as Mesembria (Nesebâr). They set up a base at Odessos (Varna), where the largest Roman ruins in Bulgaria, the great Roman Thermae complex, can still be seen (see p240).

865	917	972
Orthodox Christianity is adopted as the official state religion by Khan Boris, who retires in 889. Four years later he suppresses his ruling son Vladimir's attempts to reinstate paganism by deposing and blinding him.	Boris' second son, Tsar Simeon, leads a decisive victory over the Byzantines at the Battle of Acheloi, making the Bulgarian Empire the greatest power in Europe.	The Bulgarian capital, Veliki Preslav, is captured and burnt to the ground by the Byzantines, forcing the Bulgarians to de-camp to Ohrid, their capital until its loss several decades later to the Byzantine Empire.

By AD 46 the Romans had conquered the entire Balkan Peninsula, and the territory of modern-day Bulgaria was initially divided into the provinces of Thrace, in the south, and Moesia, in the north. To shore up vital defensive lines, the Romans built numerous military strongholds and fortified major Thracian and Greek towns along the Danube at Ruse and Bononia (Vidin), and at Debeltus (Burgas) along the Black Sea coast. Although they burned and looted the major Greek settlement of Apollonia, the Romans rebuilt it to become a vital port within the Roman Empire.

The Romans established Ulpia Serdica (Sofia) as the capital of their province of Inner Dacia (northwestern Bulgaria); the most visible reminder of their presence that still stands is the Sveti Georgi Rotunda, or Church of St George (p91). Other towns founded by the Romans, or built on existing settlements of the Thracians, Greeks and Macedonians, include Sevtopolis (Kazanlâk), Ulpia Augusta Trayana (Stara Zagora), Nikopolis-ad-Istrum (situated north of Veliko Târnovo) and Trimontium (Plovdiv), where a magnificent amphitheatre was built that's still used for performances today (see p141). By the late 3rd century AD, Ulpia Serdica had become a major regional imperial capital, where Diocletian and subsequent emperors held court.

Remnants of Roman settlements can be admired in many places, even as far west as Belogradchik. In central Bulgaria, the Romans were the first to build a real fortress on top of Tsarevets Hill in Veliko Târnovo (see p171). They built extensive walls, which partially still stand, at Hisarya (Hisar; see p196) to protect valuable fresh water sources.

Goths, Visigoths, Vandals, Huns and a distressing array of other 'barbarian' tribes began descending on the Roman provinces of Bulgaria from the 3rd century AD onwards, causing much havoc, although such raids were sporadic and short-lived.

DID YOU KNOW?

Bogomilism was a 10th-century Bulgarian heresy based on the notion of two deities, one good, one evil. A similar creed surfaced in France, where it was known as Catharism.

HOLY ALPHABET

Born in Thessaloniki in the early 9th century to a noble Byzantine family, the brothers Kiril (Cyril) and Metodii (Methodius) were scholars and monks who studied and worked throughout the Balkans. They are revered in Bulgaria for developing, around 855, the first Bulgarian alphabet, called Glagolic, which was thought to better represent the sounds of the Bulgarian language than the Greek alphabet, which had previously been in use. It was later simplified by one of their disciples, Clement, and became known as the Cyrillic alphabet. But, more importantly, they helped spread Orthodox Christianity throughout the Balkans by promoting the use of Slavic as the fourth official language of the Church (after Latin, Greek and Hebrew).

The Cyrillic alphabet is now used in Bulgaria, Russia, Macedonia, Ukraine, Belarus, Serbia and Mongolia. Bulgarians even celebrate Cyrillic Alphabet Day (also known as the Day of Bulgarian Culture) on 24 May.

1014	1018	1185–1396
Fifteen thousand Bulgarian soldiers are captured and, according to gory legend, blinded by Byzantine Emperor Basil II (later nicknamed 'the Bulgar Slayer') and sent back to Tsar Samuel.	The Bulgarian capital city of Ohrid is finally captured by the advancing Byzantine Empire, and Bulgaria loses its independence for almost 170 years.	Successfully rising up against the Byzantine Empire, aristocratic brothers Asen and Petâr establish the Second Bulgarian Empire, making Veliko Târnovo its capital city. Tsar Ivan Asen II (1218–41) expands Bulgaria's borders.

BYZANTINES & BULGARS

The Byzantine Commonwealth by Dimitri Obolensky presents a detailed and erudite survey of the development of Byzantine culture in the medieval Balkans.

In 330 the city of Constantinople (modern Istanbul) was founded by the Roman emperor Constantine the Great on the site of ancient Byzantium, and was declared the capital of the Eastern Roman Empire. The division of the empire meant that the Bulgarian provinces were now ruled from that city. By the late 4th century, the Western Roman Empire fell apart, but the East continued for another thousand years, as the Byzantine Empire. The 6th-century rule of Emperor Justinian the Great was a relatively peaceful time for Bulgaria – Sofia's original Church of Sveta Sofia (p91) was built at this time – but the following centuries saw growing numbers of Slavs, Avars and Bulgars breaching the empire's borders.

In 632 the numerous Bulgar tribes, whose territories stretched from the Black Sea to the Caspian Sea, were united under the overlordship of Khan Kubrat, and by the middle of the 7th century they had moved into the land of modern-day Bulgaria. The Byzantines, unable to cope with the vast influx, allowed them to stay. This fierce Turkic tribe settled throughout the region, subjugating and integrating with the Slavs and the remaining Thracians.

DID YOU KNOW?

The 9th-century Bulgar ruler Khan Krum 'The Dreadful' earned his sobriquet from his fierceness in battle and his collection of enemy skulls – including that of Byzantine Emperor Nicephorus – which he used as wine goblets.

Khan (Tsar) Asparuh (r 681–700) was responsible for establishing what became known as the First Bulgarian Empire (681–1018), creating a capital at Pliska, near modern-day Shumen. The empire expanded south and west under Khan Tervel (r 701–718) and was revered for repelling an Arab advance on Constantinople.

Conflict between Byzantium and the Bulgars continued over the centuries, with Khan Krum 'The Dreadful' (r 803–814) besieging Constantinople after the Byzantines burnt down Pliska.

Golden Times

The 9th century was Bulgaria's apogee in many ways, with several tsars expanding the kingdom's territory: Khan Omurtag (r 814–831) captured Hungary in 829, and by the end of Khan Presian's reign (r 837–852) the Bulgarian state encompassed a huge swath of southeastern Europe, including modern-day Romania, Moldova and Macedonia.

In 865 Tsar Boris I (r 852–889) tried to unify the fledgling Bulgar-Slav Empire by converting it to Christianity. At about this time, an independent church was established and a Slavonic alphabet devised by two monks, Kiril and Metodii, known in English as Cyril and Methodius (see the boxed text, p35).

The Legend of Basil the Bulgar-Slayer by Paul Stephenson offers a scholarly reinterpretation of the medieval Byzantine emperor and his campaigns in Bulgaria.

Boris retired to a monastery in 889, leaving his son Vladimir in control, but was roused out of retirement by Vladimir's attempts to restore paganism. Boris deposed his son, blinding him as extra punishment, and his younger brother Simeon (r 893–927) ascended the throne. The empire reached its zenith under Tsar Simeon, who transferred the capital to Veliki Preslav and ushered in a cultural golden age. The Bulgarian Empire, which stretched

1204	1381–95	1396
Tsar Kaloyan gains papal support for the expansion of the Bulgarian Empire by converting to Roman Catholicism, but most Bulgarians remain loyal to the Orthodox Church. Kaloyan is murdered in a coup in 1207; the old religion is restored in 1232.	As the Bulgarian tsar's powers grow ever weaker, the brothers John and Constantine Dragash establish a short-lived independent principality based in Velbâzhd (Kyustendil), covering southeastern Bulgaria and Macedonia.	Bulgaria's last native king, Tsar Ivan Shishman (1371–96), is defeated and the whole of Bulgaria is finally incorporated into the expansive Ottoman Empire, ushering in 500 years of harsh, feudal rule from Constantinople.

from the Adriatic Sea to the Aegean Sea and to the Dnieper River (northeast of Bulgaria) was the largest and most powerful in Europe at that time, and the powerful Bulgarian army routed the invading Byzantines at the Battle of Acheloi (near Nesebâr) in 917.

Decline & Fall

Tsar Peter's reign (r 927–968) was long and peaceful, but internal conflicts led to its decline. In 971 Preslav fell to the Byzantines and Tsar Samuel (r 978–1014) moved the capital to Ohrid (in modern-day Macedonia). At the Battle of Belasitsa in 1014, the Byzantines defeated the Bulgars; according to gory (but probably fanciful) legend, Emperor Basil II ('the Bulgar Slayer') ordered 15,000 Bulgarian soldiers to be blinded and marched back to Samuel, who promptly expired from grief (he actually died some months after the battle). In 1018 Ohrid fell, and Bulgaria officially became part of the Byzantine Empire.

In 1185 two aristocratic brothers, Asen and Petâr, led a general uprising against the Byzantines and the Second Bulgarian Empire (1185–1396) was founded, with Veliko Târnovo as the capital.

In 1204 the Byzantines fell victim to the forces of the Fourth Crusade, whose leader, Baldwin of Flanders, declared himself emperor. Invading Bulgaria the following year, though, he was captured and spent the rest of his days imprisoned in a tower (which still bears his name) at the fortress in Veliko Târnovo (see p171).

(see p171)

> **DID YOU KNOW?**
>
> Peasant revolt leader Ivailo the Swineherd was crowned tsar in 1277. He claimed to be divinely inspired but was killed by the Tatars three years later, after fleeing a court coup.

LADISLAS & THE LAST CRUSADE

By the early 15th century, Bulgaria, Serbia and Transylvania had fallen to the advancing armies of the Ottoman Empire, Hungary looked vulnerable and things were looking increasingly bleak for beleaguered Byzantium. It seemed only a matter of time before the mighty Christian capital of Constantinople itself fell. It was within this desperate atmosphere that Pope Eugenius IV called for a crusade against the Turks, and in 1443 a 25,000-strong army under the leadership of King Ladislas of Hungary and Poland set sail from Venice. They scored early successes, sweeping through Serbia and taking Sofia, and in the summer of 1444, Sultan Murad II, who was facing insurrections on all sides of his empire, agreed to territorial concessions – including the return of Serbia – and a 10-year truce. The Pope and the other sponsors of the crusade were not happy with this arrangement, however, and forced Ladislas to break his agreement and continue the fight to push the Turks out of Europe altogether. It was to prove a disastrous mistake. With a smaller force, Ladislas marched across Bulgaria to Varna, hoping to meet up with a fleet carrying reinforcements. It never arrived. The sultan, with 80,000 men behind him, rushed up the coast; on 10 November 1444 they met the much smaller crusader army in the Battle of Varna. Ladislas was killed and his army almost entirely destroyed. Constantinople fell to the Turks just nine years later, and Ottoman expansion continued throughout the region. It would be centuries before the Balkans were free again.

1444	1598	1686
The Battle of Varna results in crushing defeat for an army largely composed of Hungarians and Serbs by a much larger Turkish force. It is the last battle of the last crusade against the Ottomans.	Religious and civic leaders head the First Târnovo Uprising against Turkish rule, briefly liberating Veliko Târnovo and crowning a new tsar, but the revolt is brutally crushed and thousands of Bulgarians flee over the border to Wallachia.	Major military defeats inflicted on the Turks by the Austrian army encourage widespread armed revolt in northern Bulgaria, but the Second Târnovo Uprising – as it became known – is swiftly put down.

Through skilful diplomacy, Asen's son, Tsar Ivan Asen II (r 1218–41), became the most powerful ruler in southeastern Europe and established Veliko Târnovo as an influential cultural centre. His most famous military victory was the crushing defeat of the Byzantine army at the Battle of Klokotnitsa in 1230. After the death of Tsar Ivan Asen II, the empire was weakened by Tatar and Arab invasions but in the end, internal fighting among Bulgarian leaders effectively brought an end to the unified Bulgarian state.

A Short History of Byzantium by John Julius Norwich is an absorbing overview of the medieval Byzantine Empire by one of the world's leading experts in the field.

UNDER THE YOKE

The Ottoman Turks swarmed into the northern Balkan Peninsula in 1362 and within the next 30 years they had conquered all of Bulgaria, which was subsumed into the Ottoman Empire where it remained for the next five centuries. Turkish rule meant the imposition of a harsh feudal system, and the isolation of Bulgaria from the rest of Christian Europe. Huge numbers of Bulgarians – some estimates say half the entire population – were either killed or carried off into slavery and many churches and monasteries were destroyed or closed. Numerous uprisings were put down with cruel ferocity, and many Bulgarians emigrated.

The Crusade of Varna 1443–45 by Colin Imber is a thorough academic investigation into this calamitous period, including eyewitness accounts from each side, available in English translation for the first time.

Turkish overlords settled in urban areas, forcing Bulgarians to flee into the mountains and rural regions. *Haidouks* (armed rebels) took to the hills and fought the occupiers in any way they could, while others, especially in the Rodopi region, were forced to convert to Islam, receiving exemption from tax and some rights in the law courts in return. These Pomaks, as they became known, were despised by their fellow Bulgarians, and remained a source of bitterness for centuries. Bulgarian national and cultural identity managed to survive in isolated monasteries, such as Rila, which were allowed to remain open, or were never found or controlled by the Turks. Taxes owed to the sultan by the Christian Bulgarians were oppressive, and eldest sons were routinely removed from their families to be trained for the elite janissary corps, which provided a bodyguard for the sultan.

BREAKING FREE

Bulgaria's monasteries had done much to preserve the country's history and traditions during the darkest days of Turkish rule, and nationalist sentiment had never been entirely subdued. However, the era that was to become known as the Bulgarian National Revival was prompted by the work of a monk, Paisii Hilendarski, who wrote the first complete history of the Slav-Bulgarian people in 1762. He travelled across Bulgaria reading the history to illiterate people (the authorities would not allow the publication of a Bulgarian-language book) and ignited a long-suppressed national identity. By the early 19th century, the Bulgarian economy was growing fast. Merchants in towns such as Plovdiv and Koprivshtitsa were supplying wool, wine, metals and woodcarvings to the ailing Ottoman Empire and Western Europe, and

1762	**1854–56**	**1876**
The National Revival era begins with the dissemination of Paisii Hilendarski's *Slav-Bulgarian History*, and continues into the 19th century, when Bulgarian-language education (1840s) and the Bulgarian Orthodox Church (1870) are established.	The Crimean War brings British and French troops to Bulgaria, and Varna becomes an important garrison town. The Turks are persuaded to open up Bulgaria to international trade.	The April Uprising against Ottoman rule begins in Koprivshtitsa; its quick suppression is followed by civilian massacres, causing international outrage. In November, the Turks reject Bulgarian autonomy at the Constantinople Conference.

a new educated, prosperous, urban middle class was emerging, a process that quickened further after the Crimean War, when the victorious allies persuaded Turkey to open up its empire to foreign trade.

These merchants built grand private homes and public buildings, often in the distinct National Revival style (see p54). They were decorated by woodcarvers from Tryavna and painters from Samokov, who had developed a unique Bulgarian style.

Bulgarian art, music and literature also flourished at this time, and schools with instruction in the Bulgarian language were opened. There were *chitalishta* (reading rooms) in nearly every town and village, which provided the people with a communal forum for cultural and social activities – and for political discussions. Official Turkish recognition of an autonomous Bulgarian Orthodox Church in 1870 was a crucial step towards independence.

Travels in European Turkey in 1850 by Edmund Spencer is a first-hand travelogue giving a rare insight into the later years of Ottoman rule in the Balkans.

REVOLUTION & FREEDOM

Rebel leaders, such as Georgi Rakovski, Hristo Botev and Bulgaria's iconic hero Vasil Levski (see the boxed text, p197), had been preparing a revolution against the Turks for years before the rebellion, known as the 1876 April Uprising, prematurely started at Koprivshtitsa.

The Turks brutally suppressed the uprising: an estimated 30,000 Bulgarians were massacred and 58 villages were destroyed. The largest massacre occurred in the town of Batak (see the boxed text, p163).

These atrocities caused outrage in Western Europe and led Russia to declare war on the Ottomans in 1877 after the indecisive Constantinople Conference. Major battles were fought at Pleven and Shipka Pass and about 200,000 Russian soldiers were killed throughout Bulgaria during the year-long Russo-Turkish War. As the Russian army, and its Bulgarian volunteers, crushed the Turks and advanced to within 50km of Istanbul, the Ottomans accepted defeat. It ceded 60% of the Balkan Peninsula to Bulgaria in the Treaty of San Stefano, signed on 3 March 1878.

However, fearing the creation of a powerful Russian ally in the Balkans, the powers of Western Europe reversed these gains at the Treaty of Berlin, signed 13 July 1878. They decided that the area between the Stara Planina ranges and the Danube, plus Sofia, would become the independent principality of Bulgaria. The Thracian Plain and Rodopi Mountains to the south would become Eastern Rumelia and, bizarrely, were placed under Ottoman stewardship. The Aegean Thracian plain and Macedonia were returned outright to Turkey. The legacy of the Treaty of Berlin carved up the region irrespective of ethnicity and left every Balkan nation feeling cheated and angry. These redefined borders have haunted the peninsula ever since: between 1878 and WWII the Balkan countries, including Bulgaria, fought six wars over border issues.

The Balkans 1804–1999: Nationalism, War and the Great Powers by Misha Glenny explores the historic background to the ethnic strife and conflicts that have beset the region.

1877–78	1878	1885
Russo-Turkish War; the Russian army, headed by Tsar Alexander II, invades Bulgaria and inflicts a heavy defeat on the forces of the Ottoman Empire, forcing the Turks to sign the Treaty of San Stefano, ceding 60% of the Balkan Peninsula to Bulgaria.	Only four months after the gains of San Stefano, the Western European powers carve Bulgaria up at the Treaty of Berlin, fearing a 'Big Bulgaria' will be too powerful a Russian ally.	Bulgaria is reunited with its Ottoman-controlled lands in a bloodless coup. The Turks prepare for war and Serbia invades Bulgaria, but is soon defeated. The country's new borders are internationally recognised.

THE MACEDONIAN QUESTION   *Christopher Deliso*

For many Bulgarians, there is no question: Macedonians are simply Bulgarians in denial, their country, really a part of the Bulgarian state, unfairly detached by bad luck and Great-Powers intrigues. No wonder Bulgaria's self-proclaimed Macedonian minority is now having such a tough time gaining acceptance.

Since the medieval Bulgarian Empire included much of today's Republic of Macedonia (as well as modern Greece's Macedonian province), 19th-century Bulgarian nationalism preached that Macedonia should be retaken, once the Turks were overthrown. After the 1877–78 Russo-Turkish War, Bulgaria was awarded much of both Macedonia and Thrace by the Treaty of San Stefano. However, the Great Powers, fearing Russia's Balkan expansion, forced a new peace conference. The resulting Treaty of Berlin drastically reduced San Stefano's proposed borders, causing great resentment and feeding decades of strife.

In August 1903, unending Turkish atrocities against Macedonia's Christian populations provoked the Ilinden Uprising, which created the Balkans' first republic, in the Macedonian mountain town of Krushevo. Although the Turks soon crushed the rebellion, both Macedonians and Bulgarians consider it essential to their national heritage.

While both governments agreed to joint celebrations of Ilinden Day (2 August), Bulgaria has taken a hardline attitude towards its Macedonian minority, propelled by inflammatory media reports and ultranationalists' rhetoric. Indeed, despite being the first country to recognise the independent Macedonian state after it peacefully separated from Yugoslavia in 1991, Bulgaria doesn't recognise the Macedonian identity, language or church.

For many Macedonians and Bulgarians, the Pirin Mountain region is considered part of the geographical Macedonia, the subregion 'Pirin Macedonia'. However, this doesn't mean (as Bulgarian journalists and politicians darkly intone) a threat of annexation by the Macedonian state. 'We just want to live in peace, in a truly multiethnic and democratic country', says 34-year-old Stojko Stojkov, a co-president of OMO-Ilinden, a group representing Bulgaria's Macedonian minority.

OMO-Ilinden has repeatedly tried and failed to become a political party. Bulgarian law requires candidate groups to provide a list of at least 5000 members – including their addresses and telephone and ID numbers. This information proved useful in December 2006 when the Bulgarian government ordered all 6000 members of OMO-Ilinden to be rounded up for police interrogation. While this Stalinesque decision conjured up dark images of Bulgaria's communist and nationalist past, it was ignored by the European Union, which welcomed Bulgaria into its club on 1 January 2007. Police later intimidated Macedonians attending the annual commemoration of revolutionary Yane Sandanski at his tomb at Rozhen Monastery. Small provocations still occur.

While the Strasbourg-based European Court of Human Rights has ruled in OMO-Ilinden's favour, and the Council of Europe has also condemned the Bulgarian government's heavy-handed approach, in Bulgaria itself, says Stojkov, 'only the Bulgarian Helsinki Human Rights Committee supports us'.

At the time of writing, the Bulgarian Supreme Court had just denied OMO-Ilinden's appeal of a lower court's ruling against it. Nevertheless, Stojkov's confident things will eventually improve. 'Bulgaria is in the European Union now – they have to allow us to represent ourselves. The only question is how and when.'

1908	1912–13	1919
Prince Ferdinand takes advantage of political chaos in Turkey to declare full independence from Ottoman suzerainty. Bulgaria upgrades its status from a principality to a kingdom, and Ferdinand is crowned tsar.	Bulgaria and its neighbours fight Turkey in the First Balkan War (1912), reclaiming more territory from the Ottoman Empire. The allies fall out over the spoils and Bulgaria is defeated by Greece and Serbia in the Second Balkan War (1913).	The Treaty of Neuilly punishes Bulgaria for its German alliance in WWI, granting huge swaths of land to its neighbours and saddling the government with crippling and humiliating reparation payments.

The Nascent State

On 16 April 1879 the first Bulgarian national assembly was convened at Veliko Târnovo in order to adopt a constitution, and on 26 June of that year Alexander Battenberg, a German prince, was elected head of state. On 6 September 1885 the principality of Bulgaria and Eastern Rumelia were reunified after a bloodless coup. This contravention of the Treaty of Berlin angered the central European powers and Turkish troops advanced to the southern border of the reunified Bulgaria.

Serbia, supported by the Austro-Hungarian Empire, suddenly declared war on Bulgaria. Heroic Bulgarian border guards defied the odds and repelled advancing Serbian troops while the Bulgarian army hurriedly moved from the Turkish border to the western front. Eventually, the Bulgarians defeated the Serbs and advanced deep within Serbian territory. Austria intervened, calling for a ceasefire, and the Great Powers recognised the reunified Bulgaria.

THE WAR YEARS

Alexander was forced to abdicate in 1886 and was replaced by Prince (later King) Ferdinand of the Saxe-Coburg-Gotha family. Around this time the prime minister, Stefan Stambolov, accelerated the country's economic development and two Bulgarian political parties were founded that would wield enormous influence in the years ahead. These were the Social Democrats, forerunner to the communists, and the Agrarian Union, which represented the peasantry.

King Ferdinand I declared Bulgaria's complete independence from Ottoman control on 22 September 1908. But only four years later, the First Balkan War broke out when Bulgaria, Greece and Serbia declared war on Turkey. Although these states succeeded in largely pushing the Turks out of the Balkans, squabbling among the victors, especially over claims to Macedonia, led to the Second Balkan War (1913), from which Bulgaria emerged a loser.

Bulgaria entered WWI on the side of the Central Powers (which ironically included Turkey) in 1915. Facing widespread opposition to his pro-German policies, Ferdinand abdicated three years later in favour of his son, Boris III.

Between Wars

In the 1919 Treaty of Neuilly, Bulgaria lost Aegean Thrace to Greece, the southern Dobrudzha to Romania, and was saddled with humiliating and crippling war reparations. The interwar period was marked by political and social unrest, and the ruling Agrarian Party's radical agenda and willingness to renounce territorial claims to Macedonia resulted in a right-wing military coup in 1923, while in 1925 communist terrorists tried, unsuccessfully, to kill Boris III at Sofia's Sveta Nedelya Cathedral, murdering 123 people in the process. The 1930s saw the rise of the right-wing Zveno group, which staged a coup d'état in 1934, and after 1935, Tsar Boris assumed dictatorial powers.

DID YOU KNOW?

The Russian Tsar, Alexander II, known to Bulgarians as Tsar Osvoboditel (Tsar Liberator) for freeing Bulgaria from the Ottoman Empire, abolished serfdom in his empire in 1861. He was assassinated in 1881.

Crown of Thorns: The Reign of King Boris III of Bulgaria by Stephane Groueff tells the intriguing story of Bulgaria's war-time monarch.

DID YOU KNOW?

Communist leader Georgi Dimitrov first found fame when he was accused, along with three others, of starting the infamous Reichstag fire in Berlin in 1933. Stalin later secured a deal for his release.

1923	1940	1941
Prime Minister Aleksander Stambolyiski is assassinated in a bloody coup by right-wing military supporters of Macedonian revolutionaries. A communist uprising that year is brutally repressed and the communist party is banned.	The Southern Dobrudzha region, occupied by Romania since the end of the Balkan Wars, is finally returned to Bulgaria for a nominal fee and Bulgarian troops make a triumphant entry into Balchik and other towns.	After declaring neutrality at the start of WWII, Bulgaria is persuaded to join the Axis powers after German troops are stationed along the Danube, and declares war on Britain and France, but not on the Soviet Union.

World War II

At the beginning of WWII Bulgaria declared its neutrality. However, by 1941 German troops advancing towards Greece were stationed along the Danube on Bulgaria's northern border with Romania. To avoid a war it could not win, and tempted by Hitler's offer of Macedonia in return for assistance, the militarily weak Bulgarian government decided to join the Axis. Bulgaria allowed the Nazis into the country and officially declared war on Britain and France, but it refused to accede to demands that it declare war on Russia. Spurred by public opinion, the Bulgarian government also held back from handing over the country's 50,000 Jews to the Third Reich. Tsar Boris III died suddenly on 28 August 1943, one week after meeting Hitler, prompting the inevitable conspiracy theories about murder, through slow-acting poison, though current research has found no evidence of this. Boris' infant son succeeded him as Tsar Simeon II.

During the winter of 1943–44, Allied air raids inflicted heavy damage on Sofia and other major towns in central Bulgaria. A hastily formed coalition government sought a separate peace with the Allies, but to no avail. Then Russia declared war and invaded Bulgaria. On 9 September 1944 the Fatherland Front, a resistance group coalition that included communists, assumed power. Even before WWII had ended, 'people's courts' were set up around the country at which thousands of members of the wartime 'monarch-fascist' government were sent to prison or executed.

RED BULGARIA

The Fatherland Front won the November 1945 elections and the communists gained control of the new national assembly. Under leader Georgi Dimitrov, a new constitution, created on the Soviet model, proclaimed the People's Republic of Bulgaria on 15 September 1946. The royal family was forced into exile.

From the late 1940s, industrialisation and the collectivisation of agriculture was imposed, and opponents, 'class traitors' or any other awkward individuals were harshly dealt with by the strict Stalinist regime, often through the ever-popular show trials. Dimitrov's successor, Vâlko Chervenkov was known as 'Little Stalin' for his unquestioning loyalty. Under Todor Zhivkov, Bulgaria's leader from 1954 to 1989, the country prospered under Soviet protection, which included cheap oil, electricity and other necessities. However, this boon came at a price, and the Bulgarian secret police had an especially fearsome reputation for their handling of dissidents, at home or abroad, and were even rumoured to have been plotting the assassination of Pope John Paul II. A ruthless nationalism came to the fore in the 1980s, when Turks, Pomaks and Roma were pressured into adopting Bulgarian names. Riots and a mass exodus of ethnic Turks resulted.

Beyond Hitler's Grasp: The Heroic Rescue of Bulgaria's Jews by Michael Bar-Zohar is a thought-provoking account of the heroism of ordinary Bulgarians in protecting their Jewish neighbours from the Nazis during WWII.

The Diary of Georgi Dimitrov, 1933–1949, edited by Ivo Banac, gives a revealing insight into the mind of Bulgaria's first communist ruler and his relationship with Stalin.

Voices from the Gulag: Life and Death in Communist Bulgaria, edited by Tzvetan Todorov, is a collection of first-hand accounts from inmates, guards and bureaucrats of the horrors of the communist system.

1945–46	1957	1958
After scoring victories in the 1945 elections, the communists gain power under their leader Georgi Dimitrov. In 1946 the People's Republic of Bulgaria is proclaimed with backing from the Soviet Union.	The first hotel opens in the planned package beach resort of Golden Sands (Zlatni Pyasâtsi), marking the start of mass tourism in Bulgaria. In the 1960s, it becomes a popular holiday destination for tourists from across the Eastern Bloc.	The communist government initiates a mass collectivisation of agriculture in a programme known as 'The Great Leap Forward', intending to fulfil its five-year plan for modernisation in just three years.

THE RETURN OF DEMOCRACY

By 1989 *perestroika* was sending shock waves throughout Eastern Europe. On 10 November 1989 an internal Communist Party coup led to the resignation of the ageing Zhivkov, and the Communist Party agreed to relinquish its monopoly on power, changing its name to the Bulgarian Socialist Party (BSP). In opposition, a coalition of 16 different groups formed the Union of Democratic Forces (UDF). However, the BSP comfortably won the first parliamentary elections in June 1990, so Bulgaria had the dubious honour of being the first country from the former Soviet Bloc to elect communists back into power.

However, the BSP soon lost favour with the electorate, and the UDF managed a narrow victory in the October 1991 parliamentary elections. Within a year, though, their government had collapsed. After a caretaker government of technocrats was similarly unable to deal with the financial disarray, the BSP again captured, in overwhelming fashion, the December 1994 parliamentary elections. Meanwhile, Zhelyu Zhelev of the UDF became the new Bulgarian head of state after the first democratic presidential elections in January 1992.

The mid-1990s was a period of economic chaos, marked by hyperinflation and a sharp drop in living standards, which included the return of bread lines and fuel shortages, while legitimised criminal networks flaunted their new-found wealth.

The election of liberal lawyer Petâr Stoyanov of the UDF as president in November 1996, coupled with the resignation of the unpopular socialist prime minister Zhan Videnov, signalled that the electorate was finally fed up. Nationwide protests and highway blockades eventually forced the discredited BSP to agree to new parliamentary elections.

April 1997 ushered in the seventh change of government in as many years. Ivan Kostov of the United Democratic Forces (UDF), a coalition that included the other UDF, became prime minister and promised to combat corruption and attract foreign investment while adhering to market reforms. But like leaders of all former communist countries, Kostov had to make harsh economic decisions, which pleased the International Monetary Fund (IMF) and EU, but not the voters.

DID YOU KNOW?

The body of communist leader Georgi Dimitrov, who died in 1949, lay embalmed in Sofia until 1990. His mausoleum was dynamited in 1999.

Into the 21st Century

In June 2001 the Bulgarian electorate made history by voting in their former king as prime minister – the first ex-monarch to return to power in Eastern Europe. Simeon Saxe-Coburg, or Simeon II as he is still often known, had formed his party, the National Movement Simeon II (NMSII), only two months before the election. Saxe-Coburg had lived most of his life in Spain and although he did not actually run for a parliamentary seat, the rules still allowed him to become prime minister.

DID YOU KNOW?

Former king, prime minister and NMSII party leader Simeon Saxe-Coburg is a distant relative of Queen Elizabeth II.

1978	1981	1984
In a murky scenario that could have been written by Ian Fleming, Bulgarian dissident Georgi Markov is assassinated in London with a poisoned umbrella tip by an agent of the Bulgarian secret service.	Bulgaria celebrates the 1300th anniversary of the founding of the Bulgarian state, spending lavish amounts of money on nationwide celebrations and the building of public monuments.	A nationalistic campaign begins, aimed at forcing the country's ethnic Turkish population to adopt Bulgarian names and assimilate into mainstream Bulgarian society. A mass exodus of Turks ensues.

The party won exactly half the seats in parliament and entered into a coalition with the Turkish Movement for Rights and Freedoms (MRF), the party with the smallest number of elected representatives. The new government raised the minimum wage from 85 lv to 100 lv per month and promised a turnaround in Bulgaria's economic fortunes, pushing for both NATO and EU membership.

However, in a major upset just five months after the new government took office, Petâr Stoyanov, regarded as one of Bulgaria's most popular politicians, was beaten by the Socialist Party leader Georgi Parvanov in the presidential elections. Anyone looking for consistency in Bulgarian politics will be sorely disappointed.

BULGARIA TODAY

Low wages, unemployment and the growth of organised crime, among other things, led to disillusionment with the NMSII, and at the general election of 2005 the BSP was returned as the biggest party. After weeks of stalemate, it finally formed a coalition government with the NMSII and the Turkish MRF party, with the BSP's Sergei Stanishev as prime minister. Turnout for the vote was low, and there was much criticism of the government's decision to offer competition prizes, including cars, as an incentive for people who did turn up at the polling booths. In 2006, Georgi Parvanov won another five-year term as president, in a landslide against a nationalist candidate who opposed EU entry.

Imagining The Balkans by Maria Todorova is an insightful read challenging what the author sees as the historically entrenched, negative images of this 'troubled' corner of Europe.

Bulgaria's entry into NATO in 2004, along with a number of other former Warsaw Pact countries, was welcomed by a Bulgarian population keen to engage with the wider world, and in January 2007 the country, along with neighbouring Romania, finally joined the EU, introducing a third alphabet (Cyrillic) into the multilingual organisation. Already, though, there have been problems, with EU criticism, and threats of fines, over Bulgaria's tardiness in supplying a list of areas to be included in the pan-European Natura 2000 network of protected ecological areas (see p72) and the state of waste management in Sofia; the EU will now supply 80% of the money needed for a new waste recycling plant. The government, meanwhile, scored a small victory after winning the right to call the European common currency the 'Evro' rather than the 'Euro' in Bulgaria, in keeping with local pronunciation.

Discontent over low wages has increased since Bulgaria joined the EU, and 2007 saw a succession of long, drawn-out strikes. Teachers, demanding as much as a 100% wage increase, took industrial action over the summer, and all the teachers in five major cities, including Varna and Burgas, resigned en masse in protest at wages that are among the lowest in Europe. Bulgaria's current minimum wage is just 220 lv (€110) per month.

Corruption continues to be a hot topic, especially around the vast construction projects shooting up in the big tourist resorts. There have been

1989–90	1990	1996–97
Democratic changes sweeping through Eastern Europe reach Bulgaria: Todor Zhivkov's communist regime collapses, but the first free parliamentary elections are won by the Bulgarian Socialist Party, the new name for the old communist party.	After the collapse of the communist regime, elections are held in Bulgaria for the first time and the socialist candidate, Zhelyu Zhelev becomes the country's first democratically elected president.	Massive inflation, widespread corruption and plummeting wages cause an economic crisis, making Bulgaria the poorest country in Europe. The socialist government collapses; elections bring a democratic coalition to power.

numerous campaigns spearheaded by environmentalists against what they see as thoughtless overdevelopment of pristine and supposedly protected areas of the country, all in the name of big business and big money. Organised crime, meanwhile, prompts sighs of exasperation from people who have lost trust in their government to combat it. Bulgaria has become a hub for human trafficking and the drug trade into Europe.

Painful memories of the country's totalitarian past were once again dragged up in the run-up to local elections in 2007, with numerous politicians, including the current president, 'outed' as state security collaborators under the communist regime. What effect all this will have on the government's future, though, is uncertain, but there is a great deal of disenchantment with politicians in general. Far-right nationalism entered the mainstream political arena at the 2005 elections, with 12 members of the ultranationalist Ataka party entering parliament, and wherever they go, controversy is sure to follow.

One of the biggest talking points of recent years was resolved in 2007, when the five Bulgarian nurses imprisoned in Libya since 1999, on charges that they deliberately infected children in their care with HIV, were finally released. The nurses had been sentenced to death, but direct intervention by the EU and France brought the affair to wider world attention.

See www.parliament.bg for more information, in English, on the workings, personnel and policies of the Bulgarian Parliament. More still can be found at www.government.bg.

2001

Bulgaria's former king, the charismatic Simeon Saxe-Coburg, exiled by the communists as a child, is elected prime minister just months after founding a new political party, the National Movement Simeon II.

2004

Bulgaria finally puts its communist past behind it and, along with several other former Warsaw Pact nations, joins NATO. Bulgarian troops are posted overseas in peacekeeping roles.

2007

On 1 January, Bulgaria joins the EU, introducing the Cyrillic alphabet to the polyglot organisation. The Bulgarian government comes under increasing pressure to deal more firmly with organised crime and environmental problems.

The Culture

THE NATIONAL PSYCHE

Living on the edge of Europe, Bulgarians have a fierce pride in their own often tempestuous history and their centuries of struggle against foreign occupation. As the country continues to integrate into the wider world and welcome more foreign tourists, though, many have come to question what exactly it means to be Bulgarian, and are frustrated at the country's lack of a tangible international image. EU membership has provided a confidence boost as people begin to feel more a part of the European mainstream; at the same time they are looking ever more keenly at their own identity. The recent spate of Thracian archaeological discoveries has encouraged interest in this period, which lost out to the study of Slav history during the communist era, and many want Bulgaria's Thracian heritage to be the nation's international trademark.

For a Bulgarian odyssey, read Dani Valent's fascinating account of travelling through her grandparents' home country for the first time. See www.lonelyplanet .com/bulgarianodyssey

Regrettably, Bulgaria and its people remain something of an enigma to most Westerners, but increasing tourism is slowly putting this to rights. Warm and open to strangers, Bulgarians are a welcoming and hospitable people, with an often worldly wise, cynical outlook on life: decades of totalitarian rule and corruption and uneven economic fortunes since have taught them not to expect much of politicians and bureaucrats. Family and friends are of paramount importance and regional loyalties – and rivalries – are often strong, too, although that doesn't diminish their national sensibilities, especially when an international football match is in the offing.

DAILY LIFE

As elsewhere in Eastern Europe, Bulgaria is still largely a conservative and traditional society, and rural life goes on much as it has done for the last century or so, although even the remotest areas are beginning to see the effects of foreign investment as ramshackle old houses are snapped up by developers for holiday homes and construction projects shoot up in and around the more popular areas. Many welcome the extra income brought into these once poor areas, though others lament the social dislocation and environmental damage of overdevelopment.

Things are of course very different in the cities, where Western boutiques, tacky casinos and strip clubs have proliferated, and racks of porn magazines openly decorate every newsstand alongside children's comics and daily newspapers. The gay scene, on the other hand, is still very discreet and mostly confined to Sofia.

All Bulgarians, though, are very proud of their education: the literacy rate in Bulgaria is over 98%, one of the highest in the world. Family life, too, is important: private events such as christenings, weddings, house-warmings and birthdays are celebrated with gusto, as are public festivals and holidays. The severe decline in the birth rate over recent years has resulted in many one-child families, poor maternity leave and low pay having dissuaded many people from starting large families. Since Bulgaria joined the EU, people have been far less patient with poor levels of pay and services, especially as the cost of living rises.

ECONOMY

Bulgaria's transition to a free-market economy after the fall of communism was a painful period in the country's history, characterised by hyperinflation and high unemployment. Things stabilised after the lev was pegged to the Deutschmark in 1997 and subsequently to the Euro in 2002, and the country has experienced an economic upturn since joining the EU in January 2007. Foreign investment and tourism are at all-time highs, fuelling a major construction boom, especially on the Black Sea coast. In fact, the demand has been so great that workers have had to be brought in from as far away as Ukraine to complete building projects.

However, despite the healthy economy and Bulgaria's top-10 ranking in the World Bank's list of best reforming economies in the world, serious problems remain. Bulgaria is the poorest country in the EU, and average wages hover around €200 a month, among the lowest on the continent. In 2007 there were a succession of strikes by nurses, medical staff, miners, public transport drivers and teachers demanding wage increases of up to 100%. With record consumer price inflation reaching 12%, this is unlikely to happen, but now that Bulgaria is a fully fledged EU member, people are far less content with low pay.

It has been estimated, too, that the so-called 'grey economy' – undeclared incomes, 'contract-free' workers and fiddled tax returns – makes up as much as 35% of the economy as a whole, prompting calls for tax cuts and a reduction in VAT (Value Added Tax).

POPULATION

Bulgaria is a small nation of just under 7.5 million people, some 70% of whom now live in urban centres, including Sofia, which is the largest city by far, and (in order of population size) Plovdiv, Varna, Burgas, Ruse, Stara Zagora, Pleven and Sliven. Around 14% of Bulgarians call the capital home.

Bulgaria's population is falling at a faster rate than any other nation in Europe due to a decreasing birth rate, a child mortality rate three times the European average and emigration spurred on by high unemployment, low wages and, since 2007, the opening up of labour markets in other EU member states. It has been estimated that around 1.5 million people have left the country since 1989.

Bulgarians are of Slavic origin and constitute roughly 85% of the population. The largest minority groups are the Turks (9%) and the Roma (4.5%), while the remainder belong to tiny ethnic groups such as the Armenians, Wallachs and Circassians, as well as small numbers of Jews and ethnic Greeks and Russians. Greek populations are found in places such as Sozopol and Sandanski. Most of Bulgaria's 757,000 Turks live in the northeast and in the foothills of the eastern Rodopi Mountains, especially, of course, towards the Turkish border.

The Rodopi Mountains area is home to about 200,000 Pomaks, the descendants of Slavs who converted to Islam during the Ottoman occupation in the 15th century. In the past, they have been subjected to the same assimilatory pressures as the Turks. Some villages in the Rodopis, such as Borino, are almost entirely Pomak.

At the outbreak of WWII, about 50,000 Jews lived in Bulgaria. Although forced to assemble in provincial labour camps, none were turned over to the Nazis despite the fact that the Bulgarian government had formed an alliance with Germany. After the war most Jews left for Israel; only about 5000 still remain in Bulgaria, most in Sofia.

The Orient Within by Mary Neuberger investigates the story of Bulgaria's Muslim minority population, their relationship with the modern state and ideas of national identity.

MULTICULTURALISM

Although it's been invaded, conquered and occupied by countless foreign powers throughout its long history, Bulgaria remains a fairly homogenous nation, with some 85% of the population declaring themselves Bulgarian.

YES OR NO?

Bulgarians shake their head in a curved, almost bouncy, motion to indicate 'yes', and nod their heads to mean 'no' – it's confusing at first, then fun. Just try to think that a shake is sweeping the floor clean ('yes, come in') and a nod is slamming a garage door shut ('no, go away fool!'). To add to the confusion, some Bulgarians may do the opposite to 'help' confused foreigners. If there is any doubt, ask *da ili ne?* (yes or no?).

In 1985 the communists mounted a programme to assimilate the country's Turkish inhabitants by forcing them to accept Bulgarian names. Mosques were also closed down and even wearing Turkish dress and speaking Turkish in public were banned. Mass protests erupted, and in early 1989 about 300,000 Turkish Bulgarians and Pomaks left for Turkey (though many subsequently returned to Bulgaria when the repressive policies were overturned).

Relations between Bulgarians and the ethnic Turkish minority have improved since, and the 2005 election resulted in a coalition government led by the Bulgarian Socialist Party, including the Turkish Movement for Rights and Freedoms party – the third biggest party in parliament. However, racial tensions remain, and the far-right Ataka party, with its aggressively nationalistic rhetoric, hasn't exactly soothed the situation.

Bulgaria's Roma suffer disproportionate rates of unemployment, social deprivation, illiteracy, poverty and prejudice, and public attitudes towards them are rarely sympathetic. They tend to live in ghettos and can be seen begging on the streets all over the country. Along with other East and Central European nations, Bulgaria signed up to the Decade of Roma Inclusion (www.romadecade.org) programme in 2005, which attempts to improve conditions for Roma populations. Some success in providing employment has been claimed, but it remains to be seen if any lasting good comes out of it. In the meantime, the Roma are often subject to abuse. Violent attacks on Roma youths by skinheads in the Roma-dominated Sofia suburb of Krasna Polyana in 2007 led to armed riots, which in turn resulted in the ultra-nationalist Bulgarian People's Union calling for a National Guard of patriotic volunteers to be formed to protect citizens from such menace. It's an ongoing social problem with no easy answers.

Holidays of the Bulgarians in Myths and Legends by Nikolay Nikov is a fascinating account of the traditions and customs associated with all the major festivals.

One topic that excites massive controversy is the 'Macedonian question'. The historical region of Macedonia covered areas of modern-day northern Greece and southwestern Bulgaria, as well as the Republic of Macedonia itself. In 1945 the inhabitants of the Pirin region were named a Macedonian ethnic minority, and there were plans to merge Bulgaria and Macedonia into one country, though all this came to nothing in the end and by the 1960s the ethnic minority status was rescinded. The majority of people living in the Pirin region regard themselves first and foremost as Bulgarian, but movements for regional autonomy such as the Internal Macedonian Revolutionary Organisation (IMRO) still exist (see the boxed text, p40).

MEDIA

Press freedom is a touchy topic in Bulgaria and the country has been criticised by international bodies such as the Paris-based Reporters Without Borders (RSF). In 2007, their annual Press Freedom listings ranked Bulgaria at 51 (down from number 35 in 2006), making the country one of only two EU nations outside the top 50. It has been claimed that reporters are often obstructed or even attacked in the course of their duties, and in 2007 a court dropped charges against police officers who had beaten up a press photographer as he tried to take pictures of a well-known gangster.

In 2000, the Rupert Murdoch–owned Balkan News Corporation launched BTV, the country's first private commercial channel, and in 2003, Nova TV became Bulgaria's second commercial TV channel. In addition, there are now several privately run satellite TV channels, such as 7-Dni, and more than 130 radio stations. Bulgaria National TV (BNT) is the state public broadcaster, operating Kanal 1 and the satellite channel TV Bulgaria.

RELIGION

Orthodox Christianity has been the official religion since 865, though modern Bulgaria is a secular state that allows freedom of religion. The vast majority of the population – around 83% – still professes adherence to the Bulgarian Orthodox Church, although only a fraction of this number actually attends church services on a regular basis. Major holy days do draw out the crowds, however, and attending an Orthodox service is an unforgettable experience for visitors. Worshippers light candles and kiss icons as bearded, golden-robed priests sing and swing their incense burners.

Some 12% of the population is Muslim – ethnic Turks, Pomaks and most Roma. Over the centuries the Islam practised in Bulgaria has incorporated various Bulgarian traditions and Christian beliefs and has become known as Balkan Islam.

There's also a small Jewish population – Judaism arrived in Bulgaria with refugees from Catholic Spain in the 15th century, and is still practised at synagogues in Sofia and Vidin.

Other Christian denominations, including Roman Catholics, Protestants and Armenian Orthodox, account for just under 2% of the nation.

DID YOU KNOW?

Dunovism, founded in Bulgaria after WWI by Peter Dunov, is a religion combining Orthodox Christianity with yoga, meditation and belief in reincarnation.

WOMEN IN BULGARIA

Bulgarian culture has a strong macho edge to it, and although there have been improvements in the status of women in the workplace over recent years, old-fashioned attitudes are still daily facts of life. Pouting, scantily clad women are popular motifs used for advertising everything from alcohol to shopping centres, while a profusion of sleazy strip clubs and escort agencies has appeared in the big cities, colourfully touted in tourist magazines alongside reviews of restaurants and museums.

Women have made it into the top levels of national politics, business, the media and other competitive areas of employment, but most Bulgarian women are still expected to put raising a family before any other commitments. The country's dramatic population decline and very low birth rate, though, have finally prompted the government to act, and better-paid maternity leave and improved childcare are now offered in an effort to both encourage family life and help women back to work sooner after childbirth.

ARTS

Bulgaria has an ancient tradition of icon painting and these religious images are still the most accessible and memorable of Bulgarian art. Five centuries of Turkish rule suppressed much of native Bulgarian culture, but the National Revival of the late 18th to 19th centuries saw a creative blossoming as writers and artists strove to reignite the national consciousness. During the communist era, however, most Bulgarians with artistic, literary, theatrical or musical talents were trained in the former Soviet Union and therefore heavily influenced by the Russians. These days, artistic activity in Bulgaria is at an all-time high.

CHRISTO & JEANNE-CLAUDE

Undoubtedly the most internationally famous living Bulgarian artist is Christo Javacheff, known simply as Christo. Born in Gabrovo in 1935, he studied at Sofia's Fine Arts Academy in the 1950s and met his French-born wife, Jeanne-Claude, in Paris in 1958. They have worked in collaboration since 1961, when they created their first outdoor temporary installation, *Stacked Oil Barrels,* at Cologne Harbour. Since then, the couple, who moved to New York in 1964, have made a name for themselves with their (usually) temporary, large-scale architectural artworks, often involving wrapping famous buildings in fabric or polypropylene sheeting to highlight their basic forms. In 1985 they created *The Pont Neuf Wrapped,* covering the Parisian landmark in golden fabric for 14 days, while in 1995 the Reichstag in Berlin was covered entirely with silver fabric. More recently, *The Gates* was unveiled in New York's Central Park in 2005, an impressive installation consisting of 7503 vinyl gates spread over 32km of walkways. Christo and Jeanne-Claude are still working on major projects around the world, and current schemes still in the planning stage include *The Mastaba,* a gigantic stack of 390,500 barrels to be built in the desert in the UAE. For the latest news, see www.christojeanneclaude.net.

Painting & Sculpture

Most of Bulgaria's earliest artists painted on the walls of homes, churches and monasteries. The most famous was unquestionably Zahari Zograf (1810–53), who painted magnificent murals that can still be admired in the monasteries at Rila, Troyan and Bachkovo. Many of Zograf's works were inspired by medieval Bulgarian art, though they display a more human (if often gory and sadistic) spirit, with naked sinners being inventively tortured by demons (a common and seemingly much-relished motif) alongside the prettier scenes of angels and saints.

Famous Bulgarian artists of the last 150 years include Vladimir Dimitrov, often referred to as 'The Master', Georgi Mashev, Michail Lutov, Zlatyu Boyadjiev and Ivan Angelov. You can see their work in museums and galleries around the country. Contemporary Bulgarian artists include the renowned sculptor Asen Botev and the abstract painter Kolyo Karamfilov. Without doubt, though, the most widely recognised modern Bulgarian artist is Christo (see the boxed text, above).

Bulgarian sculpture developed in the 19th and 20th centuries, and one of the leading lights of the period was Andrei Nikolov (1878–1959), who was influenced by contemporary French styles. His home in Sofia is now a cultural centre and hotel (p103). He designed the stone lion outside Sofia's Tomb of the Unknown Soldier (p91) and more examples of his naturalistic sculptures are on show in the city's National Art Gallery (p90). The works of his contemporary, Ivan Lazarov (1889–1952), were more nationalistic, inspired by the bravery of soldiers and ordinary Bulgarians in wartime. Contemporary sculptors who have enjoyed great success include Georgi Chapkunov, who created the Sofia Monument (p87), Kroum Damianov and Bozhidar Kozarev.

Literature

The first recognised literary work written in Bulgarian was probably *Slav-Bulgarian History* by Paisii Hilendarski (1722–73), an enormously influential work that led to a national revival of Bulgarian cultural heritage and identity from the mid-18th century on.

Bulgaria's most revered author was Ivan Vazov (1850–1921), who wrote *Under the Yoke,* a stirring novel based on the 1876 April Uprising against the Turks. He is commemorated with two house-museums, in Sopot and

Sofia. Other famous literary figures immortalised in museums throughout Bulgaria include Nikola Vaptsarov (in Bansko), Yordan Yovkov (Dobrich) and Dimcho Debelyanov and Lyuben Karavelov (Koprivshtitsa).

Elias Canetti (1905–94) is probably the best internationally known Bulgarian writer of the 20th century. He was born into a Jewish family in Ruse, though lived most of his life in England, writing in German. His most famous work was *Die Blendung* (Auto-da-Fé), published in 1935. He won the Nobel Prize for Literature in 1981.

Less well known overseas, but still held in high regard, is Bogomil Rainov (1919–2007), who wrote several popular novels, such as *There is Nothing Finer Than Bad Weather,* a Cold War spy story from the other side of the Iron Curtain, made into a film in 1971. Other authors, whose works are available in translation, include the poet Blaga Dimitrova (1922–2003) – also vice president of Bulgaria in 1992–93 – and Georgi Gospodinov (b 1968), whose rambling *Natural Novel* (2005) ranges over topics including toilet graffiti, housing estates and bees.

DID YOU KNOW?

The first Bulgarian-language publishing house was founded by Hristo Danov in Plovdiv in 1855. It's now a museum.

Music
OPERA & CHORAL
Bulgaria has an impressive musical tradition, and musical academies continue to produce world-class opera stars such as Boris Hristov, Raina Kabaivanska and Orlin Anastassov.

Emanuil Manolov (1860–1902) wrote the first Bulgarian opera, *Siromahkinia,* based on a work by Ivan Vazov, while Pancho Vladigerov (1899–1978) is acknowledged as Bulgaria's greatest internationally renowned classical composer.

Bulgarian ecclesiastic music dates back to the 9th century and conveys the mysticism of chronicles, fables and legends. To hear Orthodox chants sung by a choir of up to 100 people is a moving experience. Dobri Hristov (1875–1941) was one of Bulgaria's most celebrated composers of church and choral music, and wrote his major choral work, *Liturgy No 1,* for the Seven Saints ensemble, Bulgaria's best-known sacred-music vocal group, based in Sofia's Sveti Sedmochislenitsi Church. The Sofia Boys Choir, formed in 1968, has also performed around the world to great acclaim.

Learn more about Seven Saints, Bulgaria's leading sacred-music vocal ensemble, at www.thesevensaints.com

TRADITIONAL
Alongside the scholarly Byzantine traditions maintained in Orthodox church music is the Turkish influence evident in the folk songs and dances of the rural villages. As in many peasant cultures, Bulgarian women are not given access to musical instruments, so they usually perform the vocal parts. They often practise singing while weaving and doing household chores. Bulgarian female singing is polyphonic, featuring many voices and shifting melodies, and women from villages in the Pirin Mountains are renowned for their unique singing style. Some of the more famous performers include Koyna Stoyanova and Yanka Rupkina.

During the communist era, Bulgarian village music was transformed into a sophisticated art form and communicated worldwide by groups such as the Philip Kutev National Folk Ensemble and recordings such as *Le Mystère des Voix Bulgares.*

DID YOU KNOW?

Music from *Le Mystère des Voix Bulgares* was included in the capsule aboard the *Voyager 2* space probe in the hope of reaching alien ears.

CONTEMPORARY
The most distinctive sound in Bulgarian contemporary music is the spirited, warbling, pop-folk idiom known as *chalga*. Bands usually feature a scantily clad female lead vocalist and play jazzed-up traditional Balkan tunes on instruments such as the electric guitar, clarinet and synthesizer. Some of the

---

RECOMMENDED LISTENING

▪ **Bulgarian Folk Songs and Dances featuring Petko Radev and Petko Dachev** (2000) – a top-selling collection of traditional tunes

▪ **Twin Kingdoms** (2001) by Georgi Andreev – the music from the colourful stage show (see below)

▪ **Orthodox Chants** (2004) by Orlin Anastassov and the Seven Saints Choir – sacred sounds from the young opera star and the highly respected church vocal group

▪ **Diva** (2006) by Azis – pop-folk from Bulgaria's most flamboyant transvestite

▪ **Best Ballads** (2007) by Emilia – the biggest hits of one of Bulgaria's top *chalga* stars

▪ **Contact** (2004) by the Balkan Horses Band – innovative prog-rock played with traditional Balkan instruments

▪ **Bulgarian Impressions** (2000) by Pancho Vladigerov – some of the composer's most popular works

---

biggest names in contemporary *chalga* include Gloria, Emilia and, especially, Azis (real name Vassil Boyanov), one of Bulgaria's most recognisable and most unlikely stars. A gay, white-bearded, transvestite Roma, his concerts regularly attract thousands of fans. Also popular is the experimental band Isihia, which incorporates traditional elements into its music, and the progressive-rock combo Balkan Horses Band, an international ensemble whose members come from Bulgaria, Macedonia, Turkey and other countries in the region.

See www.balkanhorses band.com for background information and details of upcoming gigs by the popular cross-cultural prog-rock group.

Other Bulgarian artists worth looking out for are Akaga, who play a mix of folk and techno; Grafa, the so-called 'prince of ballads'; and Stoian Iankulov and Elitsa, who represented Bulgaria at the 2007 Eurovision Song Contest.

Theatre

Every city and major town has at least one theatre, many of them built during the communist era, offering Bulgarian and foreign plays, classical music and operas.

Perhaps more accessible to foreign visitors, musical theatre has also taken off in recent years. The most successful theatre group is the National Art Dance Company, which made its debut at the National Palace of Culture (NDK) in Sofia in 2000 with *Twin Kingdoms,* a contemporary take on Bulgaria's folk-cultural heritage by composer Georgi Andreev. It uses traditional Bulgarian instruments and a variety of musical influences, ranging from baroque to Byzantine and even Balinese styles, to tell a lavish fairy tale of abducted maidens, dragons and witches. This show also has the distinction of being the first-ever Bulgarian production staged on Broadway. The company's other shows include the Gypsy legend–inspired *Aramii* and *Are You Ready?,* a more up-to-date show combining rap, hip-hop, Gypsy music and traditional Bulgarian tunes. Shows are staged across Bulgaria and the troupe often performs overseas. Visit www.neshkaart.com for details.

Another show worth seeing if you get the chance is *This is Bulgaria,* a lively musical romp through the nation's history staged by Bulgare (www .bulgare.net).

Note that most theatres close during July and August, while Sofia's National Palace of Culture (p103) offers a year-round programme of international acts.

Cinema

Few Bulgarian films, even those that receive international accolades, get seen overseas. However, recent well-received movies include *Stolen Eyes* (2004), about the fraught relationship between a Christian man and his Muslim girlfriend during the troubled 1980s; *Monkeys in Winter* (2006), chronicling the woe-filled lives and loves of three women living at different periods in Bulgaria over the last four decades; and the downbeat but award-winning *Lady Zee* (2005), about the delicate issues of race, poverty and social exclusion in modern Bulgaria. (There aren't a lot of laughs in Bulgarian cinema.) *Investigation* (2006), a joint Bulgarian-Dutch-German murder mystery directed by Iglika Trifonova, won awards for Best Bulgarian Feature Film and Best Balkan Film at the 2007 Sofia International Film Festival (www.cinema.bg/sff).

Esteemed Bulgarian directors include Peter Popzlatev, Ivanka Grabcheva, Mariana Evstatieva and Ivan Nitchev, who directed the joint German-Bulgarian movie *Journey to Jerusalem* (2003), a sensitive drama about two German-Jewish children fleeing persecution who get stranded at Sofia train station.

Foreign films – such as *The Cherry Orchard* (1999), *The Contractor* (2007), and *Return to House on Haunted Hill* (2007) – are sometimes shot in Bulgaria because of the cheap labour, reliable weather and varied backdrops.

Traditional Crafts

Bulgarian carpets, rugs and traditional costumes were first made as early as the 9th century, but were most popular and creative during the Bulgarian National Revival period. Sadly, weaving is a dying art, practised only by a dwindling band of elderly ladies who still work on handmade looms in a few remote villages such as Chiprovtsi, Kotel and Koprivshtitsa.

Carpets and rugs made in the southern Rodopi Mountains are thick, woollen and practical, while in western Bulgaria they're often delicate, colourful and more decorative. The carpet-making industry began in Chiprovtsi around the late 17th century, with patterns based mainly on geometric abstract shapes. The more popular designs featuring birds and flowers, commonly seen in tourist shops today, were developed in the 19th century.

Woodcarving reached its peak during the National Revival period. While weaving was practised mostly by women, woodcarving was almost exclusively a male domain. Men would spend hours designing and creating wooden furniture and traditional flutes and pipes. More experienced carvers produced intricately carved ceilings (which can be seen in homes and museums in Koprivshtitsa, Kotel, Tryavna and Plovdiv) and iconostases and altars in churches and monasteries.

The craft is still practised in Koprivshtitsa, Teteven and Lovech, but the most famous town in Bulgaria for woodcarving is undoubtedly Tryavna (see the boxed text, p184). One of the best places to admire woodcarvers at work is the Etâr Ethnographic Village Museum (p187) near Gabrovo.

Another ancient Bulgarian craft is pottery; the most famous design is the so-called 'Troyanska kapka' pattern, which literally means 'Troyan droplet', after its town of origin and the runny pattern made by the paint. Everything from plates and bowls to jugs and honey pots are made with this design; blue, brown and green are the most common colours. Bulgarians still use this Troyan ware in the home, though fancier pieces are made for the tourist trade. It's sold all across the country and makes a perfect souvenir.

Princes Amongst Men: Journeys with Gypsy Musicians by Garth Cartwright is a sympathetic introduction to the lives and musical traditions of Roma across the Balkans.

For a round-up of Bulgarian movies, actors and other statistics relating to the country's cinema industry, visit www.bgmovies.info.

Fairy Tales by Ran Bossilek (translated by Terry Whalen and Filipina Filipova) is an engaging collection of simple, age-old fables and stories.

Architecture

The most obvious product of the prodigious and creative Bulgarian National Revival era is the unique architectural style of homes seen throughout the country. These were either built side-by-side along narrow cobblestone streets, as in Plovdiv, or surrounded by pretty gardens, as in Arbanasi.

DID YOU KNOW?

During the Ottoman occupation, by law Christian churches had to be built below ground-level to be as unobtrusive as possible. Many 'sunken' churches from that period can be seen today.

The wood-and-stone homes were usually painted brown and white (though some were more colourful), and featured bay windows and tiled roofs. Ceilings were often intricately carved and/or painted with bright murals and rooms would have several small fireplaces and low doors.

Architectural designs and styles of furniture differed from one region to another. The colour, shape and size of the typical home in Melnik contrasts significantly with those found in Arbanasi. Some of the most stunning examples of National Revival–period homes can also be appreciated in traditional villages such as Koprivshtitsa, Tryavna and Shiroka Lŭka. There are also examples among the old towns of Plovdiv and Veliko Târnovo, and at the re-created Etâr Ethnographic Village Museum (p187) near Gabrovo.

The most prodigious architect of the National Revival era was Nikola Fichev (1800–81), also known as Master Kolyo Ficheto. He built bridges, churches and fountains across central Bulgaria, including the bridge at Byala, the bell tower at Preobrazhenski Monastery (p182) and the Holy Trinity Church in Svishtov. A museum is dedicated to him in his birthplace of Dryanovo.

SPORT

Football (soccer) is by far the most popular Bulgarian spectator sport, and the Sofia-based team, Levski, is the current Bulgarian champion. Football games normally take place on weekends and the season lasts from late August to late May, with a winter break in January and February.

For all you want to know about the national sport, see www.bulgarian-football.com

The high point for the Bulgarian national side was the 1994 World Cup, in which it finished in a very respectable fourth place. Since then, however, the team's performance has been disappointing, and it failed to qualify for the 2002 and 2006 World Cups.

The men's national volleyball team has had rather more success recently, winning the bronze at the 2006 World Championships in Japan and being currently ranked fourth in the world league.

Bulgarian tennis came to the fore through the 1990s with the remarkable Maleeva sisters, Magdalena, Katerina and Manuela, who all became WTA Top 10 players, with Manuela reaching the world number-three spot. They have all now retired and today run the Maleeva Tennis Club (p94) in Sofia.

Other sports in which the country has had some international success include basketball, Greco-Roman wrestling and weightlifting.

Food & Drink

Fresh fruit, vegetables and dairy produce form the basis of Bulgarian cuisine, and besides home-grown Balkan traditions, it has been heavily influenced by Greek and Turkish cookery. When it comes to meat, pork is king, while veal, chicken and tripe are also popular. Duck, rabbit and venison feature in many traditional recipes and fish is plentiful along the Black Sea coast, but less common elsewhere.

STAPLES & SPECIALITIES

Breakfast is rarely more than a coffee and a cigarette for most Bulgarians, but those with more time may partake of cheese, salami and even cakes. Lunch again is normally a small, casual meal, while dinner is the main meal of the day, often of two or three courses, including grilled meat, salad and soup.

DID YOU KNOW?

The bacteria used to make yoghurt is called *Lactobacillus bulgaricus*, named in honour of its Bulgarian origins.

Popular Bulgarian dishes with a Turkish influence include the omnipresent *kebabche* (grilled spicy meat sausages) and *kyufte* (basically the same thing, but round and flat). Salads are an essential part of most Bulgarian meals, normally eaten as a starter, but some are so large that they could be a full meal in themselves. *Shopska* salad, which is made with chopped tomatoes, cucumbers, green peppers and onions, covered with feta cheese, is so popular, it's regarded as a national dish, while *snezhanka* ('Snow White') salad is made with cucumbers and plain yoghurt, with garlic, dill and crushed walnuts. *Tarator* (chilled cucumber and yoghurt soup) is a delicious and refreshing summertime dish (see the boxed text, p56). Bread is a staple of Bulgarian meals and it will be brought to you, almost always at a small extra cost, whether you ask for it or not, when you order a main meal.

Offal, in various forms, is a distressingly common feature of many a restaurant menu.

Some tasty regional specialities are *patatnik* (a hearty cheese and potato omelette; Rodopi region), *kapama* (meat, rice and sauerkraut simmered and served in a clay pot; around Bansko), *mlechnik* (similar to crème caramel; Rodopi region) and *midi tzigane* (mussels sautéed with a spicy cheese-and-mustard sauce; along the Black Sea coast).

Popular desserts of Turkish origin include baklava, made with honey and pistachios, and *lokum* (Turkish delight). *Mlechna banitsa* is a sweet pastry made with milk and eggs, and is one of the best Bulgarian desserts, while ice cream features on menus everywhere.

TASTY TRAVEL

Grilled meat and cheese feature on virtually every Bulgarian restaurant menu, and are sometimes combined, as in the *kyufte tatarsko* (seasoned pork burger filled with melted cheese). Considering that there are only two traditional kinds of Bulgarian cheese, *sirene* ('white', similar to feta) and *kashkaval* ('yellow', hard cheese), it's amazing how much Bulgarians make out of these traditional ingredients. *Pârzheni kartofi sâs sirene* (white cheese–topped fried potatoes) is a regular side dish in many cafés and restaurants.

We dare you...

Bulgarians are very keen on using up the parts of animals most Western abattoirs would throw away, but if you have the stomach for it, you might like to try, well, stomach soup *(shkembe chorba)* for a start, or maybe some brain *(mozâk)* or tongue *(ezik)*, which come in various forms, including in omelettes. Spleens and intestines also turn up in soups and grills.

COOL AS A CUCUMBER

There is perhaps no more typical or evocative Bulgarian dish than *tarator,* the chilled soup made with diced cucumbers, diluted yoghurt, garlic, dill, salt, vegetable oil and crushed walnuts. Served everywhere as a starter during the hot summer months, it was originally created as a simple yet refreshing meal that could be made in large quantities and kept longer than cooked food. Its preparation is a matter of pride, and slight variations exist around the country; some chefs do away with the walnuts, for example, and others substitute olive oil for the vegetable oil, but if the cucumbers have been grated, or, unforgivably, replaced with lettuce or some other ingredient, then it's simply not the real thing. Oh, and please, never ask for hot *tarator*!

DRINKS

Bulgarians are caffeine addicts, and slurp their way through little cups of coffee morning, noon and night at kiosks, cafés and bars across the country. While you might encounter some instant coffee, good espresso coffee is available everywhere and *Spetema* is a reliable local brand. Smarter places also offer cappuccinos, though in cheaper outlets this might simply be instant coffee with a dollop of sprayed cream on top. If you're looking for a caffè latte and a squashy sofa, international chains can now be found in Sofia and other big cities.

Tea is mostly of the *bilkov* (herbal) and *plodov* (fruit) variety. If you want the real, black tea, ask for *cheren chai*. This will normally come with a slice of lemon; if you'd prefer milk, ask for *chai s'mlyako*.

For a cooling, refreshing beverage at any time of year, *ayran* is hard to beat. It's a chilled, slightly salty, thin yoghurt drink that makes an ideal accompaniment to light meals. Another local speciality, though perhaps more of an acquired taste, is *boza*, a thick malty drink made with millet.

Beer *(pivo* or *bira)* is another staple beverage in Bulgaria, and is sold everywhere, either in bottles or in draught *(nalivna)* form, which is generally cheaper. Leading nationwide brands are Zagorka, Kamenitsa, Ariana and Shumensko, while there are several regional brews, such as Burgasko (from Burgas) and Pirinsko (from Blagoevgrad), which are rarely available far beyond their home areas.

Bulgaria produces huge quantities of both white and red vino (wine), which varies greatly in quality. For more information see p63.

The national spirit is *rakia* (a clear and potent kind of brandy, usually made from grapes, although versions made from plums or apricots can also be found). Slivenska Perla, Manastirska, Burgas-63 and Simeon I are just a few of the many brands available. It's drunk as an aperitif, and served with ice in restaurants and bars, which often devote a whole page on their menus to a list of the regional *rakias* on offer.

Whisky, gin and vodka made in Bulgaria are a lot cheaper than the imported brand names, but in general are probably best left to the Bulgarians. Better quality Bulgarian vodkas include Flirt and Mary Jane.

CELEBRATIONS

Festivals throughout Bulgaria invariably involve eating and drinking, and there are often particular meals prepared for each holiday. One age-old custom is the baking of special loaves of bread, for example for saints' days, each marked with a distinctive design and used in some elaborate ritual; you'll see these displayed in ethnographic museums. On 28 February (Horse Easter), for example, women in rural communities traditionally bake bread in the shape of horseshoes, which are then fed to horses and new brides to ensure fertility. St George's Day (6 May), also known as Gergyovden, originated as an ancient pagan festival to do with sheep farming, and is one of the most important rural festivals, especially in eastern Bulgaria, involving a big, ritual meal of lamb and bread.

At Easter (called Velikden, or Pasha) a traditional bread is baked, containing whole eggs that have been dyed red. The bread is broken – never sliced – by the eldest member of the family, and pieces are distributed to all family members present. Other celebrations throughout the year are also marked with bread in many forms, including snakes (Jeremiah or Snake Day, 1 May) and crosses (Krastovden or Holy Cross Day, 14 September), or decorated with patterns such as beehives (Prokopi Pchelar or Procopius the Beekeeper Day, 8 July) and bunches of grapes (Preobrazhenie or Transfiguration Day, 6 August). In age-old tradition, Preobrazhenie was the first day on which Bulgarians ate the new crop of grapes, while eating blackberries (once known as devil's grapes) on this day was regarded as taboo.

One rather cheerful time to be anywhere near a winery is 1 February, when the Trifon Zarezan festival takes place to honour the patron saint of vineyards, St Trifon. On this day, wine producers start pruning their vines, and pour wine on the vine roots in the hope of a bountiful harvest. The grower who has produced the largest quantity of wine is declared 'king' and is driven around in an open cart. Plenty of tasting and drinking is also undertaken (all in the name of tradition, of course).

WHERE TO EAT & DRINK

Most outlets providing seating describe themselves as restaurants, while a *mehana* (tavern) is a more traditional restaurant, often decorated in a rustic style, and offering only authentic Bulgarian cuisine. Some of these, of course, are tourist traps, luring foreign tourists with noisy 'folk shows' and waiters in fancy dress, though the real places provide a pleasant atmosphere to linger over good local food. Look out for those frequented by locals and steer clear of any that employ touts to harangue passers-by.

Cafés are cheaper affairs and include basic cafeterias serving precooked Bulgarian food, soups and salads, although more often they will only serve beverages and simple snacks. In the cities, small basic cafés or snack bars offer drinks and snacks, sometimes with a few chairs outside, or just a table to lean on. These are popular with office workers and teenagers grabbing a quick coffee and a sandwich. Look out for signs reading закуска (*zakuska*; breakfast).

In the big cities, most restaurants will offer menus in English and, occasionally, French or German, while restaurants in coastal resorts such as Sunny Beach (Slânchev Bryag) and Albena will have multilingual menus featuring Swedish, Finnish and several other languages spoken by international tourists. Restaurant bills will usually be 'rounded up', and a service charge of 10% is sometimes added. If it isn't, a small tip is expected.

Most restaurants are open daily from about 11am to 11pm, although outside the big towns some may close on one or two days of the week. Cafés and street kiosks usually have longer opening hours, roughly 9am to 11pm in cities, although many open earlier to offer a quick breakfast to people hurrying to work.

Quick Eats

Bulgarians are great snackers and in big towns you will see old ladies on the streets or in parks selling *semki* (sunflower seeds) wrapped in paper cones, or homemade bread rolls from sacks. Both go for around 0.50 lv. In the colder months, steamed corn-on-the-cob is proffered by street vendors, while *banitsa* (cheese pasty), *byurek* (essentially the same, but with egg added), *palachinki*

The Bulgarian National Cuisine In My Home by Sonia Kapsazova is a handy, widely available book with easy-to-follow recipes.

(pancakes) and other sweet and savoury pastry products are always popular, and are widely available, most reliably at stalls outside bus and train stations. Prices are normally around 1 lv to 2 lv.

Western fast-food outlets can be found all over Bulgaria, and there are plenty of takeaway places selling pizzas, Turkish-style doner kebabs and the like. Trops Kâshta and BMS are two nationwide cafeteria chains serving cheap, traditional nosh such as *kebabche* and moussaka.

VEGETARIANS & VEGANS

Vegetarianism remains an alien concept to most Bulgarians, but it's relatively easy to follow a meat-free diet here. On the down side, variety may be lacking, and those with an aversion to cheese may find their options very limited. Most restaurants offer a dozen or more salads, which are sometimes large enough for a main course. Omelettes, vegetarian pizzas and pasta dishes are common, but note that 'vegetarian' meals may simply mean that they include vegetables (as well as meat) or fish. Sometimes this designation doesn't seem to mean anything at all. Vegans will have a much harder time: Kibea Health Food Restaurant in Sofia (p101) is probably the only place in Bulgaria serving genuine vegan dishes.

Other tasty vegetarian meals and snacks include *sirene po shopski* (cheese, eggs and tomatoes baked in a clay pot), *gyuvech* (potatoes, tomatoes, aubergine, onions and carrots baked in a clay pot), *mish-mash* (scrambled eggs with peppers, tomatoes and cheese), *kashkaval pane* (fried breaded cheese), *chuska byurek* (fried, breaded peppers stuffed with egg, cheese and parsley), *bob chorba* (bean soup) and the ever-popular *banitsa*.

If you're looking for a quick and easy Bulgarian recipe, www.findbgfood.com gives instructions for several popular dishes.

EATING WITH KIDS

Most restaurants in Bulgaria welcome families with young children, although few offer specific children's menus and fewer still will have such things as highchairs for babies. The more modern, Western-style restaurants such as the Happy Bar & Grill chain serve up dependable and recognisable food of the sausage-and-chips variety, while pizzas, in various sizes, are available almost everywhere. Similarly, you'll have no problem finding sweets, chocolates, crisps and other treats, while chocolate and jam-filled croissants are a popular local snack. Larger supermarkets will normally have a good supply of baby food and formula. See p284 for further information on travelling with children.

HABITS & CUSTOMS

Dining out in Bulgaria is normally a casual and convivial experience, and the usual Western table manners prevail. Few Bulgarian restaurants, however, have smoke-free zones, and nonsmokers will have to put up with their fellow diners puffing away before, after and even during their meals: if you can, it's best to sit outside.

Traditional Bulgarian Cooking by Atanas Slavov gives more than 140 recipes you might like to try out, including all the favourites such as kavarma, banitsa and shopska salad.

Breakfast, if eaten at all, is almost invariably eaten at home. Lunch is a light meal, while dinner is often the time for family get-togethers, and is a longer, more sociable affair. Bulgarians tend to eat dinner quite late, and restaurants fill up after about 9pm; you'll have trouble getting a seat at popular places after this time. For a quiet meal, aim to eat dinner around 6.30pm to 7pm.

EAT YOUR WORDS

If you want to know the difference between *kebabche* and *kyufte,* or are looking for a meal without meat, you'll first need to learn the Cyrillic alphabet. For language guidelines, see p309.

DOS & DON'TS

Bulgarians are by and large a laid-back lot when it comes to behaviour at the table, although the usual Western rules of 'good manners' still apply when dining out. Obviously, these standards will vary according to where you are eating: street-bar patrons won't be shocked if you use your fingers to eat, for example, but it would certainly draw attention in a smart restaurant.

- *Molya* is the word used to attract the attention of a waiter.
- If service is good (and not included in the bill), leave a tip of 10%.
- If you're invited to dine at a Bulgarian home, it's traditional to bring flowers (an odd number – even numbers are for funerals).
- *Rakia* is drunk as an aperitif, so don't order one to go with your main meal, or, even worse, with your dessert.
- In most restaurants, the main dish, eg grilled chicken, will come without trimmings and you will have to order side dishes *(garnitura)* such as potatoes separately, but ask what's included first.

Useful Phrases

Can you recommend a ...?
Можете ли да пре-поръчате ...?   *mo*-zhe-te lee da pre-po-*ruh*-cha-te ...?
  bar
  бар   bar
  café
  кафене   ka-fe-*ne*
  pub
  кръчма   kruhch-*ma*
  restaurant
  ресторант   res-to-*rant*
  tavern
  механа   me-ha-*na*

Where would you go for ...?
Къде ходите да ...?   kuh-*de ho*-dee-te da ...?
  a cheap meal
  хапнете евтино   *hap*-ne-te *ev*-tee-no
  local specialities
  опитате местните специалитети   o-*pee*-ta-te *mest*-nee-te spe-tsee-a-lee-*te*-tee

I'd like to reserve a table for ...
Бих искал да запазя маса за ...   beeh *ee*-skal da za-*pa*-zya *ma*-sa za ...
  (two) people
  двама (души)   *dva*-ma (*doo*-shee)
  (eight) o'clock
  осем часа   o-sem cha-*suh*

Are you still serving food?
  Сервирате ли все още?   ser-*vee*-ra-te lee vse osh-te?
I'm a vegetarian.
  Вегетарианец съм.   ve-ge-ta-ree-*a*-nets suhm
Is it cooked in meat stock?
  В месен бульон ли е приготвено?   v me-sen bu-*lyon* lee e pree-*got*-ve-no?
What's in that dish?
  Какво има в това ястие?   kak-*vo ee*-ma f to-*va ya*-stee-e?
I'd like a local speciality.
  Може ли местен специалитет.   *mo*-zhe lee *me*-sten spe-tsee-a-lee-*tet*

I'd like the set menu, please.
Може ли пълното меню. *mo·*zhe lee *puhl·*no·to me·*nyu*

What are the daily specials?
Какви са специалитетите за деня? kak·*vee* sa spe·tsee·a·lee·*te·*tee·te za de·*nya*?

What would you recommend?
Какво ще ми препоръчате? kak·*vo* shte mee pre·po·*ruh*·cha·te?

I'd like (a/the) ..., please.
Дайте ми ..., моля. *dai·*te mee ..., *mol·*yuh
  bill
  сметката *smet·*ka·ta
  drink list
  листата с напитките *lees·*ta·ta s na·*peet·*kee·te
  menu (in English)
  менюто (на английски) me·*nyoo·*to (na an·*gleey·*skee)
  (non)smoking section
  маса за (не)пушачи *ma·*sa za (ne·)poo·*sha·*chee
  table for (five)
  маса за (пет) човека *ma·*sa za (pet) cho·*ve·*ka
  that dish
  онова блюдо o·no·*va blyoo·*do

Bon appétit!
Добър апетит! do·*buhr* a·pe·*tit!*

Cheers!
Наздраве! naz·*dra·*ve!

That was delicious!
Това беше много вкусно! to·*va* be·she *mno·*go *vkoos·*no!

I'd like ..., please.
Моля, ако обичате ... *mol·*yuh, *a·*ko o·*bee·*cha·te ...
  a cup of tea/coffee
  чаша чай/кафе *cha·*sha chay/ka·*fe*
  with (milk)
  с мляко s (*mlya·*ko)
  without (sugar)
  без (захар) bez (*za·*har)
  decaffeinated
  без кофеин bez ko·fe·*een*
  iced coffee
  айскафе *ais·*ka·fe
  strong coffee
  силно кафе *seel·*no ka·*fe*
  Turkish coffee
  турско кафе *toor·*sko ka·*fe*
  Viennese coffee
  виенско кафе vee·*en·*sko ka·*fe*
  weak coffee
  слабо кафе *sla·*bo ka·*fe*

a bottle/glass of ... wine
бутилка/чаша ... вино boo·*teel·*ka/*cha·*sha ... *vee·*no
  dessert
  десертно de·*sert·*no
  red
  червено cher·*ve·*no

sparkling
шумящо   shoo·*myash*·to
white
бяло   *bya*·lo

a ... of beer
... бира   ... *bee*·ra
  glass
  чаша   *cha*·sha
  jug
  кана   *ka*·na
  large bottle
  голяма бутилка   go·*lya*·ma boo·*teel*·ka
  small bottle
  малка бутилка   *mal*·ka boo·*teel*·ka

DID YOU KNOW?

Although it might seem one of the most 'traditional' Bulgarian dishes, the origins of *shopska* salad are unclear, and it may have been created as recently as the 1950s.

Food Glossary
BASICS

хляб	hlyab	bread
краве масло	kra·ve *mas*·lo	butter
сирене	*see*·re·ne	cheese
шоколад	sho·ko·*lat*	chocolate
яйца	yay·*tsa*	eggs
мед	met	honey
мляко	mlya·ko	milk
пипер	*pee*·per	pepper
ориз	o·*rees*	rice
сол	sol	salt
захар	*za*·har	sugar
кисело мляко	*kee*·se·lo *mlya*·ko	yogurt

MEAT

пиле	*pee*·le	chicken
рива	*ree*·ba	fish
шунка	*shun*·ka	ham
агнешко месо	*ag*·nesh·ko me·*so*	lamb
свинско	*sveen*·sko	pork
скариди	ska·*ree*·dee	shrimp
език	e·*zeek*	tongue
телешко	*te*·lesh·ko	veal

VEGETABLES

син домат	seen do·*mat*	aubergine/eggplant
(зелен) боб	(ze·*len*) bob	(green) beans
зеле	*ze*·le	cabbage
морков	*mor*·kof	carrot
карфиол	kar·fee·*ol*	cauliflower
целина	*tse*·lee·na	celery
краставица	*kras*·ta·vee·tsa	cucumber
маруля	ma·*ru*·lya	lettuce
гъби	*guh*·bee	mushrooms
лук	luk	onions
грах	grah	peas
картоф	kar·*tof*	potato
домат	do·*mat*	tomato

SOUPS & SALADS

таратор	ta·ra·*tor*	chilled cucumber soup
шкембе чорба	shkem·be *chor*·ba	tripe soup
шопска салата	*shop*·ska sa·*la*·ta	*shopska* salad
боб	bob	bean soup

FRUIT

ябълка	*ya*·buhl·ka	apple
кайсия	kay·*see*·ya	apricot
банан	ba·*nan*	banana
смокиня	smo·*ki*·nya	fig
грозде	*groz*·de	grapes
лимон	lee·*mon*	lemon
портокал	por·to·*kal*	orange
праскова	*pras*·ko·va	peach
круша	*kru*·sha	pear
слива	*sli*·va	plum
ягода	*ya*·go·da	strawberry

DRINKS

бира	*bee*·ra	beer
ракия	ra·*kee*·ya	brandy (local)
шампанско	sham·*pan*·sko	champagne
кафе	ka·*fe*	coffee
плодов сок	*plo*·dof sok	fruit juice
минерална вода	mee·ne·*ral*·na vo·*da*	mineral water
газирана ...	ga·*zee*·ra·na ...	sparkling ...
негазирана ...	ne·ga·*zee*·ra·na ...	still ...
портокалов сок	por·to·*ka*·lov sok	orange juice
безалкохолна	bez·al·ko·*hol*·na	soft drink
напитка	na·*peet*·ka	
чай	chai	tea
вино	*vee*·no	wine

Bulgarian Wine

Bulgaria's varied climates and grape varietals, along with its rich soil, have made the country legendary for its wine since Thracian times, as glittering ancient gold and silver vessels that depict bacchic merrymaking attest. Modern devotees of Bulgarian wine include Winston Churchill, who regularly ordered barrels of the local red from Melnik, a lovable little hamlet in the country's deep southwest, and centre of one of the best wine producing areas in the Balkans.

While the mass quantities produced during Soviet times have diminished as the country continues to make the transition to a free-market economy, a new emphasis on quality and foreign know-how are already bearing fruit, as a new standard of Bulgarian wine becomes increasingly known – and available – across the globe.

Wine-loving travellers setting out to see the country will find plenty of opportunities to get into Bulgarian wine, ranging from gourmet urban restaurants with the chic top brands, to wine cellars dug out of cliffs and little roadside stands. Just remember to indulge liberally – it's a time-honoured part of the Bulgaria experience.

DID YOU KNOW?

Thanks to its Thracian forerunners, Bulgaria is one of the world's oldest winemaking lands.

HISTORY OF WINEMAKING IN BULGARIA

The origins of Bulgarian wine are shrouded in the mists of time, actually predating the modern state and even the Bulgarians themselves. The wine tradition here is so ancient and mythical that it can only be spoken of in divine company; Dionysus, the god of wine and revelry, adopted into the Greek pantheon but of Thracian stock, is represented on gold and silver drinking vessels depicting wine bacchanalias dug up by archaeologists in Bulgarian Thrace. Ancient poet Homer, presumably a bit of a tippler himself, sung the praises of Thracian wine almost 3000 years ago, retelling in *The Iliad* that Achaeans besieging Troy frequently ordered up black wine from the Thracians. Back then, wine was thick and sweet, and drunk diluted with water; drinking it straight was seen as fit only for a Scythian. Oenologists today consider that many of Bulgaria's seminal grapes, including the northern Gamza, and Mavrud and Melnishka from the south, probably derive from Thracian times.

Bulgaria's white wines emerged with the arrival of the Romans, who cultivated vineyards in the Black Sea regions of Pomorie and Nesebâr, according to another ancient poet, Ovid. With the 9th-century adoption of Christianity, winemaking continued under the care of monks – even though cranky King Krum tried to stamp it out (see the boxed text, p64). He was unsuccessful and, during the medieval Bulgarian kingdoms, vineyards flourished. After all, even in Christianity there was room for wine, the 'blood of Christ', and the Bulgarian monks even enforced new quality standards.

DID YOU KNOW?

Winston Churchill was one of history's many famous lovers of Melnik red wine.

The excellence of Bulgarian wine was noted by Western 'guests' such as crusading count Geoffrey De Villehardouin, who in 1205 allegedly decided to spare the southern town of Asenograd – still today a major centre of winemaking – because of his fondness for the local libation. In the 14th and 15th centuries, Bulgarian wine was traded widely in Europe. During the middle Ottoman centuries, winemaking decreased but the situation improved during the National Revival period of the 18th and 19th centuries, when a new affluence bred sophisticated tastes. The grand aristocratic mansions that you see today also served as wine salons for entertaining

A ROYAL CASE OF SOUR GRAPES

Around the year 802, a teetotalling warlord by the name of Krum came to power in Bulgaria. A fierce and ambitious chap, Khan Krum sought to expand Bulgaria's borders at the expense of the Byzantine Empire, bringing about a savage war of attrition. The decade of war with the Byzantines involved offensives and counter-offensives, generous burning and pillaging, subterfuge and the slaughter of untold hapless civilians. It resulted in the Bulgars almost taking Constantinople and the victorious Krum, according to legend, drinking from the skull of the first of three Byzantine emperors he defeated, Nikephoros I.

The question remains: what was Krum drinking from said silver-lined skull? For aside from his martial success, the stern ruler was also known for his strict and unprecedented legal code, meant to enforce law and order across Bulgaria. Severe punishments were meted out for drunkenness and, tradition states, Khan Krum even ordered the wholesale destruction of vineyards.

Krum, however, did not last long, dying in 814 while preparing to attack the Byzantine capital, and the edict against winemaking died with him. Monks kept the traditions alive, building the earliest recorded cool cellars for storing the lovingly made holy elixir.

Nowadays, the sour-grapes king may well be turning in his grave, and not only because to-day's Bulgarian state is significantly smaller than the territory he fought ferociously to create; his ambivalent legacy is also wryly commemorated in a popular white wine, 'Khan Krum', produced near Shumen in east-central Bulgaria.

esteemed guests, and some, such as the Kordopoulov House in Melnik (see the boxed text, p68), were the property of wine merchants themselves.

The national euphoria at freedom, following the Russo-Turkish War in 1878, would be tempered for vintners a few years later, with devastating outbreaks of phylloxera (caused by a root-devouring aphid), which decimated vineyards. French experts were called in around the turn of the 20th century; their recommendations about what styles to concentrate on in particular – Mavrud and Pamid in the south, Gamza in the north – would have lasting importance, shaping the production patterns that still exist today. The foreign experts, consulted again during the following two decades, also urged Bulgarian vintners to plant popular varietals, such as Cabernet Sauvignon and Riesling; again, their advice would prove auspicious.

Even before communism came in 1944, Bulgarian planters had started working in collectives. With the Soviet nationalisation of the industry, the state monopoly, Vinprom, made Bulgaria one of the world's biggest wine-producing countries – though the market was mostly limited to within the USSR. Bulgarian independence in 1990 brought both new opportunities for foreign investment and know-how, and also new problems involving property decentralisation – an issue that still vexes. Yet as the 1990s drew to a close, Bulgarian wine was appearing increasingly on foreign supermarket shelves.

State of the Industry

It hasn't been an unmitigated success story for the industry, however; Bulgarian wineries still need to develop the more lucrative export market for high-end wines. While partially a problem of perception for marketers to sort out, it's also caused by unresolved issues from Bulgaria's communist past. In 1996, Bulgarian vintners were exporting almost 30 million litres to Britain; 10 years later, however, that figure had waned to under 3 million litres. While 'devastating competition from California and the southern hemisphere' has been one reason for this, reported the *Financial Times* in a candid August 2007 article, the main problem involves denationalisation issues; the precious soil needed to grow the best grapes hasn't been freed up, as selling land tracts belonging in pieces to several owners requires them all to agree on a sale, and all too often, they don't.

To build vineyards of profitable sizes and qualities requires foreign financial muscle and expertise. One success story here, according to the *Financial Times*, is Bessa Valley Vineyard near Pazardzhik, acquired by funds manager Dr Carl Heinz Hauptmann and the splendidly named Count Stephan von Neipperg, whose family pedigree for winemaking in France extends back 800 years. Today, Bessa Valley is one of the few Bulgarian wines to have cracked the £4.99 barrier on the British shelves, its Enira Merlot now going for almost 10 quid. With the help of foreign know-how and capital, Bulgarian wine can indeed be recognised as the world-class product Bulgarians have always believed it to be.

KEY WORDS

Degustatsija na vino: it's Bulgarian for wine tasting.

WINEMAKING REGIONS

Bulgaria is officially divided into five wine-producing regions, each with its own unique microclimate and grape varietals. Visiting them all is possible, though unless you're going on a prearranged and specific wine tour, it will take time to do so comprehensively. A summary of the regions and their characteristics follows, along with a short list of unique wineries in each. Contact the individual wineries if you'd like to arrange a tour.

Northern (Danube Plain)

The Danube gives Bulgaria's fertile northern plains a cool, Continental climate. The northern wine region comprises the area between this river and the Stara Planina mountain range that runs across central Bulgaria, hemmed in by the Serbian border to the west and the eastern Dobrudzha Valley. It boasts 35% of Bulgaria's vineyards.

The north is most known for Gamza, a light red dinner wine. Well-known foreign reds, such as Cabernet Sauvignon and Merlot, are crafted here, as are whites such as Chardonnay, Riesling and Sauvignon Blanc. Other common northern wines include Muscat Ottonel, Aligoté and Pamid.

THE ART OF TASTING

Wine tasting is an art, a complex exercise that requires years of practice and, of course, unusually juxtaposed vocabulary. If you can conceptualise, however, you can learn how to impress in certain company.

1. Colour

Look through the wine, with the light behind it. Then tilt the glass slightly, and look through it towards a pale background. Clarity is the first category, and easy (good wines don't have floating particles), but colour, the second, is more complex. Most basically, deep colour indicates a strong wine. Colour also reveals the types of grapes used, and even the wine's age (in reds, a blue tint indicates youth, whereas an orange hue indicates age).

2. Smell

Swirl the wine, then smell it in one inhalation. The swirling summons up the wine's full bouquet. With eyes closed, concentrate on which of the 11 main smells associated with wine you pick up; they range from fruits to plants, herbs and spices, and more.

3. Taste

Now sip and swill the liquid around in your mouth; simultaneously, draw in some air to bring out the flavour. There are four possible flavours: bitter, acid, salty and sweet. Now swallow the wine, and wait; a fine wine should leave an aftertaste.

WINERIES

Vinprom Rousse Winery (☎ 082-311 487; www.vinpromrousse.com in Bulgarian; ul Treti Mart 44, Ruse) Ruse's largest winery derives from the former Soviet monopoly. Following a 1998 privatisation it's modernised admirably, devoting energy and modern methods to developing quality white wines characteristic of the Danubian valley. It's especially known for the light local red, Gamza, but also produces quality Chardonnay, Sauvignon Blanc, Igni Blanc and Welschriesling, among others.

Lovico Suhindol (☎ 061-362 411; www.lovico.net; ul Rositsa 156, Suhindol) In Suhindol village near Veliko Târnovo, this venerable winery was founded in 1909 and was Bulgaria's first cooperative. It now produces over 6 million litres of wine and brandy per year. It specialises in the deep purple, slightly spicy Gamza (best after two or three years of ageing), Cabernet Sauvignon, Chardonnay and Muscat.

The official site for Bulgarian wines is www.bulgarianwines.org.

Eastern (Black Sea Coastal)

Bulgaria's narrow eastern winemaking region runs down the Black Sea coast, between Romania to the north and the border with Turkey to the south. More than half of the country's white grape varietals are cultivated here, with the long summers and mild autumns ensuring ideal conditions for the sugars necessary for white wine to develop in the grapes. The east accounts for 30 percent of Bulgaria's vineyards, with major centres being in Targovishte, Preslav and Strandja. Among the best known wines created here are Dimyat, Traminer, Riesling, Muscat Ottonel, Sauvignon Blanc and Gewürztraminer.

WINERIES

Chateau Euxinograde (☎ 052-393 165; www.euxinograde.com; Varna) Housed in the former royal palace north of Varna on the Black Sea, this winery was established in 1891 by Prince Battenberg; snatched later by the communists, from 1944 to 1989 it catered to high officials of the party. The 90-hectare Euxinograde complex offers no ordinary wine tour; the stately palace features elaborate period furnishings, botanical gardens with rare plants, and the impressive old wine collections of Prince Ferdinand and Tsar Boris III, which includes astonishing treasures such as a Chateau Margaux from 1904.

The winery is known for its delicate Riesling and rich yet mild Traminer, a favourite white wine of Bulgarian connoisseurs, along with its beloved French-style brandy, Euxignac.

LVK-Vinprom Targovishte (☎ 060-164 751; bul 29 Yanuari 8, Targovishte) An illustrious microregion for winemaking is Targovishte, near Veliko Târnovo, and its wines have won numerous prizes at international fairs. LVK-Vinprom is the largest area vintner and you can visit the winery and its vineyards bursting with grapes at nearby Kralevo. Targovishte wines, both red and white, sparkle and are good dinner wines.

Domaine Boyar (☎ 02-969 7980; www.domaineboyar.com; Zlaten Rog 20-22, Sofia) This leading winery emerged soon after the demise of communism, and has become one of Bulgaria's top exporters to the West. The results of the considerable investments in modern technology and techniques have been numerous awards at international fairs, and a very competitive position among all producers in Eastern and Central Europe. In 2005 it boosted its elite image by becoming the official importer of champagnes drunk in the narrowest of circles – the royal families of Britain, Sweden, Spain and Monaco.

With vineyards in both the eastern Black Sea region and on the Thracian plain, Domaine Boyar produces the best of both Bulgaria's whites and reds. The winery offers a tasting tour to eastern vineyards near Shumen. Professional guides inform about the winery's history, and Bulgarian winemaking in general, and of course serve you the winery's spectacular Chardonnay (among others).

The Valley of Roses (Sub-Balkan)

A small but significant winemaking area is in the Valley of Roses, just south of the Stara Planina mountain range and north of Plovdiv. Known more for its historic production of rose oil, the rich fields of the region are ideal for the production of dry whites, the Misket being the most unique white variety, produced from a grape that grows better here than anywhere else in Bulgaria.

Thracian Lowland (South Bulgarian)

The Thracian lowlands, beginning south of the Stara Planina range and extending to the Sakar Mountain and Maritsa River, are protected from the cold northern air by the mountains and have hot, dry summers. One important subregion, the Bessa Valley, has a history of winemaking going back to the 5th-century BC Thracian Bessi tribe. This region produces one of Bulgaria's most famous wines, Mavrud, a famous local red that ages well. It also produces Merlot, Cabernet Sauvignon, Muscatel and Pamid.

WINERIES

Bessa Valley Winery (☎ 0889499992; www.bessavalley.com; Ognyanovo village) This impressive, foreign-owned winery has attracted international attention for its Merlot, Syrah, Petit Verdot and Cabernet Sauvignons, crafted from select, hand-picked grapes aged in French oak barrels. Tasting tours involve also seeing the impressive facilities, which include an enormous rotunda and arched pergola; the limestone cellar walls are flecked with the fossils of ancient sea creatures.

Bessa Valley's flagship brand, Enira, combines Merlot (80%) and Cabernet Sauvignon (20%); the wine retains a complex bouquet, both spicy and redolent of fruits. The innovative Enira (2004 vintage) took first prize at Bulgaria's prestigious Vinaria competition. The well-organised winery tour, involving sampling of three wines accompanied by cheeses and meats, lasts two hours and costs 12 lv.

Todoroff Wine Cellars (02-985 4785; www.todoroff-wines.com) Now one of Bulgaria's premier wineries, in Brestovitsa, 15km southwest of Plovdiv, this winery was created over the ruins of a neglected communist-era one in 1999 by Ivan Todoroff, lover of the arts and wine. While he wished only to create a small winery sufficient for himself and his friends, word spread and demand grew. Now, while remaining very much a boutique place, Todoroff Wine Cellars is one of Bulgarian wines' most revered names. It's especially known for its juicy, red Mavrud, one of two truly representative Bulgarian varieties (along with Melnik wine from the southwest). Todoroff's 'Mystery of Thrace' is a deep red with an intriguing bouquet, combining the aromas of cherry and vanilla, oak and spice. Vineyard tours may also include sampling traditional cuisine, spa hotel accommodation and even grape picking.

DID YOU KNOW?

No Man's Land wine, produced by Damianitza, is made from grapes grown in the once forbidden border-zone fields between Bulgaria and Greece.

Struma River Valley (Pirin Mountains)

Although Bulgaria's southwestern corner accounts for only 6% of the country's vineyards, its wines are among the best. This area bounded by the River Struma and Pirin Mountains is geographically known as Pirin

---

WHERE TO STICK IT

People are used to dropping coins into wishing wells. But what about a wishing wall?

Tranquil Melnik, in Bulgaria's southwestern Pirin region, is famous for both its winemaking tradition and its National Revival–era houses. The two unite at the magnificent cliffside **Kordopoulov House** (p135), once owned by a prosperous 18th-century vintner. This marvellously furnished house-museum, said to be the biggest in the Balkans, still produces its own wine, storing it in a labyrinthine cellar where, at the end, rows of glittering coins have been stuck into the soft stone comprising the dug-out cellar wall. The coins are gestures of good wishes from many happy visitors, hoping for a future of good crops and good rains, to keep Melnik's rich red wines flowing for future enjoyment. If you share this warm sentiment (and after a glass or two of the house wine, you will be feeling very warm indeed), stick a coin of your own into the wall.

Macedonia, and indeed the arid, Mediterranean climate and soil are similar to those of the neighbouring Republic of Macedonia to the west and the Greek province of Macedonia to the south. It's the hottest part of the country, with very dry summers and mild winters.

The most famous wine here is Melnik's signature red, the Shiroka Melnishka Loza, while Cabernet Sauvignon and Merlot are also produced. Melnik wines, still stored in catacomb-like cellars dug out of chalky cliffs, are full-bodied and improve with age. Another unique local variety, the Keratzuda, is unique to Kresna, a village between Blagoevgrad and Sandanski.

WINERIES

Damianitza (☎ 0746-300 90; www.damianitza.bg) The leading producer of the famed Melnik wine, Damianitza dates from 1940 but was privatised in 1997 and subsequently modernised. Damianitza has been innovative, fashioning new tastes by combining the local Melnik grape with Cabernet Sauvignon, creating Ruen, and similarly combining Nebbiolo and Syrah varietals to create Rubin, a unique Damianitza wine now regarded as one of Bulgaria's best. Signature wines include the ReDark and Unicato, hearty, barrel-aged reds full of character.

Environment

THE LAND

Bulgaria covers just under 111,000 sq km at the heart of the Balkan Peninsula, and in that relatively small area encompasses an amazing variety of landscapes and landforms. About one-third of Bulgaria's terrain is mountainous and the country boasts seven distinct mountain ranges, each with a unique range of flora and fauna, and all covered with well-marked walking trails.

From the northern border with Romania, a windswept fertile plain gradually slopes south as far as the Stara Planina mountains, the longest mountain range in the Balkans, which virtually splits the country in half. To the south, the Sredna Gora mountains are separated from the main range by a fault in which the Valley of Roses lies.

Mt Musala (2925m), in the rugged and floriferous Rila Mountains south of Sofia, is almost equalled in height by Mt Vihren (2915m) in the wild Pirin Mountains further south. The Rila Mountains' sharply glaciated massifs, with their bare rocky peaks, steep forested valleys and glacial lakes, are the geographical core of the Balkans and a paradise for hikers (and, in parts, skiers). The Rodopi Mountains stretch along the Greek border east of the Rila and Pirin Mountains and spill over into Greece. The fascinating Yagodina and Trigrad caves (p162) are geological must-sees in the Rodopis, while Melnik's (p134) dramatic and unique sand pyramids are one of the more unusual highlights of the Pirin region.

The Thracian plain opens onto the Black Sea coast. The 378km-long coast is lined with beaches and also features coastal lakes near Burgas, spectacular cliffs near Kaliakra and several gaping bays. In addition to the mighty Danube, which forms much of the border with Romania, the major rivers include the Yantra, which meanders its way through the town of Veliko Târnovo; the Iskâr, which stretches from south of Samokov to the Danube, past Sofia; and the Maritsa, which crawls through Plovdiv.

WILDLIFE

Though not an especially large country, Bulgaria packs in a huge and diverse array of flora and fauna, helped by the varied climate and topography, relatively small human population, and the fact that almost a third of the country is forested. However, all environmental groups believe that the

---

RESPONSIBLE TRAVEL

Everyone travelling to Bulgaria can minimise the impact of their visit. Try to conserve water and electricity, respect traditions in villages, and leave ruins as they are. In addition, don't litter and don't destroy flora and fauna. Driving is often an ideal way to get around, but please bear in mind that traffic and air and noise pollution are increasing problems in Bulgaria.

One local organisation promoting sustainable alternative tourism is the **Bulgarian Association for Alternative Tourism** (BAAT; ☎ 02-980 7685; www.baatbg.org), which publishes the excellent *Bulgaria Bed & Breakfasts Guidebook*, a compendium of family-run guesthouses and off-the-beaten-track itinerary ideas. **Zig Zag Holidays** (☎/fax 02-980 5102; www.zigzagbg.com) is a leading tour operator running ecologically sensitive trips and activities (see p86). It also sells BAAT's guidebook. The **Bulgarian Association for Rural & Ecological Tourism** (BARET; ☎ 02-979 3363; baret@aster.net) is a major national NGO promoting village and country regions and the development of sustainable rural tourism.

future of Bulgaria's ecology is at a critical stage and that local and international action is urgently needed before the environmental damage already caused becomes irreversible.

Animals

Visit www.panda.org /bulgaria to see what environmental projects and campaigns the World Wide Fund For Nature (WWF) is currently involved in.

Bulgaria is home to some 56,000 kinds of animal, including almost 400 species of birds (about 75% of all species found in Europe), 36 types of reptiles, over 200 species of freshwater and saltwater fish (of which about half are found along the Black Sea coast of Bulgaria) and 27,000 types of insect.

Many larger animals are elusive and live in the hills and mountains, some way from urban centres, but if you are keen to see some natural fauna, join an organised tour (see p301 and p304). Alternatively, hike in the Strandzha Nature Park (p227); the Rusenski Lom Nature Park (p273), home to 67 species of mammals (about two-thirds of those found in Bulgaria); the Rila National Park (p116); or the Pirin National Park (p124), where 42 species of animals, such as the European brown bear, deer and wild goats thrive.

Bird-lovers can admire plenty of our feathered friends at Burgas Lakes (p220), the largest wetland complex in the country, and home to about 60% of all bird species in Bulgaria; the Ropotamo Nature Reserve (p224), with more than 200 species of birds; Lake Srebârna (p274), also with over 200 bird species; the Strandzha Nature Park (p227), with almost 70% of all bird species found in Bulgaria; and the Rusenski Lom Nature Park (p273), home to 170 species of water birds. White storks, black storks, Dalmatian pelicans, sandpipers, corncrakes and pygmy cormorants are some of the species that can be seen in these areas.

ENDANGERED SPECIES

Included in the official list of the endangered animals of Bulgaria are seals and dolphins, both of which were hunted ruthlessly in the past (dolphin hunting was banned in Bulgaria in 1966) but can still be seen in sadly decreasing numbers off the northern part of the Black Sea coast.

Bulgaria has one of the largest brown bear populations in Europe (the last estimate was around 1000 individuals), and numbers are increasing, thanks to a ban on hunting, although farmers are still allowed to apply for hunting licences in areas where bears have attacked livestock. There are thought to be around 200 bears in the southeastern Rodopis, and 15 even live on Mt Vitosha, on the outskirts of the capital city. However, unless you're on a wildlife-spotting tour, you're extremely unlikely to see a bear, let alone get close enough to be mauled by one; if you are confronted, don't run (they're faster than you) but instead, back away slowly, discarding clothing or food items for the bear to investigate, and, ahem, hope for the best.

The cruel practice of 'dancing' bears was officially banned in 1993, and rescued bears now live in the **Dancing Bears Park** (☎ 0887866189; www .vierpfoten.org; ☷ 10am-6pm Apr & May, to 8pm Jun-Sep, to 4pm Oct & Nov) in Belitsa, in the Rila Mountains. Located around 33km northeast of Bansko (and 12km outside the village of Belitsa itself), the park is the largest of its kind in Europe, and visitors are welcome to join guided tours. You will need your own transport to visit. The park is dependent on donations, and it costs €10 for basic care for just one bear for one day, so anything you can spare will be appreciated. As well as helping these abused animals, the park also provides employment in a poor region of the country and it is hoped that this will become a significant ecotourism draw in the future.

There are thought to be around 2000 wolves in the country, and lynxes, previously presumed extinct, were officially 'rediscovered' in 2003, though exact numbers of these elusive creatures are uncertain. Again, you'll be very lucky to see these animals in the wild.

Rare insects include the Bulgarian Emerald dragonfly, only discovered in 1999. It is thought only to inhabit a small area of the Eastern Rodopi mountains and neighbouring areas of Greece and Turkey.

Various species of rare birds, including Egyptian vultures, lesser kestrels and great eagle owls, are protected in the Rusenski Lom Nature Park, while small cormorants, Ferruginous ducks and Dalmatian pelicans thrive in the Srebârna Nature Reserve. The Imperial eagle is one of Bulgaria's most threatened birds – only around 18 pairs are believed to exist in the wild today – while the distinctive-looking Tengmalm's owl is another scarce species. Saker falcons have been brought close to extinction in Bulgaria, due to the illegal falconry trade and egg collectors.

Plants

Of Bulgaria's 10,000 or so plant species, 31 are endangered. About 250 are endemic and many have indigenous names, such as Bulgarian blackberry and Rodopi tulip. The *silivriak*, with its small pink flowers, grew all over Europe before the last Ice Age, but is now found only in southern Bulgaria, particularly in the Rodopi Mountains, where it's reasonably abundant. The wonderfully named Splendid Tulip, with its large red flowers, is extremely rare, and was only discovered in 1976, near Yambol. It has been found nowhere else, and you'll be very lucky to spot it: only around 20 plants are known to exist.

Squeezed between the mighty Stara Planina and Sredna Gora ranges, the Valley of Roses was, until recently, the source of 70% of the world's supply of rose oil. Roses are still grown there extensively, and can be seen and enjoyed most of the year.

Forests are also protected in the national parks and reserves. The Strandzha Nature Park (p227) contains vast areas of oaks and beeches. The Unesco-protected Pirin National Park (p124) boasts about 1100 species of flora, and the Central Balkan National Park (www.centralbalkan nationalpark.org) encompasses ancient fir, spruce and hornbeam forests and mountain meadows, and supports some 2340 plant species, several of which are found nowhere else.

DID YOU KNOW?

The *silivriak* is also known as the Orpheus flower; legend says that its flowers were stained pink with the blood of the divine musician after he was hacked to pieces by the frenzied Bacchantes.

NATIONAL PARKS

The Bulgarian government has officially established three national parks – Rila, Pirin and Central Balkan – where the flora, fauna and environment are (in theory) protected. Besides the three officially protected national parks, which do not include any towns or villages, Bulgaria has 10 'nature parks', which do include permanent settlements, and nature reserves, which are unique managed ecosystems. The latter category receives the strictest protection, and access is often regulated or even prohibited. Confusingly, the term national park is regularly used to describe parks in any of these categories. Throughout this book we have followed the usual local usage for park names. For further information about the parks and reserves, visit www.bulgariannationalparks.org.

Environmental groups continue to lobby the Bulgarian government to expand areas already under protection and create new parks and reserves, especially in the unprotected Rodopi Mountains and along the Black Sea coast.

National Park/ Reserve	Features	Activities	Best time to visit	Page
Central Balkan National Park	mountains, forests, waterfalls & canyons; wolves, otters, wild cats, rare birds & bats	hiking, caving & horse riding	May-Sep	p71
Pirin National Park	mountains & lakes; bears, deer & birds	hiking	Jun-Sep	p124
Rila National Park	alpine forests & pastures; deer, wild goats & eagles	hiking	Jun-Sep	p116
Ropotamo Nature Reserve	marshes & sand dunes; rare birds	boat trips & hiking	Apr-Jul	p224
Rusenski Lom Nature Park	river banks, valleys & mountains; rare birds; rock churches	bird-watching & caving	Jun-Sep	p273
Strandzha Nature Park	varied forest & beaches; birds & mammals; archaeological ruins	hiking & bird-watching	Jun-Aug	p227
Vitosha Nature Park	mountain trails	hiking & skiing	Apr-Aug & Dec-Jan	p109
Vrachanski Balkan Nature Park	forest, varied tree life & caves	hiking & caving	Jun-Sep	p266

ENVIRONMENTAL ISSUES

Like most postcommunist countries, the lure of fast cash has often outweighed ecologically sustainable development. Logging, poaching and insensitive development continue in protected areas and excessive and harmful air and water pollution is infrequently controlled. Finite fossil fuels, such as coal, are still used for generating electricity, and farmers continually (and illegally) clear land by burning, which causes many devastating fires each summer.

Tourism & Transport Development

The big money to be made in Bulgaria's growing tourism industry has resulted in a spate of huge construction projects, notably along the Black Sea coast and in the skiing resorts, and accusations of corruption and thoughtless profiteering have been thrown at the developers and officials involved by concerned environmentalists. Large swaths of the coastline seem to be disappearing under a sea of concrete and cranes as local municipalities and private developers try to grab more land and yet more holiday home complexes, hotels and marinas are constructed.

In 2006, the government agreed to allow investors to develop Bulgaria's longest natural, untouched beach – Kamchiiski Pyasâtsi, near Shkorpilovtsi – for tourism development, in return for agricultural land elsewhere, while in 2007 there was an uproar when the Supreme Court rescinded Strandzha Nature Park's protected status, which allowed a hotel complex to be built inside the park – Tsarevo Municipality and the investment company, Krash 2000, had claimed the park's borders were unclear, even though they are clearly marked on official maps. The Bulgarian Parliament eventually overturned the decision, after initially refusing to respond to petitions and demonstrations, and pleas from international bodies such as the World Wide Fund for Nature (WWF).

In 2003 a highly controversial new ski centre was opened in the heart of the (supposedly) protected Pirin National Park, near Bansko. Thousands of hectares of trees were felled, and huge disruption was caused to the natural habitat. Outraged environmentalists feared that it might set a precedent for the development of more ski runs in Pirin National Park and other protected mountain ranges, and they were right. After years of opposition, the go-ahead was finally given in 2007 for the so-called Super-Borovets mega ski resort, which will encompass the towns of Samokov and Beli Iskâr as well as expand Borovets itself. There will be 19 new ski runs, with a combined length of 42km, as well as hotels and holiday apartments. The scale of the project has been heavily criticised by environmental campaigners.

One bone of contention through 2007 has been the Natura 2000 scheme (www.natura.org), the European network of protected nature sites. The Bulgarian government came in for criticism domestically, and, more importantly, from the EU, for its tardiness to supply the full list of areas to be included on time, and its apparent unwillingness to comply with its legal obligations; the government removed half the areas to be listed, citing, astonishingly, the 'interest of investors' in supposedly protected areas around the Black Sea coast and the mountains, when only scientific criteria were to be used. Under threats of fines, the government has relented, and more sites have now been submitted for protected listing.

Visit www.bluelink.net, the best website for environmental news, with details of current campaigns and projects and lots of useful links.

Nuclear Energy

Bulgaria's only nuclear power plant – at Kozlodui (www.kznpp.org) near the Danube, about 200km north of Sofia – was once rated as one of the world's most dangerous nuclear facilities. Since opening in 1974, minor accidents have periodically forced partial shutdowns, leading to power cuts across the country. Massive pressure and financial aid from the EU convinced the Bulgarian authorities to close two of the facility's reactors in December 2002, and to carry out vital upgrades. Independent safety checks in 2003 praised its 'high technical standards', and it is now regarded as one of the safest in Europe. It remains an important supplier of the country's electricity, but four more reactors are due to close in 2009, and the plant itself should finally go offline in 2013.

Kozlodui will be replaced with another nuclear plant at Belene (www .belene-npp.com). The government gave the go-ahead for its construction in 2004, but the project has been dogged by controversy and protests from environmentalists, who claim the building of this facility in an earthquake-prone area poses particular dangers, but after much discussion the EU finally agreed to the plans in late 2007 and Belene is expected to start generating power in 2014.

Pollution

Pollution from effluent along the Black Sea coast continues to be an issue, while another big concern is the Danube, which is often heavily polluted before it even reaches Bulgaria (see the boxed text, p261). Bulgaria's coal-fired power stations also pose environmental hazards. The largest, Maritsa East 2, near Stara Zagora, has been behind schedule in its efforts to meet strict EU emission standards by 2008 and is working to upgrade its facilities. There have also been worries about maintaining energy supplies once the Kozlodui nuclear plant closes down in 2013.

For details of the campaign against the proposed gold mine in the Rodopi Mountains, visit www .cyanidefreerhodopi.org.

The ageing Kremikovtsi steel plant outside Sofia has also been grappling with long-standing pollution problems, and is attempting to modernise its facilities in order to meet EU guidelines on emissions by 2011, but huge investments are needed.

The proposed construction of the open-pit Ada Tepe gold mine near Krumovgrad in the Rodopis has been highly controversial, with campaigners protesting that the cyanide-leaching process used to extract the gold would pose huge health risks to the local population. Thracian archaeological remains have already been bulldozed on top of Ada Tepe hill in preparation for the pit, but continuing objections have delayed the opening.

Environmental Organisations

The Bulgarian Green Party (www.greenparty.bg) was one of the first opposition parties to be formed in the wake of the collapse of the communist government in December 1989, and though initially scoring some success, it has performed poorly in subsequent elections.

Anyone with genuine interest in a specific ecological issue can contact one or more of the following organisations. Apart from Neophron, these groups do not, however, provide tourist information or offer tours. For some companies that offer environmental tours, see p304.

The Balkani Wildlife Society (www.balkani.org) is active in environmental conservation programmes around the country and in raising public awareness of wildlife issues.

Bulgarian Association for Alternative Tourism (BAAT; ☎ 02-980 7685; www.baatbg.org; bul Stamboliyski 20-V, Sofia) The biggest tourist nongovernment organisation (NGO) in Bulgaria supports small businesses and organisations involved in sustainable tourism development across the country.

Bulgarian Biodiversity Foundation (☎ 02-931 6183; www.bbf.biodiversity.bg) A nonprofit organisation active in the conservation of Bulgaria's natural heritage and promoting sustainable development.

Bulgarian Society for the Protection of Birds (BSPB; ☎ 02-971 5855; www.bspb.org) The BSPB helps to protect bird life and their habitats and proudly claims to have reintroduced an extinct species, the cinereous vulture. It's part of BirdLife International.

Ekoglasnost (☎ 02-986 2221) The local Friends of the Earth affiliate in Sofia.

Green Balkans (☎ 032-626 977; www.greenbalkans.org) Based in Plovdiv, Green Balkans is a major nature conservation NGO comprising four regional societies, organising campaigns and promoting biodiversity in Bulgaria and the Balkan peninsula.

Neophron (☎ 052-650 230; www.neophron.com; PO Box 492, Varna) Based in Varna, Neophron is an ecological tour agency run by the BSPB, offering bird-watching, bear-watching and botany trips around Bulgaria.

Za Zemiata (☎ 02-943 1123; www.zazemiata.org) 'For the Earth' is an environmental NGO that coordinates various campaigns on issues including pollution and sustainable energy.

Activities

Bulgaria's mountainous, heavily forested terrain makes for great hiking, mountaineering and skiing, while on the Black Sea coast, you can indulge in an array of water sports from paragliding to scuba diving, although these tend to be confined to the big package-holiday resorts. In addition, travel agencies organise a wide range of activity and special-interest holidays, including bird-watching, wildlife-spotting, botanical and archaeological tours.

HIKING

Hiking has long been a hugely popular activity in Bulgaria, and with distinctive mountain ranges covering a third of the country, and some 37,000km of marked trails to follow, it's easy to see why. The trans-European hiking trails E3, E4 and E8 all cross through Bulgaria. The E3 trail, which begins in Spain, follows the crest of the Stara Planina range from Belogradchik eastwards to the coast at Cape Ermine, and is well signposted along the way. If you want to go the whole way, count on taking around 20 days or so. The E4 and E8 trails both pass through Rila National Park and offer varied scenery and difficulty.

Walkers are well supported, with numerous *hizhas* (mountain huts) along the more popular tracks, as well as in real wilderness areas. It's one of the more positive legacies of the old communist regime, which believed that hiking was a healthy and productive proletarian pastime.

The standard of accommodation at these huts varies greatly, ranging from the simplest wooden shacks with only the most rudimentary of facilities for an overnight stop, to cosy hostels with kitchens, cafés and even shops attached. These huts only provide the basics and are not intended for lengthy stays.

If you intend doing some serious walking, you will need a detailed map of the region you're visiting. The main publisher of hiking maps is Kartografia, which produces *Pirin* (1:55,000), *Rila* (1:55,000) and separate maps for the east and west Rodopis (both 1:100,000). All are printed in English, German and Bulgarian and cost about 6 lv to 8 lv each. Maps of the central and west Rodopi Mountains (both 1:100,000) are issued by YEO-Rhodope and contain marked trails and details of sights and accommodation in the area. The handy *Troyan Balkan* map (1:65,000) covers the Stara Planina.

SAFETY GUIDELINES FOR WALKING

Before embarking on a walking trip, consider the following points to ensure a safe and enjoyable experience:

- Pay any fees and possess any permits required by local authorities.
- Be sure you are healthy and feel comfortable walking for a sustained period.
- Obtain reliable information about physical and environmental conditions along your intended route (eg from park authorities).
- Be aware of local laws, regulations and etiquette about wildlife and the environment.
- Walk only in regions, and on trails within your realm of experience.
- Be aware that weather conditions and terrain vary significantly from one region, or even from one trail to another. Seasonal changes can significantly alter any trail. These differences influence the way walkers dress and the equipment they carry.
- Ask before you set out about the environmental characteristics that can affect your walk and how local, experienced walkers deal with these considerations.

The Rila Mountains are a rugged, rocky, heavily forested range with plunging glacial valleys and rich plant life. One of the most attractive and accessible walking routes heads into the Maliovitsa range, south of the small town of the same name and based around soaring Mt Maliovitsa (2729m). Happily, one of Bulgaria's more comfortable mountain huts, Hizha Rilski Ezera, is along this route.

Another relatively easy and very pleasant walk runs along the Rilska *reka* (Rilska river) towards the magnificent Rila Monastery, passing through Kiril Meadow along the way.

Visit www.bulgarian nationalparks.org for comprehensive information on Bulgaria's three national parks.

The Pirins offer some of the very finest walking country in Bulgaria. It's an alpine landscape of glacial valleys and lakes, and the climate is blessed with a moderating Mediterranean influence.

The Sredna Gora is the highest, most visited section of the Stara Planina, with hundreds of marked tracks and the largest number of *hizhas*. The Stara Planina is noted for its sudden weather changes, and some of Bulgaria's highest rainfalls and strongest winds have been recorded here, so be prepared. September is the most amenable month for walking. Camping out is discouraged at all times, due to bears and adverse weather.

Travel agencies running organised hiking trips include **Zig Zag Holidays** (Map p88; ☎ 02-980 5102; www.zigzagbg.com; bul Stamboliyski 20-V, Sofia), which offers tailor-made trips as well as standard trips, such as its five-day hike in the Rodopi Mountains (€169 per person in a group of four) – challenging but suitable for most people of average fitness, with four to six hours hiking each day. The price includes four nights full-board accommodation. Its 11-day 'Alpine Moods of Bulgaria' trip (€350 per person in a group of six) is meant for more experienced hikers and includes the E4 trail in the Rila and Pirin Mountains.

Balkan Trek (☎ 02-973 3595; www.balkantrek.com) also runs guided hiking tours in the Pirin, Rila and Balkan mountain ranges; see the website for departures dates and prices.

Mountain Adventures in Bulgaria (www.bghike.com) is a specialist company running guided hiking and trekking excursions that is happy to make tailor-made arrangements if you have any special interests or limited time. Its nine-day hike round the Rila Mountains costs €380 per person including full-board accommodation.

Walking Softly Adventures (☎ 1888 743 0723; www.walkingsoftly.com) is a US-based company that runs hiking tours all over the world. Its 10-night Mountains of Bulgaria trip costs US$3150 per person.

MOUNTAINEERING

With seven major mountain ranges squeezed into such a small geographical area, Bulgaria is a paradise for climbers. The **Bulgarian Climbing & Mountaineering Federation** (☎ 02-987 1798; www.bfka.org) in Sofia is the main organisation worth contacting for information, advice and details of guides. Also in Sofia, **Club Extreme** (www.clubextreme.org) offers the services of professional guides. Prices vary and are dependent on where and when you want to go. Shops such as Stenata (p104) can provide gear, which will probably work out cheaper than in Western Europe.

The most popular areas for mountaineering are the Rila, Pirin and Stara Planina mountain ranges. The Rila Mountains (p115) are the highest range in the country boasting well over a hundred alpine peaks more than 1000m in height, including the highest peak in Bulgaria, Mt Musala (2925m), and some 180 clear, burbling streams and placid lakes. Mt Maliovitsa (2729m), reached from the town of Maliovitsa, is one of the prime climbing peaks here. Note that snow and low temperatures persist at higher levels even into summer.

TOP HIZHAS

- Hizha Rilski Ezera (Rila Mountains; p123)
- Hizha Vihren (Pirin Mountains; p133)
- Hizha Kuker (Vitosha Nature Park; p111)
- Hizha Banderitsa (Pirin Mountains; p133)
- Hizha Kamenitsa (Pirin Mountains; p133)
- Hizha Skakavitsa (Rila Mountains; p123)

The sparsely inhabited Pirin Mountains (p124) are another alpine range in the southwest, with three peaks above 2900m and almost a hundred above 2500m. It's a typical alpine landscape of cirques and ridges. The mountains were named after the Slavic god of thunder, Perun, who is said to have once lived atop the highest peak here, Mt Vihren (2915m). The northern face of Vihren is the most popular climb in this region and can be reached via Bansko (p127).

The 550km-long Balkan Range (or Stara Planina; literally 'Old Mountains') cuts right across the country from Serbia almost as far as the Black Sea, and acts as a climatic barrier between the north and south of Bulgaria, with the northern side significantly colder. It's a huge, diverse area, covering 10% of Bulgaria's territory. Due to its relatively easy access (from Vratsa) and the variety of routes offered, the most frequented section of this mighty range is the Vratsa Rocks in the far west, the largest limestone climbing area in Bulgaria. Mt Botev (2376m), inside the Central Balkan National Park, is another popular climb, with easy access from Karlovo.

Odysseia-In (below) and Zig Zag Holidays (p75) in Sofia are the best people to contact for a wide array of guided climbing trips; contact them for current itineraries and costs.

ROCK CLIMBING

Another outdoor activity that has become very popular in Bulgaria is rock climbing, and there are numerous locations around the country where you can indulge in a bit of clambering, either independently, or with a qualified guide – essential for some of the tougher areas. A good place to start is www .climbingguidebg.com, which has lots of information, advice and links.

The main area for rock climbing is around Vratsa (p265) where there are some 333 identified climbing routes and a variety of climbing conditions including alpine, sport and ice climbing. The area of Vratsata, on the road to the Ledenika Cave, is a popular spot, with permanent bolts attached to the rock face.

Other areas include the Pirin Mountains, with 31 alpine and traditional climbing routes, although these are only suitable for experienced climbers. The north face of Mt Vihren, to the south of Bansko, is particularly challenging. Maliovitsa (p122), in the Rila Mountains, is home to the Central Mountain School, which offers rock climbing activities and guides in the Maliovitsa range. Again, these are quite serious climbs, and safety nets are provided. The Vitosha mountain range and the Stara Planina are the other main areas for rock climbing, with many different routes for climbers of varying abilities.

A number of tour agencies offer guided climbing trips. The most experienced are the hearty outdoors folk at **Odysseia-In** (Map p88; ☎ 02-989 0538; www.odysseia-in.com; 1st fl, bul Stamboliyski 20-V, Sofia) who offer three-day rock-climbing trips in various areas, according to your own abilities and preferences, for €235 per person, for a group of two. The price for individuals is €375.

Join author Robert Reid as he takes to the Bulgarian mountains, picking up hitchhiking weightlifters, metal-heads and grandmothers along the way. Visit www.lonelyplanet .com/bulgarianhitchhikers

RESPONSIBLE HIKING

To help preserve the ecology and beauty of Bulgaria, consider the following tips when hiking.

Rubbish

- Carry out all your rubbish. Don't overlook easily forgotten items, such as silver paper, orange peel, cigarette butts and plastic wrappers. Empty packaging should be stored in a dedicated rubbish bag. Make an effort to carry out rubbish left by others.
- Never bury your rubbish: digging disturbs soil and ground cover and encourages erosion. Buried rubbish will likely be dug up by animals, who may be injured or poisoned by it. It may also take years to decompose.
- Sanitary napkins, tampons, condoms and toilet paper should be carried out despite the inconvenience. They burn and decompose poorly.

Human Waste Disposal

- Contamination of water sources by human faeces can lead to the transmission of all sorts of nasties. Where there is a toilet, please use it. Where there is none, bury your waste. Dig a small hole 15cm (6in) deep and at least 100m (320ft) from any watercourse. Cover the waste with soil and a rock. In snow, dig down to the soil.
- Ensure that these guidelines are applied to a portable toilet tent if one is being used by a large trekking party.

Washing

- Don't use detergents or toothpaste in or near watercourses, even if they are biodegradable.
- For personal washing, use biodegradable soap and a water container (or even a lightweight, portable basin) at least 50m (160ft) away from the watercourse. Disperse the waste water widely to allow the soil to filter it fully.
- Wash cooking utensils 50m (160ft) from watercourses using a scourer, sand or snow instead of detergent.

Erosion

- Hillsides and mountain slopes, especially at high altitudes, are prone to erosion. Stick to existing trails/tracks and avoid short cuts.
- Avoid removing the plant life that keeps topsoils in place.

Trapezitsa (Map p172; ☎ 062-621 593; www.trapezitsa-1902.hit.bg; ul Stefan Stambolov 79, Veliko Târnovo) offers a number of itineraries, including to the nearby Sveta Troitsa area as well as artificial walls to practice on.

Bulgarian Mountain Tours (☎ 01516-480 699; www.bulgarianmountaintours.com) is an excellent UK-based company that organises a variety of outdoorsy activities in Bulgaria such as walking, rock climbing, fishing and bird-watching. It also arranges accommodation.

SKIING

If there's one outdoor activity that Bulgaria is famous for, it's skiing. There has been massive investment in developing resorts in the country in recent years, and environmentalists have been highly critical of some of the more ambitious schemes (see p72).

Bansko (p127) is the number one resort in the country, with the most modern facilities, the longest snow season and the biggest international profile, attracting tourists from all over the world. It has also seen the heaviest investment, with numerous hotels and holiday apartments being built. There are now two ski centres – Chalin Valog (1100m to 1600m) and Shiligarnika (1700m to 2500m), roughly 10km from town and accessed from Bansko by gondola. All abilities are well catered for. Snow cover here lasts from December to May, helped in part by the use of artificial snow cannons. There's also a 5km cross-country ski track, and plenty of areas for snowboarding.

See www.bulgariaski .com for comprehensive information about the country's skiing resorts and snow reports.

Pamporovo (p156) likewise is experiencing rapid expansion. It's sited at 1650m, with 25km of trails and is said to be the sunniest resort in the country. It's an attractive, family-friendly place and great for beginners. The more experienced will be drawn towards the giant slalom run and, most difficult of all, the infamous 1100m-long Wall. The 'town' itself, though, such as it is, is pretty bland. Nearby Chepelare (p155) is quieter, but it has 30km of cross-country tracks and some of the longest runs in Bulgaria. The Mechi Chal 1 (3150m) is a black level run used for international competitions while Mechi Chal 2 (5250m) is a combined red/green slope. Both of these resorts are to be linked up into the vast Perelik project, creating one vast ski centre with 28km of new trails. It is due to open by December 2008.

Bulgaria's oldest resort, Borovets (p120) was founded in 1896 and although the infrastructure at present doesn't compare with nearby Bansko, it has 45km of trails and has a well-regarded ski school. In 2007, the go-ahead was finally given for the highly controversial 'Super Borovets' ski development, planned as part of Bulgaria's unsuccessful attempt to stage the 2014 Winter Olympic Games. This enormous project will turn a large swath of the countryside into a year-round tourist resort, with numerous other activities as well as skiing on offer, including golf courses and swimming pools. The mega resort will have 33 runs and 60km of tracks. It is expected to take around 15 years to complete.

Just 10km from Sofia, Vitosha (p109) is a convenient destination for weekending city folk and has slopes to suit all levels of skiers and snowboarders. Other, smaller (and cheaper) ski resorts include the new centre at Momchilovtsi (p158), Govedartsi (p122) and Maliovitsa (p122), which are mainly patronised by Bulgarian holidaymakers.

The **Bulgarian Extreme & Freestyle Skiing Association** (www.befsa.com) organises events such as the annual Big Mountain competition at Bansko. It also offers freestyle skiing excursions to remote, undeveloped locations if you want to escape the crowds.

BIRD-WATCHING, BOTANY & BEARS

Bulgaria is a haven for all kinds of wildlife, including such elusive creatures as brown bears and wolves, plus 400 species of birds (around 75% of the European total). Bird-watching is a popular hobby and several companies run bird-watching tours. The nesting period (May to June) and migration period (September to October) are the best times to come. The Via Pontica, which passes over Bulgaria, is one of Europe's major migratory routes for birds, while Atanasovsko Lake, north of Burgas, is the country's most important reserve, frequented by 314 different species.

Based in Sofia, Spatia Wildlife (www.spatia wildlife.com) runs specialised botany and dragonfly-spotting tours around Bulgaria.

Neophron (☎ 052-650 230; www.neophron.com; PO Box 492, Varna) runs 10- to 14-day guided birding trips across the country, which can be combined with botany and bear-watching tours. It's run by professional ornithologists, and raises funds for the **Bulgarian Society for the Protection of Birds** (www.bspb.org).

Birdwatching Bulgaria (☎ 02-400 1055; www.birdwatchingbulgaria.com) runs numerous birding trips throughout the year, headed by professional, English-speaking guides. For those with minimal time, the one-day trip around Sofia (€80) takes in Vitosha Nature Park (p109) and/or Dragoman Marsh, some 35km west of the capital, where possible sightings include ferruginous ducks, sedge

Visit www.cometobg.com
for details about wildlife
photography tours
around Bulgaria run
by the knowledgeable
Emil Enchev.

warblers and black woodpeckers. More dedicated bird-watchers can book onto longer tours, such as the eight-day Southern Bulgaria tour (€680 per person full board, for a group of two) where you'll have the chance to spot rarer species including the Squacco heron and Imperial eagle. The company also offers bear-watching tours and specialised excursions concentrating on botany; see the website for the full list of options.

Also worth a look is **Pelican Lake Guesthouse** (www.srebrnabirding.com) near Lake Srebârna (p274), where you'll find Bulgaria's only breeding colony of Dalmatian Pelicans. The British owners will be happy to arrange tours.

WATER SPORTS

The big Black Sea package resorts such as Sunny Beach (Slânchev Bryag), Golden Sands (Zlatni Pyasâtsi) and Albena offer all the usual organised watery fun, with numerous outlets offering jet-skiing, water-skiing, parasailing and windsurfing along the beaches. Often these are quite casual affairs set up at various points along the shoreline. Albena (p249) probably has the most comprehensive setup.

Visit www.vierpfoten.org,
the website of the Four
Paws Foundation, for
news of the Dancing Bear
Park in Belitsa.

There's a growing number of diving outlets along the coast, and most are in the big resorts, although a major new complex is currently being planned near Tsarevo. As well as standard training courses and boat dives, there's also the opportunity to explore some WWII wrecks off Kaliakra Cape.

Harry's Diving Center (☎ 052-321 766; todorharbaliev@hotmail.com) in Golden Sands (p248) is a PADI-certified outfit offering reef dives offshore and wreck dives off Kaliakra Cape.

Albena Diving Centre (☎ 0888980409; ☯ 9am-6pm), based at Hotel Laguna Beach in Albena (p250), offers a similar setup, with similar prices.

Angel Divers (Map p230; ☎ 0889427355; www.angel-divers.com), with kiosks at Nesebâr harbour and on Sveti Vlas beach, runs (amongst other things) four-day PADI-certified open-water courses and wreck-diving trips off Sozopol.

CYCLING & MOTORBIKING

Though not advisable as a means of getting around cities, cycling is an excellent way of exploring some of the more off-the-beaten-track areas of Bulgaria's wild and wonderful countryside. Hostels sometimes offer bike rental to guests, but there are surprisingly few businesses that rent out bikes – the Black Sea coast resorts are probably the best places for this – so it's a good idea to either bring your own, or book onto a guided tour.

Motoroads (off Map p84; ☎ 0885370298; www.motoroads.com; Mladost 2, bl 279, office 1, Sofia 1799) in Sofia has a good choice of motorcycles for rent from €40 per day (plus €300 security deposit) and organises a series of motorbike trips: a quick three-day riding tour of the Rila, Pirin and Rodopi Mountains costs €460 per person for two, including accommodation, or €270 for a self-guided trip.

Odysseia-In (Map p88; ☎ 02-989 0538; www.odysseia-in.com; 1st fl, bul Stamboliyski 20-V, Sofia) runs eight-day mountain-biking trips through the Rodopis, covering around 50km per day (€590 per person, groups of six to nine).

Cycling Bulgaria (☎ 02-400 1080; www.cyclingbulgaria.com) is another big outfit offering interesting excursions such as the eight-day Monastery Cycling Tour (€415) taking in some of Bulgaria's smaller monasteries.

Cross the Line (Map p88; ☎ 02-987 9089; www.crossthelinebg.com; ul Tsar Samuil 38, Sofia) offers guided cycling trips and many other activities. Its seven-day Black Sea Coast trip, running from Balchik to Sozopol, costs €499 per person (includes transport and full-board accommodation). Hiking, climbing, canyoning and other outdoor trips are also available.

HORSE RIDING

Seeing the open countryside from atop a horse can be a magical experience, and there are several companies around the country offering horse-riding tours in some of the most spectacular areas such as the Balkan range, the Pirin Mountains and the Black Sea coast. One of the most comprehensive companies is **Horse Riding Bulgaria** (☎ 02-400 3095; www.horseridingbulgaria.com), which runs an array of adventures including eight-day treks in the Western Balkan range, based around Koprivshtitsa (p191) for €695 per person, and around Strandzha Nature Park (p227) for €750.

SOFIA

Sofia СОФИЯ

By far Bulgaria's biggest city, Sofia (*So*-fia) is one of Europe's most compact and walkable capital cities, although it's still one of the least known by foreign travellers. It's usually bypassed by tourists heading to the coast or the ski resorts, but they're missing out on something special. Sofia has a young and dynamic vibe, like a city waking up after decades of slumber, and is becoming a confident and cosmopolitan European capital. The old east-meets-west feel is still here, with a scattering of onion-domed churches, Ottoman mosques and Red Army monuments topped with air-punching Soviet soldiers, but these days they share the skyline with glitzy shopping malls, five-star hotels and the best bars and clubs the country has to offer.

Although no grand metropolis, Sofia is nevertheless an attractive and cultured city with plenty to keep you busy for several days or more. Museums, art galleries, theatres, fine restaurants, they're all here. Sofia is also a surprisingly green city, with huge swaths of parkland within the city boundaries and the ski slopes and hiking trails of mighty Mt Vitosha right on the doorstep.

The city has certainly developed quickly over recent years and a new affluence is apparent in the trendy international boutiques, upmarket hotels and less savoury casinos and flashy cars with blacked-out windows, but there are also great inequalities. Hard-up pensioners and disabled people begging on the street are, sadly, not an uncommon sight, but most Sofians have hope for the future of their city as one of the EU's newest capitals.

HIGHLIGHTS

- **Golden glow**
  Cast an eye over the stunning Thracian treasures on display at the Archaeological Museum (p91)

- **Woodland wandering**
  Escape the crowds and get lost in the wilds of Yuzhen Park (p92)

- **Magnificent murals**
  Ponder eternity amongst the sacred artwork of the medieval Boyana Church (p108)

- **Up the workers**
  Get close to more recent history at the towering Monument to the Soviet Army (p92)

- **Engage your brain**
  Join the locals in a competitive game of chess in the City Garden (p90)

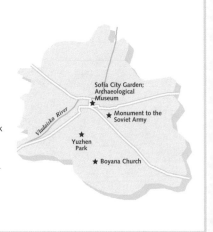

Sofia City Garden;
Archaeological
Museum ★

★ Monument to the
Soviet Army

Vladaiska River

★
Yuzhen
Park

★ Boyana Church

| TELEPHONE CODE: 02 | POPULATION: 1.3 MILLION |

HISTORY

The Thracian Serdi tribe settled the Sofia region as far back as the 8th century BC, and the area was briefly occupied by the Macedonians in the 4th century BC. However, the city as we know it today was founded by the Romans, who conquered the region in AD 29 and built the town of Ulpia Serdica. In the late 3rd century AD, Serdica became a major regional imperial capital, reaching a zenith in the early 4th century under Emperor Constantine the Great. The Sveti Georgi Rotunda is the most prominent reminder of the Roman era still standing.

The Bulgar king Khan Krum swung by in AD 809 and made it one of the main towns of his empire. The Byzantines occupied it in the 11th century, and it was during the Second Bulgarian Empire (1185–1396) that the name of the city was changed (for the last time) to Sofia, after the Church of Sveta Sofia, which still stands, albeit much rebuilt. Sadly, few monuments survive from this crucial period; the most important, and most precious to all Bulgarians, is the lovely Boyana Church.

The Ottomans, sweeping through the Balkans, captured the city in 1382, and held it for nearly 500 years. Sofia became the regional capital and a major market town. The Ottomans built baths and mosques, such as the Banya Bashi Mosque, but many churches were destroyed or abandoned; the tiny Church of Sveta Petka Samardjiiska is a very rare survivor.

The city declined during the feudal unrest of the mid-19th century, and it was in Sofia that the celebrated anti-Turkish rebel Vasil Levski was hanged in 1873, after first being interrogated and tortured in the building that later became the Royal Palace. After the liberation of the city from the Turks in early 1878, Sofia officially became the capital of Bulgaria on 4 April 1879. The new roads and railway lines linking Sofia with the rest of Europe and the Balkans soon boosted the city's fortunes. However, Bulgaria picked the wrong side during WWII so, tragically, much of the city's heritage was destroyed during bombing raids.

The Red Army 'liberated' Sofia in 1944 – the monument (p92) to their arrival still soars near Borisova Gradina – and a People's Republic was set up after the war. Socialist architects set to work in the following years, rebuilding the heavily damaged city on the Soviet model, complete with high-rise housing blocks in the suburbs and monstrous monuments in the city centre, such as the old Party House which dominates pl Nezavisimost. Some of the more distasteful reminders of the communist era, such as the mausoleum of postwar leader Georgi Dimitrov, have been swept away, while others have been allowed to slowly decay since the fall of the communist government in 1989.

High unemployment and declining living standards blighted the 1990s, but while serious problems still exist, EU membership in 2007 does seem to have brought a new dynamism and sense of stability to the city, which is experiencing something of a building boom. As more international companies set up offices, and more foreign citizens choose to settle here, it's a trend that looks set to continue.

ORIENTATION

At the heart of Sofia is pl Sveta Nedelya, dominated by the great cathedral of the same name. To the north, bul Maria Luisa runs past the Central Hali Shopping Centre and the Banya Bashi Mosque towards the central train and bus stations. To the south, bul Vitosha, Sofia's partly pedestrianised main shopping street, heads towards the National Palace of Culture (NDK) and on to Yuzhen Park.

East of pl Sveta Nedelya you'll come upon pl Nezavisimost (also known as The Largo) and bul Tsar Osvoboditel, watched over by the former Royal Palace. Continuing down bul Tsar Osvoboditel, you'll pass pl Narodno Sabranie and the parliament building on the way to the huge park of Borisova Gradina.

See p107 for details on getting to and from the airport.

Maps

The *Sofia City Map* (1:19,000), published by Domino, and Datamap's *Sofia City Plan* (1:20,000), both printed in English, are widely available. The *Sofia City Info Guide* (see p85) also includes a good tourist map of the city centre. All bookshops listed in the next section sell maps of Sofia and other places in Bulgaria, as do stalls at pl Slaveikov. One of the best sources of maps, especially for hiking, is **Odysseia-In** (Map p88; ☎ 989 0538; www.odysseia-in.com; 1st fl, bul Stamboliyski 20-V); also see p86.

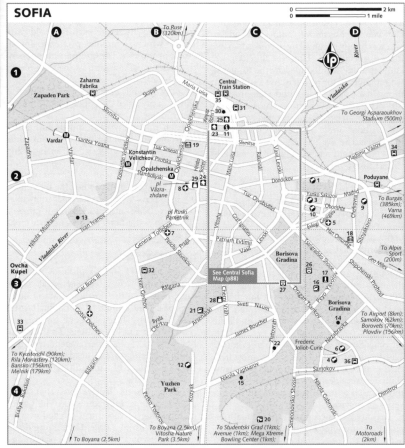

INFORMATION
Bookshops
Booktrading (Map p88; ☎ 981 0448; ul Graf Ignatiev 15; ⏱ 8.30am-8.30pm Mon-Sat, 10am-8pm Sun) Stocks a fair selection of English-language novels as well as books on Bulgarian history, cuisine and topics of general interest.

Helikon (Map p88; ☎ 987 1919; bul Patriarh Evtimii 68; ⏱ 9.30am-8.30pm Mon-Sat, 10am-8.30pm Sun) Welcoming modern bookshop selling a good range of English-language fiction plus books on Bulgaria in various languages.

Knigomaniya (Map p84; ☎ 980 5214; 3rd fl, Mall of Sofia, bul Stamboliyski 101) Has a good stock of English-language fiction and nonfiction, plus maps, guidebooks and tourist-oriented books on Bulgaria. It also sells magazines and Bulgarian pop-music CDs.

Open-Air Bookmarket (Map p88; pl Slaveikov) Dozens of bookstalls crowd this square daily, selling mostly Bulgarian novels and technical manuals, but plenty of books on Bulgarian history, culture and cuisine are available in foreign languages, as well as some second-hand English novels.

Cultural Centres
American Cultural Center (Map p84; ☎ 937 5306; ul Kozyak 16; ⏱ 2-5pm Tue-Fri)

British Council (Map p88; ☎ 942 4344; www.british council.org/bulgaria; ul Krakra 7; ⏱ 9am-5pm Mon-Fri)

French Cultural Institute (Map p88; ☎ 937 7922; www.institutfrance.bg; ul Dyakon Ignatiy 2; ⏱ 11am-6pm Mon-Fri, 10am-1pm Sat)

Goethe Institute (Map p88; ☎ 939 0100; ul Budapeshta 1; ⏱ 9am-noon & 3-5pm Mon-Fri)

Emergency
Ambulance (☎ 150)
Fire (☎ 160)
Mountain Rescue (Aleko ☎ 967 455; Cherni Vrâh ☎ 967 1128)
Police (☎ 166)
Traffic Police (☎ 866 5060)

Internet Access
BTC Centre (Map p88; ul General Gurko; per hr 0.80 lv; ⌚ 24hr) Offers several computers in a modern, office-style environment.
Bulgaria-Korea Internet Plaza (Map p88; NDK Underpass; 45mins 0.30 lv, per hr thereafter 1.60 lv; ⌚ 9am-8pm Mon-Fri) Probably the cheapest internet centre in Sofia, with a dozen or so computers.
Site Internet Cafe (Map p88; ☎ 986 0896; bul Vitosha 45; per hr 3 lv; ⌚ 24hr) One of the more central and more reliable internet centres, with a nonsmoking room. Insomniacs can take advantage of the all-night rate (from 10.30pm to 8.30am) of 10 lv, which includes a soft drink and a coffee.

Internet Resources
www.easysofia.com Information about hotels, restaurants, clubs, bars and more.
www.programata.bg Comprehensive eating, drinking and clubbing information.
www.sofia.bg Official municipal website, with business information.
www.sofiacityguide.com Website of the invaluable *Sofia City Info Guide* (right).
www.sofia-life.com Bar and restaurant reviews, plus details of some shops and attractions.

Media
Programata (www.programata.bg; free) A useful, widely available weekly listings magazine, with details of cinemas, restaurants and clubs. It's only in Bulgarian, but the website is in English.

Sofia City Info Guide (free) An excellent source of information, published monthly. It includes basic practical information and reviews of hotels, restaurants, clubs and shops. It's available at hotel reception desks and some travel agencies.
Sofia Echo (www.sofiaecho.com; 2.40 lv) An English-language newspaper published each Friday and available at some central newsstands. Mainly aimed at the expat business community, it also has restaurant and entertainment reviews useful for visitors.
Sofia In Your Pocket (free) Another handy quarterly magazine, with eating, sleeping and sightseeing reviews and practical information on the city.
Sofia – The Insider's Guide (free) A pleasingly opinionated quarterly publication featuring background information and advice for visitors, as well as restaurant and entertainment reviews. Available at some hotels and travel agencies.

Medical Services
Apteka Sveta Nedelya (Map p88; ☎ 987 5089; pl Sveta Nedelya 5; ⌚ 24hr) Pharmacy.
Dento (Map p84; ☎ 958 4841; www.dento-bg.com; ul Atanasov 11) English-, French- and Italian-speaking dentists.
International Medical Centre (Map p84; ☎ 944 9326; ul Gogol 28) The IMC has English- and French-speaking doctors who will make house calls at any time. It also deals with paediatrics and dental care.
Pirogov Hospital (Map p84; ☎ 915 4411; bul Gen Totleben 21) Sofia's main public hospital for emergencies.
Poliklinika Torax (Map p84; ☎ 91 285; www.thorax.bg; bul Stamboliyski 57) A competent, privately run clinic with English-speaking staff.

Money
The Foreign Exchange Office has numerous outlets on bul Vitosha, bul Maria Luisa and bul Stamboliyski.

SOFIA IN...

One Day
Head straight to Sofia's most impressive sight, the **Aleksander Nevski Memorial Church** (p91). While you're there, visit the Aleksander Nevski Crypt to see the colourful Museum of Icons. Carry on to **Borisova Gradina** (p92) for a leisurely stroll among the trees, and cast an eye over Sofia's socialist past at the **Monument to the Soviet Army** (p92) on the way. In the evening, drop by **Pri Kmeta** (p102) for a beer or two.

Three Days
Follow the above itinerary, and on the second day admire the treasures on show at the **Archaeological Museum** (p91) and the **National Art Gallery** (p90). On the next day, relax in **Yuzhen Park** (p92) and have a meal at the excellent **Manastirska Magernitsa** (p101).

One Week
After the above itinerary, go to Boyana to see the **National Museum of History** (p108) and the lovely **Boyana Church** (p108). Take a look round the **National Museum of Military History** (p94) and take a day trip out to **Koprivshtitsa** (p191).

Biochim Commercial Bank (Map p88; ul Alabin)
Unicredit Bulbank (Map p88; cnr ul Lavele & ul Todor Alexandrov)
United Bulgarian Bank (Map p88; ul Sveta Sofia)

Post
Central Post Office (Map p88; ul General Gurko 6; ⏱ 7.30am-8.30pm)

Telephone
BTC Centre (Map p88; ul General Gurko; ⏱ 24hr) Modern communications centre run by the Bulgarian Telecommunications Company, with booths for local and international calls and internet access.

Toilets
Central Hali Shopping Centre (Map p88; bul Maria Luisa; admission free)
NDK Underpass (Map p88; Yuzhen Park; admission 0.30 lv)
Public Toilets (Map p88; bul Maria Luisa; admission 0.40 lv) Beside Banya Bashi Mosque.
Tsum Retail Centre (Map p88; bul Maria Luisa; admission free)

Tourist Information
National Tourist Information Centre (Map p88; ☎ 987 9778; www.bulgariatravel.org; ul Sveta Sofia; ⏱ 9am-5pm Mon-Fri) Bright modern tourist office with helpful, English-speaking staff and glossy brochures for destinations around Bulgaria.
Zig Zag Holidays (Map p88; ☎ 980 5102; www.zig zagbg.com; bul Stamboliyski 20-V, enter from ul Lavele; ⏱ 8.30am-7.30pm Mon-Sat) Although essentially a

private travel agency, Zig Zag is happy to provide tourist information, and sells a range of maps and books. It charges a reasonable 5 lv for detailed consultations, though this fee is deducted if you book a tour (eg hiking or climbing) or accommodation with the agency.

Travel Agencies
Alexander Tour (Map p88; ☎ /fax 983 3322; www .alexandertour.com; ul Pop Bogomil 44) An upmarket outfit offering numerous tours all over Bulgaria, including bird-watching, archaeology and wine tours.
Balkan Tourist (Map p88; ☎ 986 5849; www.balkan tourist.bg; bul Tsar Osvoboditel 4) Inside the old Bulgaria Grand Hotel, this efficient agency books domestic and international air tickets.
Odysseia-In Travel Agency (Map p88; ☎ 989 0538; www.odysseia-in.com; 1st fl, bul Stamboliyski 20-V, enter from ul Lavele) Odysseia-In can book you on hiking, skiing, climbing, bird-watching and numerous other trips across the country. It deals with groups; individuals should contact Zig Zag Holidays (left) on the ground floor of the same building.

DANGERS & ANNOYANCES
The main danger you are likely to face in Sofia comes from the often dreadful traffic; pedestrian crossings and traffic lights don't mean much to many drivers, so be extra careful when crossing roads. Note that traffic lanes and pedestrian areas are marked only by faint painted lines on the cobbles around pl Aleksander Nevski and pl Narodno Sabranie, and although a large section of bul Vitosha is now off-limits to private cars, you should still

watch out for trams and for vehicles zipping out of the side streets.

As always, be careful with bags, wallets and purses on crowded public transport and particularly in busy areas such as the Ladies' Market and pl Sveta Nedelya.

SIGHTS

Most of Sofia's sights are handily located in the compact city centre, and you won't have to do too much walking to get round them all. Further afield, the suburb of Boyana (p108) is the location of the city's biggest museum and its most revered church.

Around Ploshtad Sveta Nedelya

SVETA NEDELYA CATHEDRAL

This magnificent domed **church** (Map p88; pl Sveta Nedelya) is one of the city's major landmarks. Built between 1856 and 1863 on the foundations of several older churches, the cathedral's interior is covered with rich, Byzantine-style murals of saints. A glass case to the right of the iconostasis holds the body of Sveti Kral Stefan Milotin, a medieval king of Serbia, wrapped in a velvet robe. The bones are said to have miraculous healing powers. A small plaque near the southern entrance explains, in English, how the cathedral was blown up by communists on 16 April 1925 in an attempt to assassinate Tsar Boris III. Over 120 people were killed in the attack, including most of the cabinet, but Boris escaped unharmed.

SOFIA MONUMENT

Erected in 2001 on the site where a gigantic statue of Lenin once stood, this 24m-high **monument** (Map p88; bul Maria Luisa) was created as a new civic symbol for the city. The bronze female figure at the top of the column, holding the wreath of victory in her right hand and balancing an owl on her left arm, represents Sofia, personification of wisdom and fate.

North of Ploshtad Sveta Nedelya

SVETA PETKA SAMARDJIISKA CHURCH

This tiny **church** (Map p88; admission 2 lv; 🕑 7am-6pm) is incongruously located in the underpass below the Tsum Retail Centre. Named in honour of St Peter of the Saddlers, the church was built during the early years of Ottoman rule (late 14th century), which explains its sunken profile and inconspicuous exterior. Inside there

are some 16th-century murals, but nothing is explained in any language. It's rumoured that the Bulgarian freedom fighter and national icon Vasil Levski is buried here.

MINERAL BATHS

The **Mineral Baths** (Map p88; ul Triaditsa) – also known as the Turkish Baths – was built between 1911 and 1913. With its elegant striped façade and ceramic decorations recalling the designs of Nesebâr's medieval churches, it's one of Sofia's architectural gems, but it fell into dereliction in the 1990s and has been undergoing sporadic restoration for over a decade. When restoration is finally complete, it will house a new civic museum, although no date has been set for this. The centrepiece of the little square between the baths and the Banya Bashi Mosque, known as pl Banski, is a modern fountain, while a smart **drinking-fountain complex** has been constructed just behind the baths, where locals fill up their bottles with free streaming mineral water.

BANYA BASHI MOSQUE

Sofia's only working **mosque** (Map p88; bul Maria Luisa) was built in 1576 by the celebrated Ottoman architect Kodja Mimar Sinan, who also designed the Selim II Mosque in Edirne, Turkey. It's certainly an eye-catching edifice and the red brick minaret makes a convenient landmark. At the rear of the building is a small, recently excavated section of the bathhouse that once joined onto the mosque and a hot-water drinking fountain. Visitors are welcome outside prayer times if modestly dressed.

SOFIA SYNAGOGUE

Sofia's grand **synagogue** (Map p88; ☎ 983 1273; www.sofiasynagogue.com; ul Ekzarh Yosif 16) was designed in a flamboyant Moorish style by the Austrian architect Friedrich Gruenanger, and was consecrated in 1909. Built to accommodate up to 1170 worshippers, it is the largest Sephardic synagogue in Europe, and its 2250kg brass chandelier is the biggest in Bulgaria. However, visitors are only admitted if invited or of the Jewish faith.

NATIONAL POLYTECHNIC MUSEUM

One of Sofia's less visited attractions, this small **museum** (Map p84; ☎ 931 3004; ul Opalchenska 66; admission 3 lv; 🕑 9am-5pm Mon-Fri) is nevertheless

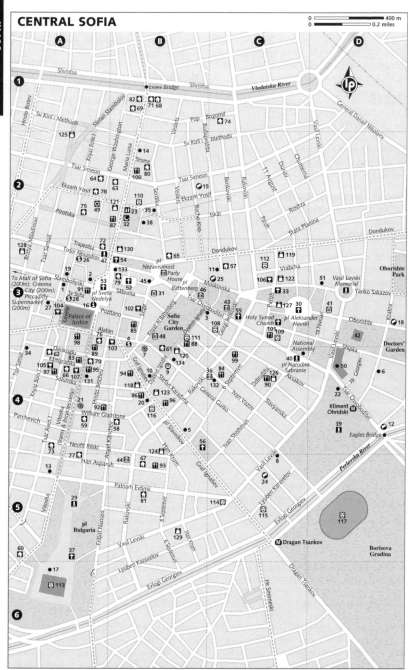

CENTRAL SOFIA

a treasure trove for anyone interested in the history of science and technology. On show is a varied (though not always well labelled) collection covering such subjects as photography, radio and time measurement. A gleaming, perfectly restored 1928 Ford Model A is parked just inside, while other displays include atomic clocks, typewriters, early movie cameras and mechanical pianos. Look for the Bulgarian-made freeze-dried 'space food', which includes a packet of powdered *tarator*.

Around Ploshtad Battenberg

ROYAL PALACE

Originally built as the headquarters of the Ottoman police force, it was at the **palace** (Map p88; pl Battenberg 1) that Bulgaria's national hero, Vasil Levski, was tried and tortured before his public execution in 1873. After the Liberation, the building was remodelled in Viennese style and in 1887, apparently undeterred by its grisly recent past, Prince Alexander Battenberg moved in and it became the official residence of Bulgaria's royal family until the communist takeover. These days it houses the National Art Gallery and the Ethnographical Museum, while the shaded park at the rear contains an odd assemblage of statues.

Occupying the east wing of the palace, the **National Art Gallery** (☎ 980 3325; admission 4 lv; ☽ 10am-6pm Tue, Wed & Fri-Sun, to 7pm Thu) holds one of the country's most comprehensive collections of Bulgarian art, with several galleries full of mainly 19th- and 20th-century paintings and sculptures. All the big names are represented, including the ubiquitous Vladimir Dimitrov, whose orange, Madonna-like *Harvester* hangs in the former royal music room. Other standouts include Goshka Datsov's *The Dream of Mary Magdalene* and Georgi Mashev's creepy *Outcast*. Anton Mitov's paintings of early-20th-century Sofia, such as *Vegetable Market at Sofia*, offer a fascinating insight into local history. On the floor above, a warren of corridors and small rooms forms a display space for Bulgarian sculpture, featuring marble, bronze and terracotta portraits by Ivan Lazarov, Vaska Emmanouilova and Andrei Nikolov, whose marble head, *Yearning*, is among the highlights.

Spread over two floors, the **Ethnographical Museum** (☎ 987 4191; admission 3 lv, guided tour 10 lv; ☽ 10am-5.30pm Tue-Sun) has a permanent collection of regional costumes and crafts, although most of the space is usually occupied by long-term temporary exhibitions on topics of varying interest, such as traditional festivals, carpet-making, or, as was the case through 2007, provincial bread stamps. (Everything is captioned in English.) Some rooms are in poor condition, but others, with their marble fireplaces, mirrors and ornate plasterwork, are worth pausing over; note the lobster, fish and dead duck on the ceiling of what was once presumably a royal dining room.

The exit from the museum leads directly into the Centre of Folk Arts & Crafts souvenir shop (p105).

NATIONAL MUSEUM OF NATURAL HISTORY

You can almost sense the ghosts of generations of school parties dutifully trooping through the musty halls of this old-fashioned **museum** (Map p88; ☎ 987 4195; ul Tsar Osvoboditel 1; admission 2 lv; ☽ 10am-6pm). The didactic collection of animal, plant and mineral specimens is vast, although there's little labelling in anything but Bulgarian. Rocks, crystals and minerals grace the ground floor, while on the next two floors you can browse cases full of stuffed birds and animals, including a brown bear dangling a Nazi hunting medal from its claw and some threadbare apes, lions and tigers. Pickled fish and cases of dried insects complete the collection.

SVETI NIKOLAI RUSSIAN CHURCH

This gorgeous **church** (Map p88; ul Tsar Osvoboditel; ☽ 7.45am-6.30pm) with its glittering mosaic exterior was built between 1912 and 1914 for Sofia's Russian community, and named in honour of St Nikolai, the 'miracle worker'. Like the Aleksander Nevski Church, the design is strongly influenced by Russian architecture, most notably in its five golden onion domes. The surprisingly cramped interior features colourful murals and icons painted between the 11th and 14th centuries. Bishop Serafim (1881–1950), one of Bulgaria's most revered spiritual leaders, lies entombed in the crypt (accessed by a separate door to the left of the main entrance). Sitting in a flower-filled garden, the church is one of the most photographed sites in the capital.

SOFIA CITY GARDEN

Take a break from pounding the city streets and rest up in this leafy **garden** (Map p88), with its cafés, swings, flowerbeds and lovely fountain, where old men gather to play chess. Until its sudden and unceremonious demolition in 1999, the mausoleum of Bulgaria's first communist ruler, Georgi Dimitrov, squatted at the northern end of the park facing the Royal Palace. It has since been replaced by some shrubbery.

SOFIA MUNICIPAL GALLERY OF ART

Originally built as a casino, this chunky building at the southern end of the City

Garden is now an avant-garde **art gallery** (Map p88; ☎ 987 2181; ul General Gurko 1; admission free; ⏰ 10am-6pm Tue-Sat, 11am-5pm Sun). It stages rotating exhibitions of mostly contemporary Bulgarian and international art over two floors.

ARCHAEOLOGICAL MUSEUM

The Buyuk Djami (Great Mosque), with its nine lead-covered domes, was built in 1496, and since 1899 it has housed Sofia's fascinating **Archaeological Museum** (Map p88; ☎ 988 2406; ul Sâborna 2; admission 10 lv; ⏰ 10am-6pm Tue-Sun). Thracian and Roman tombstones fill up much of the ground floor, along with weaponry and jewellery. Among the more eye-catching artefacts are a 3rd-century AD bronze head of the Emperor Gordianus; a stone plaque showing gladiatorial fights in the circus, now under the Arena di Serdica hotel (p100); and the original 4th-century AD mosaic floor from the apse of the Church of Sveta Sofia (right). On show upstairs are the remarkable finds unearthed near Shipka in 2004, including the 4th-century BC gold burial mask of a Thracian king, and a magnificent bronze head with coloured glass eyes and fine copper eyelashes, thought to be of King Sevt. On the gallery level, the walls are lined with icons and frescoes removed from churches around Bulgaria. The wall facing the main entrance, meanwhile, is dominated by an early-20th-century reproduction of the Madara Horseman figure; the slightly more weathered original can be seen near Shumen (p169). Everything in the museum is labelled in English.

PRESIDENCY

The Bulgarian president's **office** (Map p88; pl Nezavisimost) occupies the eastern end of the grey, monolithic building that also houses the Sheraton Hotel. It's not open to the public, but the **changing of the guard** ceremony (on the hour) is a spectacle not to be missed, as soldiers in raffish Ruritanian uniforms stomp their way to their sentry boxes.

SVETI GEORGI ROTUNDA

Regarded as the oldest preserved building in Sofia, the **Sveti Georgi Rotunda** (Map p88), in the courtyard between the Sheraton Hotel and the Presidency, dates from the 4th century AD. This circular Roman structure, also known as the Church of St George, was largely rebuilt in the 6th century after being knocked about

---

TOP PICKS: FREE ATTRACTIONS

- Aleksander Nevski Memorial Church (below)
- Borisova Gradina (p92)
- Mondays at the National Gallery for Foreign Art (p92)
- Sofia Municipal Gallery of Art (opposite)

---

by invading Huns and in the 16th century was converted into a mosque. It was badly damaged by bombing during WWII and only fully opened to visitors again in 1998 after much restoration. The murals inside were painted on three layers between the 10th and 14th centuries.

Inside the entrance there's a small explanation in English about the church. You're also allowed to wander around the unlabelled Roman ruins behind the church.

Around Ploshtad Aleksander Nevski

ALEKSANDER NEVSKI MEMORIAL CHURCH

One of *the* symbols not just of Sofia but of Bulgaria itself, this massive, awe-inspiring **church** (Map p88; pl Aleksander Nevski) was built between 1882 and 1912 in memory of the 200,000 Russian soldiers who died fighting for Bulgaria's independence during the Russo-Turkish War (1877–78).

Designed by the esteemed Russian architect AN Pomerantsev, the church was built in the neo-Byzantine style favoured in Russia at the time and adorned with mosaics and gold-laden domes. The cavernous, incense-scented interior is decorated with naturalistic murals, pendulous chandeliers and elaborate onyx and alabaster thrones.

A door to the left of the main entrance leads to the **Aleksander Nevski Crypt** (Museum of Icons; ☎ 981 5775; admission 4 lv; ⏰ 10am-5.30pm Tue-Sat). It displays Bulgaria's biggest and best collection of religious icons from the last millennium, brought here from churches all over the country.

CHURCH OF SVETA SOFIA

There has been a church on this site since the mid-4th century, although the **Church of Sveta Sofia** (Map p88; ul Parizh) as it stands today is a much-restored 6th-century foundation, making it the oldest Orthodox church in the Bulgarian capital, to which it eventually gave its name. The church fell victim to invading hordes, fires and earthquakes several times over the centuries, and after a devastating 1858 earthquake, the building, then used as a mosque, was abandoned. The present, rather sober, red-brick structure is mostly 19th century, and was restored as a church in the early 20th century. Outside stands the **Tomb of the Unknown Soldier**, with its eternal flame and stone lion, and on the northern side of the church is a simple monument commemorating Tsar Boris III's role in the rescue of Bulgaria's Jews.

SOFIA UNIVERSITY BOTANIC GARDEN
Easily overlooked near the Vasil Levski Memorial, the **Botanic Garden** (Map p88; ul Moskovska; admission 1 lv; ⏰ 10am-6pm Tue-Sun) is a small, well-manicured plant collection, which includes a glasshouse filled with palms and cacti, a rose garden and various trees and flowers (labelled in Bulgarian and Latin).

NATIONAL GALLERY FOR FOREIGN ART
An eclectic assemblage of international artworks is on display in this huge **gallery** (Map p88; ☎ 988 4922; www.foreignartgallery.org; ul 19 Fevruari 1; admission 4 lv, Mon free, guided tours 15 lv; ⏰ 11am-6pm Wed-Mon), and although you won't find any world-class treasures here, there are a few big names and plenty of little-known artists to discover. On the ground floor you can browse Indian woodcarvings, Burmese Buddhas, African tribal art and colourful Japanese prints. Upstairs are several galleries of European paintings, mostly by long-forgotten artists, while highpoints include a Van Dyck portrait, minor sketches by Renoir, Matisse and Degas, and a *Last Supper* attributed to Palma Vecchio. There are also some small bronzes by the 16th-century German Master Conrad Meit and bronze studies for *The Burgesses of Calais* by Rodin. Works of minor artists worth seeking out include Albert Andre's everyday scenes (such as *The Small Restaurant)* and Henry Moret's Impressionistic landscapes.

South of Ploshtad Aleksander Nevski
MONUMENT TO THE SOVIET ARMY
Near the entrance to Borisova Gradina, this giant **monument** (Map p88) was built to commemorate the 10th anniversary of the Russian 'liberation' of Bulgaria in 1944 and is a prime example of the forceful socialist-

realism of the period. The place of honour goes to a Red Army soldier atop a column, surrounded by animated cast-iron sculptural groups depicting determined, gun-waving soldiers and grateful, child-caressing members of the proletariat.

BORISOVA GRADINA
Lying southeast of the city centre, Sofia's most attractive expanse of greenery is home to the **Vasil Levski Stadium** (Map p88), **CSKA Stadium** (Map p84) and **Maria Luisa Pool** (Map p84; ☎ 963 0054; ⏰ 9am-8pm summer), as well as bike tracks and tennis courts. It's laid out with countless statues and flowerbeds, and is a relaxing place to take a leisurely stroll on a sunny Sunday afternoon. The eastern end of the park is dominated by a gigantic communist monument built in 1956 and known as the **Mound of Brotherhood** (Map p84), featuring a 42m-high obelisk and socialist-realist icons including a pair of partisan fighters, dramatically gesturing comrades clutching Kalashnikovs, and smiling, stoic workers. It has long been neglected by the authorities, and several of the socialist heroes are now missing limbs and gaining coats of graffiti, but small groups of pensioners come on occasion to lay flowers in remembrance of the red old days.

YUZHEN PARK
South of bul Bålgaria, behind the NDK, **Yuzhen Park** (Map p84) is a vast green sprawl, filled with trees and shady pathways, and is the closest you'll come to open countryside within the city. It's wilder, less managed, more peaceful and less populated than Borisova Gradina and has some superb, uninterrupted views towards Mt Vitosha. A sparkling stream bubbles through it, and there is a handful of discreet bars and cafés that are not always easy to find, but it's a satisfying place to get lost in and explore for yourself.

NATIONAL PALACE OF CULTURE (NDK)
Bulevard Vitosha leads down to the **National Palace of Culture** (NDK; Map p88), the city's vast concert hall (see p103), which watches over an elongated park known as pl Bulgaria. There are some kiosks and sociable bars here for those in search of a cheap alfresco beer, as well as carts selling popcorn and ice cream. It's also a favourite venue for Sofia's skateboarding teens. At the northern end of the park is the disintegrating **1300 Years Monument**, built in

1981 to celebrate the anniversary of the creation of the First Bulgarian Empire. It has been falling to pieces and fenced off for years, and nobody seems to want to take responsibility for the renovation – or more likely, the demolition – of this unloved monstrosity.

Nearby is the **memorial and chapel** dedicated to the victims of the communist regime, with a plaque bearing some 10,000 names. Behind it is a section of the Berlin Wall.

Steps just in front of the NDK building lead down into a gloomy **underpass** crammed with cheap clothes shops and cafés.

PEYO YAVOROV HOUSE-MUSEUM

The Romantic poet and revolutionary Peyo Yavorov (1878–1914; see the boxed text, below) briefly lived in the small apartment in this house, now a low-key **museum** (Map p88; ☎ 987 3414; 2nd fl, ul Rakovski 136; admission 1 lv; ⏰ 10am-5pm Mon-Wed & Fri, 1-5pm Thu). The three rooms here have been restored to their original appearance, although there are worrying cracks everywhere. Ghoulish mementos include the dress Yavorov's wife, Lora, was wearing when she killed herself in the study, Yavorov's death-mask and several photographs of the unhappy couple. Ring the doorbell for admittance.

SVETI SEDMOCHISLENITSI CHURCH

Set in a leafy garden just off the main road, the **Church of the Seven Saints** (Map p88; ul Graf Ignatiev; ⏰ 7am-7pm), as it's known in its more tongue-friendly translation, is dedicated to Sts Cyril and Methodius and their five disciples. Originally built as a mosque in 1528, it had already fallen into disuse by the time the Russians came along in 1878 and turned it into an arms depot. After a brief spell as a prison, the structure was restored and remod-elled in a style termed Bulgarian National Romanticism, and consecrated as a church in 1903. Inside, the walls are covered in traditional murals of saints, while an image of the Trinity decorates the huge central dome. The gilded iconostasis includes icons painted by Anton Mitov and Stefan Ivanov.

The church is perhaps best known for its links with the choral group The Seven Saints Choir (see p51). CDs of its music are available at the little counter inside.

IVAN VAZOV HOUSE-MUSEUM

Bulgaria's best-loved author, Ivan Vazov (1850–1921), lived at this house, now a **museum** (Map p88; ☎ 988 1270; ul Ivan Vazov 10; admission 1 lv; ⏰ 1-5pm Tue-Thu, 11am-5pm Fri & Sat), from 1895 until his death. Vazov wrote *Under the Yoke*, a classic of Bulgarian literature based around the 1876 April Uprising against the Turks. Several rooms have been restored to their early-20th-century appearance, and in the study, you can even meet Vazov's beloved pet dog, Bobby, whom Vazov had stuffed after he was run down by a tram. Downstairs, there's a small exhibition of photographs and documents, though labelling is only in Bulgarian. You'll need to ring the doorbell to gain admittance.

East of Ploshtad Aleksander Nevski
DOCTORS' GARDEN

Just behind the National Library (Map p88), in one of the smartest residential areas in town, this neat, secluded and well-maintained park is a pleasant place to catch your breath. At the centre is a big, pyramidal monument dedicated to the medics who died in the Russo-Turkish War (1877–78). Also here is an outdoor lapidarium featuring lots of Roman architectural fragments dug up around Sofia.

PEYO YAVOROV

One of Bulgaria's most admired lyric poets, Peyo Yavorov's turbulent life story sounds like it could have come from the pages of a lost Puccini opera. He was born in Chirpan in 1878 and by his early 20s his moody writing style had won him acclaim in the highest literary circles. He was already a celebrated literary figure in Sofia when he joined the guerrillas fighting the Turks in Macedonia, later continuing the fight in the First Balkan War. His girlfriend Mina Todorova (whose parents had forbidden her relationship with the restless poet) died of consumption in Paris in 1910, and it was at her funeral that he met his next love, Lora Karavelova, who lived with him at the house on ul Rakovski that now holds a museum dedicated to his memory. However, theirs was a stormy marriage and Lora, jealous of her husband's supposed affairs with other women, shot herself in 1913. Yavorov, a now broken and penniless man, shot himself a year later.

NATIONAL MUSEUM OF MILITARY HISTORY
Don't be put off by the rusting army trucks in the overgrown front yard – this **museum** (Map p84; ☎ 946 1806; ul Cherkovna 92; admission 2 lv, guided tour 10 lv; ☺ 10am-6pm Wed-Sun) is among the most interesting and best presented in Sofia. Displays over three floors tell the story of warfare in Bulgaria from the time of the Thracians onwards, with extensive labelling and information boards in English. Most space goes to the period from the 1876 April Uprising through to WWI, with cases filled with weaponry, rebel flags and a seemingly endless parade of uniforms and personal belongings of soldiers. Among the more striking are the shaggy-fur flying costume, resembling a traditional Kuker outfit, worn by a Lt Simeon Petrov during the First Balkan War, and the pint-sized tunic of Nikola Kostov, a 10-year-old WWI 'volunteer'. Exhibits from WWII and the communist period follow, with the final gallery concentrating on the Bulgarian army's current peace-keeping role within NATO. An additional ticket (2 lv) is required for the 4th-floor galleries, which hold a collection of foreign decorations awarded to Bulgarian leaders and, if you haven't had your fill, yet more uniforms and guns.

The rear yard is home to an impressive assemblage of defunct, Soviet-made military hardware including Scud missile launchers, tanks and MiG fighters. Everything is labelled in English. The museum entrance is on ul Han Omurtag.

ACTIVITIES
There are a number of gyms, pools and sports centres around Sofia. For details about hiking, skiing and other popular activities, see Vitosha Nature Park (p109).

Bowling
The **Mega Xtreme Bowling Center** (off Map p84; ☎ 969 2600; ul Stefanov 12, Studentski Grad; per game 3-5 lv; ☺ 10am-4am) is a vast, state-of-the-art complex featuring an 18-lane bowling alley, pool tables and a disco with live music Friday and Saturday nights. To get there, catch minibus 7 from bul Maria Luisa.

Fitness
One of the most advanced gyms in town is **Sparta Fitness & Spinning** (Map p84; ☎ 963 1337; www.spartabg.com; bul Arsenalski 4; full-day pass 20 lv; ☺ 7am-

11pm Mon-Fri, 9am-9pm Sat & Sun). Besides the well-equipped gym, there's a sauna, pool and spa area. Yoga and Pilates classes, massages and more are available. A one-hour massage costs around 30 lv.

Paintballing
Paintballing has become a popular pastime around Sofia. **Paintball Bulgaria** (☎ 928 1125; www.paintballbulgaria.com; per game 15.99 lv; ☺ 10am-7pm) offers sessions around Mt Vitosha. The price includes equipment and 100 balls. Reservations are essential.

Swimming
If you need to cool off, go for a dip at **Spartak** (Map p84; ☎ 866 5973; bul Arsenalski 4; adult/child 4/3 lv; ☺ 7am-10pm Mon-Fri, 9am-8pm Sat & Sun) near the City Center Sofia mall. It's a big place with an Olympic-sized indoor pool and summer-only outdoor pool with a 'beach'. The Sparta Fitness & Spinning centre is on the same site.

Tennis
Run by the Maleeva sisters, a trio of ex-pro tennis players, the **Maleeva Tennis Club** (Map p84; ☎ 962 2288; www.maleevaclub.com; bul Nikola Vaptsarov) has both outdoor and indoor courts (per hour from 13/28 lv), as well as squash courts (45 minutes from 14 lv). Individual tennis coaching costs 26 lv per hour. Other facilities include a spa and sauna, and a 30-minute massage costs around 18 lv. See the website for a full price list.

WALKING TOUR
Fortunately, most of Sofia's attractions are easily accessible on foot. Allow most of the day to fully appreciate the best of what the city has to offer.

Start from outside the magnificent **Sveta Nedelya Cathedral** (**1**; p87) and walk north up bul Maria Luisa, past the **Tsum Retail Centre** (**2**; p104) and its shops, to the **Banya Bashi Mosque** (**3**; p87). Walk through the square behind the mosque for a view of the **Mineral Baths** (**4**; p87). Cross the road and turn right on ul Ekzarh Yosif to get to the **drinking fountains** (**5**; p87), a good place to fill your water bottle with fresh mineral water.

Continue southeast on ul Serdika, emerging on the eastern end of pl Nezavisimost. Cross over to the **Presidency** (**6**; p91) where you can witness the Changing of the Guard

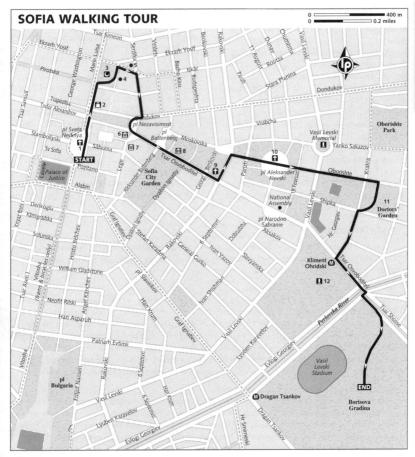

SOFIA WALKING TOUR

ceremony. Stop by the **Archaeological Museum** (**7**; p91) just opposite, which holds some of Bulgaria's greatest Thracian treasures. Follow the yellow brick road (bul Tsar Osvoboditel), and admire the grandeur of the former Royal Palace, which now hosts the **National Art Gallery** (**8**; p90). Carry on eastwards, past the glittery **Sveti Nikolai Russian Church** (**9**; p90). Cross ul Rakovski and you'll see pl Aleksander Nevski, dominated by the awesome **Aleksandri Nevski Memorial Church** (**10**; p91).

Head east again, crossing bul Vasil Levski onto ul Oborishte, until you come to the secluded **Doctors' Garden** (**11**; p93). From here, walk down ul Krakra to bul Tsar Osvoboditel, stopping to take in the immense, socialist-

WALK FACTS

Start Sveta Nedelya Cathedral
Finish Borisova Gradina
Distance 2.5km
Duration 1½ hours

realist **Monument to the Soviet Army** (**12**; p92). Just beyond this, you'll cross the dinky Eagles Bridge, which spans the unassuming stream-like trickle known rather grandly as the Perlovska River. You'll then come upon the entrance to the vast Borisova Gradina, where you can relax under the horse-chestnut trees or refresh yourself with a beer at one of the outdoor cafés.

COURSES

Kibea Health Centre (Map p88; ☎ 988 0193; www .kibea.net; Kibea Health Food Restaurant, ul Valkovich 2a) Nutritional healing courses can be followed here. Three- to five-day courses, in English, start at €150, and cover various aspects of nutritional science.

Sofia University (Map p88; ☎ 971 7162; www .deo.uni-sofia.bg; bul Tsar Osvoboditel) Bulgarian language courses for foreigners are offered by the university. One-to-one courses cost 220 lv for 20 hours' tuition; group courses cost 200 lv per person for 20 hours. Summertime classes in Bulgarian language and folklore are also offered; the intensive two-week course costs 430 lv.

TanguerIN (Map p84; ☎ 0888373940; www.tanguerin .com; ul Zlatovrah 51) Fancy learning the tango in Sofia? This friendly studio in the Lozenets district runs private one-hour classes for 30 lv (more than one couple 20 lv) on weekday evenings. Longer courses are also available; see the website for details.

SOFIA FOR CHILDREN

Sofia has few obvious attractions for children, but you can try the following places.

Although looking a little sad and dated these days, with a collection of bedraggled animals, the **Sofia Zoo** (Map p84; ☎ 962 0449; bul Simeonovsko Shosse; admission 1 lv; ⏰ 9am-5pm) does have a few play areas for children, and a couple of simple cafés. It's free for children under seven years old.

Young speed fans (over eight years old) can take the wheel of a motorised go-kart and

---

A SOFIAN SPEAKS

We asked Georgi Dimitrov, a 28-year-old project manager at the sustainable travel agency Odysseia-In, for his thoughts on his home city and how he sees Bulgarian tourism developing in the future.

What is Sofia like as a place to live?
I think Sofia is becoming a harder place to live; due to the increasing traffic and the ever-greater concentration of business and industry in the city, it gets very crowded during the week. There's more space to breathe in summer, though, when most people head to the Black Sea for their holidays. I still live [in Sofia] because I have a big family here, and I have a great job. There's also a big advantage living next door to Vitosha Nature Park, and Rila National Park is just 80km away, so Sofia is a handy gateway for keen mountaineers like myself. Sofia also has [a] good social life, which you can hardly find anywhere else in Bulgaria, and a big variety of bars and restaurants.

What do you get up to in your spare time?
I like going to bars and cinemas on the weekends, or cycling round the city's quieter streets. I often spend time in the parks…my favourite is Yuzhen Park, but Borisova Gradina has some wild areas for cycling too, and a very refreshing swimming pool, the Maria Luisa pool – a cool escape from the burning heat of August in Sofia! I like hiking in Vitosha Nature Park with my family, too. There are many pathways, fascinating nature and interesting churches like Boyana Church and Dragalevtsi Monastery. Vitosha is also great in winter for skiing and snowshoeing, which is real fun!

Why should travellers spend time in Sofia, and what are its best attractions?
Sofia alone is an interesting destination. Nearly all the highlights are concentrated in the centre, so you can explore on foot, and there are a number of attractive little parks where you can get away from the noise of the city. I'd recommend visiting the thermal springs opposite the Hali [shopping centre], where you can experience the 'real Sofia' and meet some of the locals, and a visit to one of the city's churches on a Sunday for the Orthodox liturgy.

How do you see tourism developing in Bulgaria, and what would you say are the country's unique selling points?
Unfortunately, at present tourism development in Bulgaria is far from sustainable. There is recognition in the tourism sector of the need for sustainable development, but it's held back by a lack of motivation and knowledge, and there is still much to be done when it comes to tourism infrastructure. However, Bulgaria is a land with great historical heritage, fascinating nature and friendly people, and it's a country where you can still get a sense of the traditional, sustainable lifestyle that has been largely forgotten elsewhere on the Continent. Bulgaria offers great hiking, biking and skiing, authentic folklore festivals, good beer and very good wine!

zoom around the twisting, 1km-long track at **Karting Sport** (Map p84; ☎ 920 1447; www.karting -bg.com; bul Vardar 3a; per lap 2 lv; ☯ 9am-9pm May-Sep, 10am-6pm Oct-Apr), a modern speedway circuit in the Krasna Polyana district. Take bus 11 or tram 11 or 22 to get here.

Kids and adults can enjoy active, outdoorsy fun at **Kokolandia** (Map p84; ☎ 831 3095; www.kokolandia.com; ul Nezabravka; admission from around 3 lv; ☯ 9am-9pm May-Oct), an adventure park inside Borisova Gradina. Divided into three increasingly challenging areas, it offers rope-climbing, tree-top obstacle courses (harnesses provided), rock-climbing walls and a minigolf course. The first zone is suitable for children aged five to 10, while the third is for over-18s only.

Play areas can also be found in Borisova Gradina, which has wide open green spaces that young children might enjoy. Older siblings might prefer a game of bowls at Mega Xtreme Bowling Center (p94) or a spot of tennis at the Maleeva Tennis Club (p94). There are no reliable baby-sitting agencies working with foreign tourists, although some top-end hotels may be able to provide such services.

TOURS

Almost everything worth seeing in Sofia is accessible on foot, so unless you're seriously pressed for time there's little point taking an organised tour around the city.

Rila Monastery (p117) is awkward to visit in one day by public transport from Sofia, so an organised tour may be more convenient. However, renting a car or even chartering a taxi for the day may be cheaper for a group of two to four people, and will certainly be more flexible. For details about renting cars and hiring taxis, see p301.

The following companies offer tours in and around Sofia:

Eurotours (Map p84; ☎ 931 1500; basement, central train station; ☯ 6am-7pm Mon-Fri, to 4pm Sat & Sun) Offers various day trips by car, including tours to Rila Monastery for around €70. The cost is per car, seating up to four people.

Tourist Service (TUI; Map p84; ☎ 832 4032; www .tourist-service.com; ul Klokotnitsa 1; ☯ 9am-6pm Mon-Sat) Opposite the Princess Hotel, the TUI runs three-hour tours by car around Sofia (from €35 per person for a party of two) and 'folkloric evenings' of music, food and dance (from €70). Other day trips, which include lunch, go to Rila Monastery (€90) and Koprivshtitsa (€90). Prices for

larger groups (in a minivan) work out slightly cheaper per person.

Zig Zag Holidays (Map p88; ☎ 980 5102; www.zig zagbg.com; bul Stamboliyski 20-V; ☯ 8.30am-7.30pm Mon-Sat) Offers all sorts of tailor-made outdoor activities, including hiking, climbing, caving and biking trips. It offers day trips to Rila Monastery (€67) and walking tours of Sofia (€25). Prices are per person, for groups of up to three. Entrance is on ul Lavele.

FESTIVALS & EVENTS

Sofia International Film Festival (www.cinema.bg /sff) Movie buffs descend on the capital each March.

Sofia International Folklore Festival Takes places in and around the city for five days in late August.

Sofia Fest Includes cultural events, concerts and exhibits held at various galleries and museums, as well as the Church of Sveta Sofia, around 14 to 18 September.

St Sofia's Day The city's patron saint is honoured with services at churches across the capital on 17 September.

Cinemania An international, month-long celebration of independent filmmaking held in the NDK in November.

SLEEPING

Unsurprisingly, accommodation in Sofia tends to be more expensive than anywhere else in Bulgaria, with prices at most establishments now comparable to those in Western European cities. Over recent years there has been a surge in the number of top-end hotels, but fortunately for budget travellers, Sofia also has a growing number of modern, good-quality hostels. Note that the majority of places quote prices in euros, though of course you can also pay in leva.

Budget
HOSTELS

Hostel Turisticheska Spalnya (Map p88; ☎ 983 6181; www.ts-hostel.com; ul Tsar Simeon 63; dm/d from €9/14) This bright, clean hostel is in a great central location and offers pleasant, high-ceilinged dorms of between three and five beds, as well as a double room and modern bathrooms.

Sofia Backpackers' Inn (Map p88; ☎ 983 1672; www .sofiabackpackersinn.dir.bg; ul Struma 6; dm/d incl breakfast from €9/25; ☒ ☐) Small, friendly hostel, with English-speaking staff, on a quiet side street off bul Maria Luisa. There are a couple of slightly cramped four- and six-bed dorms, one double and a comfy TV lounge with a balcony, and the price includes unlimited tea and coffee. Parking is available for bikes and motorcycles (2 lv per day).

SOFIA

Art Hostel (Map p88; ☎ 987 0545; www.art-hostel .com; ul Angel Kánchev 21a; dm incl breakfast €10; 💻) This bohemian hostel stands out from the crowd with its summertime art exhibitions, live music and more. Accommodation consists of a couple of small dorms (one with bathroom) plus summer-only 'basic accommodation' (ie space for your sleeping bag on the floor) for €5. A communal kitchen and peaceful little garden are available to guests, too.

Internet Hostel Sofia (Map p88; ☎ 0888384828; 2nd fl, ul Alabin 50a; dm/s/d/apt incl breakfast from €10/18 /26/40; 💻) A great deal in a very central location just off bul Vitosha. Rooms are large and clean, with five- and six-bed dorms (no bunks) and an apartment, sleeping up to four, with private kitchen. There's also a communal kitchen, laundry service and bicycle hire. Not immediately obvious from street level, the entrance is inside an arcade a couple of doors down from a McDonald's.

Hostel Mostel (Map p88; ☎ 0889223296; www .hostelmostel.com; ul Denkoglu 2; dm/s/d incl breakfast €10/25/30; 🅿 💻) Popular Mostel has six- and eight-bed dorms, either with shared or private bathrooms, as well as a single and a couple of doubles; guests have use of a kitchen and cosy lounge. If you're just looking for a bare bed to lay down your sleeping bag, it's yours for €7. Free pick-ups from the bus and train stations are available.

MAKING A DIFFERENCE

Like any other big European city, Sofia has its social problems, and beggars are a common feature on the streets. Many are elderly, struggling to exist on very low pensions and have resorted to selling flowers, singing, playing an instrument or simply sitting beside a battered old pair of bathroom scales where passers-by can weigh themselves for a few stotinki. Anything you can spare will be greatly appreciated. Beware, though, the professional beggars who pretend to be mentally or physically disabled, and gangs of children. Another way to help out is to book into private rooms, usually rented out by pensioners with little other means of support. The much-needed cash will go straight into their pockets, and be spent locally.

Sofia Guesthouse (Map p88; ☎ 981 3656; www.sofia quest.com; bul Patriarh Evtimii 27; dm/d/q €10/30/36; 💻) Newish, central hostel with clean dorms and a couple of private rooms sleeping between two and four people. It offers free pick-ups from the bus and train stations (€5 from the airport) and various day trips.

PRIVATE ROOMS
Sofia has plenty of private rooms available to foreign tourists, usually offering a much better deal than the city's few budget hotels.

Eurotours (Map p88; ☎ 931 1500; www.eurotours.bg; basement, central train station; ☽ 6am-7pm Mon-Fri, to 4pm Sat & Sun) This agency in the basement of the central train station offers rooms from as little as €12 per person, although these are likely to be some way from the centre.

Zig Zag Holidays (Map p88; ☎ 980 5102; www.zig zagbg.com; bul Stamboliyski 20-V; ☽ 8.30am-7.30pm Mon-Sat) Arranges rooms with a shared bathroom in private homes. Singles cost €15 to €18 and doubles €24 to €30, including breakfast.

Alma Tours (Map p88; ☎ 986 5691; www.almatour .net; bul Stamboliyski 27; ☽ 9am-6pm Mon-Sat) Arranges single/double rooms in private homes around the city centre for €16/20.

Wasteels (Map p84; ☎ 931 1117; www.wasteels.bg; central train station; ☽ 9am-6pm Mon-Fri) Friendly and professional outfit that can book private rooms for €20, and hotel rooms starting at around €50.

HOTELS
Good-quality budget hotels are a bit of a rarity in Sofia, and the cheaper places that do exist are often either squalid dives best avoided or in awkward-to-reach locations – private rooms or hostels are a much better deal. These listed here are among the more reliable.

Hotel Maya (Map p88; ☎ 980 2796; 2nd fl, ul Trapezitsa 4; r 30-40 lv) Remarkably good value for such a central location, the Maya feels more like a set of old-fashioned rooms in a private home (which is what it is, basically), presided over by a chatty but non-English-speaking landlady. All rooms have TV and fridges, though individual bathrooms are detached, and there is one double with private bathroom (40 lv). The entrance is inside the courtyard that's just past the small art supplies shop.

Hotel Edona (Map p88; ☎ 983 2036; bul Slivnitsa 172; s/d 30/40 lv, with bathroom 40/60 lv) Basic-but-clean hotel overlooking the Lions Bridge just off bul Maria Luisa. Rooms are plain, with tiled floors and minimal furnishing, though all come with TVs, and it's handy for the central bus and train stations.

Hotel Enny (Map p88; ☎ 983 4395; ul Pop Bogomil 46; s/d/tr with shared bathroom 30/40/60 lv, s/d with bath 40/50 lv, d with bath & toilet 60 lv) The Enny is a neat, quiet place that offers reasonable value for budget-conscious travellers, although some rooms, especially the singles, are small and you don't even get a fan for this price. It's well signposted from bul Maria Luisa.

Midrange

Hotel Ametist (Map p88; ☎ 983 5475; ul Tsar Simeon 67; s/d/tr 48/60/72 lv) The location, just round the corner from the Central Hali Shopping Centre, is convenient and rooms are clean and comfortable and come with TVs and fridges, although bathrooms are tiny. Rooms 102 and 202, on the corner, are slightly bigger and have balconies.

Red Bed & Breakfast (Map p88; ☎ 988 8188; www .redbandb.com; ul Lyuben Karavelov 15; s/d from €25/40) Attached to the Red House cultural centre (p103), in an unusual Italianate building designed for the sculptor Andrei Nikolov, this six-room hotel is a unique place to stay. All rooms are decorated in different styles and colours, though none have private bathrooms.

Hotel Pop Bogomil (Map p88; ☎ 983 1165; www .bulgariabedandbreakfast.com; ul Pop Bogomil 5; r €32-40; ⓟ) This small hotel has 10 clean and comfy rooms, all individually decorated. It's handy enough for the central train and bus stations, though a little out of the way for anything else.

Hotel Niky (Map p88; ☎ 953 0110; www.hotel-niky .com; ul Neofit Rilski 16; s/d/ste from €35/40/55; ⓟ ✸) Offering excellent value and a good city-centre location, the Niky has comfortable rooms and gleaming bathrooms, as well as a communal garden and restaurant. Suites all come with kitchenettes with microwave ovens, fridges and tea- and coffee-making facilities. It's a very popular place and frequently full. Advance reservations are recommended.

Hotel Aris (Map p84; ☎ 931 3177; www.hotel-aris.com; ul Knyaz Boris I 203; s/d/tr from €40/50/60; ✸) Hidden away on a cobbled street in the shadow of the Princess Hotel, the Aris is a neat, modern hotel with smallish but comfortable rooms featuring the standard three-star amenities,

including TVs and fridges. It's a quiet spot, not far from the bus and train stations.

Sun Hotel (Map p88; ☎ 983 3670; www.sun hotel-bg.com; bul Maria Luisa 89; s/d/ste €49/59/90; ✸) Opposite the Hotel Lion, this well-kept hotel in a renovated 19th-century building is one of the smarter establishments in this area. It's handy for the central train and bus stations, but not so convenient for the sights. Rooms are small but clean and functional.

Scotty's Boutique Hotel (Map p88; ☎ 983 6777; scottyshotel@yahoo.com; ul Ekzarh Yosif 11; s/d from €50/60; ⓟ ✸) Opposite the synagogue, Scotty's is a small, stylish, gay-friendly hotel with just nine rooms, all individually designed and named after international cities – such as the Cape Town Room, kitted out with zebra-print details. Breakfast, delivered to your room, is €5 extra.

Hotel Lion (Map p88; ☎ 917 8400; www.hotel-lion.net; bul Maria Luisa 60; s/d/ste €58/70/96; ✸) Facing the Lions Bridge, this is a grand old building in a lively location. Rooms are large, modern and come in a variety of shapes and styles, some with striking arched windows.

Hotel Central (Map p84; ☎ 981 2364; www.central -hotel.com; bul Hristo Botev 52; s/d/ste from €65/80/120; ✸) The Central is a clean-cut business hotel sitting on a busy main road just west of the city centre. Rooms are neat, if a bit small, but it has a restful atmosphere, and weekend discounts of between 10% and 20% make it good value.

Hotel Diter (Map p88; ☎ 989 8998; www.diterhotel .com; ul Han Asparuh 65; s/d Sun-Thu €65/85, Fri & Sat €55/75; ✸) The Diter is a small, homely hotel set in a restored 19th-century building on a quiet backstreet, though still within easy walking distance of the centre. The bright, orange rooms are comfortable and bathrooms are large and shiny.

Hotel Sveta Sofia (Map p88; ☎ 981 2634; www.sveta sofia-alexanders.com; ul Pirotska 18; s/d €75/85; ⓟ ✸) Enjoying a superb location on the busy, pedestrianised ul Pirotska, Sveta Sofia has a slightly snooty atmosphere, but rooms are attractively furnished and there's a good restaurant on site. Weekend and long-stay discounts are on offer.

Kolikovski Hotel (Map p88; ☎ 933 3000; www .kolikovski.com; ul Hristo Belchev 42; s/d/ste incl breakfast from €80/90/120; ✸ 🖳) Occupying a bright, attractively renovated building on a side street near the NDK, the Kolikovski offers a range of rooms, including 'business class' (with a free bottle of wine thrown in) and some spacious suites – the one on the 5th floor comes with kitchenette and terrace.

Hotel Arte (Map p88; ☎ 402 7100; www.artehotelbg .com; bul Dondukov 5; d/ste from €85/110; P ✂) One of the newer city-centre hotels, Arte is a friendly place with stylish rooms, all with flat-screen TVs, fridges and wi-fi connections. Suites have a sofa bed that can be pulled out to accommodate an extra two people. Breakfast is an additional €10.

Art'Otel (Map p88; ☎ 980 6000; www.artotel.biz; ul William Gladstone 44; s/d from €95/100; P ✂) Tucked down a narrow side street off bul Vitosha and housed in a tastefully renovated 1930s building, Art'Otel has 22 spacious rooms with bright bathrooms. In keeping with its name, there are contemporary artworks dotted throughout the building.

Top End

Princess Hotel (Map p84; ☎ 933 8888; bul Maria Luisa 131; s/d/ste from €97/117/155; P ✂ ✂ ✂) With over 600 rooms, this gigantic place has a justifiable claim to be the biggest hotel in the Balkans. Rooms are comfy and spacious and top-notch facilities include a gym, sauna, pool and shops. Size really does matter here, and the hotel also encompasses Bulgaria's biggest casino. It's convenient for the train and bus stations, though not for anything else.

Hotel Les Fleurs (Map p88; ☎ 810 0800; www.les fleurshotel.com; bul Vitosha 21; s/d/ste from €140/180/230; P ✂ ✂) Slap bang in the middle of Sofia's main shopping street, this *très chic* boutique hotel opened in 2007. The unmissable façade is decorated with outsize blooms, and the flowery motif is continued in the large, carefully styled, nonsmoking rooms.

Central Park Hotel (Map p88; ☎ 805 8888; www .centralparkhotel.bg; bul Vitosha 106; s/d/ste from €150 /170/220; P ✂ ✂) Overlooking the NDK, this towering four-star hotel is a classy, newish option offering large, airy rooms with some great views. There's a very good restaurant and the hotel offers a baby-sitting service.

ourpick **Arena di Serdica** (Map p88; ☎ 819 9191; www.arenadiserdica.com; ul Budapeshta 2-4; s/d/ste from €190/210/240; P ✂) What might have been just another glassy, upscale hotel received a public-relations boost when the remains of Sofia's long-sought-after Roman amphitheatre were uncovered during construction in 2004; the curving walls have been preserved

below the foyer, and visitors are welcome. The rooms themselves are contemporary and stylish, with king-size beds, minibars and rather smart bathrooms. There's also a Roman-style steam bath and gym. Summer rates (July and August) are marginally cheaper.

Grand Hotel Sofia (Map p88; ☎ 811 0800; www .grandhotelsofia.bg; ul General Gurko 1; s/d/ste Mon-Thu from €290/310/490, s/d Fri-Sun from €155/170; P ✂ ✂) Right in the heart of the city, the Grand is a swanky, 109-room, glass-and-granite affair looming over the southern edge of the City Garden. It's an upscale place, with uniformed doormen and lots of marble, and the spacious rooms are fitted with the latest mod cons. Facilities include a fitness centre, a couple of restaurants, some boutiques and a café.

Sheraton Sofia Hotel Balkan (Map p88; ☎ 981 6541; www.luxurycollection.com/sofia; pl Sveta Nedelya 5; s/d/ste from €310/320/420; P ✂ ✂) This grand old Sofian landmark represents the epitome of luxury. Marble floors, glittering chandeliers and large, elegantly furnished rooms provide a level of opulence that would please the most demanding guests. The official rates are startlingly high, but discounts are frequently available.

EATING

Compared with the rest of Bulgaria, Sofia is gourmet heaven, with an unrivalled range of international cuisines represented and new, quality restaurants springing up all the time. It also has countless snack bars, fast-food outlets and cafés dotted across town.

Bulgarian Restaurants

Trops Kâshta (Map p88; bul Maria Luisa 26; mains 2-4 lv; ⏱ 8am-9pm) There are several branches of this budget cafeteria around town, offering Bulgarian favourites such as *kebabche* (grilled spicy meat sausages) and moussaka. The menu is in Bulgarian only, but you can point at whatever takes your fancy and trust to luck. Best to get here early as popular items get snapped up and the remainder get cold.

Pri Yafata (Map p88; ☎ 980 1727; ul Solunska 28; mains 6-15 lv; ⏱ 10am-midnight) Another traditional-style place with agricultural tools, rifles, *chergas* (patterned rugs) and other rustic reminders adorning the walls. Hearty dishes of duck, rabbit, pork and chicken are on the lengthy menu, which also includes plenty of vegetarian options. It's a very popular place, and reservations are advisable for the evenings, which regularly feature live music.

ourpick Manastirska Magernitsa (Map p88; ☎ 980 3883; ul Han Asparuh 67; mains 7-10 lv; 🕙 11am-2am) Set in the courtyard of a 19th-century townhouse and decked out like an old-fashioned *mehana* (tavern), this is among the best places in the city to sample some first-class, traditional Bulgarian cuisine. The menu is enormous and encompasses recipes collected from monasteries and villages all over the country, with dishes such as 'drunken rabbit' stewed in wine and 'quails in a nest', as well as salads, grills, fish, chicken, pork and game options. There's also an extensive wine list, which includes some pricey vintage bottles.

International Restaurants

Dream House (Map p88; ☎ 980 8163; 1st fl, ul Alabin 50a; mains 3-4 lv; 🕙 11am-10pm) Although not the easiest place to find – look for the door on the left inside the small shopping arcade and climb the stairs – this vegetarian restaurant is well worth seeking out. The menu includes dishes such as grilled tofu, algae soup and various stir-fries. There's an all-you-can-eat buffet on Sundays (5 lv) and beer and wine are available.

Pizza Troll (pizzas 3-10 lv, mains 6-18 lv) bul Vitosha 27 (Map p88; ☎ 981 5833; 🕙 24hr); pl Slaveikov 6a (Map p88; ☎ 980 4553; 🕙 8am-midnight) Dozens of pizzas fill the menu pages at these bright and cheery outlets. Those who've tired of cheese can choose from plenty of pasta, chicken and fish dishes, too.

Happy Bar & Grill (Map p88; ☎ 980 7353; pl Sveta Nedelya 4; mains 5-10 lv; 🕙 24hr) Big branch of the dependable nationwide chain offering a menu of fairly standard but tasty salads and grills. You can sit outside and watch the sports channels on the numerous silent TVs, or inside among the Planet Hollywood–style mess of movie posters, guitars and saxophones, while friendly, microskirted waitstaff flit between the tables. It's packed out in the evenings.

Victoria (Map p88; ☎ 986 3200; bul Tsar Osvoboditel 7; mains 5-12 lv; 🕙 24hr) In the shady courtyard of a grand neoclassical building next to the Officers' Club, Victoria is a big hit with locals who drop by throughout the day for the excellent pizzas. Pasta and chicken dishes also feature.

Kibea Health Food Restaurant (Map p88; ☎ 980 3067; ul Valkovich 2a; mains 6-10 lv; 🕙 noon-11pm Mon-Sat)

Kibea offers a refreshingly different menu of mostly vegetarian and vegan dishes such as barley risotto with squash, although a limited choice of chicken and fish dishes are sometimes available, too. It's probably the only restaurant in Bulgaria to completely ban smoking, and there's a bookshop downstairs.

Spaghetti Company (Map p88; ☎ 926 0427; bul Dondukov 1; mains 6-15 lv; 🕙 10am-midnight) Discreetly located in the courtyard at the back of the Tsum Retail Centre, this Italian restaurant has become a popular spot for lunchtime business meetings. It serves up some good, if relatively expensive, pasta dishes, and offers a short wine list.

Olive's (Map p88; ☎ 986 0902; ul Graf Ignatiev 12; mains 8-15 lv; 🕙 10am-3am) Walls splashed with vintage advertising posters and mock newspapers for menus give Olive's a quirky twist, and the international cuisine on offer is excellent, featuring dishes such as chorizo sausages, chicken skewers, pasta, steaks and burgers. It gets very crowded at night.

Egur-Egur (Map p88; ☎ 989 3383; ul Dobrudzha 10; mains 8-20 lv; 🕙 noon-midnight) Hearty Armenian cuisine is served up at this convivial restaurant, with plenty of kebabs, steaks, stews and other meaty offerings available (though there's also a decent range of vegetarian dishes).

Tambuktu (Map p88; ☎ 988 1234; ul Aksakov 10; mains 8-30 lv; 🕙 noon-midnight) One of the very few restaurants in Sofia specialising in seafood, this is a big, bright and slightly tacky-looking place, dressed up with lurid maritime knick-knacks. However, the fish and crustaceans on the large menu are expertly cooked.

Background (Map p88; ☎ 986 3529; bul Vitosha 14; mains 9-20 lv; 🕙 10am-midnight) Attractive courtyard restaurant offering an upmarket menu (in English) featuring things such as duck in port sauce, tagliatelle with truffles and chicken breasts with roasted brie. The food is good, but it's a little let down by slow service.

Cafés

In summer, cafés seem to occupy every piece of garden and footpath in Sofia. Some are just basic spots for a coffee and a sandwich, while others offer a more refined setting for cocktails and cakes. Most cafés are open from about 8am to midnight.

Cafe de Sofi (Map p88; ul Pirotska; cakes from 2.50 lv) This sociable summer outdoor café beside

SOFIA

the Central Hali Shopping Center makes a handy pit stop for drinks and snacks.

Cafe Theatre (Map p88; ul Vasil Levski; cakes from 3 lv) Beside the imposing Ivan Vazov National Theatre, this summer-only pavement café is a pleasant spot for drinks and cakes.

Toba & Co (Map p88; ☎ 989 4696; ul Moskovska 6; snacks from 3 lv; 8.30am-6am) Hidden away in what was once Tsar Ferdinand's butterfly house, in the gardens at the rear of the Royal Palace, this discreet café is a charming spot to indulge in an alfresco cocktail, as well as ice cream and cakes.

Club Lavazza (Map p88; ☎ 987 3433; bul Vitosha 13; mains 6-8 lv) A chic, continental-style spot for coffee and cocktails, Lavazza also offers a brief food menu. It gets very smoky indoors, but in summer there's outdoor seating.

Quick Eats

There are plenty of kiosks around town where you can buy tasty local fast food such as *banitsa* (cheese pasties) and *palachinki* (pancakes), as well as the inevitable hot dogs and burgers.

Sladak Svyat (Map p88; ul Alabin; banitsa from 0.60 lv; 6.30am-9pm) Typical simple bakery serving up a tasty selection of *banitsa*, bread rolls, cakes and other street-snack fare.

Bakehouse (Map p88; ul Ivan Vazov 12; snacks from 1 lv; 7am-8pm Mon-Fri, 9am-6pm Sat) Another good place to pick up a variety of *banitsa* and other cheap street eats.

Central Hali Shopping Centre (Map p88; bul Maria Luisa 25; 7am-midnight) There are several outlets in the upstairs food court in this market complex (see p104) that sell cheap fast food such as kebabs, pizzas and ice cream, as well as beer at half the price of the snazzier bar downstairs. Despite the official opening hours, the food court closes down by about 9pm.

Self-Catering

An abundance of fresh fruit and veg can be yours at the Central Hali (Map p88), the Ladies' Market (Map p88) and the stalls (Map p88) along ul Graf Ignatiev (outside the Sveti Sedmochislenitsi Church). For everything else, try Bonjour Supermarket (Map p88) or the branches of Piccadilly Supermarket (off Map p88), which can be found in the basements of the Mall of Sofia and the City Center Sofia shopping malls.

DRINKING

There's a seemingly inexhaustible supply of watering holes all over Sofia. The cheapest places to grab a beer are the kiosks in the city's parks; if you're looking for a more sophisticated ambience, the city centre has plenty of swish new bars.

Pri Kmeta (Map p88; ☎ 981 3399; ul Parizh 2; noon-4am) 'At the Mayor's' is a convivial microbrewery serving its own 'Kmetsko' beer, which is available in litre and, for the very thirsty, metre-length measures. There are seats at ground level, but the cellar beer hall, with its gleaming copper vats, is more atmospheric, and hosts regular live music events.

Upstairs (Map p88; ☎ 989 9896; bul Vitosha 18; 10am-2am) Join the 'in-crowd' on the 1st-floor terrace stools of Upstairs and look down on the shoppers and trams of bul Vitosha over a cocktail or two, or lounge on the sofas inside. It's all good.

Buddha Bar (Map p88; ☎ 989 5006; ul Lege 15a; 24hr) Very hip, very trendy and very crowded, this Buddha-bedecked drinking spot also serves food, and has a nightly disco from around 9pm.

Exit (Map p88; ☎ 0888140133; ul Lavele 16; 8am-2am) This modern and fashionable bar/diner is a popular gay venue, with a DJ party every evening.

Sofia also has its share of Irish pubs, frequented by expats knocking back overpriced imported beers and stouts. These include **JJ Murphy's** (Map p88; ☎ 980 2870; ul Kârnigradska 6; noon-12.30am), **Dublin** (Map p88; ☎ 943 4004; ul Alabin 54; 24hr) and **Irish Harp** (Map p88; ☎ 989 9276; ul Sveta Sofia 7; 10am-midnight), which offers live music and satellite TV showing international football matches.

ENTERTAINMENT

If you read Bulgarian, or at least can decipher some of the Cyrillic, *Programata* is the most comprehensive source of entertainment listings; otherwise check out its excellent English-language website, www .programata.bg. You can book tickets online at www.ticketpro.bg.

Nightclubs

Some clubs charge admission fees of anywhere between 2 lv and 15 lv, mostly late at night and on weekends when live bands are playing. Studentski Grad is home to several of Sofia's trendier clubs; ask around for the latest venues.

Social Jazz Club (Map p88; ☎ 0884622220; www .socialjazzclub.com; pl Slaveikov 4; ☻ 10pm-4am Mon-Sat) The place to go to catch some quality live jazz, with a programme of leading international acts.

Swingin' Hall (Map p84; ☎ 963 0696; bul Dragan Tsankov 8; ☻ 9pm-4am Tue-Sun) Huge club offering an eclectic programme of live music each night, ranging from jazz and blues to rock and folk pop.

Avenue (off Map p84; ☎ 0888400435; ul Atanas Manchev 1a, Studentski Grad; ☻ 24hr) One of the more popular student joints, Avenue plays both Western songs and Bulgarian *chalga* (folk pop) music.

Chervilo (Map p88; ☎ 981 6633; bul Tsar Osvoboditel 9; ☻ 10.30pm-6am Tue-Sat) The live music, guest DJs and themed party nights at 'Lipstick' draw in Sofia's young and fashionable set at night, and it also has a pleasant terrace for sitting out with a drink or two.

Cinemas

As well as a couple of modern multiplexes, Sofia has several smaller cinemas dotted around town. Most screen recent English-language films with Bulgarian subtitles, although cartoons and children's films are normally dubbed into Bulgarian. Tickets cost anything from 4 lv to 12 lv, depending on the comfort of the theatres and the times of the sessions.

Cinema City (Map p84; ☎ 929 2929; www.cinema city.bg; Mall of Sofia, bul Stamboliyski 101; tickets 4-7 lv) Modern, multiscreen cinema on the top floor of the Mall of Sofia, showing the latest Hollywood releases.

Cineplex (Map p84; ☎ 964 3007; www.cineplex.bg; City Center Sofia, bul Arsenalski 2; tickets 4-10 lv) Another state-of-the-art multiscreen cinema inside the City Center Sofia mall, offering the same fare as Cinema City.

Odeon (Map p88; ☎ 989 2469; bul Patriarh Evtimii 1; tickets 4-6 lv) Snubs modernity by showing only classic old films, which run for months at a time.

Dom Na Kinoto (Map p88; ☎ 980 3911; ul Ekzarh Yosif 37; tickets 4-5 lv) Mainly shows Bulgarian-language and art-house films.

Theatre & Music

Ticket prices at these venues vary enormously. For the Opera House or the National Theatre,

they might cost anything from 10 lv to 30 lv; shows at the NDK vary much more, with tickets costing from 30 lv to 70 lv for international acts and around 10 lv to 30 lv for local ones.

National Opera House (Map p88; ☎ 987 1366; www .operasofia.com; ul Vrabcha 1; ☻ ticket office 9.30am-6.30pm) Bulgaria's best divas strut the boards here and artists from around the world often perform in the well-staged productions.

National Palace of Culture (NDK; Map p88; ☎ 916 6369; www.ndk.bg; pl Bulgaria; ☻ ticket office 9am-7pm) The NDK (as it's usually called) has 15 halls and is easily the country's largest cultural complex. It maintains a regular programme of events in summer (when most other theatres in Sofia are closed) and offers an eclectic range of shows throughout the year (recently featured artists have included George Michael and Chuck Berry).

Bulgaria Hall (Map p88; ☎ 987 7656; ul Aksakov 1; ☻ ticket office 9.30am-6pm) The home of the excellent Sofia Philharmonic Orchestra, this is the place to come for classical music concerts.

Ivan Vazov National Theatre (Map p88; ☎ 811 9219; www.nationaltheatre.bg; ul Dyakon Ignatiy 5; ☻ Sep-Jun) The National Theatre Company stages dramatic performances in this grand old building.

Red House (Map p88; ☎ 988 8188; www.redhouse -sofia.org; ul Lyuben Karavelov 15) Occupying a unique, early-20th-century mansion, this avant-garde institution hosts everything from political and cultural debates (in various languages) to poetry readings and dance performances. Many events are free; check the website for the current programme. There's also a hotel here (p99).

Sport

Football (soccer) is Bulgaria's main sporting passion, and Sofia alone has four teams. The main clubs are **CSKA** (☎ 963 3477), which plays at the CSKA Stadium (Map p84) in Borisova Gradina and **Levski** (☎ 989 2156), based at the Georgi Asparoukhov Stadium (off Map p84; bul Vladimir Vazov, Poduyane). Lokomotiv and Slavia are Sofia's two smaller teams.

No other spectator sport comes anywhere near to the popularity enjoyed by football, although basketball has a keen, if relatively small, following. The main teams are, again, named **CSKA** (☎ 898 593; www.cskabasket.net) and **Levski** (☎ 983 7893; www.levskibasket.com).

The **Vasil Levski Stadium** (Map p88; ☎ 988 5030; Borisova Gradina) is the main venue for international football matches, athletics and other big sporting events.

SHOPPING

Bulevard Vitosha is Sofia's main shopping street, mostly featuring international brand-name boutiques interspersed with restaurants. More shops cluster along ul Graf Ignatiev, while ul Pirotska is a central pedestrian mall lined with cheaper shops selling clothes, shoes and household goods. Sofia now also has a couple of sleek, ultramodern shopping malls, housing international fashion chains, cinemas and coffee bars. Street stalls and markets are the best places to seek souvenirs.

Camping & Skiing Equipment

Stenata (Map p88; ☎ 980 5491; www.stenata.com; ul Bratia Miladinovi 5; ⌚ 10am-8pm) The best place in town to buy hiking, climbing and camping equipment, including backpacks, tents and sleeping bags, but it doesn't hire gear.

Alpin Sport (off Map p84; ☎ 0886456600; www.alpinsport-bg.com; off ul Geo Milev, Slatina; ⌚ 10am-7pm) Slightly out of the way, near the Akademik Stadium in the eastern Slatina neighbourhood, this shop nevertheless has an excellent stock of skiing, camping and climbing equipment.

Clothing

Denyl (Map p88; ☎ 987 3119; www.denyl.com; pl Slaveikov 7; ⌚ 9am-8pm Mon-Sat, 10am-5pm Sun) One of several branches of the nationwide men's clothing chain in Sofia, offering a range of fairly conservative suits and shirts for the office plus some casual wear.

Mirela Bratova (Map p88; ☎ 980 7156; ul Ivan Shishman 4; ⌚ 10.30am-8pm Mon-Fri, to 6pm Sat) Stylish women's fashions designed by Sofia couturier Mirela Bratova are on display at this little shop, including a selection of knitted dresses.

Kanela (Map p88; ☎ 0888413749; ul Neofit Rilski 59; ⌚ 10am-7pm Mon-Fri, to 4pm Sat) Small boutique selling a small and changeable selection of women's clothes by young local designers, as well as a range of jewellery.

Markets & Shopping Centres

Central Hali Shopping Centre (Map p88; ☎ 917 6106; bul Maria Luisa 25; ⌚ 7am-midnight) This elegant, covered market hall, built in 1911, has three floors of shops and cafés. Stalls on the ground floor sell varied produce, including fruit, vegetables, pastries, wine and cheese. Upstairs there's a cheap food court and more shops. The centre also holds a pharmacy, post office, bank and ATMs. Despite the posted opening times, the place is invariably closed before 10pm.

City Center Sofia (Map p84; ☎ 865 7285; www.ccs-mall.com; bul Arsenalski 2; ⌚ 10am-10pm) Modern shopping mall with three floors of shops, including Bulgaria's only Marks & Spencer. It also holds a supermarket, cinema, restaurants and a newsstand selling international papers and magazines.

Mall of Sofia (Map p84; ☎ 929 3377; www.mallofsofia.com; bul Stamboliyski 101; ⌚ 10am-10pm) The city's newest, biggest and busiest shopping centre, filled with international brand-name stores and coffee bars. There's a big supermarket in the basement, and a cinema, IMAX screen and food court on the top floor.

Tsum Retail Centre (Map p88; ☎ 951 5266; bul Maria Luisa 2; ⌚ 10am-9pm Mon-Sat, 11am-8pm Sun) The former all-in-one state department store is now an upmarket shopping mall, with five floors of pricier shops such as Laura Ashley and Tommy Hilfiger. However, it feels staid compared with the city's more modern malls and often seems to have more staff than customers.

Ladies' Market (Map p88; ul Stefan Stambolov; ⌚ from 7am) The 'Zhenski Pazar' stretches several blocks along a street between ul Ekzarh Yosif and bul Slivnitsa. It's Sofia's biggest fresh-produce market, with all kinds of fruit and vegetables on sale. Other stalls sell clothes, shoes, car parts, kitchen utensils and pretty much anything else you can think of. You can buy traditional Troyanska kapka pottery much more cheaply here than in souvenir shops. It's great fun to wander around, but it does get very crowded, so watch your belongings.

Music

Tapes and CDs of Bulgarian music can be bought at souvenir shops such as those listed in the next section, and sometimes more cheaply at stalls in the underpass below the NDK, where you can also find Western and Middle Eastern pop music.

Bulgarski Kompositor (Map p88; ul Ivan Vazov 2; ⌚ 10am-6pm Mon-Fri) Opposite the Ivan Vazov Theatre, this small shop has a good choice of classical and folk music CDs, as well as sheet music.

Alexandra Video (Map p88; ☎ 810 2256; cnr ul Graf Ignatiev & ul Solunska; ⏰ 10am-9.30pm) This bright chain store has a mixed collection of jazz, folk and pop CDs, with more space given to DVDs of Hollywood films, comics and some English-language books.

Souvenirs

Traditzia (Map p88; ☎ 981 7765; www.traditzia.bg; bul Vasil Levski 36; ⏰ 11am-7pm Tue-Sat) Everything in this wonderful little store is made by 'socially art excluded artisans' from the Roma and Turkish ethnic minorities and by people with disabilities whom this project aims to help become self-sufficient. On sale is a selection of traditional and contemporary Bulgarian handicrafts such as ceramics, glassware, carpets and textiles.

Centre of Folk Arts & Crafts (Map p88; ☎ 988 6416; pl Battenberg; ⏰ 10am-6pm) Inside the former Royal Palace, this shop offers a huge selection of folk art, including colourful hand-woven rugs from Chiprovtsi, Troyan pottery, woodcarvings, silver jewellery and rose-oil products, as well as books and CDs of Bulgarian music. However, prices tend to be on the high side. There's another branch on ul Parizh.

Art Gallery Paris (☎ 980 8093; www.gallery-paris.com; ul Parizh 8; ⏰ 11am-7pm Mon-Fri) This welcoming little art gallery showcases, and sells, the works of contemporary Bulgarian artists, with an ever-changing stock of prints, paintings and sculptures on offer.

Artists sell paintings, mainly of traditional rural scenes, near the Mineral Baths and around pl Aleksander Nevski, where you'll also find stalls selling reproduction religious icons, jewellery, souvenirs and embroidery. But be wary of the ancient coins, Soviet and Nazi paraphernalia and other 'antiques': there are some genuine items here, but most of it's fake, and prices are very much aimed at tourists. The underpass below pl Nezavisimost has several decent souvenir shops selling the usual array of postcards, paintings and books, and there are more in the underpass below the Tsum Retail Shopping Centre.

GETTING THERE & AWAY
Air

For information about international flights to and from Sofia, see p296.

The only domestic flights within Bulgaria are between Sofia and the Black Sea coast. Bulgaria Air flies daily to Varna (single/return around €105/160), with two or three daily flights between July and September. Bulgaria Air also flies between the capital and Burgas (single/return around €80/130). See p301 for domestic airline contact details.

Bus

The pleasingly modern **Central Bus Station** (Tsentralna Avtogara; Map p84; ☎ 090 021 000; www .centralbusstation-sofia.com; bul Maria Luisa 100), right beside the train station, is a bright, well-organised place that handles services to most big towns in Bulgaria as well as international destinations. There are dozens of counters for individual private companies, as well as an information desk and computer screens, touch-screen monitors giving details of departures, and an **OK-Supertrans taxi desk** (⏰ 6am-10pm). There are cafés and shops upstairs. At the time of research, just a couple of companies were still operating from the scruffy, semi-derelict bus terminal on the opposite side of bul Maria Luisa.

Departures are less frequent between November and April. The schedules below are for the summer:

Destination	Fare	Duration	Frequency
Albena	18 lv	8hr	3-4 daily
Bansko	12 lv	3hr	5-6 daily
Blagoevgrad	7 lv	2hr	about hourly
Burgas	20 lv	7-8hr	7-10 daily
Dobrich	29 lv	7-8hr	3-4 daily
Haskovo	14 lv	6hr	12-14 daily
Kazanlâk	10 lv	3½hr	6 daily
Lovech	12 lv	3hr	7-8 daily
Nesebâr	28 lv	7hr	7-10 daily
Pleven	9 lv	2½hr	hourly
Plovdiv	11 lv	2½hr	several hourly
Ruse	16 lv	5hr	hourly
Sandanski	9 lv	3½hr	8-9 daily
Shumen	21 lv	6hr	hourly
Sliven	16 lv	5hr	hourly
Smolyan	18 lv	3½hr	6-7 daily
Stara Zagora	13 lv	4hr	hourly
Sveti Vlas	28 lv	8hr	5 daily
Varna	25 lv	7-8hr	every 45min
Veliko Târnovo	14 lv	4hr	hourly
Vidin	14 lv	5hr	hourly

From the far smaller **Ovcha Kupel bus station** (Map p84; ☎ 955 5362; bul Tsar Boris III) – sometimes called the Zapad (West) station – a few buses head south, eg to Bansko, Blagoevgrad and Sandanski (although more buses to these places leave from the Central Bus Station). There are also regular buses to Dupnitsa (4 lv,

1½ hours) and Kyustendil (6 lv, two hours). If you're heading to the Rila Monastery in summer, it's worth ringing the station to ask about any direct buses. Tickets for services departing from this station must be bought at counters inside. Ovcha Kupel bus station is linked to the city centre by bus 60, tram 5 and taxi (about 4 lv one way).

From tiny **Yug bus station** (Map p84; ☎ 720 063; bul Dragan Tsankov 23), buses and minibuses leave for Samokov (4 lv, one hour, every 30 minutes 7am to 7.30pm). The station also offers an unreliable daily service (9am) direct to Maliovitsa (7 lv, two hours).

From the ramshackle **Poduyane bus station** (Map p84; ☎ 847 4262; ul Todorini Kukli) – aka Iztok (East) station – buses leave infrequently for small towns in central Bulgaria (schedule below).

Destination	Fare	Duration	Departure Times
Gabrovo	15 lv	3½hr	7.45am
Lovech	8 lv	3hr	7.45am
Teteven	9 lv	2½hr	8.30am, 9am & 5pm
Troyan	9 lv	3hr	9.45am, 2pm & 5pm

INTERNATIONAL

Some agencies operate at the Central Bus Station, offering services to Istanbul (40 to 45 lv, 18 hours), Athens (108 lv, 12 hours) and elsewhere, although most are now found at the **Trafik Market** (☎ 981 2979), immediately in front of the central train station. There are numerous kiosks here representing all the major companies such as **Eurolines** (☎ 981 0998) and **Group** (☎ 980 6586), which sells tickets on buses to destinations all over Europe, including Paris (190 lv), Rome (180 lv), London (260 lv), Copenhagen (250 lv) and many cities in Germany.

Eurotours (Map p84; ☎ 931 1500; basement, central train station) also sells tickets for international destinations, including twice-daily trips to Belgrade (38 lv, eight hours).

Matpu-96 (Map p84; ☎ 981 5653; Trafik Market) offers some of the best services to Greece and other Balkan countries, including Macedonia and Serbia. There is another office at ul Damyan Gruev 23.

It pays to shop around though, as different companies offer different prices.

Train

The **central train station** (Map p84; ☎ 931 1111) is a massive concrete hive that has recently undergone a facelift, though it's still far from cheerful or user-friendly – if Franz Kafka had turned his hand to architecture, this might have been the result.

Destinations for all domestic and international services are listed on timetables in Cyrillic, but departures (for the following two hours) and arrivals (for the previous two hours) are listed in English on a large computer screen on the ground floor. Directions and signs around the station are sometimes translated into French. There's a small information counter in the foyer, but nobody here speaks foreign languages. Other facilities include a post office, left-luggage office, simple cafés, a *very* basic hotel and accommodation agencies. The rates at the foreign exchange offices are very poor indeed, so best wait until you get into town.

Same-day tickets for destinations along the lines to Vidin, Ruse and Varna are sold at counters on the ground floor; same-day tickets to other destinations are sold in the gloomy basement, accessed via an unsigned flight of stairs obscured by another set of stairs that heads up to some snack bars. Counters are open 24 hours, but normally only a few are staffed and queues are long, so don't turn up at the last moment to purchase your ticket, and allow some extra time to work out the confusing system of platforms (ПЕРОН; indicated with Roman numerals) and tracks (КОЛОВОЗ). Advance tickets, seat reservations and sleepers for domestic services are available from a separate downstairs office (open 6am to 7.30pm Monday to Friday and 7am to 2.30pm Saturday).

The central train station is easy to reach from pl Sveta Nedelya on Trams 1, 2 and 7; by taxi (about 3 lv one way); or on foot (about 20 minutes).

All tickets for international trains, and advance tickets for domestic services, can be bought at one of several **Rila Bureaux** (www .bdz-rila.com; central train station Map p84; ☎ 932 3346; ✆ 6.30am-11pm; NDK Underpass Map p88; ☎ 965 8402; ✆ 7am-7pm Mon-Fri, to 2pm Sat; ul General Gurko Map p88; ☎ 987 0777; ul General Gurko 5; ✆ 7am-7pm Mon-Fri, to 2pm Sat). Staff at these offices usually speak some English.

Major domestic services to and from Sofia are listed in the table, opposite.

More information about the schedules and fares for other services to and from Sofia are included in the relevant Getting There & Away sections throughout this book. For more information about international services to and from Sofia, see p299.

DOMESTIC TRAIN SERVICES TO/FROM SOFIA

Destination	1st-/2nd-class fare	Duration	Number of trains (daily)
Burgas	19.60/15.70 lv (fast), 23.30/18.20 lv (express)	7–8hr	6 fast & 1 express
Gorna			6 fast, 1 express & 3 slow
Oryakhovitsa	13.60/10.90 lv (fast), 16.60/13.40 lv (express)	3–6hr	(for Veliko Tărnovo)
Plovdiv	8.40/6.70 lv (fast), 10.90/8.80 lv (express)	2½–3½hr	7 fast, 3 express & 8 slow
Ruse	18.10/14.50 lv	7hr	4 fast
Sandanski	9.50/7.60 lv	4hr	3 fast
Varna	23.60/19 lv (fast), 27.30/22 lv (express)	8–9hr	6 fast & 1 express
Vidin	12.90/10.30 lv (fast)	5–7hr	4 fast & 1 slow

GETTING AROUND
To/From the Airport

Sofia airport (☎ 937 2211; www.sofia-airport.bg) is located 12km southeast of the city centre. Minibus 30 shuttles between the airport and pl Nezavisimost for a flat fare of 1.50 lv; you can pick it up outside the Sheraton Hotel. Less convenient are bus 84 from Terminal 1 and bus 284 from Terminal 2 (which handles the bulk of international flights), both of which take a slow and meandering route before depositing you opposite Sofia University.

When you emerge into the arrivals hall you will immediately be greeted by taxi drivers offering you a ride into town, at often ridiculously inflated rates; bypass these and instead head to the reputable **OK-Supertrans taxi** (☎ 973 2121) office counter, where you can book an official, meter-equipped taxi. They will give you a slip of paper with the three-digit code of your cab, which will normally be immediately available. If there happen to be none available, you can try to negotiate an unmetered rate with one of the other taxis, but check the price carefully first. A taxi (using the meter) from the airport to the city centre should cost no more than 10 lv.

Car & Motorcycle

Frequent public transport, cheap taxis and horrendous traffic all provide little or no incentive to drive a private or rented car around Sofia. If you wish to explore further afield, though, a car would certainly come in handy. For more details about renting a car, see p302. Rental outlets include:

Avis (☎ 945 9224; www.avis.bg; Sofia airport)

Eurodollar (Map p88; ☎ 875 779; bul Vitosha 25)

Hertz Central (Map p88; ☎ 980 2467; ul Rakovski 135a);
Sofia airport (☎ 945 9217)

Sixt (☎ 945 9276; Sofia airport)

Tourist Service (Map p84; ☎ 981 7253; www.tourist
-service.com; ul Klokotnitsa 1)

Public Transport

The various forms of public transport – trams, buses, minibuses and trolleybuses, as well as the underground metro – run from 5am to 11.30pm every day.

A ticket on any bus, tram or trolleybus within Sofia costs 0.70 lv, or 0.80 lv from the driver. Most drivers on public transport sell tickets – make sure you have the right change – but it's far easier and quicker, especially during peak times, to buy tickets from kiosks at stops along the route before boarding.

If you plan to use public transport frequently, buy a strip of 10 tickets (6 lv) or a pass for one day (3 lv) or one month (37 lv), which are valid for all trams, buses and trolleybuses (but not the metro). All tickets must be validated by inserting them in the small machine on board; once punched, tickets are nontransferable. Inspectors will issue on-the-spot fines (7.50 lv) if you don't have a ticket; unwary foreigners are a favourite target. Don't forget to buy an extra ticket for each piece of oversized luggage, too – officially, this means anything exceeding 60cm x 40cm x 40cm.

Probably the most useful trams for visitors are 1 and 7, which link the central train station with bul Vitosha, via pl Sveta Nedelya. Public transport routes for buses, trams and trolleybuses are indicated on Domino's *Sofia City Map,* and tram routes are marked on the excellent (free) map inside the *Sofia City Info Guide.*

Buses for Boyana, Zlatni Mostove and Aleko depart from the Hladilnika bus terminal. It is near the southern terminus of Trams 2, 4, 9 and 12 from pl Sveta Nedelya. (From the final tram stop, walk through the tiny park to the bus stop on the main road.)

Private minibuses, known as *marshroutki,* are a popular and efficient alternative to public transport, but cost slightly more

SOFIA

(1.50 lv per trip). Destinations and fares are indicated (in Cyrillic) on the front of the minibus; pay the driver upon boarding. There are 49 routes in operation, with most services running between the city centre and the outlying suburbs. Routes of interest to travellers include 30, which goes to the airport; 5, which goes to the central train station; 21, which runs to Boyana; and 41, to Simeonovo.

At the time of research, Sofia's metro system (www.metropolitan.bg) had only one line, running between the western residential suburb of Obelya and the city centre (Serdica station), although construction was underway on expanding the line, which will eventually cross the city to the southeastern suburb of Mladost. The first of the new stations, including one near Sofia University, should be in operation by 2008. Metro tickets cost 0.70 lv per trip and cannot be used on other forms of public transport.

Taxi

Taxis are an affordable and easier alternative to public transport. By law, taxis must use meters, but those that wait around the airport, luxury hotels and within 100m of pl Sveta Nedelya will often try to negotiate an unmetered fare – which, of course, will be considerably more than the metered fare. All official taxis are yellow, have fares per kilometre displayed in the window, and have obvious taxi signs (in English or Bulgarian) on top. Never accept a lift in a private, unlicenced vehicle, because you will (at best) pay too much or (at worst) be robbed.

The rates per kilometre may range enormously from one taxi company to another, but the standard rate is 0.59 lv per minute in the daytime, 0.70 lv per minute at night.

In the very unlikely event that you can't find a taxi, you can order one by ringing **OK-Supertrans** (☎ 973 2121) or **Yes Taxi** (☎ 91 119). You will need to speak Bulgarian.

AROUND SOFIA

The places mentioned here are accessible from Sofia by public transport, but beyond Boyana, it's worth staying at least one night to avoid excessive travel and to really appreciate the surroundings.

BOYANA БОЯНА
☎ 02
Boyana is a peaceful and prosperous suburb of Sofia, lying around 8km south of the city centre. Once a favourite retreat for communist leaders and apparatchiks, these days it's home to Sofia's wealthy elite and two of the capital's major attractions. However, besides these there's little else to detain you.

Sights
NATIONAL MUSEUM OF HISTORY
Housed in the former presidential palace, the **National Museum of History** (☎ 955 7604; www .historymuseum.org; ul Vitoshko Lale 16; admission 10 lv, Boyana Church 12 lv, guided tour 20 lv; 9.30am-5.30pm) is Bulgaria's most hyped museum, though it's hardly in the most convenient of locations, and unless a coach party happens to turn up, you may have the place to yourself. However, it does occupy quite a stunning setting, and as a bonus you get to see the overblown splendour in which the old communist leadership once lived and held court.

A grand stairway sweeps up to the 1st floor, where the exhibitions begin. The star of the show is undoubtedly the fabulous 4th-century-BC Thracian gold treasure from Panagyurishte, with its *rhyta* (drinking cups) in the form of animal heads. Frustratingly though, this, along with other major exhibits, seems to spend a lot of time on loan abroad. There are more Thracian and Roman artefacts on display, as well as Greek pottery from the Black Sea region and lots of reproductions of treasures kept elsewhere. Also on this floor is a large, 16th-century fresco from a church in Arbanasi showing demons gleefully torturing naked sinners, and uniforms and paraphernalia from the 1876 April Uprising.

Upstairs, you can look over a gallery of icons and traditional folk costumes; temporary exhibitions are also held here. Outside, there's a collection of ancient tombstones on show alongside a few Russian MiG fighters.

BOYANA CHURCH
The tiny, 13th-century **Boyana Church** (☎ 959 0939; www.boyanachurch.org; ul Boyansko Ezero 3; admission 10 lv, with National Museum of History 12 lv; 9am-5pm Tue-Sun) is around 2km south of the museum. It's on Unesco's World Heritage list and is Bulgaria's most cherished and revered historic monument. The 90 murals, which date from 1259, are rare survivors from that period,

and are among the very finest examples of Bulgarian medieval artwork. They include the oldest known portrait of St John of Rila, along with representations of King Konstantin Asen and Queen Irina. Decades of painstaking restoration were finally completed in 2006, so visitors can now enjoy the church in all its glory. Taking photos of the interior is not permitted.

Getting There & Away

Minibus 21 runs to Boyana from the city centre (pick it up on bul Vasil Levski). It will drop you right outside the gates of the museum and also connects the museum with Boyana Church. You can also take bus 63 from pl Ruski Pametnik, or bus 64 from the Hladilnika terminal. Signs advertising the museum line the motorway, but it's not easy to spot the building, which is set back from the road behind a screen of trees. A taxi (about 6 lv one way) from the city centre to the museum is probably the easiest option of all; for the museum, ask for the 'Residentsia Boyana'.

VITOSHA NATURE PARK
ПРИРОДЕН ПАРК ВИТОША
☎ 02

The Mt Vitosha range, 23km long and 13km wide, lies just south of the city; it's sometimes referred to as the 'lungs of Sofia' for the refreshing breezes it deflects onto the often polluted capital. The mountain is part of the 22,726-hectare **Vitosha Nature Park** (www .park-vitosha.org), the oldest of its kind in Bulgaria (created in 1934). The highest point is Mt Cherni Vrâh (Black Peak; 2290m), the fourth-highest peak in Bulgaria, where temperatures in January can fall to –8ºC.

As well as being a popular ski resort in winter, the nature park is popular with hikers, picnickers and sightseers on summer weekends, and receives around 1.5 million visitors a year. There are dozens of clearly marked hiking trails, a few hotels, cafés and restaurants and numerous huts and chalets that can be booked through the Bulgarian Tourist Union (see p282).

Aleko Алеко
elevation 1800m

Aleko was named in honour of the renowned writer Aleko Konstantinov, who kick-started the hiking craze back in 1895 when he led a party of 300 fellow outdoors enthusiasts to the top of Mt Cherni Vrâh. On summer weekends, the area is crammed with picnicking families and hikers.

Zlatni Mostove Златни Мостове
elevation 1400m

Zlatni Mostove (Golden Bridges) takes its name from the bubbly little stream here, known as the Stone River, which was once a popular site for gold-panning. The trail of mammoth boulders running along its length was dumped here by glaciers during the Ice Age. It's another very popular spot on summer weekends, but at other times you may have the place to yourself. It's accessible cheaply by bus 261 from Ovcha Kupel bus station every 20 minutes on Saturday and Sunday, less frequently on weekdays. A taxi from the city centre will cost about 20 lv one way.

Dragalevtsi Драгалевци

A two-person **chairlift** starts about 5km (by road) up from the centre of Dragalevtsi village (though it's about 3km on foot if you take the obvious short cut up the hill). One chairlift (2 lv, 20 minutes) goes as far as Bai Krâstyo, from where another (2 lv, 15 minutes) carries on to Goli Vrâh (1837m). Both lifts operate year-round, but most reliably from about 8.30am to 6.30pm, Friday to Sunday.

A pleasant option is to take the chairlift to Goli Vrâh, walk to Aleko (30 minutes) and catch the gondola down to Simeonovo (or vice versa).

From the start of the chairlift, a well-marked trail (about 1km) leads to **Dragalevtsi Monastery**. Probably the oldest extant monastery in Bulgaria, it was built around 1345, but abandoned only 40 years later. The monastery contains colourful murals and is revered as one of the many hiding places of the ubiquitous anti-Turkish rebel leader Vasil Levski.

Ploshtad Tsar Ivan Aleksandâr in Dragalevtsi village has a number of cafés and traditional restaurants. There are also places to eat and drink along the road from the village to the chairlift.

Buses 64 and 93 from the Hladilnika terminal go to the village centre; bus 93 continues on to the chairlift.

Simeonovo Симеоново

Take a gondola to the mountains from Simeonovo (3/5 lv one way/return, 30 minutes). It operates Friday to Sunday from

SOFIA

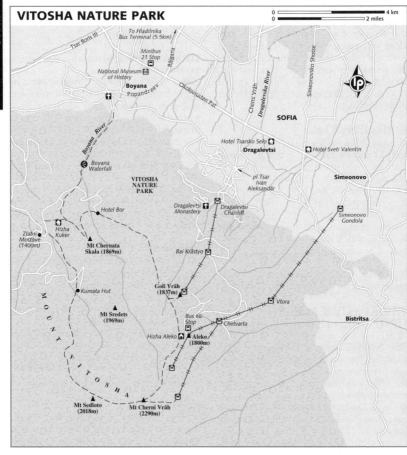

VITOSHA NATURE PARK

9am to 6.30pm (1 October to 31 March) and 8.30am to 6pm (1 May to 30 September). You can jump off at the junctions of Vtora or Chetvarta, from where hiking trails lead deep into the park – and then continue the trip later with the same ticket. Bus 123 from the Hladilnika terminal goes directly to the gondola station.

Activities
HIKING
The best map is probably *Vitosha Turisticheska Karta* (1:50,000), printed in Cyrillic and available at bookshops around central Sofia.

Some of the shorter and more popular hikes around the park:

Aleko–Goli Vrâh A short trail (30 minutes) between the top of the gondola from Simeonovo and the chairlift from Dragalevtsi.

Aleko–Mt Cherni Vrâh A popular, but steep, 90 minutes on foot. Alternatively, take the chairlift from Aleko to within 30 minutes' walk of the summit.

Aleko–Zlatni Mostove Follow the trail to Goli Vrâh, skirt around Mt Sredets (1969m) and pass Hotel Bor; about three hours.

Boyana Church–Zlatni Mostove At the church, ask for directions to the path that hugs the Boyana River and leads to the 15m-high Boyana Waterfall (best in winter). From there, obvious paths lead to Zlatni Mostove; about three hours in total.

Dragalevtsi Chairlift–Goli Vrâh Follow the chairlift from the bottom; a three-hour steep climb.

Zlatni Mostove–Mt Cherni Vrâh A challenging hike, via Kumata Hut and Mt Sedloto (2018m); about three hours.

SKIING

At 1800m above sea level, Mt Vitosha is Bulgaria's highest ski resort and its six slopes are only 22km from the centre of Sofia. There is rarely enough snow here before mid-December, but the season can often last into April.

The 29km of alpine ski runs (the longest is about 5km) range from easy to very difficult, and start as high as Mt Cherni Vrâh. Cross-country skiing is ideal along the 15km of trails, and snowboarding is also possible. As well as the Simeonovo gondola and Dragalevtsi chair-lift there is a handful of other chairlifts and draglifts. A one-day lift pass costs 25 lv.

However, Mt Vitosha gets very crowded on weekends, the slopes are not always well maintained and the quantity and quality of ski equipment for hire is not great because so many locals use their own gear. The ski-rental shop at the start of the Simeonovo gondola and the Aleko Ski Centre at Aleko both charge about €14 per day for a set of ski gear. A snowboard and boots also cost €14 per day, and a sledge €4.

The ski school at Aleko caters mainly to Bulgarians but instructors are multilingual. Five-day ski courses (four hours per day) are offered for €70. The website www .skivitosha.com may be useful for those who read Bulgarian.

Sleeping & Eating

In Vitosha Nature Park there are several modern hotels, which are usually much cheaper than those in the city centre. Ideally, though, you'll need your own transport to stay out here. Hikers can stay at any of the numerous mountain huts.

Hizha Aleko (☎ 967 1113; dm 10 lv, s/d with shared bathroom 15/25 lv) This hut offers a number of basic rooms with two to eight beds.

Hizha Kuker (☎ 955 4955; www.kukerbg.com; r from 25 lv; 🖳) One of the newer, more comfortable 'huts', this one has 10 rooms with bathrooms and an on-site restaurant.

Hotel Sveti Valentin (☎ 860 1399; www.hotels valentin.com; bul Simeonovsko Shosse 80; s/d/tr €49/54/69; 🅿 🔄 🖳) A modern, reasonably priced option in Simeonovo, the Sveti Valentin has a wide range of rooms available and a pleasant garden restaurant. Lunch and dinner can be arranged for between €6 to €10 extra.

Hotel Tsarsko Selo (☎ 816 0101; www.tsarskoselo.com; Oklovrusten Pat; s/d/apt from €80/100/130; 🅿 🔄 🖳) At the base of Mt Vitosha, this vast, upmarket hotel complex offers a variety of large rooms and villas (€108). On-site facilities include a restaurant, gym, sauna, Turkish bath, indoor and outdoor pools and even a football pitch; there's also a casino. The hotel has its own airport shuttle bus, too.

Getting There & Away

To Aleko, bus 66 (2.50 lv) departs from Sofia's Hladilnika terminal 10 times a day between 8am and 7.45pm on Saturday and Sunday, and four times a day on weekdays. Minibus 41 runs from Sofia city centre to Simeonovo (1.50 lv).

KYUSTENDIL КЮСТЕНДИЛ
☎ 078 / pop 56,500

Kyustendil, 90km southwest of Sofia, has been famous for its curative mineral springs since Thracian times, although it was the Romans who built up the site into a major city, which they called Pautalia, in the 2nd century AD. Under the Byzantines it was renamed Velbâzhd, growing into an important religious and military centre, and in the late 14th century it briefly became the seat of an independent principality, ruled over by the brothers John and Constantine Dragash. The town's present name derives from the Turkish for 'Constantine's Land'.

The sunny climate and mineral springs still draw tourists from across Bulgaria, and it's an agreeable, relaxed provincial town with a café-filled pedestrian centre and a handful of sights worth a look. For visitors, Kyustendil is a common transit point for travel to and from Macedonia, and a relatively easy day trip from Sofia.

Bulevard Bulgaria is the shady pedestrian lane that links the train station (and adjacent bus station) with pl Velbâzhd, the central square.

Sights

Although small, the two-roomed **City History Museum** (☎ 26 396; bul Bulgaria 55; admission free; ☽ 10am-noon & 1-5pm Mon-Fri) houses an intriguing array of archaeological artefacts from the locality, including Neolithic tools, some impressive Thracian armour excavated from a burial mound, and a reconstructed Thracian chariot. Votive tablets and statuettes of Zeus and Hera from Roman-era temples and medieval jewellery are also on display.

The **Vladimir Dimitrov Art Gallery** (☎ 22 503; ul Patriarh Evtimii 20; admission 1 lv; ☺ 9am-noon & 2-6pm Tue-Sun) is about 150m north of pl Velbâzhd, just off ul Han Krum. It houses over 200 works of art over two floors, mostly by Dimitrov, also known as 'The Master', who grew up in Kyustendil. A number of self-portraits are on show, along with many examples of his favourite images of young maidens surrounded by fruit and flowers. Labelling is in Bulgarian only.

On the southern side of pl Velbâzhd is the **Metropolitan Church of the Assumption** (ul Demokratsiya), an unusual wooden structure built slightly below ground level in 1816 and sporting three squat octagonal towers, which let in light to the dark interior, with its carved wooden pulpit, iconostasis and murals painted by Ivan Dospevski. It's set in pretty gardens, with a separate belltower at the front.

Also worth a look is the 16th-century **Ahmed Bey Mosque** (ul Stefan Karadzha), about 300m east of pl Velbâzhd. No longer a place of worship, it occasionally hosts archaeological exhibitions. It perches on top of the scant, largely rebuilt ruins of the 2nd-century-AD **Roman thermae**, located below present ground level and not accessible to visitors (though you can look over the railings).

On top of the forested **Hisarlâk Hill**, about 2km south of pl Velbâzhd, are ruins of the 2nd-century **ancient fortress** from the Roman city of Pautalia.

Sleeping & Eating

Hotel Velbâzhd (☎ 520 246; pautalia_tours@esnet.bg; bul Bulgaria 46; s/d unrenovated 20/35 lv, renovated 50/60 lv; P) Close to the bus and train stations, this concrete tower is divided into older and newer sections. The old rooms are pretty basic, though still clean and reasonably comfortable, but it's worth paying more for the 'renovated' rooms. All rooms have TVs, fridges and balconies, and rates include breakfast. The hotel also offers various balneological treatments.

Hotel Lavega (☎ 523 488; ul Tsar Asen 18; s/d 27/34 lv) Close to the Roman thermae, the Lavega is a neat, small guesthouse with a few basic rooms above a café of the same name.

The main pedestrian thoroughfare, bul Bulgaria, is lined with numerous restaurants, including **Gostilinitsa Batenberg** (☎ 50 344; bul Bulgaria; mains from 3 lv), a few steps north of pl Velbâzhd, which offers an English menu of grills, salads, omelettes and sausage-and-chips type dishes.

Getting There & Away

Buses leave from the Ovcha Kupel bus station in Sofia (6 lv, two hours) every 30 minutes for the **Kyustendil bus station** (☎ 22 626). From Kyustendil, six daily buses go to Blagoevgrad, eight depart for Dupnitsa and one travels to Plovdiv. Buses also leave daily for Skopje in Macedonia (around 30 lv, 11.30am). Tickets are sold at the **Matpu-96** (☎ 50 245) counter. From the adjacent **train station** (☎ 26 041), two fast trains (1st/2nd class, 6.80/5.40 lv; two hours 20 minutes) and three slow passenger trains travel every day to Sofia.

Southern Bulgaria

With spectacular and infinitely varied nature just waiting to be explored, and some of Bulgaria's greatest spiritual and cultural attractions, the south is a truly fascinating region that should be placed high on the itinerary of every traveller. From the stunning Rila Monastery and the fabled Seven Rila Lakes, strung out like jewels in the mountains beyond it, to the dynamic cultural capital of Plovdiv, southern Bulgaria offers something for everyone. Its striking landscapes range from the sandstone 'pyramids' of Melnik, where you can sample the country's best wine in splendid serenity, to the rugged Pirin Mountains and the gentler Rodopi range, together home of Bulgaria's best ski resorts.

The legacy of southern Bulgaria's colourful and complex history of ancient civilisations – from the mysterious Thracians and the Macedonians to Romans, Slavs, Byzantines and Turks – is also abundantly evident, in Plovdiv's grand Roman amphitheatre, the enthralling medieval monastery of Bachkovo, numerous Ottoman mosques and other sites attesting to a glorious past.

SOUTHERN BULGARIA

HIGHLIGHTS

▪ **Hit the powder**
  Ski Bansko (p127) and Borovets (p120),
  Bulgaria's baddest winter resorts

▪ **Liquid pleasure**
  Sample Bulgaria's best wine beneath
  sandstone cliffs in little Melnik (p134)

▪ **Get some action**
  Dive in to Plovdiv's Bohemian old town and
  partake in its vibrant nightlife (p138)

▪ **Marvel and repent**
  Make a pilgrimage to the spellbinding
  monasteries of Rila (p117) and Bachkovo
  (p153), and consider their vivid frescoes
  of eternal damnation

▪ **Indolent enjoyment**
  Cleanse yourself with the spa waters and
  massage therapies of the Devin spa resort
  (p160), deep in the rolling Rodopi Mountains

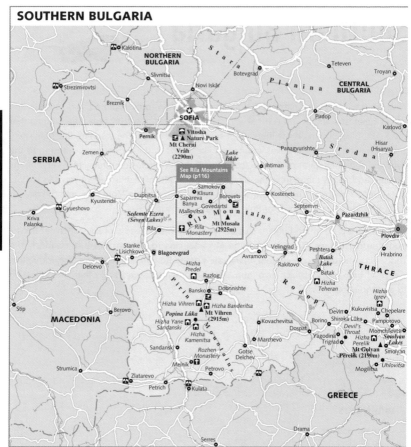

SOUTHERN BULGARIA

HISTORY

The vastness of southern Bulgaria and its mountainous geography have graced it with great historical diversity. It was the stomping ground of the ancient Thracians, an enigmatic, warlike group of tribes that left no written records in their own language, but once dominated large parts of modern-day Bulgaria, northeastern Greece and today's European Turkey. Thracian customs and beliefs have been passed down to us in Greek, and indeed their mystery religion, which found its supreme expression at the Temple of the Great Gods on the Greek island of Samothraki, influenced antique religion, attracting initiates even from Macedonian and Egyptian royalty.

Today's 'Bulgarian Thrace' – the section between the Sredna Gora Mountains, the Rodopi Mountains and the Black Sea coast – was the birthplace of the legendary Spartacus, the slave leader, and Orpheus, the tragic, semimythical inventor of music. Some two-thirds of the historical Thrace lie in Bulgaria, with Greek and Turkey splitting the remainder. Although the Thracians have long died out, there is a certain proud, earthy toughness common to the differing inhabitants of these three parts of Thrace that might, just perhaps, express the spirit of that long-lost civilisation.

In the deep south of Bulgaria, the sparsely populated Rodopi Mountains, dotted with

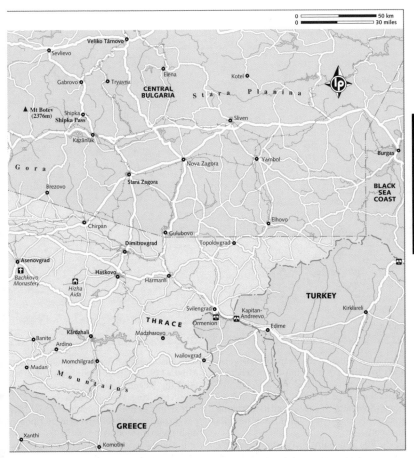

tiny, unvisited villages, attest to the more recent Ottoman legacy. The Muslim populations of Turks and Pomaks (Bulgarian Slavs who converted to Islam to win special benefits during Ottoman times) are evidenced here by minarets that pierce the boundless sky in villages unchanged over the centuries.

On the other side, in the western region of Pirin, towns such as Sandanski and Gotse Delchev preserve the names of heroic revolutionaries who fought against the Ottomans at the turn of the 19th century to free Macedonia from Turkish oppression. The issue of the similarities and differences of Bulgarian and Macedonian national iden-

tities and history remain controversial topics to this day, something you may experience while travelling in this region.

RILA MOUNTAINS
РИЛА ПЛАНИНА

'Mountains of Water' was the ancient Thracian name for this compact, majestic set of peaks covering 2629 sq km – a reference to the 180 lakes, streams and springs gushing with pure alpine aqua. These waters give the range famous attractions such as the small but stunning **Sedemte Ezera (Seven Lakes)**, and entice hikers and day-tripping travellers

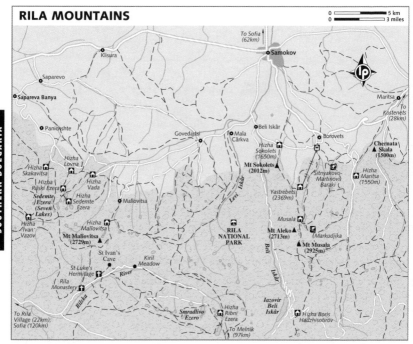

RILA MOUNTAINS

from Sofia. A hiking trail from the lakes also leads to Bulgaria's most important religious shrine, the captivating Rila Monastery, which draws throngs of devout Bulgarians and curious foreigners to gaze upon its dramatic architecture and vivid, wall-to-wall frescoes and icons.

The Rila Mountains also include Bulgaria's biggest ski resorts, Bansko and Borovets, and new access roads that will substantially reduce the driving time to Sofia are sure to expedite their expansion. Now increasingly popular for skiing (and partying) with foreign groups from Britain, Israel, Russia and beyond, these resorts are growing at the expense of the natural environment; lovers of untouched natural beauty are encouraged to come before Bulgaria catches up with more developed winter resort countries.

Despite the inevitable incursions of modern development, the permanently open **Rila National Park** (www.rilanationalpark.org) remains a sanctuary for wildlife and flora, comprising 144 sq km of forest and 130 sq km of alpine pastures. Its fir trees, beechwoods and other conifers provide a peaceful habitat for deer,

wild goats, eagles, falcons and more. Mount Musala (2925m), near Borovets, is Bulgaria's (and the Balkans') highest peak, and offers excellent hiking. Mountain huts *(hizhas)* provide simple accommodation (from about 10 lv per person), sometimes serving meals (though do bring extra food).

Invaluable printed resources for hikers include Julian Perry's *The Mountains of Bulgaria*, which details an extensive north–south trek (part of the trans-European E4 trek) across the Rila Mountains. It starts at Klisura and finishes at Hizha Predel, near Razlog, and takes from seven to 10 days. For serious hiking, you'll need Kartografia's *Rila* map (1:55,000), with place names in Cyrillic.

RILA VILLAGE РИЛА

The jumping-off point for Bulgaria's most sacred Orthodox shrine, this village 22km east of Rila Monastery is a sleepy place that just keeps up a pulse with its small faculty of tourism. Most monastery-bound buses connect here, however, and Rila does offer more inexpensive accommodation options than the monastery, as well as several foreign exchange offices and ATMs. Along with a BulBank ATM machine near the bus station, there's an OBB Bank ATM between the village supermarket and Kafe Djoana, a sort of landmark on the corner of pl Vazhrajdane and facing you when entering Rila from the west.

Sleeping & Eating

Hotel Orbita (☎ 07054-2167; s/d 25/40 lv; P ☑) The remodelled rooms here are basic but clean and contain good-sized bathrooms. It's reasonably good value, with a passable restaurant and not nearly as glum as the communist-era façade and lobby would seem to indicate. To find Hotel Orbita go to the right of the square past the OBB Bank ATM and walk about 30m.

Kafe-restoran Boyka Lazarova (☎ 0885628401; ul Doktor Spas Stoychev; mains 3-5 lv; ☺ 7.30am-midnight) Better eating, however, is actually found in a rudimentary café amusingly set in a time-worn school (now housing the tourism faculty). It serves inexpensive salads and grills in a pop-music environment. To get there, take the uphill street on the left of the square (when you're facing Kafe Djoana), proceed about 100m and turn left up the narrow stairway at the school. It's inside the building, straight ahead.

Kafe Djoana (pl Vazhrajdane 2; ☺ 7am-1am) A small, bright place on the square, good for an evening drink, and attracting a young local crowd.

Getting There & Away

From Dupnitsa, buses serve Rila village at 10am, 11am and 4pm. From Rila village, they depart for Dupnitsa at 6.20am, 8.40am and 3pm. Hourly buses between Rila village and Blagoevgrad operate between 6.20am and 7pm (1.50 lv, 45 minutes), and buses to Sofia leave at 6.20am and 3.30pm.

Buses leave Rila village for the monastery at 7.40am, 12.40pm and 3.50pm and return at 9am, 3pm and 5pm (1.30 lv).

RILA MONASTERY

☎ 07054 / elevation 1147m

Bulgaria's largest and most renowned monastery emerges abruptly out of a forested valley in the Rila Mountains. It's a major attraction for both Bulgarian pilgrims and foreign tourists. On summer weekends, the hordes descend and parking can be tough. In the

low season, however, the monastery provides much more solitude. Staying over at a nearby hotel or camping ground, or even at the monastery itself, allows you to experience Rila's photogenic early mornings and late evenings. You can also hike in the surrounding mountains (see p119).

Rila Monastery was founded in AD 927 by Ivan Rilski, leader of a monastic colony of hermits. Originally built 3km to the northeast, it was moved to its current location in 1335. By the 14th century's end, Rila Monastery was a powerful feudal fiefdom and, while plundered early in the 15th century, was restored in 1469, after Rilski's sacred relics were returned from Veliko Târnovo. The monastery helped preserve Bulgarian culture and religion during the Ottoman centuries, despite being destroyed by them often over the years.

An accident, however, caused Rila's greatest modern catastrophe: a fire in 1833 nearly engulfed all of the monastery's buildings. So many donations were received afterwards from various patrons that rebuilding commenced within a year – clearly indicating the monastery's importance and reverence to Bulgarians. It was proclaimed a national museum in 1961 by the communist government, and made a Unesco World Heritage site in 1983.

Monastery Grounds

The monastery compound, open from about 6am to 10pm, includes a main church and two museums, guest rooms and a post office. Photos are prohibited inside the church but are allowed elsewhere. Souvenir shops selling religious paraphernalia and Rila holy water are also enclosed within the monastery's high walls.

Cars and buses usually park near the western Dupnitsa gate. The eastern entrance is known as the Samokov gate. Some historical details in English, French and German fill notice boards at both entrances.

Within the monastery's walls, four levels of colourful balconies – with monastic cells, storerooms, a refectory and kitchen – surround the large courtyard, where stands the magnificent **Church of Rozhdestvo Bogorodichno** (Church of the Nativity), Bulgaria's grandest monastery church. Built between 1834 and 1837, the structure is crowned by three great domes. Its outside walls are covered with frescoes both vivid and harrowing (or humorous, depending on your disposition), depicting hell, where demons with whips, chains and pitchforks torture sinners in various states of woe and undress. The happier paintings, depicting the virtuous accompanied by angels and saints, indicate the moral lesson that stern church fathers wished to impart. The celebrated Zahari Zograf, most eminent of the many painters involved, signed his work. The gilded and intricately carved wood iconostasis was created by master artisans from Samokov and Bansko.

Considering the fierceness of the church's caretaker, it's best to take the prohibitions against skimpy clothing seriously. Long shorts are fine, but more revealing attire is forbidden. Luckily, a few sporting green tunics lie at the ready, helping you conceal whatever amount of nudity you choose to bring onto the premises. Photography, prohibited inside the church itself, is allowed outside, meaning you can snap away at the devilish frescoes and church architecture without fear.

After the church, see the **museum** (admission 8 lv; 8am-5pm), in the compound's southeastern corner. Its collected 18th- and 19th-century ecclesiastical paraphernalia, prints and Bibles are punctuated by the astonishing **Rila Cross**, a double-sided crucifix carved over a 12-year period by a certain Brother Raphael, between 1790 and 1802. It's incised in miniature with 140 biblical scenes and inscriptions, and about 650 human figures. Not surprisingly, Raphael eventually ended up beatifically blind after so much staring through a magnifying glass. To protect visitors from the same fate the monastery also exhibits blown-up photos of the cross, revealing just how detailed this work is. Despite the numerous foreign visitors, however, the labelling is in Bulgarian only (the available English-language booklet will help).

Beside the Samokov gate in the northeast of the monastic compound is the **Ethnographic Museum** (admission 8 lv; 8am-5pm), displaying regional folk costumes, textiles and crafts. Again, labelling is in Bulgarian only.

Other sites include the 23m-high stone **Hreliova Tower** (1335), named after a significant benefactor. The only part of the monastery remaining from that time, it's close to the Samokov gate. The monastery's **kitchen**, built in 1816, is at courtyard level in the northern wing. The 22m-high chimney, caked with centuries' worth of soot, cuts through all storeys, with 10 rows of arches crowned by a small dome. Thousands of

pilgrims were once fed here simultaneously, with food prepared in giant cauldrons – one of which could fit an entire cow.

Finally, walk up to the **upper balcony** for outstanding views of the surrounding Rila Mountains.

Sleeping

Most accommodation is within 100m of the Samokov gate. The monastery also provides relatively spartan accommodation for those desiring the full Rila experience. Rila village (p117) and Kiril Meadow (opposite) provide alternative accommodation options.

Zodiak Camping (2291; camping sites per person 10 lv, s/d bungalows 15/25 lv) A run-down camping ground with an idyllic setting along the river, 1.6km past the monastery along the road to Kiril Meadow, the Zodiak also offers a good restaurant.

Hotel Rilets (2106; fax 3363; s/d incl breakfast from 25/33 lv; P) The large and outdated Rilets has many rooms; the renovated ones are worth the higher price (singles/doubles 35/45 lv). You'll probably want private transportation, however, as the hotel's down a 500m-long access road starting 1.2km past the monastery, on the road to Kiril Meadow. There's an average, on-site restaurant.

Rila Monastery (2208; r per person 30 lv) Rooms in the older western wing have three or four beds, and are sparsely furnished but clean. The communal facilities have toilets, but no showers. The nicer new rooms include bathrooms with showers. In summer, the latter rooms can be booked by midday, so call ahead or arrive early. The reception office (in the southern wing) handles bookings.

Hotel Tsarev Vrah (/fax 2280; s/d with bathroom 40/60 lv) The renovated Tsarev Vrah has decent rooms; most balconies offer forest views, and from some you can see the monastery. It's signposted about 150m from Samokov gate.

Eating

Most restaurants are near the Samokov gate. Rila's local delicacy is *pasturvka* (trout); menu prices are usually per 100g.

Restaurant Drushlyavitsa (0888278756; mains 3-12 lv; 8am-10pm) Outside the Samokov gate, this fine place has outdoor tables overlooking a little brook, and serves traditional Bulgarian cuisine.

Rila Restaurant (0488-90 418; mains 5-12 lv; 8am-midnight) The Rila offers similar fare to Drushlyavitsa, but is more atmospheric, set in a 120-year-old building.

The popular little **bakery** (☺ dawn-dusk), next to the Rila Restaurant, sells hot, deep-fried doughnuts, bread and all-natural sheep's-milk yoghurt.

Getting There & Away

The most common starting points for trips to Rila Monastery are Sofia and the town of Blagoevgrad, administrative capital of southwestern (Pirin) Bulgaria (see p127). In Sofia, you can ask at the **Ovcha Kupel bus station** (☎ 02-955 5362) about direct buses, though it's more likely you'll need to connect in Rila village first. The same is true for journeys from Blagoevgrad.

Buses leave Rila village for the monastery at 7.40am, 12.40pm and 3.50pm and return at 9am, 3pm and 5pm. (In summer, the 3pm service may continue to Sofia, but not always.) From Dupnitsa, buses to Rila Monastery leave at 6.40am and 2.15pm and return from the monastery at 9.40am and 5.15pm.

A day trip from Sofia by bus involves taking any bus leaving before 8am to Dupnitsa (1½ hours) from the central bus station or Ovcha Kupel bus station. Then take the 10am or 11am bus to Rila village, and from there the 12.40pm bus to the monastery. You'll then return on the 5.15pm bus to Dupnitsa, and from there take one of the hourly buses (or trains) back to Sofia.

Buses to Rila village from Blagoevgrad run four or five times daily, the last leaving at 8pm. A day trip to the monastery from Blagoevgrad is also possible, though again you'll have to start early.

If you really need to accelerate things, take a taxi from Rila village to the monastery (about 15 lv). Rila village has several taxis, and usually one or two wait at the monastery.

Full-day tours of Rila Monastery from Sofia cost from around €60 to €70 per person for a group of two people, or less for larger groups (see p97). The resort hotels at Bansko and Borovets also offer organised day trips to the monastery, among other places, though prices fluctuate considerably.

AROUND RILA MONASTERY
St Luke's Hermitage & St Ivan's Cave

About 3.7km northeast of Rila Monastery, on the road to Kiril Meadow, a left-hand trail leads to St Luke's Hermitage; look for Sveti Ivan's picture by the steps. Built in 1798, the hermitage features a large courtyard and the **Church of Sveti Luka**. Take the trail for about 15 minutes to St Ivan's Cave, where Ivan Rilski lived and is buried. Legend states that anyone able to pass through the aperture in the cave's roof has not sinned; the generous size of the hole would seem to indicate that gluttony is the only significant one of the seven deadly sins.

Kiril Meadow Кирилова Ливада

Continue 7km northeast of Rila Monastery to reach Kiril Meadow, a gorgeous area with pine trees, picnic spots, cafés and stunning views of the craggy cliffs. It's an easy, and mostly shady, walk, and there's a **guesthouse** (☎ 076-3268; r 25 lv, bungalows 50 lv) offering simple rooms with shared bathrooms, and bungalows with five beds and a private bathroom. It's an excellent alternative for those seeking spiritual reflection amidst tranquil nature rather than at the busy monastery.

SAMOKOV САМОКОВ
☎ 0722 / pop 27,503

You have to pass Samokov, 62km southeast of Sofia, to reach Borovets ski resort, and indeed most of the locals employed at Borovets do seem to live here. It's a small and somewhat gritty town, with history but few sites, though the Borovets expansion projects will bring Samokov closer to the action and, hopefully, smarten it up a bit.

In the 14th century, Samokov became a centre for iron mining. Five centuries later, the Samokov School of Icon Painting and Woodcarving brought the town cultural fame; soon thereafter it became known for some eccentric political ideas when the local council established the famous but ultimately unsuccessful Samokov Commune (1910–12). As Bulgaria's first socialist organisation, the commune sought to improve workers' rights and education.

Samokov's foreign exchange offices are near the bus station, which contains food, and even clothing shops.

Sights

Near the bus station is the **Bairakli Mosque** (admission 1 lv; ☺ 9am-6pm Tue-Fri), built in the 1840s. It doesn't function, but does have some wonderfully ornate murals, and an unusually cut minaret.

SOUTHERN BULGARIA

The **History Museum** (☎ 22 194; ul Liubcho Baramov 4; admission 2 lv; ⊙ 8am-noon & 1-5pm Mon-Fri) contains archaeological and ethnographical displays, models of engines and furnaces, displays on the town's icon-painting heritage and the printing press that produced Samokov's first Bulgarian-language magazines in 1844. The upstairs photo gallery is devoted to the old town and 19th- and early-20th-century family photos. It's a few metres west of the square.

The **Sarafska Kâshta Museum** (☎ 22 221; ul Knyaz Dondukov 11; admission 1 lv; ⊙ 9am-noon & 1-5pm Mon-Fri), 200m north of the History Museum, dates from 1860 and contains period furnishings.

Sleeping & Eating

Samokov's proximity to Borovets means hotel prices in winter are approximately 25% higher than those given here. The hotels also have restaurants.

Hotel Koala (☎ 350 783; ul Hristo Zagrafski 25; s/d/tr 15/22/32 lv; P) This small place on a side street 1km northeast of the bus station has six large, bright and well-furnished rooms.

Hotel-Restaurant Sonata (☎ 27 534; ul Petâr Beron 4; s/d/tr 36/48/60 lv; P) A fairly new and central hotel with clean, cosy rooms that include TVs and fridges, the Sonata offers additional half- and full-board options (10 lv or 20 lv extra). The hotel runs guided fishing and biking trips, rents bikes and contains a children's playground.

Mehana Golyamata Cheshma (☎ 66 617; ul Tûrgovska; mains 6-10 lv; ⊙ 10am-1am Mon-Sat) Near the bus station, this place serves salads, grills and fish dishes. It's named after the adjacent 17th-century drinking fountain.

Getting There & Away

Buses and minibuses to Samokov (4 lv, one hour) depart every 30 minutes between 7am and 7.30pm from Sofia's Yug bus station. From the **Samokov bus station** (☎ 66 540; ul Tûrgovska), minibuses serve Borovets (1.20 lv, 20 minutes), Govedartsi and Malîovitsa. Buses to Dupnitsa (3.50 lv, one hour) leave at 7.30am, 2.20pm and 5pm.

BOROVETS БОРОВЕЦ
☎ 07503 / elevation 1350m

Although it's been overtaken by Bansko for the title of Bulgaria's biggest ski resort, Borovets still draws big crowds (both locals and foreign package tourists), and is con-

tending to reclaim its old position with the so-called 'Super Borovets' project planning to expand it significantly.

Borovets is one of Bulgaria's oldest ski resorts, as the slightly faded and worn state of the structures and lifts attests. However, unlike built-up Bansko, a town of 10,000 people, Borovets is simply a resort; most accommodation and services literally spill off the mountain. Out of ski season, when the shuttered restaurants offer only last season's chalk-scrawled menus out front, it can feel eerily empty. However, the thick pine forests all around are excellent for summer hikes, and the mountain air is very crisp and refreshing.

Information

Borovets' hotels spread over several kilometres of the main resort; however, the following year-round places all occupy the small, curving main street, which starts from the Samokov–Kostenets road and ends at the mountain's base. There's no real tourist information office, so get information about hiking, guided tours and other activities through the big hotels or ski shops.

Foreign exchange offices and ATMs exist in central Borovets. The larger hotels also have lobby ATMs and wireless internet.

Bulgariaski.com has information on snow conditions, accommodation and news at all of Bulgaria's ski resorts; the **Bulgarian Extreme & Freestyle Skiing Association** (www.befsa.com) lists organised competitions, demonstrations and excursions in Borovets and elsewhere.

Activities
SKIING

Only 70km from Sofia, Borovets sits under Mt Musala (2925m). It has twice hosted World Cup Alpine ski rounds, and usually gets about 1.5m of snow in winter. The 45km of ski runs, which include Bulgaria's longest, occupy the main areas of Markudjika, Yastrebets and Sitnyakovo-Martinovi Baraki. The four cross-country trails total about 19km, and start about 2km from Borovets.

Borovets is too far for a day trip from Sofia by bus; however, this will change when the Sofia–Borovets direct highway, which will cut travel time to 35 minutes, is completed. While nearby Samokov (p119), Govedartsi (p122) and Malîovitsa (p122) offer more budget accommodation than Borovets itself,

SOUTHERN BULGARIA

TOP PICKS: SKI RESORTS

- Bansko (p127)
- Borovets (opposite)
- Pamporovo (p156)
- Chepelare (p155)
- Maliovitsa (p122)

---

prices rise everywhere during winter. Shops rent ski equipment, from 50 lv to 60 lv per day. Well-qualified, multilingual instructors provide training for 300 lv (four hours per day for six days, including a lift pass and ski gear). Guests at the big hotels can get cheaper training from in-house instructors.

Borovets has three chairlifts, 10 draglifts and a gondola from the Borosports complex in Borovets to Yastrebets, costing 10/15 lv one way/return. A one-day lift pass costs 60 lv. With one, you can board a minibus to the slopes for free from the main hotels. Borovets also has decent snowboarding, with gear going for about 50 lv per day. Lessons cost about 120 lv for six hours.

HIKING

Borovets is an ideal base for eastern Rila Mountain hiking. Trails are marked, and some simply follow established ski runs – good news since the hiking trails around Borovets are not marked on Kartografia's *Rila* map.

Some short and popular hikes are:

Borovets–Chernata Skala Take the road towards Kostenets, and follow the signs pointing south to Hizha Maritsa; three hours (easy).

Borovets–Hizha Maritsa From the Borovets to Chernata Skala road, continue along the southern road; 4½ hours (moderately difficult).

Borovets–Hizha Sokolets Follow the road through Borovets – 2½ hours (easy). Another trail (1½ hours) from Hizha Sokolets heads south to Mt Sokolets (2021m).

OTHER ACTIVITIES

Horse riding is available in summer from outside the Hotel Rila, and costs around 40 lv for two hours, while **Hotel Samokov** (☎ 2581; www.samokov.com) has an indoor **swimming pool** (admission 4 lv), bowling alley and fitness centre, and offers saunas and massages. These facilities are open daily in winter, and on weekends in summer.

The major hotels all offer **excursions** to places such as Plovdiv, Sofia and Rila Monastery (at varying prices).

Sleeping

Independent travellers planning to ski (and sleep in) Borovets should book three to six months ahead for midrange or top-end hotels. The low-season rates listed here increase by 25% in winter. Borovets' streets are unnamed and few, so addresses don't really exist. For cheaper accommodation, try Samokov (opposite), Govedartsi (p122) and Maliovitsa (p123).

Flora Hotel (☎ 2520; hotel-flora@gbs.com.bg; s/d/ste from 60/80/75 lv; **P** **🍴** **🖥**) After some recent revitalisation, the now four-star Flora boasts a swimming pool, spa and 'Irish pub'. It's a more intimate alternative to the behemoth Rila and Samokov, while boasting similar amenities. Rooms are plain but clean, with balconies, and the restaurant's fine.

Alpin Hotel (☎ 32 201; www.alpin-hotel.bg; d/q 67/80 lv; **P** **🍴** **🖥**) On the mountain's base opposite Hotel Rila, this nice modern place has small but comfortable rooms with all the mod cons, and a sparkling lobby bar.

Hotel Rila (☎ 2441; www.borovets-bg.com; s/d/apt 90/120/160 lv; **P** **🖥** **🐕**) The gigantic Rila, opposite the mountain near the main road's upper end, has impressive facilities such as a fitness centre, tennis court, two restaurants, shops and a nightclub. The slightly worn rooms were once very modern but even now are just fine. Upper-floor rooms facing the mountain offer wonderful views from their balconies. While you wouldn't usually expect skiers to be packing heat, the Rila takes no chances with its prowling team of surly, black-clad armed guards, menacingly noticeable when guests are fewer out of season.

Hotel Samokov (☎ 2581; www.samokov.com; s/d/ste from 90/120/220 lv; **P** **🖥** **🐕**) Halfway down the main road from the mountain, the gargantuan Samokov has three restaurants, a nightclub, shopping centre, gym, bowling alley and ski school. The comfortable modern rooms have balconies, but are even more characterless than the Rila's.

Villa Stresov (☎ 02-980 4292; www.villastresov.com; d from €100, whole villa from €480; **P** **🍴**) This large, Swiss-style villa has four double rooms, sleeping up to eight people, a fully fitted kitchen, a garden and all the mod cons. Rent it all, or just pay for one, two or three bedrooms. There's a two-night minimum stay.

SOUTHERN BULGARIA

Eating

Borovets' main streets feature cafés, bars and restaurants heavy on 'English steaks' and cocktails reminiscent of gauche seaside summer holidays. Without the package tourists after winter, however, most close.

La Bomba (☎ 483; mains 5-9 lv; 🕑 8am-1am) Opposite the Hotel Rila, La Bomba serves pizzas and steak-and-chips style dishes.

Black Tiger (☎ 0898580483; mains 6-9 lv; 🕑 9am-1am) A simple place playing punchy Bulgarian music, the Black Tiger goes for the well-lacquered ski lodge look, and is popular with locals even out of high season, serving good *mehana* (tavern) fare. It's behind La Bomba on the mountain's base.

Alpin Restaurant (mains 8-12 lv) The Alpin Hotel's (p121) restaurant offers a varied, if touristy, menu of pizzas, grills and barbecue meals.

Getting There & Away

There's not (yet) direct public transport between Sofia and Borovets, but that will probably change with the Sofia–Borovets road's completion. For now, take a bus from Sofia to Samokov (4 lv, one hour) and then a minibus to Borovets (1.20 lv, 20 minutes). Minibuses from Samokov leave every 30 to 45 minutes between 7am and 7pm. Borovets has no bus station; minibuses from Samokov stop outside Borovets' Hotel Samokov.

Alternatively, if you're coming on a long-haul bus passing by Borovets, such as the Blagoevgrad–Plovdiv service, the driver may leave you on the side of the road; from here, it's a 1km uphill walk into town.

Taxis are a good option for out-of-town travel; note, however, that taxi rides within Borovets itself during ski season start at a staggering 10 lv (for out-of-town journeys, normal rates always apply).

Borovets has several taxi companies; a good bet is **Boro Taxi** (☎ 0888707785), led by the affable Slaveyko Spasov, who speaks English, German and Russian, and who bears an uncanny resemblance to American comic actor Leslie Nielsen. Examples of his base fares from Borovets include: Samokov (10 lv); Maliovitsa (30 lv); Dupnitsa (50 lv); Sofia (70 lv); Septembri (50 lv); and Plovdiv (100 lv). An international trip west to the first town in Macedonia (Kriva Palanka) also costs 100 lv – worth mentioning, since travelling this relatively short distance via public transportation would require at least four different buses and most of a day.

GOVEDARTSI ГОВЕДАРЦИ
☎ 07125 / elevation 1200m

Govedartsi, 13km southwest of Samokov, is an alternative, and cheaper base to Borovets for local hiking, or for skiing at Borovets. It's also where the marked trails listed in Kartografia's *Rila* map start.

Number 53 Hotel (kokojambazki@hotmail.com; d with shared bathroom 20 lv) has large, airy and bright rooms, with a garden, sauna, bar and restaurant. It's 300m east of the bus stop on the Samokov–Maliovitsa road.

Kalina Hotel (☎ 2643; kalina-hotel@top.bg; s/d 20/40 lv), 150m up from the town square and bus stop, offers small but comfortable rooms. There's a restaurant-bar and garden barbecue. The friendly owners love discussing local history and folklore.

From Samokov, six or seven daily minibuses serve Govedartsi (2 lv, 20 minutes).

MALIOVITSA МАЛЬОВИЦА
elevation 1750m

At the foot of the Rila Mountains 13km southwest of Govedartsi, little Maliovitsa (Mali-*ov*-itsa) is a more low-key ski resort than Borovets (though this will change someday as Borovets continues to expand and encroach). It's also a popular summertime base for rock climbing, mountain climbing and hiking, with rich bird life. Day trips from Sofia require private transport, so if you're bussing it from there you'll probably be sleeping over.

Activities
SKIING

Skiing in Maliovitsa is cheaper than at Borovets, but not nearly as challenging. The **Central Mountain School** (☎ 07125-2270) rents equipment for 5 lv to 8 lv per person per day depending on quality. Other local shops charge about 15 lv per day. The village's one draglift costs 8 lv per person per day.

CLIMBING & WATER SPORTS

In summer, the Central Mountain School offers **rock climbing** and **mountain climbing** activi-

---

THE WHITE BROTHERHOOD

This exotic Bulgarian cult, also known as Dunovism (after the priest who started it in 1918), follows an eclectic set of rituals such as yoga, sun-worshipping and vegetarianism, amalgamating Orthodox Christianity and Hinduism, among other religions. Followers meet at the Seven Rila Lakes each August; check with the Odysseia-In Travel Agency (p86) or the National Tourist Information Centre (p86) in Sofia for the exact dates. Note that cult members often fill up the Hizha Sedemte Ezera and Hizha Rilski Ezera huts for a week or more in August for their inscrutable evening rituals, though the unwashed masses can still enter the huts during daylight hours to witness the pilgrimage.

---

ties for about 30 lv to 50 lv per person per day, including a guide, but not transport or equipment (they're available at the school).

Between March and June, and in September and October, the Central Mountain School runs **kayaking** and **rafting** trips on local rivers.

HIKING

Hiking from Maliovitsa involves a network of *hizhas* that lead to and from what seem to be foreign visitors' favourite southwestern natural attraction, the **Seven Rila Lakes** *(Sedemte Rilski Ezera)*. These glittering turquoise lakes, small but exquisitely beautiful, are strung out like jewels across rolling meadows in the central Rila Mountains. While Maliovitsa's hiking trails heading there are well-marked, consider buying Kartografia's detailed *Rila* map.

Reaching the lakes, and their *hizha* accommodation, is done in various ways. From Maliovitsa, first hike (about one hour) to **Hizha Maliovitsa** (2050m). The barracks-like rooms have between four and 20 beds, and there's cheap camping as well. The café has basic meals, or, bring your own food and use the kitchen.

From Hizha Maliovitsa, it's a seven-hour hike to Hizha Sedemte Ezera, an older hut with simple dormitories. Alternatively, a little further north you'll find **Hizha Rilski Ezera** (☎ 0701-50 513), up at 2150m. The Rila Mountains' best *hizha*, it offers dorm beds

and rooms with a shared/private bathroom from around 30/35 lv per person, including breakfast and dinner, plus a café. Reservations aren't necessary, except during August's grand convocation of the mystical White Brotherhood (see the boxed text, left).

From the Seven Lakes, it's an easy, downhill one-hour walk to **Hizha Skakavitsa** (☎ 0701-50 513) at 1985m, and its lovely waterfall; alternatively, head for the Rila Monastery (a six- to seven-hour hike).

Another route to the Seven Rila Lakes from Maliovitsa is via Hizha Vada and Hizha Lovna, bypassing Hizha Maliovitsa.

Alternatively, reach the lakes from **Sapareva Banya** (take a bus from Dupnitsa), further to the west, or from Hizha Pionerska (1500m). To reach this hut from Sapareva Banya, walk 13km up the steep road, hire a taxi (best done from Dupnitsa), or organise a transfer (about 30/35 lv for one/two people) with Sofia-based **Zig Zag Holidays** (p86). From the hut, it's a three-hour hike to Hizha Rilski Ezera.

Sleeping & Eating

Guesthouse Dzhambazki (☎ 07125-2361; info@house-djambazki.com; s/d/apt from 12/24/44 lv; **P**) This cosy place has comfortable rooms, some with balconies, plus a sauna and bike rental.

Hotel Maliovitsa (☎ /fax 07125-2222; d/tr/q incl breakfast from 20/30/40 lv; **P**) This large hotel above the central car park has rooms nicer than the hotel's façade and corridors might suggest, plus a restaurant, bar, ski school and kids' playground.

Central Mountain School (☎ 07125-2270; d from 25 lv; **P**) Located near the central car park, the school offers basic accommodation and a restaurant.

Getting There & Away

In Sofia, call the **Yug bus station** (p105) to see if the daily, direct 9am minibus to Maliovitsa (6 lv, two hours) is running. Alternatively, catch a bus to Samokov and get a minibus to Maliovitsa (3 lv, 45 minutes) at 8.15am or 4.15pm. Minibuses return to Samokov at 9am and 5pm, and (theoretically) to Sofia at about midday. From Blagoevgrad, take a regular bus passing through Samokov and then catch the Maliovitsa minibus from there.

PIRIN MOUNTAINS
ПИРИН
ПЛАНИНА

The stark Pirin Mountains, with peaks surpassing 2900m, rise dramatically out of Bulgaria's southwestern corner; their dark, portentous appearance has affected human imagination since well before the ancient Slavic tribes named the mountains after their god of thunder and storms, Perun. Over the centuries, these mountains and their life-giving waters – some 230 springs and 186 lakes – have attracted Macedonians, Greeks, Slavs and Turks, among others. While their average height is relatively low, at 1033m, over 100 Pirin peaks exceed 2000m, and 12 are higher than 2700m. The highest, Mt Vihren (2915m), is near Bansko.

Some 40,447 hectares of the Pirin range constitute the **Pirin National Park** (www.pirin-np.com in Bulgarian), Bulgaria's largest, permanently open and free to enter. The gate is only 1.8km southwest of Bansko, the country's premier ski resort. The park's been a Unesco World Heritage site since 1983, protecting a varied and unique landscape, home to 1100 species of flora, 102 types of birds and 42 species of mammals, such as bears, deer and wild goats. The Bansko-based **Pirin National Park office** (☎ /fax 07443-2428; ul Bulgaria 4) offers key information for longer hikes in the mountains.

Besides skiing at Bansko and hiking in the national park, visitors to the Pirin region can enjoy some of Bulgaria's best wine at the offbeat village of Melnik, clustered with 18th- and 19th-century houses, or take in the waters at mineral baths near Sandanski, legendary birthplace of Roman slave revolt leader Spartacus, and even indulge in some nightlife at Pirin's provincial capital and a major university town, Blagoevgrad.

BLAGOEVGRAD БЛАГОЕВГРАД
☎ 073 / pop 69,572

About 100km straight south of Sofia, Blagoevgrad (Bla-*go*-evgrad) is more than just the Pirin region's administrative capital; it's a friendly, liveable place filled with grand squares, vibrant cafés and clubs frequented by 16,000 Bulgarian (and foreign) young people studying at the **Neofit**

Rilski Southwest University (☎ 827 177) and the **American University of Bulgaria** (☎ 825 241; www .aubg.bg). On the road between Sandanski and Sofia, Blagoevgrad makes a useful base for day trips or longer forays to places such as Rila Monastery, Bansko, Sandanski and Melnik. It's also a stop on the Sofia–Thessaloniki–Athens international train line.

Known in Ottoman times as Gorna Dzhumaya, the city's large Turkish population was displaced after the Balkan Wars of 1912–13. It was renamed Blagoevgrad by the communists in 1950, after the 19th-century Bulgarian Marxist, Dimitar Blagoev, whose statue stands on the square near the American university.

Orientation

Blagoevgrad's adjacent train station and two bus stations are on Sveti Dimitâr Solunski, about 2km from the centre (taxis costs around 3 lv).

East of the small river bisecting Blagoevgrad is Varosha, the old quarter; behind and to the southeast are a forested park and botanical gardens. Most of the action, however, is on the river's western side, around three large and pedestrianised adjoining squares, pl Bulgaria, pl Makedonia and pl Georgi Izmirliev Makedoncheto. They contain most of the shops, cafés, restaurants and clubs. Rising from the far end of the latter square is the American University of Bulgaria, beyond an enormous fountain; at the time of writing, however, the university was preparing to move across to pl Bulgaria. The state university, Neofit Rilski Southwest University (known to students simply by the Bulgarian-language name, *Yugozapaden*) is 3km west of the centre.

Information

Foreign exchange offices line ul Tsar Ivan Shishman, hugging the river on the western bank. A First East International Bank stands on a laneway southwest of pl Makedonia, while the Bank of Piraeus is on the corner of pedestrianised ul Todor Aleksandrov and ul Kralli Marko. There's also a DSK Bank ATM on pl Bulgaria, next to the popular Underground nightclub.

Escapenet (☎ 0899879042; ul Petko Petkov 2; per hr 1 lv; ☼ 10.30am-10.30pm Mon-Sat) A centrally located internet café.

Post office (ul Mitropolit Boris) Combined with the telephone centre.

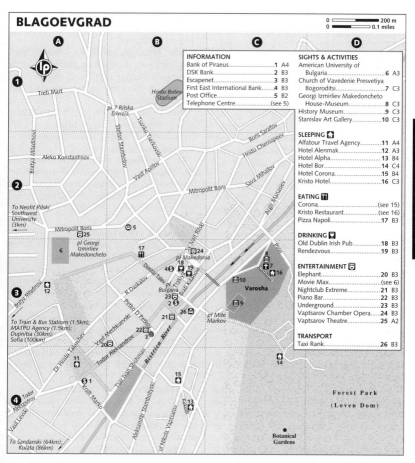

BLAGOEVGRAD

0 — 200 m
0 — 0.1 miles

INFORMATION	
Bank of Piraeus	1 A4
DSK Bank	2 B3
Escapenet	3 B3
First East International Bank	4 B3
Post Office	5 B2
Telephone Centre	(see 5)

SIGHTS & ACTIVITIES	
American University of Bulgaria	6 A3
Church of Vavedenie Presvetiya Bogoroditsi	7 C3
Georgi Izmirliev Makedoncheto House-Museum	8 C3
History Museum	9 C3
Stanislav Art Gallery	10 C3

SLEEPING	
Alfatour Travel Agency	11 A4
Hotel Alenmak	12 A3
Hotel Alpha	13 B4
Hotel Bor	14 C4
Hotel Corona	15 B4
Kristo Hotel	16 C3

EATING	
Corona	(see 15)
Kristo Restaurant	(see 16)
Pizza Napoli	17 B3

DRINKING	
Old Dublin Irish Pub	18 B3
Rendezvous	19 B3

ENTERTAINMENT	
Elephant	20 B3
Movie Max	(see 6)
Nightclub Extreme	21 B3
Piano Bar	22 B3
Underground	23 B3
Vaptsarov Chamber Opera	24 B3
Vaptsarov Theatre	25 A2

TRANSPORT	
Taxi Rank	26 B3

SOUTHERN BULGARIA

Sights

The **History Museum** (☎ 823 557; bul Aleksandâr Stamboliyski; admission 3 lv; 9am-noon & 3-6pm Mon-Fri), in a modern building near Varosha, exhibits roughly 160,000 religious relics, archaeological artefacts and traditional costumes, and displays on the military history of Macedonia (from the Bulgarian point of view). The natural history section contains Bulgaria's biggest stuffed bird and animal collection.

Between Forest Park and bul Aleksandâr Stamboliyski, which runs parallel to the river on its eastern bank, is the old quarter, **Varosha**. Several renovated Bulgarian National Revival–period homes, including the **Georgi Izmirliev Makedoncheto House-Museum**, and art galleries such as the **Stanislav Art Gallery**, are

on Varosha's relaxing cobblestone streets. Opening hours are erratic, however.

In a small, serene garden under the Kristo Hotel, the **Church of Vavedenie Presvetiya Bogoroditsi** (Church of the Annunciation of the Virgin; ☎ 884 795; ul Komitrov; 6.30am-8pm), built in 1844, has a richly frescoed portico and unique black-and-white chequered façade, with an extraordinary painting of the circle of life that includes continents and astrological symbols. There are also attractive murals and icons inside.

A steep road (700m) from Varosha leads to **Forest Park** (*Loven Dom*), a shady and popular place with good views. Towards the park's southern edge are the small **Botanical Gardens**.

Sleeping

Alfatour Travel Agency (☎ 885 049; alfazdr@abv.bg; ul Krali Marko 4) can arrange centrally located private rooms from 20 lv per person.

Hotel Korona (☎ 831 350; www.hotel-crown.com; ul Nikola Vaptsarov 16; d/apt incl breakfast from 40/50 lv; **P**) This new place near the Hotel Alpha offers good value. The spacious, modern rooms have TV, minibar, air conditioning and double beds. There's a glossy bar and downstairs restaurant (guests get a 20% discount). Reception workers, however, don't all speak English, and though the hotel claims to have internet, no one seems to know how to make it work.

Hotel Alpha (☎ 831 122; alphablg@hotmail.com; ul Kukush 7; d/apt from 40/50 lv; **P** 🖳) Although the rooms at this established and popular place are slightly smaller and less posh than the Korona's, service is friendlier and more professional. Rooms are clean, with modern bathrooms, and the attractive lobby bar has a wireless connection.

Hotel Alenmak (☎ 884 076; pl Georgi Izmirliev Makedoncheto; d 50 lv; **P**) At the time of writing this glum communist throwback was being reincarnated as a posh five-star hotel with spa centre. Till then, it remains an overpriced dinosaur.

Kristo Hotel (☎ 880 444; hotel_kristo@abv.bg; ul Komitrov; s/d/apt incl breakfast 50/60/70 lv; **P** 🔀) With white walls bedecked with wood-framed windows and flowering balconies, the Kristo offers plenty of old-town atmosphere. The cosy, well furnished rooms have nice views, and many have fireplaces. The hotel's *mehana* (see right) is excellent as well. The triple combination (adjoining church, hotel, restaurant) makes the Kristo popular for weekend weddings.

Hotel Bor (☎ 884 075; fax 885 078; hotel_bor@yahoo .com; Loven Dom; d/apt 60/100 lv; **P** 🔀) In the forested hills above Varosha, this refurbished hotel offers two restaurants, indoor pool, Jacuzzi, sauna, steam bath and fitness centre. While rooms are smart, the Bor's peaceful location is its best asset. Although you can walk there in 10 minutes via a steep and winding stepped path through the woods, driving or taking a taxi over the bridge and up the winding ul Pirin (about 1km) is a better idea.

Eating

Blagoevgrad's dining is mainly to be found around the main squares or in the hotel restaurants. The busy cafés and nightclubs are packed with Blagoevgrad's irrepressible student population.

Kristo Restaurant (☎ 880 444; ul Komitrov; mains 4-6 lv) The Kristo Hotel's restaurant has outdoor seating overlooking the Church of Vavedenie Presvetiya Bogoroditsi, and serves good salads and grilled meats.

Pizza Napoli (☎ 34 649; pl Hristo Botev 4; mains 5-8 lv; ☽ 8am-midnight) This place has an attractive square-side setting, and serves good pizzas, pasta and grills.

Restaurant Korona (☎ 831 350; www.hotel-crown .com; ul Nikola Vaptsarov 16; mains 2-5 lv; ☽ 7am-midnight) The Hotel Korona's restaurant does good grills such as *tatarsko kiofte* (hamburger stuffed with melted cheese), though service is slow.

Drinking & Entertainment

Old Dublin Irish Pub (ul Trakiya 3; ☽ 8am-2am) What a Bulgarian university town would be without an Irish pub finds no definitive answer in this big, well-furnished establishment playing techno instead of jigs and reels. Nevertheless, the Old Dublin is popular with students, and is the only place with any sort of pub ambience. It also serves good bar snacks and full meals.

Rendezvous (ul Brati Kitanovi 5; ☽ 7.30am-midnight) A slick, central café for a morning coffee or evening drink.

Underground (☎ 0888552578; pl Bulgaria; ☽ 9pm-4am) This very popular student place serves unusual cocktails and features a dimly lit and subterranean brick-walled bar. Underground usually plays house music and R&B.

Piano Bar (☎ 0898828828; ul Petko Petkov; ☽ 10pm-4am) Although the drinks are expensive at this stylish after-hours club, it's very good when live rock or jazz bands are playing.

Nightclub Extreme (☎ 832340; ul Koritarov; ☽ 11pm-5am) A very popular, slightly Eurotrash, central discotheque near the river.

Elephant (☎ 0896624343; ul Pere Toshe 6; ☽ 6pm-4am) Located off the pedestrianised ul Todor Aleksandrov, Elephant is a more chilled-out alternative to the club scene here, also playing house music.

For Hollywood blockbusters, visit the widescreen **Movie Max** (American University complex, pl Georgi Izmirliev Makedoncheto). The respected **Vaptsarov Theatre** (☎ 823 475; pl Georgi Izmirliev Makedoncheto) and the **Vaptsarov Chamber Opera** (☎ 820 703; pl Makedonia) offer more edifying entertainment, but close during August.

Getting There & Away

Buses leave from the well-organised and helpful **main bus station** (☎ 884 009), known as the *tsentralna aftogara*, and from the adjacent **Chastna Aftogara** (☎ 831 132), which has buses to Sofia, Sandanski, Gotse Delchev, Petrich, Dupnitsa and Plovdiv. Ascertain which station you need when buying the ticket. The main bus station also has a **left-luggage office** (⏱ 6am-7pm,per bag 0.50 lv).

Buses travel hourly (6.30am to 6pm) from Blagoevgrad to Sofia (7 lv, two hours) via Dupnitsa, but more come through en route to/from Kulata or Sandanski. There are 10 daily buses to Sandanski (4 lv, 1½ hours), six to Bansko (5 lv, two hours) and one direct bus to Melnik daily at 11am (5 lv, two hours). Buses to Rila village (1.50 lv, 45 minutes) leave hourly between 7am and 8pm. Two daily buses serve Plovdiv (10 lv, three hours).

Bus 2, which stops outside the History Museum, serves the bus/train stations; alternatively, a taxi from the centre costs around 3 lv.

The **train station** (☎ 885 695) is on the line between Sofia and Kulata. From/to Sofia, there are five daily fast trains (1st/2nd class 7.10/5.70 lv, 2½ hours), and one slow train, via Dupnitsa. Three of these fast trains continue to Sandanski (1st/2nd class 4.90/3.90 lv, two hours) and Kulata (1st/2nd class 5.60/4.50 lv, 2½ hours); two continue on to Thessaloniki in Greece, leaving Blagoevgrad at 9.12am and 7.42pm (20 lv, four hours).

BANSKO БАНСКО

☎ 07443 / pop 9740 / elevation 930m

Bansko is the big daddy of Bulgarian ski resorts, continually bulldozing new trails and roads, increasing hotel occupancy, and enhancing its entertainment options; indeed, with over 100 hotels and *pensions*, the once-quiet village now has more beds than permanent residents. In winter, hordes of Brits, Russians, Israelis, Germans, Bulgarians and others bear down to ski (and party) in this sunny yet snow-filled resort. However, in summer things are quieter and you will see old women in traditional dress chatting on their doorsteps.

Built in the 10th century over an ancient Thracian settlement, Bansko became wealthy by the mid-18th century, well-positioned on the caravan route between the Aegean coast and Danubian Europe. Eminent traders, craftsmen, icon painters and woodcarvers hailed from Bansko, as did Otets Paisii Hilendarski, the 18th-century monk who helped create Bulgarian ethnic nationalism with his literary work and travels.

Bansko's considerable ties with this past include several museums and more than 150 cultural monuments, most from the 19th-century National Revival period. These stone-and-timber houses were buttressed by fortress-style walls, with hidden escape routes, protecting their inhabitants from the rapacious Turks. As elsewhere in Bulgaria, many have been reincarnated as *mehanas* or guesthouses, and there's an old quarter with lovely (and slightly hazardous) cobblestone lanes.

Orientation

Bansko's adjacent bus and train stations are north of the centre, a 15-minute walk to the main square, pl Nikola Vaptsarov. The large ul Pirin connects this square with pl Vûzhrazhdane, dominated by the mammoth Paisii Hilendarski Monument, dedicated to the literary monk. Shops and cafés line the pedestrian mall, ul Tsar Simeon.

In winter, the action shifts away from the centre almost completely, to the area around the ski gondola and its terminus up at Baderishka Polyana. Restaurants, cafés and wintertime nightlife are concentrated near the gondola area, around the convergence of ul Pirin and ul Giorgi Nastev.

Information

Accommodation-seekers and those wanting to be informed should head to the centrally located **Tourist Information Center** (☎ 88 580; infocenter@bansko.bg; pl Nikola Vaptsarov 1; ⏱ 9am-5pm), where the very helpful Tanya Stancheva can find accommodation for all budgets, and advise on cultural and outdoors activities. Here maps of Bansko town are sold (4 lv), with hotels, restaurants and banks listed on the front, and the Pirin National Park map on the back; the similarly priced winter map features Bansko's ski trails, gondola and lifts on the back instead.

Biochim Bank (☎ 88 387; ul Tsar Simeon 56) Bank with an ATM, across from the post office and telephone centre.

DSK Bank (☎ 88 120; ul Tsar Simeon 57) Also has an ATM.

Internet Club Zonata (ul Bulgaria 22)

SOUTHERN BULGARIA

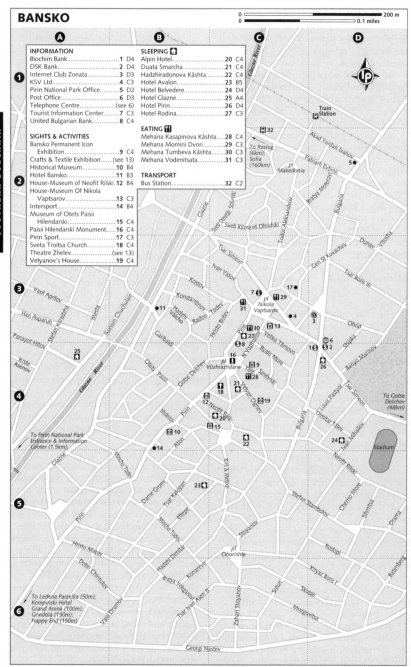

BANSKO

0 — 200 m
0 — 0.1 miles

INFORMATION
Biochim Bank...........................1 D4
DSK Bank................................2 D4
Internet Club Zonata..............3 D3
KSV Ltd.................................4 C3
Pirin National Park Office........5 D2
Post Office.............................6 D3
Telephone Centre..................(see 6)
Tourist Information Center.......7 C3
United Bulgarian Bank.............8 C4

SIGHTS & ACTIVITIES
Bansko Permanent Icon
   Exhibition.............................9 C4
Crafts & Textile Exhibition......(see 13)
Historical Museum..................10 B4
Hotel Bansko........................11 B3
House-Museum of Neofit Rilski.12 B4
House-Museum Of Nikola
   Vaptsarov............................13 C3
Intersport.............................14 B4
Museum of Otets Paisii
   Hilendarski.........................15 C4
Paisii Hilendarski Monument....16 C4
Pirin Sport...........................17 C3
Sveta Troitsa Church..............18 C4
Theatre Zhelev....................(see 13)
Velyanov's House..................19 C4

SLEEPING
Alpin Hotel...........................20 C4
Duata Smarcha.....................21 C4
Hadzhiradonova Kâshta..........22 C4
Hotel Avalon........................23 B5
Hotel Belvedere....................24 D4
Hotel Glazne........................25 A4
Hotel Pirin...........................26 D4
Hotel Rodina........................27 C3

EATING
Mehana Kasapinova Kâshta.....28 C4
Mehana Momini Dvori.............29 C3
Mehana Tumbeva Kâshta........30 C3
Mehana Vodenitsata..............31 C3

TRANSPORT
Bus Station...........................32 C2

KSV Ltd (ul Tsar Simeon) Exchange office near the supermarket.

Pirin National Park Office (☎ /fax 88 202; www .pirin-np.com; ul Bulgaria 4) Informs about long treks in the Pirin Mountains.

United Bulgarian Bank (ul Pirin) Next to Rodina Hotel; has an ATM and foreign currency exchange.

www.bansko.bg Official municipal website; also in English.

www.bulgariaski.com Invaluable resource on skiing in Bansko and all other Bulgarian resorts.

Sights

The **House-Museum of Nikola Vaptsarov** (☎ 8304; pl Nikola Vaptsarov; admission 3 lv; ☼ 8am-noon & 2-5.30pm) is where Nikola Vaptsarov (1909–42), a respected antifascist poet and activist, was born. Influenced by communist ideology while a student, his populist writings led Vaptsarov to be arrested and tortured by the wartime fascist government; he wrote his most famous poem, in fact, while awaiting execution. Period décor in the museum's rooms, plus photographs, documents and Vaptsarov's personal belongings are exhibited, while a short video, followed by an audio tape (English, French or German) provides background.

The attached **Crafts & Textile Exhibition** sells traditional arts, crafts and textiles from Bansko and the Pirin region; ask at the Vaptsarov Museum if it's not open. The adjacent **Theatre Zhelev** (admission free; ☼ 9am-noon & 2-5.45pm) contains landscape paintings by local artist Tenio Zhelev. They are for sale (but expensive).

Velyanov's House (☎ 4181; ul Velyan Ognev 5; admission 3 lv; ☼ 9am-noon & 2-5pm Mon-Fri) features elaborately painted scenes and woodcarvings from the 'Bansko School' of carving, icon and fresco painting. The **Bansko Permanent Icon Exhibition** (☎ 88 273; ul Yane Sandanski 3; admission 3 lv; ☼ 9am-noon & 2-5pm Mon-Fri) has more Bansko School creations. Both museums can be opened on weekends by prior arrangement.

Housed in a former schoolhouse, the **House-Museum of Neofit Rilski** (☎ 2540; admission 3 lv; ul Pirin 17; ☼ 9am-noon & 2-5pm Mon-Fri) exhibits manuscripts by, and photos of, Rilski (1793–1881), the father of Bulgarian secular education, who created an early Bulgarian grammar textbook (1835), and a Bulgarian–Greek dictionary.

The **Sveta Troitsa Church** (pl Vûzhrazhdane; ☼ 7am-7pm), built in 1835, is surrounded by a 1m thick and 4m high stone wall. It features magnificent wooden floors and faded murals. Within its grounds stands Bansko's

major landmark: the 30m-high **clock tower**, built in 1850. Until Sofia's Alexander Nevsky Cathedral was completed in 1912, this was Bulgaria's largest church.

At the time of writing, two new museums were opening: the first, the **Historical Museum** (☎ 88 304; ul Aton 3; admission 3 lv; ☼ 9am-noon & 2-5pm), also known as Radonova Kâshta after the building in which it's housed, contains, believe it or not, finds dating back to 6000 BC, as well as antique, medieval and 19th-century National Revival–period items.

The second new museum, the **Museum of Otets Paisii Hilendarski** (☎ 88 304; ul Otets Paisii 21; ☼ 9am-noon & 2-5pm) commemorates the life of this local monk, author and instigator of Bulgarian nationalism. The museum's chapel includes a replica of the room at the Serbian Hilandarski Monastery on Greece's Mt Athos, where Paisii wrote his seminal and fulsome narrative of the history of the Bulgarian nation.

Activities

SKIING

Nestled up at 1000m, at the base of rugged Mt Vihren (2915m), Bansko enjoys long snowy winters. With slopes ranging from 1800m to 2560m, Bansko boasts Bulgaria's most consistent skiing conditions. The snow, often 2m thick between mid-December and mid-April, sometimes lasts until mid-May. Lifts and slopes are modern and well maintained and the resort has snowmaking equipment that works at above-freezing temperatures.

Bansko also boasts a state-of-the-art gondola (carrying eight persons). The trip lasts 20 minutes and takes skiers directly from town and onto the slopes at **Baderishka Polyana**, now full of pubs, restaurants and ski schools. A second gondola, plying the same route, will open by 2009. From Baderishka Polyana, another chairlift accesses more trails at Shiligarnika, which has four chairlifts and four draglifts. Bansko has a total of seven chairlifts and 16 draglifts.

Chalin Vrag I and II are the most famous of Bansko's 15 (and counting) ski runs, which total 67km, along with 8km of cross-country trails. The total trail coverage comprises 35% for beginners, 40% for intermediates, and 25% advanced. There's no freestyle helicopter skiing at Bansko, though veering off some trails brings you into wide open, untouched mountainside

SOUTHERN BULGARIA

where you're essentially taking your life into your own hands. There's also a half-pipe for snowboarders.

An all-day Bansko lift pass costs 60 lv, though note prices rise each year.

Pirin Sport (☎ 8537; ul Gen St Kovachev 8) rents ski equipment (from about 45 lv per day) and snowboarding gear, and provides instructors for both sports. Similar services are provided by **Intersport** (☎ 4876; ul Pirin 71), **Alpin Hotel** (☎ 8075; ul Neofit Rilski 6) and **Hotel Bansko** (☎ 4275; bansko@bg400.bg; ul Glazne 37), among many others. Hotel Bansko and Intersport rent mountain bikes in summer.

OTHER ACTIVITIES

A fun side activity is ice skating at the new skating rink, **Ledena Parzelka** (ul Pirin; ☺ 9am-10pm, Dec-Apr), as it's known in Bulgarian. Skate rental is 5 lv; another 5 lv gets you 90 minutes of skating time. Alternatively, pay 15 lv for an all-day skating pass.

There's a hot **mineral water bath** in Dobrinishte, 6km south of Bansko, and numerous local summertime **hiking** opportunities; see the Bansko Tourist Information Center (p127) for more information.

Festivals & Events

St Theodor's Day (15 March) Celebrated with horse racing; in Dobrinishte.
Celebration of Bansko Traditions (17-24 May) Folklore, dancing and the like.
Pirin Sings Folk Festival (August) Held annually, with a larger version occurring every four years (the next is in 2009). The festival unites thousands of folk musicians and dancers from the Pirin region.
International Jazz Festival (around 7-15 August) Attracts Bulgarian and foreign artists; most events are held on an open-air stage at pl Nikola Vaptsarov and in the Theatre Zhelev.
Bansko Day (5 October)

Sleeping

Bansko has over 100 choices of accommodation, ranging from simple private rooms to five-star luxury hotels. Discreet camping is possible in the nearby Pirin National Park (p124). While most foreigners come on package tours, independent bookings are possible; the Tourist Information Center (p127), which finds rooms for all budgets, is happy to help. Book well in advance for the ski season, when rates are at least 25% higher than those listed

here (and even higher during the Christmas and New Year's holidays).

Duata Smarcha (☎ 2632; ul Velyan Ognev 2; s/d incl breakfast from 16/32 lv) The lovely garden setting of this popular *pension* encloses a well-run, friendly place with airy rooms and traditional home-cooked meals.

Hadzhiradonova Kâshta (☎ 8276; ul Buirov 7; s/d from 20/30 lv) An atmospheric house with large, traditionally furnished rooms with sheepskin bedspreads and spotless bathrooms, the Hadzhiradonova overlooks a pretty courtyard.

Alpin Hotel (☎ 8075; ul Neofit Rilski 6; s/d from 20/30 lv) The Alpin offers clean and simple rooms; less exciting than the Hadzhiradonova but also good value.

Hotel Belvedere (☎ 8083; fax 8082; ul Ivan Mihailov 28; r 40 lv; ℗) Set on a residential street in east Bansko, the Swiss-chalet style Belvedere has modern, well-maintained rooms with balconies, plus restaurant and bar.

Hotel Rodina (☎ 8106; fax 8472; ul Pirin 7; s/d/apt 50/64/120 lv) The Rodina is a cosy and central place that, despite the lacklustre lobby area, has nice if simple rooms. The hotel offers sauna and massage, plus a restaurant and tavern.

Hotel Pirin (☎ 8051; www.hotelpirin.bansko.bg; ul Tsar Simeon 68; s/d/apt incl breakfast from 60/80/100 lv; ℗ ▯) The large and slightly timeworn Pirin, opposite the post office, has smart, comfortable rooms, ample facilities and an attractive garden. Remarkably, it offers 'smoker's rooms' – so assert yourself if you'd rather not have a room smelling like stale smoke.

Hotel Glazne (☎ 88 022; www.glazne.bansko.bg; ul Panapot Hitov 2; s/d 62/84 lv) There's a certain elegance to the Glazne, on the river's western bank. Rooms are smart and well done, and the service and restaurant are excellent.

Hotel Avalon (☎ 88 399; www.avalonhotel-bulgaria .com; ul Eltepe 4; s/d/tr €36/50/60; ℗ ▯) A friendly, British-run place popular with budget travellers, the Avalon has well-done, airy rooms, some with Jacuzzi, plus a restaurant serving French and Italian fare. The owners also organise local excursions.

Kempinski Hotel Grand Arena (☎ 88 888, 88 565; www.kempinski-bansko.com; ul Pirin 96; s, d & ste from 360 lv; ℗ ▨ ▯) This global giant enjoys – but of course – a prime location, close to the gondola and winter nightlife, and boasts luxurious rooms with all expected amenities, prompt, efficient service and excellent facilities.

Eating & Drinking

Bansko's traditional *mehanas* offer regional delicacies and excellent local wine. Some places close out of season.

Mehana Tumbeva Kâshta (☎ 0899888993; ul Pirin 7; mains 3-7 lv; ☺ 8am-midnight) A small and friendly bar and grill offering meat specialities and lighter fare, the Tumbeva Kâshta rests in a secluded garden (the cosy interior functions in winter).

Mehana Momini Dvori (☎ 88 239; pl Nikola Vaptsarov 2; mains 4-5 lv; ☺ 8am-midnight) This *mehana* overlooking pl Nikola Vaptsarov offers pizzas, salads, barbecued dishes and more, and has outdoor seating also.

Mehana Kasapinova Kâshta (☎ 3500; ul Yane Sandanski 4; mains 4-10 lv; ☺ 8am-1am) Excellent local food and wine is served in a traditional setting at the Kasapinova. Nice touches include the colourful local rugs, clay pitchers of wine and a cosy fireplace.

Mehana Vodenitsata (☎ 84 019; cnr ul Hristo Botev & ul Ivan Vazov; mains 6-8 lv; ☺ 11am-midnight) A traditional Bulgarian restaurant offering hearty portions and live music, the Vodenitsata is popular with locals and visitors alike.

Happy End (☺ 11am-late) They forgot the '-ing', but never mind: this grand bar-disco, capable of containing 400 ruddy skiers for après-ski activity, is a wintertime favourite, opposite the gondola. Numerous other bars and nightclubs are in the general area as well.

Getting There & Away

From Sofia (12 lv, three hours), 15 daily buses travel to the **Bansko bus station** (☎ 88 420; ul Patriarh Evtimii), most via Blagoevgrad; from the latter to Bansko, it's 5 lv. Several more buses travelling to Gotse Delchev also stop at Bansko.

From Bansko, four or five daily buses go to Blagoevgrad, and two more depart for Plovdiv (9 lv, 3½ hours), at 7.10am and 8.20am. Between mid-June and mid-September, private minibuses (3 lv) run to Hizha Banderitsa (see Hiking in the Pirin Mountains, p133), leaving at 8.30am, 2.15pm and 5pm, and returning at 9.30am, 3pm and 6pm.

The coolest route to Bansko, however, is by train; the narrow-gauge rail route from Septemvri to Dobrinishte crosses the mountains and reaches the Bansko **train station** (☎ 8232; Akad Yordan Ivanov) in five hours (5 lv, four daily). Among the stops is Avramovo – the highest Balkan train station. Taking the leisurely, visually stunning ride to Septemvri also brings you onto the main Sofia–Plovdiv line, allowing connections to these cities and other major destinations. Four daily trains depart Bansko for Septemvri, at 6.59am, 10.14am, 3.21pm and 6.40pm. The amusingly inactive ticket office asks you to buy tickets only 10 minutes in advance of departure time.

SANDANSKI САНДАНСКИ
☎ 0746 / pop 27,390

Sandanski, 65km south of Blagoevgrad, is known to most travellers as merely the connection point for Melnik, 17km to the southeast. However, it's a likeable, laid-back place, a notable spa centre and perhaps Bulgaria's sunniest town. Like Blagoevgrad, it's on the Sofia–Thessaloniki–Athens international train line, and so its numerous restaurants, bars and clubs are popular with visitors from south of the border as well. Indeed, rather than a town of no consequence, it's a town of no consequences for the hordes of Greek sex tourists looking for something discreet and affordable on the side.

On the less lurid side, Sandanski makes a great alternative base for Pirin Mountain hikes (see p133), and has numerous wineries in the arid surrounding villages. Sandanski's curative mineral springs, useful against ills such as bronchitis and asthma, attract local and foreign visitors alike.

The Thracians first settled here, in about 2000 BC. Macedonians and Romans followed. Sandanski may have been the birthplace of Spartacus, leader of the legendary slave revolt against the Romans in Sicily in 74 BC. Almost completely destroyed in the 6th century AD by barbarians, the subsequently rebuilt Sandanski became important during the First Bulgarian Empire (681–1018). Once known as Sveti Vrach, it was renamed in 1949 after Macedonian freedom fighter Yane Sandanski.

Orientation

The train station is 5km west of town. The bus station, on ul Hristo Smirnenski, is a five-minute walk from the centre. Head straight

SOUTHERN BULGARIA

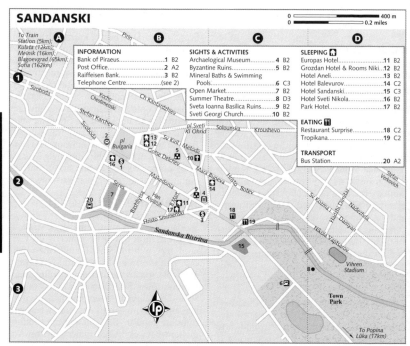

SANDANSKI

INFORMATION		SIGHTS & ACTIVITIES		SLEEPING	
Bank of Piraeus	1 B2	Archaeological Museum	4 B2	Europas Hotel	11 B2
Post Office	2 A2	Byzantine Ruins	5 B2	Grozdan Hotel & Rooms Niki	12 B2
Raiffeisen Bank	3 B2	Mineral Baths & Swimming		Hotel Aneli	13 B2
Telephone Centre	(see 2)	Pools	6 C3	Hotel Balevurov	14 C2
		Open Market	7 B2	Hotel Sandanski	15 C3
		Summer Theatre	8 D3	Hotel Sveti Nikola	16 B2
		Sveta Ioanna Basilica Ruins	9 B2	Park Hotel	17 B2
		Sveti Georgi Church	10 B2		
				EATING	
				Restaurant Surprise	18 C2
				Tropikana	19 C2
				TRANSPORT	
				Bus Station	20 A2

northeast from the bus station to reach the central pl Bulgaria, or follow ul Hristo Smirnenski eastwards, through the open market, until it reaches the long east–west bul Makedonia, the main street for banks/ATMs, foreign exchange offices, shopping and cafés. Turn left here towards pl Bulgaria, site of the post office and telephone centre.

Sights & Activities

The centrally located **Archaeological Museum** (☎ 23 188; bul Makedonia 55), built over a Roman villa's remains, contains tombstones and votive tablets, plus the original villa's mosaic floor. Sandanski's apparent link to Spartacus is explained (in Bulgarian), and items from the adjacent ruins of the 5th-century **Sveta Ioanna Basilica** are also displayed. The basilica ruins themselves are small, but fun to wander around. Much less prominent **Byzantine ruins** are up on ul Mara Buneva, possibly including a baptistry, though there are no descriptions and not much is visible.

The **Sveti Georgi Church** (ul Sveti Kiril i Metodii 10; 8am-6pm), built in 1861, is Sandanski's only surviving National Revival–era church.

The large **Town Park** contains over 200 species of Mediterranean plants, surrounding **mineral baths and swimming pools** (admission 1.50 lv; 9am-7pm summer) where locals unwind, a small **lake** with paddle boats and a **Summer Theatre**. A lazy stream runs through the park, and is crossed by a rocking bridge.

Just outside of Sandanski itself, there are more mineral baths; ask at your hotel for details.

Festivals & Events

St Vasil's Day Folk Concert (1 January)

Sandanski Celebrations Thursday after Orthodox Easter Sunday.

Pirin Folk National Festival (early September) Features dancing and music.

Young Red Wine Festival (early December) Merry festival of the grape.

Sleeping

Although **Grozdan Hotel** (☎ 32 918; ul Gotse Delchev 4; s/d/tr 25/35/50 lv) and **Rooms Niki** (☎ 0888259633; ul Gotse Delchev 4; d/tr 35/50 lv) share the same address and prices, they're independently run. Both have simple, clean and spacious rooms. However,

Grozdan has friendlier, English-speaking staff, and unlike Niki offers single rooms.

Hotel Balevurov (☎ 30 013; fax 24 024; ul Mara Buneva 14; tw/d 25/30 lv; **P** 🐾) This quiet place near the Archaeological Museum has clean rooms; twin rooms have separate, but large bathrooms.

Europas Hotel (☎ 30 166; ul 8 Mart 11; s/d 29/40 lv; 🐾) A central and reasonably priced option, the Europas has snug, clean rooms; most have balconies.

Hotel Aneli (☎ 31 844; www.aneli.hit.bg; ul Gotse Delchev 1; d/apt 30/50 lv) This budget favourite is on the square; the simple, clean rooms have modern bathrooms.

Hotel Sveti Nikola (☎ 33 035; www.hotelsvetinikola .com; bul Makedonia 1; s/d/ste 58/78/136 lv; **P** 🐾 🖳 🛒) The splendidly located Sveti Nikola, right on lively pl Bulgaria, borders on luxurious and has an international clientele. The comfortable rooms are complemented by the facilities (sports centre, casino, nightclub, 10m by 5m indoor pool and lobby bar), which include the inevitable Greek taverna.

Park Hotel (☎ 30 206; www.parkhotelsandanski.com; ul Hristo Smirnenski 13; s/d 74/97 lv; 🐾 🖳) This new hotel on the road between the bus station and bul Makedonia is perhaps Sandanski's most elegant. The pretty and posh rooms have all the mod cons (including wireless internet), wood furniture and soft, understated décor. Service is friendly and professional, and there's both a small spa centre and a well-regarded restaurant.

Hotel Sandanski (☎ 31 165; www.interhotel sandanski.com; bul Makedonia; s/d/apt 110/140/220 lv; **P** 🗙 🐾 🛒) This 300-room giant is Sandanski's leading spa treatment centre, with hydrotherapy, weight-loss, antistress and aromatherapy programmes. There's also tennis, a *pétanque* pitch and gymnastics classes, plus restaurants, cafés, bars and a nightclub.

Eating

Aside from the hotel restaurants, eateries and cafés line bul Makedonia.

Tropikana (☎ 0898726578; bul Makedonia 73; mains 4-7 lv) Near the park entrance, the Tropikana does traditional Bulgarian dishes, and has outdoor seating.

Restaurant Surprise (☎ 31 202; bul Makedonia 63; mains 5-8 lv; ☾ lunch & dinner) Right on the main strip, Surprise has a varied menu and outdoor seating.

Getting There & Away

From the **bus station** (☎ 22 130; ul Hristo Smirnenski) buses to Sofia (10 lv, 3½ hours, six to eight daily) travel via Blagoevgrad (4 lv, 1½ hours) and Dupnitsa. Buses go to Melnik (1.70 lv, 40 minutes), and then Rozhen, at 7.40am, 11.40am, 3.30pm and 5.30pm. They return to Sandanski at 1pm, 4pm and 5pm. Check in Melnik for times of morning buses to Sandanski. Store luggage in the ticket booth (0.50 lv per bag).

HIKING IN THE PIRIN MOUNTAINS

A network of marked hiking trails (13 primary and 17 secondary) link 13 huts and shelters throughout the park. The primary trails are described and mapped in the Bulgarian Ministry of Environment's detailed map (1:55,000) in the *National Park Pirin* leaflet printed in English; get it at the **National Park office** (☎/fax 07443-2428; ul Bulgaria 4), or from souvenir shops.

Kartografia's widely available *Pirin* map (1:55,000) is the only accurate and detailed hiking map of the whole mountain range. The numerous marked trails delineated range from Bansko to Melnik and Sandanski. Also, Domino's *Bansko* map includes a small but detailed map in English of 12 hiking trails. These trails include Bansko to **Hizha Banderitsa** (☎ 07443-8279), 2km south-west of Shiligarnika, and Bansko to **Hizha Vihren** (☎ 07443-8279), 2km further up. Both offer convenient bases for hikes to nearby **caves** and **lakes**, such as Hizha Vihren to Mt Vihren (about three hours one way).

From Sandanski, a popular, three-hour hike leads to the glorious **Popina Lûka** region, with lakes, waterfalls and pine forests. Hikers can stay at **Hizha Kamenitsa** (☎ 0746-30 385) or **Hizha Yane Sandanski** (☎ 0746-30 385). Half-board at either costs around 25 lv. Julian Perry's *The Mountains of Bulgaria* describes a hike across the entire Pirin Mountains from Hizha Predel (at the end of the Rila Mountains hike) to Petrovo village near the Greek border. It's a tough, seven- to 10-day hike (longer if the weather is bad). You'll want to buy the above maps, not rely on the book's.

SOUTHERN BULGARIA

SOUTHERN BULGARIA

Sandanski is on the Sofia–Thessaloniki–Athens international train line. The **train station** (☎ 22 213) is 5km west of town. From Sofia, three fast trains (1st/2nd class 9/6.80 lv, 3½ hours) travel here daily via Blagoevgrad and Dupnitsa, continuing to the Greek border at Kulata. Two daily international trains leave for Thessaloniki at 10.12am and 8.42pm (15 lv, three hours).

Taxis serve Melnik, Rozhen Monastery, Kulata and other local destinations.

MELNIK МЕЛНИК
☎ 07437 / pop 240

While clever marketers aim to enhance little Melnik's charm by calling it 'Bulgaria's smallest town', it's actually just a tiny, though very appealing village tucked beneath sandstone cliffs, and cluttered with white National Revival–era stone houses with overhanging, Macedonian-style wood balconies. Melnik has historically been a centre of wine production, and here you can sample some of Bulgaria's best and most unique wines, and tour house-museums where the village's vintners once lived. For more information on local wineries, see p68 and opposite.

About 20km north of the Greek border, Melnik is also notable for its unusual environmental surroundings. The yellow-white mixture of clay and sand in the surrounding hills has, over the centuries, eroded into bizarre formations, resembling pyramids and giant mushrooms. Melnik's also a good base

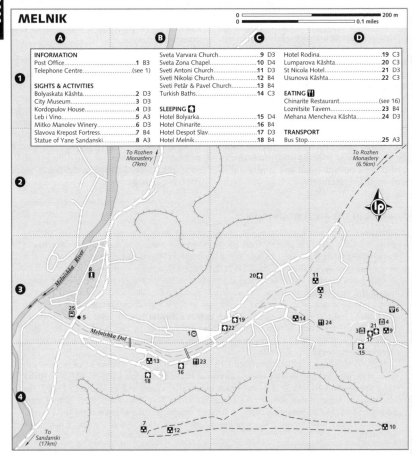

MELNIK

0 ————————— 200 m
0 ————————— 0.1 miles

INFORMATION	Sveta Varvara Church.................9 D3	Hotel Rodina..................................19 C3
Post Office..........................1 B3	Sveta Zona Chapel.....................10 D4	Lumparova Kâshta.....................20 C3
Telephone Centre.................(see 1)	Sveti Antoni Church...................11 D3	St Nicola Hotel............................21 D3
	Sveti Nikolai Church..................12 B4	Usunova Kâshta..........................22 C3
SIGHTS & ACTIVITIES	Sveti Petâr & Pavel Church.........13 B4	
Bolyaskata Kâshta...................2 D3	Turkish Baths.............................14 C3	**EATING** 🍴
City Museum..........................3 D3		Chinarite Restaurant..............(see 16)
Kordopulov House...................4 D3	**SLEEPING** 🛏	Loznitsite Tavern..........................23 B4
Leb i Vino.............................5 A3	Hotel Bolyarka..........................15 D4	Mehana Mencheva Kâshta.........24 D3
Mitko Manolev Winery.............6 D3	Hotel Chinarite.........................16 B4	
Slavova Krepost Fortress...........7 B4	Hotel Despot Slav.....................17 D3	**TRANSPORT**
Statue of Yane Sandanski...........8 A3	Hotel Melnik............................18 B4	Bus Stop......................................25 A3

for exploring the southern Pirin Mountains (see the boxed text, p133) and, though seeing its main attractions requires one day, you may well enjoy lingering on in Melnik's lazy sunshine and quietude, as there are nice places to stay and eat. There are no banks or ATMs, however.

History

The Melnik area was first settled by the Thracian Medi tribe, to which the legendary Spartacus belonged. It was later settled by Romans, then by proto-Bulgarians between the 7th and 9th centuries AD. The name Melnik probably comes from the Old Slavonic *mel*, 'sandy chalk', abundant in the surrounding cliffs.

In the early 13th century, Melnik fell under the rule of Despot Alexei Slav, who ran a personal fiefdom from here, while building several monasteries and a large fortress (some remains survive). Melnik became an educational and cultural centre, and its jewellery, woodcarving and ceramics were famous throughout Europe, while Melnik's celebrated red wine was traded as far away as modern-day Croatia and Venice.

Although Melnik declined after the 14th-century Ottoman invasion, it prospered during the Bulgarian National Revival period in the late 18th and early 19th centuries. Many traditional houses were built, often over ruined Roman and medieval homes. Until a century ago, Melnik was a thriving commercial centre with some 20,000 inhabitants, but with the 1912–13 Balkan Wars, it was largely burned and the town's Greek population was forcibly removed by the Greek army. Since then, Melnik has been significantly restored and rebuilt.

Orientation & Information

Melnik's bus stop, along the main east–west road connecting it with Sandanski and Rozhen Monastery, is on the village's western edge, opposite the municipal building. The two main streets run east–west along both sides of the Melnishka River's often-dry tributary. Walking paths and goat tracks run parallel to the valley, leading to the homes and ruins. Drivers should park off the main road and walk into Melnik.

Paradoxically, Melnik's increasing tourism means services for locals have declined.

With house prices skyrocketing, and very few children still being raised here, Melnik's old schoolhouse was put up for sale, and even the doctor's office and pharmacy have closed. Melnik has neither internet café nor ATMs. Only the **post office** (7.30am-noon & 1-4.30pm) lingers on.

On a happier note, a tourist information office (dubbed 'Euro-Information Center') was to open at the time of writing, and be based in the municipality building opposite the bus stop, where the informative cultural organisation Leb i Vino (see the boxed text, p136) also dwells.

Sights & Activities

WINERIES

Melnik's wines have been celebrated for over 600 years. The locally grown grapes produce a superb dark red wine, known as the Shiroka Mehichka Loza and widely sold. Shops and stands dot Melnik's cobblestone paths, with bottles of quality reds and whites going for 3 lv to 4 lv and up.

To participate, visit the numerous hotels and restaurants that advertise wine tasting. Unfortunately, some old favourites have closed, so for the most atmospheric adventure in *degustatsia* (wine tasting), clamber up the hillside to the **Mitko Manolev Winery** (0887545795; 9am-midnight). Also known as Mitko *Sheshtaka* ('the Six-Fingered') it's basically a cellar dug into the rocks, and an informal hut with tables and chairs outside, for sampling (and buying) both red and white wine. It's along the hillside trail between the Bolyaskata Kâshta ruins and the Kordopulov House. There are certainly worse things than whiling away the hours in the sunshine with a glass of Melnik red, and the views of the town and cliffs from up here are wonderful as well.

MUSEUMS

Melnik's grand old houses, many jutting out from cliffs, feature handsome wood balconies and spacious upper quarters, with cool stone basements for wine storage. Officially, all buildings here must be built and/or renovated in the Bulgarian National Revival–period style, and painted brown and white.

According to the proud caretaker, it's the Balkans' biggest house-museum; in any case, the **Kordopulov House** (265; admission 2 lv; 8am-8pm), built in 1754 and former home of one of Melnik's foremost wine merchants,

---

IN SEARCH OF SONG

If you've been hunting for a place that allows you to dive into traditional Bulgarian culture, then look no further than Melnik. Run by the husband-and-wife team of Yane Kamenarov and Elena Georgieva-Kamenarova, Leb i Vino ('Bread and Wine') is a cultural organisation that aims to celebrate the musical and cultural heritage of the Pirin region. Through visiting local villages and interacting with sagacious elders, Yane and Elena have collected the knowledge and artistry of everything from singing and wool dying to instrument making and carpet weaving.

While their primary goal is to keep traditional Pirin culture alive and to transmit it to future generations, they also provide lessons and tours so visitors can enjoy a unique and intimate experience of, as Elena says, 'the real traditions that are slowly disappearing' as the modern world continues to encroach on rural Bulgarian life.

The lessons and trips offered by Leb i Vino are varied and flexible. For example, someone interested in learning to weave traditional blankets might spend some hours at the loom with Eleni, and then visit a village to see it done for real; likewise with a *gayda* (Balkan bagpipe) lesson from Yane.

While prices fluctuate depending on the activities, weaving, dying, or tambura or *gayda* lessons cost around 50 lv per hour, while a full 'folklore programme' involving exhibitions of traditional dances, songs and costumes costs 150 lv per hour.

Yane and Elena have an informative English-language website (www.lebivino.com) and can be contacted through it or by phone (☎ 0887803143). Their shop, signposted as 'Folklore Art Center', is in the municipality building opposite the bus stop, and is generally open from 7am to 10pm, unless they're in the villages.

---

is a truly impressive structure. The lovely sitting rooms have been carefully restored, and boast 19th-century murals, stained-glass windows and exquisite carved wooden ceilings, plus couches along the walls, bedecked with colourful pillows.

Downstairs, the house's enormous wine cellar includes 180m of illuminated, labyrinthine passageways. It's fun to explore; look out at the end for the wall full of glittering coins, which well-wishers have managed to stick into the soft cave surface – a gesture of goodwill and hope that the crops will be good and the rains will fall. If you share these sentiments, stick a stotinka of your own into the wall. You can taste, and buy, the house wine here. The Kordopulov House is the four-storey building on the cliff face at the street's end, south of the creek.

Not always open and without many attractions, the **City Museum** (☎ 229; admission by donation; 🕙 9am-7pm Mon-Fri) features local traditional costumes, ceramics and jewellery. The early-20th-century photos of old Melnik are fascinating. The museum is signposted before the Hotel Despot Slav.

RUINS

The 10th-century **Bolyaskata Kâshta**, one of Bulgaria's oldest homes, is ruined except for some partially standing walls. You can peer

into it and also enjoy the great views. Nearby is the ruined 19th-century **Sveti Antoni Church** (also not signposted).

At its peak, Melnik had around 70 churches; only 40, mostly ruined ones survive. A signposted path opposite the Hotel Rodina leads to the ruined **Sveti Nikolai Church** (1756), and to the ruins of Despot Slav's **Slavova Krepost Fortress**. Both are visible from the Bolyaskata Kâshta ruins, or from near the Lumparova Kâshta Hotel. The trail then heads east along the ridge about 300m to the ruined **Sveta Zona Chapel**.

The **Turkish Baths**, easy to miss and difficult to recognise, are just before the Mehana Mencheva Kâshta tavern. **Sveti Petâr & Pavel Church**, built in 1840, is down from the Hotel Melnik's car park. Just below the Kordopulov House, the 15th-century **Sveta Varvara Church** has retained its walls and floor, and displays icons where visitors light candles.

To visit the closed churches, find caretaker Yancho, usually at Sveti Nikolai Church.

Festivals & Events

First among Melnik's wine-making festivities is the **Trifon Zarezan Festival** (1 February), dedicated to Sveti Trifon, patron saint of the vine. Events also occur during grape-picking season (first two weeks of October). There's also a **folklore festival** on 1 April.

Finally, the cultural organisation **Leb i Vino** (see the boxed text, opposite) offers lessons in traditional Pirin crafts, singing and instrument playing, which can involve trips to unvisited villages where these still-living traditions can be experienced in 'raw' form.

Sleeping

Private rooms cost around 15 lv to 20 lv per person; all are clean but with shared bathrooms. English-language 'Rooms to Sleep' signs are prominent.

Hotel Rodina (☎ 08869472020; s/d/ste 15/30/45 lv) North of the creek bed, the Rodina has clean and modern rooms, though not the town's most atmospheric. It's good value, however, and has a restaurant.

Lumparova Kâshta (☎ 0888804512; r per person 20 lv; P) Behind the village, the cosy rooms here have balconies with fantastic views, and attractive décor and beds. There's traditional food and wine tasting, too. It's up a steep path starting behind Usunova Kâshta.

Usunova Kâshta (☎ 270; s/d incl breakfast 20/40 lv) The well restored Usunova, once an Ottoman prison, now has a happier function. Kindly old Ivan Usunov, who was born here, inherited the house from his grandfather. He can open the restaurant, but only for groups of 10 or more. The simple but well maintained rooms are ensconced within the hotel's central courtyard and are painted a dazzling white.

Hotel Melnik (☎ 272; d/apt 30/100 lv; P) A huge and slightly dated, faux-traditional place high up, the Melnik offers great views. It's a bit musty, though the rooms are fine, and come with TV and fridge.

Hotel Despot Slav (☎ /fax 248; s/d/tr incl breakfast 40/50/60 lv) One of Melnik's nicest and most traditional places, the Despot Slav is on Melnik's far end and has large, handsome rooms with lovely furnishings. The attached *mehana* is similarly atmospheric.

Hotel Chinarite (☎ 0887992191; www.varvarabg.com; s/d 40/60 lv) This small hotel, known for its adjoining restaurant (see right), offers clean, modern rooms and has friendly staff. Wine tastings are held in the small wine cellar adjoining the restaurant.

St Nicola Hotel (☎ 286; stnicola@datacom.bg; d/apt from 40/90 lv; P 🕿) Just above the Despot Slav, the St Nicola offers excellent value. Rooms are large, cheery and tastefully furnished, and the apartment has a sun terrace, lounge,

kitchen and big bathroom. There's a tasty restaurant, serving the famous house wine. Ask (politely) for laundry service.

Hotel Bolyarka (☎ 383; www.bolyarka.hit.bg; d/apt 60/80 lv; P 🕿) One of Melnik's finest hotels, this new place opposite the Hotel Despot Slav has gracious and helpful owners, who run an excellent on-site restaurant. Rooms are cheerful and well decorated; the apartments include a fireplace.

Eating

Most of Melnik's best eating (all around 6 lv to 10 lv for main courses) is at hotel restaurants: the Mehana Despot Slav has traditional décor and hearty portions, while the St Nicola Hotel's restaurant above it offers a cosy setting and food fuelled by its famous wine. The Hotel Bolyarka Tavern has a lovely stone-and-wood traditional interior, plus a summer garden. It serves traditional Melnik *banitsa* (a flaky cheese pasty), part of a lengthy menu including roast lamb and pork specialities.

Chinarite Restaurant (☎ 0887992191; mains 5-8 lv) and **Loznitsite Tavern** (☎ 283; mains 5-8 lv) are next door to each other midway up the main road, by the bridge. The former also serves homemade Melnik *banitsa* and has a small wine cellar for tasting, while the latter has an inviting, vine-covered outdoor setting, and good Bulgarian fare.

Mehana Mencheva Kâshta (☎ 339; mains 6-11 lv; 🕙 10am-11.30pm) This tiny tavern, popular with locals, serves authentic Bulgarian dishes and fresh local specialities such as river trout.

Getting There & Away

Bus schedules between Melnik and Sofia are unpredictable. One daily bus usually leaves Melnik for Sofia (10 lv, four hours) at 6am and returns to Melnik from Sofia at about 10am. A bus to Blagoevgrad (5 lv, two hours) leaves at 4pm. Buses from Sandanski (p133) to Melnik, continuing another 7km to Rozhen, leave Melnik at 8.16am, 12.21pm and 4.06pm, and return from Rozhen at 9am, 1.10pm and 7.27pm. Melnik has no taxis.

ROZHEN MONASTERY

The **Rozhen Monastery** (admission free; 🕙 7am-7pm), also known as the Birth of Virgin Mary Monastery, stands 7km north of Melnik and was originally built in 1217. Rebuilt in the late 16th century, it was destroyed by the Turks soon after. Today's monastery, mostly built between 1732 and the end of the 18th century, has also undergone significant modern renovations. Photography and video cameras are prohibited inside the monastery.

The **Nativity of the Virgin Church**, originally built in 1600, contains wonderful stained-glass windows, 200-year-old murals, woodcarvings and iconostases. Murals also occupy the 2nd-floor **refectory**. The monastery enjoys a great setting over Melnik's unique cliffs, and has a vine-covered courtyard.

About 200m before the monastery car park is the (closed) **Sveti Kiril & Metodii Church**; in front of it is the grave of Yane Sandanski (1872–1915), one of the most important Macedonian revolutionary leaders. The locally popular **Rozhen Fair** of traditional culture is held on 8 September.

Hotel Rozhena (☎ 07437-211; s/d incl breakfast 30/40 lv; Ⓟ) has simple but comfortable rooms with TV and bathroom, and more luxurious double apartments. A sauna and gym are available, and there's a restaurant.

There are *mehanas* near the bus stop. The café by the monastery car park sells drinks and snacks.

Getting There & Away

It's 7.2km from Melnik to the monastery, including the steep 800m uphill bit from Rozhen village. Buses from Sandanski to Melnik continue to Rozhen village. Alternatively, hike (6.5km) from Melnik up the track by the Bolyaskata Kâshta ruins along the creek bed, then look for the English-language signs. The trail has no shade so, in summer, avoid midday walking and take water.

BULGARIAN THRACE

The vast territory of the ancient Thracian tribes, now encompassed by modern Bulgaria, Greece and Turkey, is still a wild, sparsely populated region of varied and dramatic landscapes and remote villages. However, its one major urban centre, Plovdiv, is Bulgaria's second-biggest – and arguably its best – city, and an important transport hub. Just south of it, striking Bachkovo Monastery lies among wooded hills and vineyards (for more information on local wineries, see p67). The largely unvisited east has a marked Turkish influence, and is Bulgaria's main tobacco-growing country; however, tourism here remains largely undeveloped.

PLOVDIV ПЛОВДИВ
☎ 032 / pop 346,760

With its innumerable art galleries, winding cobbled streets and bohemian cafés, it would be no exaggeration to call today's Plovdiv (*Plov*-div) the Paris of the Balkans. Bulgaria's second city equals Sofia in things cultural and is a determined rival in nightlife as well. Being a smaller and less stressful city than Sofia, Plovdiv is also great for walking, offering most of the capital's amenities without its traffic or crime. Plovdiv is also a major university town, something that enhances its lively, exuberant spirit and guarantees great nightlife.

Plovdiv's appeal derives first from its lovely old town, the *Stariot Grad*, largely restored to its mid-19th-century appearance and full of winding cobblestone streets. It's literally packed with atmospheric house-museums and art galleries and, unlike many other cities with 'old towns', has eminent artists still living and working within its tranquil confines. The old town also boasts Thracian, Roman, Byzantine and Bulgarian antiquities, the most impressive being the Roman amphitheatres – the best preserved in the Balkans, and still used for thrilling performances.

Plovdiv's modern centre, sprawling below the old town, features a shop-lined pedestrian mall, ul Knyaz Aleksandâr, which leads to a splendid square with gushing fountain. The nearby Tsar Simeon Garden is a shady, popular spot for relaxing. Plovdiv's cafés and bars are widespread, though one concentration of popular places is found in the Kapana district, northwest of the old town.

Plovdiv's always been one of Bulgaria's wealthiest and most cosmopolitan cities, and it's also Bulgaria's second-largest road and railway hub and economic centre. Although often used by travellers merely as a stopover between Bulgaria and Greece or Turkey, Plovdiv repays a longer visit and will certainly draw you in if you let it.

History

The ubiquitous Thracians settled Plovdiv around 5000 BC. Their fortress, at Nebet Tepe in the old town, was called Eumolpias. Philip II of Macedon (father of Alexander the Great) extended the settlement, humbly naming it Philipopolis in 342 BC. He re-fortified the existing Thracian fortress, making Philipopolis an important military centre. However, the city whose ruins remain today was only created after AD 46, when the Romans arrived, building streets, towers and aqueducts for the new city, Trimontium. Unfortunately, Goths and Huns plundered and destroyed it in the mid-3rd century and in AD 447 respectively, and Trimontium languished. The proto-Bulgar Khan Krum seized it in 815 and renamed it Pupulden, making it an important strategic outpost of the First Bulgarian Empire (681–1018).

Pupulden, or Philipopolis as the Byzantines called it, was controlled by Constantinople, Bulgars and even Latin Crusaders over the following centuries. The Ottomans conquered in 1365, rebuilding and renaming the city Filibe (a bastardisation of the Greek name, Philipopolis). The city thrived during Turkish rule and its merchants grew wealthy. Some of Bulgaria's finest and most lavish townhouses were built here during the Bulgarian National Revival period. In 1855, Hristo Danov founded Bulgaria's first publishing house in Plovdiv.

Shockingly, the 1878 Congress of Berlin that followed the Russo-Turkish War decreed that Plovdiv would remain Ottoman, as capital of the Eastern Rumelia province, while most of Bulgaria was freed. Only in 1885 did Plovdiv join the state – missing its likely opportunity to become Bulgaria's capital.

Plovdiv today is a centre of business and regional transport, with its international trade fairs (held since the late 19th century) being among the Balkans' biggest.

Orientation

Plovdiv's central train station, Rodopi bus station and main Yug bus station are all adjacent on the southern side of town. From here, several broad streets radiate northwards, including bul Ruski and ul Ivan Vazov, which runs towards the city's main square, pl Tsentralen. Plovdiv's main pedestrianised thoroughfare, ul Knyaz Aleksandâr, runs north from here to pl Dzhumaya, and the enormous Dzhumaya Mosque, continuing north to the Maritsa River as ul Rayko Daskalov. Plovdiv's centre is south of the river; modern (and expensive) suburbs lie to the north. The old town is east of major thoroughfare bul Tsar Boris Obedinitel, which runs north–south over the river, partially through a tunnel dug under the old town.

Like Rome, Plovdiv boasts seven hills, though one was flattened during the communist era and only four are impressive: Nebet Tepe, with ruins of a Thracian fort, and standing above the old town; Sahat Tepe (Clock Hill), crowned with a clock tower; Bunardjika (the 'Hill of the Liberators') to the west; and Djendem ('Hill of the Youth') in the southwest.

Although central bookstalls and bookshops sell city maps such as Domino's *Plovdiv* (1:11,500), free maps from hotels, hostels and the tourist information centre should suffice.

Information

BOOKSHOPS

Litera (Map p142; ☎ 625 300; ul Tsaribrod 1; ☼ 8.30am-8.30pm Mon-Fri, 10am-7pm Sat & Sun) A bookshop opposite the Dzhumaya Mosque; has English-language travel books about Bulgaria, including a few Lonely Planet guides.

INTERNET ACCESS

Internet centres around pedestrianised ul Knyaz Aleksandâr are open 24 hours and charge from 1 lv to 2 lv per hour.
Internet Café Speed (Map p142; 2nd fl, bul Maria Luisa 1)
Internet Fantasy (Map p142; ul Knyaz Aleksandâr 31)
Zeon Internet Cafe (Map p142; pl 19 Novemvri; ☼ 24hr)

MEDICAL SERVICES

Klinika Medicus Alpha (Map p140; ☎ 634 463; www.medicusalpha.com; ul Veliko Târnovo 21; ☼ 24hr) A modern medical centre with many different specialists.
Polyclinic DKC 4 (off Map p140; ☎ 0888566478; ul Gergana 7) Friendly, British-trained GP Dr Plamen Todorov speaks excellent English and comes highly recommended by local expats. He provides basic medical examinations (15 lv) and can order blood tests, write prescriptions and refer you to specialists if necessary. Call in advance for an appointment.

MONEY

Foreign exchange offices line ul Knyaz Aleksandâr and ul Ivan Vazov. Several exchange offices will also change travellers cheques, and some give credit card cash advances. Most close on Sunday, and rates vary. ATMs are found widely, with many around pl Dzhumaya and ul Knyaz Aleksandâr, though not in the old town's upper reaches.

POST

Main post office (Map p140; pl Tsentralen)

TELEPHONE

Telephone centre (Map p140; pl Tsentralen; ☼ 6am-11pm) Inside the post office.

SOUTHERN BULGARIA

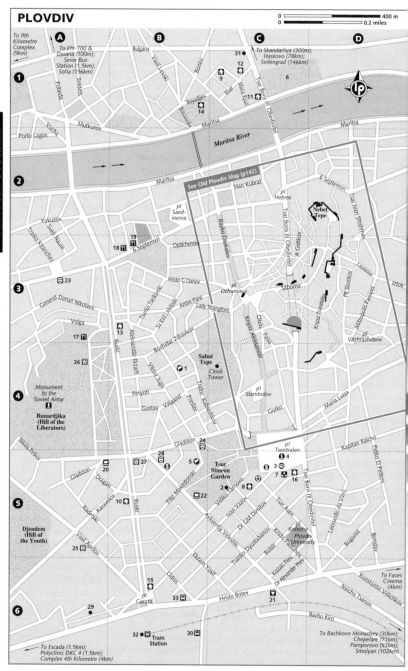

PLOVDIV

0 ——————— 400 m
0 ——————— 0.2 miles

To 9th
Kilometre
Complex
(9km)

To Efir-100 &
Djoana (100m);
Sever Bus
Station (1.5km);
Sofia (156km)

Bulgaria

To Skandarliya (300m);
Haskovo (78km);
Svilengrad (146km)

Maritsa River

See Old Plovdiv Map (p142)

Han Kubrat

pl
Hebros

Nebet
Tepe

pl
Saed-
inenie

pl
Vázhrazhdane

Monument
to the
Soviet Army

**Bunardjika
(Hill of the
Liberators)**

**Sahat
Tepe**

Clock
Tower

pl
Stambolov

pl
Tsentralen

Tsar
Simeon
Garden

**Djendem
(Hill of
the Youth)**

Kolezha
Plovdiv
University

pl
Garata

To Faces
Cinema
(4km)

To Escada (1.5km);
Polyclinic DKC 4 (1.5km);
Complex 4th Kilometre (4km)

**Train
Station**

To Bachkovo Monastery (30km);
Chepelare (71km);
Pamporovo (83km);
Smolyan (102km)

INFORMATION					
Greek Consulate	**1** B4	Hotel Maritsa	**11** C1	ENTERTAINMENT 🖸	
Klinika Medicus Alpha	**2** C5	Hotel Nord	**12** C1	Flamingo Cinema	**23** A3
Main Post Office	**3** C5	Noviz Hotel	**13** B3	Luki Cinema	**24** B4
Telephone Centre	(see 3)	Novotel	**14** B1	Nai Club	**25** A5
Tourist Information Center	**4** C5	Trakiya Hotel	**15** B6	Open-Air Theatre	**26** A4
Turkish Consulate	**5** B5	Trimontium Princess		Palmite	**27** B5
		Hotel	**16** C5	Plovdiv Opera House	**28** B5
SIGHTS & ACTIVITIES		**EATING** 🍴		**TRANSPORT**	
International Plovdiv		Malåk Bunardzhik	**17** A3	Avis	(see 14)
Fairgrounds	**6** C1	Ristorante Da Lino	**18** B3	Etap	(see 33)
Roman Forum	**7** C5	XIX Vek	**19** B3	Rila Bureau	**29** A6
				Rodopi Bus Station	**30** B6
SLEEPING 🏠		**DRINKING** 🍸 🍷		S & Z Rent-a-Car	**31** C1
Esperantsa	**8** C5	Planet Club	**20** A5	Tourist Service Rent-a-Car	(see 16)
Hotel Avion	**9** C1	Plazma Light	**21** C6	Union-Ivkoni Vesna 61	**32** B6
Hotel Leipzig	**10** B5	Simfoniya	**22** B5	Yug Bus Station	**33** B6

TOURIST INFORMATION

The *Plovdiv Guide* and *Programata* are free, weekly magazines, listing local bars, restaurants and clubs. The latter is Bulgarian-only, though its website (www.programata.bg) is in English too. You can also try the municipal website www.plovdiv.bg and www.plovdivcityguide.com for more useful local information.

Tourist Information Centre (Map p140; ☎/fax 656 794; tic@plovdiv.bg; pl Tsentralen 1; ⏰ 9am-7pm) Well-informed Franz and colleagues provide maps, find local accommodation and more. It's by the post office.

Usit Colours (Map p142; ☎ 622 530; www.usitcolours.bg in Bulgarian; ul Konstantin Stoilov 12; ⏰ 9am-5pm) The friendly Plovdiv branch of this international network issues ISIC cards for foreign students, provides a list of cafés, shops, restaurants and bars where a student discount applies, and books plane and bus tickets.

Sights

RUINS

Plovdiv's magnificent 2nd-century AD **Roman Amphitheatre** (Map p142; ul Hemus; admission 3 lv; ⏰ 8am-6pm), built by Emperor Trajan was, incredibly enough, only uncovered during a freak landslide in 1972. At its peak, the structure held about 6000 spectators. Now largely restored, it once again hosts large-scale special events and concerts. Visitors can admire the amphitheatre from several lookouts along ul Hemus, or from the cafés situated above. There's an unsigned shortcut from above the Church of Sveta Bogoroditsa along ul T Samodomov; enter through the passageway into the Academy of Music, Dance and Fine Arts on the right-hand side. Alternatively, you can pay the entrance fee and explore the marble seats and stage.

The once huge **Roman Stadium** (Map p142) is mostly hidden under the pedestrian mall and buildings; alas, a visionary plan to reconstruct the street with a glass walkway and so reveal the whole structure, remains unrealised. For now, 12 rows of the northern section have been restored, and are visible from the street. Above the ruins, a modern bronze statue of the city's founder – the 4th-century BC king of Macedon, Philip II – stands on a column.

Just down the steps at the overpass near pl Tsentralen, ruins of the **Roman Forum** (Map p140), are still being excavated; peer over the fence along the main road. Adjacent to the tourist information centre, the remains of a **Roman Odeon** (Map p142) have been partially restored. There's a tiny, reconstructed amphitheatre and some original columns. It's used for occasional performances.

Some 203m high in the old town, a hill contains sparse **ruins of Eumolpias** (Map p142), a Thracian settlement from about 5000 BC. The fortress and surrounding town enjoyed a strategic position, and it was later bolstered by Macedonians, Romans, Byzantines, Bulgarians and Turks, who named it Nebet Tepe (Prayer Hill). While the remaining rubble is rather formless, the site does offer great views. The hill is best reached from ul Dr Chomakov (the continuation of ul Sâborna). Partially restored remains of a 13th-century reservoir are also here.

MUSEUMS

Plovdiv's fascinating **Ethnographical Museum** (Map p142; ☎ 625 654; ul Dr Chomakov 2; admission 4 lv; ⏰ 9am-5pm) houses some 40,000 exhibits, including folk costumes and musical instruments,

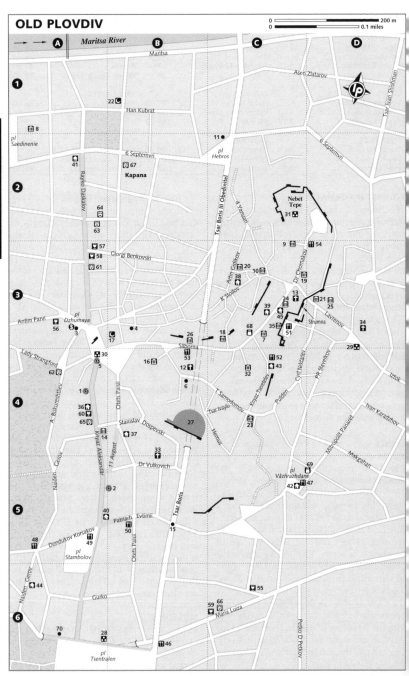

OLD PLOVDIV

SOUTHERN BULGARIA

INFORMATION

Internet Café Speed....................**1** A4
Internet Fantasy..........................**2** B5
Litera..**3** A3
USIT Colours...................................**4** B3
Zeon Internet Cafe.........................**5** A4

SIGHTS & ACTIVITIES

Academy of Music, Dance and Fine Arts..............................**6** B4
Apteka...**7** C3
Archaeological Museum..............**8** A1
Atanas Krastev House (Red Pony Art Gallery)...........................**9** C3
Balabanov House.......................**10** C3
Center for Contemporary Art (Chifte Banya).......................**11** C2
Church of Sveta Bogoroditsa.....**12** B4
Church of Sveti Konstantin & Elena....................................**13** C3
City Art Gallery..........................**14** A4
Cultural Center Thrakart............**15** B5
Danov House.............................**16** B4
Dzhumaya Mosque...................**17** B3
Encho Pironkov City Gallery of Fine Arts..............................**18** C3
Ethnographical Museum...........**19** C3
Hindlian House..........................**20** C3
Historical Museum....................**21** D3
Imaret Mosque..........................**22** B1
Lamartine House.......................**23** C4
Museum of History...................(see 8)
Museum of Icons......................**24** C3
Nedkovich House.....................**25** D3
Philipopolis Art Gallery.............**26** B3
Roman Amphitheatre...............**27** B4
Roman Odeon...........................**28** A6
Roman Ruins............................**29** D3
Roman Stadium........................**30** A4
Ruins of Eumolpias...................**31** C2
State Gallery of Fine Arts..........**32** C4
Statue of Philip II of Macedon..(see 30)
Sveta Marina Church................**33** B4
Sveta Nedelya Church..............**34** D3
Zlatyu Boyadjiev House............**35** C3

SLEEPING

Accommodation Agency..........**36** A4
Dali Art Hotel............................**37** B4
Hebros Hotel.............................**38** C3
Hikers Hostel............................**39** C3
Hotel Bulgaria...........................**40** A5
Hotel Elit...................................**41** A2
Hotel Renaissance....................**42** C5
Old Town Residence................**43** C4
PBI Hostel.................................**44** A6
Plovdiv Guest House................**45** C3

EATING

Art Cafe Philipopolis...............(see 26)
Café Avenue..............................**46** B6
Café Starino..............................**47** C5
Café Taksim Tepe...................(see 68)
Dayana......................................**48** A5
Dreams......................................**49** A5
Gusto...**50** B5
Hebros Hotel Restaurant.........(see 38)
King's Stables...........................**51** C3
Puldin Restaurant.....................**52** C4
Restaurant Kambanata.............**53** B4
Restaurant Rahat Tepe.............**54** D3

DRINKING

Art Bar Maria Luisa...................**55** C6
Fashion Café.............................**56** A3
Makalali.....................................**57** A3
Naylona.....................................**58** A3
Remix Music Club.....................**59** C6
Sky Bar......................................**60** A4

ENTERTAINMENT

Caligula...................................(see 60)
Enjoy Club 69............................**61** A3
Gepi..**62** A4
Infinity......................................**63** A2
King's Stables Café.................(see 51)
Marmalad..................................**64** A2
Nikolai Masalitinov Dramatic Theatre.....................................**65** A4
Paparazi....................................**66** C6
Petnoto.....................................**67** B2

SHOPPING

Antique Shops...........................**68** C3
Ponedelnik Pazar (Monday Market)..................................**69** D5

TRANSPORT

Plovdiv Airport Travel Agency....**70** A6

jewellery and examples of traditional crafts such as weaving, metalworking, winemaking and beekeeping. Traditional tools ranging from grape-crushers and wine-measures to apparatuses used for distilling attar of roses are also displayed. Upstairs, the restored 19th-century rooms have nice touches such as carved wooden ceilings. The most renowned Bulgarian National Revival–period home in Plovdiv, it was built in 1847 and owned by the eminent Agir Koyoumdjioglou, later becoming a girls' boarding school and a tobacco and flour warehouse.

The **Historical Museum** (Map p142; ☎ 623 378; ul Lavrenov 1; admission 2 lv; 9am-noon & 1-5.30pm Mon-Sat), also called the Museum of Revival & The National Liberation, concentrates on the 1876 April Uprising and the Batak massacre (see the boxed text, p163). Built in 1848 by Dimitâr Georgiadi, it's also called the *Georgiadi Kâshta*.

Due to reopen in 2008, the **Archaeological Museum** (Map p142; ☎ 624 339; pl Saedinenie 1) displays Thracian and Roman pottery and jewellery, and ecclesiastical artefacts, icons and liturgical paraphernalia. Hopefully the museum will exhibit its collection of 60,000 archaeological items upon reopening.

Housed within the Archaeological Museum, the **Museum of History** (Map p142; ☎ 629 409; pl Saedinenie 1; admission 2 lv; 9am-5pm Mon-Sat) chronicles the 1885 Unification of Bulgaria through documents, photographs and belongings of the protagonists.

Visible through floor-to-ceiling windows in the Tsar Obedinitel underpass, **Cultural Center Thrakart** (Map p142; ☎ 631 303; Podlez Arhaeologiski; 9am-7pm) contains extensive Roman floor mosaics and various artefacts from Roman (and earlier) times. Concerts are performed on the centre's small stage.

Apteka (Old Hippocrates Pharmacy; Map p142; ☎ 624 594; ul Sâborna 16; 9am-5pm) is a rarely open museum of pharmacy.

HOUSE-MUSEUMS

Plovdiv's 19th-century 'baroque' style house is typified by an overhanging upper storey with jutting eaves, a columned portico and brightly painted façade. The interior rooms feature finely carved woodwork, painted wall decorations and ornamental niches. Most also display art or other exhibits.

Once owned by merchant Stepan Hindlian, **Hindlian House** (Map p142; ☎ 628 998; ul Artin Gidikov 4; admission 3 lv; 9am-5pm Mon-Fri), built in 1835, is one of Plovdiv's most opulent. It's full of exquisite period furniture and walls painted with real and imaginary landscapes of Venice, Alexandria and Constantinople. These scenes, which took six months to complete, impressed visitors by showing the locales of the owner's overseas trading empire. The magnificent panelled ceilings and 'Oriental style' marble bathroom, with its high, domed ceiling and skylight are other highlights. The small **courtyard garden** is lovely, too.

In the Hindlian House cellar, the so-called **Wine from Bulgaria Museum & Oenology Collection** (☎ 635 376; ☽ 10am-5.30pm Tue-Sat) conducts wine tastings (10 lv per person for three wines). A braver endeavour, the full tasting of 10 wines, costs 40 lv. Specialist courses are also offered.

The **Danov House** (Map p142; ☎ 629 405; ul Mitropolit Paisii 2; admission 2 lv; ☽ 9am-12.30pm & 2-5pm Mon-Sat), dedicated to renowned writer and publisher Hristo Danov and several other Bulgarian authors, contains a re-creation of a bookshop and a National Revival–era classroom. There's an old printing press, and the **gardens** offer wonderful views. Enter through a wall up the laneway leading to the Church of Sveta Bogoroditsa.

Once owned by Luka Balabanov, a wealthy 19th-century merchant, the **Balabanov House** (Map p142; ☎ 627 082; ul Dr K Stoilov 57; admission 3 lv; ☽ 9am-7.30pm) was completely rebuilt in 1980 according to the original blueprints. It contains modern paintings and gorgeous antique furniture.

Built in 1830, the elegant **Lamartine House** (Map p142; ☎ 631 776; ul Knyaz Tseretelev 19; open by special arrangement), also called the Georgi Mavridi House, belongs to the Union of Bulgarian Writers. The building is named after the French poet, Alphonse de Lamartine, who stayed for three days in 1833, during his 'travels in the Orient'.

The **Nedkovich House** (Map p142; ☎ 626 216; ul Lavrenov; admission 3 lv; ☽ 9.30am-noon & 1-6pm), dating from 1863, has a lovely, leafy courtyard that sometimes hosts art shows, but alas, the house is poorly lit inside. The highlights are the ornate wood ceiling and flowery wall paintings.

ART GALLERIES

Plovdiv's large and thriving artistic community continues creating and sustaining the city's many galleries – already bursting with the fruits of 200 years of Bulgarian painting.

On 28 September each year, the magical **Night of the Galleries** sees every Plovdiv gallery open, for free, from 8pm to 3am.

Encho Pironkov City Gallery of Fine Arts (Map p142; ul Vasil Konchev 1; admission 1 lv; ☽ 9am-12.30pm & 1-5.30pm Mon-Fri, 10am-5.30pm Sat) displays Bulgarian modern art. It's down a small laneway downhill from ul Sâborna.

Zlatyu Boyadjiev House (Map p142; ☎ 635 308; ul Sâborna 18; admission 3 lv; ☽ 9am-noon & 1-6pm Apr-Sep, 8.30am-noon & 12.30-5pm Mon-Fri Oct-Mar), opposite Hikers Hostel (see p148) in the old town, contains paintings by Plovdiv native Zlatyu Boyadjiev (1903–76), many idealising the Bulgarian peasantry; some cover entire walls.

The **State Gallery of Fine Arts** (Map p142; ☎ 635 322; ul Sâborna 14a; admission 3 lv, free admission Tue; ☽ 9am-12.30pm & 1-5.30pm Mon-Fri, 10am-5.30pm Sat), occupying a mansion from 1846, contains outstanding works by 19th- and 20th-century Masters such as Goshka Datsov, Konstantin Velichkov and Nikolai Rainov. Look out also for Georgi Mashev and Master Vladimir Dimitrov's works.

The **Philipopolis Art Gallery** (Map p142; ☎ 622 742; ul Sâborna 29; admission 2 lv; ☽ 10am-6pm) is Bulgaria's first private art gallery and occupies the well-restored Hadzhi Aleko house (1865). It boasts works by 19th- and 20th-century Bulgarian Masters such as Vladimir Dimitrov, Anton Mitov and Dimitar Gyudzhenov. Hospitable owner Stefan Maletzov happily provides background information and encourages you to take photos.

Beside the Church of Sveti Konstantin & Elena, the small **Museum of Icons** (Map p142; ☎ 626 086; ul Sâborna 22; admission 2 lv; ☽ 9am-12.30pm & 1-5.30pm) has a sublime display of (15th century and up) icons.

The **City Art Gallery** (Map p142; ☎ 624 221; ul Knyaz Aleksandâr 15; admission 2 lv; ☽ 9am-12.30pm & 1-5.30pm Mon-Fri, 10am-5.30pm Sat), another branch of the State Gallery of Fine Arts, holds small, temporary exhibitions of abstract art.

The **Atanas Krastev House** (Red Pony Art Gallery; Map p142; ☎ 625 792; ul Dr Chomakov 5a; admission 1 lv; ☽ 10am-6pm Mar-Nov) was where local painter and conservationist Atanas Krastev lived until his death in 2003. His self-portraits and personal collection of (mostly) abstract 20th-century Bulgarian paintings are displayed. The cosy, well-furnished house is strewn with personal mementoes, and the terrace offers superb views. The garden also houses exhibits. Buy paintings by living legend Dimitar Kirov (see the boxed text, opposite) here.

THE MASTER & THE BALLERINA

Born in Istanbul in 1935 to a sculptor father, the gifted Dimitar Kirov was painting by the age of seven. Still working and living today in Plovdiv's old town, with Rosalia, his wife of 44 years – and one of modern Bulgaria's greatest ballerinas – Dimitar may well be the spirit of old Plovdiv personified. This living master of Bulgarian painting and mosaic art considers himself 'the last of an era', after the passing a few years ago of his best friend and fellow painter, Giorgi Bozhilov, nicknamed *Slon* ('the elephant').

With a faint smile peeking out of his beard, and kindly eyes set behind thick glasses, the laconic artist bedecked in a fedora hat and puffing on a cigar is truly a larger-than-life personality from another era. As he recalls the things that inspired him to create, his comments are animated by interjections from slender Rosalia, whose delicate beauty is still obvious, and who, though retired, still moves with the unmistakable half-steps of the ballerina.

The Kirovs have wonderful stories of the Bolshoi Theatre (where Rosalia was dancing when they decided to marry), of travelling the world with the Plovdiv Opera and of participating in the bohemian abstract art scene in Paris in the 1960s. Still, it was Plovdiv that initially inspired Dimitar and it was Plovdiv that called him back. When Parisian gallery owners, recognising the young painter's talent, asked him to stay, he told them no: 'I wanted to live in my country,' says Dimitar, 'and I'm still very proud of my decision to stay here.'

What inspires Dimitar most about Plovdiv? 'This city has 8000 years of culture,' he says, using a barely relatable Bulgarian idiom, 'and this beats me in the ankle.' What he means to say is that the city uplifts him: 'Old Plovdiv is a place you take energy from – it itself is my inspiration.'

Rosalia features prominently in his paintings. For her birthday in 2007, the painter threw his wife a party – an entire exhibition of portraits of her, displayed in the garden of the Atanas Krastev House gallery.

The couple's spacious home in the heart of old Plovdiv is perhaps the greatest museum you'll never see. Closed to the public, it contains hundreds of paintings and mosaics by this phenomenally prolific artist, clustered, jumbled and hung everywhere in a riotous outburst of colour. Bedrooms, living rooms and even a basement crypt are all filled to bursting with art, and not only Kirov's: works by other Bulgarian Masters, such as the great Vladimir Dimitrov – who also happened to be Rosalia's uncle – abound, and there are even works by Salvador Dalí, whose portrait Dimitar sketched in Paris.

Dimitar himself, puffing on his Cuban and resting amidst the wonderful mayhem of his art, is remarkably placid. He lets his wife do the talking.

'Before he was in a darker mood,' she says with her wonderfully warm smile. 'But now he's very happy, and everything's a celebration.'

You can see the works of Dimitar Kirov at art galleries around Plovdiv, and even buy them at the **Atanas Krastev House/Red Pony Art Gallery** (Map p142; ☎ 625 792; ul Dr Chomakov 5a; admission 1 lv; 10am-6pm Mar-Nov).

The **Center for Contemporary Art** (Map p142; ☎ 638 868; Chifte Banya; admission 3 lv; 1-6pm Tue-Sun) is housed on pl Hebros in the Chifte Banya, an old Turkish bath, and hosts contemporary works.

RELIGIOUS BUILDINGS

The huge, three-aisle **Church of Sveta Bogoroditsa** (Map p142; ☎ 623 265; ul Sâborna 1; 7am-7pm) stands atop a grand series of stone stairs at the old town's base. With its unmistakable pink and blue belltower, this church (built in 1844 on the site of a 9th-century shrine) contains icons and murals, including one depicting a sword-wielding Turkish soldier harassing chained and lamenting Bulgarian peasants.

The **Church of Sveti Konstantin & Elena** (Map p142; ul Sâborna 24), Plovdiv's oldest, was built over a late Roman church. It's dedicated to Constantine the Great, the 4th-century emperor who made Orthodox Christianity the state religion, and his mother, Sveta Helena. The current church, however, dates mostly to 1832. The wonderful iconostasis was painted by Zahari Zograf between 1836 and 1840, and the covered portico features sumptuous frescoes.

Originally built in 1561, **Sveta Marina Church** (Map p142; ul Dr Vulkovich 7) was burnt down 50 years later, rebuilt in 1783, and repaired in 1856. See the 17m-high pagoda-shaped wooden bell tower (1870), and the intricate, 170-year-old iconostasis.

The grand, reopened **Sveta Nedelya Church** (Map p142; ☎ 623 270; ul PR Slaveikov 40; 8am-5pm), built in 1578 and renovated in the 1830s, contains exquisite, carved walnut iconostases and now faded wall murals from the mid-1800s.

The **Dzhumaya Mosque** (Map p142; pl Dzhumaya), currently undergoing heavy renovation, is one of the Balkans' oldest, dating from the mid-15th century. This enormous structure with a 23m minaret was the largest of Plovdiv's more than 50 Ottoman-era mosques. Another Ottoman structure, the **Imaret Mosque** (Map p142) is open; note the unusual minaret. It's between the Hotel Elit and the river.

Walking Tour

Plovdiv's major sites can be seen in one day, though to really enjoy the numerous museums, mansions and churches, allow more time. The following tour follows a compre-

---

WALK FACTS

Start pl Stambolov
Finish Hindlian House
Distance 2.5km
Duration 1½ hours

OLD PLOVDIV WALKING TOUR

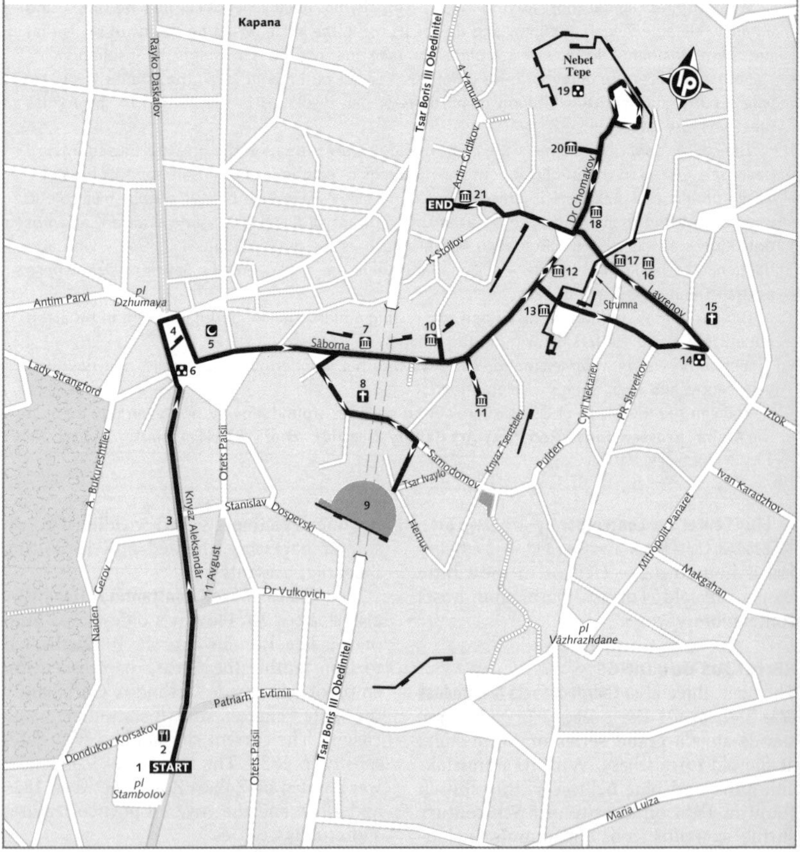

hensive route passing the major sites, most in the upper old town.

Note that this is no place for high heels: the large and irregular cobblestones, particularly in the upper half, make wearing sneakers or other low, comfortable shoes imperative.

Start at **pl Stambolov (1)**, perhaps with a morning coffee at **Dreams (2)** café, beside the square's grand fountain. Continue north down the chic pedestrian mall, ul Knyaz Aleksandâr, for some window (or real) **shopping (3)**. Continue to the next square, pl Dzhumaya; before **Dzhumaya Mosque (5)**, you will see the underground ruins of the **Roman stadium (6)**, and the unmissable modern **statue of Philip II of Macedon (4)** overhead.

Leaving the mosque to your left, proceed up ul Sâborna, the main old town thoroughfare. Soon you'll see, on the right, the enormous set of stone stairs leading to the **Church of Sveta Bogoroditsa**, before climbing up, however, visit the **Philipopolis Art Gallery (7)** opposite. Then, after seeing the church, follow the street behind it (ul T Samodomov) leaving the large Academy of Music, Dance and Fine Arts to your right; enter the academy's small gate to gaze down on the magnificent **Roman amphitheatre (9)** below.

Retracing your steps, continue up ul Sâborna towards more art galleries and house-museums. The first (down a stairway to the left on ul Vasil Konchev) is the **Encho Pironkov City Gallery of Fine Arts (10)**; the second, further up ul Sâborna on the right-hand side, is the **State Gallery of Fine Arts (11)**. Further up ul Sâborna on the right is the **Zlatu Boyadjiev House (13)** and, on the opposite corner of a small street leading southeast, the **Museum of Icons (12)**.

Take the small street bisecting them right to admire some **Roman ruins (14)** and, turning left on ul Lavrenov, the **Sveta Nedelya Church (15)**. Continuing northwest up this street, see the **Historical Museum (17)** and **Nedkovich House (16)**, before passing under a walled gate and back onto the main street, ul Sâborna, which now becomes ul Dr Chomakov; turn right, and immediately you'll see the **Ethnographical Museum (18)**. Continuing uphill from here brings you to **Nebet Tepe** and the **ruins of Eumolpias (19)**, site of the original Thracian hill settlement. From here, double back to find, on your right, the **Atanas Krastev House/ Red Pony Art Gallery (20)**. Continue down-

hill, taking your first right to reach the **Hindlian House (21)**; if it's open, celebrate your industriousness in the wine-tasting room downstairs.

Festivals & Events
International Plovdiv Fair (mid-May & late September) Week-long festival held in the massive fairgrounds (Map p140; ☎ 553 146; bul Tsar Boris III Obedinitel 37), located north of the river.

Cultural Month Festival (late May–mid-July) Performances and exhibits of opera, literature, painting and events celebrating the greatness of Bulgarian history.

Verdi Festival (early June) Two-week festival of opera concerts in the Roman amphitheatre, featuring Bulgarian and international singers.

International Festival of Chamber Music (mid-June) Ten-day festival.

International Folklore Festival (end July–early August) Folklore groups perform on the pedestrian mall for free by afternoon; evening shows performed in amphitheatre.

Thracia Summer Music Festival (www.geocities.com /thracia_festival; August) Regional traditional music, performed in the Balabanov House and the Ethnographic Museum; events also happen in Stara Zagora, Chirpan and other southern towns.

City Holiday (6 September) Celebration of the Day of National Unification (Narodni Saedinenie), ratified in Plovdiv in 1885. Unusually, officials shampoo the city's monument before the event.

Jazz Festival (September) Acclaimed international festival.

Sleeping
While the fairs are on, in May and September, prices increase substantially.

BUDGET
Campers can choose between the **Complex 4th Kilometre** (off Map p140; ☎ 951 360; camping sites per person 3 lv; bungalows 28-38 lv; ☺ year-round) and the **9th Kilometre Complex** (☎ 632 992; www .leipzig.bg; bul Pazardzhikoshose; camping sites per person 3 lv, tents 3 lv, bungalow 20 lv; r renovated 32 lv, r unrenovated 25 lv; ☺ year-round). The former (also called Gorski Kat Camping), is a shady, loud place about 4km west on the old Sofia Highway. A restaurant-bar and water park is also there. Take bus 4, 18 or 44 west along bul Bulgaria, or bus 222 from the train station to this terminus and walk another 200m. The latter camping ground, owned by Plovdiv's Hotel Leipzig, is snazzier, with a restaurant and 24-hour bar. There's also a large outdoor swimming pool. Take a taxi (about 10 lv).

Hikers Hostel (Map p142; ☎ 0896764854; www.hikers
-hostel.org; ul Sâborna 53; tent/dm/s/d with shared bathroom
12/20/43/48 lv, all incl breakfast; 💻) The ideal place for
independent travellers to chill in Plovdiv's old
town, Hikers has comfy couches, outside tables,
and sleeping choices ranging from tents and
dorms to lofts and private rooms. The friendly,
helpful staff all have different specialities: Petar
is the hiking expert, Neli the queen of nightlife,
and master of hospitality Natcho is the all-
around problem-solver. There's free wireless
internet, a computer, and laundry service (4 lv).
There's also a private room and extra dorm in
an apartment block near Dzhumaya Mosque,
and discounted bookings at hostels in Sofia and
Veliko Târnovo can be arranged.

Plovdiv Guest House (Map p142; ☎ 622 432; www
.plovdivguest.com; ul Sâborna 20; dm/s/d with shared bathroom 20/30/60 lv; 💻) If the Hikers Hostel is full,
try this new place across the street. Its clean
and bright dorms have 10, eight and four beds,
and there's one spacious attic double. Dorms
feature their own self-contained and modern
bathroom/shower. The atmosphere is slightly
formal, though an upcoming outdoor café
out the back, above the ancient Roman wall,
should improve the vibe.

PBI Hostel (Map p142; ☎ 638 467; hostel@pbihostel
.com; ul Naiden Gerov 13; dm 20 lv; 💻) Plovdiv's
oldest hostel has a central location, near pl
Stambolov, but is showing its wear, and has indifferent service. PBI offers internet and a bar,
and the owner speaks English and Japanese.

Trakiya Hotel (Map p140; ☎ 624 101; ul Ivan Vazov 84;
s/d 30/60 lv) This small hotel 100m from the train
station has basic, clean rooms (with fan), and
they are quiet despite the noisy location and
popular bar downstairs.

Hotel Leipzig (Map p140; ☎ 654 080; www.leipzig.bg;
bul Ruski 70; s/d unrenovated 36/50 lv, renovated 52/64 lv; P)
Renovations continue at this ageing yet popular
high-rise, which boasts a 'Cuban' lobby bar, restaurant, beauty salon and wireless internet, to go
with decent rooms (try a renovated one). Some
have great views of the Hill of the Liberators.

For private accommodation, try the
Tourist Information Centre (see p141), or
the **Accommodation Agency** (Map p142; ☎ 272 778; ul
Knyaz Aleksandâr 28; r per person 22 lv; ⏰ 9am-5pm Mon-Sat)
or **Esperantsa** (Map p140; ☎ 260 653; ul Ivan Vazov 14; r
per person 22 lv; ⏰ 9am-5pm Mon-Sat).

MIDRANGE & TOP END

Hotel Elit (Map p142; ☎ 624 537; ul Rayko Daskalov 53;
d/ste 60/100 lv; ✴) The modern and reasonably

central Elit is on the corner of bul 6 Septemvri,
just west of the Kapana bar district. The rooms
are insulated from road noise, and it's clean
and comfortable. The suites, however, are really glorified doubles.

Hotel Avion (Map p140; ☎ 967 451; www.hotelavion
.info; ul Han Presian 13-15; s/d/ste incl breakfast 64/115/154 lv;
P ✴) The Avion is a small, modern hotel
on a quiet side street north of the Maritsa,
offering smartly furnished doubles and suites.
Rooms have nice wood floors and a back garden, and service is gracious.

Hotel Bulgaria (Map p142; ☎ 633 599; www.hotel
bulgaria.net; ul Patriarh Evtimii 13; s/d incl breakfast from
70/130 lv; P ✴) On the central pl Stambolov,
the Bulgaria has a worn, yet stately demean-
our. Rooms are bright and modern, with good
bathrooms and double-glazed windows that
block street noise.

Dali Art Hotel (Map p142; ☎ 621 530; www
.arthoteldali.com; ul Otets Paisii 11; d/ste/apt incl breakfast
90/110/132 lv) This intimate new boutique hotel
off the mall has eight rooms, including two
apartments, with appropriately minimalist
décor. However, it's most distinguished by
its friendly and relaxed staff, who give you the
feeling of being in a home-away-from-home.
Indeed, after only three years, the Dali boasts
a 40% repeat visitor rate.

Hotel Maritsa (Map p140; ☎ 952 735; fax 652 899;
www.victoria-group.net; bul Tsar Boris III Obedinitel 42;
s/d/apt 90/160/280 lv; P ✴ 💻) Opposite the fairgrounds, the Maritsa is a lavish, renovated
four-star hotel, offering attractive doubles
with big bathrooms and suites sumptuously
decorated in an ornate, vaguely French style.
Facilities include a gym, business centre, restaurant and casino. It's popular with large
weekend wedding parties.

Hotel Nord (Map p140; ☎ 907 959; www.hotelnord
-bg.com; ul Ibar 33; s/d/ste 100/120/140 lv; ✴) Opposite
the Hotel Maritsa, this cosy place has bright,
clean rooms and attentive staff. However, it
doesn't offer the amenities of the larger and
similarly priced hotels nearby.

our pick **Hotel Renaissance** (Map p142; ☎ /fax
266 966; www.renaissance-bg.com; pl Vâzhrazhdane 1; s/d
incl breakfast from 100/160 lv; P ✴ 💻) This lovely
new boutique hotel has an enviable location
between the old town and the main square.
It aims to recreate, with its intricate, hand-
painted walls in the traditional Plovdiv style
and handsome wood floors, the experience of
being in a National Revival–era mansion at
its peak. All rooms are unique and differently

priced. Friendly, English-speaking owner Dimitar Vassilev is a fount of local knowledge; ask him to show you the Ottoman-era property documents that accompanied the house. If going by taxi, tell the driver to take you to the adjoining Café Starino (see p150), the well-known local landmark.

The Old Town Residence (Map p142; ☎ 620 789; ul Knyaz Tseretelev 11; www.theoldtownresidence.com; d 100 lv, apt from 150 lv) This magnificent place with ornate, arched columns and elegant period furnishings is undoubtedly the old town's most romantic and regal hotel. It offers six doubles and three sumptuous apartments, and has an equally posh restaurant and bar (where noisy weddings are sometimes held on weekends). There are excellent views from the restaurant terrace. It's absolutely unbeatable for old-world ambience.

Noviz Hotel (Map p140; ☎ 631 281; www.noviz.com; bul Ruski 55; s/d/ste 100/140/170 lv; P ✷) While the Noviz is a small place, it's friendly and the rooms are large and well furnished. What people come for, however, is the excellent and inexpensive massage therapy; there's also a sauna and refreshing cold pool.

Hebros Hotel (Map p142; ☎ 260 180; www.hebros -hotel.com; ul Konstantin Stoilov 51a; s/d/apt from 135/156/186 lv; P ✷) One of Plovdiv's most characterful hotels, this 200-year-old house is filled with antique furniture, all six rooms being individually decorated with National Revival–era flair. The bathrooms are sparklingly modern and there's also a Jacuzzi, sauna and well-regarded restaurant (see p150).

Trimontium Princess Hotel (Map p140; ☎ 605 000; www.trimontium-princess.com; pl Tsentralen; s/d/apt from 176/215/293 lv; P ✷ ▯) The grand old Trimontium seeks to be to Plovdiv what the Grand Bretagne is to Athens or the Moskva to Belgrade, though this old-world elegance is more apparent in the public areas than the rooms. The huge lobby bar has marble floors, wedding-cake curtains and heavy leather chairs, where pipe-smoking people converse in various languages. Amenities include two restaurants, a bar, nightclub, fitness centre and hairdressers. The rooms, however, while certainly nice, are not nearly as striking as those found at some of Plovdiv's smaller hotels.

Novotel (Map p140; ☎ 934 444; www.novotelpdv.bg; ul Boyadjiev 2; s/d/ste 176/235/352 lv; P ✷ ▯ ▤) Currently Plovdiv's only five-star hotel, the enormous Novotel is in a modern, north-side high-rise. Rooms are large and comfortable, with all amenities, and there's a bar, restaurant, nightclub and minispa centre with indoor pool, and clay tennis courts outdoors. However, there's a certain sad anonymity to it common to similarly impersonal business hotels.

Eating

Restaurant Rahat Tepe (Map p142; ☎ 624 454; ul Dr Chomakov; mains 2-5 lv) Way up in the old town, the outdoors Rahat Tepe serves simple meals such as salads, beef kebabs and fried fish.

King's Stables (Map p142; ☎ 0898542787; ul Sâborna; mains 4-7 lv; ✆ 9am-2am) The sprawling, summer-only King's Stables, opposite the Hikers Hostel, occupies a rolling hill ending in Roman walls. Offerings range from breakfast crepes to hearty meat dishes such as Thracian *gouviech* (melting cheese and sausage with seasonings cooked in a clay pot). It also features that relative rarity in Bulgaria – friendly service. The restaurant has two adjacent cafés.

Dayana (Map p142; ☎ 623 027; ul Dondukov Korsakov 3; mains 5-9 lv; ✆ 9am-late) This big place off the pedestrian mall, popular with locals and foreigners alike, has a huge (and colourful) menu strong on grilled meats. The staff seem overworked, so service can be slow.

Gusto (Map p142; ☎ 623 711; ul Otets Paisii 26; mains 5-9 lv; ✆ 9am-1am) Across the road from the Hotel Bulgaria, the friendly Gusto has diner-style booths upstairs and cosy tables downstairs, both with classy décor. While it's arguably not even the best thing served, pasta accompanied by wine seems the most popular choice.

Djoana (off Map p140; ☎ 961 909; cnr Pobeda & Dunav; mains 5-9 lv; ✆ 24hr) This big and often full *taverna*-style place north of the river is great for a hearty grilled meat and beer dinner.

Efir-100 (off Map p140; ☎ 961 117; cnr Pobeda & Dunav; mains 5-9 lv; ✆ 9am-late) Adjoining Djoana, and serving similar grilled meat specialities, this busy place (pronounced *efir-sto* in Bulgarian) has an eclectic, jungle-like décor. Entrées range from common standbys such as *shopska* salad and chicken *shishle* to more unknown commodities like 'dinosaur's tail on fire'.

Restaurant Kambanata (Map p142; ☎ 260 665; ul Sâborna 2b; mains 5-10 lv; ✆ 9am-midnight) Beneath the Church of Sveta Bogoroditsa, the Kambanata has tables set in ascending rows for watching live music. The food, however, is more prosaic, and somewhat overpriced, and they don't do breakfasts.

Skandarliya (off Map p140; ☎ 955 093; bul Dunav 29; mains 5-10 lv; ✆ 9am-late) Another north-side eatery, and Plovdiv's best place for Serbian *skara* (grilled meats), with an extensive wine list.

Malâk Bunardzhik (Map p140; ☎ 446 140; ul Volga 1; mains 5-10 lv) Quality Bulgarian cuisine is served at this popular place with garden dining and live music most nights.

XIX Vek (19th Century; Map p140; ☎ 653 882; ul Tsar Kaloyan 1; mains 6-10 lv; ⏰ 7am-midnight) Pronounced *devetnaystee vek*, this local favourite in a garden near the pedestrian mall offers traditional *satch* (a stew baked in a clay pots) dishes, charcoal-grilled shish kebabs and more. Its walls are decorated with traditional implements and décor reminiscent of a 19th-century village.

Ristorante Da Lino (Map p140; ☎ 631 751; bul 6 Septemvri 135; mains 8-15 lv) Plovdiv's best place for Italian food, Da Lino occupies a converted monastery; however, prices are high and portions are small.

Puldin Restaurant (Map p142; ☎ 631 720; ul Knyaz Tseretelev 8; mains 8-15 lv; ⏰ 9am-midnight) The magical Puldin is one of Plovdiv's most atmospheric restaurants. In one dining room, the famous whirling dervishes of the Ottoman Empire once whirled themselves into ecstatic exhaustion, while in the cellar hall Byzantine-era walls and Roman artefacts predominate. Although expensive, the décor alone makes it worthwhile.

Hebros Hotel Restaurant (Map p142; ☎ 625 929; ul K Stoilov 51; mains 11-18 lv) The upscale garden restaurant of the upmarket Hebros Hotel does excellent, and innovative Bulgarian cuisine, such as rabbit with plums, trout, pork with blue cheese and more.

CAFÉS

Café Starino (Map p142; pl Vâzhrazhdane; ⏰ 8am-2am) One of Plovdiv's oldest and most atmospheric cafés, this dark, weathered place next to the Hotel Renaissance (p148) has a thick bar and pillowy, Ottoman-style bench-tables on the upper section. Behind the antique, handpainted walls are even older, Turkish-era sections. The Starino attracts mostly a subdued, local crowd.

Café Taksim Tepe (Map p142; ul Sâborna 47; ⏰ 10am-midnight) With its patio setting overlooking Plovdiv's old red roofs, this tiny place has a relaxing vibe and (sometimes) plays ragtime and jazz. Despite the allusive name, it doesn't serve Turkish coffee.

Art Cafe Philipopolis (Map p142; ☎ 624 851; ul Sâborna 29; ⏰ 10am-midnight) Adjacent to the Philipopolis Art Gallery, the café has a garden section with views, while indoors there's

a nonsmoking section. Light breakfasts and lunches are served, along with coffees and cocktails, though the musical offerings (the rock ballads of Bryan Adams and Aerosmith, over and over) could hardly be called arty.

Dreams (Map p142; ☎ 627 142; pl Stambolov; sandwiches around 2 lv; ⏰ 9am-11pm) This excellent and very popular café on pl Stambolov is the perfect place to relax before the square's giant gushing fountain on a balmy summer's day. It serves surprisingly good cakes, along with numerous alcoholic and nonalcoholic drinks. There's also a spacious upstairs hall.

Café Avenue (☎ 626 526; bul Maria Luisa 12; ⏰ 7.30am-1.30am) Very popular with locally known personalities, black-clad businessmen and students too, this fashionable, dressed-up café plays retro, house and dance music.

Drinking

Plovdiv's nightspots are widespread. However, several good places occupy the district called Kapana, meaning 'the trap', referring to its inextricably tight streets for drivers, which includes the areas north of pl Dzhumaya, between ul Rayko Daskalov to the west and bul Tsar Boris Obedinitel to the east.

Art Bar Maria Luisa (Map p142; bul Maria Luisa 15; ⏰ 8am-4am) Too pretty to be just a dive bar, the Maria Luisa has dedicated owners who keep adapting the décor to suit their whims. The colourful downstairs is particularly stylish, vaguely reminiscent of 1920's Paris. This little place has a dedicated local following.

Makalali (Map p142; ul Giorgi Benkovski 7, Kapana; ⏰ 9am-4am) While the African tribal theme is somewhat less obvious than the owners might think, Makalali is still a good, and often busy place, with a big cocktail menu, cool lighting and Fashion TV aspirations to go with its ambient house music.

Remix Music Club (Map p142; ☎ 0898607010; bul Maria Luisa 43a; ⏰ 9am-late) This very chic new place is a chill spot for a daytime coffee, but gets loud at night when the beautiful people show up. It's full of colour and plasma screens, and smooth seats from some postmodern hair salon.

Planet Club (Map p140; ☎ 643 221; Ivan Andonov 5; ⏰ 9am-2am) Don't be put off by the black windows on the big black Jeeps out front; the Planet is not really a Mafia bar, just a slick, fashionable place with an ultramodern interior and occasional wild excess (see the photos upon entry).

Simfoniya (Map p140; ☎ 630 333; Tsar Simeon Garden; ☼ 24hr) At the western end of the park, Simfoniya is a busy bar-café with drinks (and cakes).

Sky Bar (Map p142; ☎ 633 377; ul Knyaz Aleksandâr 30; ☼ 24hr) You can't beat the Sky Bar, located atop one of Plovdiv's tallest buildings, for panoramic evening or night-time views in the company of a cold drink.

Fashion Café (Map p142; ☎ 632 131; ul Antim Parvi; ☼ 8am-4pm) In the shopping centre west of Dzhumaya Mosque, this popular place offers mixed musical styles and is popular with students, especially by night.

Plazma Light (Map p140; ☎ 033 055; Botev 82; ☼ 24hr) A very, very chic new bar with a nightclub behind, Plazma Light is one of the prime places to chill out to house music, with detached, island-like bars set in a sea of cream-and-black décor. Shiny screens and shiny people complete the mesmerizing effect.

Naylona (Map p142; ☎ 0889496750; ul Giorgi Benkovski 8, Kapana; ☼ noon-4am) They say that the owners of this Kapana dive bar purposefully didn't fix the roof, so that the rain would trickle in; whatever the story, this damp, bare-bones place usually playing classic (and other) rock remains the unwashed, long-haired antithesis of Plovdiv style.

Escada (off Map p140; ☎ 643 204; ul Tsaravets 22a; ☼ 7am-2am) The smooth modern look of this café/bar/restaurant with striped couches, a long bar and canopied outdoor seating is reminiscent of the smart Grecian cafés of Thessaloniki. It's good for a light lunch and has an upstairs nightclub. It's 2km west of the train station.

Entertainment
DISCOS & NIGHTCLUBS

Paparazi (Map p142; ☎ 0888715657; bul Maria Luisa 43; ☼ 11pm-6am) Plovdiv's longest-running nightclub, Paparazi has three big halls for DJ-driven house music, *chalga* (Bulgarian pop music) and hip-hop.

Enjoy Club 69 (Map p142; ☎ 0888699688; Evlogi Giorgiev 1; ☼ 11pm-6am) This scantily clad *chalga* club somehow combines brick-wall décor and plasma video screens, attracting students and wanna-be mafiosi as well.

King's Stables Café (Map p142; ☎ 0898542787; ul Sâborna) This summer-only outdoor café has two parts: a lower area beside the restaurant, with live music stage, and a funky upper bar (the 'second stage'), offering a short list of well-made cocktails. A DJ here spins chilled-out tracks, sometimes accompanied by wafting, pungent incense.

Petnoto (Map p142; ☎ 0898542787; ul Ioakim Gruev 36, Kapana; ☼ 8am-6am) The pinstriped Petnoto combines a bar, small restaurant and a music stage where Bulgarian bands and DJs perform.

Marmalad (Map p142; ☎ 631 834; ul Bratya Pulievi 3, Kapana; ☼ 9am-2am) This two-floor place is one of Kapana's best for live music. The upper floor is a bar, and the lower one a club where nationally known rock bands perform on Thursday. Tuesday features a piano bar, karaoke's on Wednesday, and DJs play on weekends.

Palmite (Map p140; ☎ 0889909536; ul Gladstone 15; ☼ 10am-6am) Translated as 'the Palms', this pumping *chalga* club shares its entrance with a fitness club and features male strippers (Thursday) and student nights (Sunday).

Nai Club (Map p140; ☎ 647 484; bul Vasil Aprilov 13a; ☼ 10pm-late) Bulgarian folk-pop blares out at this popular club; notably, there are frequent live performances, if you've been yearning to see the starlets of *chalga* in the flesh.

Infinity (Map p142; ☎ 0888281431; Bratya Pulievi 4, Kapana; ☼ 10am-late) Varied music is played at this studenty late club in Kapana.

Gepi (Map p142; ☎ 0888924301; Lady Strangford 5; ☼ 8am-4am) Live salsa, jazz, hip-hop and rock concerts happen at this slightly underground place with a bright, visually arresting lamp-lit interior.

Caligula (Map p142; ☎ 626 867; ul Knyaz Aleksandâr 30; ☼ 10am-8am) Plovdiv's only gay club is, Bulgarian men only half-jokingly say, a nice place to meet girls. Whatever the case, the mixed crowd comes not only for the greased-up male pole dancers, but for the live music, DJs and neighbouring facilities (the Sky Bar is in the same complex).

CINEMAS
See recent foreign films in original languages (with Bulgarian subtitles) at **Luki Cinema** (Map p140; ☎ 629 070; ul Gladston 1), **Flamingo Cinema** (Map p140; ☎ 644 004; bul 6 Septemvri 128) or **Faces Cinema** (off Map p140; ☎ 683 310; bul Saedinenie, Trakiya District).

THEATRE & OPERA
Roman Amphitheatre (Map p142) The amphitheatre hosts Plovdiv's annual Verdi Festival (June), as well as other summertime opera, ballet and music performances.

Open-air Theatre (Map p140; Bunardjika) This theatre has summertime traditional music and dance performances.

Nikolai Masalitinov Dramatic Theatre (Map p142; ☎ 224 867; ul Knyaz Aleksandâr 38) One of Bulgaria's top theatres, it features anything from Shakespeare to Ibsen (most performances are in Bulgarian).

Plovdiv Opera House (Map p140; ☎ 632 231; opera@thracia.net; ul Avksentiy Veleshki) Classic and modern European operas are performed in Bulgarian at this venerable hall.

Shopping

Trendy clothes and shoe stores line the pedestrian mall, ul Knyaz Aleksandâr. Where this street meets pl Dzhumaya, south of the mosque, silver jewellery, icons and paintings are sold outside. Continuing up ul Sâborna, you'll find several antique shops. Paintings by Bulgarian artists are sold in various cafés and galleries.

Finally, the busy Ponedelnik Pazar (Monday Market), over by pl Vazhrajdane and the Hotel Renaissance, displays fresh fruits and vegetables (and the Bulgarians who buy them).

Getting There & Away

AIR

Only charter flights use Plovdiv airport; the **Plovdiv Airport travel agency** (Map p142; ☎ 633 081; ul Gladston 4) can therefore only book domestic and international flights to and from Sofia.

BUS

Plovdiv's three bus stations include the **Yug bus station** (Map p140; ☎ 626 937), diagonally opposite the train station, and a 15-minute walk from the centre (a taxi costs 3 lv to 5 lv). Alternatively, local buses (0.60 lv) stop across the main street outside the station, on bul Hristo Botev. From the Yug bus station, public and private buses go to the destinations listed.

Destination	Fare	Duration	Frequency
Bansko	7.50 lv	3½hr	2 daily
Blagoevgrad	7 lv	3hr	3 daily
Burgas (private)	15 lv	4hr	2 daily
Haskovo	4 lv	1hr	5 daily
Hisar	2.20 lv	1hr	12 daily
Karlovo	2.80 lv	1½hr	half-hourly
Ruse (private)	13 lv	6hr	1 daily
Sliven	10 lv	3hr	5 daily
Sofia	9 lv	2½hr	half-hourly
Stara Zagora	4.80 lv	1½hr	4 daily
Varna	15 lv	7hr	2 daily
Veliko Târnovo (private)	11 lv	4½hr	3 daily

In summer, one or two daily buses leave this station for the Black Sea (Kiten, Ahtopol, Albena and Nesebâr).

From **Rodopi bus station** (Map p140; ☎ 777 607), through the underpass by the train station, 13 daily buses serve Haskovo and Karlovo and hourly buses (between 6am and 7pm) go to Smolyan (7.50 lv, 2½ hours), via Bachkovo (2.70 lv, one hour), Chepelare and Pamporovo.

The **Sever bus station** (off Map p140; ☎ 553 705), in the northern suburbs, has one daily bus to Pleven (10 lv), Ruse (12 lv), Troyan (7 lv) and Koprivshtitsa (6 lv).

Union-Ivkoni Vesna 61 (Map p140; ☎ 628 365; train station underpass; ☒ 8am-6pm) offers buses to international destinations, including Paris (180 lv), Rome (170 lv), Vienna (110 lv) and Amsterdam (170 lv).

Etap (Map p140; ☎ 632 082; Yug bus station) sells bus tickets to Istanbul (25 lv), Athens (95 lv) and more.

TRAIN

Plovdiv, along the major Sofia–Burgas line, has many trains; the main ones are given here.

Destination	1st-/2nd-class fare	Duration	Number of trains (daily)
Burgas	13.60/10 lv*	4hr*	6
Hisar	4.50/3.50 lv	2hr	3
Karlovo	4.30/3.30 lv	2hr	5
Sofia	9/6.50 lv*	2½hr*	14
Svilengrad	7.50/5.30 lv	3½hr	3

*denotes express trains

Plovdiv's **train station** (Map p140; ☎ 632 720; bul Hristo Botev) is well organised, though the platforms aren't numbered and the staff do not speak English. Computer screens at the station entrance and in the underpass leading to the platforms list recent arrivals and upcoming departures. You can store luggage here (2 lv per bag for 24 hours); the office is always open.

For international tickets see the **Rila Bureau** (Map p140; ☎ 446 120; ☒ 8am-6.30pm Mon-Sat), on a side street paralleling bul Hristo Botev. For information about international trains here, see p299.

Getting Around

Plovdiv is best experienced on foot. Much of the old town is off-limits to cars anyway, so with a taxi your most likely 'final destination' will be outside the Church of Sveta Bogoroditsa on ul Sâborna, where all cars must turn back (at night the street is usually open). Although taxi drivers conscientiously use meters, a few offenders charge rates as opprobrious as 4 lv per kilometre; the daytime base rate should be around 0.52 lv per kilometre, and at night, 0.59 lv.

For car rental, **Tourist Service Rent-a-Car** (Map p140; ☎ 623 496; Trimontium Princess Hotel) and **Avis** (Map p140; ☎ 934 481; Novotel) are well known but expensive; travel agencies along the mall or the tourist information centre can find better prices. For example, **S & Z Rent-a-Car** (Map p140; ☎ 967 410; bul Tsar Boris Obedinitel 26) rents from 30 lv per day.

AROUND PLOVDIV
Bachkovo Monastery
About 30km south of Plovdiv is the magnificent **Bachkovo Monastery** (admission free; ☺ 6am-10pm), founded in 1083 by Georgian brothers Gregory and Abasius Bakuriani, aristocrats then in Byzantine military service. The monastery flourished during the Second Bulgarian Empire (1185–1396), but was ransacked by the Turks in the 15th and 16th centuries. Major reconstructions began in the mid-17th century. Bachkovo's now Bulgaria's second-largest monastery, after Rila.

In the courtyard, the **Church of Sveta Bogoroditsa** (1604) contains frescoes by Zahari Zograf from the early 1850s. Other highlights include the 17th-century iconostasis, more 19th-century murals and a much-cherished icon of the Virgin, allegedly painted by St Luke, though actually dating from the 14th century. Pilgrims regularly come here to pray before the silver-encased icon.

The monastery's southern side houses the former **refectory**, built in 1601. The walls are filled with stunning frescoes relating the monastery's history. A gate beside the refectory leads to a (rarely open) little courtyard; this leads to the **Church of Sveti Nikolai**, built in 1836. During the 1840s, Zograf painted the superb *Last Judgment* inside the chapel; note the condemned, nervous-looking Turks on the right and Zograf's self-portrait (no beard) in the upper-left corner.

Around 50m from the monastery entrance, the restored **Ossuary** features wonderful medieval murals, but remains closed.

A prominent explanation board provides monastic history (in English, French and German), and a map of **hiking trails** to nearby villages. The helpful guidebook (15 lv) is available at the monastery's shop.

SLEEPING & EATING
The monastery offers austere older rooms with shared bathrooms, and newer ones with their own bathrooms, for 20 lv per person and 40 lv per person, respectively. Enquire upstairs in the reception office.

Echo Hotel (☎ 048-981 068; d incl breakfast 50 lv) On the other side of the road, and river, from the monastery turn-off, this small place offers quiet, comfortable rooms.

Restaurant Vodopada (mains 4-7 lv; ☺ 9am-10pm) The best place to eat nearby, this is a charming courtyard restaurant, ranged around a waterfall and fish-pool, serving good grills and salads.

GETTING THERE & AWAY
Take any of the regular buses to Smolyan from Plovdiv's Rodopi bus station (3 lv), disembark at the turn-off about 1.2km south of Bachkovo village and walk about 500m uphill. There are also direct buses half-hourly.

HASKOVO ХАСКОВО
☎ 038 / pop 78,450
Little-visited Haskovo has a distinct Turkish influence and is a staging post for journeys to Greece or Turkey via Svilengrad. For information on hiking from Haskovo, see the boxed text on p157.

Information
Bulgarian Post Bank (ul Otets Paisii)
Hebros Bank (ul Rakovski)
Internet Club (ul San Stefano; per hr 1 lv)

Sights
The **Historical Museum** (☎ 24 505; pl Svoboda; admission 1 lv) exhibits agricultural implements, folk costumes and archaeological finds. The museum keeps erratic hours.

The **Ezhi Dzhumaya Mosque** (ul San Stefano), built in the late 14th century, is probably Bulgaria's oldest mosque.

Sleeping & Eating
Hotel Aida (☎ 665 164; pl Svoboda; d 29 lv) This large, central old hotel has decent rooms and a fairly good restaurant.

Hotel Oasis (☎ /fax 663 248; ul Rakovski 10; s/d 40/84 lv) The Oasis, about 150m north of pl Svoboda, has smarter rooms than the Aida.

Hotel Central (☎ 660 333; ul Varna 1; d incl breakfast 48 lv; ⌨) On a central pedestrian street, this place has bright, airy rooms.

SOUTHERN BULGARIA

SOUTHERN BULGARIA

HASKOVO

0 ____ 200 m
0 ____ 0.1 miles

To Stara Zagora (61km);
Plovdiv (78km)

INFORMATION	
Bulgarian Post Bank	1 B3
Hebros Bank	2 B2
Internet Club	3 C3
Post Office	4 A3
Telephone Centre	(see 4)

SIGHTS & ACTIVITIES	
Ezhi Dzhumaya Mosque	5 C3
Historical Museum	6 C2

SLEEPING	
Hotel Aida	7 B2
Hotel Central	8 B2
Hotel Oasis	9 B2

EATING	
Restaurant Vesta	10 C3

TRANSPORT	
Bus Station	11 D3

Saedinenie
Hadzhi Dimitâr
Georgi Kirkov
Rakovski
Ivan Dinov Dramatic Theatre
Otets Paisii
1000 Years Monument
Preslav
M. Drinov
Rise
Burgas
Veliko Târnovo
Varna
pl Svoboda
Patriarh Evtimii
Veliko Târnovo
Aton
Stefan Karadzhi
Saedinenie
Pirin
San Stefano
Tsar Kaloyan
Haskovska River
Bulgaria
To Kârdzhali (54km)
To Train Station (1km); Svilengrad (68km)

Cafés and bars line the pedestrian mall. For pizzas, grills and salads, try **Restaurant Vesta** (☎ 35 730; ul San Stefano 20; mains 4-6 lv; 9am-midnight).

Getting There & Away

From the **bus station** (☎ 24 218; ul Saedinenie) a dozen public and private buses depart daily for Sofia (12 lv, six to seven hours), five serve Plovdiv (4 lv, one hour) and several depart daily for Varna, Burgas, Gabrovo, Kazanlâk, Stara Zagora and Svilengrad (the border with Greece and Turkey). Companies at the station, such as **ABAP** (☎ 0888375811), offer daily services to Istanbul (about 30 lv).

RODOPI MOUNTAINS
РОДОПИ
ПЛАНИНА

Vast stretches of serene pine forests, perilously steep gorges and hundreds of remarkable caves characterise the enthralling Rodopi (rod-*oh*-pee) Mountains, which cover some 15,000 sq km of territory from east to west, spilling across into Greece. In fact, much of the border between the two countries is determined by the Rodopi range (85% of which is in Bulgaria).

Being relatively remote compared with the Rila and Pirin mountain ranges further to the west, the Rodopi Mountains see far fewer foreign visitors, with the exception of the major ski resorts of Pamporovo (p156) and Chepelare (opposite), and the spa town of Devin (p160). Outside of these areas, however, the region remains one of the wildest in Bulgaria, an endless expanse of majestic, thickly packed conifer forests where over 200 bird species and brown bears, wild goats and wolves dwell. The Rodopi Mountains are exceptionally rich in wildflowers, including indigenous violets, tulips and the unique *silivriak* – a fragile white flower said to have sprung up from the blood of Orpheus, the semidivine father of music, after he was torn to pieces by the frenzied Bacchantes.

Despite being sparsely populated, this mountain range named after a Thracian god,

Rhodopa, is dotted with hundreds of tiny villages where life has changed little in centuries. This is particularly so for the numerous, and quite conservative Muslim villages populated by Turks and Pomaks (Slavic Christians who converted to Islam to win benefits during the Ottoman occupation). The Rodopi area fell to the Turks in 1371 and suffered harshly under their rule, the most appalling episode being the massacre at Batak (see p163) in 1876. Today, relations between the various ethnic and religious groups are normal, though Bulgarians are nervous about rising Turkish nationalism here, manifested in low-level vandalism and other provocations, as well as more large-scale political power grabs.

Along with winter skiing, summertime outdoor activities such as hiking, horse riding and caving are all excellent here. The Batak and Dospat Lakes also providing opportunities for boating and fishing. There are over 700 mapped caves in the Rodopi Mountains, the most spectacular being near Trigrad (p162) and Yagodina (p163), though others, such as the partially underwater Golubovitsa (p159), are still being discovered. While the range's average height is only 785m, the highest peak – Mt Golyan Perelik, near Smolyan – rises to 2190m.

CHEPELARE ЧЕПЕЛАРЕ

☎ 03051 / pop 3000 / elevation 1150m

A laid-back, unprepossessing village and ski centre, modest Chepelare plans to link up to the far larger and louder Pamporovo, 6km down the road. In summer, the nearby mountains offer excellent hiking (see the boxed text, p157). Chepelare is supposedly undergoing EU-sponsored beautifications, though little progress is evident, partly because it has fewer old houses than more well-known traditional villages.

Information

The combined post office and telephone centre, near the square, has internet.

Chepelare.com The informative municipal website has ski information.

Hebros Bank (ul Vasil Dechev) About 300m down the main street from the square.

Tourist Information Centre (☎ 2110; tic@infotel .bg; ul Dicho Petrov 1; ⏰ 8.30am-12.30pm & 1.30-6pm) A fairly helpful place 100m up from the square, on a side street, the centre provides detailed brochures about hiking routes, skiing and other activities.

www.orbita.bgcatalog.com Has snow reports, advice and accommodation information for all Bulgarian ski resorts.

Sights

Also called the Cave Museum, the **Museum of Speleology & Karst** (☎ 3051; ul Shina Andreeva 9a; admission 3 lv; ⏰ 9am-noon & 1.30-5pm Mon-Fri) is unique in Bulgaria and, possibly, the Balkans. Minerals, bottled bats, remains of ancient cave-dwelling animals such as lions and bears, are exhibited, along with displays on the Trigrad and Yagodina caves. A tape in English and German gives explanations. The museum's in the Hotel Pesternika building, 200m up from the bus station on the hillside.

At time of writing, a **Museum of Ski & Sport** was scheduled to open, with displays devoted to the history of Chepelare skiing; consult the Tourist Information Centre.

Activities

SKIING

Chepelare is a humbler, more family-friendly place than Bulgaria's big ski resorts. However, it does offer world-class skiing: the two most famous trails, Mechi Chal I (3150m) a black-level, Super Giant Slalom course, and Mechi Chal II (5250m) are among Bulgaria's longest, and have hosted international competitions. Chepelare's three main trails equal 11.4km; a fourth, gently sloping trail is, so the tourist office humorously states, 'suitable for women and children'.

In fact, Chepelare's most famous native is a female athlete: Ekaterina Dafovska, biathlon gold medallist of 1998's Nagano Winter Olympics. Her success prompted local leaders to open an academy for skiing, snowboarding and, oddly enough, table tennis. The school (not for tourists) aims to train future Olympians.

The chairlift 1.5km south on the Pamporovo road, is signposted. At the time of writing, two new chairlifts were being installed. Chepelare also offers 30km of cross-country skiing. Hire gear at **Orion Ski** (☎ /fax 2142), by the lift, though note few instructors are available. Chepelare has a ski factory, and you can buy cheap, good-quality ski gear.

Sleeping & Eating

The tourist offices in Chepelare or Smolyan can book private rooms in Chepelare (from 20 lv per person with shared bathroom). Hotel prices increase significantly in winter.

SOUTHERN BULGARIA

Hotel Phoenix (☎ 3408; ul Murgavets 4; s/d 15/30 lv) About 200m up ul Vasil Dechev from the square, the Phoenix offers simple, spotless rooms with TV, along with a traditional restaurant.

Hotel Savov (☎ 2036; ul Vasil Dechev 7; d/tr/apt from 30/40/50 lv; P) Opposite the Hebros Bank, this comfortable place offers large, airy doubles, and apartments with sitting areas. The restaurant is popular and good.

Hotel Gergana (☎ 4201; ul Hristo Botev 75; d incl breakfast from 30 lv; P) The Gergana, along the Plovdiv road, is a cosy, family-run place with simple, clean rooms. Home-cooked traditional cuisine is served at the hotel restaurant.

More Chepelare hotels, signposted along the Plovdiv–Smolyan road, require private transport to reach.

ourpick Pelelanovska Konak (☎ 2176; ul Dimitar Chichovski 10; mains 5-8 lv; ☼ 11am-1am Mon-Sat) This traditional Rodopean *mehana* may be in the back streets, across the river, but it's well worth seeking out. Tucked inside a little enclosure, it has cosy outdoor seating and a spacious, hunting-lodge interior with pelts and antlers on the walls. The enormous menu, strong on local dishes, includes the 'chef's special' *satch*, a riotous mixture of various meats, cheese and vegetables baked in a clay pot. Service is friendly and attentive.

Getting There & Away

The bus station is across a footbridge, 200m northeast of the square. Buses leave hourly for Smolyan (3 lv, one hour), via Pamporovo. Regular services between Plovdiv (6 lv, 90 minutes) and Madan, and Plovdiv and Smolyan, also stop in Chepelare.

PAMPOROVO ПАМПОРОВО

☎ 3095 / elevation 1650m

Pamporovo (Pam-*por*-ovo), 6km south of Chepelare, is one of Bulgaria's four major ski resorts. As with Bansko, rampant expansion has left the place – full of cranes, stacked building supplies and the skeletons of characterless, identical luxury apartments – looking like one monstrous construction site. However, unlike Bansko, there's no settlement – just a decentralised resort. Pamporovo is increasingly popular and thus more expensive, also expanding deeper into the forests, with almost 30km of new trails connecting Pamporovo with Chepelare (the 35,000 sq km 'Perelik

project') being planned at the time of writing – dismaying local environmentalists.

Although there's good nearby hiking, most of Pamporovo closes in summer. Other nearby villages have more atmospheric accommodation – making Pamporovo only recommendable if you're on a planned ski holiday. Otherwise, you can pass it by without feeling much guilt. The main cultural event for locals, the **Rozhen Folk Festival** (late August) occurs in the Rozhen fields between Pamporovo and Progled.

Orientation

The T-junction of the roads to Smolyan, Chepelare and Devin (via Shiroka Lûka) is Pamporovo's central point. From here, the amoeba-like resort spreads for 4km along several roads. Most hotels, restaurants and shops in remote parts are closed from May to October, but everything around the central Hotel Perelik is open year-round.

Information

Try www.bulgariaski.com for updated snow reports, advice and accommodation information for all Bulgarian ski resorts.

Activities
SKIING

Nestled in Bulgaria's deep south, Pamporovo and Chepelare boast over 250 days of sunshine a year. With significant snowfall between mid-December and mid-April, skiing conditions are often ideal.

Pamporovo's facilities are comparatively new and the slopes well maintained; however, the resort sprawls, so private transport is helpful. In winter, accommodation for independent skiers and travellers is scarce. If you're skiing here, consider cheaper accommodation options in Chepelare (p155), Momchilovtsi (p158), Smolyan (p159) and Shiroka Lûka (p160).

Pamporovo's eight downhill ski runs total 25km, and are complemented by 25km of cross-country trails and four training slopes. At least three new trails are being gouged out of the mountains between Pamporovo and Stoykite. The resort is at 1620m, with the highest trailhead rising to 1937m. Of Pamporovo's original five chairlifts and nine draglifts, a few operate during summer. Chairlifts cost 10/15 lv one way/return and a day pass costs about

---

HIKING IN THE RODOPI MOUNTAINS

Exploring the idyllic, forested region around Chepelare, Smolyan, Shiroka Lŭka and Devin is the high point for nature lovers in the Rodopi region. First, get the English-language *West Rhodopean Region* or *Western Rhodope Mountains* maps (1:100,000) from the tourist offices in Pamporovo, Chepelare or Smolyan. They detail hiking trails of three to five hours, plus five mountain biking routes. Kartografia also has an excellent *Rodopi* map (1:100,000).

Julian Perry's *The Mountains of Bulgaria* describes (but with poor maps) a five- to seven-day trek from Hizha Studenents, near Pamporovo, to Hizha Rodoposki Partizanin, near Hrabrino, about 14km southwest of Plovdiv. *Hizhas* are available.

For shorter hikes, base yourself in Shiroka Lŭka or nearby Devin. Nine marked trails, including one to Chepelare, via Kukuvitsa (two to three hours one way) and another to Mt Golyam Perelik (five to six hours), begin here. Other excellent hikes along marked trails include:

Batak to Hizha Teheran About four hours.

Chepelare to Hizha Igrev About three hours. From there, continue to Shiroka Lŭka (three hours) or Pamporovo (seven hours).

Haskovo to Hizha Aida Twenty-six kilometres west by road (four to five hours).

Pamporovo to Progled An (easy) five-hour return trip across the lovely Rozhen fields.

Smolyan to Hizha Smolyanski Ezera About three hours one way.

SOUTHERN BULGARIA

---

50 lv. Minibuses from the hotels to the lifts are free if you have a lift pass.

Pamporovo offers trails for beginners and ample instructors speaking English or German, plus a children's ski kindergarten. Most instructors charge about 200 lv per person for 12 to 24 hours' group training, spread over six to 12 days.

Over a dozen ski shops rent gear, including the **Sport Shop** (☎ 0888552354) in the Hotel Perelik complex. A full set of equipment costs 40 lv to 60 lv per day. Pamporovo is ideal for snowboarding; visit the popular British-run **Snow Shack** (snowshack_uk@yahoo.co.uk) in the Hotel Markony complex for snowboarding gear and/or training courses.

OTHER ACTIVITIES

In summer, Pamporovo Sports Services, in the Pamporovo Shopping Centre between Hotel Perelik and Hotel Murgavets, arranges **mountain bikes** (6 lv per hour), **hiking guides** (from 15 lv per hour) and **tennis** courts and equipment. Around the central T-junction, **horse riding** is offered (20 lv to 25 lv per hour). For **hiking**, see the boxed text above.

Sleeping & Eating

It's useless describing Pamporovo accommodation in depth, as most foreign visitors come on prearranged package tours, or on day trips from Plovdiv. In winter, the hotels' rates are 25% higher than those quoted here.

Hotel Perelik (☎ 8405; pamporovo@bsbg.net; www .pamporovoresort.org; s/d from 40/50 lv; P ⚷ ⚑) This monolith was being renovated (again) at the time of writing, and will soon offer smarter and more expensive rooms, plus the old facilities (a bowling alley, shops, restaurants and disco).

Hotel Murgavets (☎ 8317; s/d/apt from 60/100/120 lv; P ⚷ ⚑) A giant hotel next to Hotel Perelik, with large comfortable rooms; facilities include a gym, health and beauty centre and kids' playground.

Hotel Finlandia (☎ 8374; s/d from 90/120 lv; P ⚑) The four-star Finlandia has clean, classy rooms plus a nightclub, health centre and ski school with English- and German-speaking instructors; there's also a kindergarten for depositing unnecessary baggage while on the slopes. The price includes compulsory half-board.

Pamporovo's numerous bars, cafés and restaurants offer varied, though inevitably touristy and overpriced food – for authentic Bulgarian cuisine, try the less frequented local villages.

Getting There & Away

The hourly Smolyan–Chepelare buses pass Pamporovo, as do the regular Smolyan–Plovdiv, and Smolyan–Sofia buses. A few daily buses from Sofia go directly to Pamporovo (14 lv, four hours) and up to eight leave from Plovdiv (8 lv, two hours). The bus stop is at the 'Ski Lift No 1' chairlift at the central T-junction.

MOMCHILOVTSI МОМЧИЛОВЦИ
☎ 03023 / pop 3000 / elevation 1100m

Much smaller and more peaceful than Pamporovo, little Momchilovtsi (Mom-*chil*-ov-tsi) occupies a mountainside about 3km up from the main Chepelare–Smolyan road. Several solitude-seeking Bulgarian painters and writers live here, and expensive holiday villas belonging to the Sofia elite are also found in Momchilovtsi. It's an alternative and cheaper base to Chepelare or Pamporovo, and a relaxing place for summer hikes.

The new **Center for Mountain Sport & Tourism Momchilovtsi** (☎ 2823; www.momchilovtsi.hit.bg), on the square, provides local information and assistance for outdoor activities. It finds private rooms and hotel accommodation (from 8 lv and 20 lv per person, respectively). The centre rents ski equipment (15 lv to 18 lv per day) and provides ski instruction (18 lv per hour for individuals, or 15 lv per hour if in a group) as well as free transport to the ski run, 10km away at the **Momchilovtsi Fun Park**. The one ski trail here is elementary, though snowboarders will have more fun on the several jumps.

In summer the centre organises **rock climbing** trips and rents **mountain bikes** (10 lv per day).

If it's closed, the centre can open the **Historical & Ethnographical Museum** (☎ 2272; ul Byalo More), where traditional crafts by local artists and weavers are sold.

Usually sleepy Momchilovtsi comes alive for the four-day celebration of the **Sveti Konstantin & Elena holiday** (21 May).

Several signposted *pensions* are along the main road about 500m south of the square; try the **Rodopchanka Hotel** (☎ 2863; ul Byalo More 40; d/apt 48/72 lv).

Shadravana Restaurant, in the park below the square, offers Bulgarian dishes, and there are a few other cafés around.

Buses between Smolyan's eastern Ustovo bus station (1.40 lv, 45 minutes, 11 daily) and Banite, and Plovdiv and Banite, regularly pass through Momchilovtsi.

SMOLYAN СМОЛЯН
☎ 0301 / pop 34,300 / elevation 1000m

The longest and highest town in Bulgaria, Smolyan is actually an amalgamation of four villages, and the southern Rodopi Mountains'
administrative centre. The steep and forested mountains rise abruptly on its southern flank, lending a lovely backdrop to a town that's otherwise slightly timeworn and gritty. As in most of the Rodopi region, there's a notable Pomak Muslim population here.

Smolyan, first settled by Thracians around 700 BC, is an alternative place to stay for skiing Pamporovo and Chepelare, though certainly not the most beautiful one. It's the transport hub for villages such as Shiroka Lûka and Devin. Smolyan is also a base for exploring the seven **Smolyan Lakes**, the **caves** of Golubovitsa, partially underwater, and Uhlovitsa, with its bizarre rock formations (see the boxed text, opposite).

For **hiking** information, see the boxed text on p157.

Orientation
The 10km-long Smolyan overlaps, from west to east, the villages of Ezerovo, Smolyan, Raikovo and Ustovo. The partially pedestrianised main street, bul Bulgaria, has ATMs, a post office, and cafés and restaurants on its western end. The concrete, and often eerily deserted civic centre complex, is further east, opposite the forlorn Hotel Smolyan; here, too, are the main post office, a couple of banks and a supermarket, café and restaurant.

Information
Regional Association of Rhodope Municipalities (☎ 62 056; bul Bulgaria 14) Near the tourist office; represents the 20 local districts and has local arts and crafts information or organises tours or guides.

Tourist Information Center (☎ 62 530; www.rodopi-bg.com; ⏰ 9am-noon & 1-6pm Mon-Fri, 10am-2pm Sat) Beside the Hotel Kiparis, this very helpful English-speaking centre has plenty of brochures and local information.

Sights
HISTORICAL MUSEUM
Smolyan's **Historical Museum** (☎ 62 727; Dicho Petrov 3; admission 5 lv; ⏰ 9am-noon & 1-5pm Mon-Sat), up behind the civic centre, has exhibits including Palaeolithic artefacts and Thracian armour and weaponry. Rodopi weaving and woodcarving, plus numerous traditional musical instruments and folk costumes (most notably the fantastical Kuker outfits worn at New Year celebrations) are also shown. Upstairs contains photos and models of traditional buildings.

SOUTHERN BULGARIA

SMOLYAN'S MYSTERIOUS CAVES

In ancient times, the road to hell was paved with water; so, too, in today's Bulgaria. Although not exactly replicating the voyage to Hades along the River Styx, the journey into the recently discovered **Golubovitsa Cave** is a thrilling and similarly aquatic one. Located 3km south of Uhlovitsa Cave (see below), off the road between Smolyan and Mogilitsa, the cave is accessible by boat, as the first 25m or so is completely underwater. After that, you walk, accompanied by lantern and a guide, and for daredevils, there's even a way down by rope.

Golubovitsa tours are arranged by the **Marsalitsa Club** (mursalitsa@abv.beg; Mogilitsa village). Contact either Aleksei Kodzhebashev (☎ 0887630274) or Aleksander Inev (☎ 0889293070) to arrange a guided tour, which costs 14 lv per person, and includes boots, lanterns and other equipment (including the boat). See the English- and Bulgarian-language website www.arda-tour. org for photos and more information.

The more established **Uhlovitsa Cave** (admission 4 lv; ⏲ 10am-4pm daily summer, Wed-Sun winter), about 3km northeast of Mogilitsa, boasts numerous waterfalls (most spectacular in winter) and some bizarre formations, but requires private transport; check with the Marsalitsa Club or Smolyan Tourist Information Center for more details.

SMOLYAN ART GALLERY

Opposite the museum, the **Art Gallery** (☎ 62 328; Dicho Petrov 7; admission 5 lv; ⏲ 9am-noon & 1.30-5pm Tue-Sun) boasts some 1800 paintings, sketches and sculptures by local, national and foreign artists.

PLANETARIUM

Bulgaria's biggest **planetarium** (☎ 83 074; bul Bulgaria 20; admission 5 lv), about 200m west of Hotel Smolyan, offers a spectacular show (35 to 40 minutes) with commentary in English, French or German at 2pm from Monday to Saturday, and in Bulgarian at 3pm from Monday to Saturday, and Sunday at 11am and 3pm. The foreign-language shows are for groups of five or more; otherwise, you'll pay 15 lv for a solo viewing.

Sleeping

The tourist office finds private rooms (about 22 lv per person).

Three Fir Trees House (☎ 38 228; dreitannen@mbox .digsys.bg; ul Srednogorec 1; s/d 24/34 lv; 🖳) This place is 200m east of the main bus station, with well-maintained rooms. It's signposted, down the steps from bul Bulgaria. Bathrooms are shared. There's an excellent, varied breakfast (5 lv), and the helpful, multilingual owner arranges tours and rental cars, plus a cheap laundry service.

Hotel Babylon (☎ /fax 63 268; ul Han Presian 22; d/tw/apt 36/52/70 lv) This central place offers large, two-room apartments with comfortable lounge, plus a downstairs bar and res-taurant. It's behind the little park, above bul Bulgaria.

Hotel Smolyan (☎ 62 053; www.hotelsmolyan.com; bul Bulgaria 3; s/d/apt from 36/52/80 lv; P 🖳) This antiquated ex-communist hotel facing the civic centre has clean but forlorn rooms; some have balconies overlooking Smolyan's lovely forests.

Hotel Kiparis A (☎ 64 040; www.hotelkiparis.com; bul Bulgaria 3a; s/d/apt 42/62/102 lv) A relatively new hotel located between the tourist office and Hotel Smolyan, it's a vast improvement on its neighbour with bright, modern rooms.

Eating & Drinking

Starata Kâshta (ul Studenska 2; mains 4-7 lv; ⏲ 4.30pm-2am) Also known as the Pamporovata Kâshta, this place offers a short menu of grills and salads. The attractive National Revival–style house (built in 1840) has a few rough-hewn, log cabin–style outdoor tables and benches. It's up the steps from bul Bulgaria.

Rodopski Kat (bul Bulgaria 3; mains 5-8 lv; ⏲ 7am-2am) This new restaurant, wedged between the Hotel Smolyan and Hotel Kiparis, is excellent for traditional Rodopean fare.

Riben Dar (☎ 63 220; ul Snezhanka 16; mains 6-10 lv) In the western neighbourhood of Nevyasta, this is the place for delicious fresh fish, such as Rodopi Mountain trout. Take a taxi (3 lv to 5 lv).

Club Venus (bul Bulgaria 11; ⏲ 24hr) Sleepy Smolyan's best entertainment spot, the Venus is popular at night, and serves good food. There's a wi-fi hotspot, too.

Getting There & Away

Most buses to/from Smolyan use the **main bus station** (☎ 63 104; bul Bulgaria) at Smolyan's western end. Four daily buses serve Sofia (18 lv, 3½ hours) and hourly buses serve Plovdiv (11 lv, 2½ to three hours), via Chepelare (3 lv, one hour) and Pamporovo (2 lv, 30 minutes). From this station, buses also serve Shiroka Lûka and Devin (4.50 lv, 90 minutes, three to four daily), for Trigrad and Yagodina Caves.

From near the station, local buses 2 and 3 (0.60 lv, every 20 minutes) serve the centre /Hotel Smolyan. Walk left out of the station and turn left up a double set of stairs; after 50m, you'll see the stop on the left. The taxi rank is further down the street. By taxi, it's around 2.50 lv to the Hotel Smolyan/Tourist Information Center.

Alternatively, if you're heading out on the Smolyan–Pamporovo–Chepelare–Plovdiv road, minibuses conveniently go from Hotel Smolyan's car park – saving you the trip back to the bus station. They leave every hour on the hour between 8am and 5pm.

Some 10km east, the **Ustovo bus station** (☎ 64 585; ul Trakia) serves less-visited eastern villages such as Momchilovtsi (1.40 lv, 45 minutes), as well as Kardzhali (9 lv, four hours, two daily). Local buses 3, 8, 9, 11, 14 and 18 travel between the main bus station and Ustovo station, via the Hotel Smolyan. The ticket offices at both stations close for lunch from 12.30pm to 1.30pm and, though kind, the workers don't speak English.

SHIROKA LÛKA ШИРОКА ЛЪКА
☎ 03030 / pop 1500

Tiny Shiroka Lûka, hugging the forested road between Smolyan and Devin, is famed for its three arching bridges and 19th-century National Revival homes. This hamlet has few services, but does have a **tourist office** (☎ 233; www.rhodope.net; ☼ 9am-5pm) near the square, providing general information and maps, including the useful *Western Rhodope Mountains* map (1:100,000). Staff can book private rooms in Shiroka Lûka and surrounding villages, such as tiny Gela (7km north), legendary birthplace of Orpheus. For local hiking information, see the boxed text on p157.

The village's sites include the **Church of the Assumption**, built in less than 40 days in 1834. Its uproarious outdoor fresco depicts a funeral procession followed by dancing demons; more sedate icons and murals are inside,

with the iconostasis chronicling the story of Adam and Eve. The **Ethnographical Museum** in the Kalenjievi Kâshta house generally opens only for organised bus tours.

Shiroka Lûka is renowned for traditional Rodopean music; see the week-long **music festival** in mid-April. The **Kukeri** (first Sunday in March) is a classic seasonal festival with likely pagan roots, when locals don frightening masks, bells and elaborate costumes for a spring cleaning of evil spirits.

The local tourist office, and the Smolyan and Chepelare ones, books private rooms in Shiroka Lûka.

Guesthouse Vasilka (☎ 666; sharkov@hotmail .com; r from 30 lv; **P**), at the village's peak, offers simple rooms with balconies and home-cooked meals.

Hotel Margarita (☎ 693; d/apt incl breakfast from 40/60 lv; **P**) is along the main road west of the creek, and has fine rooms.

Restaurant Shiroka Lûka (☎ 318; mains 4-8 lv; ☼ 11am-midnight Mon-Sat), in the centre, is the village's only real restaurant, but the food doesn't match the idyllic surroundings.

Buses between Smolyan and Devin pass six to eight times daily. Alternatively, take a taxi from Devin (around 20 lv).

DEVIN ДЕВИН
☎ 03041

One of Bulgaria's best spa towns, placid Devin is somewhat dated though it does offer solitude, services and one or two café-bars. Still, it's the kind of place where unworried mothers leave their baby carriages outside the shop while browsing, and the only noise you'll hear at night is the far-off baying of hounds.

Devin's famous for producing Bulgaria's premier brand of bottled mineral water, and for its balneological resort; indeed, plenty of wealthy Sofians (driven in black Jeeps with tinted windows) frequently come for discreet, five-star luxury treatment. However, the slightly faded town hardly resembles a resort, and you can take in the waters inexpensively outdoors, hike the lovely local eco-path and stay in budget accommodation. Devin also makes a handy base for visiting nearby caves.

Information

Even if the municipal tourist office reopens someday, you're best off heading straight to **Travel Escape** (☎ 2411, 0896734204; cnr ul Osvobozhdenie

& ul Orpheas), run by the very helpful and experienced Irina Ilieva, who converses in five languages. Irina both finds local private accommodation and organises local outdoors activities (see right).

The **Internet Club** (ul Orfei), in the House of Culture, has slow connections.

A couple of ATMs are along the main street, others by the House of Culture and Orpheas Spa & Resort.

Sights & Activities

A comically gruff reception awaits visitors at the little **Devin Museum** (ul Orfei; admission 1 lv; 10am-12.30pm & 1.30-5.30pm Mon-Sat), which exhibits Rodopi folk arts and crafts, ancient and medieval coins, and colourful minerals from local mountains. Prominently positioned reproductions of salacious 19th-century paintings depict wicked Turks whipping Bulgarian women, hurling Bulgarians babies and carrying off slaves. The roomful of traditional implements and machinery, however, is quite interesting, and also displays the *gayda* (Balkan bagpipe) of Bai Mihail (see the boxed text, p162). In winter the museum operates only in afternoons.

The belltower of the **Church of Sveti Duh** (Church of the Holy Spirit), built in 1937, tolls out the hours from high over the houses of Devin. The church is not particularly traditional, but contains many icons and a wood-burning stove.

If you seek the Devin spa experience, but don't want to pay at the big hotels, bathe with the locals at the outdoor **mineral baths** (5 lv per person), 4km west of town in a gorgeous wooded setting between steep hills. Boasting a large bath and a smaller one for kids, this well-kept facility includes a café and nearby restaurant. There's a sand volleyball court and inexpensive massages are available. In summer, the baths work 24 hours, in winter, according to demand. To go by taxi, ask for *Struilitsa Parking* (the car park of the baths). The 10-minute trip costs 3 lv.

Continue 30 seconds down the road, leaving the baths on your left, to the **Devin eco-path**. Part of the EU-funded Beautiful Bulgaria project, this lovely trail follows the Vacha River through lush countryside, eventually winding uphill into the mountain. A sort of triangular loop, beginning and ending at the baths, takes in the ruined **Devinsko Kale** (Devin Castle), where locals once made a desperate

last stand against the Turkish onslaught. The whole hike takes about three hours. There are a couple of picnic tables along the way.

Irina Ilieva of **Travel Escape** can arrange guided **hiking** and **caving** tours. Multiday **horse riding** to the Greek border, with stopovers in mountain huts along the way, is another of the enjoyable local activities arranged here. Irina has info on an intriguing nearby traditional farm, just opening at the time of writing, and on how to obtain the rare, endemic *mursalski* tea – racily called the 'Bulgarian Viagra'.

Sleeping

Private rooms (from 15 lv per person) can be arranged by Irina Ilieva of **Travel Escape** (2411, 0896734204; cnr ul Osvobozhdenie & ul Orpheas; 9am-5pm).

Paunovata Kushta (2628; paunovatakashta@vbs_bg.com; ul Stara Planina 3; s/d 20/30 lv) This is a new guesthouse, 100m up the road going immediately left after the bus station, then up the hill and over the bridge. It has clean and comfortable rooms; ring ahead as there's not always someone there.

Hotel Elite (2240; ul Undola 2; s/d/apt 50/70/80 lv;) On the central pedestrian street, the Elite has large, well-kept rooms with gleaming modern bathrooms; doubles have bathtubs. The basement mini-spa includes sauna, Jacuzzi and massage rooms.

Villa Ismena (4872; fax 3917; ul Goritsa 441; s/d/apt 55/85/160 lv;) At the top of a steep road, the signposted Ismena is a modern villa offering quality rooms with smart décor, balconies and sparkling bathrooms. The restaurant's terrace has views, and the modest spa centre does various therapeutic programmes.

Spa Hotel Devin (2513; www.spadevin.com; ul Druzhba 2; s/d/apt from 66/110/160 lv;) One of Devin's most popular places, this hotel has breezy and cheerful rooms, a very good restaurant (see p162), and arguably offers therapeutic treatments equal to or better than the snazzier (and much pricier) new five-star Orpheus. The hydrotherapy centre includes swimming pools, Jacuzzis and various therapeutic and 'antistress' programmes. There's a café-*sladkarnitsa* (sweet shop) and casino. During summer, various outdoors activities are organised.

Orpheus Spa & Resort (2041; fax 6245; www.orpheus-spa.com; Tzvetan Zangov 14; s/d/ste 116/137/214 lv) Sofia's upper strata finds itself drawn as if by

SOUTHERN BULGARIA

magnetic attraction to this giant gingerbread mansion, its centre dominated by a gigantic pool over which an enormous faux crystal improbably rises. Fortunately, the wealthy guests' desire for discretion means the hotel, behind the pedestrian mall, has not ruined Devin's solitude. Rooms are luxurious, and the spa centre revels in exotic treatments involving gold dust, diamonds and caviar. There's a fitness centre, Jacuzzi, pool, tennis courts and a football pitch. The hotel's two restaurants include a lavishly decorated Turkish one (see below).

Eating & Drinking

Oriental Restaurant (☎ 2041; fax 6245; www.orpheus -spa.com; Tzvetan Zangov 14) In the Orpheus resort, the Oriental serves Turkish kebabs and is decorated with the requisite couches, pillows and gauze.

Complex Struilitsa (☎ 0888838971; mains 5-7 lv; ☺ 10.30am-midnight) This restaurant by the public mineral baths is up a short trail that veers left above the car park, in the forest. It does Bulgarian grills and salads and has a lovely terrace.

Bulgarsko Selo Restaurant (☎ 2513; www.spadevin .com; ul Druzhba; mains 7-15 lv; ☺ 8am-midnight) In the Spa Hotel Devin, this place does reasonably priced meat dishes, and more expensive regional specialities. The cosy folk décor is enhanced by the open oven, where you can watch the chef roasting huge, crunchy slabs of bread. The restaurant is also the definite winner of the prize for most hysterical English-language entrée title – 'girl spittle'.

In town, the Royal Café, within the unmissable obshtina (municipality) building, is good for a drink. The nightclub below it attracts a fairly juvenile crowd.

Getting There & Away

From **Devin bus station** (☎ 2077) buses serve Smolyan (4.60 lv, 1½ hours, six daily), Plovdiv (7 lv, three hours, four daily) and Yagodina (3.80 lv, 40 minutes, 8am Monday to Saturday). A daily bus to Sofia (12 lv, four hours) leaves at 6.45am. Alternatively, catch a bus to Plovdiv, which has numerous bus and train connections to the capital. All Smolyan-bound buses stop in Shiroka Lûka.

AROUND DEVIN
The Caves of Trigrad & Yagodina

The most accessible and developed Rodopi caves are south of Devin, near Trigrad and Yagodina. Admission to both caves includes a guided tour, in Bulgarian only.

The **Trigrad Cave** (☎ 0889052208; admission 3 lv; ☺ 9am-5pm May-Sep, shorter hr rest of year), also called the Devil's Throat Cave (Dyavolskoto Gurlo Peshtera) has extensive and speleologically significant grottoes. The mandatory, 20-minute guided tour requires three or four tourists; you can stay longer, under the caretaker's supervision. As you descend, you can hear (but unfortunately not see) a 45m-high waterfall. Exiting involves a somewhat daunting set of steep steps. You may see a (harmless) bat or two flitting about.

Trigrad village is 2.3km south of the road from the cave entrance. **Guesthouse Silivryak**

THE ENCHANTED PIPE OF BAI MIHAIL

Near the end of WWI, a young man from Chepelare named Mihail was dispatched to the front, along with six fellow Rodopean friends. Bulgaria had been at war almost continuously for six years, and the exhausted, dismayed young men resolved to desert. However, they were caught by the military police, and condemned to death for treason.

When told to make his final request before being executed, Mihail said: 'Just bring me my *gayda* so I can play one last song.' The goatskin bagpipe was duly brought, and Mihail struck up a traditional old Rodopi tune. When the homesick, weeping soldiers started to sing along, the commander, realising he'd have a mutiny on his hands if he went through with the executions, ordered the sentences to be commuted. 'Bai' (an affectionate Rodopi term, translated roughly as 'uncle') Mihail went on to live out the rest of his long and distinguished life in Devin, as one of the leading local personalities (and musicians) of this quiet mountain settlement.

Today, the memory of this beloved Rodopi elder is preserved in popular legends and tales. And, while it's no longer played, the enchanted pipe of Bai Mihail can still be seen, in a glass case at the Devin Museum.

SOUTHERN BULGARIA

(☎ 03040-220; s/d 15/30 lv; P), above the square, has six cosy rooms, and the owner, Kosta Hadjiiski, is the cave boss, and thus a knowledgeable and experienced caver. Devin and Smolyan provide more accommodation options; alternatively, try the Muslim village, Borino, which has 17 daily buses to Devin (2.50 lv, 30 minutes). The friendly **Family-Hotel Royal** (☎ 03042-2830; s/d from 10/20 lv; P) is the best Borino option. From Trigrad, you can hike to Yagodina (about 2½ hours).

The spectacular, 8km **Yagodina Cave** (☎ 03419-200; admission 4 lv; ☽ 9am-5pm May-Sep, shorter hr rest of yr) is the longest known Rodopi cave and, with its many abysses and labyrinthine tunnels, also one of Bulgaria's deepest. The 45-minute tour highlights the remarkable stalagmites and stalactites, which resemble curtains, and mentions the Neolithic settlers who lived here 8000 years ago. Visitor numbers permitting, tours leave on the hour every hour between 9am and 4pm, except at midday. From 1 October to 1 May, at least six visitors are required for the tour; otherwise, you pay 15 lv. In summer, 10 visitors (or 25 lv) are required. Remember that no matter how hot it may be, caves are chilly, so pack extra clothes.

Family-Hotel Yagodina (☎ 03419-310; s/d from 15/30 lv; P) is a small, modern place with comfortable, clean rooms and balconies. The cave is 6.4km south of the turn-off along the Smolyan–Dospat road, and 3km south of Yagodina.

You can hike to Trigrad or ask for directions in Yagodina to the **South Rodopi Ecotrail**; contact the tourist office in **Smolyan** (☎ 0301-62 530) or **Shiroka Lûka** (☎ 03030-233) for details.

BATAK БАТАК
☎ 03553 / pop 4500
Although Batak is most famous in modern Bulgarian lore for its bloody history (see the boxed text, right), this quiet, depressed town is today mostly known for the Batak Lake, great for summertime fishing and swimming. Boats can be rented near Hotel Panorama, and local hiking information is given in the boxed text on p157.

Sights
The Church of Sveti Nedelya, the Ethnological Museum and the History Museum are Batak's major (and adjacent) attractions. The ticket costs 2 lv (admission free on Thursday). Visit

THE MASSACRE AT BATAK
During the 1876 April Uprising most of the population of Batak fought against the Turks under the leadership of Peter Goranov. They successfully held the Turks at bay for nine days before the aggressors eventually gained control. In brutal retaliation, the Turks burned down the village and massacred almost every citizen (between 5000 and 6000 people). The massacre was reported in the English press and (eventually) acknowledged and denounced by the British government. It was the catalyst for the Russo-Turkish War that started a year later.

the History Museum first to ensure the other two are unlocked.

On the square, the **History Museum** (☎ 2339; pl Osvodozhenie; ☽ 9am-noon & 2-5pm Mon-Sat) contains graphic displays about the 1876 April Uprising, the Batak Massacre and the Russo-Turkish War. The downstairs crypt lists locals who fought the Turks.

The **Church of Sveti Nedelya** (☽ 9am-noon & 2-6pm Tue-Sat), built in 1813, was the final refuge for 2000 locals who fought the Turks in 1876. Signs of the subsequent massacre, such as bullet holes and a macabre, half-covered tomb with dozens of skulls, are gruesomely evident. The **Ethnological Museum** (☽ 9am-noon & 2-6pm Tue-Sat), one of Batak's few National Revival–period houses, contains late-19th-century costumes.

Sleeping & Eating
Batak itself has no hotels, but several line the lake's southwestern shore. The gigantic **International Youth Tourist Centre** (☎ 3385; s/d/apt incl breakfast 30/40/50 lv; P ⚥), also known as the Orbita Hotel, has tennis and basketball courts, rents bikes and organises excursions.

These hotels, and several cafés and restaurants, line the 1.2km-long access road, which starts about 7km west of Batak along the Rakitovo road. The larger hotels are open year-round, but some cafés and restaurants only operate on weekends, especially during winter.

Getting There & Away
Four daily buses connect Batak with Plovdiv. The three daily buses between Batak and Velingrad pass the turn-off to the lake.

Central Bulgaria

Bulgaria's central heartland, divided in two by the rolling Stara Planina mountain range, is the place of greatest importance to the country's turbulent modern history and the people and events that shaped the nation. Reminders of this past abound in gorgeous towns such as Lovech and Koprivshtitsa, filled with National Revival–period architecture, and at sites of key military victories such as the Shipka Pass. Stunning artistic achievements including the vivid church frescoes of the monasteries at Dryanovo and Troyan and the incredibly detailed masterwork of the 19th-century Tryavna school of woodcarvers attest to the vitality of Bulgarian tradition, and the region's innumerable house-museums preserve the spirit (and wonderful worldly goods) of the freedom fighters and other eminent Bulgarians of yesteryear.

The natural beauty of central Bulgaria, which can be experienced through hiking, climbing, caving, horseback riding and other outdoor activities, has everything to do with its mountain ranges – the Stara Planina and the Sredna Gora, sprawling just to the southeast – and the waterfalls, cliffs, caves and rivers that run through them. At the same time, the lowlands beckon with romantic locales such as the Valley of Roses, near Kazanlåk, long famous for its rose oil production.

For many visitors, however, the distilled essence of the central Bulgaria experience comes down to one place: Veliko Târnovo, the magnificent former capital of the Bulgarian tsars, built along rolling hills and bisected by a river, with one of the most impressive fortresses in Europe standing proudly over it. Târnovo's exuberant existence as host to Bulgaria's second-largest university also allows it to boast the best nightlife in central Bulgaria.

HIGHLIGHTS

- **Magical atmosphere**
  Absorb the fairy-tale castle, churches and old quarters of Veliko Târnovo (p170)

- **Powerful paintings**
  See the frescoes of legendary Zahari Zograf at Troyan Monastery (p190)

- **Age-old artistry**
  Marvel at the hand-carved wood iconostases of the 'Tryavna school' in the pretty town of Tryavna (p183)

- **Mountain meandering**
  Hike Bulgaria's grand 'old mountains' – Stara Planina (p188)

- **Pure Balkans**
  Dive into the dusty, garrulous open market in ethnically mixed Kazanlåk (p198)

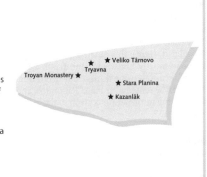

SHUMEN ШУМЕН
☎ 054 / pop 86,660

There's an awful lot of concrete in Shumen, but it does make its own beer, Shumensko Pivo. Not only that, this somewhat faded but friendly industrial city full of communist memorials is crowned by a striking medieval fortress, and has a surprisingly wide range of eateries and drinking spots. Several museums, a park and a lengthy pedestrian mall where the locals stroll and sip coffee round out the local attractions.

Recent additions on the sleeping scene have also brought fancier, though still quite affordable, accommodation to town, making Shumen an even more comfortable base for day trips to the towns of Veliki Preslav, Madara (p169) and even Kotel (p209). The city's location, at the base of a low spur of the Stara Planina ranges, about halfway between the Black Sea coast and the Danube, also means it's within a couple of hours' drive of several unique destinations.

For information on local winery tours, see p66.

History
Thracians and then Romans originally settled and fortified Shumen. After the migration of the Turkic Bulgars in the 6th century, nearby Veliki Preslav and Pliska became the centres of the medieval Bulgarian kingdom. In 1388, the Ottomans captured Shumen, renaming it Chumla. It became an important market town and, in the final days of Ottoman domination, part of the Turks' strategic quadrangle (along with Ruse, Silistra and Varna) of towns fortified to defend against Russian advances in 1877. Reminders of Ottoman multi-ethnicity remain with Shumen's minority Jewish, Armenian and Muslim communities.

Orientation
The bus station and adjacent train station are at Shumen's eastern end. The long pedestrian mall, bul Slavyanski, stretches from the city park to the main square, pl Osvobozhdenie. Most services, cafés and restaurants are on or around the mall and square.

Information
Biochim Commercial Bank (bul Slavyanski)

Helikon (☎ 800 103; bul Slavyanski 88; ☷ 9am-8pm) Has a few English-language books on Bulgaria and maps.

Internet Café (ul Hristo Botev)

Post office (pl Osvobozhdenie; ☷ 7am-10pm Mon-Fri)

SG Ekspres Bank (pl Osvobozhdenie; ☷ 8.30am-4.30pm Mon-Fri) Has an ATM and does Western Union money transfers.

Telephone centre Inside the post office.

Unicredit Bulbank (bul Slavyanski; ☷ 8am-6pm Mon-Fri)

United Bulgarian Bank (ul Tsar Osvoboditel)

Sights
SHUMEN FORTRESS
Towering over the city from a steep hillside, the **Shumen Fortress** (☎ 858 051; adult/student 3/1.50 lv; ☷ 8am-7pm Apr-Oct, 8.30am-5pm Nov-Mar) dates originally to the early Iron Age. It was augmented and reinforced by the Thracians in the 5th century BC, and between the 2nd and 4th centuries AD, the Romans added towers and more walls. It was again fortified later on by the Byzantines, who made it an important garrison. During the Second Bulgarian Empire (1185–1396), the fortress was one of northeast Bulgaria's most significant settlements, renowned for its pottery and metalwork. However, invading Ottomans in the late 14th century burnt and looted the fortress.

Wandering the fortress is fun, with notice boards dotted around the site. A yellowing information booklet (2 lv) is also available at the gate. The fortress is about 5.5km up from the mosque. A taxi costs about 3.50 lv one way.

From the fortress entrance, a 3km path leads to the gigantic Creators of the Bulgarian State Monument, which then brings you to the city centre.

CREATORS OF THE BULGARIAN STATE MONUMENT
This massive, Soviet-era hilltop monument was built in 1981 to commemorate the First Bulgarian Empire's 1300th anniversary. To get here on foot, climb the staircase behind the History Museum. The 3km path leads from the equally communist **Partisan's Monument**. The circuitous 5km road going there starts along ul Sv Karel Shkorpil at the History Museum. Go by taxi (3.50 lv one way), and then just walk back down the steps leading to the city centre.

Shumen's **Information Centre** (☎ 852 598; admission 3 lv; ☷ 8.30am-5pm winter, 8am-7pm summer), about 300m from the Creators of the Bulgarian State Monument, has information about the structure and surrounding flora. A 3km path passes the Information Centre and car park, finishing at Shumen Fortress.

CENTRAL BULGARIA

CENTRAL BULGARIA

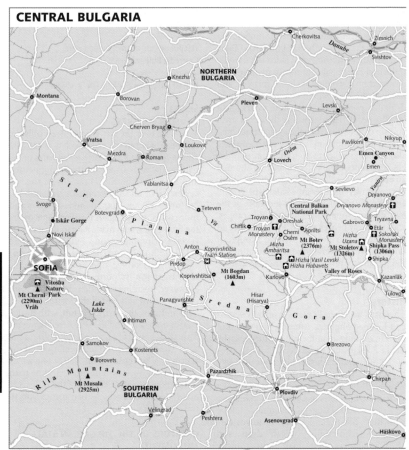

CENTRAL BULGARIA

TOMBUL MOSQUE

Arguably Bulgaria's most beautiful mosque, and definitely the largest still in use, Shumen's **Tombul Mosque** (☎ 856 823; ul Doiran; admission 2 lv; ☻ 9am-6pm) was built in 1744. Also called the Sherif Halili Pasha Mosque, its Turkish nickname, *tombul* (plump) refers to the shape of its 25m-high dome. The 40m-high minaret has 99 steps. According to local Muslim belief, the courtyard fountain gushes sacred water. An informative leaflet (in English and French) is available.

The ruins of the **Bezisten**, a 16th-century Turkish covered market, are just down the road from the mosque; however, they are closed for renovations (at time of research, no completion date could be found).

HISTORY MUSEUM

This brick **museum** (☎ 857 487; bul Slavyanski 17; admission 2 lv; ☻ 9am-5pm Mon-Fri) on the main road exhibits numerous Thracian and Roman artefacts from Madara, Veliki Preslav and Pliska. Ancient coins, icons and a scale model of the Shumen Fortress as it was in its heyday are also on display.

MUSEUM COMPLEX OF PANCHO VLADIGEROV

One of several National Revival and early-20th-century baroque houses dotted along the cobblestone western section of ul Tsar Osvoboditel is the **Museum Complex of Pancho Vladigerov** (☎ 852 123; ul Tsar Osvoboditel 136; admission 1.50 lv; ☻ 9am-5pm Mon-Fri), commemorating

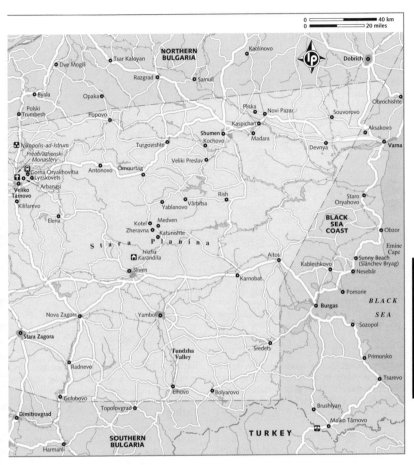

CENTRAL BULGARIA

Bulgaria's most renowned composer and pianist. The handsome structures include a library, set around a shady courtyard garden.

PRIPODEN PARK

Also known as Kyoshkovete Park, this large, 3930-hectare park on Shumen's western edge has some modest, shaded **hiking trails**. You'll see and hear the humming of the city's most famous product being made at the nearby Shumensko Pivo Brewery.

Festivals & Events

Days of Shumen Cultural Festival Mid-May
Folklore Festival August
Watermelon Festival Last Sunday in August

Sleeping

Hotel Pazara (☎ 0887292756; ul Maritsa 15; d 30-40 lv; ✗) The plain Pazara, just north of bul Simeon Veliki, is simply a set of clean but characterless rooms (some with shared bathrooms), but nothing else. It's a 10-minute walk from pl Osvobozhdenie. When on ul Maritsa, look above Bistro Stives (you'll see the Coke sign), go in through the gates and take the staircase up.

Hotel Madara (☎ 800 180; fax 877 078; pl Osvobozhdenie; s/d 30/40 lv) Rearing up from the far end of the square, the monstrous Madara is a communist relic with very basic rooms.

Acktion Center Complex (☎ 801 081; www.acktion center.com; ul Vasil Drumev 12; s/d/apt 38/42/68 lv) Surprisingly situated right in the centre, the

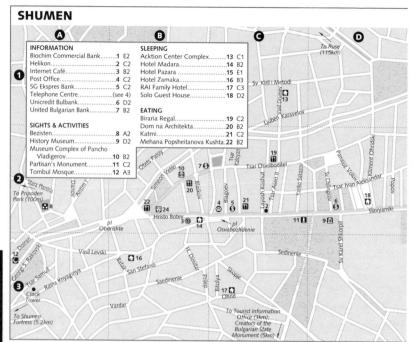

SHUMEN

INFORMATION	
Biochim Commercial Bank	1 E2
Helikon	2 C2
Internet Café	3 B2
Post Office	4 C2
SG Ekspres Bank	5 C2
Telephone Centre	(see 4)
Unicredit Bulbank	6 D2
United Bulgarian Bank	7 B2

SIGHTS & ACTIVITIES	
Bezisten	8 A2
History Museum	9 D2
Museum Complex of Pancho Vladigerov	10 B2
Partisan's Monument	11 C2
Tombul Mosque	12 A3

SLEEPING	
Acktion Center Complex	13 C1
Hotel Madara	14 B2
Hotel Pazara	15 E1
Hotel Zamaka	16 B3
RAI Family Hotel	17 C3
Solo Guest House	18 D2

EATING	
Biraria Regal	19 C2
Dom na Architekta	20 B2
Katmi	21 C2
Mehana Popsheitanova Kushta	22 B2

Acktion Center has 11 rooms and five apartments, all done in a snazzy modern style, which management swears is Italian. With facilities like a manicurist, hairdresser and cosmetics salon, it appeals to those requiring some pampering.

Solo Guest House (☎ 981 571; www.hotelsolo-bg.com; ul Panaiot Volov 2; s/d 40/50 lv) This brand new guesthouse has an excellent central location and well-kept rooms with all mod cons and room service. Although it's pitched at business travellers, Solo's reasonable rates means it's also a nice find for those travelling, well, solo.

RAI Family Hotel (☎ 802 670; www.hotel-rai.eu; ul Ohrid 26a; s/d/apt 40/55/85 lv) Another new hotel, the RAI has a quiet setting near the Shumensko Plato Nature Park. Rooms are spacious and well done, with all amenities including hydromassage showers, a fitness centre and a solarium.

Hotel Zamaka (☎ 800 409; www.zamakbg.com; ul Vasil Levski 17; s/d/apt 40/60/85 lv) This lovely new hotel in a quiet residential neighbourhood just west from the main square has friendly staff and cosy rooms, set around a garden courtyard with a traditional restaurant. As

with the Solo, décor does not astonish but is modern, clean and well kept. All expected amenities, including wireless internet.

Eating

Shumen's best traditional restaurants are located along ul Tsar Osvoboditel, near the main square.

Katmi (pl Osvobozhdenie 12; pancakes 2 lv; ⏲ 7.30am-8pm) This local take-away institution, off a side entrance on the square, offers delicious *palachinki* (pancakes) – much better than the usual Balkan crepe – with a choice of 122 different combinations. A pancake with all-natural blueberry and strawberry jam is especially tasty.

Mehana Popsheitanova Kushta (☎ 802 222; ul Tsar Osvoboditel 158; mains 4-7 lv; ⏲ 11am-2am) This wood-framed traditional restaurant has big outdoor benches and big portions, too. Try the chicken *shishle* 'special' (skewered chicken interspersed with cooked red peppers, onions, tomatoes and a little mushroom on the side).

Biraria Regal (☎ 802 301; ul Tsar Osvoboditel 108; mains 5-7 lv; ⏲ 8am-2am) Like the Dom na Architekta,

DRINKING
10th Town Café.....................23 E2

ENTERTAINMENT
Biraria Guinness....................24 B2
Club Retro.............................25 F2
Nightclub Colosseum.............26 E1

TRANSPORT
Bus Station............................27 F2

CENTRAL BULGARIA

café offers that relative rarity in the Balkans, a room for nonsmokers, plus a summer garden.

Club Retro (☎ 832 742; City Park; ☒ 8am-1am) This café in the park is good for a relaxing coffee by day, or for cocktails at night. There's salsa dancing on Fridays.

Nightclub Colosseum (☎ 830 444; ul Simeon Veliki; admission 2 lv; ☒ 10pm-4am Mon-Sat) Drunken Bulgarians, aerosol cans and a lighter might seem a dangerous combination, but there are even hotter things besides 6ft-high flames inside this big student nightclub. Different theme nights range from student nights to DJ parties and retro.

Getting There & Away

From the **bus station** (☎ 830 890; ul Rilski Pohod), buses go to Burgas (13 lv, three hours, four daily), Ruse (7 lv, two hours, three daily), Dobrich (13 lv, two hours, four daily), Silistra (6 lv, 2½ hours, three daily), Veliko Târnovo (11 lv, two hours, several daily), Madara (1.50 lv, 20 minutes, five daily) and Veliki Preslav (1 lv to 1.30 lv, 30 to 60 minutes, three daily). There are also buses to Sofia (21 lv, six hours, hourly) and Varna (8 lv, 1½ hours, nine daily). Private buses, such as those operated by **Etap Adress** (☎ 830 670), also stop in Shumen on the route between Sofia and Varna.

From the **train station** (☎ 860 155; pl Garov) daily trains (including one express) go to Varna (3.90 lv, two hours, nine daily), and fast trains serve Sofia (10.70 lv, four to seven hours, two daily). There are services to both Ruse (7 lv, three hours, daily) and Plovdiv (13 lv, six hours, daily). A couple of trains stop at Madara. The station has a **left-luggage office** (☒ 24hr) inside.

Taxis wait outside both the bus and train stations, and are easy to find in town.

this traditional *mehana* (tavern) further east on ul Tsar Osvoboditel enjoys a leafy garden setting and offers a good selection of grills and salads.

Dom na Architekta (☎ 088938585; ul Tsar Osvoboditel 145; mains 5-8 lv; ☒ 8am-1am) This wood-and-stone traditional tavern has great Bulgarian specialities, served in a balmy back garden in summer, moving indoors in front of a crackling fire in winter.

Drinking & Entertainment

Numerous good cafés line the leafy pedestrian mall of ul Slavyanski; other popular places off this main strip are listed following.

Biraria Guinness (☎ 872 218; ul Hristo Botev 18; ☒ 10am-5am Mon-Fri, 5pm-5am Sat & Sun) This beer hall across from Mehana Popsheitanova Kushta is a popular nightspot with locals, going well into the wee hours.

10th Town Café (☎ 0899838344; ul Tsar Osvoboditel 53; ☒ 7am-midnight Mon-Fri, 10am-midnight Sat & Sun) The name of this sleek café refers to Shumen's rank among Bulgarian cities. It aspires, with its wireless connection, colourful décor and Spanish coffee, to scale new cosmopolitan heights. The

AROUND SHUMEN

Madara Мадара
☎ 05313 / pop 1400

An important town for the mysterious Thracians around 7000 years ago, this village, 16km east of Shumen, was also settled during the Roman occupation. It's most famous today for the Madara Horseman, a grand rock carving from the early Bulgar khanate of the 8th century.

SIGHTS

The **Madara National Historical & Archaeological Reserve** (☎ 2095; adult/student 4/1 lv; ☒ 8.30am-7.30pm)

surrounds the so-called Madara Horseman (*Madarski Konnik*). Carved into a cliff 23m above the ground, the bas-relief features a mounted figure spearing a lion and followed by a dog. It was an early-8th-century creation, made to commemorate the victorious Khan Tervel, and, more profoundly, the creation of the First Bulgarian Empire (681–1018). As Bulgaria's only known medieval rock carving, it's listed as a Unesco World Heritage site. Since the permanent scaffolding hides more of the bas-relief the closer you get, it's not necessary to climb all the way to the figure to get the best views.

North of the horseman, a 373-step stairway hewn out of rock leads to the 130m-high clifftop and the ruined **Madara Fortress**, built during the Second Bulgarian Empire (1185–1396) to protect the capitals, Pliska and Veliki Preslav. There are sweeping views from above.

At the reserve's entrance gate you can pick up the *Madara* booklet (2 lv, in English or German), which explains the site and gives information on the popular hiking trails to the nearby **tombs** and **caves**.

FESTIVALS & EVENTS
Madara Horseman Music Days Festival Held in the reserve on four successive Thursdays from mid-June to mid-July.

SLEEPING & EATING
Camping Madara (☎ 5313; camp site per person 7 lv, cabins 20 lv), a shady and peaceful camping spot 500m from the horseman has a small restaurant, while **Hizha Madarski Konnik** (☎ 2091; dm 17 lv) offers dorm rooms.

GETTING THERE & AWAY
Public transport to Madara is limited, and the horseman is 3km up a steep road from the village. Several daily trains between Shumen and Varna stop at Madara. Buses to Madara from Shumen are infrequent, so get a bus from Shumen to Kaspichan (five daily), then a minibus to Madara from there. A taxi from Shumen costs 25 lv return, including waiting time. There are no taxis in Madara.

VELIKO TÂRNOVO
ВЕЛИКО ТЪРНОВО
☎ 062 / pop 75,000
The evocative capital of the medieval Bulgarian tsars, sublime Veliko Târnovo is

dramatically set amidst an amphitheatre of forested hills, divided by the ribboning Yantra River. Commanding pride of place is the magisterial, well-restored Tsarevets Fortress, citadel of the Second Bulgarian Empire. It is complemented by scores of churches and other ruins, many of which are still being unearthed.

Overgrown Trapezitsa Hill, one time residence of Bulgaria's kings, is especially exciting in this regard, and clambering up to it you will encounter teams of local helpers digging away at numerous church foundations and washing colourful Byzantine ceramic plates. Since there's much work to be done still, chances are good that Trapezitsa will yield many more treasures.

As the site of Bulgaria's most prestigious university, Veliko Târnovo also boasts a revved-up nightlife of which many larger towns would be jealous. There's great food and drink, too, with the best places enjoying stunning views of the river and castle. The old-world ambience of the Varosha quarter, with its terracotta rooftops and lounging cats, makes for wonderful leisurely walks in a place where you can feel the spirit of a bygone time.

As one of the main stops on the Bucharest–Istanbul express train, Veliko Târnovo is also a favourite with backpackers, as the ever-increasing number of youth hostels attests. However, it's also popular with weekending Bulgarians drawn by its romantic ambience and European tour groups peering over the sites. Certainly, it's one of the 'obligatory' destinations for getting the full Bulgarian experience, but Târnovo is well worth it, and will probably draw you in for at least a few days.

For more information on local wineries, see p66 and p66.

History
The strategic geography of Târnovo's hills led them to be settled from the earliest times. Neolithic people in 5500 BC, and Thracian tribes three millennia later, inhabited Tsarevets Hill (on which the fortress stands today) and Trapezitsa Hill opposite. The Romans built the fortress's first walls and, in the 6th century AD, Byzantine Emperor Justinian created a citadel. Slavic tribes captured the town in the 7th century.

Under the leadership of brothers Asen and Petâr, Târnovgrad became a centre of rebellion against the Byzantine rulers. With the foundation of the Second Bulgarian Empire in 1185, Târnovgrad would become second only to Constantinople in importance, and trade and culture flourished for the next 200 years.

On 17 July 1393, the Ottomans captured Târnovgrad, destroying the fortress on the hill. No longer very strategic in the middle of a vast empire, the town was allowed to stagnate through Ottoman times until Bulgarian nationalism asserted itself during the mid-19th century. In 1877, during the Russo-Turkish War, the Russian General Gurko liberated Târnovgrad from the Turks. Because of its importance during the Second Bulgarian Empire, Veliko Târnovo (as it was renamed) was the location for writing Bulgaria's Constitution in 1879, and was where the independence of the Bulgarian state was officially proclaimed in 1908.

Orientation

Veliko Târnovo is based along a ridge above the Yantra River (probably derived from the Thracian word *yatrus* meaning 'quick flowing'). The river winds in a horseshoe bend between four hills: Tsarevets, site of the fortress; Momina Krepost, several kilometres to the east; Trapezitsa; and Sveta Gora (Holy Mountain).

The centre of town runs along ul Nezavisimost and ul Stefan Stambolov, between the post office and a huge underpass. Where ul Rakovski branches up from the latter street is where you'll find the traditional crafts shopping quarter, Samovodska Charshiya; above that is the quiet old town, Varosha. Târnovo's modern part, generally unvisited by tourists, spreads out to the west and southwest from ul Vasil Levski.

MAPS

Find the *Infoguide Veliko Turnovo* booklet (5 lv), packed with practical and cultural information in English, at the Tourist Information Centre and most bookstalls. Local monasteries are chronicled in *The V Turnovo Monasteries: A Guide* (4 lv). The Domino *Veliko Târnovo* map of town also includes maps of Tsarevets Fortress and Arbanasi.

Information

BOOKSHOPS

Knisharnitsa Apoloniya (☎ 620 287; ul Stefan Stambolov 65; ☼ 9am-7.30pm Mon-Sat, 10am-6.30pm Sun) Central bookstore with maps, Lonely Planet guides and other English-language travel books.

INTERNET ACCESS

Most hotels and hostels have wi-fi connections, and sometimes computers.
I-Net Internet Centre (off ul Hristo Botev; per hr 1.50 lv) Under Mustang Food restaurant.

LAUNDRY

Ladybird (ul Hadji Dmitâr 25; ☼ 9am-5pm Mon-Fri, 10am-6pm Sat & Sun) Same-day service; 5 lv per load.

MEDICAL SERVICES

Hospital Stefan Cherkezov (☎ 626 841; ul Nish 1) A modern hospital with an emergency room and English-speaking doctors, in the new part of town.

MONEY

Foreign exchange offices are plentiful. The following banks have ATMs:
Alpha Bank (ul Stefan Stambolov) Near the corner where the main road forks down to ul Gurko.
First East International Bank (ul Stefan Stambolov 1).
United Bulgarian Bank (ul Hristo Botev 3) Near the Cinema Poltava complex.

POST

Main post office (ul Hristo Botev 1; ☼ 7am-10pm)

TELEPHONE

Telephone centre Inside the post office.

TOURIST INFORMATION

Tourist Information Centre (TIC; ☎ 622 148; fax 600 768; tic_vt@mobikom.com; ul Hristo Botev 5; ☼ 9am-6pm Mon-Sat) Helpful English-speaking staff assist with everything from basic info and excursions to booking private rooms and onward travel. It stocks leaflets from many hotels and hostels.

Sights

TSAREVETS FORTRESS

The inescapable symbol of this proud medieval town, this reconstructed fortress dominates the skyline, and is one of Bulgaria's most beloved monuments. The **Tsarevets Museum-Reserve** (☎ 638 841; adult/child 4/2 lv; ☼ 8am-6pm Apr-Oct, 9am-5pm Nov-Mar) is located on Tsarevets Hill, which has been settled since time immemorial

CENTRAL BULGARIA

VELIKO TÂRNOVO

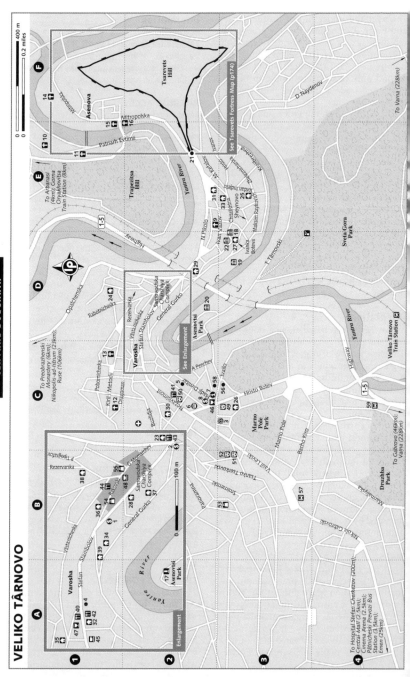

INFORMATION			
Alpha Bank	1 B1	Veliko Târnovo Archaeological	
First East International Bank	2 C2	Museum	22 D3
I-Net Internet Centre	3 C3		
Knisharitsa Apoloniya	4 A1	**SLEEPING** 🏠	
Ladybird	5 C2	Grand Hotel Yantra	23 C2
Main Post Office	6 C2	Hikers Hostel	24 D1
Telephone Centre	(see 6)	Hostel Mostel	25 E3
Tourist Information Centre	7 C2	Hotel Allegro	26 C3
United Bulgarian Bank	8 C2	Hotel Boliari	27 D3
		Hotel Bolyarski	28 B2
SIGHTS & ACTIVITIES		Hotel Kiev	29 D2
Church of Sveta Bogoroditsa	9 E2	Hotel Premier	30 C2
Church of Sveti Dimitâr	10 E1	Hotel Studio	31 E2
Church of Sveti Georgi	11 E1	Hotel Trapezitsa	32 A1
Church of Sveti Kiril i		Hotel Tsarevets	33 E3
Metodii	12 C1	Hotel-Mehana Gurko	34 B1
Church of Sveti Nikolai	13 C1	Kâshata Private Flats	35 A1
Church of Sveti Petar &		Loft Hostel	36 B1
Pavel	14 F1	Nomads Hostel	37 B2
Church of the Assumption	15 E1	Pink Bakery	38 B1
Forty Martyrs Church	16 E2	Villa Tashkov	39 B1
Monument of the Asens	17 A2		
Museum of National Revival &		**EATING** 🍴	
Constituent Assembly	18 D3	Ego Pizza & Grill	40 A1
Sarafkina Kâshta	19 D3	Ego Pizza & Grill	41 C2
State Art Museum	20 D2	Hotel-Mehana Gurko	(see 34)
Trapezitsa	(see 32)	Restaurant Hotel Studio	(see 31)
Tsarevets Fortress Entrance	21 E2	Shtastlivetsa	42 A1
		Starata Mehana	43 C2

Stratilat	44	B1
DRINKING 🍸 🍷		
Café Aqua	45	A1
City Pub	46	C2
Pepy's Bar	47	A1
Shekerdzinitsa	48	B2
Ulitsata	(see 32)	
ENTERTAINMENT 🎭		
Bally	49	C3
Deep Café Club	50	C2
Jack	51	B3
Konstantin Kisimov Dramatic		
Theatre	52	B3
Scream Dance Club	(see 41)	
SHOPPING 🛍		
Gorgona	53	B3
Icons Krasimir Ivanov	54	B1
Magazin za Manasta	55	B1
TRANSPORT		
Etap Adress	56	C3
Minibuses For Gorna		
Oryakhovitsa		
Train Station	57	B3
Rila Bureau	58	C2
Yug Bus Station	59	C4

CENTRAL BULGARIA

due to its strategic location. Thracians and Romans used it as a defensive position, but the Byzantines built the first significant fortress here between the 5th and 7th centuries. The fortress was rebuilt and fortified by the Slavs and Bulgars between the 8th and 10th centuries, and again by the Byzantines in the early 12th century. When Târnovgrad became the Second Bulgarian Empire's capital, the fortress was truly magnificent, but with the Turkish invasion in 1393, it was sacked and destroyed. Tourists can thank the Soviets for returning it to a semblance of its former glory (although some archaeologists grumble about the faithfulness of the restoration).

The remains of over 400 houses, 18 churches and numerous monasteries, dwellings, shops, gates and towers have so far been uncovered. The Patriarch's Complex and Baldwin Tower have received the most restoration, and there is plenty of random rubble lying about. Not much English-language information is provided, but guided English-language tours (10 lv) can be arranged by enquiring at the Tourist Information Centre.

Entering the structure, pass through two gates and veer left (northeast) for the fortress walls, some of which were once 12m high and 10m thick. Further along the walls are the unrecognisable remains of a 12th-century **monastery**, various **dwellings & workshops** and two

churches. To the north lie remains of a 13th-century **monastery**, and **Execution Rock**, from which traitors were pushed into the Yantra River. Alleged traitor Patriarch Joachim III was the most famous figure to take the plunge, in 1300.

The complex's eastern path is unremarkable, so return to the middle, using the hill-top Patriarch's Complex as a landmark. Past one of several modern bells (used in the sound and light show; see the boxed text, p175) are a ruined **nobleman's dwelling** and two **churches** to the left (east).

Below the Patriarch's Complex are the foundations of the **Royal Palace**, from where 22 successive kings ruled Bulgaria. Once covering 4500 sq metres, the palace included an appropriately enormous (about 30m by 10m) throne and Roman columns, probably transferred from nearby Nikopolis-ad-Istrum.

From the palace, head west to the main path and up the steps to the **Patriarch's Complex**, also called the Church of the Blessed Saviour. Once about 3000 sq metres in size, it was probably built about 1235, but has been extensively restored. The views of the city from the front steps are more impressive than the modern murals inside, depicting 14th- and 15th-century Bulgarian history.

Returning towards the main entrance, veer left along the path hugging the southern

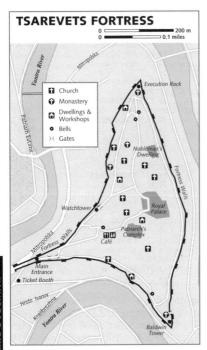

TSAREVETS FORTRESS

Church
Monastery
Dwellings & Workshops
Bells
Gates

Yantra River
Mitropolska
Execution Rock
Patriarh Evtimii
Nobleman's Dwelling
Fortress Walls
Watchtower
Royal Palace
Mitropolska Fortress Walls
Patriarch's Complex
Café
Main Entrance
Ticket Booth
Hristo Ivanov
Kralitrehna
Yantra River
Baldwin Tower

CENTRAL BULGARIA

wall. At its end is the restored **Baldwin Tower**, where Baldwin I of Flanders – the perfidious Crusader who led the sack of Christian Byzantium in 1204 – got his just desserts, imprisoned and executed after his defeat by the Bulgarians a year later. There are great views from the top.

SARAFKINA KÂSHTA

Built in 1861 by a rich Turkish merchant and moneylender, this fine five-storey National Revival–period style **house-museum** (☎ 635 802; ul Gurko 88; adult/student 4/2 lv; 9am-noon & 1-6pm Mon-Fri) displays antique ceramics, metalwork, woodcarvings and jewellery, and has some fascinating exhibits about traditional costumes and breadmaking. Revival-period furniture fills the upper floor, along with vintage family photos on the walls.

MUSEUM OF NATIONAL REVIVAL & CONSTITUENT ASSEMBLY

This **museum** (☎ 629 821; ul Ivan Vazov; admission 4 lv; 8am-6pm Wed-Mon), in a former Turkish town hall built in 1872, was where Bulgaria's first

National Assembly was held seven years later to write the country's first constitution.

The ground floor contains numerous costumes, books and photos about Veliko Târnovo's history. The former assembly hall, upstairs, displays portraits of local personages of note. The basement has classic old town photos, and some valuable icons.

VELIKO TÂRNOVO ARCHAEOLOGICAL MUSEUM

Housed in a grand old building with a colonnaded terrace and courtyard full of Roman sculptures, the **archaeological museum** (☎ 634 946; ul Ivan Vazov; adult/under 7yr 4/2 lv; 8am-6pm Tue-Sun) contains Roman artefacts from Nikopolis-ad-Istrum and more Roman pottery and statues from elsewhere. Medieval Bulgarian exhibits include huge murals of the tsars, while there's also some ancient gold from nearby Neolithic settlements.

CHURCHES

Most of Veliko Târnovo's numerous churches are closed on Wednesdays.

The **Forty Martyrs Church** (ul Mitropolska; 9am-6pm Thu-Tue), in the old Asenova quarter, was originally built in 1230 to celebrate Tsar Asen II's victory over the Byzantines. It was used as a royal mausoleum, and then as a mosque by the Turks.

Across from it is the tiny **Church of the Assumption**, built in 1923 over a ruined 14th-century church. The church is usually closed, but it's very pretty with blue-painted bas-reliefs decorating its sides.

Two blocks north, the late-13th-century **Church of Sveti Petar & Pavel** (☎ 638 841; ul Mitropolska; adult/concession 4/2 lv; 9am-5pm) features three layers of remarkable 11th- and 17th-century murals. This is the most interesting of the churches, mainly as there are some surviving early-11th-century wall paintings. The best preserved is in the corner to the left of the altar, where Jesus on the cross is being comforted by the Virgin Mary.

Across the river, enclosed by a high wall, is Târnovo's oldest church, the beautifully proportioned **Church of Sveti Dimitâr** (ul Patriarh Evtimii; admission 4 lv; by arrangement). Built in the so-called Târnovo style, it was named after St Dimitrios, patron saint of Thessaloniki in northern Greece. During the church's consecration in 1185, Tsars Asen and Petâr proclaimed an uprising against Byzantine rule, which would create the Second Bulgarian Empire (1185–1396). It's often closed, but a warden at the Church of Sveti Petar & Pavel can open it on request.

The nearby **Church of Sveti Georgi** (☎ 620 481; ul Patriarh Evtimii; admission 4 lv; ✆ by arrangement), probably built in 1612 on medieval church ruins, was initially destroyed by the Ottoman invaders, but restored during their rule in the early 18th century. It boats impressive murals inside. The Tsarevets Fortress ticket office arranges visits.

There are also notable frescoes at the **Church of Sveta Bogoroditsa** (✆ 9am-5pm), the town's main cathedral. Located just off ul Ivan Vazov, the church's large green neo-Byzantine domes distinguish it on the old town's skyline.

Up in Varosha, visit the **Church of Sveti Nikolai** (ul Vâstanicheska; ✆ 9am-5pm), built in 1879. After, follow the steps on the left (western) side, and turn left along ul Kiril i Metodii to the **Sveti Kiril i Metodii Church** (✆ 9am-5pm), which has an elegant tower.

STATE ART MUSEUM

Dramatically situated in a tight bend of the Yantra River, the **State Art Museum** (☎ 638 941; Asenovtsi Park; adult/student 3/1 lv; ✆ 10am-5pm Tue-Sun) contains paintings of Veliko Târnovo and the region by numerous artists. The 2nd floor exhibits more artworks, mostly on permanent loan from galleries in Silistra, Dobrich and Ruse. Guided tours (in English and French) are available for about 5 lv extra per person; entry is free on Thursdays.

Nearby, the **Monument of the Asens** is an awe-inspiring commemoration of the establishment of the Second Bulgarian Empire in 1185; there are great views over the town and river.

Activities

Numerous local operators offer **hiking**, **mountain biking**, **horse riding** and **caving**; for more information contact the Tourist Information Centre (p171). The helpful staff provide special hiking maps and can link you with the right people. The Centre also offers the useful *Climbing Guide*, good for serious rock climbers.

Rock-climbing trips and training at nearby massifs can be arranged at **Trapezitsa** (☎ /fax 635 823; www.trapezitsa-1902.hit.bg; ul Stefan Stambolov 79; ✆ 9am-noon & 1-6pm Mon-Fri) based in the eponymous hotel.

Festivals & Events

Holiday of Amateur Art Activities (early May) Also known as the Balkan Folk Festival, it's held over a period of 10 days.

International Festival of Religious Music (June) This new festival presents Bulgarian, Romanian and other choral singers in the fortress; ask at the Tourist Information Centre (p171) for details.

International Folklore Festival (late June–mid-July) Three-week festival with over 300 acts from Bulgaria and other Balkan countries. Details are usually available from mid-April (☎ 630 223).

Sleeping

There's been a veritable explosion in accommodation options in Veliko Târnovo over the past couple of years, though thankfully this hasn't damaged the town's aesthetic allure, as hotels tend to blend in with their surroundings. The proliferation of youth hostels, in particular, guarantees competitive prices and a wide range of free services. Boutique hotels are also seeing plenty of opportunity in romantic Târnovo.

THE SOUND & LIGHT SHOW

Târnovo rocks out with medieval flair during the Sound & Light Show, a nocturnal event that sees the whole of Tsarevets Hill lit up in great flashes of colour and rumbling music, a spectacular homage to the Second Bulgarian Empire. The show doesn't happen unless a certain number of people have bought tickets, but during the summer it happens most nights, as there are always tour groups in town. The show is 40 minutes long and apparently relates the rise and fall of the Second Bulgarian Empire (although for most people it will just be a pretty array of flashing lights set to music).

To find out if the show is happening, ring the organisers on ☎ 636 828 or ask the Tourist Information Centre (p171) or your hotel to check for you. Alternatively, turn up at the fortress and hope the show is on, or do what most locals and visitors do: listen for the bells, and look for the laser beams. Starting time is anywhere from 8pm to 9.30pm depending on the time of year.

BUDGET

The Tourist Information Centre (p171) finds private rooms (25 lv to 35 lv for a single/double). For atmosphere, stay near the Samovodska Charshiya Complex (p178) in the Varosha district, along the lower (southeastern) end of ul Gurko, or near Tsarevets Fortress.

Hikers Hostel (☎ 0889691661, 0887098279; www .hikershostel.org; ul Rezervoarska 91; tent/dm/d incl breakfast 12/20/50 lv; ▯) Târnovo's most laid-back hostel, Hikers is run by the energetic Toshe Hristov, who is constantly transferring guests or taking them on day trips. Simple but clean dorms (one with four beds, the other with 10), plus one double room are on offer; the patio also has two tents. The upper balcony, outfitted with couches, has great views and when the Sound & Light Show (see p175) is on it's fun to watch the far-off spectacle from here with a cold beer. The hostel, which has laundry service, free wireless internet and computers, is a five-minute uphill walk from the Samovodska Charshiya Complex. Call for free pick-up from the train or bus stations.

Hostel Mostel (☎ 0897859359; www.hostelmostel .com; ul Jordan Indjeto 10; tent/dm/d incl breakfast & dinner 14/20/60 lv) The famous Sofia-based Hostel Mostel has made a splash in Târnovo with this big, new place, set in a renovated 170-year-old house just 150m from Tsarevets Fortress. The hostel offers clean, very modern dorm rooms and doubles with sparkling bathrooms. The back garden has a BBQ, and a downstairs 'party room' is in the works. They even throw in free dinner and a glass of beer. Call for free pick-ups from the train or bus stations.

Loft Hostel (☎ 603 521; www.thelofthostel.com; ul Kapitan Diado Nikola 2a; dm/d/apt 16/40/80 lv) Adjacent to the Samovodska Charshiya Complex, this new hostel tucked into a side lane offers two dorms, a double and a small apartment. It's colourfully painted and has a spacious common room, and internet and laundry service are available. Call in advance as there's not always someone around.

Nomads Hostel (☎ 603 092; www.nomadshostel.com; ul Gurko 27; dm/d 18/25 lv) Another new and central budget place, Nomads offers all the same amenities as the other hostels and has a relaxing balcony with views. It arranges both day trips and evening jaunts, and has no fixed check-out time.

Hotel Trapezitsa (☎ 622 061; ul Stefan Stambolov 79; s/apt 28/54 lv) This very central place overlooking the river and town is starting to show its age and a certain indifference, but is still good value. Rooms are small but clean. The ones away from the street have great views over the river and town.

Kâshata Private Flats (☎ 604 129; www.the-house .hit.bg; pl Slaveikov 4; 1-/2-person apt 35/50 lv, 4-person apt 80 lv) Why hit the hotels when you can hire your own flat? Kâshata (The House), centrally located off the main street, offers well-equipped and good quality self-contained apartments.

Pink Bakery (☎ 601 362; www.the-pink-bakery.com; ul Reservarska 5; d/apt 40/70 lv) Nestled in the lower section of Varosha, this offbeat guesthouse in an unmissable pink building is a friendly and relaxing place run by two Brits, with colourful, slightly camp décor and bedding. Bathrooms are shared, but modern. There's also a spacious self-contained apartment with air conditioning, satellite TV and bright furnishings.

MIDRANGE

Hotel Kiev (☎ 600 571; kiev@abv.bg; pl Velchova Zavera 4; s/d 50/75 lv; ☒) This central hotel with an imposing façade and old-world lobby bar has breezy, tastefully decorated rooms. There aren't a lot of extras, but management is friendly and helpful.

Hotel Boliari (☎ 606 002; www.boliarihotel.com; ul Ivanka Boteva 2; s/d/ste 66/88/99 lv) This unassuming new boutique hotel between the Church of Sts Konstantin & Helena and the fortress has attractive rooms with handsome wood furnishings. It has a small café at reception and is a friendly, quiet place.

Hotel Bolyarski (☎ 613 200; www.bolyarski.com; ul Stefan Stambolov 53a; s/d 70/120 lv, apt 180-220 lv; ☒) Eight years in the making, the new Bolyarski has a phenomenal location on the bluff on ul Stambolov, with views of the town and river from its long café patio and rooms. Its modern, well-kept rooms are pitched at business travellers, though if you don't mind having no view, the 40 lv singles are practically budget. You pay extra for the fitness centre, swimming pool and Jacuzzi, however, and the service can be hit-or-miss.

Hotel-Mehana Gurko (☎ 627 838; www.hotel-gurko .com; ul Gurko 33; s/d 80/110 lv; ☒ ▯) The spacious, air-conditioned rooms at this old town place are individually decorated and offer great views. The traditional restaurant attached offers good Bulgarian cuisine.

Villa Tashkov (☎ 635 801; www.tashkoff.com; ul Gurko 19; d from 80 lv, entire villa 200 lv) Call in advance for this gorgeous, centrally located villa, which

can be rented in part or in full. The rooms
are fully equipped, and there's a daily cleaning
service. Reception is at ul Stambolisky 13.

Hotel Tsarevets (☎ 601 885; ul Chitalistna 23;
s/d 90/110 lv; P ✷ ☐) Also close to the fortress, the Tsarevets delights with its friendly
service and comfortable, well-kept rooms
with, TVs, internet and minibars. Ask about
multiday discounts.

our pick Hotel Studio (☎ 604 010; www.studiohotel-vt
.com; ul Todor Lefterov 4; s 100-110 lv, d 130-160 lv) This
chic new boutique hotel, run by suave Ivan
Velchev (the 'man in black'), is characterised
by understated, black-and-white décor with
the occasional splash of red. It has an enviable
location 25m from Tsarevets Fortress, and a
drink on the rooftop patio offers views of the
fortress, Arbanasi, Trapezitsa Hill, Sveta Gora
Hill and the town of Târnovo – an unmatched
panorama. The hotel's posh downstairs bar-
restaurant (right) offers imaginative cuisine
and minimalist cool.

TOP END

Hotel Allegro (☎ 602 332; www.veliko-tarnovo.net
/alegro; ul Todor Svetoslav 15; s/d 82-95/109-123 lv; ✷ ☐)
The new-town Allegro, located between
Marno Pole Park and the Tourist Information
Centre, is nevertheless only a 10-minute walk
from the old town. It has friendly service and
spotless rooms, some quite large, with all mod
cons and modern art. There's a breezy garden
restaurant as well.

Grand Hotel Yantra (☎ 600 607; www.yantrabg.com; ul
Opalchanska 2; s/d/ste 98/138/170 lv) This opulent new
place is one of Târnovo's smartest top-end
destinations. Service is excellent and rooms are
sumptuously decorated; some suites even have
fireplaces. It lacks the intimacy of smaller places
and attracts business conferences, though.
There's also an art gallery and casino.

Hotel Premier (☎ 615 555; hotel.premier@abv.bg; ul
Sava Penev 1; s/d 140/200 lv, ste 240-480 lv; P ✷ ☐ ☎)
For those craving the safety of internation-
ally certified luxury, Târnovo's Hotel Premier
(part of the Best Western chain) awaits. It's
located on a side street near the post office, a
10-minute walk from the old town. Facilities
include a pool, sauna, spa treatments and
(they claim) Bulgaria's biggest Jacuzzi.

Eating

Veliko Târnovo has some good restaurants
and cafés; for atmosphere, try those with terraces overlooking the river and gorge.

Stratilat (☎ 635 313; ul Rakovski 11; mains 5-7 lv) The
large outside terrace makes this a popular
place for a coffee, light meal or dessert from
the morning till night.

Starata Mehana (ul Stefan Stambolov; mains 5-8 lv)
Another dramatic location is found here,
with great views and traditional, good-value
cooking.

Hotel-Mehana Gurko (☎ 627 838; ul Gurko 33; mains
5-8 lv) The traditional *mehana* of the Hotel
Gurko (opposite) has traditional décor and
hearty Bulgarian specialities.

Ego Pizza & Grill (☎ 601 804; ul Nezavisimost 17; mains
5-9 lv; ✷ 9am-midnight) Located upstairs from
Scream Dance Club, this spacious place has an
outdoor balcony with excellent views. Massive
salads, Bulgarian cuisine, Serbian mixed grills
and more obscure Chinese and Mexican
dishes are on offer. A second location, right
beside the popular Pepy's Bar has a more snug
bistro feel and friendly, gorgeous staff.

our pick Shtastlivetsa (☎ 600 656; ul Stefan
Stambolov 79; mains 5-10 lv; ✷ 11am-1am) Hands
down the most popular place in town for
both locals and foreigners, the 'Lucky Man'
(as the impossible-to-pronounce name means
in Bulgarian) has a great menu of inventive
meat dishes, baked-pot specials, nourishing
pizzas and (at lunchtime) delicious soups. It's
good value, considering the high quality. The
service is generally good, though sometimes
comically formal.

Restaurant Hotel Studio (☎ 604 010; www.studio
hotel-vt.com; ul Todor Lefterov 4; mains 7-12 lv; ✷ 9am-11pm)
This new gourmet eatery at the boutique Hotel
Studio (left) has elegant black décor and a
back-lit, well-equipped bar, winning you over
even before the baked camembert in almond
and wild berries sauce or Black Sea bluefish
arrive. Dress up.

Drinking

Shekerdzinitsa (☎ 0898563490; ul Giorgi Momarchev 13;
✷ 9am-6pm Tue-Sun) This lovely little café with
traditional furnishings in the old market
is the place to go for real Turkish coffee –
appealingly prepared the old-school way, in
a diminutive copper pot run across a basin
of heated sand.

Ulitsata (☎ 603 252; ul Stefan Stambolov 79) To one
side of the Hotel Trapezitsa, this is one of
Târnovo's busiest and friendliest cafés, with
nice views from the terrace.

our pick Pepy's Bar (☎ 603 041; pl Slaveikov; ✷ 10am-
3am) If you were an expat in Târnovo, Pepy's

might well be your local. The dark-lit, popular bar doesn't put on airs like the more studenty places; it's just a cosy, chilled-out nightspot with subdued style.

City Pub (☎ 637 824; ul Hristo Botev 15) This popular, big British-style pub near the post office and TIC is a bit gimmicky, but usually lively with local students.

Café Aqua (☎ 623 567; ul Nezavisimost 3) Lounge over a coffee and *slatka* (sweet) until late in the evening at this central café, which has a breezy balcony overlooking the gorge.

Entertainment

Veliko Târnovo's nightlife is buzzing year-round; in summer, there's a big foreign presence, when the backpacker *internationale* descends, while the town's 20,000 vivacious university students flesh out the clubs during the rest of the year.

Jack (☎ 0887203016; ul Magistraka 5; ☒ 10pm-4am) This pumping student club for knavish lads and short-skirted girls is named for the American whisky, and is especially popular on weekends with house music and dancing.

Scream Dance Club (☎ 0897938266; ul Nezavisimost 17; ☒ 10pm-4am) Another of Târnovo's popular clubs, Scream is slightly more tasteless but equally studenty.

Deep Café Club (☎ 321 645; ul Nezavisimost 23; ☒ 8am-1am) This small, eccentrically lit subterranean bar-verging-on-club caters to a young crowd with hip-hop and house music.

Bally (☎ 0885565666; ul Hristo Botev 2; ☒ 8pm-5am) This new club playing hip-hop and techno has both its supporters and detractors. With its large central dance floor, it can seem empty unless there's a weekend crowd.

The latest Hollywood films are on at **Cinema Arena** (tickets 6 lv; ☒ 10am-midnight) in the new shopping centre, Central Mall (right), which also has a nightclub, bowling alley and casino. (A taxi is the easiest way to get there.) In addition to the mall, the new town, little-visited by tourists, is where many students reside and thus also offers heavy-duty entertainment during term.

For a spot of theatre, try the **Konstantin Kisimov Dramatic Theatre** (☎ 623 526; ul Vasil Levski). The Tourist Information Centre (p171) can tell you what's on.

Shopping

Roughly opposite the Hotel Bolyarski, ul Rakovski veers upwards from the main road, ul Stambolov. On and behind it is the **Samovodska Charshiya Complex**, the town's historic centre of craftsmanship; blacksmiths, potters and gunsmiths, among other artisans, still practise their trades here. The numerous bookshops and purveyors of antiques, jewellery and art are also housed in appealing Bulgarian National Revival houses. It's a great place for shopping, or just a stroll, as is the equally appealing old residential quarter of Varosha just above it.

At the beginning of ul Rakovski, a prominent map signposts the name and location of each shop in the *charshiya*, in both Bulgarian and English. The following two are only a couple of the many unique shops around.

Magazin za Manasta (ul Giorgi Momarchev 14; ☒ 9am-7pm) You'll recognise this cosy shop from the sign out front reading 'hand-made jewelry', and the walls lined with brightly coloured glass and silver beads. Buy them by the piece, or choose from the many unique necklaces.

Icons Krasimir Ivanov (☎ 0885060544; cnr ul Rakovski & ul Kapitan Diado Nikola; icons 60-400 lv; ☒ 10am-7pm) Krasimir Ivanov has been painting icons since the fall of communism, when religious art was allowed again. His detailed ink sketches of old Târnovo (20 lv), displayed outside the shop are another excellent take-home memento. The shop doubles as Krasimir's workshop, so you can watch him painstakingly painting while you browse.

For camping, climbing, skiing and biking gear, you'll want to visit **Gorgona** (☎ 601 400 www.gorgona-shop.com; ul Zelenka 2; ☒ 10am-1pm & 2-7pm Mon-Fri, 10am-2pm Sat).

The eastside **Central Mall** (☎ 674 040; www.mallvt.eu; ul Oborishte 18; ☒ 10am-8pm) is Bulgaria's most modern shopping centre to be found outside of Sofia.

Getting There & Away
BUS

Two bus stations serve Veliko Târnovo, both out of the centre. **Pâtnicheski Prevozi bus station** (Zapad bus station; ☎ 640 908; ul Nikola Gabrovski 74) is about 4km from the centre and is the main terminus for buses from elsewhere in Bulgaria. Local buses 10, 12, 14, 70 and 110 go there, along ul Vasil Levski. There's also a **left-luggage office** (☒ 7.30am-4.30pm). From here, buses serve Gabrovo (3.50 lv, 40 minutes, half-hourly), as well as Elena (2 lv, 30 minutes, six daily), Kazanlâk (5 lv, 2½ hours, five daily) Ruse (6 lv, two hours, eight daily), Sliven (4 lv, two hours, seven daily), Burgas (14 lv, four hours, four daily) and Plovdiv (14 lv, four hours, four daily). Daily buses serve Troyan (4 lv, two hours), Karlovo (7 lv, four hours) and Pleven (6 lv, two hours).

The somewhat more central **Yug bus station** (☎ 620 014; ul Hristo Botev) has many daily buses to Sofia (11 lv, four hours) and the Black Sea cities of Varna (11 lv, four hours) and Burgas (14 lv, 3½ hours). From here, several daily buses also serve Shumen (5 lv, three hours).

Under the Hotel Etâr, **Etap Adress** (☎ 630 564; ul Ivaylo 2) has hourly buses to Sofia (15 lv, 3½ hours) and Varna (15 lv, four hours), plus two daily buses to Dobrich (13 lv, four hours), one to Kavarna (15 lv, 4½ hours) via Albena and Balchik and one to Shumen (8 lv, two hours).

To reach Romania by bus, go first to Ruse, from where three daily minibuses make the three-hour trip to Bucharest.

TRAIN

The **Veliko Târnovo train station** (☎ 620 065), 1.5km west of town, runs three daily trains to Plovdiv (10.10 lv, five hours) via Stara Zagora (4.80 lv, two hours). Trains also serve Sliven (7 lv, three hours, six daily), Burgas (11.40 lv, five hours, three daily), Varna (11.80 lv, five hours, three daily) and Sofia (12.80 lv, 4½ hours, six daily). There are five daily trains to Gabrovo (change at Tsareva Livada) and regular trains to Târnovo's other train station, at Gorna Oryakhovitsa. From the Veliko Târnovo station, buses 10, 12, 14, 70 and 110 go to the centre. A taxi from the station to the centre should cost around 3 lv to 5 lv.

Gorna Oryakhovitsa train station (☎ 826 118), 8.5km from town, is along the main line between Sofia and Varna and has daily services to/from Sofia, via Pleven, (10 lv, five hours, eight daily) and Varna (9.10 lv, four hours, three daily) and 11 trains to Ruse (6 lv, two hours). There are also six daily connections to Stara Zagora (7 lv, four hours), and 10 to Shumen (7 lv, four hours).

You can get to this station from Veliko Târnovo by catching a minibus from opposite the market along ul Vasil Levski, by taking bus 14 from the Pâtnicheski Prevozi bus station, or by bus 10 from the centre. Taxis cost about 8 lv to 9 lv.

International

To reserve international or domestic tickets, visit **Rila Bureau** (☎ 622 042; ul Tsar Kaloyan 2a; ☻ 8am–noon & 1-4.30pm Mon-Fri), located behind the Tourist Information Centre. A daily train to Bucharest (22.93 lv, six hours) in Romania leaves Veliko Târnovo train station at 10.42am, stopping at Gorna Oryakhovitsa and continuing north from there at 12.22pm. A night train from Târnovo goes to Istanbul, Turkey (35.85 lv, 62.32 lv with sleeper car, 11 hours) at 7.55pm. You can also reach Thessaloniki in northern Greece via an evening train from Gorna Oryakhovitsa (41.95 lv, 63.42 lv with sleeper car, 14 hours).

Getting Around

Most people will find walking both sufficient and enjoyable for getting around in Veliko Târnovo. Taxis are good for zipping around the central areas – try **Toptaxi** (☎ 631 111; fares 1-3.30 lv) – but sometimes refuse to drive in the old quarters, especially Varosha, due to the narrowness of the streets. If staying in a hostel in such a neighbourhood, therefore, you're better off taking advantage of the free pick-up services offered. Hiring taxis (at fixed metered rates) for local destinations such as Arbanasi, or chartering them (for negotiable rates) to places further afield is more feasible.

For car rental, ask at the Tourist Information Centre for the best offers (usually around 40 lv per day, including insurance, but not petrol).

AROUND VELIKO TÂRNOVO

Arbanasi Арбанаси
☎ 062 / pop 1500

Just 4km from Veliko Târnovo, Arbanasi is a historic monastery-village with some lovely architecture, traditional accommodation and hearty cuisine, horseback riding and hiking. Although opulent villas for wealthy Sofians have gone up in recent years, Arbanasi is still far from being overrun, with a bucolic air and leafy surroundings. Nearly 90 churches, homes and monasteries here are state-protected cultural monuments.

Founded by Christians from Albania in the 15th century (medieval Albanians were often called 'Arvanauts'), Arbanasi enjoyed a bit of luck when Ottoman Sultan Süleyman I bequeathed it to a son-in-law in 1538, making it exempt from taxation. Local artisans and traders did business far and wide, with Greece, Russia and India, and the village became a summer getaway for the Ottoman elite. In 1798, however, Arbanasi was mostly destroyed by the infamous Turkish *kurdjali* gangs.

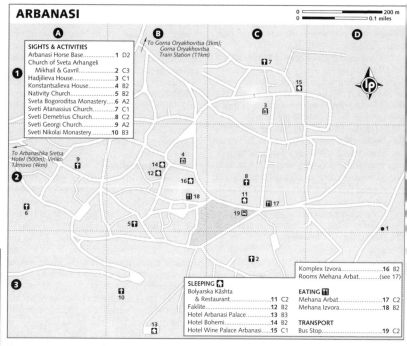

ARBANASI

SIGHTS & ACTIVITIES
Arbanasi Horse Base...................1 D2
Church of Sveta Arhangeli
  Mikhail & Gavril....................2 C3
Hadjilieva House........................3 C1
Konstantsalieva House...............4 B2
Nativity Church.........................5 B2
Sveta Bogoroditsa Monastery....6 A2
Sveti Atanassius Church............7 C1
Sveti Demetrius Church..............8 C2
Sveti Georgi Church...................9 A2
Sveti Nikolai Monastery...........10 B3

To Gorna Oryakhovitsa (3km);
Gorna Oryakhovitsa
Train Station (11km)

To Arbanashka Sretsa
Hotel (500m); Veliko
Târnovo (4km)

SLEEPING
Bolyarska Kâshta
  & Restaurant.......................11 C2
Faklite.....................................12 B2
Hotel Arbanasi Palace...............13 B3
Hotel Bohemi...........................14 B2
Hotel Wine Palace Arbanasi.....15 C1
Komplex Izvora........................16 B2
Rooms Mehana Arbat............(see 17)

EATING
Mehana Arbat..........................17 C2
Mehana Izvora.........................18 B2

TRANSPORT
Bus Stop..................................19 C2

ORIENTATION & INFORMATION

Relaxing Arbanasi has plenty of open space and a network of nameless streets, though most of the action is centred on one or two on the central square, where a Unicredit Bulbank ATM machine also stands.

The Arbanasi municipal **website** (www .arbanassi.org) contains information about the town's history, accommodation and eating, and local activities.

SIGHTS

Arbanasi's three major sites, two churches and one house-museum, are all covered by the same ticket (4 lv). Each operates from 9.30am to 6pm daily, though they're usually closed between 1 October and 31 March. Double-check first in Veliko Târnovo with the **Museums Department** (☎ 062-349 460) before off-season visits. At any time of the year, you may also want to first get the book *Arbanasi: A Guide* (3 lv) at a bookstore in Târnovo.

During the 16th and 17th centuries, benevolent Turkish rulers condoned church-building in Arbanasi. The village's oldest remaining church, the **Nativity Church**, boasts a stunning,

kaleidoscopic frescoed interior, with paintings (created between 1632 and 1649) covering every inch of space in the five chambers; the hand-carved central iconostasis is also magnificent. Over 3500 figures are depicted in some 2000 scenes throughout the church, which also boasts lavish wood iconostases created by eminent carvers from Tryavna.

The 16th-century **Church of Sveta Arhangeli Mikhail & Gavril**, built on the ruins of a medieval church, also contains impressive frescoes, including one from Thessaloniki in Greece and another from Bucharest in Romania. Since the interior is rather dark, these are best viewed on a sunny day. The wooden iconostases were also carved by experts from the Tryavna school of woodcarving.

The final major site, the gorgeous, 17th-century **Konstantsalieva House**, was later rebuilt in the Bulgarian National Revival style. It contains period furniture in the upstairs rooms, while the ground floor has a souvenir shop with embroidery and more for sale.

At the time of writing another unique site, the **Hadjilieva House**, was closed but scheduled to be re-opened soon, so check when you're there. Other sites include the unsignposted **Sveti Demetrius Church**, and the pretty **Sveti Atanassius Church**, probably built in 1667, which has a cemetery.

There are also three 17th-century working monasteries: **Sveti Georgi Church**, the **Sveta Bogoroditsa Monastery** (☎ 620 322) and the **Sveti Nikolai Monastery** (☎ 650 345). All are usually open.

ACTIVITIES

The **Arbanasi Horse Base** (☎ 623 668), on the village's eastern edge, does guided horseback riding trips in the lush hills around Arbanasi. Phone to ask about current programmes and costs, or consult the Tourist Information Centre (p171) in Veliko Târnovo. It also hosts a riding tournament each June.

SLEEPING

Arbanasi is much quieter than Veliko Târnovo, and its traditional guesthouses, and a few more lavish hotels, will appeal to those looking for peace and quiet. Some places close in winter. Private rooms are also available; ask at the shops at the bus stop or in the restaurants.

Faklite (☎ 604 496; s/d 20/32 lv) Faklite (the torches) offers huge and atmospheric rooms with bathroom in a traditional villa. The main house, not the one with modern-style rooms beyond the garden, is the place to be.

Rooms Mehana Arbat (☎ 631 811; s/d incl breakfast 35/45 lv) These new rooms offered by the central Mehana Arbat (right), just upstairs from the restaurant, have lovely doubles with weathered wood floors and traditional furnishings. Bathrooms are simple but modern.

Arbanashka Sretsa Hotel (☎ 601 370; s/d 48/88 lv; ☒) This new guesthouse with cosy, traditional style rooms is set off on a small dirt drive just before the centre. There are good views from the on-site restaurant patio as well as a small swimming pool.

Hotel Wine Palace Arbanasi (☎ 630 176; s/d/ste incl breakfast 48/68/108 lv; P ☒ ☐ ☒) This expansive place, which has an outdoor pool and well-kept grounds, offers excellent value considering the luxury of the well-appointed rooms, which come with all modern conveniences and bathtubs. Many of the rooms have spacious balconies. As the name suggests, the restaurant includes a winery where numerous exemplary Bulgarian wines can be sampled.

Bolyarska Kâshta & Restaurant (☎ 620 484; www.boliarska.com; s/d/apt incl breakfast 50/65/90 lv) Only metres from the square and bus stop, this hotel offers spacious rooms and a lovely garden. A fountain feeds terraced pools along the rooms, creating the soothing sound of gurgling water. The hotel overlooks the St Demetrius Church.

Hotel Bohemi (☎ 620 484; www.arbanassivt.hit.bg; d/apt 65/90 lv) Small but comfortable rooms are on offer at this established place in the centre. The large apartments' amenities include a crackling fireplace.

Hotel Arbanasi Palace (☎ 630 176; s/d/ste 77-104/122-144/126-198 lv; P ☒ ☐ ☒) Looking somewhat grey and battered on the outside, the Arbanasi Palace nevertheless has a five-star interior with a seemingly endless labyrinth of marble halls. The stunning view out over the valley towards Veliko Târnovo from the restaurant balcony, and from many of the rooms, is no doubt what inspired its original creation – it was originally built as the grand residence of former communist leader Todor Zhivkov.

Komplex Izvora (☎ 601 205; www.izvora.hit.bg; s/d 100/140 lv, ste 180-280 lv; P ☒ ☒) The Izvora sprawls to include a hotel, *mehana* with garden setting and barbecue, swimming pool and pens of odour-bearing farm animals, which are fascinating for children. You're paying for accoutrements such as a spa centre, however, as the double rooms are just standard. However, the nice wood-floored suites are more aesthetically pleasing.

EATING

Mehana Izvora (☎ 627 917; mains 6-8 lv) A 17th-century, well-decked-out residence houses this popular tavern. It also has a swimming pool and playground, and folk music is provided (at no extra cost) in the evening if there are enough customers.

Mehana Arbat (☎ 631 811; mains 6-9 lv) Probably the most atmospheric place in town, this cosy main-street *mehana* serves excellent grilled meats, both quick bites and specialities requiring 18 hours of slow roasting. There's also now a new upstairs Vino Bar for drinks in the evening.

GETTING THERE & AWAY

On ul Vasil Levski in Veliko Târnovo, opposite the market, minibuses depart for Gorna Oryakhovitsa train station when full (about every 30 minutes). Ask the driver if it's possible to detour through Arbanasi. If not, disembark at the turn-off to Arbanasi along the way, and walk (about 700m) to the village. A taxi from Veliko Târnovo costs about 5 lv to 6 lv one way. Taxis in Arbanasi will take you back.

Preobrazhenski Monastery

Preobrazhenski Monastir (☎ 623 076), or the Monastery of the Transfiguration, is located high in a forest about 7km north of Veliko Târnovo. Originally built in 1360, it's Bulgaria's fourth largest monastery and offers fantastic views. Despite being destroyed by the Turks in the late 14th century, it was rebuilt in 1825, about 500m from the original site, but later damaged by landslides. To the sides of the main church you will see massive rocks that tumbled down the hill and miraculously just missed the building. The monastery's churches boast murals painted between 1849 and 1851 by the renowned Zahari Zograf. While the best are now in Veliko Târnovo's Archaeological Museum (p174), a restoration program now underway has brightened up the remaining age-blackened frescoes, making a visit here very worthwhile. You may also see (and hear!) the enormous barrels of fermenting plum brandy in the courtyard being made by the rascally monks.

Bus 10 from Veliko Târnovo goes past the monastery. It will leave you at a turn-off on the road headed to Ruse. From here, it's a shady, uphill 3km walk. A taxi from Veliko Târnovo costs about 6 lv one way.

Emen Емен

The 3km-long **Emen Canyon**, along the Negovanka River, is the only one of its kind in Bulgaria. Some 25 hectares of land here exist as a protected reserve for species of butterflies, fish, birds and bats. The reserve also includes the 10m-high **Momin Skok Waterfall**, at its best in spring.

Hiking the **Negovanka Ecotrail**, which runs in a loop in and around the canyon, is the main attraction at Emen. The trail is signposted from Emen village. Veliko Târnovo's Tourist Information Office (p171) can provide more details and/or maps.

Emen village and the canyon are 25km west of Veliko Târnovo, and are accessible by the bus from Veliko Târnovo to Pavlikeni, which leaves Târnovo's Pâtnicheski Prevozi bus station at 8.30am and 6pm.

Nikopolis-ad-Istrum
Никополис-ад-Иструм

Built in AD 102 under Emperor Trayan, but destroyed by the Slavs in the late 6th century, this former Roman city has extensive **ruins** (admission 4 lv; ☉ 8am-6pm) that include streets, towers, gates, the city square and the town hall. While many local treasures were looted long ago, some of the best finds are housed in Veliko Târnovo's Archaeological Museum (p174); visiting both site and museum is thus recommended for archaeology buffs.

If driving from Veliko Târnovo, head north towards Ruse and take the signposted turn-off to the left (west) after about 20km. This access road, however, is rough in parts. By bus, take the same route (towards Ruse), and ask the driver to stop at the turn-off to Nikyup; from there it's a 4km signposted walk to the ruins. In high summer, check in advance to ensure the site will be open, as archaeological work is ongoing; either the tourist office in Veliko Târnovo (p171) or the relevant **authority** (☎ 062-624 474) can inform you.

DRYANOVO MONASTERY
☎ 0676

Originally dating from the 12th century, this **monastery** (☎ 5253; admission free; ☉ 7am-8pm), tucked beneath limestone cliffs about 6km from the town of Dryanovo (Dry-an-ovo), has a turbulent history. It was alternately destroyed by the Turks and rebuilt by Bulgarians several times over a period of about 500 years. Like many other monasteries, it provided sanctuary to the revolutionary leader, Vasil Levski, and his men. Later, during the Russo-Turkish War (1877–78), more than 100 locals made a valiant last stand against the Turks, for some nine days. The Turks eventually won out, burning the place down yet again. The villagers' hopeless bravery is commemorated with a **mausoleum** in the monastery grounds.

The monks of Dryanovo have a reputation for friendliness and are happy to chat with visitors. Accommodation (see opposite) is usually available, but call in advance just to be sure.

Inside the Komplex Vodopadi (opposite) is a **Historical Museum** (☎ 2097; admission 3 lv;

9am-noon & 12.30-3.30pm Mon-Fri, 9.45am-3.45pm Sat & Sun), devoted mostly to the 1876 April Uprising and the Russo-Turkish War. The macabre collection of skulls draws attention immediately. Downstairs are artefacts from nearby caves, including Bacho Kiro, and some icons.

From the bridge near the car park, a 400m path leads through lush forest to the 1200m-long **Bacho Kiro cave** (☎ 2332; admission 3 lv; 9am-6pm Apr-Oct, 10am-4pm Nov-Mar), inhabited during the Palaeolithic era. It is a long, well-lit cave, and guided tours are offered, though aren't really necessary.

Hikers will enjoy the **Dryanovo Ecotrail**, a well-marked, circular path that starts and finishes near the monastery. The hike takes about four hours, and passes through lush, hilly forests. To find the trailhead, ask at the Bacho Kiro cave or at the Mehana Mecha Dupka, which is in the woods just behind the monastery, about 50m from the start of the trail leading to the cave.

The **tourist office** (☎ 2106) in Dryanovo or the **Bacho Kiro Tourist Society** (☎ 2332) can arrange local rock-climbing and caving trips.

Sleeping & Eating

Simple rooms are offered in the **monastery** (☎ 5253; per person with shared bathroom 10 lv).

Komplex Vodopadi (☎ 2314; d/apt 40/50 lv) This place, virtually attached to the monastery, offers several small but clean rooms. Many of them have balconies overlooking the monastery.

Mehana Andyka (☎ 2230; mains 5-9 lv; 9am-1am) This relaxing restaurant has a lovely wooded setting between cliffs, about 300m before the cave entrance, and does good grilled meats and salads.

Getting There & Away

Buses travelling between Veliko Târnovo and Gabrovo can leave you at the turn-off to the monastery (4km south of Dryanovo), from where you'll have to walk the last 1.5km. Car parking costs 2 lv.

TRYAVNA ТРЯВНА
☎ 0677 / pop 12,200

Once just a day trip and now a tourist draw, Tryavna (40km southwest of Veliko Târnovo) has been impressively renovated thanks to EU largesse. The National Revival–period homes, stone bridges and cobblestone streets are all aesthetically appealing, as is the sight of the main church selectively floodlit at night. Tryavna is most famous for its craftsmanship, and particularly for the eminent Tryavna school of religious wood-carving that existed during Ottoman times. However, despite its plethora of exhibitions and churches, Tryavna has not become simply a museum town; a school for woodcarving still exists, attended by young Bulgarians eager to continue this important aspect of their national heritage.

Orientation

The bus station and train station are 100m apart and west of ul Angel Kânchev, the main road running through the old town. Get local maps either at Tryavna train station or at shops (either on ul Angel Kânchev, or opposite the Hotel Tryavna on the main square). The town's few services, including an ATM and some restaurants, are located around this square.

Information

Bulgarian Post Bank (Post Office Bldg, ul Angel Kânchev 22) The best place to change money; there's also an ATM.
DCK Bank (Municipal Bldg) ATM only, on the side of the municipality building.
Internet Centre (ul Angel Kânchev 15) The local internet café.
Tourist office (☎ 2247; www.tryavna.bg; ul Angel Kânchev 22; 9am-noon & 2-5pm Mon-Fri) In the post office building; can help with bus and train schedules, and arrange private rooms.

Sights

A two- to three-hour walking tour will suffice to see all of Tryavna's sights. From the bus station, head east (away from the train line) and then turn right along ul Angel Kânchev to reach the impressive **St Georgi Church** (ul Angel Kânchev 128; 7.30am-12.30pm & 2.30-5.30pm) on the left. Completed in 1852, it features some beautiful icons and carvings. Further on the right is the **Angel Kânchev House-Museum** (☎ 2278; ul Angel Kânchev 39; admission 2 lv; 8am-6pm Apr-Oct, to 5pm Nov-Mar). Built in 1805, it contains exhibits about revolutionary hero Kânchev, and the liberation of Tryavna during the Russo-Turkish War.

Walk over the bridge, past the shady park and head right (still along ul Angel Kânchev) to pl Kapitan Dyado Nikola. First built in 1814 in National Revival–period

---

WOODCARVING

During the Bulgarian National Revival period, Tryavna became renowned for the quality and quantity of its woodcarvings, often intricately chiselled from local walnut, birch, poplar and oak trees. Many carvings from Tryavna were used to decorate monasteries in Gabrovo, Veliko Târnovo, Arbanasi and Rila, and carvers were sought after by builders and house owners as far away as Serbia, Turkey and modern-day Iran.

By the early 19th century, over 40 workshops in Tryavna were churning out wooden cradles, frames, icons, friezes, doors and crosses. Each design was individual, but most included the type of ornate and detailed flower motifs that became known as the Tryavna school of woodcarving. Some of the most beautiful exhibits include the 'sun ceiling' inside the Daskalov House in Tryavna, which is also home to the Museum of Woodcarving & Icon Painting (below).

In an attempt to resurrect the tradition, courses in the Tryavna school of woodcarving are offered to tourists. Courses for one/two/three days (six hours per day) cost 35/60/80 lv, and can be arranged through the tourist office (p183). Every even-numbered year, the school also hosts the International Woodcarving Competition. Details are available from the tourist office in Tryavna.

---

style, this large square is dominated by a **clock tower** (1844) that chimes loudly on the hour. Facing this square is **Staroto Shkolo**, the town's old school. Built in 1836, it's now been fully restored and houses the **Tryavna Museum School of Painting** (☎ 2517, 2039; adult /student 2/1 lv; ☯ 9am-7pm). Also overlooking the square is the slate-roofed **St Archangel Michael's Church** (admission free; ☯ 8am-4.30pm), Tryavna's oldest church, which is magically lit at night. Burnt down by the Turks but rebuilt in 1819, it boasts intricate Tryavna school woodcarvings. Its **Museum of Icons** (admission 1 lv; ☯ 9am-5pm) illustrates the history of Bulgarian icon painting.

Across the stone **Arch Bridge** (1844) is ul PR Slaveikov, one of Bulgaria's nicest cobblestone streets. On the left-hand side is **Daskalov House** (☎ 2166; ul PR Slaveikov 27a; adult /student 2/1 lv; ☯ 9am-6pm Apr-Oct, to 5pm Nov-Mar). Completed in 1808, this walled home with garden also contains the intriguing and unique **Museum of Woodcarving & Icon Painting**. It features some superb examples of the Tryavna school of woodcarving, as well as icons and antique copper implements.

Housed in a former chapel, Tryavna's second, larger **Museum of Icons** (☎ 3753; ul Breza 1; admission 2 lv; ☯ 9am-4.30pm summer, 10am-6pm winter) contains over 160 religious icons from the erstwhile collections of famous local families. The museum is beyond the train line, and signposted from ul PR Slaveikov.

Back on this street, the **Slaveikov House-Museum** (☎ 2166; ul PR Slaveikov 50; admission 2 lv; ☯ 8am-noon & 1-6pm Wed-Sun) is dedicated to Petko Slaveikov and his son Pencho, re-

nowned poets who lived here for many years. Further down on the left is the **Summer Garden Kalinchev House** (☎ 3694; ul PR Slaveikov 45; admission 1.50 lv; ☯ 9am-1pm & 2-6pm Mon-Fri). This house, built in 1830, features a charming courtyard **café** (☯ 8am-11pm) and contains (but is not currently exhibiting) 500 works by Bulgarian artists, including Kalinchev. More paintings, drawings and sculptures are displayed next door at the **Ivan Kolev House** (☎ 3777; ul PR Slaveikov 47; admission 2 lv; ☯ 9am-1pm & 2-6pm Mon-Fri).

Sleeping

Along the first 200m of ul Angel Kânchev after the bus station you will see offers of rooms for rent. The tourist office can also arrange private rooms (including in the old town) for about 20 lv to 25 lv per person, including breakfast.

Hotel Tigara (☎ 2469; ul D Gorov 7a; s/d 25/30 lv) The Tiger Hotel is a friendly place near the Hotel Tryavna. This family-run hotel is hospitable, and the best value in town. The best of the clean and comfortable rooms are the newer ones at the back. Breakfast costs 4 lv.

Hotel Tryavna (☎ 3448; fax 2598; ul Angel Kânchev 46; s/d 35/50 lv) This refurbished large hotel has an excellent location and very modern, though fairly standard, accommodation aimed at the business traveller market. There are two restaurants, a fitness centre and a garden café.

Komplex Brâshlyan (☎ 3019; bungalows 36 lv, d 40-90 lv) The Brâshlyan overlooks the town from a shady spot north of the centre. The bigger rooms have huge leather sofas and balconies, and there's a restaurant and outdoor deck for evening drinks. Cross the tracks past the old bridge, and head up and right.

Zograf Inn (☎ 4970/80; zograf@mbox.dgsys.bg; ul PR Slaveikov 1; s/d/apt 38/56/90 lv; 🖳) In the heart of historic Tryavna, the Zograf occupies an old building complete with a traditional *mehana*. The rooms are spotless and good value, though more indifferently modern than the building itself would lead you to expect. Internet provided is cable. Note rates rise slightly on weekends.

Hotel Seasons (☎ 2285; www.tryavna.bg/web /seasons; ul Kâncho Skorchev 11; s/d/ste 38/56/90 lv; 🅿 🖳 🏊) Tryavna's luxury option includes a large outdoor pool, sauna and Jacuzzi. The breezy, spacious rooms are the best in town, though you'll need to get up there by car to beat the steep hill. The professional staff organise walking tours in the nearby hills for guests.

Hotel Family (☎/fax 4691; ul Angel Kânchev 40; s/d 40/55 lv) Clean and smart rooms are found at this family-run place, most with balconies.

Hotel Ralitsa (☎ 2262; fax 2402; hotelralica@mbox .digsys.bg; ul Kaleto; s/d incl breakfast 40/60 lv) This three-star place is south of town, set amidst hills and best reached by taxi or private car. The rooms are spacious, and most doubles feature a balcony with great views. A good restaurant is attached.

Eating & Drinking

Gostilintsa (ul PR Slaveikov 35; mains 5-7 lv) Almost diagonally opposite the Starata Loza, this classy place is uninvitingly located behind a wooden door. The service is excellent, the meals are not too expensive and the menu is in English.

Zograf Mehana (ul PR Slaveikov 1; mains 5-8 lv) The traditional-style restaurant in the hotel of the same name is just off the main square and serves a reliable range of Bulgarian staples.

Restaurant Tryavienski Kut (☎ 2033; ul Angel Kânchev; mains 5-8 lv; 🕑 8am-midnight) This atmospheric restaurant in an imposing National Revival–style house has worn wooden floors and carved ceilings, and a good range of homemade Bulgarian cooking.

Starata Loza (☎ 4501; ul PR Slaveikov 44; mains 6-12 lv) The Old Vine features eccentric traditional décor (wood carvings on the interior, wine casks sticking out of the walls) and has a big menu of inventive Bulgarian fare, plus 27 kinds of *rakia* (fruit brandy). The specials,

such as pork stuffed with onions, sausage, mushrooms and walnut (11 lv) are expensive, but worth it. It's on the cobblestone street opposite the entrance to Daskalov House.

Slatkarnitsa Enitsa (☎ 6789; ul PR Slaveikov 25; 🕑 9am-9pm) There are tasty cakes and a corner for kids at this local sweet shop in the middle of town.

Bar Kokoracia (☎ 6811; ul Han Asparuh 1; 🕑 6pm-2am weekdays, to 4am weekends) This cool place with red paper lanterns and house music is the best watering hole in town.

Getting There & Away

Most public transport to Tryavna goes via Gabrovo; frequent minibuses connect the two (2 lv, 30 minutes). From other points of origin, you'll need to connect in Gabrovo. By train, Tryavna is along a spur track, and has nine passenger trains daily (3 lv, 50 minutes). It's one of the closest stops to Veliko Târnovo and thus easy to see before or after visiting that town.

GABROVO ГАБРОВО

☎ 066 / pop 64,340

A long and somewhat dusty town on the north–south road that crosses the Stara Planina, Gabrovo is not particularly remarkable in itself, but it is close to intriguing places, such as the artisans' village of Etâr, and has several local hiking opportunities. Its natives have an amusing old reputation for miserliness that makes them the butt of numerous jokes (they invented the one stotinka coin, says one). Despite the dig, Gabrovo's good-natured citizens have taken the initiative by creating a museum of humour; they also organise a biennial festival dedicated to the comic self-deprecation they've mastered.

The *Gabrovo* map, published by Domino and available in town, details 10 mountain-bike routes (ranging from 9km to 58km), which pass local villages, monasteries and ancient ruins. These trails are also excellent for hiking (see the boxed text, p188).

Information

Foreign exchange offices and ATMs are on ul Radetska.

Bulgarka Natural Park Directorate (☎ 808 857; www.ppbulgarka.nug.bg; ul Minzuhar 1) Provides information on hiking opportunities in Bulgarka Natural Park.

Internet Era (ul Skobelevska)

Matrix Internet Club (Hotel Balkan complex, ul Emanuil Manolov 14)

Tourist office (☎ /fax 828 483; did@globcom.net; pl Vŭzhrazhdane; ☼ 9am-5pm Mon-Fri) Provides brochures and general info, arranges private accommodation rooms, and can rent mountain bikes and advise about mountain-bike routes and hiking trails.

Sights

Certainly one of Bulgaria's more unusual museums is the **House of Humour & Satire** (☎ 807 228; www.humorhouse.bg; ul Bryanska 68; adult/student/child 4/2/2 lv, guided tour 6 lv; ☼ 9am-6pm summer, 9am-6pm Mon-Sat winter). This huge, ugly building has four floors, but ideas relating to humour run out by the 2nd floor – a fact that's funny in itself.

The upper floors contain unrelated art and fascinating masks from around the world. Most items are labelled in English; tours are in English, French or German.

There's a small number of **National Revival–period homes** on the eastern side of town, immediately behind the dominant (but rarely open) **Sveta Troitsa Church**. If you want to fill in some time, the quaint **Sveta Bogoroditsa Church** (ul Dyustabanov) is mildly interesting. The **Museum of Education** (☎ 804 071; ul Aprilovska 13) is accessible through the stunning courtyard in the Aprilov School. Also worth a peek is the **art gallery** (ul Sv Kiril i Metodii).

Festivals & Events

In May during odd-numbered years, Gabrovo hosts the **Biennial Festival of International Humour & Satire**, part of the annual **May Festivities of Culture**.

Other festivals include the **Balkan Youth Festival** in August and the **Days of Chamber Music** in September.

Sleeping & Eating

Like the town itself, accommodation in Gabrovo is neither here nor there. Considering the superior options in nearby Tryavna (p183) and Etâr (opposite), there's no real need to linger here. However, if you'd like to stay over, the tourist office can find private rooms (20 lv to 25 lv per person including breakfast).

Hotel Balkan (☎ 801 911; fax 801 057; ul Emanuil Manolov 14; s/d/ste 80/90/110 lv; P) This old mainstay has been admirably modernised, offering clean but unexciting rooms that are still better than many provincial hotels.

Tri Lovetsa (ul Emanuil Manolov 14; mains 5-7 lv) This tavern across from the Hotel Balkan does good traditional-style Bulgarian specialities, and has a breezy terrace for summer dining.

Gusto Pizza & Grill (mains 5-8 lv) This place inside the Hotel Balkan does decent Italian and Bulgarian food as well as pizza.

Old Gabrovo, on the eastern side of the River Yantra, has several restaurants and cafés, including **Restaurant Cafe VMRO** (mains 3-5 lv) and the more expensive **Strannopriemnitsa Inn** (mains 6-9 lv). Cafés line ul Dyustabanov and the footbridge along ul Aprilovska.

Getting There & Away

From the **bus station** (☎ 805 566; ul Stefan Karadzha) three daily buses serve Varna, Sliven, Burgas, Stara Zagora (8 lv, two hours) and Plovdiv (10 lv, three hours). Five or six daily buses go to Pleven, and there's a service to Sofia (9 lv, 3½ hours, daily). Buses also leave hourly for Tryavna and Veliko Târnovo (via the Dryanovo Monastery; 4 lv, one hour), crossing the mountains at Shipka Pass for Shipka village (2 lv, 50 minutes) and Kazanlâk (5 lv, 1½ hours).

The **train station** (☎ 827 127; pl Garov) has trains on a spur track of the Veliko Târnovo–Kazanlâk line. Services to both towns are infrequent, however.

ETÂR ЕТЪР
☎ 066

This complex of traditional artisans just 8km southeast of Gabrovo is a fun place for shopping, or just wandering and watching the craftsmen at work. It also offers nearby hiking. Cumulatively known as the **Etâr Ethnographic Village Museum** (☎ 801 831; www.etar.hit.bg; admission 7 lv; ☑ 8.30am-6pm), the market complex contains nearly 50 shops and workshops clustered along narrow lanes. It's set all by itself in a 7-hectare, tree-lined spot along the Gabrovo–Shipka road. Etâr's 19th-century National Revival–period style buildings house the workshops of bakers, cartwrights, cobblers, furriers, glass workers, hatters, jewellers, leather workers, millers, potters, weavers and more. True, it's all a bit precious, but there are quality goods produced, and if you're looking to take home a memento of bygone days in the Balkans, you could do worse than to shop at Etâr. Intriguingly, some of the workshops are powered by water from a stream running through the complex.

Enter the complex either on the northern side (near the Hotel Strannopriemnitsa), at the central administration building, or on the far southern side, near the large car park. A multi-entry, one-day ticket is usually required, and guided tours (in English, French or German) are available for another 7 lv per person (minimum of five people).

Fair Day (14 October) features traditional dance and music, played on instruments such as locally-made *kavals* (wooden flutes).

Domino's *Gabrovo* map (available in Gabrovo and sometimes elsewhere) includes a detailed Etâr map, though it's not really necessary as wandering aimlessly is part of the fun here.

Besides the market, there's also excellent **hiking** to be had in the lush, hilly forests around Etâr. A large map standing opposite the entrance to the ethnographic village details some 15 different trails through the nearby **Bulgarka Natural Park**, plus the time required to hike them. Some trails can be done as day hikes, allowing you to park at Etâr and return there afterwards. However, those planning more extensive hikes that involve sleeping in mountain huts should first consult the **Bulgarka Natural Park Directorate** (☎ 808 857; www.ppbulgarka.nug.bg; ul Minzuhar 1) in Gabrovo.

Sleeping

Hotel Strannopriemnitsa (☎ 801 831; s/d incl breakfast 36/60 lv) At the northern (Gabrovo) end of the complex, this hotel is decent value, though singles are tiny. The doubles have balconies with views (of the less interesting part of the complex).

Hotel Perla (☎ 801 984; d 42 lv) This friendly place offers the best value around, with spacious rooms that boast shiny bathrooms and balconies. Breakfast is 3 lv extra.

Eating

Restaurant Strannopriemnitsa (mains 6-8 lv) Part of the Hotel Strannopriemnitsa, this hunting lodge–style *mehana* (replete with wall-mounted deer antlers) has better décor than food. The service is good, however, and the outdoor tables overlook the grass and trees.

Renaissance Tavern (mains 7-10 lv) Inevitably, due to its location within the complex, the Renaissance charges more than most village restaurants, but the food is good and the setting enhances the overall Etâr experience.

HIKING IN THE STARA PLANINA

With an average height of little more than 700m, the Stara Planina (Old Mountain) range is not high, particularly compared with the Rila and Pirin Mountains. Nonetheless it is vast, covering 11,500 sq km (about 10% of Bulgaria) and, at close to 550km long, it extends almost the entire length of the country. Nearly 30 peaks are over 2000m high and the mountains feed one-third of Bulgaria's major rivers. The highest point is Mt Botev (2376m), north of Karlovo.

The Mountains of Bulgaria by Julian Perry describes the strenuous 25-day (650km to 700km) trek across the entire range. This trek – which starts at Berkovitsa, near the border with Serbia, and finishes at Emine Cape, about 20km northeast of Nesebâr on the Black Sea coast – is part of the trans-European E3 trek. The text in Perry's book is detailed, but the maps are poor, so buy the Stara Planina map, published by Kartografia and available at bookshops in Sofia. The Troyan Balkan map, available from the tourist office in Gabrovo (p186), is detailed, but specific to the Troyan and Apriltsi regions.

Some of the more interesting hikes along marked trails:

Cherni Osêm to Hizha Ambaritsa Four hours.
Dryanovo Ecotrail Four hours; see p183.
Etâr to Sokolski Monastery One hour, then continue to Shipka Pass (extra two to three hours – steep).
Gabrovo to Hizha Uzana Four hours.
Karlovo to Hizha Hubavets Two hours, or continue to Hizha Vasil Levski (another two to three hours) and Mt Botev (further two to three hours).
Shipka Monastery to Shipka Pass Two hours.
Sliven to Hizha Karandila Three hours.

The complex's little bakery sells basic takeaway food, such as glazed *simit* buns (a local speciality) and cheese pies, while the *sladkarnitsa* (sweet shop) offers a tempting and very colourful range of traditional sweets, including *lokum* (Turkish delight) and halvas.

Getting There & Away

From Gabrovo, take buses 1, 7 or 8 from ul Aprilov (2 lv, 15 minutes). Alternatively, catch the hourly Gabrovo–Kazanlâk bus, and bail at the turn-off; from here, walk 2km to reach Etâr. A taxi from Gabrovo costs about 7 lv one way. From Etâr, a taxi to Tryavna (about 20 lv) saves the trouble of bussing via Gabrovo. If you're driving, Etâr can also be done as a day trip from Veliko Târnovo, Arbanasi or Dryanovo (among other places).

LOVECH ЛОВЕЧ
☎ 068 / pop 41,050

Popular with weekending locals but less visited by foreign travellers, Lovech is a quiet, well-restored traditional village along the Osêm River, 35km south of Pleven. In the old quarter of Varosha, over 150 National Revival–period structures have been restored, and the covered bridge over the river is the photogenic symbol of the town.

Lovech was significant as a military outpost and trade centre during the Thracian and Roman eras, and again during the Second Bulgarian Empire. During the Ottoman occupation, however, it would reach its peak, though precariously playing with fire as the surreptitious headquarters of the Bulgarian Central Revolutionary Committee during the mid-19th century.

Orientation & Information

The adjacent bus and train stations are far enough from the centre to dissuade walking. Either take a taxi or walk along ul Tsacho Shishkov, veer to the right and follow the signs to the *centrum*. At the road's end, turn left along ul Bulgaria to reach the modern town, where the banks, foreign exchange offices and post office surround the main square, pl Dimitrov. Alternatively, to reach the old town, turn right past colourful, renovated buildings, and the Hotel Lovech, to the covered footbridge and nearby vehicle bridge.

Sights

Just past the Hotel Lovech is the **pokritiyat most** (covered footbridge) – the Balkans' only such structure. Built in 1872, and completely restored twice since, it once again features its original wooden design. Arts and crafts shops, as well as cafés, are found within. Passing the square beyond the bridge brings you to the **Art Gallery** (☎ 23 937; ul Vasil Levski 9; admission free; ⏱ 9am-noon & 1-6pm Mon-Sat), with works by local and other Bulgarian artists exhibited.

Extensive ruins of the **Hisar Fortress** (admission free; ⏱ 8am-6pm) are visible from all over the old town. Here the treaty with the Turks that lead to the creation of the Second Bulgarian Empire was signed. There are great views from the fortress, which is fun to explore. From Varosha, it's a 10- to 15-minute uphill walk.

From near the art gallery, follow the cobblestoned ul Hristo Ivanov Golemia uphill about 100m to the **Ethnographical Museum** (☎ 27 720; ul Hristo Ivanov Golemia; admission 3 lv; ⏱ 8am-noon & 2-5pm Mon-Sat). The two mid-19th-century buildings contain fascinating exhibits and period furniture, plus a cellar full of wine-making equipment. Leaflets with explanations in English, French or German are available.

About 50m further up, the **Vasil Levski Museum** (☎ 27 990; admission 2 lv; ⏱ 9am-5pm Mon-Fri) contains extensive displays about the revered revolutionary. Another 50m uphill is the renovated Byzantine **Sveta Bogoroditsa Church**, which is not always open.

From the church, follow the steps past more renovated National Revival homes leading to **Stratesh Hill**, where lilacs blossom and a stern **Vasil Levski statue** stands.

Sleeping

Hotel Tsariana (☎ 600 995; tsariana@mbox.digsys.bg; pl Todor Kirkov 10; s/d 24/36 lv) The refurbished Tsariana on Varosha's square has good rates and fine, though not terribly atmospheric, rooms.

Hotel Varosha 2003 (☎ 22 277; ul Ivan Drasov 23; s/d /ste/apt incl breakfast 30/40/50/60 lv; P) This recently renovated hotel on the river is very popular, and deservedly so. Its five spacious and well-equipped rooms lend a feeling of cosiness, enhanced by the hospitality of the owners, who serve breakfast in the garden and offer nourishing evening meals.

Hotel Lovech (☎ 604 717; ul Târgovska 12; s/d 30/46 lv) In Lovech centre by the footbridge, this old standby has been admirably renovated, and is a well-run and friendly place.

Hotel Oasis (☎ 26 239; ul NV Drasov 17; s/d 30/50 lv) Another riverfront hotel, the well-furnished Oasis is signposted 100m from the vehicle bridge. A decent restaurant, often featuring live music, is attached.

Eating

Mehana Gallereya (ul Vasil Levski; mains 4-7 lv) Located beside the eponymous Art Gallery, this *mehana* features a large courtyard, good service and very tasty food.

Mehana Billaya (ul Marni Poplukanov; mains 5-8 lv) Up the cobbled street from the Gallereya, the Billaya is equally atmospheric, if you don't mind the loud live music during the evenings.

Cafés and brasseries are found on pl Todor Kirkov in Varosha. A popular new watering hole, Power's Irish Pub, is located near the covered bridge.

Getting There & Away

From the **bus station** (☎ 603 618), hourly buses serve Troyan (4 lv, 45 minutes) from 7am to 7pm. Three daily buses serve Burgas (22 lv, six hours), Sliven (19 lv, four to five hours), Teteven (6 lv, 1¾ hours) and Veliko Târnovo (7 lv, two hours); more frequent buses cross the Stara Planina to Shipka (10 lv, 2½ hours, four daily) and Kazanlâk (12 lv, 3½ hours, four daily). Buses also leave hourly for Pleven (5 lv, one hour). Daily buses serve Sofia (14 lv, three hours, six daily), and one or two daily buses serve Vratsa (11 lv, three hours) in northern Bulgaria, via Cherven Bryag.

From the **train station** (☎ 634 935), three daily trains serve both Troyan (2.40 lv, one hour) and Levski (2.80 lv, 1 hour); from the latter, change for Sofia and the important railway hub of Gorna Oryakhovitsa (to get to Veliko Târnovo, among other places).

TROYAN ТРОЯН
☎ 0670 / pop 23,100

Troyan, associated mostly with its famous nearby monastery, is a laid-back, slightly faded town with crisp, clean mountain air. The grand, Soviet-era main square has a relaxed atmosphere and several well-frequented cafés. There's also a notable Pomak Muslim population. Although there's not much else to the place, it makes a good base for seeing the Troyan Monastery, Oreshak, Lovech and Karlovo. Troyan's also close to some excellent Stara Planina hiking paths.

Millennia ago, the Thracians first made Troyan strategically significant. Much later, during the Bulgarian National Revival period, it became famous for woodcarving, metalwork and particularly pottery. Examples of these crafts can be admired at the charming museum in Troyan, or bought at Oreshak.

Orientation

From the bus and train stations, cross the Bely Osâm River by walking 300m over the footbridge along ul Zahari Stoyanov to reach the centre. From here, turn right and walk along the mall, ul General Kartsov, to Troyan's main square, pl Vûzhrazhdane. The narrow main road, ul Vasil Levski, starts north of the square and hugs the river.

Information

The Troyan **tourist office** (☎ 35 064; infotroyan@ yahoo.com; ul Vasil Levski 133; 🕑 8am-8pm summer, 9am-5pm Mon-Fri winter) can find private accommodation, provide maps, and arrange activities, such as horse riding, as well as car rental from about 40 lv per day.

Sights

The impressive **Museum of Folk Craft & Applied Arts** (☎ 62 063; pl Vûzhrazhdane; admission 2 lv; 🕑 9am-5pm Mon-Fri) by the bridge comprises 10 halls exhibiting local textiles, woodcarving, metalwork, weaving, pottery and ceramics, as well as some archaeological artefacts. The adjoining **History Museum**, included in the admission cost, is also worth a look.

Activities

Horse riding (15 lv per person per hour) at local villages can be arranged by the tourist centre, which also assists with renting **mountain bikes** (per hour/day 1/8 lv); there are five designated mountain-bike routes, including to Troyan Monastery (right) and the nearby town of Chiflik. Guides (40 lv per day), who speak French, German or English, are available for local tours and **hikes**.

Sleeping & Eating

The tourist office can arrange rooms in private homes in Troyan as well as in nearby villages, such as Oreshak (opposite), for about 15 lv per person, usually with breakfast. It also offers apartments in central Troyan with kitchen facilities, sitting room and bathroom (40 lv to 50 lv per double).

Hotel Panorama (☎ 622 930; hotelpanoramatr@ mail.bg; Park Kâpincho; s/d 30/40 lv) The renovated Panorama, located in the hillside park above town, offers clean and decent rooms in a relaxed setting. Taxis to the hotel cost about 2 lv from the bus station or town centre.

Hotel Nunki (☎ 622 160; ul Minko Radkovski) Under renovation at the time of research (but due to re-open soon), the rooms here promise to be large, quiet and traditionally furnished, with good, modern bathrooms. The hotel's restaurant offers good value and tasty food. The Nunki is at the start of the bridge (from where the road leads to Troyan Monastery), about 100m across from the tourist office.

Troyan Plaza Hotel (☎ 64 399; www.troyanplaza .com; ul PR Slaveykov 54; s/d/ste incl breakfast 70/90/110 lv; 🅿 🖳) Troyan's classiest place, the four-star Troyan Plaza has all the expected amenities, including two restaurants and a spa centre. It can arrange activities such as horse-riding, archery and shooting.

Café Antik (☎ 60 910; Ploshtad Vûzhrazhdane; mains 7-12 lv; 🕑 7am-midnight) This café-restaurant, located behind the folk museum and with relaxing views of the river, is a good bet for coffee on the terrace when it's warm out, or a shot of the very strong Troyan brandy when it's cold. It also does some inventive (though relatively expensive) meat dishes.

A couple of cafés and pizza places are also found on the corner of ul Vasil Levski and pl Vûzhrazhdane.

Getting There & Away

From the Troyan **bus station** (☎ 62 172), one daily bus serves Sofia (7 lv, three hours), at 2pm; buses passing through Lovech (2 lv, 45 minutes, hourly) have immediate connections to Pleven. Three daily buses serve Chiflik (2.60 lv, 50 minutes). For Troyan Monastery, take the hourly bus for Cherny Osâm and ask to disembark at the gates (the bus goes right past). Troyan is at the end of a spur track south of Lovech, complicating travel by train.

AROUND TROYAN
Troyan Monastery

Only 10km southeast of Troyan is Bulgaria's third-largest **monastery** (admission free, photos 5 lv, video 15 lv; 🕑 6am-10pm), after Rila (p117) and Bachkovo (p153). Troyan stands out for its powerful and searching frescoes, painted by Bulgarian master Zahari Zograf, regarded as the leading mural artist of the Bulgarian National Revival period. One of the highlights of central Bulgaria, it can nevertheless be seen in an hour or two.

Some of this 16th-century monastery survived numerous attacks by the Turks between the 16th and 18th centuries, but most of today's monastery dates to 1835. All of the striking murals inside the **Church of the Holy Virgin** were painted in the 1840s by Zahari Zograf. The church is poorly lit, except for the rows of candles lit mostly by devout old ladies visiting, so it's hard to see the detail of the frescoes inside, though restoration work to brighten them up is happily underway. The very best of Zograf's frescoes, however, are outside on the back wall. They depict Judgment Day, the apocalypse and hell, with the seven-headed fire-breathing dragon and demonic torture of sinners in hell aptly illustrating the vivid old Bulgarian ecclesiastical imagination.

The monastery is also renowned for its hand-carved wood altar and iconostasis, crafted in the mid-19th century by master carvers from Tryavna. The highlight for most, though, is the legendary Three-Handed Holy Virgin, only seen in public during the annual monastery celebrations on **Virgin Mary's Day** (15 August).

The 19th-century revolutionary leader, Vasil Levski, formed and trained insurgents at the monastery and urged the monks themselves to take up arms against the Turks in 1876. This history is highlighted in the small, separate **museum** (admission 4 lv) on the 3rd floor. The museum door is usually locked, but staff at the reception office inside the gate can open it.

Troyan Monastery is not as touristy as famous Rila Monastery (p117), though it's getting there, and several cafés, restaurants, souvenir shops and art galleries are gathered around it.

Monk Nektarii at the **reception office** (☎ 0896668015) handles room bookings. Rooms are basic but expensive (doubles 60 lv), reflecting the monastery's increasing popularity, so book ahead.

Monastirska Bara (☎ 0888798591; mains 2-5 lv; ⊗ 8am-midnight) is a decent and cheap *mehana* next to the monastery. Service can be a bit rough, though, and the modern Bulgarian pop playing doesn't really enhance the hallowed atmosphere of the monastery.

GETTING THERE & AWAY
Every hour, a bus between Troyan and Cherni Osêm stops at the monastery gates. A taxi from central Troyan to the monastery costs about 7 lv for a one-way trip. Most taxi drivers will agree to return in an hour or two to take you back to Troyan.

Oreshak Орешак
Only 6km southeast of Troyan is Oreshak, home of the **National Fair and Exhibition of Arts & Crafts Complex** (☎ 06952-2317; ⊗ 8am-6pm Tue-Sun). This complex displays and sells embroidery, pottery, ceramics, weaving, woodcarving and metalwork. It's the best place in the Stara Planina region for buying authentic, locally made souvenirs at reasonable prices. The week-long annual fair in mid-August is held at the complex. The village bubbles over again during the **Festival of the Plums and Plum Brandy** (late September).

Oreshak offers an alternative, and more scenic, accommodation option to Troyan, and is not far (4km) by bus or on foot from the Troyan Monastery. The tourist office in Troyan (see opposite) can arrange private rooms for about 20 lv per person including breakfast. Some of these private homes also can cook up large servings of traditional meals, though at additional cost.

An hourly bus (2 lv, 20 minutes) leaves Troyan bus station for Cherni Osêm, and stops at Oreshak and the Troyan Monastery.

KOPRIVSHTITSA КОПРИВЩИЦА
☎ 07184 / pop 2900
This unique museum-village, nestled in wooded hills between Karlovo and Sofia, is a perfectly – and deliberately – preserved hamlet filled with Bulgarian National Revival–period architecture, cobblestone streets, and bridges that arc gently over a lovely brook. Nearly 400 buildings of architectural and historical significance are protected by government decree, some of them restored churches and house-museums containing fascinating collections of décor and implements from yesteryear.

Because much of Koprivshtitsa (Ko-*priv-shti-tsa*) is filled with rambling, overgrown lanes, it's also a very safe and fun place for children to scamper around in. Some of the traditional homes function as guesthouses or restaurants, most loaded with traditional ambience, making Koprivshtitsa a romantic getaway, too. And, while the inevitable busloads of tour groups add to the gentrified sense of being in a giant open-air museum, the muddiness of the lanes after the rain, and the garrulous, bemused old locals keep Koprivshtitsa from being too precious for its own good.

CENTRAL BULGARIA

History

Koprivshtitsa was first settled at the end of the 14th century by Bulgarians of various social stations fleeing the Turkish invasion of Veliko Târnovo. Sheep, cattle and goat herding developed the local economy, and a wealthy merchant class arose. Sacked by brigands in 1793, 1804 and 1809, Koprivshtitsa was rebuilt during the mid-19th century. The population subsequently reached about 12,000 – thus becoming almost as big as Sofia was at the time.

Koprivshtitsa is most famous in Bulgarian history, however, as the place where Todor Kableshkov (or Georgi Tihanek, according to some sources) proclaimed the national uprising against the Turks on 20 April 1876, from the tiny bridge now known as the Kalachev Bridge (also called Kableshkov Bridge), itself dating from 1813. This noble, if somewhat foolhardy, event has lent its name to the village's main square, dominated by the 1876 April Uprising Mausoleum.

After 1878 and independence from the Turks, many of Koprivshtitsa's merchants and intellectuals left their mountain redoubts for the cities, leaving the village essentially unchanged to this day. In 1952, the communist Bulgarian government declared the village a town-museum, and later, in 1971, a 'historical reserve'.

Orientation

From the bus stop, walk along the river (keeping it on your right) to reach the main square, pl 20 April, which houses the Tourist Information Centre. Most of the historical sites and museums are in the small streets above the square.

Information

DSK Bank (next to the bus stop) is the town's only bank. It has an ATM and money exchange. There is an OBB Bank ATM right off the main square, next to the Mehana 20 April on ul Hadzhi Nencho Palaveev. The post office and telephone centre are located across from the town hall on ul Lyuben Karavelov.

Hadzhi Nencho Palaveev Cultural Centre
(☎ 2034; ul Hadzhi Nencho Palaveev 78) Information on local festivals or cultural events is available here, or at the tourist office.

Heroes Internet Club (ul Hadzhi Nencho Palaveev; per hr 1.50 lv; 🕒 9am-midnight)

Tourist Information Centre (☎ /fax 2191; www .koprivshtitsa.info; pl 20 April; 🕒 10am-1pm & 2-7pm) This very helpful and friendly centre, a small maroon building on the main square, provides local information and can organise private accommodation.

Sights
HOUSE-MUSEUMS

Koprivshtitsa boasts six house-museums, of which some are closed either on Monday or Tuesday (all operate Wednesday through Sunday). A combined ticket for all six museums (adults/students 5/3 lv) is available at the souvenir shop Kupchinitsa two doors up the hill from the Tourist Information Centre; most of the museums also sell tickets.

Karavelov House (☎ 2176; ul Hadzhi Nencho Palaveev 39; 🕒 9.30am-5.30pm Wed-Mon) was occupied by the parents of the eminent Lyuben Karavelov (1834–79), a journalist and printer who worked for expatriate Bulgarian revolutionary groups based in Russia, Serbia and Romania. He was also the first chairman of the Bulgarian Central Revolutionary Committee. A printing press where various seditious newspapers of Karavelov's were produced is among the exhibits. The three separate buildings were constructed between 1810 and 1835.

Oslekov House (☎ 2555; ul Gereniloto 4; 🕒 9.30am-5.30pm Wed-Mon) was built by Oslekov, a rich merchant who was killed in the line of duty during the 1876 April Uprising. Oslekov House was built between 1853 and 1856, and is arguably the best example of Bulgarian National Revival–period architecture in Koprivshtitsa, with a triple-arched entrance, spacious interior, stylish furniture and brightly coloured walls. Woodcarved ceilings, collections of 19th-century costumes, paintings and jewellery add to the experience. Several woodcarvings, some of which were bought during Oslekov's extensive travels, are also on display.

Debelyanov House (☎ 2077; ul Dimcho Debelyanov 6; 🕒 9.30am-5.30pm Tue-Sun) is dedicated to Dimcho Debelyanov (1887–1916), a great poet who penned outstanding works before tragically dying in WWI. Built in 1830, the house features a pretty garden and numerous displays about Debelyanov, but the expected period furniture is scarce and the ceilings low. Debelyanov's grave can be seen in the grounds of the Church of Uspenie Bogorodichno (p194).

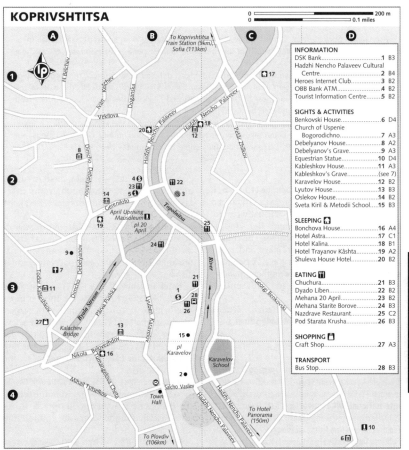

KOPRIVSHTITSA

0 — 200 m
0 — 0.1 miles

INFORMATION
DSK Bank...1 B3
Hadzhi Nencho Palaveev Cultural
    Centre...2 B4
Heroes Internet Club.........................3 B2
OBB Bank ATM...................................4 B2
Tourist Information Centre.............5 B2

SIGHTS & ACTIVITIES
Benkovski House.................................6 D4
Church of Usenie
    Bogorodichno................................7 A3
Debelyanov House..............................8 A2
Debelyanov's Grave............................9 A3
Equestrian Statue..............................10 D4
Kableshkov House.............................11 A3
Kableshkov's Grave.....................(see 7)
Karavelov House................................12 B2
Lyutov House......................................13 B3
Oslekov House...................................14 B2
Sveta Kiril & Metodii School.........15 B3

SLEEPING
Bonchova House...............................16 A4
Hotel Astra...17 C1
Hotel Kalina......................................18 B1
Hotel Trayanov Kâshta..................19 A2
Shuleva House Hotel......................20 B2

EATING
Chuchura...21 B3
Dyado Liben.......................................22 B3
Mehana 20 April...............................23 B2
Mehana Starite Borove...................24 B3
Nazdrave Restaurant.......................25 C2
Pod Starata Krusha..........................26 B3

SHOPPING
Craft Shop...27 A3

TRANSPORT
Bus Stop..28 B3

CENTRAL BULGARIA

A well-travelled man of means, Todor Kableshkov (1851–76) is revered as having (probably) been the person who fired the first shot in anger to start the 1876 uprising against the Turks. His former home, the glorious **Kableshkov House** (☎ 2054; ul Todor Kableshkov 8; ⏰ 9.30am-5.30pm Tue-Sun), dates back to 1845 and has numerous exhibits about the April Uprising. Kableshkov's grave can also be seen in the grounds of the Church of Uspenie Bogorodichno (p194).

Also called Topalov House, after the original owner, **Lyutov House** (☎ 2134; ul Nikola Belovezhdov 2; ⏰ 9.30am-5.30pm Wed-Mon) was built in 1854 in a style that mimicked Plovdiv's characteristic baroque houses. It's

Koprivshtitsa's best-preserved house-museum, featuring a lavish salon with intricately carved ceilings; the landscapes painted on them were created by Mr Lyutov himself. The lower floor contains an exhibit of locally made felt cloths.

Built in 1831 on a southeastern hillside, **Benkovski House** (☎ 2030; ul Georgi Benkovski 5; ⏰ 9.30am-5.30pm Wed-Mon) is associated with the dashing Georgi Benkovski (1843–76), a rebel cavalry commander who led many successful battles until dying in a Turkish ambush. Above the house, and easy to spot from the village centre, is a huge **equestrian statue** of Benkovski on horseback; climb up to it for the excellent views over the entire valley.

CENTRAL BULGARIA

HIKING IN THE SREDNA GORA

The Sredna Gora (Central Range) mountains are spread over 6000 sq km from Iskâr Gorge (near Sofia) to the Tundzha Valley (south of Yambol). The highest peak is Mt Bogdan (1603m) near Koprivshtitsa.

The Mountains of Bulgaria by Julian Perry provides a detailed description of the popular two- or three-day hike from Hisar (Hisarya) to Koprivshtitsa (or vice versa). No dedicated map of the Sredna Gora is available, but most of the mountains and hiking routes are included in the map of Stara Planina that is published by Kartografia.

The map of Koprivshtitsa, published by Domino and available in the village, includes a small, but clear, map with five enticing hiking routes around the surrounding hills. One trail (about four hours one way) leads to Mt Bogdan, and a hut where hikers can stay overnight.

OTHER SIGHTS

The **Church of Uspenie Bogorodichno** (Church of the Dormition of the Virgin) on ul Dimcho Debelyanov, built in 1817, is usually closed, but visitors can peer through the window and wander around the gardens. The church grounds contain **Kableshkov's grave**, and, in the upper section, **Debelyanov's grave**. A poignant statue features Debelyanov's mother anxiously awaiting his return, and reads 'I die and am yet born again in light.'

Beside the park along ul Hadzhi Nencho Palaveev is the **Sveta Kiril & Metodii School**, built in 1837.

Festivals & Events

Re-enactment of the 1876 April Uprising (1-2 May) The fateful historical events of the 1876 April Uprising are re-enacted in full costume by locals who prepare for weeks.

International Folk Festival (next festival summer 2010) Held every five years; folk dancers from all over the country converge here for the occasion.

Folklore Days Festival (mid-August) Traditional Bulgarian music and dance troupes perform throughout the town.

Sleeping

Most of the year, Koprivshtitsa's supply of accommodation outweighs demand and thus means there is a lot to choose from, and at reasonable rates. The quality of private rooms is good, though they don't always have bathrooms within the room. The **Tourist Information Centre** (☎ /fax 2191; koprivshtitsa@hotmail.com; pl 20 April) can arrange private rooms from 25 lv per person during the summer, and less at other times.

Shuleva House Hotel (☎ 2091; ul Hadzhi Nencho Palaveev 37; s/d/apt 18/24/40 lv) This hotel with large, simple and clean rooms is good value, and staff are friendly.

Bonchova House (☎ 2614; ul Tumangelova Cheta 26; d/apt 20/50 lv) Close to the Kalachev Bridge, this cosy new place has two bright, modern rooms and an apartment; the common room is relaxing and has a working fireplace. Breakfast is 5 lv extra.

Hotel Kalina (☎ 2032; ul Hadzhi Nencho Palaveev 15; s/d 36/50 lv) The three-star Kalina has a certain amount of class, with spotless rooms and professional service. Rates are good value, and it also has a nice garden.

Hotel Trayanov Kâshta (☎ 3750; ul Gereniloto 5; d/tr/apt 40/50/60 lv) Perhaps the most atmospheric place in town, this house with garden inside an enclosed courtyard has only a few rooms, which are nevertheless traditionally furnished and colourful. The upstairs balcony overlooking the back lawn is a great place for an evening drink.

Hotel Panorama (☎ 2035; ul Georgi Benkovski 40; s/d/f 45/60/80 lv) Although it's 400m from the centre, the Panorama is a very good option. It has lovely views, and the rooms are comfortable and well furnished.

Hotel Astra (☎ 2364; hotel_astra@hotmail.com; ul Hadzhi Nencho Palaveev 11; s/d 45/60 lv) Set beautifully in a garden, the Astra is a popular place with large and well-kept rooms.

Eating

Dyado Liben (☎ 2109; ul Hadzhi Nencho Palaveev 47; mains 2.50-6 lv; ⏱ 11am-midnight) Astonishingly big, this traditional restaurant housed in a mansion dating from 1852 is a wonderfully atmospheric – and inexpensive – place for a hearty evening meal. Management says it can seat 100 people, all in a warren of halls graced with ornate painted walls and heavy, worn wood floors. There's even a circular room where tables orbit a huge, column-like traditional stove extending from floor to ceiling. Find it just across the bridge leading from the main square inside the facing courtyard.

Pod Starata Krusha (☎ 2163; ul Hadzhi Nencho Palaveev 56; mains 4-6 lv) Right next to the bus station, this cosy little tavern is a nice choice for a traditional evening meal or a quick breakfast (it even has Turkish coffee) before your bus departs. Renowned Targovista wine from the Veliko Târnovo area is served, accompanied by traditional Bulgarian music.

Chuchura (☎ 2712; ul Hadzhi Nencho Palaveev 66; mains 4-7 lv) Another restaurant over near the bus stop, the Chuchura's terrace makes a fine spot for alfresco dining. Food is good and there's a small hotel attached, too.

Mehana Starite Borove (pl 20 April; mains 4-7 lv) The best place for a summertime drink, the Starite Borove is hidden along a laneway near the main square, close to the shady park. The food is decent, but not as good as some of the other places.

Nazdrave Restaurant (☎ 087624816; bul Hadzhi Nencho Palaveev 53; mains 4-7 lv) This cosy place on the opposite bank of the river is good for an evening meal, and has a relaxing summertime terrace – better than sitting indoors when the loud and decidedly non-traditional Bulgarian pop blares from the TV. The Nazdrave is also a great breakfast nook, with crepes accompanied by local strawberry jam and, if you can handle the sourness, very thick, village-fresh *ovcho kiselo mlyako* (sheep's-milk yoghurt).

Mehana 20 April (☎ 0899368220; pl 20 April; mains 5-7 lv; ⏰ 8am-midnight) This friendly place, on the edge of the square of the same name and close to the Tourist Information Centre, offers a short menu of traditional Koprivshtitsa dishes, as well as deliciously done freshwater fish. Dining is enjoyed indoors or (much better) in an attractive back courtyard.

Shopping

The souvenir shops surrounding the main square are fairly generic. If you want a specific memento of Koprivshtitsa, snatch up a felt-cloth carpet or bag; examples are on display inside Lyutov House (p193). At the **Craft Shop** (☎ 2191; ul Dimcho Debelyanov; ⏰ 10am-4pm Mon-Sat), visitors can see locals producing felt-cloth products, some of which are sold next door.

Keep an eye out for Neli Keremicheva, the woman usually found under a slanting umbrella at the beginning of the square; she sells delicious local blueberry and strawberry jam, as well as *kiselo mlyako* so thick it won't budge when held upside down.

Getting There & Away

Especially considering its significance as a tourist destination, Koprivshtitsa seems rather poorly served by public transport. The train station is some 9km north of the village itself, thus necessitating a shuttle bus (1 lv, 15 minutes). These buses are theoretically timetabled to meet incoming trains, while bringing passengers from Koprivshtitsa to meet outgoing ones. However, if the shuttle bus doesn't come, as has been known to happen, there are no taxis, and the incredibly unhelpful station masters have no phone. With no mobile phone coverage in this remote area, you're left to soldier on to the narrow main road and walk the 8km to town. Good luck!

If you do decide to come by train, there are services from Sofia (5 lv, 2½ hours, four daily) and connections can be made there or in Karlovo for Plovdiv and other points in the country. There's also a daily train to Burgas (11 lv, five hours).

Alternatively, in the centre of Koprivshtitsa the little bus stop has a posted list of train times, as well as connecting buses and long-distance bus routes. Five daily buses go to Sofia (7 lv, two hours), the first leaving at 6.45am, while the bus to Plovdiv (7 lv, two hours, daily) departs at a similarly ungodly hour (6.30am). However, note that on Sundays the Plovdiv bus leaves at a more reasonable 2pm.

HISAR ХИСАР
☎ 0337 / pop 10,000

Therapeutic mineral springs have been Hisar's (also known as Hisarya) main claim to fame ever since Roman times, when it was named Diokletianopolis, after the Emperor Diocletian. Altogether, there are 22 mineral-water springs here, said to cure many ailments; the popularity of these springs even today has ensured this sleepy mountain town's livelihood. Since it's mostly visited in summer, visiting in winter means you will have the place to yourself. The main street has some unique ruins from the days of ancient Rome, though the major reason to visit today, as it was then, is for the indolent spa therapy.

Orientation & Information

From the bus/train stations, walk (300m) down to the main road, ul Hristo Botev, leaving the ruins on your right. Then turn right onto bul Ivan Vazov to reach the town centre and the park.

A DSK Bank with ATM is on the corner of ul Hristo Botev and bul Ivan Vazov, and there's an internet café on bul General Gurko.

Sights

Hisar's **Roman walls**, later fortified by the Byzantines, are over 5m high and up to 3m thick, and are some of the best-preserved Roman ruins in all of Bulgaria. Built to protect a 30-hectare span of the town and its mineral baths from invaders, the walls escaped damage from Slavic raiders, who left this part of Bulgaria alone. The most visited section is a short walk from the bus and train stations.

More Roman ruins are found along unnamed roads heading towards the town centre from the main road. These unfenced ruins, which you can wander for free, include portions of an amphitheatre, baths and some dwellings.

The **Archaeological Museum** (☎ 62 012; ul Stamboliyski 8; admission 2 lv; ☺ 8am-noon & 1-5pm) features a scale model of the city walls as they would have originally appeared, and some photos of early excavations. Nevertheless, the displays about traditional regional costumes and agricultural and weaving equipment are more engaging. The poorly signposted museum is located past the post office, and is accessible from the main road through a pretty courtyard.

Both hotels listed below have **balneological centres**, offering all sorts of treatments, such as aromatherapy and hydrotherapy. Consultations with 'head physicians' cost from 30 lv for 30 minutes, depending on the treatment required, and include any medications, ointments or unguents the doctor is inspired to give you.

Sleeping & Eating

Both hotels are about 1km down bul General Gurko, which starts about 700m along the main road from the bus and train stations; look for the sign (in English) to Hotel Augusta. Both are close to the mineral springs.

Hotel Augusta (☎ 63 821; www.augustaspa.com; bul General Gurko 3; s 78-98 lv, d 88-138 lv; P ☐ ☒) One of Hisar's two main hotels is the Augusta, a little further down the road from the Hotel Hisar and round to the right. It has two buildings, one fully refurbished with air con and smart modern rooms, the other more basic. Both have access to the pool and spa complex.

Hotel Hisar (☎ 62 717; fax 62 634; bul General Gurko; s/d 98/118 lv; P ☒ ☐ ☒) The post-renovation prices at the Hisar have indeed risen, but get you handsome, well-maintained rooms, several restaurants, a great outdoor pool, a sauna and fitness centre, as well as a modern balneological complex.

Private rooms are generally available on bul General Gurko (look for the signs reading *stay pod naem*).

Besides the good restaurants in both hotels, several hearty, home-style *mehanas* line bul General Gurko; try the **Évropa** (bul General Gurko) or the **National** (bul General Gurko). Also, the **Tsesar** (ul Hristo Botev) serves up excellent Bulgarian grills in a rustic courtyard, decorated by a faux windmill. Chinar, near the town's church, is another popular place.

Getting There & Away

The adjoining train station and **bus station** (☎ 62 069) both have regional connections. Six daily buses go to Karlovo (2 lv, 30 minutes) and there are other connections to Sofia (13 lv, three hours, three daily) and Veliko Târnovo (12 lv, 3½ hours, four daily) via Kazanlâk (7 lv, two hours, one daily) and Gabrovo (10 lv, three hours, three daily). Regular buses between Karlovo (2 lv, 40 minutes, hourly) and Panagyurishte (3 lv, 1½ hours, two daily on Friday, Saturday and Sunday) also pass through and stop in Hisar.

There are no direct train services from Hisar to Karlovo, but several daily trains connect Hisar with Plovdiv (2.10 lv, 30 minutes).

KARLOVO КАРЛОВО

☎ 0335 / pop 24,680

Historic Karlovo, nestled in the foothills of the Stara Planina roughly equidistant from Koprivshtitsa and Kazanlâk, is not just another appealing mountain town full of National Revival–era architecture and antiquated churches; it's also venerated as the birthplace of Vasil Levski, the leader of the revolution against the Turks in the early 1870s. Although this historic link is everywhere in Karlovo, most (non-Bulgarian, at least) visitors will be rather more inspired by the town's placid atmosphere, churches and classic architecture.

Orientation & Information

Karlovo sprawls across a long hill, at the base of which are the bus and train stations. From the train station, cross the small park to where three roads go up the hill; the central one, ul

CENTRAL BULGARIA

VASIL LEVSKI

The most revered person in modern Bulgarian history may well be Vasil Levski, whose name graces myriad streets and squares, and who is immortalised in statues and museums throughout the country as 'the apostle of freedom' for his contributions to organising the national resistance to Ottoman rule.

Vasil Ivanov Kunchev was born on 18 July 1837 in Karlovo, and given the nom de guerre 'Levski' (from the Bulgarian word for lion) by his peers. He studied and worked as a monk in Stara Zagora, but in 1862 moved to Belgrade, riding an uncle's horse, to join the anti-Turkish rebellion led by Georgi Rakovski. In 1864, he formally quit from monastic life. After various misadventures the young Levski moved to Bucharest three years later, where he conspired with another revolutionary, Panaiot Hitov. In the summer of the same year Levski was dispatched by Hitov back to Karlovo, where he briefly joined the legion of yet another revered guerrilla, Lyuben Karavelov, before undertaking further conspiratorial travels in Romania and Istanbul.

From 1869 until his betrayal by a comrade to the Turks three years later, Levski travelled the Bulgarian countryside continuously, establishing revolutionary committees in places such as Stara Zagora, Sliven and Lovech. Often, remote monasteries were used to conceal rebels or communicate with the different committee members.

Against Levski's orders, enterprising fighters decided to rob an Ottoman postal courier in the autumn of 1872, provoking a Turkish crackdown designed to unravel the well-concealed revolutionary networks, especially in Lovech, where the clandestine political leadership of the freedom fighters was based. As the number of arrests multiplied, Levski undertook a desperate journey to save the organisation's documents before they could fall into the hands of the Turks. However, on 27 December 1872, he was captured by the Turks in Lovech, and hanged in Sofia on 19 February 1873.

Vasil Levski's dream for a free Bulgaria was, interestingly enough, fuelled by the ideals of liberty, equality and fraternity for all (even the non-Bulgarians in Bulgaria), as exemplified in the rhetoric of the French Revolution. Had he lived to see a liberated Bulgaria, the 'apostle of freedom' might well have sought to continue his quest to help free 'other enslaved nations', as he himself once put it – thus making him a revolutionary in the truest sense.

Vasil Levski, becomes the town's main artery later on. It stretches for 2km to the town square, pl 20 Yuli.

The bus station is about 100m up the left of the three roads from the train station, past the yellowish block of flats and to the right.

There are several foreign exchange offices and internet centres at the top end of ul Vasil Levski.

Sights & Activities

You can see Karlovo's main sights by walking up ul Vasil Levski to pl 20 Yuli. Stop first at pl Vasil Levski, where the great man is immortalised in a grand **statue** depicting him with a lion (a reference to the adopted nickname of 'lion' given to him by his peers). Turn right, and right again, to the marvellous **Sveta Bogoroditsa Church** (admission free; 7am-7pm), a pink structure that contains intricate wooden iconostases. Opposite, the similarly coloured **History Museum** (4728; ul Vŭzrozhdenska 4; admission 0.50 lv;

9am-noon & 1-5pm Tue-Sun) features significant ethnological displays.

Further up ul Vasil Levski, a small park contains the disused and closed **Kurshum Mosque**, built in 1485 during the Ottoman occupation. Continue up the mall to the town square, then head left (west) for about 300m, past the **clock tower**, to the **Vasil Levski Museum** (3489; www.vlevskimuseum-bg.org; ul Gen Kartzov 57; admission 1 lv; 8.30am-1pm & 2-5pm Mon-Fri). This set of rooms around a cobblestone courtyard contains several exhibits about Levski with explanations in English. Ask the caretaker to show you the modern shrine, where you can see a lock of Levski's hair while listening to taped religious chants in Bulgarian. A guided tour in English costs 2.50 lv per person.

Guided nature tours, walking, paragliding, cultural trips and rock climbing trips are offered by Richard and Deborah Adams of **Bulgarian Mountain Tours** (www.bulgarianmountain tours.com; Vasil Levski village), which is based in the village of Vasil Levski, a 10-minute drive southeast of Karlovo.

Sleeping

Hotel Fani (ul Vasil Levski 73; r per person 10 lv) This small, family-run place next to a popular lunchspot offers two rooms – basic, but clean and tidy. They share a bathroom; nevertheless it's still great value.

Hemus Hotel (☎ 94 597; ul Vasil Levski 87; s/d 12/16 lv) Another small family-run hotel, the Hemus has four comfortable rooms and friendly owners. Since it's not obvious, follow the street numbers or ask around.

Sherev Hotel (☎ 93 380; pl 20 Yuli; s 30-40 lv, d 60-115 lv) Enjoying Karlovo's best location, overlooking the square and its popular cafés and restaurants, the Sherev is somewhat overpriced. The unrenovated rooms are run-down, and in general it's not great value.

Eating

Ploshtad 20 Yuli has numerous restaurants and cafés; the best are on either side of the Sherev Hotel, with the **Voenen Klub** (pl 20 Yuli; mains 4-6 lv) bar-restaurant on the opposite side of the square also deserving a mention. Over near pl Sveti Nikolai, **Restaurant Dionisi** (ul Evlogi Georgiev; mains 4-7 lv) also does hearty, home-cooked fare.

Getting There & Away

From the **bus station** (☎ 93 155), eight daily buses serve Hisar (2 lv, 30 minutes), and several depart for Sofia (10 lv, three hours, two daily) and Veliko Târnovo (12.50 lv, 2½ hours, two daily). About every hour, a bus travelling to or from Plovdiv (4 lv, one hour) stops in Karlovo, not far from the Vasil Levski Museum.

The tidy **train station** (☎ 94 641) is on the line between Sofia and Burgas, going via Kazanlâk and Sliven. From Sofia, two trains (6.30 lv, 2¼ hours) stop at Karlovo. The express from Sofia continues to Burgas (10.30 lv, four hours). Six daily trains also go to Plovdiv (3 lv, two hours), but the bus is far quicker and more frequent.

KAZANLÂK КАЗАНЛЪК

☎ 0431 / pop 52,680

A bit rough around the edges, Kazanlâk is nevertheless a fascinating town where Bulgaria's various ethnic and religious groups commingle amicably. It's a place with a surprisingly active nightlife, considering the town's general scruffiness where hole-in-the-wall eateries flame roast chicken and the old Soviet apartment blocks are yellowing as if they've been smoked on too much. Nevertheless, when you throw in a rather fine square, some posh accommodation options, and glorious archaeological remains from the area's ancient Thracian civilisation, Kazanlâk becomes an interesting enough place to spend a night or two. It's also the jumping-off point for journeys across the Valley of Roses (Rozovata Dolina), a wide plain blooming with roses, responsible for over 60% of the world's supply of fragrant rose oil. Crossing the plain, one ascends to Shipka village and Shipka Pass, site of a very decisive battle in the 1877–78 Russo-Turkish War.

Originally settled as long ago as 2000 BC, the Kazanlâk area was developed by the Thracians, whose city, Sevtopolis, existed nearby. In the 4th century BC, a magnificent tomb was built, presumably for one of the Thracian kings, which still exists on the northeast side of town and is a Unesco World Heritage site. The Romans inherited the city of Sevtopolis, but modern Kazanlâk only came into being during the 14th century, as an advance guard for the protection of the Shipka Pass over the mountains just north of it. Today, the town retains considerable Ottoman spirit, with a working mosque and notable Turkish and Pomak Muslim minorities. Indeed, several of the villages in the vicinity of Kazanlâk are largely or entirely populated by such holdovers of the Ottoman empire in Bulgaria.

Orientation

Most of the action in Kazanlâk is centred on the main square, pl Sevtopolis; here and in the near vicinity are the majority of hotels, restaurants, bars and services.

It's a 10-minute walk from the bus and train stations northwards to the square. The entertaining *pazar* (open market) is five minutes northeast of the square at the corner of ul Otets Paisii and ul Slavyanska. Across from it is the town's mosque, built in Ottoman times. The town's main attraction, its Thracian Tomb, is another 10 minutes' walk further northeast on the other side of the humble Stara Reka (Old River).

Information

You'll find several ATMs on the square and especially on the section of ul 23 Pehoten

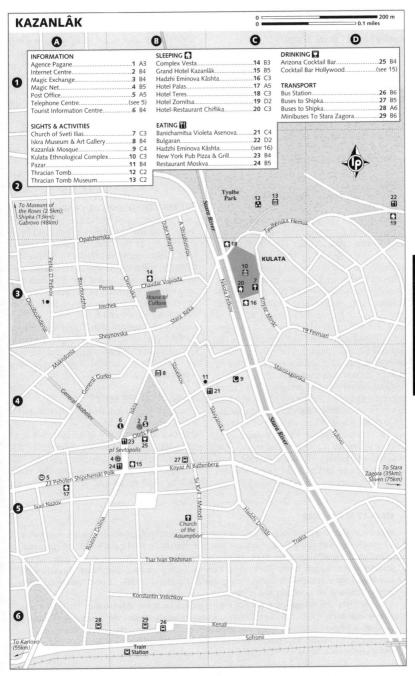

KAZANLÂK

0 — 200 m
0 — 0.1 miles

INFORMATION
Agence Pagane.............................1 A3
Internet Centre............................2 B4
Magic Exchange............................3 B4
Magic Net...................................4 B5
Post Office..................................5 A5
Telephone Centre.....................(see 5)
Tourist Information Centre............6 B4

SIGHTS & ACTIVITIES
Church of Sveti Ilias......................7 C3
Iskra Museum & Art Gallery...........8 B4
Kazanlak Mosque..........................9 C4
Kulata Ethnological Complex........10 C3
Pazar..11 B4
Thracian Tomb............................12 C2
Thracian Tomb Museum...............13 C2

SLEEPING
Complex Vesta...........................14 B3
Grand Hotel Kazanlâk..................15 B5
Hadzhi Eminova Kâshta...............16 C3
Hotel Palas................................17 A5
Hotel Teres................................18 C3
Hotel Zornitsa............................19 D2
Hotel-Restaurant Chiflika.............20 C3

EATING
Banicharnitsa Violeta Asenova.....21 C4
Bulgaran...................................22 D2
Hadzhi Eminova Kâshta............(see 16)
New York Pub Pizza & Grill..........23 B4
Restaurant Moskva......................24 B5

DRINKING
Arizona Cocktail Bar....................25 B4
Cocktail Bar Hollywood.............(see 15)

TRANSPORT
Bus Station................................26 B6
Buses to Shipka..........................27 B5
Buses to Shipka..........................28 A6
Minibuses To Stara Zagora...........29 B6

CENTRAL BULGARIA

Shipchenski Polk that runs between the square and ul Petko Stajnov.

Agence Pagane (☎ /fax 26 900; ul Petko D Petkov) Travel agency with French- and English-speaking staff; arranges hotel reservations and local tours.

Internet Centre (ul Otets Paisii) Under a video-rental store.

Magic Exchange (ul Otets Paisii) A reliable exchange office.

Magic Net (pl Sevtopolis) Under DEPO clothes shop.

Post office (ul 23 Pehoten Shipchenski Polk)

Telephone centre Inside the post office.

Tourist Information Centre (☎ 62 817; stour@kz.or bitel.bg; ul Iskra 1) Assists with hotels, excursions and general information about the town.

Sights

THRACIAN TOMB OF KAZANLÂK & MUSEUM

In hilly Tyulbe Park, just up from the Kulata Ethnological Complex, is a very large and very locked **tomb** (admission 20 lv; ☺ 10am-5pm), built in the 4th century BC for a Thracian ruler. Discovered during the construction of a bomb shelter in 1944, the tomb is now a Unesco World Heritage site. Along the *dromos* (vaulted entry corridor) is a double frieze with battle scenes. The burial chamber is 12m in diameter, and covered by a beehive dome typical of those built by the Thracians between the 3rd and 5th centuries BC. The dome contains several murals that feature events such as a funeral feast and chariot race.

Considering that you get basically the same experience from seeing the full-scale tomb replica in the nearby **museum** (☎ 64 750; admission 2 lv; ☺ 10am-6pm), most visitors choose not to cough up the 20 lv required for getting the real thing opened up, which is probably just as well. The staff who will guide you around the faux tomb are friendly and speak good English and can answer whatever questions you may have.

ISKRA MUSEUM & ART GALLERY

The town's **museum & art gallery** (☎ 23 741; ul Sv Kiril i Metodii; adult/student 2/1 lv; ☺ 9am-6pm Mon-Fri) displays extensive archaeological finds including pottery, jewellery and tools from excavations carried out at several Thracian tombs, including the one in Tyulbe Park (see left). All explanations are in Bulgarian, so the brochure (2 lv) in English, French or German is helpful.

Upstairs, numerous paintings are displayed, including those by renowned local artists such as Ivan Milev and Vasil Barakov. A printed catalogue (in English and French; 3 lv) is available.

KULATA ETHNOLOGICAL COMPLEX

Just down from Tyulbe Park and the Thracian tomb, you'll find the appealing Kulata (Tower) district, site of the **Kulata Ethnological Complex** (☎ 621 733; ul Knyaz Mirski; admission 3 lv, with rose-liquor tasting 4 lv; ☺ 8am-noon & 1-6pm). A replica of a one-storey peasant's home and wooden sheds with agricultural implements and carts are among the rustic exhibits. A courtyard leads to the two-storey House of Hadzhi Eno, built by a wealthy rose merchant in Bulgarian National Revival–period style. Some explanations in German and English are given, and you may be invited by the caretaker to sample some rose tea, liquor or jam.

MUSEUM OF THE ROSES

The grandly named Research Institute for Roses, Aromatic & Medicinal Plants houses this tiny **museum** (☎ 23 741; ul Osvobozhdenie; admission free; ☺ 9am-5pm summer). The photos and displays explain (in Bulgarian only) the 300-year-old method of cultivating the roses, picking their petals and processing the oil.

MARKET REACTIONS

Kazanlâk's sprawling *pazar* (open market), particularly vibrant on Tuesdays and Fridays, keeps alive a centuries-old Balkan tradition. Here you can find everything from horseshoes, village honey, wrenches and traditional music to wooden wine cask openers, red peppers, plastic tubs and live chickens. It's a raucous, dusty place where Kazanlâk's many peoples (Bulgarians, Turks, Pomaks and Roma) come together to barter their goods and bump shoulders as beef kebabs sizzle on nearby grills and vendors bark out prices.

For tourists, the market presents not only a unique shopping opportunity, but also a way to immerse oneself with the marvellously photogenic locals. Visitors are greeted with friendly curiosity, whether or not you speak the language, though of course the bottom line is selling – so you'll have to stand your ground when a stubborn old village crone tries to sell you a whip and a saddle for a horse you don't own.

The attached shop sells rose oils, perfumes, shampoos, liqueurs, tea bags and jams. The museum is 3km north of the centre up ul Osvobozhdenie; take a taxi (3 lv one way), or bus 3 from Kazanlâk's main square. Guided tours (rates negotiable) are available in English and French, but ring first about opening times in winter.

OPEN MARKET

Kazanlâk's **pazar** or open market (see the boxed text, opposite) is a very entertaining, dusty, all-purpose place that offers a truly characteristic Balkan shopping experience – if you happen to be around on a Tuesday or Friday, the market's busiest days, make sure to stop by.

Sleeping

Hadzhi Eminova Kâshta (☎ 62 595; bul Nikola Petkov 22; s/d/apt 20/25/40 lv) This established guesthouse offers big, traditionally furnished rooms featuring woollen quilts, and overlooking an authentic 19th-century walled compound. The one apartment is huge, and worth booking ahead. All rooms feature bathrooms, though they tend to be small, and the restaurant is excellent.

Hotel-Restaurant Chiflika (☎ 21 411; www.chiflika-bg.com; ul Knyaz Mirskia 38; s/d 38/46 lv; 😮 💻) This complex in front of the Church of Sveti Ilias has a traditional look that comes across as being somewhat contrived, and the sometimes grumpy staff haven't yet realised the kind of service required for those trying to be twee. Nevertheless, it does have rooms of a high standard and an attractive restaurant.

Complex Vesta (☎ 20 350; complexvesta@abv.bg; ul Chavdar Vojvoda 3; s/d incl breakfast 40/54 lv) Quietly set just off the road behind the House of Culture, this comfortable place has rooms with amenities such as fan, TV, fridge and balcony, and all have good modern bathrooms.

Hotel Teres (☎ 64 272; www.hotelteres.com; ul Nikola Petkov; s/d incl breakfast 48/54; P 😮 💻) This friendly new hotel is located directly below the hill of the Thracian Tomb, opposite the river. It has clean, modern and cosy rooms, a lobby bar and an adjacent restaurant.

Grand Hotel Kazanlâk (☎ 63 210; hotel_kazanlak@abv.bg; pl Sevtopolis; s/d 55/80 lv; 😮 💻) The renovated Grand Hotel Kazanlâk has well-done rooms, friendly staff and a great location on the main square. If you want to be close to the action, it's unbeatable, as the hotel has a res-

taurant, the late-night Panorama bar upstairs, and the very popular Cocktail Bar Hollywood attached to it on the square, while other bars, clubs and restaurants are all within a few metres. Those who want something quiet might be better off elsewhere.

Hotel Palas (☎ 62 311; www.hotel-palas.com; ul Petko Stajnov 9; s/d/ste incl breakfast 70/96/110 lv; P 😮 💻 🖳) This posh place on a side street just a two-minute walk from the main square offers the classiest rooms in central Kazanlâk. The spacious suites are especially enticing and great value for the price, loaded with toiletries for those compulsive hoarders of hotel freebies. The adjoining restaurant, which offers a better-than-average breakfast for guests, is well regarded by locals, too.

Hotel Zornitsa (☎ 63 939; fax 63 652; www.zornica-bg.com; s/d/ste 70/96/110 lv; P 😮 🖳) Located above the town a short walk from the Thracian Tomb, the Zornitsa is best reached from town by car or taxi. It's relaxing, with very comfortable rooms, a pool and a natural setting.

Eating

Kazanlâk's dining and nightlife scene is mostly concentrated within earshot of the central square. Since the popular places are few, they're always crowded, making the town seem perhaps more happening than it really is – though that's certainly more interesting than the alternative.

Banicharnitsa Violeta Asenova (Otets Paisii 33; banitsa 0.80 lv; 😮 6.30am-9.30pm) Kazanlâk's best breakfast nook is this tiny hole-in-the-wall place opposite the open market, serving a variety of flaky cheese (and other) pies from the *banitsa* and *byurek* family of Balkan pastry.

Restaurant Moskva (ul Sevtopolis 9; mains 3-5 lv; 😮 7.30am-11.30pm) This very busy and efficiently run place off the other side of the square is most popular at lunch, when you take a tray and get in line, choosing from a variety of Balkan specialities. It's smartly outfitted and clean, and there's also a bar.

New York Pub Pizza & Grill (☎ 62 464; pl Sevtopolis; mains 4-6 lv; 😮 10am-1am) This very popular restaurant-pub right on the square has a big menu, serving everything from pizza to fish and grills. It's not gourmet, but the locals like it.

Hadzhi Eminova Kâshta (☎ 62 595; bul Nikola Petkov 22; mains 4-7 lv) Set in the courtyard of the hotel of the same name, this well-regarded restaurant does some of Kazanlâk's best traditional cooking.

Bulgaran (☎ 64 920; mains 6-10 lv) This tourist-friendly restaurant up near the Hotel Zornitsa has a big menu of tasty Bulgarian specialities but perhaps overdoes it on the traditional-costume front, though service is friendly.

Drinking

Cocktail Bar Hollywood (☎ 0886316604; Grand Hotel Kazanlâk, pl Sevtopolis; ☿ 10am-1am) This slick and very popular curbside bar of the Grand Hotel has two rooms, disco balls, strobe lights and tiger skin couches; as stylish as it gets in Kazanlâk.

Arizona Cocktail Bar (ul Otets Paisii; ☿ 8am-4am). This popular nightspot with both an outdoor terrace and indoor bar serves over 50 different cocktails, made and transported by friendly bar hands. It usually only gets busy after midnight.

Getting There & Away

Kazanlâk's **bus station** (☎ 62 383; ul Kenali) is busy (though open only until 8pm daily), and has connections to Sofia (11 lv, 2½ hours, six daily), Veliko Târnovo (6 lv, 2½ hours), Lovech (8 lv, three hours), Karlovo (twice daily), Haskovo (7 lv, three hours) and Plovdiv (6.50 lv, two hours). About every hour, there's also a bus to Gabrovo (5 lv, 60 minutes to 90 minutes) via Shipka.

Minibuses for Stara Zagora (4 lv, 45 minutes) run half-hourly from just outside the main station where the buses congregate. Further along the road by the roundabout, town bus 6 (0.90 lv, 25 minutes, half-hourly) runs up to Shipka; there's also a stop for this bus in the centre, at the corner of Knyaz Al Battenberg and Sveti Kiril i Metodii.

The Kazanlâk **train station** (☎ 662 012; ul Sofronii) connects Sofia and Burgas, via Karlovo and Sliven. There are regular trains to Sofia (7.30 lv, 3½ hours, three daily), Burgas (7.30 lv, three hours, four daily), Karlovo (2.70 lv, one hour, six daily) and Varna (10.30 lv, five hours, three daily).

SHIPKA ШИПКА
☎ 04324 / pop 2500

The tiny mountain village of Shipka, impressively set in the foothills of steep mountains, is most famous for its proximity to the famous Shipka Pass. This, the one good route through the Stara Planina, was the site of one of the most decisive battles of the Russo-Turkish War to liberate Bulgaria from Ottoman rule. Aside from the bucolic peacefulness of the very sleepy village, the exquisite Shipka Monastery with its golden dome, and the Freedom Monument (dedicated to the soldiers who died fighting the Turks) makes this a great day trip from Kazanlâk. While this can be accomplished most easily by car, it's perfectly feasible to use buses – which will bring you up close and personal with amiable village locals, returning from town with their bags bulging with the day's shopping.

Shipka is now also world-famous for some amazing archaeological remains found here. In 2004, a 2400-year-old burial shrine for Thracian King Seutus III was uncovered nearby, containing vast amounts of Thracian gold and a unique golden mask. The site is still being excavated, while at the time of writing the loot had been triumphantly sent on tour to various world museums. While tourists can still see the physical remains of the tomb, the immense value of the gold means that its permanent residence will be in Sofia, where, even Shipka locals admit, it can be better safeguarded and preserved.

Sights
SHIPKA MONASTERY
Even before arriving in Shipka, you'll see the splendid, onion-shaped golden domes of the **Nativity Memorial Church** (admission 2 lv, photography permit 5 lv; ☿ 8.30am-7pm) glittering from amidst thick woods above the village, framed against the mountain. Part of the Shipka Monastery, and also known as the Church of St Nikolai, the magnificent structure was built in 1902 as a dedication to soldiers who died at the Shipka Pass during the Russo-Turkish War (1877–78). The design is heavily influenced by Russian architecture, and features five golden domes and 17 church bells that can be heard for several kilometres when rung. Inside the crypt Russian soldiers who perished are interred, and there are some wonderful frescoes depicting scenes from Russian history. If it's not cloudy, the church offers marvellous views of the Valley of Roses. To get there, follow the sign labelled *Hram Pametnik* for 1.2km through the village, or walk 300m up from the restaurant along the Kazanlâk–Gabrovo road.

SHIPKA PASS

About 13km along a winding road north of Shipka village is the Shipka Pass (1306m). Some 900 steps lead to the top of Mt Stoletov (1326m), dominated by the impressive, 32m-high **Freedom Monument** (admission free; 9am-5pm). It was built in 1934 as a memorial to the 7000 Russian troops and Bulgarian volunteers who, in August 1877, died while successfully repelling numerous attacks by some 27,000 Turkish soldiers desperately trying to relieve their besieged comrades in Pleven. To reach the pass from Kazanlâk or Shipka, take a bus to Haskovo, Gabrovo or Veliko Târnovo and ask the driver to let you off at the Shipka Pass (Shipchensky prokhod).

Sleeping & Eating

our pick **Hotel IT Shipka** (/fax 2112, 0896755090; www.shipkaithotel.com; ul Kolyo Adjara 12; s/d/apt 37/42/82 lv;) This brand new guesthouse located in a quiet residential area 500m east of the square has attractive, modern rooms with great views of either the Valley of Roses, or up to the mountain and the gleaming domes of the Church of St Nikolai. The hotel's little restaurant serves home-cooked Bulgarian fare, and there's even a small outdoor swimming pool. Friendly owner Ivan speaks excellent English and will gladly come to collect you from the bus stop on the main square if you ring ahead. Ivan and his wife Tosha can help arrange local hiking and other outdoor activities in the mountains.

Hotel-Restaurant Shipka (2730; Shipka Pass; r 50 lv) If you want to stay at the pass itself, this is your best bet. Although not the bargain it used to be, the hotel features well furnished rooms, some quite large with separate sitting areas. It's located about 50m up from the car park at the top of the pass.

Getting There & Away

Bus 6 runs every 30 minutes between the local bus stop near the Kazanlâk bus station and Shipka village (0.90 lv, 25 minutes). Alternatively, the hourly bus between Kazanlâk and Gabrovo stops at the village, as well as Shipka Pass, as do buses to Veliko Târnovo.

STARA ZAGORA СТАРА ЗАГОРА
042 / pop 144,150

The modern city of Stara Zagora (literally 'old behind the mountain') is an important point for national train and bus lines, though it's worth seeing for more than the time it takes to make your connection. It boasts one of Bulgaria's nicest central parks and, despite being laid out according to an uninspiring planned grid system, it is a surprisingly stylish place filled with beautiful young people luxuriating in cafés along the pedestrian malls.

Stara Zagora has a few more edifying ancient sites and a museum, but is most famous in Bulgaria as the home of Zagorka, Bulgaria's number one beer. The brewery is visible as you enter from the west, though unfortunately it doesn't conduct tours.

History

Throughout history, the salubrious climate and fertile land around Stara Zagora attracted many invaders and settlers, including the Thracians (from the 4th century BC), who called it Beroe. In around AD 100, the Romans came, creating a prosperous city they called Ulpia Augusta Trayana. Stara Zagora continued to be significant due to its strategic location during Byzantine and medieval Bulgarian times.

During the Turkish occupation, the city was destroyed often, and was abandoned altogether in the mid-13th century. After eventually regrouping, it saw fierce fighting during the Russo-Turkish War, and was again completely demolished by the Turks in 1877. Unfortunately, most of the surviving Thracian and Roman ruins were also wrecked at this time and the few surviving remnants of those eras are now largely hidden beneath the modern city. Reconstruction of Stara Zagora commenced in 1879, and here one of Bulgaria's first opera houses was opened. Today, it's very much a living city, and a thriving educational and cultural centre where visitors (mostly of the business kind) are increasing.

Orientation & Information

Foreign exchange offices line ul Tsar Simeon Veliki. Travellers cheques can be exchanged and credit cards used to obtain cash at the United Bulgarian Bank, located in a tiny mall off ul Ruski.

Post office (ul Sv Knyaz Boris I; 9am-noon & 2-5pm Mon-Fri)

Telephone centre (6am-midnight) Inside the post office.

STARA ZAGORA

0 ——— 200 m
0 ——— 0.1 miles

To Kazanlâk
(35km)

INFORMATION
Post Office..........................1 D1
Telephone Centre...............(see 1)
United Bulgarian Bank..........2 C1

SIGHTS & ACTIVITIES
City Garden.........................3 C2
Eski Mosque........................4 C2
Floor Mosaic......................(see 1)
Geo Milev Drama Theatre......5 C1
Geo Milev House-Museum......6 D2
Neolithic Dwellings Museum....7 A1
Roman Theatre.....................8 C1

SLEEPING
Hotel Ezeroto......................9 C2
Hotel Vereya......................10 C2
Hotel Zhelezhnik................11 C3

EATING
Mehana Chevermeto.............(see 9)
Restaurant Vereya...............12 C2

DRINKING
Bacardi Cocktail Bar.............(see 9)
Sobieski LABB.....................13 C2

TRANSPORT
Bus Station........................14 C3
Rila Bureau........................15 C3

To Sliven (71km);
Burgas (182km)

To Haskovo
(61km);
Plovdiv
(88km)

Train Station

Sights
OLD CITY

Built as it is on the grid of an ancient Roman city, Stara Zagora has yielded some pretty amazing discoveries. One such find, a massive **floor mosaic** dated to the 4th to 5th century AD, is displayed in the post office's eastern entrance. The room relies on natural light, however, so it's best seen on a sunny day.

The **Roman Theatre** (ul Mitropolit Metodii Kusev), often called the Antique Forum Augusta Trayana, was built in the 3rd century AD. It's in a good state and hosts popular alfresco concerts during summer. Although visitors cannot wander around the site, you can peer in from the roadside. Other ruins opposite are accessible at all hours of the day.

NEOLITHIC DWELLINGS MUSEUM

Two 8000-year-old Stone Age houses are partially preserved in a secure and airtight environment at the **Neolithic Dwellings Museum** (☎ 600 299; admission 3 lv; ☉ 9am-noon & 2-5pm Mon-Sat). These modest one-room homes were abandoned after a fire several millennia

ago, making them among the Balkans' best preserved Neolithic dwellings.

Guided tours (5 lv per group, minimum of five people) are available, and are useful for distinguishing the doors, walls and chimneys from one another. There are also the remains of handmade pottery used by the houses' prehistoric residents. The *Neolithic Dwellings: Stara Zagora* booklet (2 lv), available at the museum, offers more details.

The museum basement features exhibits of pottery, tools and jewellery from this and other excavations, but nothing is labelled in English, making the tour and/or booklet worthwhile. One of the strangest items on display, here or anywhere, is the 6000-year-old headless hedgehog.

To find the museum enter the city hospital gates, walk straight down about 100m, up the staircase and the museum is the building at the top.

GEO MILEV HOUSE-MUSEUM

This unique **house-museum** (☎ 23 450; ul Geo Milev 37; admission 2.50 lv; ☉ 9am-noon & 2-5pm Mon-Sat), set around a lovely enclosed garden, contains manuscripts and paintings by locally born Milev (1895–1925). Despite losing an eye in WWI, Milev continued to write poetry dealing with social issues, such as *Septemvri*, about the September 1923 agrarian revolution. The political sympathies of Milev's work led to it being confiscated by the authorities. The writer was arrested, put on trial, and then kidnapped by the police and murdered.

Contemporary artists also sell their work in the museum, which has a relaxing café in the garden courtyard.

ESKI MOSQUE

One of Bulgaria's oldest Muslim shrines, **Eski Mosque** (ul Tsar Simeon Veliki) dates to the 15th century, and resides along the mall. Although decidedly abandoned, it remains an interesting sight from outside and a special addition to Stara Zagora's skyline.

OTHER SIGHTS

The **City Garden** is one of Bulgaria's best: clean, with plenty of shade, new seats and functioning fountains. Behind it is the **Geo Milev Drama Theatre** (28 Mitropolit Metodii Kusev), built in 1914, where popular performances are still held.

The smaller **park** that stands between the train station and the central square features a placid pond lined with weeping willows. Paddle boats are available for rent, though it's uncertain whether the fiercely glaring sculpted crocodile at the edge of the pond is meant as some kind of warning to would-be boaters.

Sleeping

Hotel Zhelezhnik (☎ 622 158; ul Parchevich 1; d 40 lv) Just opposite the bus station, this nicely renovated old hotel has clean and modern, though quite small rooms, with just a whiff of their musty communist past lingering on. A good bet for those who need to be near the bus or train stations, but not a place that's close to the action.

Hotel Ezeroto (☎ 630 331; ezeroto@mail.bg; ul Bratya Zhekovi 60; s/d/ste 45/55/80 lv; ⊠) Located along the northern shore of a curving pond flanked by willows, the tasteful and well-furnished Ezeroto offers excellent value and, though small, boasts a nightclub, two restaurants (including the recommended Mehana Chevermeto) and the Bacardi Cocktail Bar.

Hotel Vereya (☎ 26 728, 618 600; fax 53 174; vereyatour@mbox.digsys.bg; ul Tsar Simeon Veliki 100; d 60-70 lv, apt 90-130 lv; ⊠) It's onwards and upwards for the three-star Vereya, already the poshest place in town before a recent renovation turned it into a chic modern hotel, where even the walls of the rooms are tactile. Notably, all rooms have bathtubs and two of the suites have Jacuzzis. What you're really paying for, however, is the unsurpassed location on the liveliest square in Stara Zagora, the so-called 'Complex', full of cafés and restaurants.

Eating & Drinking

Most of Stara Zagora's restaurants and cafés are located along the pedestrian sections of ul Metropolit Metodii Kusev and ul Tsar Simeon Veliki, which cross one another one block west of the City Garden.

Mehana Chevermeto (☎ 630 331; ul Bratya Zhekovi 60; mains 5-9 lv; ⊠ 7am-2am) With its traditional décor and soothing setting along a leafy pond, this restaurant of the Hotel Ezeroto has plenty of ambience and great food, too – as expected, mostly of the traditional Bulgarian kind.

Restaurant Vereya (☎ 630 666; cnr ul Metropolit Metodii Kusev & ul Tsar Simeon Veliki; mains 9-14 lv; ⊠ 9am-midnight) Close to but not part of the eponymous hotel, the Vereya aims at gourmet status and offers a wide selection of specialities, ranging from pizzas to unusual meat dishes and some innovative vegetarian options as well. Seating is both indoors and outdoors on the lively square.

Sobieski LABB (ul Tsar Simeon Veliki 102; ⊠ 7am-midnight) The most visually alluring café on ul Tsar Simeon Veliki is also the first you come to after turning right from the square (from ul Metropolit Metodii Kusev). Its stylish black-and-white décor extends to the outside benches facing the park. There are plenty of interesting drinks on offer and house music plays most of the time.

Bacardi Cocktail Bar (☎ 621 096; ul Bratya Zhekovi 60; ⊠ 7am-11pm) This cute cocktail bar attached to the Hotel Ezeroto has a shiny interior and plays candy pop music to complement the sweet cocktails; you can also sit outdoors and gaze out onto the pond.

Getting There & Away

From the **bus station** (☎ 605 349; ul Slavyanski) you can get to almost anywhere in the country. Buses go very frequently to Sofia (14 lv,

CENTRAL BULGARIA

four hours, every hour), Plovdiv (7 lv, 1½ hours), Burgas (14.90 lv, three hours, every hour) and Sliven (7 lv, 1¼ hours, hourly). There are also services to Varna (8 lv, five hours, five daily), Veliko Târnovo (10 lv, three hours, seven daily), Ruse (7.10 lv, five hours, four daily) and Kotel (9.30 lv, three hours, four daily).

For Kazanlâk (3 lv, 45 minutes), catch a bus that passes through en route to Veliko Târnovo, or get a direct minibus (which departs when full) from the bus station. Minibuses from Kazanlâk will leave you in Stara Zagora's centre. As with all big bus depots in Bulgaria, numerous private companies offer different prices and further destinations, including international lines to destinations such as Athens and Istanbul.

Stara Zagora's **train station** (☎ 626 752) is located at the southern end of ul Mitropolit Metodii Kusev, a five-minute walk from the bus station. Stara Zagora is on the major train line between Sofia and Burgas, and thus has many connections. Six daily trains serve Sofia (10.30 lv, four hours), via Plovdiv (5.10 lv, two hours). Going the other way, eastwards to Burgas (7.60 lv, two hours), six trains depart daily. Five trains daily also serve Kazanlâk (5.10 lv, one hour), Veliko Târnovo (5.70 lv, three hours) and Ruse (9.60 lv, six hours); note that for these, as for Sliven, you sometimes end up having to change trains in Tulovo (about 45 minutes east of Stara Zagora). There are also three daily services to Varna (10.90 lv, five hours).

Rila Bureau (☎ 622 724) sells advance tickets for domestic trains and tickets for all international services; it's at the train station.

SLIVEN СЛИВЕН
☎ 044 / pop 101,300

Sitting in a sort of bowl around rocky hills of up to 1000m in height, Sliven is one of the most well-known Bulgarian towns for its role in the 19th-century struggle against the Ottomans. While the most famous nearby sight, the so-called 'Blue Rocks', amounts to somewhat a case of false advertising, Sliven is still a laid-back and authentic small city with a handful of unique museums and an increasingly interesting accommodation scene. It also makes a good base for trips to relatively remote, but beautiful mountain towns such as Kotel and Medven.

The Thracians, Romans and Greeks all settled in the Sliven area, but little evidence of their civilisations remains. Sliven's modern history is inextricably linked to the *haidouks,* the anti-Turkish rebels who lived in the rocky hills nearby from the early 18th to the mid-19th centuries. Eventually uniting their cause under the leadership of Hadzhi Dimitâr and the revered Vasil Levski, they rose up successfully against their Turkish overlords. Despite the plenitude of communist concrete and decrepit apartment blocks, Sliven is worth visiting. Its friendly citizenry includes a surprisingly large number of elderly bicycle owners, and a notable Roma population, too.

Orientation & Information
Sliven's main square, pl Hadzhi Dimitâr, is where most services are located. The town hall is to the east of it, the Stefan Kirov Dramatic Theatre is to the north, and to the south is the appealing Deboya Church. The post office & telephone centre are also here.

Foreign exchange offices line the upper (southeastern) section of ul Hadzhi Dimitâr and the pedestrian mall, ul Tsar Osvoboditel. There's an **internet café** (ul Tsar Osvoboitel) inside the Voenen Klub, as well as **Spider Internet** (pl Hadzhi Dimitâr) near the Hotel Sliven in the side of the theatre building.

Sights & Activities
BLUE ROCKS
Within the folds of these magnificent rocks once hid the *haidouks,* bedevilling the Turks and making armed mischief. However, these craggy peaks a few kilometres out of town are not exactly blue, and not particularly different from other craggy peaks encountered around the world, though the air is crisp and clean and the views from above are marvellous. A **chairlift** (one way/return 5/10 lv; ⌚ 8.30am-5.30pm Tue-Sun, 12.30-5.30pm Mon) can get you up there, or you can walk (one to 1½ hours) up the hill following the chairlift. From the top of the chairlift, a path leads down about 300m to the main road; cross it and proceed another 500m through the woods to Hizha Poveda, which serves drinks and basic meals.

To reach the chairlift from Sliven, catch minibus 13 outside the train station or Hotel Sliven. Alternatively, walk about 1km uphill from the end of the route for trolleybus 18 or 20 from the city centre. Taxis are about 5 lv one way.

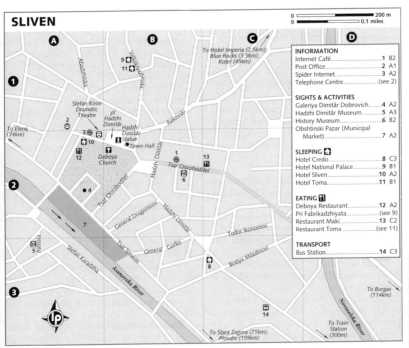

SLIVEN

CENTRAL BULGARIA

HADZHI DIMITÂR MUSEUM

This **museum** (☎ 622 496; ul Asenova 2; admission 2 lv; ☼ 9am-noon & 2-5pm Mon-Fri) dedicated to the leader of the 19th-century rebel movement is set in a lovely building and features several rooms of furniture (including antique weaving equipment) set around a cobblestone courtyard.

HISTORY MUSEUM

Along the mall, the **History Museum** (☎ 622 495; ul Tsar Osvoboditel 18; admission 2 lv; ☼ 9am-noon & 2-5pm Mon-Sat) occupies a grand old building of three floors that house archaeological and ethnological items such as coins, weapons and books. The best exhibits concern the revolutionary struggle against the Turks.

    Galeriya Dimitâr Dobrovich (☎ 622 083; ul Tsar Osvoboditel 13; admission free; ☼ 9am-12.45pm & 2-4.45pm Mon-Sat) is signposted from the centre as 'Sirak Skirnik'. This art gallery in the park displays the works of 19th- and 20th-century Bulgarian artists, including many by its namesake, Sliven-born painter Dimitâr Dobrovich. Among the works, which display strong French and Italian influences, are portraits of local luminaries and ordinary people, as well as numerous impressionistic landscape paintings (including an evocative portrayal of Veliko Târnovo). The gallery's most intriguing section, however, belongs to the **Museum of Christian Art** on the lower floor, which has a large collection of 18th- and 19th-century icons, some from the Tryavna school of icon painting. Works range from monumental wall icons to unique small pieces, the most unusual being an almost Oriental icon of the Virgin Mary surrounded by roses (1836).

OBSHTINSKI PAZAR (MUNICIPAL MARKET)

Shop with the locals at this large warren of shops, which sells everything from fruits and vegetables to electronics supplies. Clothes are shockingly cheap (€8 for a good pair of jeans), and sometimes, even stylish. Unexpectedly, an information centre on NATO and EU affairs stands in the middle of the market, educating Bulgarians about the wonders of their country's recent 'Euro-Atlantic integration'. The market's entrance is located opposite ul Tsar Simeon where it meets the park's southwestern edge.

HIKING

From the oft-closed information centre set along the road to the Blue Rocks chair-lift, marked trails head through the hills to the signposted caves used by the *haidouks*. Information (in English) about the trails is included in a mapless leaflet (1.50 lv), available at the chairlift.

For more general information about local hikes, consult the local **National Park Authority** (☎ /fax 22 926; dpp.skamani@sl.bia-bg.com). For details about hiking in the region, see p210.

Sleeping

Hotel Sliven (☎ 624 056; fax 625 112; pl Hadzhi Dimitâr; s/d 23/36 lv) This imposing communist throwback looms high in the centre of town and offers somewhat musty, worn rooms that feel like a neglected college dormitory. Nevertheless, it's the only real budget option in town and reasonably clean.

our pick Hotel Toma (☎ 623 333; www.hoteltoma.com; ul Velikoknyazhevska 27; d incl breakfast 50-60 lv; 🍴 🖳) A wonderful surprise is in store for guests at the Toma, a truly enchanting guesthouse created from a lavish 18th-century residence. This cosy and very friendly place has only six rooms, all done up in traditional style, with décor ranging from antlers and bearskins on some rooms' walls to ornate woodcarvings and sumptuous curtains in others. Rooms on the upper floor are slightly more spacious than those on the ground floor, but all are great and all have hydromassage showers, air conditioning and wireless internet access. The *coup de grace* is room 4, with an ornate painted cupola and a superb hand-carved wooden ceiling dating from the 18th century – best admired from the comfortable, big bed, which has (of course) a carved wooden frame.

Hotel Credo (☎ 625 080; ul Predel 1; d 59 lv) Not far from the centre, the Credo has clean and modern rooms, though a bit cramped and not traditional in any way. The entrance is tucked into a small street; you will see the large sign looming overhead from the main street. It's a small place, without much in the way of services, but staff are friendly and some speak English.

Hotel National Palace (☎ 662 929; www.nationalsl.bg; ul Velikoknyazhevska 29; s/d/ste/apt 68/88/90/120 lv; 🍴 🖳) Right next to the Hotel Toma, the National Palace is Sliven's best business hotel, offering classy, clean-smelling rooms with all expected amenities. The infinitesimal price difference between doubles and the more spacious studios means you might want to go for the latter. Nice touches include contemporary art in the hallways and rainbow-hued floor lighting opposite the elevators. The well-stocked restaurant, Pri Fabrikadzhiyata (below), in a courtyard setting is another plus. At the time of writing, there were plans for a fitness centre.

Hotel Imperia (☎ 667 599; www.hotelimperia.net; ul Panaiot Hitov; d/ste/apt 70/110/150 lv; 🅿 🍴 🖳) Some 3km from Sliven's centre and about 1km from the chairlift, the Imperia has sophisticated, colourful rooms with individual character and décor, along with exemplary bathrooms. There is both a swimming pool and tennis courts. This is a good option for those with transport and concentrating on Sliven's outdoor attractions.

Eating

Restaurant Maki (ul Tsar Osvoboditel; mains 4-6 lv) A large and popular restaurant just off the square, this place has a huge outdoor section for summer dining, though the interior is somewhat bland. It does good grills and salads, among other fare.

Deboya Restaurant (☎ 625 427; pl Hadzhi Dimitâr; mains 5-7 lv; 🕒 10am-midnight) The fairly cavernous Deboya is very central, located next to the Hotel Sliven's front parking. It's a popular place for pizza and traditional Bulgarian dishes.

Restaurant Toma (☎ 0886836263; ul Velikoknyazhevska 27; mains 5-7 lv) This lively *mehana* outside the Hotel Toma has a typically large menu of traditional Bulgarian specialities, including parts of animals you might never have expected could (or should) be eaten – but never mind, the food and the atmosphere are great, with live Bulgarian (and sometimes Greek) music performed nightly, and diners weaving between tables in the throes of traditional Balkan dance. Hotel Toma guests enjoy a 10% discount.

Pri Fabrikadzhiyata (☎ 662 929; ul K Irecheck 14; mains 8-14 lv) With a curious name that literally means 'at the manufacturer's place', this somewhat posh restaurant in the courtyard of the Hotel National Palace (left) serves an extensive range of good Bulgarian dishes and features somewhat bland live renditions of forgotten pop chestnuts on most nights. There's seating indoors, outdoors and (when there's enough of a crowd) in an atmospheric 18th-century house next door, which once belonged to a famous revival-period industrialist, Dobri Zheliakov. The restaurant's prices are relatively steep, though the food is good, with the roast lamb being downright succulent.

Getting There & Away

From the small **bus station** (☎ 662 629; ul Hadzhi Dimitâr), just past the massive Bila Supermarket, many daily buses and minibuses go to Stara Zagora (7 lv, one hour) and Plovdiv (9 lv, three hours). Regular buses serve Veliko Târnovo (11 lv, two hours, eight daily) and Sofia (16 lv, five hours, 10 daily). There are two daily buses to Kazanlâk (9 lv, one hour), and one to Ruse (14 lv, four hours).

Sliven's **train station** (☎ 622 614) is, like those of Stara Zagora and Plovdiv, on the busy Sofia–Burgas line and so sees a lot of action. There are daily trains to Sofia (11.90 lv, 5½ hours, three daily), Burgas (5.40 lv, 1½ hours, seven daily), Kazanlâk (4.80 lv, two hours, six daily), Stara Zagora (5.10 lv, two hours, five daily), Plovdiv (8.40 lv, four hours, three daily), Ruse (10.90 lv, seven hours, three daily) and Varna (8.40 lv, four hours, three daily). Unlike the bus station, which closes at about 8pm, the train station is open all night.

KOTEL КОТЕЛ
☎ 0453 / pop 7500

Set as if in a bowl surrounded by rolling peaks, little Kotel is a quiet and modest mountain town, though a very historic one, with its strong links to the 19th-century Bulgarian revolutionary movement. Being somewhat remote, set 49km northeast of Sliven on a forested mountain road, Kotel has not really had the fortune (or misfortune) of being discovered by tourism. It's a friendly place, where children scamper about and village elders will greet you with a smile and *dobur den* (good day). Here the crisp mountain air is permeated with the smell of wood-burning stoves in autumn, while the leafy square has just enough moss between the stones to keep your feet buoyant.

Kotel is known for having been the birthplace of numerous Bulgarian scholars, writers and revolutionaries, including Safronii Vrachanski, Georgi Rakovski and Petâr Beron. At the same time, the Turks exempted the village from onerous responsibilities such as tax payments because local artisans were contracted to outfit the Ottoman army in the mid-1800s. Kotel was home for 126 'enlight-

eners' active during the burst of revolutionary activity from 1877 to 1878. Kotel is today known for its carpets and rugs, which are made from wool in homes on wooden looms. The Kotel style predominantly features four colours: red, black, green and blue.

On 15 July 1894, a fire ravaged most of Kotel, sparing only the western Galata district. Although the houses and churches were rebuilt, the National Revival period had passed and the town is not exactly like Lovech or Koprivshtitsa – which is perhaps just why a visit here might be a relief for those past saturation point on 19th-century Bulgarian architecture.

Orientation & Information

Approaching Kotel on either of the two main entry roads, drivers will find petrol stations. For those bussing it, the station is a five-minute walk to the centre, where there is an ATM, a low-cost international telephone centre and shops.

The pink municipal building is on the square; here English-speaking tourism official Hristina Dimitrova (☎ 2030; obkotel@vip.bg) can provide information and brochures on local attractions. The official **information centre** (☎ 2334; ul Izvorska 14; ☉ 9am-7pm) is further west on the long ul Izvorska, which passes through the small Galata old town.

Sights

The **Exhibition Hall of Carpets & Woodcarving** (☎ 2613; ul Izvorska 17), 500m northwest of the bus station, exhibits and sells examples of the famed Kotel style of carpets. The town also has several museums, the best being the **History Museum** (National Revival Kotel Enlighteners; ☎ 2549; admission 4 lv; ☉ 9am-6pm), on the central square, which presents items dating from 19th-century revolutionary times, and Georgi Rakovski's mammoth mausoleum. The **Ethnographic Museum** (☎ 2315; ul Altûnlû Stoyan 5; admission 4 lv; ☉ 9am-6pm), about 200m west of the Exhibition Hall, is also worth a peek. For a more visceral connection with Bulgarian tradition, you can learn to play the *gayda* (Balkan bagpipe) and get tuition in other traditional music and dance at the **Philip Kotev School** (☎ 2215; smu_k_l@mail.bg; ul Geori Zahariev 2, 8970), which sometimes holds recitals.

The **Church of Sveta Troiitsa** (☎ 2430; ☉ 7.30am-6.30pm), located in a leafy area near the main square, is a quite large, almost Gothic-looking structure built in 1871. It has some compelling icons and frescoes, and sells the usual religious paraphernalia. The kindly caretaker heatedly denies that the curious triangle and all-seeing eye inscribed on the outside wall comprise a Masonic symbol – a question she is frequently asked by tourists. Outside the church is a fountain with cold drinking water.

Sleeping

Private rooms can be found wherever you see the *stay pod naem* sign in house windows. The tourist office or municipal officials can sometimes arrange private stays, too.

Kotel Hotel (☎ 2885; ul Izvorska 59; s/d 12/24 lv) Run-down but very cheap, the Kotel is located a bit after the tourist information centre and has simple rooms that are outdated but passable for a night.

Starata Vodenitsa (☎ 2360; d 30 lv) Certainly the best ambience in Kotel is enjoyed at this guesthouse comprising seven dark-wood, traditionally styled rooms, each with fire-

place and unique Kotel rugs. Reached from the old town along ul Krum Petrov, the place is a bit away from the centre but attracts locals, too.

Hotel Kristal (☎ 2885; ul Izvorska 59; s/d/apt inc breakfast 40/60/100 lv) This very new hotel tucked around the corner from the main square has 14 clean, bright and modern rooms and two apartments. Somewhat improbably, it also has a casino attached.

Eating

Kotel has a dearth of restaurants, with the best eatery being that at the hotel Starata Vodenitsa (mains 4 to 7 lv), where Bulgarian meat dishes are well represented.

Café Altanla Stoyan (ul Izvorska 27; ⏱ 9am-8pm) For something really offbeat, check out this tiny, ramshackle café, based in the rough-hewn original home of Altanla Stojan Voyvoda (b 1767), an obscure early freedom fighter against the Turks. None of it has been beautified or restored, the left side of the house

---

WONDERS OF NATURE: UNEXPLORED TREASURES OF THE KOTEL AREA

With its magnificent setting amidst gorgeous mountains and forests, Kotel is an ideal base for hiking, caving, bird-watching and other outdoor activities. Several villages around it, such as Zheravna, Katunishte and Medven, though smaller and less developed than Kotel, are increasingly becoming popular for their proximity to various unique and captivating natural attractions.

First of all, if coming to Kotel from Sliven, make sure to drive or take a bus that follows the mountain road, and not the plains route that runs south of the mountains. The former is a stunning and tranquil journey, where the narrow road is surrounded by almost uninterrupted thick forests, streams and occasional meadows.

These rich forests around Kotel and its villages are home to rare flora and fauna, including groves of silver firs unique in the eastern Balkans, and old woods of *orlitsa* beeches, where majestic golden eagles and other birds of prey soar overhead. Cliffside nesting areas of these eagles are found 5km west of Kotel at a place called, sensibly enough, **Eagle Rocks**.

The Kotel area is also very rich in caves, some 14 of them being located in the area between Zhelenich and Zlosten alone. **Eagle Cave**, 7km west of Kotel, is not for the squeamish, filled as it is with thousands of bats. The so-called **Fairy Cave** near Zhelenich comprises 3100m of galleries (the sixth-longest distance in Bulgaria) and features unusual stalagmite formations. Another cave at Zlosten, northeast of Kotel, is some 242m deep, the third-deepest in the country.

The most aesthetically pleasing of all local attractions, however, is near little Medven, a village that now has a few traditional guesthouses and restaurants to offer. It's best known for the sublime **Siniya Vir** (Blue Whirlpool), a crystal-clear pool of mountain water (part of the Medvenska River) into which a wispy waterfall tumbles 7m down from the cliffs that enclose the pool. It's about a 45-minute walk from the village to get there.

Unusual rock formations linked with the ancient Thracian religion are found at Yablanovo, northeast of Kotel, and at a place called Chobra Tash, 6km north of Kotel, close to the **Urushki Rocks**, a chain of bizarre limestone rocks believed to have been used as a sanctuary in the mysterious ancient Thracian religion.

For more details about the natural wonders of Kotel and environs, ask for the helpful Hristina Dimitrova at Kotel's **municipal headquarters** (☎ 0453-2030; obkotel@vip.bg).

being now a rudimentary shop with vegetables thrown around, an old-fashioned scale and sometimes a cat sitting on said scale. On the right, there are a few small tables where colourful local characters drink coffee or down shots of *rakia*.

Getting There & Away

Despite its remoteness, Kotel provides access to many places around Bulgaria. From the little **bus station** (☎ 2052), 13 daily buses and minibuses go to Sliven (5 lv, one hour), the last leaving Kotel at 6pm. Note that there are two different routes for travelling between the two places, via either the main highway on the plain, south of and parallel to the Stara Planina, or over the mountain road, which is much more beautiful and takes the same time. Ask the staff which route individual buses will take.

Travelling from Kotel through Sliven and Stara Zagora, you can also get to Plovdiv (10 lv, four hours, four daily) and Sofia (20 lv, five hours, two daily). There are also three daily buses to Shumen (7 lv, two hours) and Burgas (8 lv, two hours), and one to Ruse (10 lv, four hours). Numerous buses and minibuses serve Kotel-area villages.

Black Sea Coast

For most foreign package-tourists, the Black Sea coast *is* Bulgaria, and the big, purpose-built resorts here are becoming serious rivals to Spain and Greece in attracting international holidaymakers. Many, of course, simply fly in, splash about and fly out again without seeing anything beyond the parasols and jet skis, but independent travellers will find plenty of places to explore, including empty beaches to the south and north, the bird-filled Burgas Lakes, beautiful ancient towns such as Nesebâr and Sozopol and one of Bulgaria's most attractive cities, the unofficial regional capital of Varna. Those with their own transport will have even greater choice, with the wild Strandzha Nature Park in the south and the picturesque Kaliakra Cape and Dobrudzha region in the north theirs to discover.

More so than any other region of Bulgaria, however, the Black Sea coast has been heavily targeted by property developers in the last few years, and almost everywhere you look, construction work on massive hotels, apartment complexes and holiday homes is ongoing, scarring what were once pristine, open stretches of sand and putting pressure on local wildlife. Environmental campaigners have voiced their concerns about the pace and scale of the development, but as long as the money flows in, the building goes on.

HIGHLIGHTS

- **Sacred sights**
  Sense the centuries of devotion among Nesebâr's gorgeous churches (p231)
- **Beach party**
  Join the locals for cocktails and clubbing on Varna's pounding seaside promenade (p242)
- **Sun, sea & sand**
  Go beach-hopping between Sozopol's two sandy bays (p223)
- **Back to nature**
  Meet some new feathered friends at Burgas Lakes (p220)
- **Flowered up**
  Inhale the fragrant sea air at the botanical gardens in Balchik (p252)

Climate

In summer, the climate is warm and mild, so it's obviously the best – and the busiest – time to visit. The average temperature is a warm 23°C, but sea breezes keep it cool. During winter the temperature rarely drops below freezing, but at least once a season a storm (or three) howls in from the Black Sea and buries the coast in snow.

Media

Programata (www.programata.bg) Free weekly listings magazine, in Bulgarian only, covering bars, clubs, restaurants, cinemas and museums in Varna, Burgas and other coastal towns. Widely available in venues up and down the coast. The website is also available in English.

Summer Seaside Guide Also published by Programata, but in English and Bulgarian, this free glossy annual summertime guide carries reviews of restaurants and bars along the coast.

Sunny Times (www.sunnytimes.info) Free monthly English newspaper, aimed mainly at British expats, with a mix of local and UK news. You can pick it up at some hotel reception desks in Varna, Burgas and the big resorts.

SOUTHERN COAST

BURGAS БУРГАС

☎ 056 / pop 226,000

The gateway to some of the Black Sea coast's best beach resorts and most historic towns, Burgas (sometimes written as 'Bourgas') rarely features on the tourist itinerary in its own right. It's often compared unfavourably with the more cosmopolitan Varna, but as well as being an important industrial centre and transport hub, Burgas is a lively, unpretentious university city that makes a good base for exploring the southern coast, while its uncrowded beach, bosky seaside park and clutch of museums can happily fill a few days of anyone's time.

Burgas is at its best in summer, when the pedestrianised centre is alive with crowds of meandering, ice-cream-licking locals making their way towards the Maritime Park and the seafront, but the city's bars, clubs and theatres give it an active life beyond the transient sunny days enjoyed by the neighbouring tourist resorts.

Nature lovers also come to Burgas for the four lakes just outside the city, which are havens for abundant bird life (see p220).

History

Evidence of Bronze Age and Thracian settlements have been found in the area, while Greek colonists from Apollonia (modern-day Sozopol) expanded their territory into the Burgas region as far back as the 6th century BC. Later, the Romans came along and Emperor Vespasian founded a city here, named Deultum, in the 1st century AD. The name Burgas first appeared on maps in the 17th century, when fisher folk from the wider region settled here. The city grew quickly after the completion of the railway from Plovdiv (1890) and the development of the port (1903). Today it's a major industrial and commercial centre, home to the largest oil refinery in the Balkans.

Orientation

Burgas is pleasingly compact, so almost everything of interest is within walking distance. The train station and the Yug bus station are both located just south of the main pedestrian thoroughfare, ul Aleksandrovska, which runs northwards, via pl Troikata, to bul San Stefano. About halfway along ul Aleksandrovska, another pedestrian street, bul Aleko Bogoridi, heads eastwards towards Maritime Park.

MAPS

The *Burgas* map (1:12,000), published by Datamap, which also includes smaller maps of Sozopol, Nesebâr and Sunny Beach (Slânchev Bryag), is perhaps the most useful, but is in Cyrillic only. Domino's *Burgas* map (1:8500) is also published only in Cyrillic. Both maps are available at city bookshops and street stalls.

Information

BOOKSHOPS

Bel Canto Bookshop (ul Knyaz Al Battenberg) Small shop by the train station offering a variety of books as well as maps and postcards.

Helikon Bookshop (☎ 800 231; pl Troikata 4; ⊙ 9am-1.30pm & 2-8.30pm) On the edge of the main square, this bookshop stocks a wide range of books, including English-language novels, and local, regional and international maps.

Penguin Bookshop (☎ 830 460; ul Aleksandrovska 147) At the northern end of this road, on the corner with bul San Stefano, Penguin sells a small selection of English-language novels and books about Bulgaria.

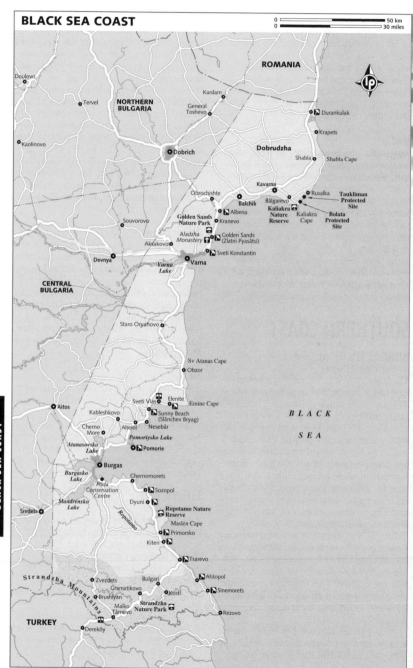

BLACK SEA COAST

0 — 50 km
0 — 30 miles

ROMANIA

Douolovo

Tervel

NORTHERN
BULGARIA

Kardam

General
Toshevo

Durankulak

Kaolinovo

Krapets

Dobrich

Dobrudzha

Shabla   Shabla Cape

Kavarna

Obrochishte   Rusalka   Taukliman
Protected
Balchik   Bălgarevo   Site
Albena   Kaliakra
Golden Sands   Nature   Kaliakra
Nature Park   Kranevo   Reserve   Cape   Bolata
Protected
Aladzha   Site
Monastery   Golden Sands
Souvorovo   (Zlatni Pyasătsi)
Aksakovo   Sveti Konstantin
Devnya   Varna
Varna
Lake

CENTRAL
BULGARIA

Staro Oryahovo

Sv Atanas Cape

Obzor

Sveti Vlas   Elenite   Emine Cape
Aitos   Kableshkovo   Sunny Beach
(Slănchev Bryag)
Cherno   Aheloi   Nesebăr
More   Pomoriysko Lake

BLACK

SEA

Atanasovsko
Lake   Pomorie

Burgasko   Burgas
Lake   Chernomorets
Poda
Conservation   Sozopol
Centre
Mandrensko   Dyuni   Ropotamo Nature
Lake   Reserve
Sredets   Maslen Cape
Primorsko
Kiten

Tsarevo

Zvezdets   Ahtopol
Gramatikovo   Bulgari
Brushlyan   Kosti   Sinemorets
Malko   Strandzha
Tărnovo   Nature Park   Rezovo

Strandzha Mountains

TURKEY   Dereköy

INTERNET ACCESS
Internet Club (cnr bul Aleko Bogoridi & ul Slavyanska; 24hr; 2 lv per hr) This subterranean outlet is the most central place to check your emails.

MEDIA
Burgas City Info Guide (www.cityinfoguide.net) Free, glossy quarterly guide published in English and German, with information on local hotels, restaurants and clubs, as well as background information on the city and surrounds. Copies are available at the tourist information centre and some hotel receptions.

MONEY
Numerous foreign exchange offices can be found along ul Aleksandrovska and ul Aleko Bogoridi. **Unicredit Bulbank** (ul Aleksandrovska) has an ATM that accepts all major credit cards. Banks that change cash and travellers cheques and have ATMs are **Central Cooperative Bank** (ul Aleksandrovska) and **Raffeisen Bank** (ul Ferdinandova).

POST
Post office (ul Tsar Petâr 2)

TRAVEL AGENCIES
Blue Sky Travel Agency (840 809; bluesky@infotel.bg; Hotel Plaza, bul Aleko Bogoridi 42) Helpful agency that can book domestic and international air tickets and arrange tours.

TOURIST INFORMATION
Burgas Museums (www.burgasmuseums.net) Website offering information on museums in and around Burgas. **Tourist Information Centre** (825 772; ul Aprilov; 9am-6.30pm Mon-Fri) Modern office with helpful, English-speaking staff, at the entrance to the underpass below ul Hristo Botev. It has plenty of brochures and leaflets on Burgas and the wider region.

Sights
STS CYRIL & METHODIUS CHURCH
The city's main **church** (ul Vûzhrazhdane; 8am-5pm) is an imposing, late-19th-century edifice, with an especially fine, intricately carved iconostasis, colourful, recently renovated murals and elaborately decorated grey marble columns. Tourists are welcome, but don't be dressed for the beach if you visit as it's still the city's chief place of worship.

ARCHAEOLOGICAL MUSEUM
Burgas' small **Archaeological Museum** (843 541; ul Aleko Bogoridi 21; adult/under 7yr 2 lv/free;

LIFE'S A BEACH
Every day during summer, lifeguards work between 8am and 6pm at the resorts and popular beaches; they usually rescue a few tourists who ignore the warnings and don't swim between the flags. It is extremely important to pay attention to these warnings on the Black Sea – there are often very strong currents at play and there are several fatalities every year.

Topless bathing is acceptable at the major resorts, but less so elsewhere.

Top Five Beaches For...
- Water sports: Albena (p249)
- Urban swimming: Varna (p242)
- Safe, shallow water: Primorsko (p225)
- 24-hour fun: Sunny Beach (Slânchev Bryag; p235)
- A low-key hideaway: Tsarevo (p226)

10am-7pm Mon-Fri, to 6pm Sat Jun–mid-Sep, 9am-5pm Mon-Fri mid-Sep–May) houses a collection of local finds ranging from the Stone Age up to the Roman era. Artefacts on show include Neolithic flint tools, a wooden canoe from the 5th century BC, Thracian jewellery and the remarkably well preserved wooden coffin of a Thracian chieftain. A separate room displays recently unearthed discoveries from a Neolithic site and a Roman necropolis outside the city, including pottery, clay idols and silver jewellery.

ETHNOGRAPHICAL MUSEUM
This **museum** (844 423; ul Slavyanska 69; adult/child 2/1.20 lv; 9am-noon & 1-6pm Mon-Sat, closed Sat mid-Sep–May) houses a collection that includes period furniture, regional costumes and exquisite jewellery, as well as displays covering the local weaving and fishing industries. Everything is labelled in Bulgarian.

NATURAL SCIENCE MUSEUM
The **Natural Science Museum** (843 239; ul Konstantin Fotinov 20; adult/under 12yr 2/1 lv; 10am-7pm Mon-Fri, to 6pm Sat Jun–mid-Sep, 9am-5pm Mon-Fri mid-Sep–May) presents a series of old-fashioned – but still informative – displays on local flora, fauna and geology. Exhibits of rocks, seashells, butterflies and beetles occupy the ground floor, while the basement holds mineral samples

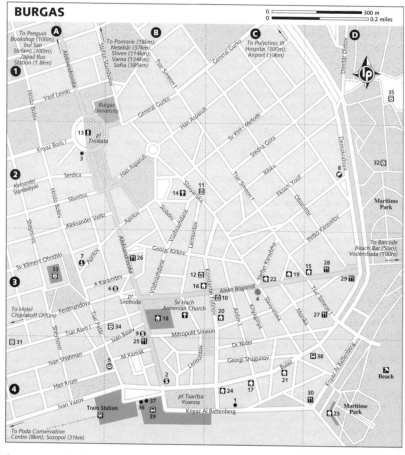

BURGAS

BLACK SEA COAST

from around Bulgaria and the rest of the world. Upstairs there's a collection of stuffed birds and animals from the locality, including rarer species such as the squacco heron and ferruginous duck.

SOVIET ARMY MONUMENT
Standing sentinel over pl Troikata is this towering concrete memorial to the Red Army, comprising a tall, slender column surmounted by a saluting Russian soldier, sculpted panels featuring Soviet soldiers in action against Nazi troops, and rejoicing Bulgarian peasants. It's in much better shape than many other similar monuments around the country, and is still a major focal point of the city; it's even illuminated at night.

MARITIME PARK
Stretching lazily along the Black Sea coast, this grassy haven – filled with manicured flower-beds, fountains, busts of Bulgarian worthies, abstract sculptures and plenty of cafés – is the pride of Burgas. At the end of bul Aleko Bogoridi, it's a relaxing place to wander on a warm summer evening and is popular with everyone from bench-warming pensioners to promenading teenagers and young families. There are some spectacular views over the sea from the terraces, and steps lead down from here towards the beach.

BEACH
Although it can't compare with the far superior beaches at the nearby resorts, or

INFORMATION		SLEEPING		ENTERTAINMENT	
Bel Canto Bookshop	**1** C4	Dimant	**15** D3	Adriana Boudevska Drama	
Blue Sky Travel Agency	(see 22)	Guesthouse Fotinov	**16** B3	Theatre	**31** A4
Central Cooperative Bank	**2** B4	Hotel Bulair	**17** C4	Alibi	**32** D2
Helikon Bookshop	**3** A2	Hotel Bulgaria	**18** B3	Burgas Opera House	**33** A3
Internet Club	**4** C3	Hotel Elite	**19** C3	Kino Trakiya	**34** B3
Post Office	**5** B4	Hotel Fors	**20** C3	Summer Theatre	**35** D1
Raffeisen Bank	**6** B3	Hotel Luxor	**21** C4		
Tourist Information Centre	**7** A3	Hotel Plaza	**22** C3	TRANSPORT	
Turkish Consulate	**8** D2	Hotel Primorets	**23** D4	Biomet	(see 18)
Unicredit Bulbank	**9** B3	TS Travel	**24** C4	Etap-Grup	(see 18)
				Karat-S	(see 37)
SIGHTS & ACTIVITIES		EATING		Left-Luggage Office	**36** B4
Archaeological Museum	**10** C3	BMS	**25** B4	NRG Travel	**37** B4
Ethnographical Museum	**11** B2	Evropa	**26** B3	Nışkılı Turızm	**38** D4
Natural Science Museum	**12** B2	London Pub & Restaurant	**27** D3	Yug Bus Station	**39** B4
Soviet Army Monument	**13** A2	Monte Christo	**28** D3		
Sts Cyril & Methodius		New Shanghai	**29** D3		
Church	**14** B2	Pri Lipite	**30** D4		

even with Varna's urban stretch of sand, Burgas beach still attracts plenty of locals on a hot summer day. It's a bit grubby at the southern end, with its long concrete pier, used as a diving platform by teenage boys and a fishing station by old men, but further on there are some smart beach bars and a couple of restaurants, and, in summer, the beach is kept clean by regular sweepers and watched over by lifeguards. There are often high winds and high waves along this coast: not great for swimming, but OK for windsurfers. Boards may be rented from the **Morski Klub** at the northern end of the beach, but nobody speaks English.

Festivals & Events

Flora Flower Exhibition (April & September) The Black Sea coast's biannual flower show.

Emil Chakarov Music Festival (early July) Internationally attended classical music festival.

Burgas Sea Song Festival (July & August) Showcases up-and-coming popular-music acts from around the country and offers new talents a chance to perform. Held in the Maritime Park.

International Folklore Festival (late August) Burgas' main festival, with shows during the evening at the Summer Theatre in Maritime Park and various locations around the city centre.

St Nicholas' Day (6 December) The patron saint of Burgas is St Nicholas (Sveti Nikolai), whose day is celebrated with gusto.

Sleeping

Few foreign tourists hang around in Burgas for longer than it takes to get the next bus or train out again, so the city's hotel scene has been slow to develop. In recent years, a few small midrange hotels have opened, but these

often fill up quickly and it's essential to book ahead in summer. Budget options are scarce and private rooms are probably the best deal. Unless stated otherwise, all hotels offer private bathroom and TV.

BUDGET

Dimant (☎ 840 779; fax 843 748; ul Tsar Simeon 15; s/d from 10/20 lv; ⏰ 8am-10pm) In the city centre, the Dimant agency has a good range of accommodation options, mostly centrally located.

TS Travel (☎ /fax 845 060; www.tstravel.net; ul Bulair 1; per person from 10 lv; ⏰ 9am-6pm Mon-Fri, to 2pm Sat & Sun) Convenient for the bus and train stations, this English-speaking agency offers fairly basic private rooms and can also book hotels.

Hotel Primorets (☎ 841 417; fax 843 137; ul Knyaz Al Battenberg 2; s/d 42/46 lv; P) The location at the bottom end of the Maritime Park is a winner, but the hotel itself is a drab leftover from the days of the People's Republic, and has a worn-out, half-forgotten air about it. However, it's still a bargain and all rooms have balconies, many with sea views.

Hotel Elite (☎ 845 780; ul Morska 35; r 45-50 lv; ❄) Well placed and with clean and comfy rooms, the Elite offers pretty good value for central Burgas, although the cheaper rooms don't have air-con. Avoid the cramped attic room.

MIDRANGE

Guesthouse Fotinov (☎ 0896002864; www.hotelfotinov.com; ul Konstantin Fotinov 22; s/d 50/60 lv; ❄) Squeezed in between the shops on a busy road right in the heart of the city, Fotinov offers plain but clean rooms, all with TV and minibar. Not the most atmospheric choice, but reasonably priced for the location.

BLACK SEA COAST

BLACK SEA COAST

HOTEL PRICES

All accommodation prices listed in this chapter (unless stated otherwise) are what you should expect to pay during the high season (July and August). During the shoulder season (May, June, September and October), room prices drop by up to 50%, so along with the continually good weather and greatly reduced crowds, this is the best time to visit.

Hotel Fors (☎ 828 852; www.hotelfors-bg.com; ul Konstantin Fotinov 17; s/d Jun-Sep 54/64 lv, Oct-May 48/58 lv; P ⊠) Another fair-priced city-centre hotel, with decent-sized rooms that are bland and functional, but perfectly comfortable nonetheless. There's a pizzeria downstairs and a basic breakfast is included in the price.

Hotel Chiplakoff (☎ 829 325; www.chiplakoff.com; ul Ferdinandova 88; s/d incl breakfast €30/35; P ⊠) A 10-minute walk west of the centre, this friendly, family-run hotel occupies an attractively restored mansion, designed by the same architect who built the city's grand train station. Rooms are large and contemporary in style, and one (No 25) has a big terrace. The original spiral staircases have been retained; there's no lift, however. There's a popular pizza restaurant downstairs.

Hotel Bulair (☎ 846 232; www.hotelbulair.com; ul Bulair 7; r Jul & Aug 65 lv, Sep-Jun 55 lv; ⊠) Very handy for the bus and train stations, this 14-room hotel occupies a converted mansion on a busy road. Rooms are neat, if unspectacular, with the usual mod cons including TVs and fridges. Breakfast is included.

Hotel Luxor (☎ 847 670; www.luxor-bs.com; ul Bulair 27; s/d/apt 85/95/125 lv; ⊠ ⬛) A little further on from Hotel Bulair, the Luxor is a vaguely Egyptian-inspired place. Rooms are comfy, fairly standard three-star fare, but the hotel also has a business centre, gym and an Italian restaurant.

TOP END

Hotel Plaza (☎ 846 294; www.plazahotel-bg.com; bul Aleko Bogoridi 42; s/d/apt 99/146/187 lv; ⊠) The snazziest place in town and in one of the best locations, the Plaza caters to business travellers, with a modern business centre and conference facilities. Rooms are comfortable, though not quite as showy as the public areas, and there's a trendy on-site restaurant. It's easy to miss though – the ground-level frontage is occupied by a couple of travel agencies.

Hotel Bulgaria (☎ 842 610; www.bulgaria-hotel.com; ul Aleksandrovska 21; s/d 118/157 lv, renovated 190/212 lv; ⊠ ⬛ ⬛) Towering 20 storeys over the southern end of the city's main pedestrian drag, this '70s monolith is certainly very convenient and has the best facilities in town, including two restaurants, a gym, pool and business centre. The renovated rooms are OK, but it's fantastically overpriced for what's on offer, and the older rooms don't even have air-con. More realistic rates are offered outside the summer months.

Eating & Drinking

There's a scattering of laid-back cafés in Maritime Park, while other inviting places for a drink or a quick bite can be found along bul Aleko Bogoridi, which also has its share of kiosks selling pizza, kebabs and ice cream. The alfresco bars on the northern end of pl Troikata make an attractive stop for an evening drink, and there are several summertime bars along the beach.

BMS (ul Aleksandrovska 20; mains 2.50-4 lv; ⏲ 10am-midnight) Cheap, self-service, cafeteria-style chain offering simple but filling fare such as sausages and stews. There are some outdoor tables and it also serves beer.

New Shanghai (☎ 843 105; bul Aleko Bogoridi 61; mains from 5 lv; ⏲ 11am-midnight) At the eastern end of the street, this always bustling, authentic Chinese restaurant serves up huge portions of all the old favourites, including sweet and sour chicken and pork noodles, as well as vegetarian dishes.

Evropa (☎ 828 845; ul Aleksandrovska 59; mains from 6 lv; ⏲ 10am-1am) Almost every restaurant in the city seems to serve pizza, but if you're in the mood for a *quattro staggione*, then Evropa is one of the better outlets, baking the freshly made pizzas in a traditional brick oven. Pasta, salads, fish and pork steaks also figure on the menu.

Vodenitsata (☎ 0897988334; Maritime Park; mains from 6 lv; ⏲ 10am-2am) Standing on the seafront overlooking the beach, 'The Water Mill' is a traditional wood-cabin affair, which is always packed out with locals. Specialities include grilled fish, barbecues, steaks and salads, and it seems to be one of the rare places along here that stays open beyond the summer months.

our pick Pri Lipite (☎ 828 500; ul Knyaz Al Battenberg 14; mains 7-18 lv; ⏲ noon-midnight) Easily the best restaurant in town, 'Under the Lime Trees' is set in the shady courtyard of a house built in 1910 for the then mayor of Burgas. It offers a huge menu of traditional Bulgarian cuisine including stewed boar, roast lamb, chicken *kavarma* (a traditional seasoned stew served in a clay pot) and veal-tail soup, as well as various yoghurt-based dishes (with all the milk and cheese coming from the restaurant's own dairy). It gets extremely busy at night, and reservations are advisable.

London Pub & Restaurant (ul Tsar Simeon 4a; mains 8-22 lv; ☯ breakfast, lunch & dinner) Catering to homesick British expats and visitors, this is a friendly place close to the seafront, offering all-day English breakfasts (9 lv), as well as mixed grills, steak-and-onion pie, chicken curry and real British tea, no less.

Monte Christo (☎ 826 006; bul Aleko Bogoridi 60; mains 9-20 lv; ☯ lunch & dinner) One of the classier options along this pizza-prone street, serving up excellent dishes such as duck breast with blueberries, salmon with peppermint sauce, and lobster. It also does some tasty appetizers: try the marinated sheep's cheese with honey and pears.

Barcode Beach Bar (☎ 0877260837; ☯ 24hr) One of the more self-consciously hip and artsy bars on the beach, offering comfy sofas, cocktails and bar snacks. Pricier than most, too.

Entertainment

In summer, nightclubs and bars materialise among the trees of Maritime Park; among the more reliable is **Alibi** (☎ 0897962262; ☯ 11pm-late), with a varied programme including 'retro nights', dance and Latino music. Live music, dance and drama performances often take place at the Summer Theatre, which was being rebuilt at the time of research.

Kino Trakiya (☎ 842 481; ul Tsar Asen I 6; tickets around 3 lv) shows recent Hollywood films every evening. For something a bit more sophisticated, find out what's on offer at the **Adriana Boudevska Drama Theatre** (☎ 846 040; ul Tsar Asen I 35) or the **Burgas Opera House** (☎ 840 789; ul Sv Kliment Ohridski 2).

Getting There & Away

AIR

Bulgaria Air links **Burgas Airport** (☎ 870 248; www .bourgas-airport.com) with Sofia (around €60/110 one way/return) every day (April through October), departing at 6.20am, and **Austrian Airlines** (www.austrianairlines.bg) flies three times

a week between Burgas and Vienna. In summer, **Wizz Air** (☎ 02-960 3888; www.wizzair.com) connects Burgas with London Luton, Budapest and Warsaw. There are a number of agencies around town, one of the handiest being the Blue Sky Travel Agency (p215).

BUS

Yug bus station (☎ 845 722), at the southern end of ul Aleksandrovska, is where most travellers will arrive or leave. It's just outside the train station and most destination signs are in English.

Buses and minibuses leave every 30 to 40 minutes throughout the day to popular places along the Black Sea coast, including Sozopol (3.50 lv, 40 minutes, every 30 minutes between 6.40am and 9.40pm), Nesebâr (2.50 lv, 40 minutes) and Sunny Beach (Slânchev Bryag; 4 lv, 45 minutes). Buses also go to Primorsko (5 lv, one hour, every 30 minutes between 6am and 7pm) and Kiten (4.60 lv, one hour, every one to 1½ hours between 6am and 8pm), but only four times a day as far as Ahtopol (6 lv, 1½ hours). Minibuses travelling directly to 'Pomorie Central' (Поморие Център; 2 lv, 25 minutes) leave every one to 1½ hours.

Each day, buses travel to Plovdiv (17 lv, four hours, 7.30am and 9.15am), Varna (9 lv, two hours, every 30 to 40 minutes), Stara Zagora (7 lv, 2½ hours, departs 10.30am) and Sliven (6 lv, two hours, about every two hours).

Two of the main intercity bus operators, **Biomet** (☎ 828 440) and **Etap-Grup** (☎ 845 857) have kiosks outside the Hotel Bulgaria. Both run several services to Sofia each day (20 lv, seven to eight hours).

Coaches to Istanbul are frequent and cheap. **NRG Travel** (☎ 844 774) and **Karat-S** (☎ 845 722), both just outside the train station, run between two and five services each day (35 lv, seven hours). **Nışıklı Turızm** (☎ 841 261; ul Bulair) has several daily departures (35 to 40 lv). Coaches depart from outside its office.

From the **Zapad bus station** (☎ 20 521; ul Maritsa 2), about 2km northwest of pl Troikata, buses leave for Malko Târnovo (7 lv, three hours, four or five daily), in the Strandzha Nature Park. Take city bus 4 from Yug bus station to get there.

TRAIN

The historic **train station** (☎ 845 022; ul Ivan Vazov) was built in 1902. Through the **ticket windows**

(☼ 8am-6pm) on the right you can buy advance tickets for domestic and international services, while same-day tickets can be bought at the **windows** (☼ 24hr) on the left. The **left-luggage office** (☼ 6am-10.45pm) is outside the station.

Seven trains travel daily between Burgas and Sofia (15.70 lv, seven to eight hours), and there are seven to Plovdiv (13.60 lv, five to six hours).

Express trains run from Burgas to Kazanlâk (7.50 lv, three hours), Stara Zagora (8.50 lv, three hours) and Sliven (5.40 lv, 1½ hours).

International tickets are also available at the **Rila Bureau** (☎ 845 242; ☼ 8am-4pm Mon-Fri, to 2.30pm Sat) inside the station.

Getting Around

If you need wheels, TS Travel (p217) offers various models from €48 per day, including unlimited kilometres and insurance (petrol not included).

BURGAS LAKES БУРГАСКИ ЕЗЕРА

The four lakes surrounding Burgas are Pomoriysko (or Pomorie), Atanasovsko, Mandrensko (Mandra) and Burgasko (Burgas). These are collectively known as the Burgas Lakes. Comprising over 9500 hectares, it's the largest wetland system in Bulgaria, and is home to some 255 bird species, representing around 67% of the country's total.

The **Poda Conservation Centre** (☎ 056-850 540; www.bspb-poda.de; admission 1 lv; ☼ 8am-6pm) opened in 1998 under the auspices of the Bulgarian Society for the Protection of Birds (BSPB) and is an admirable effort at wildlife conservation so close to the urban sprawl of Burgas.

In the **Poda Protected Area**, which surrounds the centre, bird lovers will delight in spotting numerous scarce and endangered birds, including Dalmatian pelicans, reef herons, avocets, little terns and red-breasted geese. Most birds can be seen year-round, while others are migratory, stopping over only to breed or see out the winter. The 15 kinds of mammal include Europe's smallest native species, the pygmy shrew, as well as otters and coypu, which escaped from local farms in the 1950s and now live happily unmolested in the reserve.

From the roof of the conservation centre, it is possible to observe some birds with binoculars (free of charge).

To really admire the bird life up close, go on a walk along the signposted, 2.5km **nature trail**

(admission up to 6 people 10 lv). It takes about three hours to complete and there's an explanatory leaflet in English available from the centre. It's recommended that you get a guide (English- or German-speaking), which will cost an extra 15 lv per group.

East of Burgas, the 28-sq-km **Burgasko Lake** (or Lake Vaya) is the largest sea lake in Bulgaria. It is home to pelicans throughout the year but the best time to see them is between April and October. A 1½-hour **boat trip** around this lake costs about 5 lv per person, but a minimum of six passengers is required. A guide is recommended and costs extra. For details, contact the **conservation office** (☎ 056-849 255) in Burgas, or the Poda Conservation Centre. More information is also available at www.pomonet.bg/bourgaslakes.

The *Bourgas Lakes* map (4 lv), available from the Helikon Bookshop (p213) in Burgas, is excellent. It provides maps (in Bulgarian and English) of each lake, as well as the locations of lookouts, walking trails, access roads and bird-nesting areas.

The conservation centre is poorly signposted on the left, about 8km south of Burgas on the road to Sozopol. It's accessible by taxi (about 5 lv one way), or catch bus 5, 17 or 18 from opposite the Polyclinic III hospital along bul Demokratsiya.

SOZOPOL СОЗОПОЛ

☎ 0550 / pop 4800

Ancient Sozopol, with its charming, cobbled old town crammed onto a narrow peninsula, is one of the coast's real highlights. With two superb beaches, genial atmosphere, plentiful accommodation and good transport links, it has long been a popular seaside resort and makes an excellent base for exploring the area. Although not quite as crowded and commercialised as Nesebâr, it is becoming ever more popular with international visitors. However, with prices still much lower than in Nesebâr, it's definitely worth a stopover.

History

Sozopol is the oldest settlement on the Bulgarian Black Sea coast, founded in an area already populated by Thracians in 611 BC by Greek colonists from Miletus, who called their home Apollonia Pontica, in honour of the god Apollo. One of these early settlers was the philosopher and astronomer Anaximander.

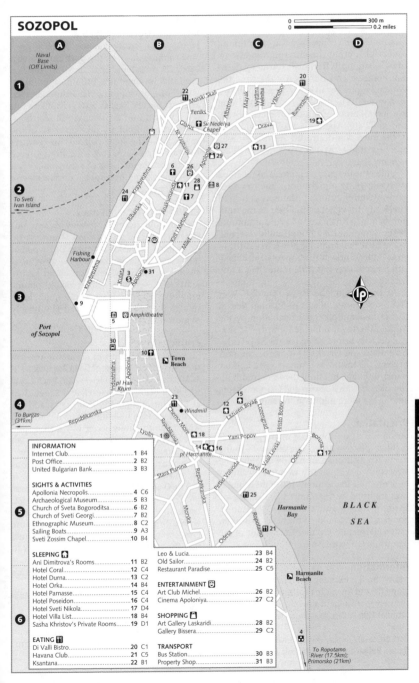

SOZOPOL

Apollonia, ruled by an elected Council of Archons, flourished by trading wine, salt, textiles, pottery and copper, among other things, with neighbouring Thracian tribes and Greek cities, enlarging its territory to cover modern-day Pomorie and Burgas. By the time the Roman Empire began expanding into the region in the 1st century BC, the city had long lost its importance as a commercial power, and in 72 BC Apollonia was sacked, most of the town was destroyed and the famous bronze statue of Apollo was taken to Rome as booty.

Under the Byzantine Empire, and renamed Sozopolis (City of Salvation), the town regained some of its former status as a civilised Greek city, though it found itself on the front line, falling to Khan Tervel in 705, recaptured by the Byzantines in 759 and finally reverting to the First Bulgarian Empire (681–1018) in 969. Under Turkish rule, Sozopol declined, and for centuries was little more than a tiny fishing village.

At the end of the Russo-Turkish War (1877–78), most citizens of Sozopol fled to Russia to avoid potential retaliation by the Turks. The town remained empty for several decades before being resettled by Turks, Bulgarians and Greeks. During the communist era, the town was promoted as a holiday resort, although not until the 1990s did it really take off, with Russians and Germans being among the more numerous foreign visitors.

Orientation

Sozopol is 31km southeast of Burgas and is divided into two areas. The old town to the north is a collection of narrow cobblestone streets lined with sturdy wooden dwellings built on stone foundations; 180 of these buildings are listed by the Ministry of Culture for their historical and cultural significance. South of the bus station is the new town, often called Harmanite. On the western side of the peninsula is a naval base.

Information

Many foreign exchange offices can be found along the old town's main streets, and around the new town's main square.

Internet Club (ul Republikanska; per hr 2 lv; ☼ 9am-11pm)

Post office (ul Apolonia; ☼ 7am-8.30pm)

United Bulgarian Bank (ul Apolonia 4)

Sights
ARCHAEOLOGICAL MUSEUM

Housed in a scruffy concrete building on a lane running down to the port, this **museum** (☎ 22 226; ul Han Krum 2; admission 3 lv; ☼ 8am-5pm, closed Sat & Sun winter) is a little disappointing given Sozopol's long and rich history, but the artefacts and dry English texts at least give you some insight into the town's past. Anchors, amphorae and pottery take up most of the space, including some painted 5th-century-BC vases, tableware imported from Greece and terracotta figurines of actors unearthed at the Apollonia necropolis, on Harmanite Beach (opposite).

ETHNOGRAPHIC MUSEUM

Scarcely bothered by the passing tourists, this **museum** (☎ 22 748; ul Kiril & Metodii 34; admission 1 lv; ☼ 8am-6pm) occupies a typical old wooden house and holds an exhibition of provincial costumes, jewellery and household knick-knacks, as well as a display of old photographs of Sozopol. It's worth a quick look, though the historic house itself is probably of most interest.

CHURCHES

Standing on the ruins of an earlier church, the 15th-century **Church of Sveta Bogoroditsa** (ul Anaksimandâr 13; admission 1 lv; ☼ 10am-1pm & 2-6pm) was built below street level, as was required at the time by the Ottoman rulers, and the modest wooden building, set on a courtyard with a giant fig tree, is one of the most picturesque in town. The church contains an exquisite wooden iconostasis, a pulpit carved with bunches of grapes and numerous icons around the walls.

The **Church of Sveti Georgi** (ul Apolonia; admission 1 lv; ☼ 9am-1pm & 3-8pm Mon-Sat, 7am-1pm & 3-8pm Sun) is another colourful, icon-filled church, with a fine painting of St George and the Dragon over the entrance. Be forewarned that the custodians here are rather keen to collect the 1 lv 'donation' for admittance from foreigners, and to enforce the dress code (no shorts).

The **Sveti Zossim Chapel** (admission free; ☼ 6am-10pm) is a small working church in the shady gardens opposite the bus station. It was built in the 13th century, on the foundations of an earlier church, to honour the patron saint of sailors.

BEACHES

The town's two beaches are attractive, though waves can be quite high. The 1km-long **Harmanite Beach** is wide and clean and offers a water slide, paddle boats, volleyball nets and beach bars. At the southern end, incongruously, archaeological excavations are continuing on the site of the ancient **Apollonia necropolis**, where a number of stone sarcophagi have been uncovered. It's off-limits to the public, but you can look down on it from the road. The **Town Beach** (or Northern Beach) is another pleasant curve of sand, but it's smaller, gets very crowded, and doesn't offer the same number of beachside cafés, restaurants and bars.

Activities

Sailing boats moored in the port offer 'panoramic cruises' around the peninsula every night in summer (adult/child around 8/5 lv), as well as day trips to Nesebâr (adult/child 40/25 lv). There are a number of boats running similar excursions, including the **Sveti Nikola** (☎ 0889521621); prices can vary according to passenger numbers.

Festivals & Events

The **Apollonia Arts Festival** (www.apollonia.dir.bg), held in the first half of September, is the highlight of Sozopol's cultural calendar and one of the most popular events along the Black Sea coast, receiving national TV coverage. It features all sorts of jazz, pop and alternative music at various venues in the old and new towns, as well as art exhibitions.

Live music, dancing and other shows are often staged through the summer at the modern **amphitheatre** near the Archaeological Museum.

Sleeping

Sozopol has an enormous number of places offering rooms. Look for signs along Republikanska in the new town and pretty much anywhere in the old town.

BUDGET

Sasha Khristov's Private Rooms (☎ 0888759174; ul Venets 17; r from 25 lv) This lovely old family home in the old town faces the art gallery at the very end of the Sozopol peninsula. It comprises good-sized rooms and a large apartment. Book ahead in summer.

Ani Dimitrova's Rooms (☎ 22 753; ul Anaksimandâr 12a; r 30-40 lv) Typical private-room setup in a large and comfortable home run by the friendly, but non-English-speaking Ani. The basic but clean rooms sleep up to four people and have private showers. Look for the hairdresser's sign reading 'Friseur Ani'.

Hotel Orka (☎ 23 977; ul Pârvi Mai 2; d/tr incl breakfast 50/66 lv; ❷) In the centre of the new town, this is a neat, family-run hotel not far from the beach. Rooms are plain but clean, with balconies, TVs and fridges.

MIDRANGE

Hotel Poseidon (☎ 24 134; ul Pârvi Mai 2a; r Jul & Aug 60 lv, Sep-Jun from 40 lv; ❷) In the new town, just off the main square, the Poseidon has small but comfortable rooms, many with balconies. It's a bargain, especially out of season.

Hotel Durna (☎ 0888705023; www.hotel-durna.com; ul Kiril & Metodii; r from 70 lv) This is the only hotel proper in Sozopol's old town. It's a smart and well-appointed place, with gorgeous sea views, overlooking the southern side of the peninsula.

Hotel Sveti Nikola (☎ 23 333; www.hotel-sveti nikola.com; ul Boruna 1; r 90 lv; ❷) On the seafront just north of Harmanite Bay, this is a bright, modern hotel with standard but comfortable rooms, all with sea-facing balconies. It's in a quiet, private spot perched on the rocks.

Hotel Villa List (☎ /fax 22 235; www.hotellist-bg.com; ul Cherno More 5; r Jul & Aug 116-125 lv, s/d Sep-Jun from 37/58 lv; ❷ ❷) With a superb setting overlooking the sea, smart rooms and great facilities, this hotel is understandably very popular, and frequently fully booked in summer. The rates, which include breakfast, vary dramatically throughout the year.

TOP END

Hotel Coral (☎ 26 266; ul Lazuren Bryag 5; s/d Jul & Aug 90/120 lv, Sep-Jun from 60/100 lv; ❷ ❷ ❷ ❷) Perched on cliffs overlooking the town beach, the Coral is a stylish complex offering bright and spacious rooms, all with balconies. It also has a spa and a nightclub.

Hotel Parnasse (☎ 24 412; www.parnasse-bg.com; ul Lazuren Bryag 3; r with/without seaview from 110/70 lv, apt 175 lv; ❷) Next to the Hotel Coral, this is a fresh-looking place with a range of rooms decked out in bright tones, and there's a sauna and spa centre.

BLACK SEA COAST

Eating

Fish, naturally enough, is the local speciality, and several reasonably priced restaurants are strung out along the port area. The best restaurants in town are on ul Morksi Skali, and are large and traditional affairs with some spectacular views.

Leo & Lucia (☎ 0878642824; ul Cherno More 1; mains 7-20 lv; ☽ 10am-midnight) Overlooking the town beach, this busy Italian restaurant serves up all the standard fare, such as pasta, pizza and gnocchi, as well as grills, steaks and fish such as grilled sea bass (18 lv).

Old Sailor (☎ 0888225385; ul Kraybrezhna 3; mains 7-25 lv; ☽ lunch & dinner) Marine-themed harbourside restaurant offering all the fishy dishes you can think of. Mussels, crabs, bluefish and shark are just some of the featured menu items, while steaks, chicken fillets and omelettes are among the alternatives.

Di Valli Bistro (☎ 0888982265; ul Morski Skali 35; mains 7-30 lv; ☽ 10am-midnight) Also known as 'The Doctor's House', this modish place offers wonderful sea views and an excellent menu of French and Italian cuisine such as risottos, lamb chops, grilled fish and scallops with caviar sauce sautéed in Cointreau.

Ksantana (☎ 22 454; ul Morski Skali 7; mains 8-15 lv; ☽ lunch & dinner) The split-level terraces of this traditional fish restaurant afford a bird's-eye view of Sveti Ivan Island from the courtyard balcony. The restaurant can be entered at both the top and bottom of the steps and can be easy to miss, with a sign only in Cyrillic.

The pedestrianised section of ul Ropotamo, alongside Harmanite Beach, is packed with cafés, restaurants and bars. They're all pretty much the same, but a couple stand out. **Restaurant Paradise** (mains 4-5 lv; ☽ lunch & dinner) has a raised, off-street eating area and serves reasonably priced steaks, fish and soup. **Havana Club** (mains 4-8 lv; ☽ lunch & dinner), specialising in pizzas, distinguishes itself from the others with a small swimming pool for customers.

Entertainment

Art Club Michel (☎ 0883352622; ul Apolonia 39; tickets about 3 lv) has live music most evenings, while the tiny **Cinema Apoloniya** (ul Apolonia; tickets 5 lv; ☽ Apr-Oct) shows modern English-language films on an outdoor screen.

Shopping

In summer, the streets in the old town are lined with stalls selling the usual array of tourist tat, but there are some better quality souvenirs to be found. **Art Gallery Laskaridi** (ul Kiril & Metodii) sells contemporary art, jewellery and pottery, as well as souvenir books about Sozopol. **Gallery Bissera** (ul Apolonia 52), set up in an old wooden barn behind the cinema, offers a similar range of local paintings and ceramics, as well as some antique oddments.

Getting There & Away

The small public **bus station** (ul Han Krum) is between the old and new towns. Buses leave for Burgas (2.10 lv, 40 minutes) about every 30 minutes between 6am and 9pm in summer, and about once an hour in the low season. Quicker and more comfortable minibuses also service this route for about the same price.

Only a couple of buses a day go directly to Ahtopol (2.50 lv, one hour), via Primorsko (1.40 lv, 20 minutes) and Kiten (1.80 lv, 30 minutes). Public buses leave up to three times a day for Shumen, Stara Zagora, Sofia and Haskovo.

Larger and more comfortable private buses arrive and depart from spots around the new town's main square. Three or four private buses go to Sofia daily, one or two depart for Plovdiv, and another one or two travel up and down the southern coast as part of the overnight Haskovo–Ahtopol service.

Getting Around

Sozopol is easy to get around on foot and there's no need to hire one of the pricey cabs from around the bus stop. If you do need a cab, get one on ul Republikanska, the main road in the new town. If you need a car, there are several travel agencies around the new town's main square, pl Harmanite, which can arrange car rental from about €40 to €45 per day, including unlimited kilometres and insurance (petrol not included). In the old town, try the **Property Shop** (☎ 22 305; ul Apolonia). In summer, you'll need to make arrangements a few days ahead.

ROPOTAMO NATURE RESERVE
НАЦОНАЛЕН РЕЗЕРВАТ РОПОТАМО

This reserve was established in 1940 to protect fragile landscapes of extensive marshes and the largest sand dunes in Bulgaria, as well as rare flora such as the endemic sand lily. The reserve also protects some 257 species of birds, reptiles such as snakes and turtles, and mullet and carp. Fishing is illegal.

At several well-signposted places along the road between Burgas and Primorsko, visitors can stop and admire some of the reserve, and wander along short **walking trails** where explanations (in English) about the local flora, fauna and natural landscapes are provided. The reserve also encompasses Thracian megaliths and tiny Sveti Toma island, which hosts Bulgaria's only wild cacti. (It's also known as Snake Island, after the indigenous water snakes that live hereabouts.)

Where the main road between Sozopol and Primorsko crosses the Ropotamo River is the major entrance to a **parkland** (admission free, parking 3 lv; ☼ dawn-dusk). There are a couple of cafés and picnic spots, and some short **hiking trails**, but most visitors come for a **boat ride** (40/70min trip per person 8/10 lv) along the river. To get to the parkland entrance by public transport, take any bus or minibus south of Sozopol, and get off at the prominent, well-signposted bridge, found around 10km or 15 minutes beyond Sozopol.

PRIMORSKO ПРИМОРСКО
☎ 0550 / pop 3100

Primorsko (meaning 'by the sea') is a busy resort 52km southeast of Burgas and popular mainly with Bulgarian families. It is far less developed than resorts to the north, although the long, crowded beach is quite attractive and the usual water sports are available, such as jet-skiing (10 minutes, 40 lv) and paddleboating (one hour, 10 lv), although the water is very shallow at low tide. Operating at Primorsko's tiny airport, **SkyDive Bulgaria** (☎ 0899868984; www .skydivebulgaria.com) is the place to go to for throwing yourself out of planes. The town centre, meanwhile, is crammed with takeaway stands and tacky souvenir stalls, but little else.

From the town square, along bul Treti Mart (the main road into town), it's a short walk south to the beach. The best shops are along ul Cherno More, which heads southeast from the square.

Sleeping

The **Demin Agency** (☎ 32 870; bus station; per person 25-35 lv) organises rooms at rates that vary according to the location and facilities. However, in summer many will demand a minimum stay of five days or more. If it's closed, call **Denka Mincheva** (☎ 0883318835) for assistance.

Spektar Palace (☎ 33 529; www.spektar-palace.com; ul Treti Mart 82; s/d/tr 60/80/110 lv; ✷ ▣) Closer to the bus station than the beach, this is one of the best hotels in town, with excellent facilities, including a small pool. Being a little out of the town centre means it's a lot quieter than most hotels.

Hotel Prima Vera (☎ 33 488; hotel_primavera@abv.bg; ul Cherno More 46; d 60 lv; ✷) A decent town centre option with modern, clean rooms and a good pizzeria downstairs. It's right in the thick of the action so some rooms may be quite noisy in summer.

Hotel Sunarita (☎ 33 222; www.sunarita.com; ul Treti Mart 29; r/apt incl breakfast Jul & Aug €40/60, Sep-Jun from €21/31; ✷) Another welcoming central hotel with unfussy, airy rooms, a sauna and a good on-site restaurant. Bikes are available for rent (one hour, 2 lv) and free pick-up from Burgas is offered for stays of seven days or more.

Eating

Kebabs, pizzas and burgers from stalls around town seem to be standard fare for most visitors, but there is a handful of decent restaurants here, too: ul Cherno More is the best place to look.

Bistro Silva (Primorsko Beach; mains from 2.50 lv; ☼ breakfast, lunch & dinner) Set right on the beach, this is a great place to grab a quick, cheap lunch. You can sit on the main wooden terrace or in an old fishing boat alongside that's fitted out with tables, and tuck into basic dishes such as moussaka and chicken and rice.

Kavaka (☎ 0889835070; ul Cherno More; mains 4-10 lv; ☼ 10am-midnight) Traditional tavern-style place doing the usual line in steaks, grills and salads, as well as some less obvious dishes such as stewed pork ribs and breaded shark.

Restaurant Chaika (☎ 32 990; ul Cherno More 40; mains 5-20 lv; ☼ 8am-midnight) One of the more modern, upscale options, serving a big menu of mostly fish dishes such as grilled mackerel, though steaks are also available.

Getting There & Away

Primorsko's bus station, 1km from the town centre, is where all public transport arrives and leaves. From here, there are buses to Kiten (1 lv, 10 minutes, roughly every 30 minutes). There are two buses to Ahtopol (3.50 lv, 45 minutes, 8am and 11.30pm) and several buses a day to Tsarevo (3 lv, 30 minutes) and Sozopol (3 lv, 35 minutes). Also, buses stop regularly at Primorsko on the way between Burgas, Sofia or Haskovo and Ahtopol or Kiten, but many of these services pass through, in either direction,

BLACK SEA COAST

late in the evening. In addition, buses travel daily to Burgas (5 lv, one hour, every 30 minutes between 6am and 7pm). About seven private buses a day also go to Sofia, and several travel to Stara Zagora, Plovdiv and Sliven via Sozopol and Burgas.

KITEN КИТЕН
☎ 0550 / pop 1020

Although not as bustling as Primorsko, the little resort of Kiten, 5km to the south, is developing quickly, with numerous hotel complexes rising up in recent years and an increasing number of foreign tourists, especially Czechs and Scandinavians, discovering its once hidden charms. Excavations have indicated evidence of Thracian and Roman settlement in the area, but there is little obvious history here today. There's no town centre as such, so all shops, restaurants and hotels are dotted along the roads between the two beaches; the biggest concentration is on ul Atliman, which is lined with restaurants and bars.

The northern **Atliman Beach** is along a horseshoe-shaped bay, one of the cleanest and prettiest along the Black Sea coast, and the hills in the background thankfully hinder all possible future development. **Morski Beach** to the south is sheltered, ideal for swimming and has plenty of beachside cafés.

Sleeping & Eating

Eos Hotel Complex (☎ 36 865; ul Petrova niva 7; r/apt 60/100 lv; 🔀 🤖) Conveniently located a short walk from the bus stop, though a little further from the beaches, the Eos is a friendly hotel with facilities including a small pool, sauna and gym. The rooms are simple, bright and clean, but not all have air-con, or even fans, so check a few out first.

Hotel Marina (☎ /fax 36 984; Kiten Marina; r/apt from 60/100 lv; P 🔀 🖳) Overlooking Kiten's pocket-sized marina and with its own scrap of private beach, this is a fresh-looking hotel with a range of bright rooms; those with sea views cost marginally more. There's a restaurant, gym and sauna, and yacht trips can be arranged. Prices fall by about a third outside the summer months.

Continental Hotel (☎ 36 131; www.continental9000 .com; r/apt incl breakfast 70/128 lv; P 🔀 🤖) Opposite the Dodo Beach hotel, this is a smaller, modern complex that has light, attractive rooms, all with balconies and most with sea views.

It also has a terrace restaurant, garden and nightclub.

Dodo Beach (☎ 36 294; www.dodo-beach.com; ul Urdoviza 8; s/d/tr incl full board from 140/190/285 lv; 🔀 🤖) With superb views over the coast, this big glass box has some of the best rooms and facilities in town, although the seemingly obligatory full-board arrangement won't be ideal for everyone.

All the hotels listed have restaurants; try **Eos Restaurant** (mains 2-3 lv) for cheap grills and salads.

Getting There & Away

The bus station is at the top end of ul Strandzha, at the junction of the roads to Primorsko and Ahtopol. Daily buses to Burgas (5.50 lv, one hour, hourly) travel via Primorsko and Sozopol (3.50 lv, 40 minutes). Direct buses to Plovdiv (15 lv to 18 lv, four to five hours) and Sofia (via Stara Zagora; 25 lv to 28 lv, seven to eight hours) leave throughout the day. All buses and minibuses travelling to or from Ahtopol will also stop in Kiten to pick up passengers.

TSAREVO ЦАРЕВО
☎ 0550 / pop 6300

Spread lazily over two small peninsulas jutting out into the Black Sea, Tsarevo is a quiet, elegant little town, once a popular holiday spot for the Bulgarian royal family. Called Vasiliko until 1934, it was renamed Tsarevo ('royal place') in honour of Tsar Boris III; the communists then renamed it Michurin (after a Soviet botanist) in 1950, and it reverted once again in 1991. The centre, on the northern peninsula, has a calm, affluent atmosphere and feels more like a real town than some of Tsarevo's seaside resort neighbours.

Orientation & Information

The post office, internet centre and cafés are found along the pedestrianised main street, ul Han Asparuh.

Tourist Information Centre (☎ 52 162; www.tzarevo .info; ul Mikhail Gerdzhikov; ⏰ 8am-noon & 1-5pm Mon-Fri, 10am-noon Sat & Sun) Friendly office with English-speaking staff and lots of brochures, leaflets and maps.

Sights

Overlooking the rocky headland at the end of ul Han Asparuh are the peaceful **Sea Gardens**, offering dramatic panoramic views across the Black Sea. Other sights of interest include the **Church of Sveti Tsar Boris-Mikhail** (ul Hristo Botev), dedicated to the former king, and the tiny **Church of the Holy Trinity**, built in 1810 above the beach, accessed by steps on the northern side of the headland. It's a small but picturesque scrap of sand with a couple of bars.

Across the wide bay, the southern peninsula is of less interest, dominated by modern apartments and holiday homes, although the headland, reached by scrambling over rocks, has Tsarevo's best **beach**. Sadly, this is no secret cove, though, as it's also occupied by the giant Serenity Bay hotel.

Sleeping & Eating

Diskos Melany (☎ 52 460; ul Mikhail Gerdzhikov 18; r 15-20 lv; 24hr) An agency on the road from the bus station into town that can arrange private rooms, but nobody speaks English. It also arranges car and bike rental and excursions.

Hotel Zebra (☎ 55 111; www.hotel-zebra.com; ul Han Asparuh 10; s/d/apt Jul & Aug 54/64/120 lv, Sep-Jun from 40/44/76 lv; P ⓧ) Near the Sea Gardens, this very modern complex offers superb value. The large, comfortable rooms all have balconies and sparkling bathrooms, and there's an outdoor pool and restaurant.

Hotel Diana (☎ 54 855; ul Hristo Botev 2; r/apt 55/100 lv; ⓧ) Another fairly new block in a central but quiet location, offering good-sized rooms with balconies.

Serenity Bay (☎ 55 300; serenity.bay@abv.bg; d/apt 90/130 lv; ⓧ) Dominating the best beach on the southern peninsula, this is a huge holiday complex popular with Scandinavian package-tour groups. It has top facilities, including a spa, but there's nothing else nearby and it looks a little out of place. All meals cost extra.

The restaurant of the **Hotel Diana** (mains 2.50-5 lv; breakfast, lunch & dinner) is a good place for cheap salads and chicken-and-chips type dishes, while fresh fish is on the menu at the harbourside **Ribarska Sreshta** (mains 4-10 lv; 7am-midnight).

Getting There & Away

Tsarevo's bus station is at the top of ul Mikhail Gerdzhikov, about 2km west of the centre. Minibuses to Burgas (6 lv, 50 minutes) run roughly every 30 minutes to one hour between 6am and 8pm via Kiten and Primorsko, and there are two daily buses to Sofia (25 lv, eight hours, 11.20am and 11.30pm).

AHTOPOL АХТОПОЛ
☎ 0550 / pop 1500

An agreeable place to enjoy some sun and sea, Ahtopol still has a quiet, remote air about it. The beach is about 800m from the town centre and below some hills, so few buildings blot the landscape. However, an €80 million marina, with room for 500 yachts, is currently being planned for the resort, so the whole character of the place may change dramatically in coming years.

The town 'centre' is based around the park where the bus stops, though the post office and administration buildings are about 500m east of this. To find the beach, walk southwest from the bus stop along ul Sveti Nikola towards the main coastal road for about 300m, and then head northwest along any laneway.

Sleeping & Eating

Coloured House (☎ 0887561258; www.colours.ahtopol.com; ul Zelenika 7; s/d/tr 39/59/69 lv; P ⓧ) Lives up to its name with a bright, multicoloured façade, though the comfy rooms aren't quite so loud.

Hotel Eskada Beach (☎ 62 035; www.hoteleskada.com; s/d Jul & Aug 56/86 lv, Sep-Jun from 40/48 lv; P ⓧ) On the seafront promenade, Eskada offers bright, stylish rooms, some with great sea views, as well as pools, a gym and a supermarket.

Hotel Lola Garden (☎ 62 020; www.lolagarden.com; ul Preobrazhenska 7; r/ste €33/46; P ⓧ) A smart central option with airy rooms. It runs various excursions and windsurfing lessons are available.

All the above hotels have their own restaurants.

Getting There & Away

Four buses a day depart from the **bus station** (☎ 0889998847) for Burgas (6 lv, 1½ hours) via Primorsko and Sozopol, while four buses go south to Sinemorets (1 lv, 10 minutes), one of which continues to Rezevo (1.50 lv, 30 minutes), the tiny village on the closed Turkish border. To cross into Turkey, you need to travel inland to Malko Târnovo.

STRANDZHA NATURE PARK ПРИРОДЕН ПАРКСТРАНДЖА
☎ 05952

In Bulgaria's southeastern corner is the remote Strandzha Nature Park, established in 1995. The 1161 sq km of rolling hills protect the country's most diverse vegetation, including vast forests of oak and beech, as well as 40 species of fish, 261 types of birds (almost 70% of those found in Bulgaria), 65 species of mammals (six are endangered) and various unexcavated Byzantine fortresses.

The park's ecotourism potential is slowly being developed, but there was public outrage in July 2007 when Bulgaria's Supreme Court declared the park's protected status void, allowing previously illegal hotel construction to continue. Parliament moved quickly to restore Strandzha's protection, and for now the park appears to have been saved from excessive development. Visiting the area is not easy without private transport, though, and don't stray too close to the Turkish border: this is an area of smugglers and suspicious border-patrol guards.

The park is ideal for **hiking** because it's sparsely populated and relatively flat. Several short hikes (1km to 8km long), and longer treks (about 20km), between the coast and the centre of the park, are detailed in the colourful *Nature Park Strandzha* map (1:70,000; 4 lv), available at the Helikon Bookshop (p213) in Burgas. The park also contains what are probably the most undeveloped stretches of sandy **beach** along the Bulgarian Black Sea coast. If you visit in early June, make sure you witness the **fire-dancing festival** (p23) in Bulgari. The website www.discoverstrandja.com is a good source of information; it also offers day trips (€57) around the main sights if you're pressed for time.

The administrative centre of the park is Malko Târnovo, an economically depressed town in the southwest. The **History Museum** (☎ 2998; mtarnovo@burgasmuseums.bg) and the **Ethnographical Museum** (☎ 2126) contain some displays about the park. For more details, contact the **park office** (☎ /fax 2963; strandjapark@yahoo.com; ul Janko Maslinov 1, Malko Târnovo).

From the Zapad bus station in Burgas, buses leave for Malko Târnovo (6.70 lv, three hours, four or five a day) via Bulgari, but transport to other villages in the park is infrequent. If you have a private vehicle, Ahtopol and Kiten are convenient bases for day trips to the park.

SINEMORETS СИНЕМОРЕЦ
☎ 0550 / pop 300
Sinemorets (Si-ne-*mor*-ets) is the Black Sea's last largely undiscovered hideaway, although

it seems that the relentless pace of development along the coastline has set it firmly in the developers' sights. Despite the presence of an enormous hotel on the village's best beach, the atmosphere of remote village life and a generally slow-paced existence remains, and it's a superb base for visiting the nearby Strandzha Nature Park and **hiking** and **bird-watching** in the surrounding countryside.

The two **beaches** are excellent – this is one of the Black Sea's best places to escape the crowds and enjoy pristine white sand and clean water.

Sleeping & Eating
Atlas Hotel (☎ 66 200; www.hotelatlas-sinemoretz.com; ul Butamya; d/apt incl breakfast from €30/60; 🛏) This modern place has light, fairly simple rooms; the apartments are spacious and come with two balconies. Prices are about a third less outside the summer months.

Asti Arthotel (☎ 65 560; www.asti-bg.com; s/d incl breakfast €40/60; P 🛏) All 26 rooms at this fresh hotel are apartments fitted with tiny kitchenettes. It's good value, and there's a tennis court, gym and restaurant on site.

Bella Vista Beach Club (☎ 66 138; r/apt incl full board €52/67; P 🛏 🛏) Overlooking Sinemorets' charming south beach, this massive place caters mainly to package tourists, although walk-in guests are welcome. Facilities are excellent, but this seems such an out-of-place venture. Weekly rates are available.

Getting There & Away
Transport to/from Sinemorets is very poor. From further up the coast you'll need to travel to Ahtopol and change there for one of the four daily minibuses to Sinemorets (1 lv, 15 minutes). There are no taxis in Sinemorets.

CENTRAL COAST

POMORIE ПОМОРИЕ
☎ 0596 / pop 14,600
Like neighbouring Nesebâr, Pomorie sits on a narrow peninsula, and until it was ravaged by fire in 1906 was almost as picturesque. There, however, the similarities end. The modern town centre has a lazy charm, but while the beach is serviceable, the water is choked with odorous seaweed. Pomorie is

BLACK SEA COAST

very much a Bulgarian resort, almost entirely bypassed by foreign tourists, but it's a relatively cheap base from which to visit Nesebâr and Burgas. The town is also famous for its salt lakes, therapeutic mud and spa treatments.

Sights & Activities

On a dusty road about 2km out of town, heading towards the main bus station, is **Sveti Georgi Monastery** (ul Knyaz Boris I). Built in 1856, it's a small complex set in pretty gardens with a quaint, icon-filled church and a belltower covered in saintly frescoes. It's also possible to stay here (see below). There are a few churches worth a look in town too, including the whitewashed **Sveta Bogoroditsa Church**, in the shady park in the town centre, while in the older part of town, with its few cobblestone streets and wooden houses, is the **Preobrazhenie Gospodne Church** (ul Han Kubrat 1; ☺ 8.30am-12.30pm & 4-10pm), dating from 1765.

It's often windy at the beach, making it ideal for **windsurfing** (per hr 10 lv), while there are several stalls along the beachfront where you can hire **scooters** (30min/1hr 5/10 lv) and **golf buggies** (30 min/1hr 15/25 lv).

Massages, mud baths, saunas, hydrotherapy and countless other treatments and programmes are available at a number of hotels.

Sleeping & Eating

Pensioners holding cardboard signs gather near the main bus station and further along ul Knyaz Boris I, offering private rooms from around 10 lv per person, and many houses on this road have accommodation signs for *svobodni stai* (Свободни стаи) in their windows.

Sveti Georgi Monastery (ul Knyaz Boris I; r 8-15 lv; (P)) If you're looking for something different, this tiny monastery rents out a few rooms. They're fairly basic, and unless you have your own transport the location's none too convenient, but it's certainly atmospheric. It doesn't take reservations – just turn up, and there'll probably be space available.

Zeus Hotel (☎ 22 770; www.zeus-pm.bg; ul Rakovski 9; s/d/apt 50/60/100 lv; (꙰)) Located in the centre of town, Zeus is one of the newer hotels, with a restaurant and bar attached. All rooms have balconies and come with fridges, TVs and kettles. Breakfast is 4 lv extra.

St George Centre (☎ 25 180; stg@pomonet.bg; ul Targovska 5; r incl breakfast 60 lv; (꙰ ▯ ꙰)) Breezy seafront complex in a quiet location, offering some surprisingly good facilities for the price, including a pool, sauna, gym, massage room and restaurant. All rooms have sea-facing balconies, and the whole complex, including the pool, is geared to the needs of disabled visitors.

Interhotel Pomorie (☎ 22 440; www.pomorie.com /ih-pomorie; ul Yavorov 3; d incl breakfast 90 lv; (P) (꙰) (▯) (꙰)) Set on a rocky outcrop on the southeastern tip of the peninsula, this hotel is the best in town. Most rooms have sea views, and there's a nightclub and a spa centre that offers numerous therapeutic treatments.

Opposite Interhotel Pomorie, **Pri Slavi** (mains 3-4 lv; ☺ lunch & dinner) is a welcoming garden café serving simple fare such as soups, salads and grills, but there's no English menu. The beachfront promenade, ul Kraybrezhna, is lined with restaurants, while better options (with multilingual menus) are found near the Preobrazhenie Gospodne Church, including **Restaurant Tsarevets** (ul Knyaz Boris I; mains 4-10 lv; ☺ lunch & dinner), which offers grilled pork, chicken and fish dishes.

Getting There & Away

There are two bus stations in Pomorie: the main bus station is about 3km outside the town centre (and accessible by local bus 1 or taxi), and the central station is in front of the town hall. From the latter, it's about 200m northeast to the beach and 100m south to the town centre.

The regular buses and minibuses between Burgas and Nesebâr and/or Sunny Beach (Slânchev Bryag) invariably stop only at the main bus station. From this station, seven or eight daily buses go to Sofia (26 lv, seven to eight hours), and several travel to Plovdiv, Sliven, Varna and Stara Zagora.

Every one to 1½ hours, daily minibuses marked 'Pomorie Central' (Поморие Център) leave from Burgas (2 lv, 30 minutes) and Sunny Beach (1.80 lv, 30 minutes), stopping at Pomorie's small central bus station.

NESEBÂR НЕСЕБЪР

☎ 0554 / pop 10,200

On a small, rocky island 37km northeast of Burgas, connected to the mainland by a narrow, artificial isthmus, pretty-as-a-postcard Nesebâr (Ne-*se*-bar) is the jewel in the Bulgarian Black Sea crown. Famous for its surprisingly numerous, albeit mostly ruined,

BLACK SEA COAST

NESEBÂR

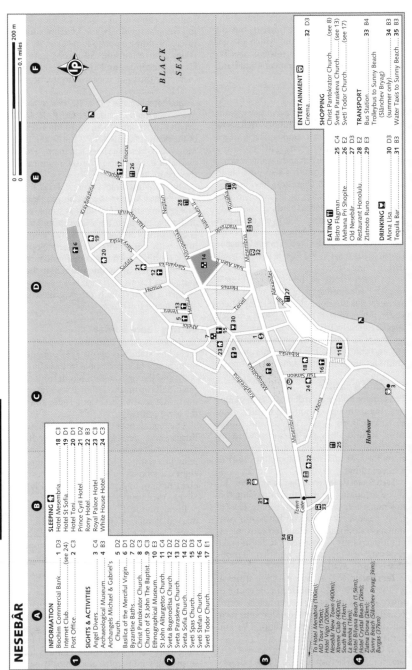

INFORMATION
Biochim Commercial Bank........1 D3
Internet Club...........................(see 24)
Post Office...............................2 C3

SIGHTS & ACTIVITIES
Angel Divers.............................3 C4
Archaeological Museum............4 B3
Archangels Michael & Gabriel's
  Church...................................5 D2
Basilica of the Merciful Virgin....6 D1
Byzantine Baths.........................7 D2
Christ Pantokrator Church..........8 C3
Church of St John The Baptist......9 C3
Ethnographical Museum...........10 E3
St John Alturgetos Church........11 C4
Sveta Bogoroditsa Church........12 D2
Sveta Paraskeva Church...........13 D2
Sveta Sofia Church...................14 D2
Sveti Spas Church....................15 D3
Sveti Stefan Church.................16 C4
Sveti Todor Church..................17 E1

SLEEPING 🛏
Hotel Mesembria.....................18 C3
Hotel St Sofia..........................19 D1
Hotel Toni...............................20 D1
Prince Cyril Hotel.....................21 D2
Rony Hotel...............................22 B3
Royal Palace Hotel...................23 C3
White House Hotel...................24 C3

EATING 🍴
Bistro Flagman........................25 C4
Mehana Pri Shopite.................26 E2
Old Nesebâr............................27 D3
Restaurant Honolulu................28 E2
Zlatnoto Runo.........................29 E3

DRINKING 🍸
Mona Lisa...............................30 D3
Tequila Bar..............................31 B3

ENTERTAINMENT 🎭
Cinema...................................32 D3

SHOPPING
Christ Pantokrator Church........(see 8)
Sveta Paraskeva Church..........(see 13)
Sveti Todor Church.................(see 17)

TRANSPORT
Bus Station.............................33 B4
Trolleybus to Sunny Beach
  (Slánchev Bryag)
  (summer only).......................34 B3
Water Taxis to Sunny Beach.....35 B3

BLACK SEA COAST

BLACK
SEA

Harbour

Town
Gate

To Hotel Mesembria (100m);
MD Tours (150m);
Hotel Vigo (200m);
Nesebâr New Town (400m);
Xtreme Club (400m);
South Beach (1km);
Hotel Bilyana Beach (1.5km);
Hotel Crystal Beach (2km);
Zlatna Diona (2km);
Sunny Beach (Slánchev Bryag; 2km);
Burgas (37km)

0   0.1 miles
0   200 m

medieval churches, it has inevitably become heavily commercialised and is virtually under siege from tour groups and souvenir sellers during the high season. Designated by Unesco as a World Heritage site, Nesebâr is a beautiful town, and also has a handful of interesting museums. Unlike Sozopol, Nesebâr has plenty of decent hotels in the old town, and with Sunny Beach (Slânchev Bryag) just across the bay, you have every conceivable water sport on hand, too.

History

It was Greek colonists who founded what became the thriving trading port of Mesembria in 512 BC, although most of their temples, gates and towers were submerged after the level of the Black Sea rose around 2000 years ago. To avoid the sorry fate of Apollonia (Sozopol), the populace of Mesembria accepted the Roman invaders in 72 BC, although the city's status as a major trading centre gradually declined.

Under Byzantine rule from AD 395, Mesembria regained its former glory as a centre of commercial, strategic and religious importance, and during the 5th and 6th centuries, several grand churches were erected and the fortifications extended. After the Bulgar invasion in 812, the town was renamed Nesebâr; over the following centuries, it passed back and forth between Byzantium and the First Bulgarian Empire (681–1018), but remained largely unscathed. It was one of the last cities still under Byzantine stewardship when Constantinople fell in 1453; the Turks took Nesebâr the same year.

Under Ottoman rule, Nesebâr continued as the seat of a Greek bishop, and existing fortifications were strengthened to defend the city against pirates. During the Bulgarian National Revival of the 18th and 19th centuries, Nesebâr prospered, and wealthy merchants built grand villas here, some of which remain today. Overshadowed by Varna and later by Burgas, Nesebâr ceased to be an active trading town from the early 20th century, and these days survives almost entirely on tourism.

Orientation

The old town is on a rocky outcrop, 850m long and 300m wide. It's connected to the new town on the mainland by a narrow causeway that goes through the 3000-year-old fortress walls, built by the Thracians and later fortified by the Greeks and Byzantines. The new town has the newest and biggest hotels, several overlooking South Beach, but all the sights are in the old town.

Probably the best available map featuring the old town is *Nesebâr, Sunny Beach and Sveti Vlas*, published by Pure Bulgaria.

Information

Every second or third shop seems to be a foreign exchange office. Many of these change travellers cheques but charge different commissions, so shop around.

Biochim Commercial Bank (ul Mesembria; ☺ 8.30am-7.45pm Mon-Fri yr-round, 11am-7.45pm Sat & Sun Apr-Oct) The only bank in town that changes travellers cheques. Also has an ATM that accepts major credit cards.

Internet Club (White House Hotel, ul Tsar Simeon 2; per hr 2.50 lv)

Post office (ul Mesembria; ☺ 8am-8pm Tue-Sat) Has a telephone centre.

Sights

A multiticket (adult/child 10/5 lv), apparently sold only at the Archaeological Museum, gives access to Sveti Stefan Church, Sveti Spas Church, the Ethnographical Museum and the Archaeological Museum. Cheaper tickets, valid for the Archaeological Museum plus one or two of the other sights, are also available.

CHURCHES

Nesebâr was once home to about 80 churches and chapels, but most are now in ruins. Characteristic of the Nesebâr style of church design are the horizontal strips of white stone and red brick, which are offset by striped blind arches resting on the vertical pilasters, the façades decorated with green ceramic discs. Except where indicated, each church is open daily during daylight hours and admission is free.

No visitor can help but be impressed by the ruins of the **Sveta Sofia Church** (ul Mitropolitska), also known as the Old Metropolitan Church. Dating as far back as the 5th century, this vast, three-nave basilica was rebuilt in the 9th century as part of a huge complex that encompassed the Bishop's palace. It remained Nesebâr's chief ecclesiastical centre until about 1257, when the church was ransacked by the Venetians. It contained three naves and

BLACK SEA COAST

boasted a spacious interior with high walls and wide windows. Today the ruins form the centrepiece of a busy plaza surrounded by cafés and artists' street stalls.

Typical of the characteristic Nesebâr construction is the well-preserved **Christ Pantokrator Church** (ul Mesembria). Built in the mid-14th century, it's decorated with green ceramic discs and intricate red brick patterns, and is topped with a sturdy belltower. An unusual feature at the eastern end is the frieze of swastikas, an ancient solar symbol. The church is now used as a commercial art gallery.

Probably the most beautiful church in old Nesebâr was the **St John Aliturgetos Church**, accessible down some steps from the end of ul Ribarska. Built in about the mid-14th century and dedicated to St John the Unbeliever, the church was mostly destroyed by an earthquake in 1913. Concerts are sometimes held here in summer.

The **Church of St John the Baptist** (ul Mitropolitska) was built in the 10th century and features some of the best-preserved murals from the 14th and 17th centuries. It's also now occupied by an art gallery.

The **Basilica of the Merciful Virgin** (ul Kraybrezhna), overlooking the sea, dates back to the 6th century; it became a monastery in the 14th century. The fortified tower alongside it was built as a response to pirate raids along the coast; eventually abandoned and partly swallowed by the sea, it was only rediscovered by archaeologists in the 1920s. Excavations are still ongoing nearby.

Sveti Spas Church (ul Aheloi; adult/child 2.50/1.50 lv; 10am-1.30pm & 2-5pm Mon-Fri, 10am-1.30pm Sat & Sun) is a small, single-nave church built in 1609; like all churches established during Ottoman rule, it had to be built below street level. Some comparatively well-preserved murals can be viewed inside.

Sveti Stefan Church (ul Ribarska; adult/child 4/2 lv; 9am-6pm Mon-Fri, 9am-1pm & 1.30-5pm Sat & Sun) is the best preserved in town, originally built in the 11th century and reconstructed 500 years later. It's a relatively large, three-nave basilica, renowned for its rare and impressive murals dating from between the 16th and 18th centuries, which cover virtually the entire interior. The Byzantine-style paintings depict scenes from the life of the Virgin as well as numerous saints, and restoration is ongoing. Also of note are the elaborate 16th-century iconostasis and the gilded 18th-century pulpit. Try to come early, as the church sees a rapid succession of large, multilingual guided tour groups throughout the day in summer.

The **Archangels Michael & Gabriel's Church** (ul Hemus) was built over the course of a few decades during the 13th and 14th centuries. It remains in relatively good condition, but is usually kept locked up. Very little is known about the origins of **Sveti Todor Church** (ul Neptun), which has been partially restored and is now an art gallery with irregular opening hours. A fine example of 13th-century architecture is the **Sveta Paraskeva Church** (ul Hemus), which has only one nave and one apse. The building is now occupied by yet another art gallery. The relatively plain, 19th-century **Sveta Bogoroditsa Church** (ul Slavyanska) is the only functioning church in town and modestly dressed visitors are welcome. (Shawls are provided at the entrance for bare-armed women.) The typically colourful interior is splashed with saintly murals, and if you *still* haven't seen enough icons, there's a small **church museum** (admission 1 lv) attached, with examples going back to the 13th century.

ARCHAEOLOGICAL MUSEUM

The **Archaeological Museum** (☎ 46 012; ul Mesembria 2; adult/child 4/2 lv; 9am-7pm Mon-Fri, 9am-1pm & 1.30-6pm Sat & Sun) has a fair collection of Hellenistic and Roman-era tombstones on the ground floor, as well as an unusual triple-image statuette of Hecate, goddess of witchcraft and fertility, from the 2nd century BC. Other exhibits include Greek pottery, Thracian gold jewellery and ancient anchors, while Hellenistic humour is on show on a bronze jug depicting Dionysus, god of wine, supporting a sozzled Silenus, god of drunkenness. The basement holds a collection of religious icons recovered from Nesebâr's numerous churches, including a 13th-century image of the Virgin.

ETHNOGRAPHICAL MUSEUM

Ignored by the shopaholics and forgotten by the tour groups is this small **museum** (☎ 46 012; ul Mesembria 28; adult/child 2/1 lv; 10am-1pm & 2-6pm Mon-Sat). Inside a typical wooden Bulgarian National Revival building (constructed in about 1840), it features regional costumes and displays about weaving. All labels are in Bulgarian and German.

BYZANTINE BATHS

Below present ground level just behind the Church of Sveti Spas are the partly excavated remains of this once huge 6th-century **Byzantine baths** complex. Though not much to look at now, in its day this was one of the region's biggest and best spas, renowned for its curative waters; allegedly the Byzantine Emperor Constantine IV dropped by and 'cured his legs' here in 680. The baths were destroyed during Khan Krum's invasion in AD 812.

BEACHES

There are a few scrappy beaches around the coast of the old town, which are popular with some locals and visitors, but they're small and rocky and the water is often choked with seaweed. Around 1.5km west of the old town is **South Beach**, a long and well managed stretch of sand that has seen some major developments over the last few years. All the usual water sports are available, including **jet-skiing** (10min 40 lv), **water-skiing** (10min 15 lv), **windsurfing** (1hr 10 lv) and **pedalos** (1hr 10 lv). The beach is lined with several giant hotel complexes, although the officially protected sand dunes at the far end should, hopefully, prevent further construction. The longer sandy shores of Sunny Beach (Slânchev Bryag), just a few kilometres up the coast, are an alternative option.

Activities

Angel Divers (☎ 0889427355; www.angel-divers.com; 🕙 9am-6pm May-Sep), located in a small booth at the ferry port, is a PADI-certified diving company offering single dives for €45, wreck diving (off Sozopol) for €90 and four-day open-water courses for €245. It has another outlet on the beach at Sveti Vlas (p236).

Tours

MD Tour (☎ 43 439; ul Christo Kudev 17), in the new town, runs all kinds of excursions, including half-day yacht cruises (adult/child including lunch €22/12), half-day jeep safaris (adult /child including lunch €30/20) and day trips to Istanbul (adult/child €45/25).

Sleeping

Unless you book in advance, accommodation in the old town can be hard to come by in the summer months, but out of season supply far outstrips demand. Private rooms are the best option for budget travellers –

ladies offering a room or two meet tourists off the bus.

BUDGET

Hotel Mesembria (☎ 0899102770; ul Ribarska 6; r 40 lv) The only real budget option in the old town, which means it's often full. The location's excellent but it's a grotty old place, and rooms don't even have fans, although they do have balconies.

Hotel Crystal Beach (☎ 46 615; off ul Ivan Vazov; r/apt 50/80 lv; 🗷) Set back from the western end of South Beach, this is the only borderline budget option here. It's an older motel-style block on an unnamed lane just off the main road. Pretty simple, but a bargain for beach bums.

MIDRANGE

Hotel Toni (☎ 42 403; ul Kraybrezhna 20; r Jul & Aug 60 lv, Sep-Jun 40 lv; 🗷) In a great spot overlooking the sea, Hotel Toni is very reasonably priced, so is regularly full in summer (when it suggests advance reservations of as much as one month). Rooms are simple but clean, and the chatty host is very helpful.

White House Hotel (☎ 42 488; www.white-house -13.8k.com; ul Tsar Simeon 2; r low/high season 50/70 lv; P 🗷 🖳) Rooms here are neat and clean, if a little cramped, and all feature TV, fridge and usually a balcony, offering good value for Nesebâr. The old town's only internet café is on the ground floor. Breakfast is 5 lv extra.

Prince Cyril Hotel (☎ 42 215; princecyril_hotel@ abv.bg; ul Slavyanska 9; r incl breakfast 70 lv; 🗷) Located on a quiet, cobbled, souvenir stall–free lane, this is a friendly place with a variety of rooms, all with TV and fridge, but not all with aircon; check a few out first and try to avoid the cramped, top-floor fan-only rooms with their sloping ceilings.

Royal Palace Hotel (☎ 46 491; www.nessebarpalace .com; ul Mitropolitska 19; s/d incl breakfast from 80/110 lv; P 🗷) Overlooking the ruins of the Byzantine baths complex, this is among the more attractive hotels in the old town, offering elegant but unfussy rooms, including some with disabled access, with fridges and TVs (though there's only one single). There's a good restaurant and summer garden on-site.

Hotel St Sofia (☎ 45 061; www.stsofiahotel.hit.bg; ul Kraybrezhna 24b; d/apt incl breakfast 85/120 lv; 🗷) Attractive three-star hotel facing the Basilica of the Merciful Virgin, with some wonderful sea views. All rooms have a TV and fridge. Prices rise in August.

Rony Hotel (☎ 44 002; www.hotelrony.com; ul Chayka 1; r/ste incl breakfast Jun–mid-Sep €50/87, mid-Sep–May €23/39; 🏊) Right behind the Archaeological Museum, the Rony is an old-style wooden villa with a dozen rooms – some of which have terraces and sea views – and a decent restaurant, too. It books up quickly in summer.

TOP END

Hotel Menabria (☎ 46 745; www.hotelmenabria.com; ul Ivan Vazov 2; s/d/apt 100/120/240 lv; 🏊 🍴) On the other side of the isthmus from the old town, the Menabria is a modern hotel built around an old wooden windmill. The location, near the road junction towards Sunny Beach can be a bit busy, traffic-wise, but the views back to town are great.

Hotel Bilyana Beach (☎ 46 645; www.bilyanabeach .com; South Beach; s/d Jul & Aug 170/180 lv, Sep-Jun from 92/122 lv; 🅿 🏊 💻 🍴) Shimmering, glassy complex right on the beach with 135 rooms and suites, all with balconies and sea views. It's a little overpriced, though it has good facilities, including a spa centre and gym.

Hotel Vigo (☎ 43 282; www.hotel-vigo.com; ul Ivan Vazov 9; r Jul & Aug from 180 lv, s/d Sep-Jun from 60/90 lv; 🅿 🏊 💻 🍴) Around 200m west of the old town on the way to South Beach, Vigo is a vast new complex with large, tastefully furnished rooms and top-class facilities including four pools, a spa centre, billiard room and gym.

Eating

It will come as no surprise to discover that all restaurants in Nesebâr are geared towards the passing tourist trade, and prices are roughly twice what you'll pay away from the coastal resorts. Freshly caught fish is, naturally, plentiful, and the cheapest places are the harbourside cafés near the bus station.

Zlatna Diona (☎ 0878345001; off ul Ivan Vazov; mains 3-7 lv; 🕙 7am-midnight) Near the Hotel Crystal Beach, the 'Golden Dune' is a cheap and cheery restaurant offering better value than the beachfront places. The English menu features grilled fish, pasta, pizza, salads and soups and the usual Bulgarian specialities.

Bistro Flagman (harbourside; mains 6-12 lv; 🕙 lunch & dinner) One of several harbourside restaurants just outside the town walls offering a fish-heavy menu, though grilled chicken, pork steaks and salads are also available. It's a pleasant place to just sit back with a Burgasko beer or two on a hot day.

ourpick Mehana Pri Shopite (☎ 0888061163; ul Neptun 12; mains 7-12 lv; 🕙 11am-midnight) Set in a traditional, tavern-style courtyard around a twisted, 300-year-old fig tree, this is a welcoming place with great food, including numerous kinds of freshly caught fish plus grills, steaks and some vegetarian options.

Old Nesebâr (☎ 0898833225; ul Ivan Alexander 11; mains 8-12 lv; 🕙 lunch & dinner) With two tiers of seating offering great sea views, this is a popular place for barbecues, grills and fish dishes. It also offers an unexpected menu of Mexican food, including reasonable stabs at fajitas and burritos.

Zlatnoto Runo (☎ 45 602; ul Rusalka 6; mains 8-20 lv; 🕙 lunch & dinner) Overlooking the sea on the southeastern end of the peninsula, the 'Golden Fleece' serves a varied menu, including roast lamb and rabbit plus some inventive seafood dishes, such as octopus with blueberry sauce and pumpkin stuffed with stewed mussels.

Restaurant Honolulu (☎ 45 505; ul Ivan Asen II 22; mains 10-20 lv; 🕙 9am-midnight) It's a long way from Waikiki Beach, but this sea-facing restaurant is a lively, sociable place to sample a range of fresh fish, including squid and octopus.

Drinking

Mona Lisa (☎ 0886677577; ul Mitropolitska; 🕙 9am-late) Facing Sveti Spas Church, this place has an outdoor terrace and a big menu of cocktails, and gets regularly packed out in the evenings.

Tequila Bar (🕙 noon-late) On a pontoon bobbing about off the northern side of the peninsula, this is an unusual, if slightly expensive, place for a drink. Open summer only.

Entertainment

There is a handful of clubs in the new town, including **Xtreme Club** (☎ 0897844867; ul Han Krum 11; 🕙 8am-late), while La Bomba, on South Beach, is a popular tourist haunt, offering regular live music and DJ parties during the summer. For livelier nightlife, head to nearby Sunny Beach (Slânchev Bryag). There's a summer-only **cinema** (☎ 445 714; ul Mesembria 20; tickets 5 lv), and free live music and dance performances regularly take place in the open-air theatre below St John Aliturgetos Church.

Shopping

Nesebâr can resemble one huge open-air market, with almost every street of the old town lined with hundreds of stalls selling all kinds

BLACK SEA COAST

of tourist tat, from cheeky t-shirts and knock-off watches to embroideries, pottery and paintings. The range on offer is impressive, but price-wise it's far better to shop almost anywhere else. If you're after something a bit different, a few of the town's many churches now operate as more upmarket souvenir shops, open daylight hours in summer only.

Sveti Todor Church (ul Neptun) This tiny church now serves as an art gallery and souvenir shop, with a range of better-quality keepsakes such as contemporary paintings, prints and studio pottery.

Christ Pantokrator Church (ul Mesembria) This church has been converted into a commercial art gallery, selling the works of local painters, mainly seascapes and views of the old town.

Sveta Paraskeva Church (ul Hemus) Another art gallery conversion, with mostly modern paintings and the odd sculpture.

Getting There & Away

Nesebâr is excellently connected to destinations both up and down the coast by public transport, and the town's bus station is on the small square at the end of the causeway, just outside the city walls. The stop before this on the mainland is for the new town. From the bus station, there are buses to nearby Sunny Beach (0.80 lv, 10 minutes, every 15 minutes), Burgas (2.50 lv, 40 minutes, every 30 minutes), Varna (8 lv, two hours, seven daily) and Sofia (28 lv, seven hours, several daily).

To get to Sunny Beach, you can also jump on the trolleybus (2 lv) or water taxi (15 lv), which leaves from an obvious spot north of the bus station about every 20 minutes between 10am and 9pm.

SUNNY BEACH (SLÂNCHEV BRYAG)
СЛЪНЧЕВ БРЯГ
☎ 0554

Bulgaria's biggest and brassiest seaside resort, the naff-sounding Sunny Beach is the Black Sea coast's hyperactive answer to the Spanish *costas*, with several kilometres of sandy beach that attracts more international sun worshippers than any other resort in the country. The beach is one of Bulgaria's finest, with every imaginable activity from minigolf to parasailing, and multilingual restaurants and pubs abound. If you're just looking for a dependable, no-worries resort to top up your tan, this is the place to come. You won't even notice that you're in a country called Bulgaria.

Sunny Beach can feel a bit insular and few people stir from the sun beds to go any further than nearby Nesebâr, but public transport connections are good if you want to explore. This is probably the most expensive place in Bulgaria, so a holiday here might not be the bargain break you envisioned: bottles of water cost as much as 3 lv on the beachfront, and restaurant prices are close to what you'd pay in Western Europe.

Orientation & Information

The main thoroughfare of Sunny Beach is the busy Varna–Burgas coastal road. Along this road, there are plentiful ATMs, market stalls, a post office, a telephone centre with an internet agency and travel agencies. Dozens of foreign exchange offices are set up here and elsewhere around the resort. Day-old copies of English, German and Swedish newspapers are sold at bookstalls.

Activities

Organised watery fun is on hand at **Aqua Paradise** (☎ 51 543; www.aquaparadise-bg.com; adult/child all day 28/16 lv, 3-7pm 20/10 lv; ☼ 10am-7pm), a huge new water park on the southern outskirts of the resort with a variety of pools, slides and chutes. A free minibus, running every 15 minutes, makes pick-ups at 10 signed stops around Sunny Beach. The smaller **Action Aquapark** (☎ 26 235; www.aquapark.bg; adult/child 26/14 lv; ☼ 10am-7pm), on the western side of Sunny Beach, offers a similar setup. Numerous water sports are available on the beach, such as **parasailing** (solo/tandem 45/80 lv), **banana boats** (per person 10 lv) and **jet-skiing** (15 min about 50 lv), as well as a range of other rather expensive diversions, including **bungee trampolines** (25 lv) and **minigolf** (per game 10 lv). In summer, weekly **shows** (tickets 25 lv) of folk music, dancing and acrobatics take place in the Hotel Majestic at the far northern end of the beach. Tickets are sold at the door.

Tours

There are several agencies on the main road near the bus station, all offering a similar range of excursions such as **yacht cruises** (57 lv), **wine-tasting trips** (65 lv), day trips to Edirne, Turkey (50 lv) and two-day trips to Istanbul (139 lv).

Sleeping

Sunny Beach is essentially a package holiday resort, so almost everyone staying here will

BLACK SEA COAST

be on a prebooked, often all-inclusive deal arranged in their home countries. Of all the coastal resorts, this is the least user-friendly for independent travellers, so if you really want to stay here, it's best to book through an agent at home. There are a few travel agencies that can book hotel rooms, but rates vary wildly. Most hotels charge an additional 'resort fee' of about €6 to €7 per person per stay.

Sunny Express (☎ 24 570; sunny-vt@abv.bg; bus station; s/d from around 50/60 lv) Helpful agency at the bus station that can book rooms at various prices in many of the resort's hotels; the cheapest will be two-star hotels, some way from the beach.

Hotel Globus (☎ 22 018; s/d incl half-board Jul & Aug €72/106; P ⊠ 🖳 🗩) Big seafront hotel in the centre of Sunny Beach offering large, bright rooms and lots of on-site diversions, including indoor and outdoor pools, a gym and spa. Prices drop by more than 50% outside high season.

Victoria Palace Hotel (☎ 25 490; www.victoria -group.net; s/d Jul & Aug 220/250 lv, Sep–Jun from 80/100 lv; P ⊠ 🖳 🗩) Colossal beachfront hotel offering every imaginable amenity, including a spa. The garish public areas appear to be following an eccentric 'Louis XIV on Safari' theme, but the large rooms have been furnished in simpler style. Offers good value out of season.

Eating

Restaurants in Sunny Beach are among the most expensive in Bulgaria. There are numerous food stalls along the beachfront where you can pick up a soggy slice of pizza for 2 lv or a burger for 5 lv, and the place is packed with restaurants, most of which employ touts to hassle passers-by. Annoyingly, even normally uniform chains such as McDonald's and Happy Bar & Grill charge two to three times more than at their branches elsewhere.

Fat Cat (mains around 10-20 lv; 🕑 24hr) On the beachfront facing the Glarus Hotel, this is a typically boisterous restaurant and pub aimed particularly at British tourists, with a menu of pizzas, steaks, pies and curries, and big screens showing Sky Sports. There's a 20% discount between 5pm and 7pm.

Chilli Peppers (pedestrian thoroughfare near Hotel Kuban; mains around 12-30 lv; 🕑 8.30am-midnight) Popular 'Wild West Barbecue' joint serving up lots of steaks, sausages and grills in a mocked-up ranch-style setting.

Steakhouse Watermill (mains from 12 lv; 🕑 lunch & dinner) On the beach just past the Neptun Beach Hotel, this place specialises, naturally enough, in steaks, with sirloin, T-bone and gammon steaks dominating the menu alongside more traditional Bulgarian grills.

Getting There & Away

The central bus station is just off the main road. City buses to Burgas (2.50 lv, 45 minutes, roughly every 30 minutes in summer) all go via Nesebâr; you can also get frequent buses to Varna (8 lv, two hours, every 30 minutes), Pomorie (1.80 lv, 30 minutes) and Sveti Vlas (0.90 lv, 30 minutes).

Most buses and minibuses use the station just off the main road, about 100m up from the Hotel Svejest. Minibuses from Burgas stop along the main road outside the station. From the bus station, buses depart roughly every hour for Sofia (28 lv, seven hours), and there are several daily services to Plovdiv and Stara Zagora.

Getting Around

Trolleybuses (2 lv) shuttle along three numbered routes every 15 to 20 minutes between 9am and 11pm. The streets around the resort are uncrowded and flat, so scooters are an ideal way of getting around. These can be rented from stalls along the beach (20 lv per hour). There are a number of car rental agencies on the main road, including **Sunny Trans** (☎ 71 082) opposite the Mariner Hotel; rates, including insurance and unlimited kilometres, start at €30 per day.

SVETI VLAS СВЕТИ ВЛАС
☎ 0554 / pop 3000

Just 5km north of Sunny Beach (Slânchev Bryag), Sveti Vlas is one of the latest holiday resort developments on the Black Sea coast. Originally settled by the Thracians, who called it Larisa, it was renamed in honour of the patron saint of cattle farmers in the 14th century, but there are few obvious signs of its history today. Instead, everywhere you look, a new multistorey hotel or apartment complex is shooting up, and in 2007 Bulgaria's first private marina, with space for 300 yachts, was completed here, along with an upmarket hotel and restaurant complex. The marina also has a new border checkpoint, making Sveti Vlas an international gateway to Bulgaria.

The 'centre' of Sveti Vlas, such as it is, revolves around the bus stop, around 250m or so uphill from the beach. Here you'll find a post office, bank and several cheap restaurants and snack bars, but little else. The main road, ul Tsar Simeon, is lined with cafés, small shops and several internet centres.

The narrow curve of sandy **beach** isn't the best the Black Sea has to offer, but compared with Sunny Beach it's mercifully uncrowded (for now). The water is shallow and there are some water sports available, including **jet-skiing** (10 mins 40 lv). The beach is bisected by the snazzy new marina complex, which encompasses a row of upscale restaurants, bars and shops.

Sleeping & Eating

Kometa-2 (☎ 68 112; www.kometa2.com; ul Vasil Levski 3; r per person 17-20 lv) Helpful but non-English-speaking agency near the bus stop that can arrange private rooms in town, as well as excursions and car rental.

Hotel Laguna (☎ 69 016; r/apt incl breakfast Jul & Aug 90/138 lv, Sep-Jun from 57/80 lv; ✲ ✲) Halfway down the unnamed lane between the bus stop and the beach, the Laguna is a decent option, though some of the apartments are a bit kitschy, with four-poster beds and gaudy artwork.

Hotel Berlin (☎ 68 875; www.hotelberlin-bg.com; r incl breakfast Jul & Aug 110 lv, s/d incl breakfast Sep-Jun from 38/50 lv; ✲ ✲) Set back from the beach, Berlin is a sparkling new hotel with bland but large rooms, all offering sea views.

Hotel Palace Marina Dinevi (☎ 33 333; s/d/apt incl breakfast €150/160/360; ✲ ✲ ✲ ✲) Part of the new marina complex, this five-star hotel is the top place to stay, with large, luxurious rooms and all the top-end facilities you'd expect for this price.

Café Teya (ul Tsar Simeon; mains 4-5 lv; ☺ breakfast, lunch & dinner) Close to the bus stop, this is one of several similar places to grab a quick bite to eat, with pizzas, omelettes and grills on the menu. It's good value for Sveti Vlas.

Old Mill (☎ 0885546326; Marina Dinevi; mains from 10 lv; ☺ lunch & dinner) At the other end of the scale, Old Mill offers a classy menu featuring dishes such as pork with fig sauce and lots of fresh fish.

Getting There & Away

In summer, there are frequent buses from Sunny Beach (Slânchev Bryag; 0.90 lv, 25 minutes, every 30 minutes) running between 6.45am and midnight. Buses make a circuitous route, with a number of stops around the resort before reaching the central square. Also in summer, there are two daily services from Sofia (28 lv, eight hours), while from the marina, boats go to Nesebâr (15 lv, 20 minutes) hourly between 9am and 8pm.

NORTHERN COAST

VARNA BAPHA
☎ 052 / pop 330,000

Bulgaria's third city and maritime capital, Varna is by far the most interesting and cosmopolitan town on the Black Sea coast, and a definite highlight of the region. A strange yet harmonious combination of port city, naval base and seaside resort, it's an appealing place to while away a few days, packed with history yet thoroughly modern, with an enormous park to amble round and a lengthy beach to lounge on. One of the most dynamic and fast-growing Bulgarian cities, it has experienced a property boom in recent years and there's a definite air of affluent swagger about the place. In the city centre you'll find Bulgaria's largest Roman baths complex and its best archaeological museum, as well as a lively cultural and restaurant scene – while every other shop-front now seems to be an estate agent touting holiday homes to British visitors.

Away from the capitalist crush, Varna has a number of less obvious attractions, including several art galleries, a dolphinarium and Bulgaria's only naval museum, while the city also makes an ideal base for day trips to nearby beach resorts such as Sveti Konstantin (p246) and Golden Sands (Zlatni Pyasâtsi; p247), and the charming towns of Balchik (p251) and Dobrich (p277). For information on local wineries, see p66.

Horror fans will no doubt remember that it was from Varna that Bram Stoker's Dracula set sail on the *Demeter*, bound for Whitby and a date with Mina Harker.

History

Remnants of an ancient Thracian civilisation dating to about 4000 BC have been found at Varna Necropolis, an area of about 100 tombs near Varna. In 585 BC, Greeks from Miletus settled in the area, founding the city of Odessos, which thrived as a major commercial centre until falling to Alexander

BLACK SEA COAST

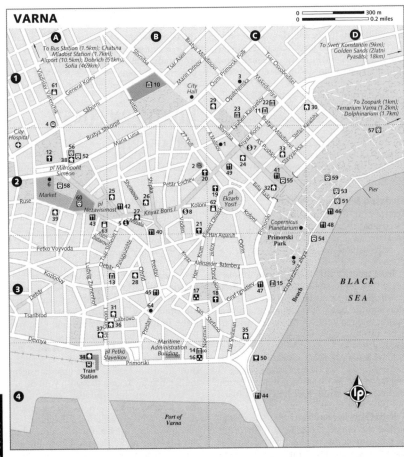

VARNA

the Great. The city didn't really regain any regional importance until the Romans conquered the area and set up a base in Odessos during the 2nd century AD.

Ransacked by the invading Avars in AD 586, the city recovered under the Byzantines as a key port city, and gained its modern name of Varna (possibly derived from the word for 'water') during the period of the First Bulgarian Empire (681–1018). It alternated between Byzantine and Bulgarian rule during the Middle Ages, and was captured by the Turks in 1393 and turned into a northern bastion of their empire. It was used by British troops as a port during the Crimean War (1853–56), after which Turkey allowed its allies Britain and France to sell their products throughout the Ottoman Empire, making Varna a great trading centre once more.

In 1866, a railway between Ruse and Varna was built, providing a direct route from the Danube to the Black Sea coast, and Varna became a major shipbuilding centre and port. In 1921, Varna was established as Bulgaria's first seaside holiday resort, and its status as the country's summertime playground was enhanced by the founding of the International Festival (see p242) in 1926, which has been going strong ever since.

Orientation

Despite its size, the centre of Varna is pleasingly compact. Ulitsa Tsar Simeon I leads from the train station into pl Nezavisimost. From this square, a short thoroughfare heads northwest, passing the domineering cathedral that towers over the market and several theatres, and turns into bul Vladislav Varenchik, which leads to the main bus station and airport. From pl Nezavisimost, another broad pedestrian mall, ul Knyaz Boris I, runs east and then northeast towards Primorski Park and the sea.

MAPS

A excellent free tourist map of the city is widely available at hotels and restaurants; if you find yourself wanting more detail, you can buy the *Varna* map (1:10,000), published by Domino in English (with a red cover), from any of the bookstalls found throughout the city and at the bus and train stations. Handily, it also includes smaller maps of Albena, Golden Sands (Zlatni Pyasâtsi) and Sveti Konstantin.

Information
BOOKSHOPS

Penguin Bookshop (☎ 623 380; pl Mitropolitska Simeon; 9am-7pm Mon-Fri, 10am-6.30pm Sat & Sun) Stocks English-language novels and books on Bulgarian history, culture, cuisine and language.

INTERNET ACCESS

Frag (pl Nezavisimost; per hr 2 lv) Subterranean internet café in the same building as the Varna Opera House.
Internet Doom (ul 27 Yuli 13; per hr 2 lv) The most central of several branches around town, just behind the St Nikolai Church.

LAUNDRY

Laundrette (ul Opalchenska 23; 8.30am-8.30pm) Offers a drop-and-collect service at very reasonable rates.

MEDIA

Varna City Info Guide Free quarterly glossy booklet, available at some hotel reception desks, with useful general information on the city and region, plus hotel, restaurant and club reviews. It also includes a handy tourist map.

MONEY

There are numerous foreign exchange offices and ATMs around the city centre.
Biochim Commercial Bank (bul Vladislav Varenchik) Near the main post office. Changes travellers cheques, provides cash advances and has an ATM.
Unicredit Bulbank (bul Slivnitsa) Changes travellers cheques, provides cash advances over the counter and has an ATM that accepts major credit cards.
United Bulgarian Bank (ul Knyaz Boris I)

POST

Main post office (ul Sâborni 36)

BLACK SEA COAST

TELEPHONE
Telephone centre (ul Sâborni 36; ☉ 7am-11pm) Inside the main post office.

TOURIST INFORMATION
Municipal Tourist Information Centre (☎ 654 518; off ul Knyaz Boris I; ☉ 9am-7pm Mon-Fri) Glass cabin set up in the middle of the street, offering a few free brochures and maps and booklets for sale.

TRAVEL AGENCIES
Balkan Tourism (☎ 618 051; www.balkantourism.bg; ul A Malinov 4) Can organise private accommodation and rental cars and book excursions.
Tourist Service (☎ 612 225; Cherno More Hotel, bul Slivnitsa 33; ☉ 9am-7pm Mon-Fri, to 2pm Sat) Rents cars and organises excursions and private rooms.

Dangers & Annoyances

Like elsewhere along the coast, some taxi drivers are prone to ripping off foreign visitors at the bus and train stations, so check the tariffs before getting in or, better still, pick up a cab on the streets away from these places, which are more likely to use their meters. Pickpockets abound, so be wary in crowded areas such as the market behind the Opera House. Varna appears to be the last refuge in Bulgaria for black-market money changers, who lurk around pl Nezavisimost. Needless to say, it's illegal to change money on the street and you're sure to end up out of pocket, so don't do it!

Sights
CATHEDRAL OF THE ASSUMPTION OF THE VIRGIN

Standing a block north of pl Nezavisimost, this large **cathedral** (☎ 225 435; pl Mitropolitska Simeon; ☉ 6am-10pm) was built between 1880 and 1886 by the architect Gencho Kunev, in celebration of the country's recent independence from Ottoman rule. Topped with golden onion domes, which alleviate the sombre, blocky appearance of its main body, the church is a much-cherished symbol of the city, second in size only to the Aleksander Nevski Memorial Church (p91) in Sofia. Note the murals (painted in 1950), colourful stained-glass windows and intricately carved bishop's throne.

ARCHAEOLOGICAL MUSEUM

The best of its kind in Bulgaria, Varna's fascinating **Archaeological Museum** (☎ 681 011; ul Maria Luisa 41; adult/child 8/2 lv; ☉ 10am-5pm Tue-Sun Apr-Oct, 10am-5pm Tue-Sat Nov-Mar) is a huge place, displaying some 100,000 objects in 39 rooms. All exhibits originate from the Varna area and are placed in chronological order, starting off with pottery and flint tools from the now-submerged Mesolithic settlements around Varna Lake.

The highlights are the 6500-year-old bangles, necklaces and earrings unearthed at the Varna Necropolis (closed to the public), about 4km west of the city, representing what is said to be the oldest worked gold found anywhere in the world. Other rooms contain Thracian jewellery, Roman-era surgical implements and Hellenistic tombstones and statues, as well as touching oddments such as a marble plaque listing, in Greek, the names of all the city's school graduates for AD 221.

Upstairs are several galleries full of religious icons dating back to the 14th century and a comprehensive collection of coins.

ROMAN THERMAE

One unmissable sight in Varna is the well-preserved ruins of the **Roman Thermae** (☎ 681 030; ul Khan Krum; adult/child 4/2 lv; ☉ 10am-5pm Tue-Sun Apr-Oct, 10am-5pm Mon-Fri Nov-Mar). The ruins are the largest in Bulgaria and the third biggest in Europe, although only a small part of the original complex (estimated to have been 7000 sq metres) still stands. The baths date from the late 2nd century AD and were probably abandoned only 100 years later.

There is no information inside the complex other than signs indicating the name of each room. You can also peer into the furnace, where slaves kept the whole thing operating.

ROMAN BATHS

The ruins described previously are termed the Roman *thermae* (Latin for 'baths') to distinguish them from the **Roman Baths** (bul Primorski), another, much smaller ablutions complex, built around the 4th century AD. There's nothing much to see other than some foundation walls, and no explanations are posted on the litter-filled site. The grounds are closed, but you can lean over the fence for a quick look.

CHURCHES

The beautiful **St Anastasios Orthodox Church** (ul Graf Ignatiev) overlooks the Roman Thermae. Built in 1602, it's one of the oldest churches

ROMAN BATHING

Like all self-respecting Roman cities, Odessos was graced with the very best public bathing facilities, and the vast *thermae* here were a visible, powerful symbol of the fruits – and engineering skill – of Roman civilisation. Far from being simply a place to wash up, the baths were an integral part of civic life. They were a place to socialise, make business deals, eavesdrop on the latest gossip, snooze, read, eat and pick up male prostitutes. All classes were allowed, though men and women were admitted at different times. Larger baths, such as the one in Odessos, had a *palaestra,* or exercise hall, where wrestling and other athletic activities took place, often accompanied by music. Bathers would then rub themselves down with oil and sweat for a while in the *sudatorium* (a kind of sauna) before scraping it off with a strigil, examples of which are on show in the Archaeological Museum (opposite). A plunge in the hot water of the *caldarium* would follow. They would then move on to the more bearable temperature of the *tepidarium,* finishing off with a dip in the icy *frigidarium*. The remains of these shallow pools can still be seen in Varna's Thermae, as well as the furnace and hypocaust system that provided underfloor heating and hot water.

n the city and features an intricately carved bishop's throne.

The quaint **St Nikolai Church** (ul Knyaz Boris I), which seems stranded along the modern mall, s worth a visit for its murals. It's always busy, and is a popular venue for weddings.

The elegant **St Sarkis Armenian Apostolic Church** (ul Han Asparuh 15) was built in 1842 and features a barrelled wooden ceiling and a wonderful collection of naive icons. It's normally closed, but the custodian will be happy to open it up for you if he's around.

St Michael the Archangel Church (ul 27 Yuli) was founded in 1865 and is historically significant as the first place where religious services were given in Bulgarian. The building also contained Varna's first school. The church is small and badly lit but there are some fine wooden icons.

THNOGRAPHIC MUSEUM

Housed in a delightful revival-era mansion built in 1860, Varna's **Ethnographic Museum** (☎ 630 588; ul Panagyurishte 22; adult/student 4/2 lv; ⏰ 10am-5pm Tue-Sun Apr-Oct, 10am-5pm Tue-Sat Nov-Mar) is one of the country's best. The ground floor contains a collection of agricultural implements and displays about weaving, wine-making and fishing from the late 19th and early 20th centuries. The 1st floor has an impressive range of costumes and jewellery, and the four rooms on the 2nd floor are furnished in period style.

HISTORY MUSEUM

Watching over the ruins of the Roman baths, Varna's ivy-covered **History Museum** (☎ 632 677; ul 8 Noemvri 3; adult/child 4/2 lv; ⏰ 10am-5pm Tue-Sun) is itself an intriguing part of the city's history. Built in 1851 as the Belgian Embassy, it subsequently became a hotel, a prison and, under the communists, a Museum of the Revolution, before taking on its present role in 1990. Displays on the ground floor include photographs of the city from the 1920s, while the basement holds an exhibition on local trades and handicrafts such as printing, weaving and brewing. More imagination has gone into the replicas of long-gone 1920s and '30s shops and offices on the 1st floor, including 'Uncle Mityu's Café', a hat shop, toy shop and lawyer's office. There's also a replica of a bedroom from the Hotel London (now the Grand Hotel Musala Palace).

NATIONAL NAVAL MUSEUM

The only one of its kind in Bulgaria, the **National Naval Museum** (☎ 632 018; bul Primorski 2; adult/child 2/1 lv; ⏰ 10am-6pm Mon-Sat) offers an introduction to the country's seagoing history from the Russo-Turkish War (1877–78) to the present day. Embedded in concrete outside the museum entrance is the **warship Druzki** (admission 1 lv; ⏰ 11am-5pm Tue, Thu & Sat), which torpedoed a Turkish cruiser during the First Balkan War in 1912. It's possible to clamber around this revered relic (ask the museum staff to open the gate). Inside the musty museum building itself is a collection of uniforms, model ships, naval insignia and displays on the *Druzki,* including an enormous torpedo, although there's little labelling in English. Anchors, artillery and helicopters can be seen rusting quietly in the grounds, while encased in glass is the yacht *Cor Coroli,* in which Georgi Georgiev became the first Bulgarian to sail single-handed around the world, in 1977.

BLACK SEA COAST

PRIMORSKI PARK
Established in 1878, this large and attractive green space overlooking the sea stretches for about 8km, and is said to be the largest of its kind in Europe. It's full of promenading families and old ladies knitting lace in summer, and there's always something going on.

Further into the park is the **Aquarium** (☎ 222 586; adult/child 2/1 lv, foreign-language lecture 24 lv; ☉ 9am-8pm). Housed in a powder-blue Art Deco building, it's an old-fashioned place with tanks filled with seahorses, piranhas and conger eels as well as some denizens of the Black Sea's depths. There's also a collection of seashells but there's no English labelling.

In the northern section, the **Zoopark** (☎ 302 528; adult/child 1/0.70 lv; ☉ 8am-8pm) is a dispiriting place featuring a range of animals, including lions, wolves, monkeys, goats and a camel, all in small concrete enclosures. There's also a solitary bear and birds kept in filthy cages. About 200m further north, the **Terrarium Varna** (☎ 302 571; adult/child 2/1.50 lv; ☉ 9am-10pm) has a collection of creepy crawlies such as spiders and scorpions.

Another 500m further north is the ugly concrete **Dolphinarium** (☎ 302 199; adult/child 20/14 lv; ☉ Tue-Sun). Apparently the only one of its kind in the Balkan regions, it presents 45-minute shows (at 10.30am, noon and 3.30pm) of dolphins performing various acrobatic tricks.

BEACH
Steps from Primorski Park lead down to the city's long, sandy beach, which is hugely popular with local sunbathers, paddlers and beach volleyball players. There are also a couple of tiny, outdoor, steaming **mineral-water pools**, although these are more popular with rheumatic pensioners than with the beachgoing set. The main attraction, though, is the long coastal lane, officially known as aleya Georgi Georgiev but more commonly referred to either as Plazhna aleya or **Kraybrezhna aleya**, which is the name we've used here. In summer, it's the centre of Varna's nightlife, lined with clubs, bars and restaurants – only a handful of which operate at other times of the year; many also change names from one season to the next. Pick up the *Summer Seaside Guide* (p213) to see what's new.

ART GALLERIES
Varna City Art Gallery (☎ 243 141; ul Lyuben Karavelov admission free; ☉ 10am-6pm Tue-Sun), also known a the Boris Georgiev Art Gallery, features two floors of 19th- and 20th-century Bulgarian art including works by Vladimir Dimitrov an David Peretz. It also hosts temporary exhibitions such as the International Print Biennial (odd-numbered years).

The **Varna Centre for Contemporary Art** (☎ 60 238; ul Knyaz Boris I 65; admission free; ☉ 10am-6pm Tue-Sun) is another gallery with a collection of idiosyncratic modern art.

Artin (☎ 614 833; ul Knyaz Boris I 57; ☉ 9.30am-7pm Mon-Fri) is an equally interesting private gallery in a charming old mansion nearby, which shows the latest work of some of the best known local artists.

Festivals & Events
Between May and October, Varna hosts th renowned **Varna Summer International Festival** (www.varnasummerfest.org). Established in 1926 the festival features outstanding events, including opera, the biennial International Ballet Competition (held in even-numbered years) and choral, jazz and folk music. Event are held at the **Open-Air Theatre** (☎ 228 38! Primorski Park) and in some of the nine halls i the massive **Festival Hall** (☎ 621 331; ul Slivnitsa, Programmes and information about buying tickets are well advertised beforehand in Varn and Sofia. The Festival Hall also hosts th **Annual International Film Festival** in late Augus and early September.

Other special events around the city includ the **Songs about Varna Competition** and the **Days o Greek Culture Festival**, both held in March.

Sleeping
Varna certainly has no shortage of accom modation, although the better (or at least, th more central) places get very busy during th summer months. Several more midrange hotel have appeared in recent years, and Varna i still the only place on the coast where you'l find backpacker hostels.

BUDGET
Private rooms are plentiful in Varna, and pen sioners with spare rooms wait around the trai station to greet new arrivals. Prices tend to b around 12 lv per person, but make sure yo don't end up in some out-of-the-way suburb **Isak** (☎ 602 318; www.accommodatebg.com; train station;

per person 12-14 lv; 7am-9pm Mon-Sat, to 6pm Sun) and
Astra Tour (605 861; train station; r per person from 12
lv, apt from 35 lv; 7am-9pm Mon-Fri, to 7pm Sat & Sun),
neighbouring agencies inside the train station,
offer private rooms around town.

Flag Hostel (0897408115; www.varnahostel.com;
1st fl, ul Sheinovo 2; dm incl breakfast €10) Varna's most
central hostel, located on a side street just off
bul Knyaz Boris I. It's a friendly place with a
young, international party atmosphere and
three six-bed dorms, modern bathrooms and
kitchen facilities.

Yo Ho Hostel (0887601691, 0887933340; www
.yohohostel.com; ul Ruse 23; dm/s/d incl breakfast €11/14/14;
) Shiver your timbers at this pirate-themed
place found just down the street from the
opera house, in a brand-new location with
four dorm rooms, two doubles and one single
room. Free internet, breakfast and pickups are
offered, and the management also organises
day trips.

Voennomorski Club (617 965; bul Vladislav
Varenchik 2; s with fan 21 lv, s/d with air-con 31/42 lv;)
The 'Naval Club' is a pale blue building fac-
ing the cathedral, offering small but comfy
rooms. However, it's an old-fashioned place,
with unsmiling, monosyllabic reception staff
and dated furnishings, giving it a kind of retro,
Warsaw Pact atmosphere. Still, the location's
good and it's a bargain.

Victorina (603 541; ul Tsar Simeon I 36; r per person
22 lv) Right by the train station and highly recommended for renting good-quality rooms in
private houses around the centre.

MIDRANGE
Hotel Astra (630 524; ul Opalchenska 9; s/d 40/60 lv;
) Not far from the centre, the Astra is a
cheery family hotel with a collection of simple
but perfectly clean and cosy rooms that are a
bargain by Varna standards.

Three Dolphins Hotel (600 911; three_dolphins@
abv.bg; ul Gabrovo 27; s/d 42/51 lv, renovated 51/60 lv;)
On a quiet side street near the train station,
this small, homely guesthouse offers fair
value. All rooms have a TV, though only the
renovated ones come with air-conditioning
and fridges.

Cherno More Hotel (612 235; www.chernomorebg
.com; bul Slivnitsa 33; s/d unrenovated 45/56 lv, r renovated
from 80 lv;) This gigantic, socialist-era
eyesore in the city centre may not look so enticing, with its tacky 'casino' sign and dark and
strangely bare foyer, but the newly renovated
rooms are bright, clean and smartly furnished,

all with balconies offering bird's-eye views of
Varna. Staff are friendly and helpful. Breakfast
is included.

Hotel Antik (632 157; www.galia-online.com/antik;
ul Ohrid 10; s/d with fan 50/58 lv, d/ste with air-con 68/90 lv;
) A neat, family-run hotel just down
the road from pl Nezavisimost. The 18 rooms
are simple but clean; all come with TVs and
minibars, and many have balconies.

Hotel Elegance (631 657; www.elegance-hotel
.com; ul Gabrovo 24; s/d/apt incl breakfast €30/50/70;)
Close to the train station, this relatively new
place is a little pricey, though rooms are
large and the apartments come with saunas.
Watch out for the huge mirror just inside
the entrance.

City Mark (655 546; www.citymark-hotel.com; pl
Nezavisimost; s/d/apt 59/79/140 lv;) Right in the
pedestrianised heart of the city, City Mark is
an attractive, modern option with some fair-
sized rooms, though the scarlet-and-silver
décor scheme can be a bit overwhelming. It's a
small and popular place, so advance bookings
are recommended.

Hotel Relax (607 847; www.hotelrelax1.com; ul
Stefan Karadzha 22; r 60 lv;) Centrally located
hotel just off bul Slivnitsa, with a small collection of homely rooms of differing sizes,
all with fridges, TV and modern bathrooms.
There's an odd setup, however, with a rival
hotel in the same courtyard, which has been
known to poach or turn away guests looking
for the original. Don't be sidetracked – the
reception for Hotel Relax is located at the very
back of the courtyard.

TOP END
Hotel Odessos (640 300; www.odessos-bg.com; bul
Slivnitsa 1; s/d with fan 85/106 lv, with air-con 110/125 lv;
) Enjoying the best location of any hotel
in town, opposite the entrance to Primorski
Park, the Odessos is an older establishment
with smallish and rather average rooms for
the price, but it's convenient for the beach
and for sightseeing. Only the pricier 'sea
view' rooms have balconies, but the cheaper
'city view' rooms are much quieter. Breakfast
is included.

Panorama Hotel (687 300; www.panoramabg.com;
bul Primorski 31; s/d/ste from 110/170/230 lv;)
The location on a grubby and busy main road
isn't ideal, but inside this is a chic, modern
hotel with good facilities including a gym
and sauna, and many of the large rooms have
panoramic sea views.

244 NORTHERN COAST •• Varna

BLACK SEA COAST

Hotel Capitol (☎ 688 000; www.capitol.bg; ul Petko Karavelov 40; s/d/apt €75/85/115; P ❖ 🖳) Stylish, friendly and located in a quiet part of town, the four-star Capitol is among the best in its price range, with a choice of good-sized rooms done out in a muted pink-and-cream décor scheme. Apartments have both shower and bath.

Grand Hotel Musala Palace (☎ 664 100; www.musala palace.bg; ul Musala 3; s/d/ste incl breakfast from €150/170/205; P ❖ 🖳) Varna's grandest and oldest hotel is this superb conversion of the Hotel London, which originally opened in 1912. There's a touch of rococo gaudiness about the public areas, but rooms are spacious and elegantly furnished, and the overall service is top-notch.

Eating

Trops Kâshta (ul Knyaz Boris I; mains 3-4 lv; ❧ 8.30am-10.30pm) This branch of the dependable nationwide self-service canteen chain is the ideal place for cheap, simple food such as sausage and beans, chicken chops and moussaka; just point at whatever takes your fancy.

Prestol (☎ 600 807; Kraybrezhna aleya; mains 3-8 lv; ❧ 10am-1am) Busy place on the seaside promenade serving cheap grills and salads in an attractive beachfront setting. Pork skewers and fish are on the menu, along with 'sausage by the metre' for the *very* hungry.

Orient Turkish Restaurant (☎ 602 380; ul Tsaribrod 1; mains 4-5 lv; ❧ lunch & dinner) Another of Varna's best, this halal place serves up delicious Turkish and Middle Eastern dishes such as shish kebabs, tabouleh and stuffed vine leaves. Despite being on a busy road, the outdoor terrace is pleasantly shielded from the traffic by some bushes.

Dom na Arkitekta (ul Musala 10; mains 4-8 lv; ❧ lunch & dinner) 'The Architect's House' is a fine old wooden National Revival–style building with a private, leafy courtyard popular with local cats. The usual grills, steaks and salads are on the menu and it's a restful place for a cold beer or two.

Morsko Konche (☎ 600 418; pl Nezavisimost; mains 4-10 lv; ❧ 8am-11.30pm) The 'Seahorse' is a cheap and cheerful pizza place with a big menu featuring all the standard varieties, as well as some inventive creations of its own: the 'exotic' pizza comes with bananas and blueberries.

Pri Yafata (☎ 609 914; Cherno More Hotel, bul Slivnitsa 33; mains 4-10 lv; ❧ noon-midnight) Folksy place offering good quality traditional Bulgarian cuisine, with dishes such as stewed pork knuckle, chicken *kavarma* and lots of salads and soups. There's live music every night.

Happy Bar & Grill (☎ 606 338; pl Nezavisimost; mains 5-10 lv; ❧ 8am-2am) Varna's home-grown, and now nationwide, chain restaurant has four branches around the city, including at this central location. The uncomplicated menu of grills, steaks and salads pulls in customers throughout the day, and the friendly waitstaff, who occasionally launch into spontaneous dance routines, certainly add to the atmosphere. There's another branch on bul Slivnitsa.

our pick **Pri Monahinite** (☎ 611 830; bul Primorski 47; mains 8-14 lv; ❧ 11am-midnight) Set in the courtyard of a little church, Pri Monahinite ('At the Nuns' Place') is a classy place for roast lamb, grilled pork and other meaty offerings. It also does good salads and has an extensive wine list.

Tambuktu (☎ 610 864; Kraybrezhna aleya; mains 8-20 lv; ❧ 9am-2am) One of the few restaurants along the seaside promenade that stay open year-round, Tambuktu is a chain seafood restaurant, serving up a vast assortment of freshly caught fish. Sea bass, lobster, prawns and many other dishes are on the menu, and there's live music in the evenings.

Mr Baba (☎ 614 629; off bul Primorski; mains 12-30 lv; ❧ 8am-midnight) The coast-long trend for novelty ship restaurants has come to Varna, with this wooden-hulled venture stranded at the end of the beach, near the port. Named after a 17th-century Ottoman admiral, it features a pricey but hearty menu of fish and steak dishes such as sea bass, trout and bluefish.

Drinking

Some of the trendiest bars are found along the beach on Kraybrezhna aleya, although most only have a brief existence in the summer sunshine and many change names from one year to the next. There are also several cafés in Primorski Park, near the entrance to the Aquarium and around the Summer Theatre. In the city centre, ul Knyaz Boris I and bul Slivnitsa are home to smarter cocktail and coffee bars.

O'Neill's Irish Pub (☎ 614 586; Cherno More Hotel, bul Slivnitsa 33; ❧ 5pm-3am) Downstairs in the vast Cherno More Hotel complex, this Irish-themed pub offers regular live music and Sky Sports coverage to go with your Guinness. It also serves food.

A-Lounge Beach (☎ 0885190180; Kraybrezhna aleya; ⏰ 9pm-3am) Swanky, summer-only beachfront bar offering live music, DJs, beach-party nights and, apparently, fashion shows. It even has a few small pools to loll around in with a cocktail in hand.

Entertainment

Varna Opera House (☎ 223 038; www.operavarna.bg; pl Nezavisimost) Bulgaria's second-most important opera house (after Sofia's) hosts performances by the Varna Opera and Philharmonic Orchestra all year except July and August.

Stoyan Bachvarov Dramatic Theatre (☎ 615 301; pl Nezavisimost 1) This theatre, located next door to the Opera House, stages dramatic plays from September through June.

Open-Air Theatre (☎ 612 803; Primorski Park) Complete with mock ivy-covered Roman arches, this theatre hosts everything from ballet to rock concerts. Details are available at the adjoining ticket office. Live music is also played most summer evenings at the temporary **Summer Theatre** (Primorski Park).

Mustang Cinema (☎ 610 333; ul Bratya Shkorpil 33; tickets 4-5 lv) and **Bulgaran Cinema** (☎ 0899333477; bul Maria Luisa 1; tickets 4-5 lv) are two of the more central places showing recent Hollywood movies.

Exit (☎ 645 050; ⏰ 10pm-6am), **4aspik** (☎ 0885 800297; ⏰ 10pm-4am), specialising in Bulgarian folk-pop, and **Copacabana** (☎ 0888281431; ⏰ 9pm-4am), with a fondness for '70s and '80s music, are just a few of the many summertime clubs along Kraybrezhna aleya.

Shopping

The pedestrian stretch of ul Knyaz Boris I has numerous small fashion boutiques, including some international chains. Reproduction icons and paintings by local artists are sold outside the Cathedral of the Assumption of the Virgin and St Nikolai Church, while there's a daily market in the park behind the Opera House, selling fruit and vegetables, books, souvenirs and clothes.

Capricorn Gallery (☎ 612 797; ul Sv Kliment Ohridski 1; ⏰ 10.30am-7pm) Just off pl Ekzarh Yosif, this interesting little gallery sells paintings and sculptures by local artists, though prices are quite high.

Blaga Blagoeva (☎ 600 613; www.blaga-blagoeva .com; bul Vladislav Varenchik 34; ⏰ 10am-7.30pm Mon-Sat, 10.30am-5.30pm Sun) Eponymous store selling the latest offerings from the highly regarded local women's fashion designer, including colourful evening dresses and knitwear.

Valentina (pl Nezavisimost; ⏰ 10am-8pm Mon-Sat, to 7pm Sun) The city centre's main department store, this ugly block has an eclectic range of goods on sale over three floors, ranging from replica Samurai swords and souvenirs to fancy soaps and clothing. It also has a café.

Getting There & Away

AIR

Varna's international **airport** (☎ 573 323; www .varna-airport.bg) is an increasingly busy place with scheduled and charter flights from all over Europe, as well as regular flights to and from Sofia. From the centre, bus 409 goes to the airport.

The local agency for bookings is the **Varna International Airport Travel Agency** (☎ 612 588; ul Knyaz Boris I 15). **Bulgaria Air** (☎ 573 416) flies between Varna and Sofia (one-way/return around €105/160) at least once every day.

BUS

Varna has two bus stations – the **central bus station** (☎ 448 349; bul Vladislav Varenchik 158) is about 2km northwest of the city centre. It's a dingy place with a couple of newsstands, a basic café and a **left luggage office** (⏰ 7am-10pm; per hr/day 0.50/4 lv). From here, services go to Athens (100 lv, 26 hours, one daily), Balchik (4 lv, one hour, 16 daily), Burgas (9 lv, two hours, five daily), Dobrich (4 lv, one hour, every 30 minutes), Istanbul (45 lv, 10 hours, two daily), Plovdiv (19 lv, six hours, two daily), Shumen (6 lv, 1½ hours, one daily), Sofia (25 lv, seven hours, 20 daily) and Veliko Târnovo (9 lv, four hours, 20 daily).

All buses to Sofia go via Shumen and Veliko Târnovo; the buses to Plovdiv go via Stara Zagora and buses south to Burgas pass through all the coastal resorts, including Sunny Beach (Slânchev Bryag) and Nesebâr.

Long-distance and international services are operated by private buses. Tickets for these can be bought at agencies in town, as well as at the bus station, but all departures are from the central bus station.

The second bus station in Varna is the **Chatsna Mladost Station** (☎ 500 039), about 200m along a road that starts almost opposite the central bus station; look for the sign in English opposite the bus station. From here, more frequent minibuses go to smaller places along the Black Sea coast, including Dobrich (4 lv, one hour, every 30 minutes), Balchik (4 lv, one hour, hourly), Kavarna (5 lv, 1½ hours, hourly), Burgas (9 lv, two hours, every 40 minutes to one hour) and Nesebâr (6 lv, 1½ hours, six daily) via Sunny Beach (5 lv, 1¼ hours).

TRAIN

The **train station** (☎ 630 414; pl Slaveikov) is a modern, well-ordered place with a recently refurbished booking hall and computer screens listing departures and arrivals in Bulgarian. Facilities include an **internet centre** (☼ 9am-noon & 1-9pm) and a **left-luggage office** (☼ 7.30am-8pm).

Varna is an important destination on the rail network and there's even a connection to Moscow via Bucharest three times a week in summer. Other destinations include Ruse (9 lv, four hours, two daily), Sofia (19 lv, eight hours, seven daily), Plovdiv (15.20 lv, six hours, four daily) and Shumen (5.10 lv, 1½ hours, nine daily).

The **Rila Bureau** (☎ 632 347; ul Preslav 13; ☼ 7am-7pm Mon-Fri, 8am-2pm Sat) sells tickets for international services and advance tickets for domestic trains.

Getting Around

The bus and train stations are on opposite sides of the city, and linked by buses 1, 22 and 41. The most useful bus for visitors is 409, which connects the airport with Golden Sands (Zlatni Pyasâtsi) every 15 minutes between 6am and 11pm. This bus passes the central bus station in Varna and Primorski Park (including the Dolphinarium) and also stops outside Sveti Konstantin. It can be caught at designated spots on bul Vladislav Varenchik near the main post office, and along bul Knyaz Boris I. Bus 109 runs between the train station and Golden Sands.

If you need a rental car, **Hertz** (☎ 510 250) and **Avis** (☎ 500 832) have offices at the international section of the airport. **Balkan Tourism** (☎ 618 052; ul A Malinov 4; ☼ 9am-6pm) in the city centre is one of the cheaper outlets, charging from €25 per day including insurance and unlimited kilometres.

SVETI KONSTANTIN
СВЕТИ КОНСТАНТИН
☎ 052

Sveti Konstantin is a small, fairly sedate beach resort about 9km northeast of Varna, with hotels attractively spaced out amongst parkland. Established in 1946 under the name of Druzhba (Friendship), it was later renamed Sveti Konstantin and Sveti Elena, but is now more commonly known simply as Sveti Konstantin. It's less commercial than other resorts and has long been popular with older holidaymakers; it still has a number of 'rest homes' for retired civil servants and trade union members, and the resort is famous for its therapeutic mineral waters and health treatments. There are several new, upscale hotels geared towards young families, but this isn't the place for water sports or raucous nightlife.

Orientation & Information

The centre of Sveti Konstantin is the road between the bus stop and beach that passes the post office and the unnamed laneway (which we've called Post Office Lane) between the post office and the Grand Hotel Varna. Another road runs eastwards from the bus stop to the Sunny Day Complex at the far end of the beach. There are no street names and hotels are poorly signposted. There is a map of the resort on a board at the bus stop, but no dedicated maps for sale; Domino's *Varna* map contains a small map of Sveti Konstantin (1:13,000).

There are dozens of foreign exchange offices, as well as the **Biochim Commercial Bank** (Post Office Lane). There's an internet centre on the ground floor of the International House of Scientists Frederic Joliot-Curie (opposite).

Sights & Activities

SV KONSTANTIN & SV ELENA MONASTERY

This tiny **church** (admission free; ☼ dawn-dusk, closed Sun am) is just off Post Office Lane. It was built below street level in the style demanded by the Ottoman rulers during the early 18th century. The church was destroyed not long after but was rebuilt in 1912. More information about the church and the general development of Sveti Konstantin is featured in a small but fascinating display (with explanations in English) on the ground floor of the International House of Scientists Frederic Joliot-Curie.

BEACH

Much of the beach is carved up into private stretches of sand appropriated by the various hotels, but there are plenty of areas accessible to nonguests too. Parasols and sun beds cost around 6 lv to 7 lv each. However, all the beaches tend to be small and bordered by jetties, breakwaters and rocky outcrops. There are no water sports available here, so if you want to windsurf or jet-ski, head for Albena or Golden Sands (Zlatni Pyasâtsi).

Tours

There are a few kiosks near the bus stop offering a range of local tours. **Beni Tur** (☎ 432 541; ☽ 10am-10pm) runs day trips to Nesebâr (33 lv), Balchik and Kaliakra Cape (26 lv) and Shumen (35 lv) among others.

Sleeping

International House of Scientists Frederic Joliot-Curie (☎ 361 161; fax 361 187; s/d 53/74 lv, renovated 84/92 lv; P ☒ ☐ ☒) Looking (and sounding) like a remnant of another era, this '60s towerblock just west of the bus stop nevertheless offers good value, and it's definitely worth the extra leva for the neater modernised rooms. It has a mineral-water pool, various balneological treatments are available and the hotel even has its own pharmacy and cactus garden.

Hotel Panorama (☎ 361 025; www.panoramahotel.bg; s/d 55/68 lv; ☒) Among the cheaper options here, the Panorama is an older establishment facing the main road, with public areas featuring chunky chandeliers and lots of grey marble. The rooms are perfectly acceptable and there are gardens at the back with steps leading down towards the beachfront area.

Estreya Palace Hotel (☎ 361 312; www.hotelestreya .com; s/d incl breakfast 80/120 lv; ☒ ☒) Nestled in secluded parkland around 200m from the beach, this is a smart hotel with large airy rooms, all with balconies. It also has a spa centre offering therapeutic treatments. Prices drop by about a third outside the summer months.

Sirius Beach Hotel (☎ 361 224; www.siriusbeach .com; s/d low season incl breakfast 120/160 lv, high season incl half-board 190/250 lv; P ☒ ☐ ☒) This flashy glass rotunda is a fairly new place, occupying a narrow curve of beach. It has a variety of bright rooms, all with balconies, and there are indoor and outdoor pools, a kids' play area and a restaurant on a mock-up ship.

Grand Hotel Varna (☎ 361 491; www.grandhotelvarna .com; s/d 210/280 lv; P ☒ ☐ ☒) The Grand Hotel, with over 300 fresh-looking rooms, certainly lives up to its name, dominating a huge complex that includes four other associated hotels and offering every conceivable amenity, including several restaurants and bars, a bowling alley, tennis courts and spa. Prices vary, and drop by almost half in May and October.

Eating

There are plenty of restaurants around Sveti Konstantin, many attached to hotels, and prices tend to be fairly reasonable compared with the bigger resorts further up the coast. The **Sparm Supermarket** (☽ 24hr) near the bus stop probably offers the best value for self-caterers.

Mehana Marina (☎ 362 616; mains 4-12 lv; ☽ lunch & dinner) A few steps up the unnamed lane running east from the bus stop, Marina is a folksy restaurant set in a courtyard planted with trees and little fountains. The menu features traditional Bulgarian cuisine such as *kebabche* (spicy grilled meat sausages), as well as lots of fish dishes, grills and German fare such as bratwurst and schnitzel.

Dolce Vita (☎ 361 491; Grand Hotel Varna; mains from 5 lv; ☽ lunch & dinner) One of the five-star hotel's clutch of excellent restaurants, this one serves up good quality Italian food, including pasta and pizza, in an attractive, civilised setting.

Sirius (Sirius Beach Hotel; mains 10-20 lv; ☽ breakfast, lunch & dinner) Certainly the resort's most eye-catching restaurant, set aboard a grounded sailing ship at the side of the Sirius Beach Hotel. Fish dishes, unsurprisingly, are the speciality here, including trout, turbot and paella.

Getting There & Away

Bus 409 travels from Varna airport to Golden Sands (Zlatni Pyasâtsi) every 15 minutes between 6am and 11pm. It stops outside the Hotel Panorama at Sveti Konstantin, from where it's a short walk down to the hotels and the beach. Every 15 to 20 minutes between 6am and 11pm, bus 8 goes directly from Varna to Sveti Konstantin, via ul Maria Luisa and the northeastern end of ul Knyaz Boris I in Varna.

Getting Around

There are better deals to be had in Varna if you want to hire a car, while bicycles can be rented at kiosks near the bus stop (15 lv per day).

GOLDEN SANDS (ZLATNI PYASÂTSI)
ЗЛАТНИ ПЯСЪЦИ
☎ 052

Golden Sands (Zlatni Pyasâtsi) might sound equally as twee as Sunny Beach, but the name is in fact an ancient one for this superb stretch of beach 18km up the coast from Varna. It was among the earliest purpose-built resorts in Bulgaria, with the first hotel opening here in 1957, though it wasn't until the late '60s that mass tourism (largely from the old Eastern Bloc) really took off. Today it's Bulgaria's second-largest coastal resort, offering around 15,000 beds clustered along, or just off, a 4km stretch of sandy beach, and some of the best nightlife on the coast. It's also a good place for diving, with a number of operators running various trips to sea.

Orientation & Information

Driving a private car into the resort costs 3 lv per vehicle, but visitors arriving by private /public bus or taxi do not have to pay any entrance fees. The resort is long, narrow and easy to get around, and there are plenty of helpful signs in English. The post office and telephone centre are near Hotel Yavor, about halfway along the resort, and there's an internet centre a few metres up from the post office.

Sights

ALADZHA MONASTERY

A major local attraction is the **Aladzha Monastery** (☎ 355 460; admission 3 lv; ☼ 9am-6pm Apr-Oct, to 4pm Tue-Sat Nov-Mar). Very little is known about this bizarre rock monastery; the cave was probably inhabited as far back as the 5th century BC, but what remains today was created during the 13th and 14th centuries. The monastery was used by monks from the Hesychast order until the 18th century, but was not discovered again until 1928.

Stairs and walkways lead to and around these astonishing caves, which were carved in the cliffside up to 40m above ground. Erosion has caused some damage to the caves, including to the monastery's murals, but it's still a remarkable place. A signposted path (600m) leads to the three-level **catacombs**, probably created in the 13th century.

To walk to the monastery from the resort, head up the road past the post office, cross the main Varna–Albena road outside the Economic & Investment Bank, and follow the signs to 'Kloster Aladja' and the markings along the obvious trail. The walk takes an hour one way and wends its way through a wonderful, shady forest, part of the 1320-hectare **Golden Sands Nature Park**.

The road (3km) is steepish in parts and starts about 500m south along the Varna–Albena road from the start of the walking trail. The infrequent bus 33 from Varna to Kranevo

drops passengers outside the front entrance of the monastery.

Activities

Near the main road, **Aquapolis** (☎ 389 999; www .aquapolis.net; adult/child 25/9 lv; ☼ 10am-7pm) is a new water park featuring lots of different pools, slides and other kid-friendly attractions, including a mini climbing wall. A minibus (1 lv, every 40 minutes) to Aquapolis picks up at various signed points around the resort. The usual water sports, such as **jet-skiing** (15min 60 lv) are available on the beach, but they're a little expensive and there's more choice in Albena. **Massages** (1hr about 30 lv) seem to be more popular with many visitors, and there are numerous tents and huts along the beach where you can get pummelled.

Hotel Palm Beach has a sports centre open to nonguests, with a pool, sauna and bowling alleys, while on the beachfront, quick thrills are offered by **bungee trampolines** (5min 10 lv) and a **ferris wheel** (adult/child 5/3 lv).

Younger kids will delight in the **children's entertainment centre**, with paddle pools, toy trains and water slides, which is near Hotel Sirena.

Diving is another popular activity and there are several outlets along the beach, including the PADI-certified **Harry's Diving Center** (☎ 321 766; todorharbaliev@hotmail.com; ☼ May-Oct). Single dives, exploring the reefs just 30m offshore, cost 80 lv, while two dives on a WWII wreck off Shabla, 80km north, cost 150 lv. A variety of other dives and courses is available, including four-day scuba courses (€300).

Tours

Dozens of agencies and stalls along the esplanade sell tours such as two-hour **yacht cruises** (30 lv per person), three-hour **fishing trips** (40 lv per person including lunch) and **bus trips** to Nesebâr (33 lv) and Balchik and Kaliakra Cape (26 lv). **Travel Plus** (☎ 0898494578), near the Kempinski Hotel, runs a wide variety of tours, including two-day trips to Istanbul (157 lv per person including lunch and hotel), cruises to Balchik (65 lv per person including lunch) and six-hour Jeep safaris (50 lv).

Sleeping

Virtually all visitors staying in Golden Sands will be on a prebooked package tour, and many of the hotels tend to be booked solid through the summer. However, there are so many hotels here that you should be able to

BLACK SEA COAST

find a room somewhere. Prices given here are for the high season (June to August).

If you haven't organised accommodation in advance, visit the **accommodation office** (☎ 355 683; Varna–Albena road; per person Jun-Aug 75-125 lv; ☼ 8.30am-8.30pm), behind the bus stop next to DSK Bank. It acts as an agent for only six of the resort's hotels, though. Prices outside the summer will be cheaper, but rates are not available in advance.

Dana Palace Hotel (☎ 383 838; dana_palace@abv.bg; s/d incl breakfast 70/90 lv; ✷ ✷) One of the cheaper hotels, set a fair way back from the beach, but offering great value with large, airy rooms, an outdoor pool, kids' playground and restaurant.

Hotel Admiral (☎ 390 200; admiral@goldensands-bg.com; r incl breakfast 250 lv; ✷ ✷) Occupying an enviable beachfront location, this huge, gleamingly white, 300-room hotel is one of the top places to stay. The large rooms all have balconies (many facing the sea), and there's an on-site nightclub and spa.

Eating

Food and drink in Golden Sands cost about twice as much as in Varna, but prices are not quite as outrageous as in Albena.

Taj Mahal (☎ 0886600030; mains around 5-7 lv; ☼ lunch & dinner) Just off the beach, near the Ferris wheel, this little place serves dishes such as chicken korma and lamb vindaloo. The lunch special (curry, rice and a beer) is good value at 10 lv and there's a free Indian dance show from 8.30pm.

Gruzhinska Kuchnya (☎ 356 850; mains 10-20 lv; ☼ lunch & dinner) For something a bit different, check out this Georgian restaurant on the beach opposite Hotel Admiral. Pork stew, lamb shish kebabs, stuffed rabbit and various veggie dishes are on the menu.

Chiflika (mains 10-20 lv; ☼ 24hr) Giant wooden barn near Hotel Astoria serving up hearty, meaty dishes, including roast pork, lamb kebabs and steaks. There's a free floorshow of traditional music and dancing every evening.

Entertainment

Golden Sands has a lively clubbing scene, with numerous venues around the resort, many inside hotels. Restaurants and bars often provide live entertainment, with everything from Bulgarian folk ensembles and mariachi bands to Elvis impersonators and Tom Jones tribute acts on the bill.

PR Club (☎ 0895500500; www.prclub-bg.com; ☼ 10.30pm-6am) On the beach near all the souvenir stalls, PR plays different music each night, with Retro Night (Thursdays) being one of the most popular. It also attracts international DJs.

Arrogance Music Factory (www.arroganceclub.com; Astera Casino & Hotel; ☼ 10pm-6am) One of the coolest nightspots in town, with four separate areas with very different styles (house and techno, R&B, chill-out lounge and folk-pop). The programme changes nightly.

If you're looking for something a little more cultural, the best you'll get are the slightly tacky shows staged at the open-air amphitheatre by the yacht harbour at the northern end of the beach. Touring dance, music and acrobatic shows take place most nights in summer and tickets (about 24 lv) are sold at the door.

Getting There & Away

There are many entrances to the resort, but the most frequently used ones are in the far south – near the Riviera Hotel complex, at the start of the road to Aladzha Monastery, and at the accommodation office and Economic & Investment Bank 500m further north – and outside the Hotel Zora in the far north.

Buses 109, 209, 309 and 409 leave Varna every 10 or 15 minutes between 6am and 11pm. The buses stop along the main Varna–Albena road at each main entrance to Golden Sands, from where it's no more than a 10-minute walk to any major hotel or the beach. Bus 9 from Varna stops at the southern entrance only, while 409 goes all the way to the Varna airport. These buses can be caught along ul Maria Luisa and the northeastern end of ul Knyaz Boris I in Varna.

Getting Around

If you're not keen on walking, the easiest option is to hop aboard the cute trolleybus (2 lv) that rumbles around the resort, with numerous signed stops. **Sixt** (☎ 0888050511; Kempinski Hotel; ☼ 9am-9pm) charges from €43 per day for car rental, including insurance.

ALBENA АЛБЕНА
☎ 0579

One of the biggest of the Black Sea coast's purpose-built resorts, Albena has been going

BLACK SEA COAST

250 NORTHERN COAST •• Albena

since 1969 and is named after the heroine of the eponymous play by Yordan Yovkov. Spread out over a wide area, and with a lovely, 4km-long beach and shallow water ideal for water sports, it's hugely popular with holiday-makers from across Europe. The downside is the horrendous prices charged for just about everything – Albena rivals Sunny Beach (Slânchev Bryag) as the most expensive place in Bulgaria.

Orientation & Information

Albena is the most organised resort in Bulgaria. There are plenty of maps along the streets (even though none of the streets have names) and multilingual staff at tourist booths. There are dozens of foreign exchange offices all over Albena, and most offer competitive rates. Along the main road, both the Biochim Commercial Bank and the SC Express Bank, at the administration building opposite the post office, change travellers cheques and offer cash advances on major credit cards. The post office has an internet centre and telephones for long-distance calls. The main shopping area is along the unnamed road between the Dobrudja and Kardam Hotels.

Entry to the resort by private car costs 3 lv; admission is free for anyone travelling by taxi, private/public bus or minibus.

Resort information and online hotel bookings are available at www.albena.bg.

Sights

The **Cultural Centre** in the middle of the resort is a lukewarm attempt to wean holidaymakers away from the beaches and clubs. It hosts regular performances of touring music, dance and folk shows (tickets about 23 lv to 25 lv), as well as 'comedy magic shows' for kids (12 lv). Posters on the centre's front door and elsewhere around the resort advertise upcoming programmes.

Away from the seafront, the small **Bolata Reserve**, a protected forest that's home to 140 rare plant and animal species, is an unexpected but welcome respite from the crowds.

Activities

Albena offers the best range of activities in the country, and adventurous and sporty types will find enough to satisfy their needs.

All kinds of water sports are available on the beach, including **jet-skiing** (10min 40 lv),

parasailing (10min 50 lv), **surfing** (board hire per hr /day 15/50 lv), **water-skiing** (10min 30 lv) and **banana boating** (10min 10 lv).

Albena Diving Centre (☎ 0888980409; ☼ 9am-6pm), based at Hotel Laguna Beach, offers diving packages (one/two/four dives 69/110/180 lv), plus a range of multiday courses, exploring wrecks and reefs off Albena, Shabla and elsewhere. A four-day scuba course costs 470 lv.

Tennis (court hire day/evening 18/20 lv) is popular and offered at a dozen or so courts all over the resort. Coaching costs from 20 lv per hour. Equipment costs extra.

Albena boasts the largest number of mineral springs in Bulgaria. The **medical centre** (☎ 62 305; Hotel Dobrudja) is the country's largest therapy centre. It offers all sorts of massages (from around 35 lv) and therapies.

Tours

Most hotels and travel agencies around Albena offer a wide range of excursions, such as **bus trips** to Balchik (adult/child 20/10 lv) and three-hour **fishing trips** (adult/child 39/19 lv). Numerous touts along the beachfront hand out leaflets for the latest tours.

Sleeping

Practically everyone visiting Albena will be on a package tour and hotels are often blockbooked by tour operators. Independent travellers may therefore struggle to find acceptably priced rooms here in summer, but if you're determined to stay, you should be able to find something somewhere. Prices following are for summer and are very changeable; for the latest deals and to make an online booking at any of the resort's hotels, see www.albena.bg. Most places close between October and April.

If you arrive without a reservation, it's worth checking out the helpful **accommodation office** (☎ 62 920; bus station; per person 90-130 lv; ☼ 8am-noon), which can organise rooms in many of the resort's hotels. If you want a private room, look for the relevant signs in English, German and Bulgarian outside homes along the main Varna–Balchik road.

Gorska Feya (☎ 62 961; camp sites 10 lv, bungalows 50-80 lv, villas 140-180 lv) Just behind the bus station, this camping ground is spread out through a shady patch of forest. It's a little remote from the centre, though a trolleybus stops outside en route to the beach, and there's an on-site shop. There's a choice of large bungalows and the newer, more attractive ones come with a

BLACK SEA COAST

TV and fridge. The two-storey 'villas' sleep between four and eight people.

Hotel Dobrudja (☎ 62 020; fax 62 216; s/d incl breakfast 91/140 lv; P ☒ 🖵 ☒) Right in the centre of Albena, though not near the beach, this vast concrete hive has unexciting but decent rooms. It has great amenities, though, including several shops, an internet café, nightclub, medical centre and a 17th-floor restaurant. It stays open longer than most hotels around here (May through November).

Hotel Dobrotitsa (☎ 62 869; fax 62 045; d/apt incl breakfast 170/180 lv; P ☒ 🖵 ☒) Another huge, central hotel, though rather more modern than the Dobrudja. The rooms are pretty standard, with TVs and fridges, and there are tennis courts and pools to keep you occupied.

Albena Beach Club (☎ 62 802; fax 62 715; r all-inclusive 210 lv; P ☒ 🖵 ☒) At the far southern end of the beach, this all-inclusive complex has airy, brightly decorated rooms and all the facilities you could ask for. It's used by package-tour groups, so advance bookings are recommended.

Eating

Albena has a profusion of restaurants serving up a vast variety of international dishes. Prices, though, are two or three times more than you would pay in Varna or anywhere else in Bulgaria (outside a couple of the other coastal resorts), so if money's an issue, check the menus before sitting down.

Bistro Dionisius (☎ 62 976; mains 5-12 lv; ⏱ lunch & dinner) At the northern tip of the beach is this slightly cheaper place, with a varied menu including omelettes, salads, fish and pizzas.

Restaurant Rai (mains 7-20 lv; ⏱ 9am-midnight) On the beachfront promenade, Rai offers a menu of Bulgarian grills and steaks, plus salads and a few fish dishes. Diners can enjoy a free 'folklore show' from 8.30pm.

Slaviansky Kât (☎ 62 103; mains 8-20 lv; ⏱ lunch & dinner) Behind the Boryana Hotel, this is a replica of a traditional tavern, with lots of meaty fare on the menu and free music and dance shows in the evenings.

Getting There & Away

The **bus station** (☎ 62 860) is about 800m from the beach, and is connected to the hotels and beach by trolleybus. Minibuses from Varna (4 lv, 45 minutes) via Golden Sands (Zlatni Pyasâtsi; 2.50 lv, 20 minutes) depart every 30 minutes between 8am and 7.30pm from a spot known as Makedonia Dom. Every 15 minutes between about 8am and 7.30pm, minibuses leave from Albena for Balchik (2 lv, 20 minutes) and for Dobrich (4 lv, 45 minutes) every 20 minutes. Three or four buses a day travel between Sofia (25 lv, eight hours) and Albena.

Getting Around

Trolleybuses (2 lv) putter along two set routes every 20 minutes between 9am and midnight. Other ways to get around include horse and cart at *very* negotiable rates, bicycles, available for rent along the beachfront (one hour/two hours/all day 5/9/20 lv), pedal-cars (one hour 12 lv), golf buggies (one hour 45 lv) and even rollerblades (one/two hours 5/9 lv).

Albena Rent-a-Car (☎ /fax 62 010; Hotel Dobrudja) charges from 70 lv per day (one day) or 55 lv per day (two to six days) including unlimited kilometres and insurance, but excluding petrol.

Plenty of predatory taxi drivers line the main roads, and may need persuasion to use their meters.

BALCHIK БАЛЧИК
☎ 0579 / pop 11,800

After the vast, artificial resorts further down the coast, Balchik is a breath of fresh sea air. A small, pretty town and fishing port huddled below white-chalk cliffs, it's a low-key holiday spot that feels like a world away from the likes of Albena, whose lights can be seen winking across the bay at night. The main attraction here is the palace, with its stunning botanical gardens, a couple of kilometres down the coast, and there are a couple of small museums to muse over. The biggest, fenced-off patch of sand (open 8.30am to 6.30pm) is in front of the Helios Hotel, just east of the centre. Otherwise, there's only one Lilliputian sliver of human-made beach crammed with parasols – the rest of the very narrow shoreline consists of rubble and boulders – although there are several concrete jetties used by some tourists for sunbathing and there are plenty of places to swim.

Although it's an easy day trip from Varna, Balchik makes a great base from which to explore attractions in the countryside, such as Dobrich (p277) and Kaliakra Cape (p255), as well as the beach resorts to the south.

History

Greek traders who settled here in the 6th century BC initially called the place Krounoi (meaning 'town of springs'), but later changed the name to Dionysopolis in honour of the god of wine. The Romans came later and fortified the town, and viticulture remained an important mainstay of the local economy. The town was rebuilt on higher ground in the 6th century AD after being destroyed by a tidal wave. In medieval times, Balchik (possibly meaning 'town of clay') thrived on the export of grain from the hinterlands. In 1913, Balchik (and the rest of the region) was annexed by Romania; it was literally sold back to Bulgaria in 1940 for 7000 'golden leva'.

Information

The post office and telephone centre are on the main square, pl Nezavisimost. There's a branch of Unicredit Bulbank with an ATM opposite the bus station, and you can change money and send/receive cash via Western Union, at **SG Expressbank** (ul Cherno More).

Internet Club (ul Primorska 29; per hr 2.40 lv; ☼ 9am-midnight) Located off pl Ribarski.

Tourist Information Centre (☎ 76 951; ul Primorska; ☼ 8am-8pm Apr-Oct, 9am-5pm Mon-Fri Nov-Mar) Hands out free basic maps and offers internet access, but is otherwise of little help.

Sights

SUMMER PALACE OF QUEEN MARIE & BOTANICAL GARDENS

Undoubtedly the prize attraction of Balchik is this lovely **palace** (☎ 72 559; adult/under 16yr 10/2 lv; ☼ 8am-8pm). It was built in 1924–26 by King Ferdinand of Romania for his English wife, Queen Marie – a granddaughter of Queen Victoria – as a place of solitude and contemplation (Balchik was then part of Romania). Marie, a follower of the Bahá'í faith, called it 'The Quiet Nest' and allegedly entertained her much younger Turkish lover here.

Far from being palatial, size-wise this is a relatively modest seaside villa, although the architecture – a blend of Bulgarian, Gothic and Islamic styles topped with a minaret – is unique. The half-dozen or so rooms on show contain original furnishings, including oil paintings by the queen, plus a curious collection of local archaeological finds such as Roman pottery and mammoth bones. The Turkish-style bathroom, with its domed ceiling, sunken bath and multicoloured glass windows, is a delight.

Beside the palace are six formal garden terraces, each representing one of the Queen's children, while behind are the extensive **botanical gardens** laid out in the 1950s and run by Sofia University. Around 600 different species of flora are featured throughout a series of themed gardens,

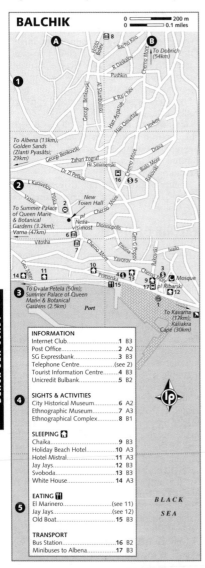

BALCHIK

0 _____ 200 m
0 _____ 0.1 miles

To Dobrich (54km)

To Albena (13km); Golden Sands (Zlanti Pyasátsi; 29km)

To Summer Palace of Queen Marie & Botanical Gardens (3.2km); Varna (47km)

To Dvata Petela (50m); Summer Palace of Queen Marie & Botanical Gardens (2.5km)

Port

To Kavarna (17km); Kaliakra Cape (30km)

Mosque

pl Ribarski

BLACK SEA

including a vast array of cacti in the 'Garden of the Gods'.

Also within the complex are a **watermill**, a classical-style **nymphaeum** and the tiny **Chapel of Sveta Bogoroditsa**. There's even a **winery**, which offers free tastings, though the bottles on sale are remarkably expensive.

If you're travelling here by bus from the southern coast, get off at the bus stop opposite the palace – either look for the tour buses and souvenir stalls, or ask the driver to drop you off at the *dvorets* (palace). The entrance here leads into the top end of the botanical gardens. The other entrance is off the seafront promenade.

OTHER SIGHTS

The three rooms of the **City Historical Museum** (☎ 72 177; ul Vitosha 3; admission 1 lv; ☼ 9am-noon & 1-5.30pm Mon-Fri) contain a small but diverse collection, including a nude marble torso of Dionysus, a headless statue of Pan, Byzantine coins and medieval pottery. The last room has a display of photographs of the town in the early 1900s, and of the front line in the Balkan War.

Opposite the Historical Museum is the **Ethnographic Museum** (☎ 72 177; ul Vitosha; admission 1 lv; ☼ 9am-noon & 1-5.30pm Mon-Fri). In a beautiful old stone house built in 1860, it features a collection of local costumes and displays relating to traditional trades and crafts such as fishing, barrel-making and woodcarving. It's not always open; contact staff at the Historical Museum if it's locked during working hours.

The **Ethnographical Complex** (☎ 72 177; ul Hristo Botev 4; admission 2 lv; ☼ 9am-noon & 1-5.30pm Mon-Fri), also known as the Bulgarian National Revival Compound, houses dry displays on publishing, literature and education, along with a restored 19th-century schoolroom and a church, originally built in 1866. From the bus station, walk north on ul Cherno More for 20 minutes and look out for the clock tower in the grounds. If you're near the port, take a taxi (about 2.50 lv) because it's a very steep walk.

Sleeping

There are a couple of agencies near the seafront that can arrange accommodation. **Chaika** (☎ 72 053; www.chaikabg.com; pl Ribarski 2) offers private rooms from €12 per person and apartments from €30, while **Svoboda** (☎ 74 707; www.svoboda-tour.com; ul Cherno More 13) has self-contained

apartments from €27 per person, and can also book hotel rooms.

Jay Jays (☎ 0887844953; jayjaysbalchik@yahoo.co.uk; ul Primorska 33; s/d from €15/18; ⌘) Run by a jolly British couple, Jay Jays has a handful of neat, simple rooms, one with bunks. There's a bar and restaurant downstairs.

Holiday Beach Hotel (☎ 77 071; www.holiday-beach.info; ul Primorska 23; s/d from 50/100 lv; P ⌘ ⌘) Smart, modern hotel just across the road from the beach. Rooms are light and spacious and have walk-out balconies with seating, most with great sea views. The open-air pool on the 1st floor is a plus.

White House (☎ 73 951; ul Geo Milev 18; s/d/ste 70/80/100 lv; P ⌘) Situated on the seafront, this is a bright and breezy place with 10 double rooms and three studio apartments, all with fridges and TVs. There's a busy restaurant at the front. Prices rise by around 50% in July and August.

Hotel Mistral (☎ 71 130; www.hotelmistralbg.com; ul Primorska 8b; s/d Jul & Aug 170/187 lv, Sep-Jun 88/98 lv; ⌘) One of the newest waterfront hotels, the Mistral is an upmarket, four-star place with large, tastefully furnished rooms, many with sea-facing balconies.

Eating

The waterfront between the port and the palace is lined with numerous restaurants, most offering fresh fish on their menus. Many provide live music in the evenings, too, so you can tuck into your grilled trout to the strains of 'Besame Mucho'.

Jay Jays (☎ 0887844953; ul Primorska 33; mains 3-8.50 lv; ☼ 8am-midnight) The restaurant of the British-run hotel (above) serves up familiar fare for hungry tourists such as bacon and eggs, burgers and, on Friday nights, fish and chips with mushy peas.

Dvata Petela (☎ 0878704340; mains 4-5 lv; ☼ 10am-midnight) The 'Two Cockerels' is one of the cheaper places on the seafront promenade, with seating on a wooden pier perched over the rocks. Pizzas, pork chops, chicken kebabs and various fish dishes are served.

Old Boat (☎ 0887998996; mains 6-15 lv; ☼ 8am-3am) With an attractive waterfront setting overlooking the harbour, this is as good a place as any for fresh fish. The grilled mackerel, shark fillet and bluefish are all good, and it also serves salads and grills.

El Marinero (☎ 71 130; mains 8-25 lv; ☼ 8am-midnight) The excellent restaurant of the Hotel

Mistral (p253) is the place to go for some classier cuisine. Fried turbot, smoked salmon, caviar and pepper steaks are among the offerings, and it does particularly good salads.

Getting There & Away

Balchik's **bus station** (☎ 74 069) is at the top of ul Cherno More, a steep 1km walk from the port. Minibuses travel from Balchik to Albena (2 lv, 20 minutes, every 30 minutes), Varna (4 lv, one hour, hourly) and Dobrich (4 lv, 45 minutes, every 45 minutes). There are also eight buses a day to Kavarna (3 lv, 30 minutes) and two to Sofia (20 lv, 10 hours). Rather more conveniently, minibuses to Albena also call at the bus stop on ul Primorska, outside the supermarket. Note that more frequent minibuses travelling from Varna to Kavarna /Shabla stop at the bus shelter opposite the bus station, although no information is posted here; ask at the bus station for times.

KAVARNA КАВАРНА
☎ 0570 / pop 16,800

Kavarna, 17km east of Balchik, is a sleepy administrative town of little interest itself, although today it's famous (in Bulgaria) as the venue for the **Kaliakra Rock Fest** (www.kaliakrarock fest.com), which attracts international acts every June, and its small beach is pleasant enough. It's also the most practical base for anyone wishing to explore the Kaliakra Cape (opposite).

The pedestrianised ul Dobrotitsa, running south from the bus station, is where you'll find the post office, banks and cafés. Halfway along, the **Church of Sveti Georgi** (ul Rakovski) is worth a quick look for its icons, modern painting of the Last Judgement, and chatty old ladies. Other (possible) sights include the **History Museum** (ul Chirakman 1), housed in an old mosque, and the **Ethnographical Revival Complex** (ul Sava Ganchev 18), although neither were open to visitors at the time of research.

The seafront is around 3km or so downhill from town, and can be reached by hourly buses from the bus station if you don't fancy the walk. Impressive white cliffs watch over the harbour and sandy beach, which is patrolled by lifeguards, and it's an agreeable place just to lounge about.

Hotel Venera (☎ 84 878; ul Chaika 6; r 18-24 lv; P), around 150m from the sea, is among the better options if you wish to stay.

There are a couple of basic beach bars, as well as some restaurants by the bus stop, including **Moryashka Sreshta** (☎ 84 820; mains 4-10 lv; ☾ lunch & dinner), which has a particular fondness for oysters – served in salads, pancakes,

---

COASTAL CONCERNS

Margarita is a tourism and business consultant who manages Villa Kibela in Krapets. She has an active interest in sustainable tourism and in promoting the wild, unspoilt attractions of this northern part of the coast. We asked her for her views on the area's current developments.

What do locals think about foreigners buying up property along the Black Sea?
They think it won't necessarily bring prosperity to rural areas, as individual buyers come mostly for short vacations and are indifferent to the local environment. The assumption is that they buy with an expectation to get a good return in the near future by re-selling. There are big investors developing real estate projects but they're unlikely to respect our cultural and natural heritage. Local property has recently become more expensive, rising about 30 to 40% in 2007.

How are all the new building developments affecting the environment?
Unfortunately, the situation from the Romanian border down to Varna is becoming critical, I would say, and local biodiversity is in danger. There are almost no fish left in Durankulak Lake, and our coastal dolphins are in danger, too. If no measures are taken, they will soon be gone.

What's the future for tourism in the region?
Green, sustainable tourism is the only way. I hope we can develop sustainable projects in our area.

What are the area's best draws for travellers?
This is an ecologically clean region, free of industry, with 15km of beautiful beach, and still rich biodiversity. In Krapets alone we have numerous swallows and storks. You can see dolphins coming close to shore when the sea is calm. We also have an amazing archaeological heritage, and many unexplored sites.

with rice and *au naturel* – as well as plenty of other fish dishes.

There are four daily buses to Balchik (3 lv, 30 minutes), one bus every 30 minutes to an hour to Dobrich (4 lv, one hour) and hourly buses to Varna (5 lv, 1¼ hours). There are a few minibuses each day to Bâlgarevo and Shabla and one or two to Rusalka and Krapets. The border with Romania is closed along the coast here.

KALIAKRA CAPE
НОС КАЛИАКРА

Kaliakra (Beautiful) Cape is a 2km-long headland (the longest along the Bulgarian coastline), about 13km southeast of Kavarna. Together with Balchik, it's a popular day trip by boat and/or bus from the southern beach resorts. Kartografia's *Northern Black Sea Coast* map provides essential details about the reserve and its attractions.

Most of the cape is part of the 687-hectare **Kaliakra Nature Reserve** (admission 3 lv; 24hr), the only reserve in Bulgaria that partially protects the Black Sea (up to 500m offshore). The reserve also protects fragile wetlands at **Bolata** and **Taukliman** (Bay of Birds), about 100 remote **caves** and over 300 species of birds. Most of the year, the official lookouts along the cape and near Rusalka are ideal spots to watch numbers of increasingly rare dolphins.

Also in the reserve are the ruins of an 8th-century **citadel**, and some ruined churches. The history of the area is explained in some

> **THE LEGEND OF KALIAKRA**
>
> According to a local myth, as the Turks advanced on Kavarna in the 14th century, a group of 40 beautiful young women, fearing a life of slavery, dishonour or worse at the hands of the Ottoman soldiers, tied their long hair together and, holding hands, threw themselves off a cliff along the Kaliakra Cape. Some displays relating to this legend can be seen in Kavarna's History Museum, and a monument at the Kaliakra Cape is dedicated to the women.

detail at the **Archaeological Museum** (admission free; 10am-6pm), wonderfully located inside a cave (look for signs to the museum).

Anyone visiting the reserve must first go to the **Nature Information Centre** (☎ 057-44 424) in Bâlgarevo village, about halfway between Kavarna and Kaliakra Cape. The centre features a display (in English) about the flora, fauna and marine life of the Black Sea.

The tiny seaside town of **Krapets**, in between the protected areas of Lakes Shabla and Durankulak, and close to several archaeological sites, makes an excellent base for exploring the region. Try **Villa Kibela** (☎ 0888880281; www .villakibela.com; r incl half-board €50-60; P), a welcoming little place that also arranges walking tours and fishing trips.

Public transport from Kavarna does not reliably go any further than Bâlgarevo, so private car is the best way to get here.

Northern Bulgaria

Although it's less visited than other parts of the country, Bulgaria's tranquil north is still well worth exploring. It's a place full of both unexpected surprises and obvious draws – such as the great River Danube, which ribbons along most of the country's border with Romania. Northern Bulgaria's major attractions include the well-preserved Roman castle overlooking the river at Vidin and the stunning prehistoric rock formations of Belogradchik; both are only about four hours away from Sofia.

Further on to the east, the enigmatic medieval monasteries at Basarbovo and Ivanovo peek out of cliffs in the vast Rusenski Lom Nature Park, while serene Lake Srebârna is a major refuge for rare species of birds (and the bird-watchers who flock to them). Magnificent neoclassical architecture and a vibrant café culture characterise the flourishing river city of Ruse, the region's capital, which is also the gateway to Bucharest in Romania, three hours to the north.

Since tourism has yet to make major inroads in Bulgaria's northern border region, it also remains an area with marvellously authentic and friendly locals, ranging from fishermen in combat fatigues to whole roving brass bands. If you're looking for a taste of the offbeat in a truly off-the-beaten-track locale, northern Bulgaria is the place to go.

HIGHLIGHTS

- **Step back in time**
  Explore Vidin's remarkably well preserved Baba Vida Museum-Fortress (opposite)

- **Natural wonders**
  Climb the huge Belogradchik rocks, seamlessly blended with the Roman Kaleto Fortress (p262)

- **Urban sophistication**
  Enjoy the Austro-Hungarian architecture and vibrant café society of Ruse (p267)

- **Get spiritual**
  Marvel at the frescoed cave churches of Basarbovo and Ivanovo in the Rusenski Lom Nature Park (p273)

- **Eco-escape**
  Gaze out on the tranquil waters of Lake Srebârna (p274), home of rare bird species, and fish the Danube at nearby Vetren

NORTHERN BULGARIA

VIDIN ВИДИН
☎ 094 / pop 69,400

The largest town in northwest Bulgaria, and a convenient place for travelling to or from Romania, Vidin enjoys an impressive setting above the balmy Danube. Although it has just one major attraction, the well-preserved Baba Vida Roman fortress, Vidin is a relaxing enough place, with most of the riverfront being taken up by little parks; these include colourful playgrounds with a certain Soviet appeal, flowers, shady trees and even a grassy strip for sunbathing above the river. The parks make Vidin a nice place for kids to scamper around, and for elders to enjoy a peaceful evening stroll. A handful of churches and museums comprises the town's cultural offerings.

Although Vidin's erstwhile commercial significance has diminished drastically since the 1990s, when UN economic sanctions on neighbouring Serbia caused trade to be rerouted further east to Ruse, a handful of cafés and restaurants keeps up a spark of life. Still, unemployment is high, and decrepit, communist-era buildings are plentiful, with the grand, and poorly lit central square and leafy streets seeming eerily empty at night. Despite its lonesome feel, however, Vidin is still a unique place and justifies an overnight stay.

History
Vidin's location on a bend in the river, east of the Stara Planina mountain range, has historically made it strategically important. The Celts, and perhaps the Thracians before them, settled there until the 3rd century BC, when the Romans built a fortress called Bononia over the Celtic settlement of Dunonia to control this key Danube crossing.

Throughout the Byzantine centuries, the Bulgars were chronically at war with the empire, and Vidin (known then as Bdin) was much contested due to its strategic importance. By 1185, when Byzantium was declining, Bulgarian brothers Peter and Asen revolted, wresting this river garrison away from Constantinople's control and beginning the Second Bulgarian Empire. A succession of notable Bulgar leaders followed, including Shishman in 1280 and his son Michail, who became tsar in 1323. During this (literally) golden period, contemporary sources attest, the imperial coffers were bursting with lucre. The Second Bulgarian Empire finally fell in

1396, with the Ottoman capture of Bdin (subsequently renamed 'Vidin').

Under the Ottomans an extensive city wall was built, and the Baba Vida Fortress strengthened. By the 16th century, Vidin was the largest town in the Bulgarian part of the Ottoman *vilayet* (province) of Eastern Rumelia, and one of the biggest Danube ports. In the late 18th century, when the Ottoman Empire began disintegrating, local *pasha* (high official) Osman Pazvantoglu declared the Vidin district independent. In 1878, during the Russo-Turkish War, Vidin was presented to the new Bulgarian state by the Romanian army. Seven years later, the Serbs tried but failed to take the city.

Orientation
From the train station and bus station across from it, turn right two blocks to the Danube and the Port Authority building (Rechna Gara). Following the water north brings you to the parks, and several restaurants, bars and hotels. From here the Baba Vida Fortress is a 20-minute walk north along the waterfront. The sprawling town square, pl Bdintsi, one block northeast of the train station, features an enormous communist-era monument, banks and shops.

Information
Foreign exchange offices, banks and several ATMs line ul Tsar Simeon Veliki and pl Bdintsi.

Cyber Zone (ul Tàrgovska 3)
Post office (☒ 7am-6.30pm Mon-Fri, 8am-1.30pm Sat) Between the square and train station.
Telephone centre (☒ 7am-6.30pm Mon-Fri, 8am-1.30pm Sat) In the post office.
Tourist Information Centre (☎ 601 421; tsviat@abv .bg; pl Bdintsi 6; ☒ 9am-6pm Mon-Fri)

Sights
BABA VIDA MUSEUM-FORTRESS
The marvellously intact **Baba Vida Museum-Fortress** (☎ 601 705; admission 2 lv, guided tour in Bulgarian or Russian 5 lv; ☒ 8.30am-5pm summer, 10am-5pm winter) stands on the riverside park's northern end, overlooking the Danube. Between the 10th and 14th centuries, the Bulgars fortified the ruined walls of the 3rd-century Roman citadel of Bononia. What you will see today dates from the 17th century, when the Ottomans upgraded its fortifications and made it an arsenal. Baba Vida escaped destruction during

NORTHERN BULGARIA

NORTHERN BULGARIA

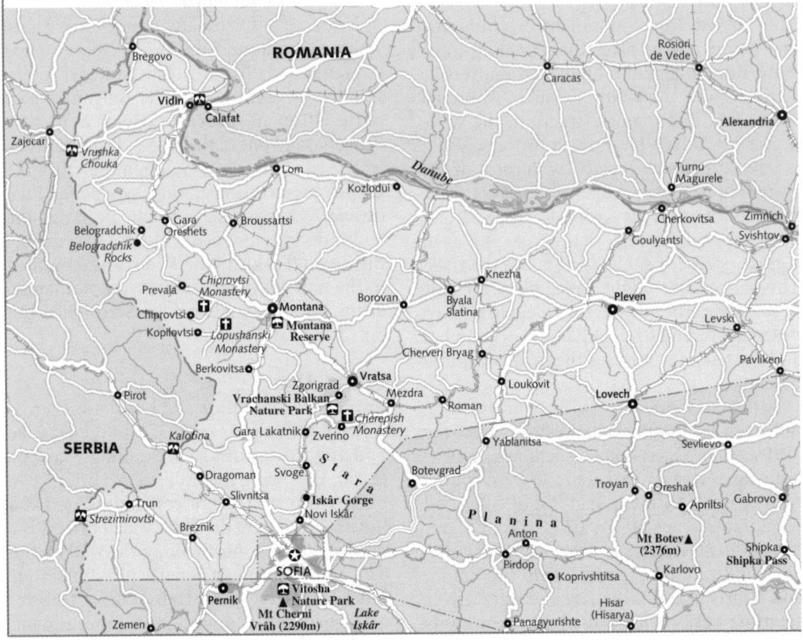

the Russo-Turkish War of 1877–78, remaining today as Bulgaria's best-preserved medieval stone fortress.

Despite its immensity (70m-long walls, with some remaining outer walls continuing several hundred metres further south), the Baba Vida is relatively empty, collected weaponry and a waxen prisoner ensconced in the dungeon being the only inhabitants. Notice boards (in French) present the history and uses of the fortress's sections. A deep moat surrounds the structure.

Between the fortress and the river is an upper patch of grass, used by locals for sunbathing. Down on the river, a tiny strip of pebbles passes for a beach; from here brave Bulgarians try rudimentary swimming in summer. However, considering the currents, boats and nearby factories, it's probably better for your health not to follow suit.

OTHER ATTRACTIONS

Vidin's main cathedral, **Sveti Velikomachenik Dimitâr** (ul Tsar Simeon Veliki; ⌚ 8am-6pm), has benefited from partial restoration work, and has nice frescoes and icons. The **Archaeological Museum** (☎ 624 421; ul Tsar Simeon Veliki 12; ⌚ 9am-noon & 1-6pm Tue-Sun), situated northwest of the square, displays Thracian and Roman jewellery and statues, plus exhibits from the Bulgarian National Revival period. The museum building was once an Ottoman *konak* (police station).

An unusual monument decrying totalitarian repression stands near the Hotel Dunav – the post-Soviet **Victims of Communism Memorial**. Further north along the river, before the fortress, is a more sanguine piece of Soviet civic architecture, the **Mother Bulgaria Monument**.

A couple of blocks inland, between the main square and the fortress, are the 18th-century **Osman Pazvantoglu Mosque** (ul Osman Pazvantoglu) and the modern **Church of Sveti Nikolai** opposite. The **Krâstata Kazarma** (☎ 23 855; ul Knyaz Boris I), housing the local history museum, is usually closed. Vidin's other religious buildings include the 17th-century **Church of Sveta Petka** and a now-abandoned **synagogue** (ul Baba Vida).

A small **contemporary art gallery** (Hudozhestvena Galeriya Nikola Petrov; admission free; ⌚ 9am-6pm Mon-Fri), named after renowned Bulgarian painter Nikola Petrov, showcases paintings by local

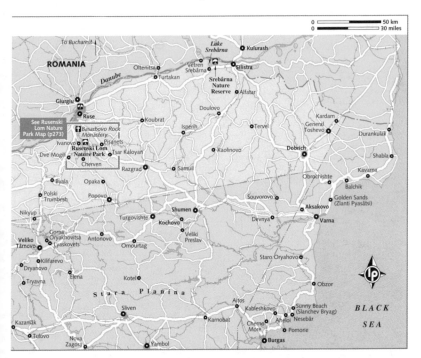

artists. It's housed in a stately white neoclassical mansion adjacent to the Hotel Bononia.

Sleeping

Hotel Dunav (☎ /fax 600 177; ul Edelvais 3; s/d 30/50 lv, with shared bathroom 18/36 lv) The Dunav is centrally located and offers Vidin's cheapest rates. Some rooms have a lived-in, musty feel, while others have slightly upgraded furnishings.

Hotel Bononia (☎ 606 031; moira_bg200@yahoo .com; ul Bdin 2; s/d 43/65 lv; ⊠) Wedged between the main square, river and park, the Bononia has a very central location and friendly staff, offering modern rooms with nice, if small bathrooms, air conditioning and TV. A ride in the hotel's spastically shuddering elevator makes you feel truly alive. The hotel also has a nourishing restaurant (see p260).

Anna Kristina Hotel (☎ 606 038; www.annakristina hotel.com; ul Baba Vida 2; d/apt from 50/150 lv; ⊠) The most luxurious place in Vidin, the Anna Kristina is also quite good value. It's set in a quiet park midway down the riverside and has a large, gated pool with bar (7 lv extra). The rooms border on posh, though the bristly carpets conflict with the chic,

raised-tile bathrooms. The eye-catching apartments have lofty ceilings and mottled painted cupolas.

Hotel Zora (☎ 606 330; www.hotelzora.hit.bg in Bulgarian; ul Naycho Tsanov 3a; s/d/apt 55/72/90 lv; ⊠) Overlooking the Sveti Velikomachenik Dimităr church, Hotel Zora is a well-kept and friendly place. All rooms have balcony, minibar, TV and even bathtubs.

Eating & Drinking

Vidin has a few decent eateries, and some cafés, though they're fairly subdued. The most popular are off the south side of the square before the Danube. There are no river views from most restaurants or cafés, thanks to the high river wall blocking views.

Pizza Vivaldi (☎ 609 334; ul Naycho Tsanov 2; mains 4-7 lv) In a garden setting under umbrellas, the Vivaldi does good pizzas and salads. It's also a relaxing place for a drink. It's not well signposted; peek inside the narrow gate halfway along ul Naycho Tsanov.

Evergreen Club (off pl Bdintsi; mains 4-7 lv) This oddly named standby is for those seeking a traditional Bulgarian *mehana* (tavern). It's

VIDIN

0 _____ 200 m
0 _____ 0.1 miles

INFORMATION
Cyber Zone.................................1 A3
Post Office..................................2 A3
Telephone Centre...................(see p259)
Tourist Information Centre.........3 B3

SIGHTS & ACTIVITIES
Archaeological Museum..............4 A2
Baba Vida Museum-Fortress Ticket
  Office.....................................5 C1
Baba Vida Museum-Fortress........6 C1
Church of Sveta Petka................7 B2
Church of Sveti Nikolai...............8 B2
Contemporary Art Gallery (Nikola
  Petrov Building)......................9 B3
Former Communist Party Building..10 A3
Krâstata Kazarma......................11 B2
Mother Bulgaria Monument.......12 C1
Osman Pazvantoglu Mosque......13 B2
St Velikomachenik Dimitâr Church..14 A3
Synagogue...............................15 B2
Victims of Communism Memorial..16 B4

SLEEPING
Anna Kristina Hotel....................17 B3
Hotel Bononia...........................18 B3
Hotel Dunav..............................19 B4
Hotel Zora.................................20 A3

EATING
Evergreen Club..........................21 A3
Pizza Vivaldi..............................22 A3
Restaurant Bononia.............(see 18)
Riben Restoran Shlepa................24 B4

DRINKING
Lyatna Terasa Panorama...........(see 27)

TRANSPORT
Alexiev Bus Station....................25 A4
Public Bus Station......................26 A4
River-Boat Terminal...................27 B4
Taxi Rank..................................28 A4

NORTHERN BULGARIA

cosy, but can get loud on weekends, when
live music plays.

Restaurant Bononia (☎ 606 012; ul Bdin 2; mains
5-11 lv; ⏰ 10am-midnight) Part of the Hotel Bononia
(see p259), this restaurant with a cavernous
interior and outer deck facing the park and
river is the place for Serbian-style *skara* (grilled
meats) prepared on an open grill. Feast on
domashna nadenitza (homemade sausages),
planena pleskavitza (hamburger stuffed with
cheese and bits of ham) or even *vratna perzhola*
(grilled pork neck).

Riben Restoran Shlepa (☎ 0887999131; fish 6-10 lv;
⏰ noon-11pm) Just because you don't swim in
the Danube doesn't mean you can't eat those
who do. This canopied boat-restaurant floating in place along the southern riverbank has

a full menu of fish, including sheatfish *(som)*,
hansen *(moruna)*, pike *(byala riba)* and trout
(pasturva), served either fried or grilled, as
well as meat standards and salads. The gentle
rocking sensation from river waves helps con-
fuse the senses into thinking you need more of
the delicious Bavarian beer. There are tables
inside and out; reserve in advance for the
upper circle seating with the best views.

Lyatna Terasa Panorama (☎ 601 321; ⏰ 8am-
1am May-Sep) On a sturdy deck above the
Port Authority building (Rechna Gara), the
'Summer Terrace' offers great river views
and a reasonable drinks selection. The
outdoors café is open when the weather's
good, while the billiards hall indoors is open
year round.

THE DANUBE

The Danube is the second-longest (472km) river in Europe. Called the Dunav by Bulgarians and other Slavic peoples, it rises in the Black Forest of southwestern Germany and empties into the Black Sea. It travels through four capital cities (Vienna, Budapest, Bratislava and Belgrade) and nine countries (Germany, Austria, Slovakia, Hungary, Serbia, Bulgaria, Romania, Moldova and Ukraine). No other river is shared by so many countries. The Danube's average depth is about 5m and the water rarely flows faster than 3km/h.

In January 2000, a tailings dam burst at a gold mine in Baia Mare, a town in Romania. About 100,000 cu metres of cyanide-contaminated water spilt into the Tisa and Danube Rivers, killing thousands of fish and birds. Described as the worst environmental disaster in Europe since Chernobyl, the spill poisoned river systems in Romania, Hungary, Bulgaria, Ukraine and Serbia. While the most affected parts are slowly starting to recover, experts believe that wildlife habitats will not return to normal before about 2010.

Getting There & Away

The **bus station** (ul Zhelezhnicharska) is on Vidin's south side, roughly opposite the train station. As elsewhere in Bulgaria, numerous small offices represent the different bus companies and sell tickets, though often you'll be buying on board. Across from this station is the **Alexiev Bus Station** (☎ 606 190; ul Zhelezhnicharska), home of the Alexiev bus line, the major company for the Sofia–Vidin route.

From these two stations 14 daily buses go to Sofia (14 lv, four hours) via Vratsa (8 lv). Six daily serve Belogradchik (4.50 lv, one hour), with one connection to Pleven (8 lv, 3½ hours).

The **train station** (☎ 606 050; ul Saedinenie) has four daily trains to Sofia, three fast (1st/2nd class 12.90/10.30 lv, four hours) and one slow (9 lv, five hours). These trains travel via Vratsa (7 lv), which has frequent connections to Mezra, for going further east to Ruse and Varna. Some trains from Vidin also stop in Gara Oreshets, the nearest train station (9km away) to Belogradchik (2nd/1st class 3.60/4.50 lv).

TO/FROM ROMANIA

With the long-anticipated bridge between Vidin and Calafat not yet begun, the 'ferry boat' (as Bulgarians, too, call it) provides the only daily service to Romania (8 lv, 15 minutes). The ferry terminal is 2km north of town; take a taxi (4 lv) from the train station's taxi rank. The boats, operated by one Bulgarian and one Romanian company, theoretically go in the morning, afternoon and evening, but won't leave unless they're full, so you might end up having to wait, though you will eventually get there.

TO/FROM SERBIA

With the discontinuation of the international bus line for Negotin in eastern Serbia, you must either backtrack to Sofia to find a Belgrade-bound bus, or take a taxi from Vidin to the Vrushka Chuka (20 lv) border, walk across and find a bus from there. Double-check at the bus station in case the bus service has resumed.

BELOGRADCHIK БЕЛОГРАДЧИК
☎ 0936 / pop 6700

The crisp mountain air and the weird and wonderful rock formations rising from a lonely hill are what draw visitors to little Belogradchik, on the eastern edge of the Stara Planina mountain range. Although somewhat forlorn, with its eternal quietude and a few rusting reminders of communist industry, Belogradchik's charms are starting to attract more visitors, with guesthouses and even a four-star hotel now under construction. Nevertheless, it's still a somewhat ornery, out-of-the-way place, where time moves slowly, even in summer.

However, if visiting Belogradchik in June, check out the town festival in honour of patron St Peter, which brings well-known Bulgarian singers, dancing, folklore and copious amounts of food and drink to the town from 25 to 30 June.

Orientation & Information

From the bus station, head uphill one block to the main square, situated at the junction of Belogradchik's three major roads. Facing you to the left stands a large board with a map listing hotels and sights. To the right, ul Treti Mart leads to the fortress (*krepost*).

LEGENDS OF THE ROCKS

For centuries, the Belogradchik rock formations have fired the imaginations of local people. These twisting, contorted pillars of stone seem to take on shapes human and animal, fluid creations that become especially inscrutable through the constant shifting of light and shadows and during the glow of sunset.

As with similar sites around the world, this anthropomorphic element has inspired numerous legends and myths about the rocks, tales that can be as bleak and beguiling as the landscape itself. One such legend retells the tragically uplifting tale of Valentina, a beautiful nun who was turned to stone. Every night, a lovesick shepherd would inflame young Valentina's passions by playing seductively on his flute beneath her window, until she finally slid down a rope from her cell. Not too long after, the cries of a child were heard in the monastery; the shepherd came for his beloved, but the monks fought fiercely to protect her. Then God pitched in, sending thunder, earthquakes and storms to destroy the convent. All of the people were turned to stone where they stood – the monks, the shepherd on his horse, and the nun Valentina with a baby in her arms.

This, the legend of the 'Madonna', and other marvellous tales of the rocks of Belogradchik are narrated on large signs within the Kaleto Fortress, right beneath the rocks. With a little imagination, you can make up your own myths, too, about these eerily lifelike wonders of nature.

There's a First East National Bank near the bus station for changing money.

An **internet café** (ul Knyaz Boris I; per hr 1 lv; 24hr) stands between the pink art gallery and the white history museum (look for the 'JAR Computers' sign). The **Tourist Information Centre** (☎ 4294; milena-tourist_centre@abv.bg; ul Poruchik Dvoryanov 5; 9am-5pm Mon-Fri) can help with accommodation and gives out maps.

Sights

BELOGRADCHIK ROCKS & KALETO FORTRESS

The massive **Belogradchik rock formations** tower over the town, at the end of a 2km-long road that passes around them. Seamlessly blended in with these bizarre wonders of nature is the **Kaleto Fortress** (admission 5 lv, guided tour 5 lv, photo/video 2/5 lv; 8am-6.30pm), built by the Romans in the 1st century BC. The fortress was later augmented and expanded with towers, walls and gates by the Byzantines and Bulgars. The remaining sections, interwoven with the rocks, date mostly from the late Ottoman period (between 1805 and 1837). There's no need to pay for the offered tour, as the fortress is fairly self-explanatory and scattered signs tell the stories and legends associated with the place (see the boxed text, above). Likewise, despite the stated ban on photos, no-one will accost you for snapping pictures; the breathtaking views of the town below and other rock formations behind are certainly great photo opportunities.

Entering the fortress is simple, but access to the highest rocks, where the best views can be had, involves narrow and steep metal ladders and is thus unsafe for small children. In any case, you can admire the ramparts, explore the defensive bunkers and peek into the dimly lit former living quarters (a torch is helpful here). These 200-million-year-old rock formations, spread over 200 hectares, have a certain Stonehenge-like quality to them and are an excellent place for solitary reflection and relaxation. A shady forest stands outside the fortress. Other impressive (but smaller) examples of rock formations are back in town, about 100m down the road from the main square (follow the track to the Nature Department of the History Museum).

Getting to the well-signposted fortress requires driving or walking 2km from the main square up ul Treti Mart. You'll pass a decrepit **Ottoman mosque** on your left-hand side. About 200 years old, the mosque has pretty floral designs above the door but is locked and derelict inside.

Outside the fortress, there's a small café patio near the ticket booth.

MUSEUMS

The **History Museum** (☎ 3469; pl 1850 Leto; admission 1 lv; 9am-noon & 2-5pm Mon-Fri), also known as Panova's House, has exhibits comprising coins, jewellery and costumes, as well as 6000 or so Kaleto artefacts. Other exhibits concentrate on mid-19th century anti-Turkish revolutionaries.

Affiliated with the history museum is the **Nature Department** (admission 4 lv), which displays unusual local flora and fauna. To get there, proceed from the Hotel Belogradchiski Skali up ul Vasil Levski, turn right, and follow the path down for 600m. From here there are great views over the Belogradchik rocks.

Sleeping & Eating

The two former state-run hotels – the Hotel Belogradchiski Skali, on the square, and the Hotel Belogradchik, one street below – have been neglected and closed, though at the time of writing the former was being transformed into a four-star hotel. New guesthouses have also opened over the past couple of years, but there are not enough restaurants to keep up with demand. Nightlife is relegated to a few café-bars on the main street and a weekend disco blaring *chalga* (Bulgarian folk-pop music).

our pick **Guesthouse Drakite** (☎ 0888713539; www .drakite.com; ul Treti Mart 37; s/d 12/24 lv) This cosy new guesthouse, 600m down from the Kaleto entrance in a quiet residential area, offers five airy, modern rooms with wood furnishings, TV and wireless internet. Three rooms have shared bathrooms, the other two having their own. Views are of the Kaleto rocks and fortress above, or of the long valley below. Friendly owner Angel Boyanov speaks excellent English and can arrange local activities, such as hiking or guided hunting and fishing tours. The Drakite is about 1km west of the centre; you can walk there (15 minutes), or phone ahead and Angel will retrieve you for free from the Belogradchik bus station or from the train station in Oreshets.

Hotel Rai (☎ 3735; s/d 25/30 lv, r with shared bathroom 20 lv) Facing the bus station, the Hotel Rai has modern if basic rooms. The staff are frequently absent, so ring ahead.

The Rocks Hotel (☎ 4002; ul Hadzhi Dimitri 1; hotel _skalite@belogradchick.info; d 30 lv) This reasonable budget option is a two-minute walk from the bus station, and around the corner from the town centre above it. The clean rooms have modern bathrooms and the restaurant downstairs is worthwhile. While reception is closed from 2pm to 5pm, banging on the restaurant door eventually rouses out a worker to check you in. Locals sometimes call the hotel by its former name, Sveti (Saint) Valentin.

Hotel Madona (☎ 5546; www.hotelmadona.hit.bg in Bulgarian; ul Hristo Botev 26; s/d 30/40 lv, with shared bathroom 25/30 lv) More like a guesthouse, the Madona

has cosy traditional-style rooms, 600m up from the main square (it's signposted). The restaurant is one of the few, and therefore one of the best, in town.

Restaurant Elit (☎ 4558; ul Yuri Gagarin 2; mains 4-6 lv; ⏰ 9am-midnight) Aside from Belogradchik's two hotel restaurants, the Elit is the only other real restaurant in town. It does some fine – and unusual – chicken specialities, as well as a variety of other Bulgarian dishes. It's an uphill walk (600m) up steep ul Vasil Levski and then off to the left.

Getting There & Away

From the desultory **bus station** (☎ 3427), three or four daily buses serve Vidin (4.50 lv, 1½ hours). A 7am bus serves Sofia (11 lv, four hours), via Montana (but not Vratsa). The three daily buses that serve the train station, 9km away at Gara Oreshets (1 lv, 20 minutes), are timed to meet the Sofia-bound train. Several daily trains from Gara Oreshets serve Vidin (3.60 lv, 30 minutes), Vratsa (6.10 lv, 20 minutes) and Sofia (8.40 lv, three hours, 30 minutes).

A taxi from Belogradchik to Gara Oreshets train station costs 5 lv. For very early morning trains, taxis wait in front of the bus depot.

CHIPROVTSI ЧИПРОВЦИ
☎ 09554 / pop 3000

Famous for its traditional carpets and unusual monastery, Chiprovtsi (*Chip*-rov-tsi) is a quiet village slowly embracing tourism, as the recent opening of new guesthouses indicates. Still, it's essentially a placid small town tucked into the foothills of the Stara Planina mountains, and even quieter than Belogradchik.

Information

The **Chiprovtsi Tourist Information Centre** (☎ 2910, 0885258405; tic.chiprovci@gmail.com), in the centre of town, provides information about local attractions and finds accommodation.

Sights
CHIPROVTSI MONASTERY

Originally built in the 15th century, probably as a Catholic church, this monastery, also known as **Sveti Ivan Rilski Monastery** (admission free; ⏰ dawn-dusk), suffered the fate of many Bulgarian churches, being burned during the Ottoman occupation when the monks sheltered rebel fighters. The structure that survives today dates from the 1830s, when it was rebuilt. The turn-off to the monastery is 5.8km northeast of Chiprovtsi village; take any bus between Montana and Chiprovtsi. From the turn-off, it's 400m to the monastery.

HISTORY MUSEUM

Local minerals, Ottoman-era exhibits and copies of murals from Chiprovtsi Monastery (the originals are in the Aleksander Nevski Memorial Church in Sofia) are displayed at this small **museum** (☎ 2194; ul Vitosha 2; admission 1 lv, free Thu; 🕑 8am-5pm Mon-Fri, 9am-5pm Sat & Sun), which also showcases traditional costumes and the renowned Chiprovtsi carpets. The caretaker offers English-language **guided tours** (per person 3 lv). The museum is above the concrete steps to the right when facing the square from the main road.

Sleeping & Eating

Neither the monastery nor the museum currently provides accommodation. The best eating is in the guesthouses' restaurants. Chiprovtsi's few cafés are centred on the main square.

Guesthouse Kipro (☎ 2974; migatas@mail.bg; Balkanska 44; s/d/apt 10/20/40 lv) A new guesthouse, the Kipro is a friendly place (though no English is spoken) decorated with traditional Bulgarian dress and tools. The owners serve good homemade meals, and even offer lessons in carpet-weaving.

Guesthouse Pavlova Kâshta (☎ 2242; office_gl@videx.bg; ul Pavleto 17; s/d 15/30 lv) Another new guesthouse built in the mid-19th century National Revival style, the Pavlova Kâshta occupies a handsome white stone building with wood shutters. Rooms are simple, though breezy and clean. The adjacent *mehana* does good Bulgarian meals.

Guesthouse Stavrovata Kâshta (☎ 2854; ul Dimitar Filipov 1; d 15 lv) This relaxing house, closed for renovation at the time of writing, has a lawn and barbecue, plus a small pool and Jacuzzi. The owners give out portions of the famous Chiprovtsi carpets as souvenirs.

Shopping

Despite being a centuries-old local tradition, Chiprovtsi's handmade woollen carpet production trade has waned. Your best bet for finding something is the museum, which offers tiny bags (about 5 lv) and small rugs (15 lv). You can also order larger items through the museum (it takes one month for delivery).

Alternately, the museum caretaker can find local weavers with products for sale.

Getting There & Away

Four or five daily buses connect Montana and Chiprovtsi. The road to Chiprovtsi from the Vratsa–Vidin highway (E79) starts 3km northwest of Montana. From the south, the turn-off is signposted 'Чипровски Манастир'; from the north, it's signposted 'Lopushanski' in English.

LOPUSHANSKI MONASTERY

Some 21km west of Montana, this small **monastery** (admission free; 🕑 8am-6pm), completed in 1853, enjoys a serene setting and boasts valuable icons painted by brothers Stanislav and Nikolai Dospevski. During the periodic rebellions against Ottoman rule, Lopushanski (also known as St John the Precursor) provided a safe haven for revolutionaries.

The monastery's **guesthouse** (☎ 095-51 350; r per person about 20 lv) is only metres from the monastery itself. The guesthouse has 20 rooms, older ones downstairs with shared bathrooms, and newer ones upstairs with bathrooms, refrigerators and smart furniture. The attached café has outdoor and indoor seating, a peaceful location and decent food.

MONTANA МОНТАНА

☎ 096 / pop 54,600

The main transport hub for Chiprovtsi or Lopushanski Monastery, this prosaic large town set between Vratsa and Vidin has nothing in common with its accidental American namesake. There are manageable rooms at the **Montana Hotel** (☎ 626 803; pl Slaveikov; s/d with TV 30/40 lv) if you choose to linger, though an overnight stay is not really warranted.

That said, one pleasant enough local diversion along the road from Montana to Lopushanski Monastery is the **Montana Reservoir**, popular for swimming and fishing. Note that there's no shade, so bring sunscreen and an umbrella (as well as fishing gear if required).

From Montana's **bus station** (☎ 623 454) buses go almost hourly to Sofia, Vratsa and Vidin. Four or five daily buses serve Chiprovtsi, Kopilovtsi, Pleven and Belogradchik. The inconvenient **train station** (☎ 623 846) is on a spur track from the major line between Sofia and Vidin.

VRATSA ВРАЦА

☎ 092 / pop 78,900

With its striking location just below a steep defile in the Vrachanska Mountains, Vratsa makes a handy base for exploring the Vrachanski Balkan Nature Park (p266), Lopushanski and Cherepish Monasteries, and other local villages. It has necessary services and elementary café life, though the town itself retains the drab concrete aesthetic of Soviet times. Nevertheless, new accommodation options existing or being built at the time of writing have increased Vratsa's viability as an overnight destination.

Orientation & Information

The centre of Vratsa is the pl Hristo Botev, crowned by a statue of the 19th-century revolutionary associated with Vratsa (see the boxed text, p266). Kiosks, shops and services congregate around this square, though most of the action is further east along the pedestrian mall (ul Hristo Botev), which finishes at the market, near the train station. Numerous banks here change money and offer ATMs.

For information, maps and advice about the Vrachanski Balkan Nature Park, visit the **Vrachanski Balkan Nature Park headquarters** (☎ 633 149; infocenter@vratsa.net; ul Ivanka Boteva 1).

Sights & Activities

HISTORICAL MUSEUM

Also called the 'Archaeological Museum', Vratsa's local **museum** (☎ 620 220; pl Hristo Botev; adult/student 5/0.50 lv; ☺ 9am-noon & 3-6.30pm Tue-Sun) displays Thracian coins and jewellery, artefacts from nearby Neolithic dwellings and Macedonia-related historical items. The museum is behind the 16th-century tower to the left (west) of Hotel Valdi Palace (right) as you face it.

ETHNOGRAPHIC COMPLEX

Closed for renovations at the time of writing, the Ethnographic Complex or **Regional Historical Museum with Art Gallery** (☎ 620 209; ul Gen Leonov; adult/student 5/0.50 lv; ☺ 8am-noon & 2-6pm Mon-Sat) is made up of structures evoking the Bulgarian National Revival, and even British Tudor, styles of architecture. Traditional costumes and objects relating to author and musician Diko Iliev are displayed. The offbeat **Museum of Carriages**, at the back, boasts an assortment of vintage buggies and carts.

A relaxing stroll takes you through the nearby museum **gardens**. The adjacent **Sveti Sofronni Vrachanski Church** (ul Gen Leonov; ☺ 8am-7pm) is also worth seeing. Get there from the central square along ul Hristo Botev, and turn right along the cobblestone lane of ul Gen Leonov.

HIKING

Relaxed hiking in the forested hills southwest of the main square, and tougher treks along the river road towards the Ledenika Cave highlight Vratsa's outdoors activities (several marked hiking trails exist). Rock climbing – for the truly fearless only – is performed on the sheer mountain cliffs that straddle the road.

Sleeping & Eating

Discreet, unofficial camping is possible in and around the Vrachanski Balkan Nature Park (p266). There are no standout restaurants in Vratsa; for eateries and cafés, try the eastern end of the pedestrian mall.

At the time of writing, the old Hotel Tourist was being resurrected as a new five-star hotel to be called Hotel Park Vratza. The hotel will be along the road to Ledenika Cave, about 300m past the Historical Museum.

Hotel Valdi Palace (☎ 624 150; pl Hristo Botev; s 35-50 lv, d 40-60 lv, apt 60-80 lv) The central Valdi, on the far eastern side of the pedestrian mall, has a startling communist appearance from without, but actually offers clean, modern rooms and friendly service within. Its restaurant is popular with locals.

our pick **Hotel Chaika** (☎ 621 369; www.chaika.net; at the gorge; d 40-50 lv, apt 70-150 lv) The spectacular location of this brand-new hotel, right at the mouth of the gorge, in itself makes it worthwhile to stay in Vratsa. A sloping-roofed place with a ski-lodge look, it boasts modern rooms with charm and spacious apartments, some with Jacuzzis. Rooms above ground level have stunning views of the enormous peaks on either side of the defile. The hotel restaurant has a relaxing summer patio, and there's even a duck pond (minus the ducks), and paddle-boats for guests. Although service is a bit frumpy and the décor not exactly chic, the Chaika makes an excellent base for hill walks, climbing and general escapist bliss. A taxi from the bus/train station costs 2 lv to 4 lv.

Restaurant Atlantik (pl Hristo Botev; mains 3 lv) This undercover and off-street complex near the

VRATSA'S TRAGIC POET

Bulgaria's most revered poet was also a revolutionary who died a tragically inspirational death. Hristo Botev was born in 1848, son of Botyo Petkov (1815–69), a teacher and one of the main figures in the Bulgarian National Revival. The father's national fervour inspired the son, who in 1863 went to study in Odessa, making contacts with like-minded Russian and Polish revolutionary thinkers. After daring to speak out against the Ottoman rule upon his return to Bulgaria four years later, Botev was exiled to Romania, where the liberation movement was bubbling along. There he befriended the great Bulgarian rebel leader, Vasil Levski, and agitated through newspaper broadsides for the national cause.

In late 1872, Levski was captured by the Ottomans and executed, causing the Bulgarian rebel movement to splinter between those who, like the impetuous young poet, urged immediate action, and a more conservative faction that feared the time was not yet ripe for a general rebellion. The latter's circumspection appeared justified when the 1876 'April Uprising' was brutally crushed by the Turks. This event deeply affected Botev, who, despite his lack of prior military training, organised a detachment to fight the Turks.

First, however, he had to escape Romania. Botev and his men hijacked an Austro-Hungarian vessel on the Danube and, after stirring the emotions of the foreign passengers with the announcement of their valiant and apparently suicidal purpose, were dropped off on the Bulgarian side of the river. They made for Vratsa and the mountains – with the Ottoman army and *bashibazouk* irregulars (mercenaries) in hot pursuit.

In the three-day battle that followed, Botev and his 200 men fought heroically, driving back the far more numerous Turks several times before being overwhelmed. During a lull in the fighting, when the poet stood to survey the enemy lines from a distance, a single bullet pierced his heart. With the death of the brave Botev, the few surviving rebels despaired and were routed. Nevertheless, historians believe that Botev's rebellion affected the course of events leading to Russia's entry into the war the following year, and thus accelerated Bulgaria's path to freedom.

Every year on 2 June, the anniversary of his death, Hristo Botev's memory is observed in a ceremony in the Vrachanska Mountains and in the Vratsa town square that bears his name.

Hotel Valdi Palace includes an internet café, a regular café, a bar and a restaurant that offers tasty food, excellent service and live music.

Getting There & Away

The **bus station** (☎ 622 558) is slightly hidden from the main road, 300m east of the train station. Buses travel to/from Sofia (8 lv, two hours) hourly (more frequently between 6am and 9am). One or two buses daily serve Gabrovo, Pleven and Lovech, plus four to Vidin.

Inside the **train station** (☎ 624 415), the **Rila Bureau** (☎ 620 562) sells tickets for international trains and advance tickets for domestic services. Five daily trains serve Sofia, six go to Montana and four to Vidin; the latter pass through Gara Oreshets, from where you can get to Belogradchik.

For more distant destinations, connecting to the nearby Mezra train station (20 minutes south) and changing there is recommended. From Mezra four daily trains serve northern Bulgarian destinations such as Pleven, Ruse (11.50 lv, seven hours) and Varna (15.70 lv), plus there's one daily to Dobrich (16.90 lv) and Silistra (18.20 lv). There are also frequent trains to Sofia (4.50 lv, two hours).

Getting Around

Vratsa itself is easily walkable, though the gorge is 2km behind the town. However, taxis are plentiful and cheap. Taxis are also useful for Ledenika Cave (below) and Cherepish Monastery (opposite).

VRACHANSKI BALKAN NATURE PARK

Numerous species of birds, 700 types of trees and about 500 caves distinguish this nature park of 288 sq km, located southwest of Vratsa. While some of the rocky outcroppings are fragile, they're still open for rock climbers and hang-gliders. Unfortunately, the park's more accessible parts are marred by abandoned hotels and a disused chairlift.

Named after the Bulgarian word for ice (*led*), the **Ledenika Cave** (guided tours per person 5 lv; ☼ 8am-6pm summer) is indeed sheathed in ice for much of the winter, but thaws out in summer, when visitors on guided tours arrive to explore it. While most come on a sunny summer afternoon, a unique time to see Ledenika is for the periodic concerts held within its chilly confines.

The cave is about 15km (or three hours on foot) from the road that starts by the former Hotel Tourist in Vratsa, where it's signposted. The hourly bus from Vratsa to Zgorigrad will leave you near the cave if you alert the driver. The cafés also have directions to the new **Vrachanski Ecotrail**.

The **park headquarters** (☎ 092-633 149; infocenter@ vratsa.net; ul Ivanka Boteva 1, Vratsa) provides information on hiking and caving expeditions.

CHEREPISH MONASTERY

The 14th-century **Cherepish Monastery** (☎ 0897 312770; admission free; ☼ 24hr), was, like Chiprovtsi's, torched, toppled and rebuilt repeatedly during the Ottoman period. Like many other monasteries, it was used by rebels as a hiding place before and during the Russo-Turkish War (1877–78).

The monastery's little **museum** displays icons and has Bulgarian-language books about the monastery and local history.

The poorly signposted monastery is 600m from the eponymous roadside restaurant on the Mezdra–Zverino route. Buses from Sofia heading towards Mezdra, Vratsa, Montana or Vidin pass the monastery; disembark at the Zverino turn-off and wait for a connecting minibus, or walk west 6km. If driving from Sofia, the most aesthetically appealing approach is definitely the scenic, if slower, road through the stunning Iskâr Gorge, via Novi Iskâr.

RUSE PYCE
☎ 082 / pop 182,500

Cultured Ruse (*roo*-seh), the fifth-biggest city in Bulgaria, is far more than just a point of passage to Romania, though for many it's just a stop on the way to or from Bucharest. Yet with its grand square enlivened by cafés and Austro-Hungarian–influenced architecture, often illuminated to great effect at night, Ruse is a very appealing and lively town with a rich and varied history. This past is abundantly displayed in several museums, and in its ruined Roman fortress, standing guard high over the Danube.

Indeed, considering that Ruse features such sites, and boasts the best dining and nightlife in northern Bulgaria, there's plenty to keep you for a few days. Ruse's also a base for visiting the nearby rock monasteries and other attractions at Rusenski Lom Nature Park (p273).

Already a key Balkan commercial transport hub, there are ambitious plans to build a new industrial zone south of Ruse, as well as a foreign-owned car factory, indicating that the city's economic importance is still growing – though such developments are not particularly encouraging for the local environment.

For more information on local wineries, see p66.

History

The Port of 60 Ships, *Sexaginta Prista*, was the grandiose name given to the key fortress built here by the Romans, around AD 69–70. From its position high on a bluff, the fortress stood guard over the Danube – the traditional border between the empire and the barbarian hordes – and ensured safe passage for commercial ships. Byzantine Emperor Justinian improved the fortress in the 6th century, but invading Slavic tribes destroyed it soon afterwards. The chronic Slavic raids caused most of Ruse's inhabitants to move to Cherven, 35km south and now within the Rusenski Lom Nature Park.

Ruse remained relatively forgotten during the First (681–1018) and Second (1185–1396) Bulgarian Empires. Its complete destruction by the invading Ottomans in the 14th century presaged, however, a period of unprecedented greatness. A reforming Turkish district governor, Midhat Pasha, rebuilt and revitalised the town, known to the Turks as Roustchouk. It developed great economic and cultural importance and, in 1866, became the first station on the first railway in the entire Ottoman Empire, linking the Danube with the Black Sea at Varna.

Ruse also became a centre for anti-Turkish agitation during the 19th-century revolutionary period, when Bucharest, just a few hours to the north, was the headquarters of the Bulgarian Central Revolutionary Committee. By the end of the Russo-Turkish War (1877–78), Ruse was the largest, most prosperous city in Bulgaria; the legacy of those halcyon days lingers on in the lovely turn-of-the-century architecture found across the city centre.

NORTHERN BULGARIA

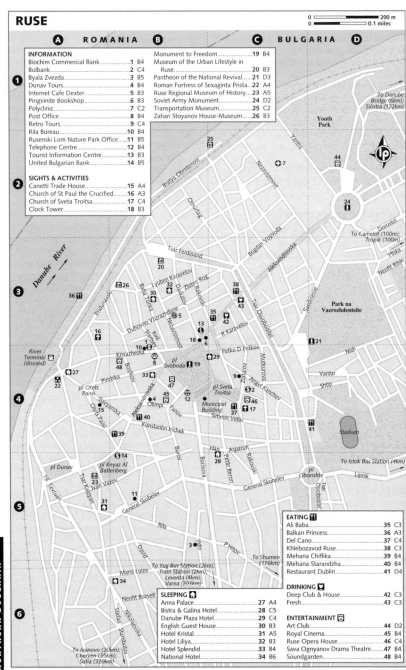

RUSE

0 ———— 200 m
0 ———— 0.1 miles

A ROMANIA **B** **C** BULGARIA **D**

To Danube
Bridge (6km);
Silistra (122km)

Youth
Park

To Camelot (100m);
Tropik (100m)

Park na
Vazrozhdentsite

River
Terminal
(disused)

Municipal
Building

Stadium

To Iztok Bus Station (4km)

pl Dunav

pl Knyaz Al
Battenberg

To Ivanovo (20km);
Cherven (35km);
Sofia (320km)

To Yug Bus Station (2km);
Train Station (2km);
Leventa (4km);
Varna (203km)

To Shumen
(116km)

Although Ruse would see its stature diminish as Sofia grew in prominence in the early 20th century, and the area suffered environmentally due to Romanian heavy industry across the river during Soviet times, a revitalisation has been occurring since the early 1990s, when UN economic sanctions on wartime Yugoslavia caused considerable economic trade to be rerouted from Vidin to Ruse.

Orientation

The heart of Ruse is the grand pl Svoboda, one of Bulgaria's biggest city squares, dominated by the huge Monument to Freedom (1908) and fountains. Some 18 streets radiate out from the square, which is bisected by Ruse's main pedestrian mall, ul Aleksandrovska, site of many shops and cafés. To the west, the arcing Danube hems in the city (unfortunately, there are few good river views). The major south-side landmark is the 206m-high TV tower, the Balkans' highest.

Information

BOOKSHOPS

Pingvinite Bookshop (☎ 829 716; ul Aleksandrovska 48; ☒ 9.30am-7pm Mon-Fri, 10am-5pm Sat) Popular local bookshop with some titles in English about Bulgaria and maps of the country.

INTERNET ACCESS

Central Ruse is now a wi-fi zone and signs highlighting this are in front of many cafés and restaurants – do bring your laptop.

Internet Café Dexter (☎ 830 205; ul Duhovno Vuzrazhdane 10; per hr 1.20 lv; ☒ 24hr)

MEDICAL SERVICES

Polyclinic (☎ 834 200; ul Nezavisimost 2) Provides basic medical services.

MONEY

Banks, ATMs and foreign exchange offices are along ul Aleksandrovska where it meets pl Svoboda.

Biochim Commercial Bank (☎ 888 113; ul Knyazheska) Near the Rila Bureau.

Bulbank (☎ 818 283; pl Sveta Troitsa 5) Just north of the opera house; changes cash and travellers cheques. The bank's ATM accepts major credit cards, as does the ATM in front of the post office.

United Bulgarian Bank (☎ 883 103; ul Aleksandrovska 6)

POST

Post office (pl Svoboda; ☒ 7am-9.45pm)

TELEPHONE

Telephone Centre (pl Svoboda; ☒ 7am-9.45pm) Inside the post office.

TOURIST INFORMATION

Rusenski Lom Nature Park office (☎ 872 397; www.lomea.org; ul Gen Skobelev 7; ☒ 8.30am-5pm Mon-Fri) Provides camping and hiking information and maps; can arrange trips to the Ivanovo Rock Monastery.

Tourist Information Centre (☎ 824 704; tic@tic .rousse.bg; ul Aleksandrovska 61; ☒ 9am-8pm Mon-Fri, 9.30am-6pm Sat & Sun) The very helpful Boris Botsev and team run one of Bulgaria's best tourist information offices, providing information about Ruse and nearby attractions, as well as accommodation assistance.

TRAVEL AGENCIES

Byala Zvezda (☎ 279 770; biala_zvezda@abv.bg; apt 25, 2nd fl, entrance B, ul Vidin 10) Local NGO organising hiking, caving, canoeing, trekking and cycling trips in Rusenski Lom Nature Park.

Dunav Tours (☎ 825 048; travel@dunavtours.bg; ul Olimpi Panov 5; ☒ 9am-5.30pm Mon-Fri) Arranges private rooms and tours, and sells tickets for long-distance buses; also runs unique eight-day Danube boat cruises to Vienna.

Retro Tours (☎ 876 108; retroturs@abv.bg; ul Angel Kânchev 14) Books air and bus tickets; can find accommodation and organise excursions to local attractions.

Rila Bureau central (☎ 876 108; ul Knyazheska 33; ☒ 9am-noon & 12.30-5pm Mon-Fri); train station (☎ 828 016; ☒ 9am-5.30pm & 9.30pm-5.30am) The central branch sells international train and bus tickets, but not to Bucharest; these are bought on the day of travel at the train station's Rila Bureau.

Sights

The **Clock Tower**, on the site of Bulgaria's first insurance company, is a popular meeting point. Located on the square at the corner of ul Alexandrovska and ul Daskalov, the clock tower stands, of course, over the Honorary Consulate of Mongolia.

CHURCHES

Behind the magnificent opera house is the Russian-style **Church of Sveta Troitsa** (pl Sveta Troitsa; admission free; ☒ 7am-6pm), Ruse's oldest surviving Ottoman-era building, built in 1632. The Turkish stipulation that no church should stand higher than a mosque led builders here, as elsewhere, to build partially underground. Large, well-preserved murals and 16th-century crosses and icons are the standouts here, as are the tower's stained-glass windows. The bell tower was a post-Ottoman addition from the late 19th century.

The **Catholic Church of St Paul the Crucified** (admission free; ☉ 7am-6pm), just off ul Pridunavski, was completed in 1892. Its original murals, stained-glass windows, chandeliers and icons survive. St Paul's was the first Bulgarian church equipped with an organ, and they still fire up the 700-pipe monster for Sunday mass.

MUSEUMS

Ruse Regional Museum of History (☎ 825 006; www.museumruse.com; ul Aleksandar Battenberg 3; ☉ 9am-5pm) is a new history museum containing prehistoric, Roman and medieval Bulgarian archaeological finds, taken from the Roman fortress and other local sites.

The unique **Transportation Museum** (☎ 803 516; ul Bratya Obretenovi 5; admission outside/indoor displays 4/2 lv; ☉ 10am-noon & 2-5pm Mon-Fri) exhibits vintage locomotives from the late 19th and early 20th centuries, as well as carriages that once belonged to Balkan luminaries such as Tsar Boris III, Tsar Ferdinand and Turkish Sultan Abdul Aziz. A photo display documents the development of communications and mass transport in Ruse.

The **Museum of the Urban Lifestyle in Ruse** (☎ 820 997; ul Tsar Ferdinand 39; admission 3 lv; ☉ 9am-noon & 1-5.30pm Mon-Sat) was built in 1866 and features early-20th-century crockery, cutlery, porcelain and costumes. The elegant furnishings date to the same period. The museum is alternatively known as the Kaliopa House. According to legend, the Turkish governor, Midhat Pasha, gave the house to his reputed mistress, Calliope, the beautiful Greek wife of the Prussian ambassador.

Revolutionary hero Zahari Stoyanov and his firearms collection, along with sabres and early photographs, are commemorated at the **Zahari Stoyanov House-Museum** (☎ 820 996; ul Pridunavski 12; adult/student 3/0.50 lv; ☉ 9am-noon & 1-5.30pm Mon-Sat).

ROMAN FORTRESS OF SEXAGINTA PRISTA

Defensive walls, a tower, some barracks and a storage area are what remain of this once great **fortress** (☎ 825 004; ul Tsar Kaloyan 2; adult/concession 2/1 lv; ☉ 9am-noon & 1-5.30pm Mon-Sat), completed in AD 70. Around 600 soldiers once stood guard here, guaranteeing safe passage for

river traders from their high bluff over the river. Stone inscriptions, decorative sculptures and tombstones are also displayed, and background information is posted in English. The friendly staff will show you around, and, if you're interested, to the somewhat more recent **German Bunker**, hewn out of bricks in WWII and still marvellously intact. Other ancient finds are kept in the cool confines of the underground bunker.

CANETTI TRADE HOUSE

The grandfather of Bulgarian Jewish writer Elias Canetti (1905–94), winner of the Nobel Prize for literature, built this fine house at ul Slavyanska 9. The cosmopolitan Canetti spoke Ladino, Bulgarian, German and English, embodying the spirit of *fin-de-siècle* Ruse, a city marked by its mixed nationalities and cultures. The house is now a private residence, so you can only look on from outside.

PARKS & MONUMENTS

The **Park na Vazrozhdentsite** (Park of the Revivalists), lined with the graves of local revolutionary heroes, is dominated by the gold-domed **Pantheon of the National Revival** (☎ 820 998; admission free; ☉ 9am-noon & 1-5.30pm). This grand achievement of Soviet monumentalism was built in 1978, to commemorate the 100th anniversary of the death of 453 Ruse-area natives who fought the Ottomans in the Russo-Turkish War. Their remains are inside.

North of the Pantheon, at the end of ul Saedinenie, is the **Soviet Army Monument**, built in 1949. Behind this is the **Youth Park**, with playgrounds, swimming pools, tennis courts and good river views.

Festivals & Events

March Music Days Festival (last two weeks of March) Features international musicians.
Golden Rebeck Folklore Festival (early June)
Ruse Jazz Bluezz Festival (September)
Days of Ruse Festival (early October) Music, dance and theatre.
Christmas Festival (15-24 December)

Sleeping
BUDGET

The **Tourist Information Centre** (☎ 824 704; tic@tic.rousse.bg; ul Aleksandrovska 61; r per person from 10 lv; ☉ 9am-8pm Mon-Fri, 9.30am-6pm Sat & Sun) can find private rooms; **Dunav Tours** (☎ 825 051; travel@dunavtours.bg; ul Olimpi Panov 5; s/d 22/35 lv;

THE DANUBE BRIDGE

Some 6km downstream from Ruse, this double-decker highway and railway bridge finished in 1954 links the city with Giurgiu on the Romanian side of the Danube. At 2.8km in length, and towering 30m above the water, it's the largest steel bridge in Europe.

In a nod to the neighbourly bickering between Bulgarians and Romanians, the Soviets named it the Friendship Bridge. Whatever filial sentiments this act may have inspired were sorely tested in the 1980s, when a Romanian chlorine-and-sodium plant caused massive air pollution and health problems in Ruse. More recently, locals suffered the misfortune of another catastrophic spill in Romania (see the boxed text, p261). In the wake of these incidents the bridge has come to denote friendship no more, but mere functionality; it's now known simply as the Danube Bridge.

🕒 9am-5.30pm Mon-Fri) can also help you, though its prices tend to be more expensive.

ourpick The English Guest House (☎ 824 120, 088326313; babatonka@gmail.com; ul Baba Tonka 24; s/d 30/45 lv) By far the best budget option in Ruse, The English Guest House has five lovely double rooms with shared, but spacious and immaculate modern bathrooms, in an artfully restored 150-year-old mansion. The guesthouse is owned and run by charismatic Englishman Steve Molyneux, who can do pick-ups from the train or bus station. There is free laundry service, sauna, wireless internet, a relaxing back garden and a lounge/kitchen with a communal fridge.

National Hotel (☎ 824 120; fax 834 915; ul Nikolaevska 51; s & d 40 lv) A 15-minute walk from pl Svoboda, the National has basic but clean rooms.

Hotel Kristal (☎ 824 333; hotel_kristal@abv.bg; ul Nikolaevska 1; s/d/t 40/56/70 lv; P 🍴 💻) The renovated but somewhat out-of-the-way Kristal attracts business travellers and tour groups. However, it's a fine, comfortable hotel with helpful staff. Rooms are clean, but bathrooms are small.

MIDRANGE

Hotel Liliya (☎ 822 900; ul Zlaten Rog 1; s/d 60/80 lv; P 🍴) The Liliya, almost down by the river off the central square, offers decent accommodation; it's nothing special for the price, but a good fallback option if others are booked. A small bar and restaurant are downstairs.

Splendid Hotel (☎ 825 972; www.splendid.rousse.bg; ul Aleksandrovska 51; s/d 68/80 lv; P 🍴) Off on a side street near the main square, the Splendid offers comfortable if unspectacular rooms.

TOP END

Bistra & Galina Hotel (☎ 823 344; www.bghotel.bg; ul Han Asparukh 8; s 90-100 lv/d 120-140 lv; 🍴) The swank Bistra & Galina has excellent rooms with all the mod cons, though the singles are small. It's part of the Best Western international chain.

Anna Palace (☎ 825 005; www.annapalace.com; ul Knyazheska 4; s/d 110/140 lv; P 🍴 💻) In a bright yellow neoclassical mansion by the river terminal, the luxurious (if a bit garish in places) Anna Palace has comfortable rooms and a professional staff. There are smaller, discounted attic singles. The hotel features one of Ruse's more elegant restaurants.

Danube Plaza Hotel (☎ 822 929; www.danubeplaza.com; pl Svoboda 5; s/d 130/200 lv; 🍴 💻) The lively Danube Plaza overlooks the square. Rooms are spacious, bathrooms large, and amenities just as expected.

Eating

Khlebozavod Ruse (ul Aleksandrovska; banitsa 0.60 lv; 🕒 8am-4pm) A busy take-away place on the pedestrian mall near bul Tsar Osvoboditel, this little shop sells an array of *banitsa* (cheese pasties) and similar morning-hours snacks.

Ali Baba (cnr Aleksandrovska & Rakovski; mains 2 lv; 🕒 8am-11pm) Quick and tasty chicken *shishle*, kebabs, falafel and meat wraps for takeaway or eating at the outdoor tables.

Del Cano (pl Sveta Troitsa 15; mains 4-6 lv) A tasty lunch spot on the square's far side.

ourpick Mehana Chiflika (☎ 828 222; ul Otets Paisii 2; mains 5-11 lv; 🕒 11am-2am) The enormous Chiflika is an excellent *mehana* with traditional furnishings, live music and a wide range of grilled meats. It's a place for hearty eaters, and the rustic charm is only enhanced by the sight of some dishes being served up on what are essentially chipped-off tree stumps.

Mehana Strandzhata (☎ 821 185; ul Konstantin Irichek 5; mains 6-9 lv; 🕒 noon-11pm) Another good spot for Bulgarian cooking, the Strandzhata has indoor seating and an enclosed outside terrace.

Restaurant Dublin (ul Tsar Osvobotidel 61; mains 6-10 lv; 🕒 11am-1am) Yes, it serves Guinness,

NORTHERN BULGARIA

but no, it's not a pub; the Dublin is in fact one of the city's better restaurants, with a big menu of inventive Bulgarian and international cuisine.

Balkan Princess (☎ 0888270297; pontoon 7, Danube waterfront; mains 6-11 lv, surcharge per person for the trip 5 lv) For Danube dining, take a supper cruise on the *Balkan Princess*, a boat-restaurant that serves plenty of fish and meat, plus cocktails and other drinks from the bar. Since the boat only sails when there's a crowd, you may be dining stationary, though there's no surcharge if so.

Leventa (☎ 862 880; www.leventa-bg.net; ul General Kutuzov; mains 10-15 lv; ◷ 11am-midnight) This gourmet eatery is not exactly central, though it is excellent. It boasts a winery, and produces an aromatic red wine characterising the vino of the Danube delta. Food is both inspired Bulgarian and international.

Drinking

Popular cafés and bars line the pedestrian mall, especially around the main square.

Fresh (cnr ul Aleksandrovska & ul Tsar Osvoboditel) This is a popular café that spills out onto the pedestrian mall.

Deep Club & House (☎ 834 712; ul Aleksandrovska) Also on ul Aleksandrovska, this cool bar with outdoor seating and a dark, eclectically decorated subterranean section plays a variety of music and is a good chill-out place.

Camelot (☎ 861 084; ul Neofit Rilski 48; ◷ 7am-11pm) and **Tropik** (Neofit Rilski 49; ◷ 7am-midnight) are next door to each other just northeast of the centre, in a suburb known for its boisterous, young population. The former has a vaguely English theme, and does good grub, while the latter is a chic and colourful outdoor café for lounging over a drink.

Entertainment

Art Club (☎ 820 948; ul Vazhrazhdane 1; ◷ 9pm-3am) Just across the park, this spacious bar is the place to go for live jazz music (Wednesday to Saturday).

Soundgarden (ul Knyazheska 16; ◷ 9am-3am) The once frequent live rock shows held here had become, at the time of writing, sadly rare; nevertheless, this weathered place between the square and the river retains its alternative edge and cultivates a pub ambience.

The **Ruse Opera House** (☎ 825 037; pl Sveta Troitsa), open since about 1890 and one of the town's finest buildings, and the **Sava Ognyanov**

Drama Theatre (pl Svoboda), are both well known for their quality productions. Buy tickets at the box offices, or through the Tourist Information Centre.

Royal Cinema (ul Olimpi Panov) screens the latest hits.

Getting There & Away

BUS

The **Yug bus station** (☎ 828 151; ul Pristanishtna), about 2.5km south of the city centre, has regular buses to Sofia (10 lv, five hours), Veliko Târnovo (5 lv, two hours), Burgas (11 lv, 4½ hours), Shumen (5.40 lv, two hours), Varna (11 lv, four hours) and Plovdiv (12 lv, six hours). Also, one or two daily public buses go to Gabrovo and Pleven, and two to Dobrich. Buses and minibuses leave for Silistra (5 lv, about two hours) every hour or so. To get to the station, take trolleybus 25 or bus 11 or 12 from ul Borisova. A taxi will cost about 2 lv to 4 lv.

The **Iztok bus station** (☎ 844 064; ul Ivan Vedur 10), 4km east of the centre, has buses to nearby destinations such as Ivanovo and Cherven in the Rusenski Lom Nature Park (opposite). Take a taxi or city bus 2 or 13, which leave from ul Gen Skobelev, near the roundabout four blocks east of ul Borisova.

To/From Romania

The Ruse-based company **Ovonesovi** (☎ 821 964) runs two minibuses to Bucharest daily, leaving the Yug bus station at 6.30am and 2pm. Tickets are 20 lv one-way or 30 lv return. Buy them either at the station or at Ovonesovi's office on pl Borisova, in front of city hall on the corner of ul Panov. These buses return from Romania at 10.30am and 4.15pm from the Hotel Horoskop on Bucharest's Piazza Uniri. A Romanian company also runs two daily buses from Ruse to Bucharest, at 11.30am and 4.30pm for similar prices.

TRAIN

The grand **train station** (☎ 820 222; ul Pristanishtna), Bulgaria's oldest, is adjacent to the Yug bus station, about 2.5km from the town's centre. It has four daily train services to both Sofia (14.50 lv, seven hours) and Veliko Târnovo (5.70 lv, two to three hours), and two more to Varna (9 lv, four hours).

For Romania, three daily trains serve Bucharest (20 lv, 3½ hours). Show up at least 30 minutes before the train departure time for customs and passport checks.

In the station, the **Rila Bureau** (☎ 828 016; ☒ 9am-5.30pm & 9pm-5.30am) sells international train tickets. It's best to buy a Bucharest ticket on the day of travel as there are sometimes delays. The train station's **left-luggage office** (☒ 6am-1.30pm & 2-8.30pm) is past the main buildings and in a smaller one up the hill.

To get to the train station, take trolleybus 25 or bus 11 or 12 from ul Borisova. A taxi costs 2 lv to 4 lv.

Getting Around

Walking central Ruse is easy enough, and plenty of taxis operate. You can also rent bicycles from **Byala Zvezda** (☎ 279 770; apt 25, 2nd fl, entrance B, ul Vidin 10; per day 25 lv). Travel agencies and hotels can advise about car rental, useful for excursions to the Rusenski Lom Nature Park.

RUSENSKI LOM NATURE PARK
ПРИРОДЕН ПАРК РУСЕНСКИ ЛОМ

This 3260-hectare nature park, sprawling south of Ruse around the Rusenski Lom, Beli Lom and Malki Lom Rivers, features unique rock monasteries and superb bird-watching. About 170 species of water birds, some endangered, live here. Among the most notable residents are the Egyptian vulture, lesser kestrel and great eagle owl. It's also home to 67 species of mammals (16 of them endangered) and 23 types of bats. The park's endless valleys and mountains (rare among the Danubian plains), were caused by unique prehistoric geological shifts.

Most visitors, however, are drawn first to the park's cliff churches. While around 40 medieval rock churches exist in and around some 300 local caves, only a handful are accessible, the most famous being those of Basarbovo and Ivanovo. The park also contains the second-longest cave in Bulgaria, the Orlova Chuka Peshtera (Eagle Peak Cave), between Tabachka and Pepelina villages. Thracian and Roman ruins are also found here.

Information

Information centre (☎ 081-162 203; Ivanovo town hall)
Rusenski Lom Nature Park office (☎ 082-872 397; www.lomea.org; ul Gen Skobelev 7, Ruse; ☒ 8.30am-5pm Mon-Fri) The *Naturpark Rusenski Lom* map, published by the Green Danube Program, is indispensable and available here or at bookstalls in Ruse.

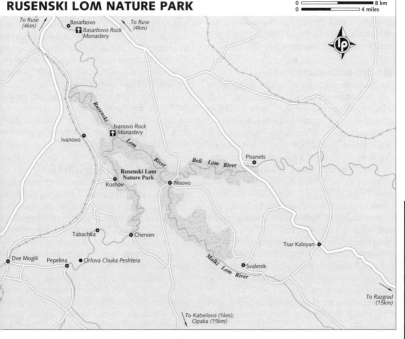

RUSENSKI LOM NATURE PARK

0 _____ 8 km
0 _____ 4 miles

To Ruse (4km)
Basarbovo
Basarbovo Rock Monastery
To Ruse (4km)
Rusenski Lom
Ivanovo Rock Monastery
Ivanovo
Lom
River
Rusenski Lom Nature Park
Koshov
Nisovo
Beli Lom River
Pisanets
Tabachka
Cherven
Tsar Kaloyan
Dve Mogili
Pepelina
Orlova Chuka Peshtera
Malki Lom River
Svalenik
To Razgrad (15km)
To Katselovo (1km); Opaka (15km)

Sights

BASARBOVO ROCK MONASTERY

The only working rock monastery in Bulgaria, Basarbovo is in the village of the same name 8km south of Ruse near the Rusenski Lom River, on the road to Ivanovo Monastery. Although the latter is more famous and thus gets more visitors, Basarbovo is also worth seeing for its striking frescoes and general aesthetic appeal, carved into a hollow in a high cliff, up a narrow rock stairway of 48 steps. Since you can park right below, it's also easier to reach for those who don't want to climb up the long wooded path at Ivanovo.

Basarbovo Monastery dates from (at least) the 15th century. Adherents of the mystical Hesychasm movement championed by the Byzantine Bishop of Thessaloniki, Gregory Palamas, flocked here. The doctrine, which emphasised inner contemplation and the attainment of spiritual tranquillity, was naturally well suited to the monastic life in remote cliff monasteries such as Basarbovo.

In 1937, the monastery was restored and strengthened by a resident monk, Hrysant, whose coffin is visible in the sepulchral chamber. Other sections of the upper part of the monastery include a small church with carved iconostasis and two monastic cells. At the time of writing, a larger, modern church was being built, just down from the cliff.

IVANOVO ROCK MONASTERY

The most famous of several former cave churches near Ivanovo village, the Sveti Arhangel Mikhail Monastery complex is also called simply the **Ivanovo Rock Monastery** (☎ 082-231 023; admission 3 lv; 🕑 8am-noon & 1-5pm Wed-Mon). This Unesco World Heritage–listed monastery is built inside a cave some 16m long, 4m wide and 38m above ground. It's about a 10-minute walk on a good trail through a forest to get there.

Built during the 13th century by Tsars Ivan Asen II and Ivan Aleksandâr, the monastery soon became a regional centre of art, culture and religion. The 14th-century murals on the walls and ceilings – regarded as some of the finest in Bulgaria – depict various saints and impassioned scenes from the Last Supper. The artists are unknown.

The monastery is signposted along a good road, about 4km east of Ivanovo and 20km south of Ruse.

CHERVEN ЧЕРВЕН

Cherven was established in the 6th century by residents of Ruse who wanted to escape chronic Slavic invasions. The town became an important religious, economic and military centre during the Second Bulgarian Empire (1185–1396). Remains of the 6th-century **citadel** (☎ 082-230 123; admission 3 lv; 🕑 8am-noon & 1-5pm Wed-Mon) are remarkably intact. Several streets, towers and churches have also been discovered, and though now a protected 'archaeological reserve', you can clamber through it easily enough. There are great views of the river valleys and hills from the top. The ruins are a short walk north of Cherven village, about 15km south of Ivanovo.

Sleeping

The nature park office in Ruse (p269) and Ivanovo's information centre (p273) provide accommodation options, such as private rooms in Cherven, Pisanets, Nisovo and Koshov (20 lv per person).

Getting There & Away

From the Iztok bus station in Ruse, four buses leave daily for Cherven, via Ivanovo and Koshov, between Monday and Friday. The best way to get to Ivanovo, however, is by train (every 30 minutes), as there are only three daily buses to Ivanovo in summer, and fewer in winter. For Pisanets, the frequent buses towards Razgrad from the Yug bus station in Ruse will work, and for Nisovo, look for a bus leaving the Iztok station for Opaka.

Ask at the Ruse Tourist Information Centre (p269) for details on getting to Basarbovo via local bus directly from the city centre. In summer, hourly buses go to Basarbovo, though in winter they are less frequent.

LAKE SREBÂRNA & AROUND

Two of Bulgaria's most important waterways unite at Lake Srebârna, a shallow (1.5m to 5m deep) lake connected to the Danube by a narrow, natural canal, and bedecked by unique types of vegetation and unusual floating islands made of reeds. The nearby village of **Vetren**, situated in tranquil isolation right on the Danube, is a good spot for fishing, boating and even swimming. There are plenty of hikes and other outdoor activities to be enjoyed amidst all the lush river verdure, and both places remain peaceful, splendid sanctuaries for nature lovers. The large

(8000-hectare) area around the lake, known simply as the **Srebârna Nature Reserve**, has been a Unesco World Heritage site since 1983.

Lake Srebârna hosts over 160 species of water birds, including colonies of endangered small cormorants, Ferruginous ducks and Dalmatian pelicans. Dedicated bird lovers are titillated, too, at the sight of the beloved red-breasted goose and lesser white-fronted goose. There are elevated lookout posts set around the lake for bird-watching, accompanied by helpful boards detailing the names of birds, amphibians and mammals (such as the river otter) found locally. Amidst all the greenery, wild raspberries grow and apple and apricot trees blossom.

Information

Neither Srebârna village nor Vetren have ATMs, though the former does have a doctor and post office (though, curiously, you can only mail letters to addresses within Bulgaria from it).

There's no real nightlife, except when the local Socialist Party Pensioners' Club tears it up at their periodic social activities. Their archrival, the Modern Club, offers dances and drinks for the (somewhat) younger set.

Sights & Activities

Bird-watching accounts for most Srebârna visitors. Guided bird-watching tours and nature walks (40 lv per group) are conducted by Englishman Mike Black of the Pelican Lake Guesthouse (see right). Mike can supply mountain bikes for local **cycling**, as well as **fishing** gear rentals (10 lv) and, crucially, free temporary permits for fly-fishing on the Danube and Lake Srebârna. Mike even arranges **boating** trips (20 lv) in local fishing caiques on the Danube from Vetren.

For walkers, there's a relatively flat, 4km-long **ecotrail** that starts from the beginning of the village and runs along the lake.

The **Museum of Natural History** (☎ 086-823 894; admission 2 lv; 9am-noon & 2-4pm Mon-Fri) is in Srebârna village. It's not spectacular, but does contain a few exhibits about local bird life and flora of interest to nature lovers.

Though unknown to tourists, the hamlet of **Vetren** is a wonderfully peaceful (if overgrown) place right on the Danube where free camping is allowed. Here you can see fishermen hard at work, with their crates of flopping fish and colourful craft lined up on the shore.

Swimming is even possible, especially on the long exposed areas where the main road terminates. Facing the river, turn left and walk for about 200m (towards the camping area) to find a suitable swimming hole. Although signs prohibit it, locals do enjoy the occasional dip. Ask locals to advise where it's safe to swim to avoid being swept away by the currents.

An unusual **summer festival** punctuates the village's offbeat appeal. Each year on 24 August, a riotous celebration is held on the riverbank to celebrate the arrival of around 100 German and Austrian kayakers and canoeists, passing through on their mad, beer-fuelled quest to paddle the length of the Danube. In honour of their feat, the village sponsors music, dancing and copious food and drink, transforming the riverbank into a couple of days of camping and festivities.

At the time of writing, still unknown **Roman ruins** had just been discovered in Vetren; enquire locally if you're interested to know what is being unearthed.

Sleeping & Eating

Srebârna village and Vetren now have several guesthouses, and some decent places to eat. Discreet camping, though technically illegal, is tolerated in the forests around Lake Srebârna. More organised free camping is on the riverbank in Vetren, on the grassy open area to the left of where the local fishing fleet pulls up its skiffs. There are basic toilets and showers, but no organised campground. A tiny canteen operates on the shore, serving soft drinks and snacks, as well as very fresh fish.

Pelican Lake Guesthouse (☎ 851 5322, 0885671058; www.srebarnabirding.com; Petko Simov 16; s/d/ste 30/50/100 lv) Owned by hospitable English couple Mike and Jerry Black (see the boxed text, p276), the cosy Pelican Lake Guesthouse has two breezy adjoining rooms with a shared, but spotless modern bathroom. Alternatively, rent out both as a suite. Mike and Jerry provide a wealth of local knowledge and activities, and bird-watching tours are free for guests. There's a relaxing back garden patio, and a good collection of English-language novels and children's books. Guests can use the guesthouse's computer for checking email. The breakfast (3 lv extra) includes Jerry's delectable homemade strawberry jam.

Hotel Pochuvin Dom Srebârna (☎ 851 5462; lubabriz@ccpro.com; s/d incl breakfast 40/60 lv; P) If Pelican Lake is full, try the Pochuvin Dom,

THANKS TO THE LAKE

After a Black Sea holiday in 2003, Englishman Mike Black and his wife Jerry took a liking to Bulgaria – so much so that they decided to move there two years later, to the placid shores of Lake Srebarna. Dedicated bird-watchers and nature lovers, the Blacks opened a small guesthouse, as several new British arrivals have done in recent years. However, unlike most, they took the trouble to study Bulgarian and learn the ways of the locals.

While there was much to like about life in the splendidly tranquil natural park, 'people weren't accustomed to picking up after themselves', recalls Mike. So, taking matters into their own hands and with the initial cooperation of a Japanese aid agency and the local authorities, the Blacks started a recycling initiative. Amazingly enough, they were even able to get local teenagers – usually the most unenthusiastic about such ventures – to join them in picking up the accumulated plastic bottles and bags that were creating a hazard for the lake's creatures and an eyesore for visitors.

Along the way, something strange happened: 'The locals started to see the value of keeping their lake clean,' says Jerry, 'and now the programme has really taken off.' The Blacks continue to get small sums from municipal authorities and, states Mike, 'sometimes even from guests, who will leave €50 in an envelope when they leave, with a note thanking us for keeping the lake clean.' For the Blacks, that has been the obvious thing to do for a special place that has given them an idyllic home, and so much unique wildlife to marvel over.

a five-room guesthouse run by the ebullient Luba Ivanova and her team of photogenic cats. Upper-storey rooms have handsome wood floors and great lake views, while lower rooms look out onto the garden and lawn. Big shared balconies stand on both levels, and the bathrooms are also shared. Guests can use the backyard *skara* (vented barbecue), and there's a wireless internet connection.

Kalimaritsa (☎ 0888234985; www.housekalimaritsa .bg; d/apt 40/60 lv) A Vetren restaurant that doubles as a guesthouse, the Kalimaritsa has six doubles and one modest apartment. The beautiful courtyard garden is bursting with grapevines and filled with traditional Bulgarian pots. The old-fashioned rooms are a bit musty, though passable. Dining is enjoyed around the courtyard and features many meats and whatever fish are in the catch of the day.

Kafe Isvor (☎ 0886432977; ul Dunav 14; mains 2-4 lv; ☺ 8am-11pm) Light lunches and drinks are served at this small café on the right-hand side of the road just after entering Srebârna village. Friendly local couple Incho and Krema run the adjacent provisions shop also.

Restoran Diva (☎ 0898751478; Dunav 19; mains 2-5 lv; ☺ 7am-1am) This fairly basic place in the centre has no architectural appeal, but does have the best food in Srebârna, from salads to grilled meats.

Restaurant Stara Kushta (☎ 0885200288; mains 3-6 lv; ☺ 6am-11pm, closed Mon) This traditional *me-*

hana, set in a handsome wood-framed house in Vetren that also provides accommodation, offers the best selection of Bulgarian dishes around. The traditional-style doubles (30 lv) have little flourishes such as colourful rugs and furnishings. It's signposted up a small dirt driveway heading towards the river. Phone ahead for either meals or rooms; the owners, the Leonova family, speak only Bulgarian.

Kafe Leshnika (☎ 851 5343; ul Liliya 1; ☺ 7am-11pm) This little café offers drinks; there's an outdoor bamboo enclosure and small interior.

Getting There & Away

There is no bus station in either Srebârna village or Vetren. Buses traversing the main Silistra–Ruse route will leave you unceremoniously in a ditch on the side of the road, 1.5km from the centre of Srebârna village. Alternatively, local bus 22 from Silistra travels several times daily into Srebârna village.

To reach Vetren, enter Srebârna village and just keep following the main street, ul Dunavska. After 4km, you'll reach Vetren, which stops at the river.

SILISTRA СИЛИСТРА

☎ 086 / pop 49,900

Little Silistra, with a bit of architecture and river views, is a low-key though intriguing town just east of Srebârna, and one of the few places on the Danube for enjoying boat trips.

While Silistra has some museums and a nice park, it has few services compared with Ruse.

Orientation & Information

The bus station is 1.5km from the main square, pl Svoboda; around it are clustered banks, foreign exchange offices, the post office, telephone centre and the new **Silistra Tourist Agency** (☎ 820 487; wfa@abv.bg), which provides local information and accommodation advice.

Sights & Activities

Silistra's prime position on the Danube has attracted a bewildering amount of invaders and occupants, from Thracians, Romans, Greeks, Bulgars, Russians, Romanians and Turks, all of whom built citadels and fortresses in or near the town. The **ruins** of the ancient Roman city of Durostorum, one of Silistra's previous incarnations, lie along the street between the mall and river.

The Turkish **Medzhitabiya Fortress** (built in 1848) is closed but the forested **park** surrounding it offers relaxed **hiking**. The fortress is 5km from town (5 lv by taxi) on the Silistra–Dobrich road, or a 3km uphill walk. The TV tower is an adjacent landmark.

The **Art Gallery** (☎ 826 838; bul Simeon Veliki 120; admission 0.50 lv, free Thu; ☺ 8am-noon & 2-6pm Mon-Fri) is in a renovated yellow building along the mall, opposite the drama theatre. The gallery contains hundreds of contemporary Bulgarian artworks, as well as Japanese engravings.

The **Archaeological Museum** (☎ 823 894; admission 1 lv; ☺ 9.30am-noon & 1-7.30pm Tue-Sat) occupies the same building as the Art Gallery, and houses artefacts from the Turkish fortress and other local sites. Costumes, jewellery and even a 3rd-century BC Thracian chariot are also displayed. The museum may move in the future, so double-check.

The MV *Bravo* offers one-hour **boat tours** (per person 5-6 lv) along the Danube several days a week. Enquire at the travel agency in the Zlatna Dobroudja Hotel.

Sleeping & Eating

Zlatna Dobroudja Hotel (☎ 821 355; fax 821 361; ul Dobroudja 2; s 40-55, lv, d 66-99 lv; ☒) This central hotel has reasonable rates given the standard of accommodation.

Hotel Drustar (☎ 812 200; www.hoteldrustar.com; Kapitan Mamarchev 10; s/d/apt 140/170/230 lv) The rooms at this new four-star place have all the mod cons, and are individually decorated and overlook the Danube. There's also a pool, and gourmet eats available at its restaurant. As if that weren't enough, the hotel also promises unimpeded impregnation for chronically childless couples. (Could we make this stuff up?)

Several cafés and restaurants are found in and around the hotel complex, including Pizzeria Zlatna Dobroudja, which offers tasty pizzas and pasta dishes from 5 lv.

Getting There & Away

Hourly buses and minibuses leave the Silistra **bus station** (☎ 820 280) for the Yug bus station in Ruse (5.50 lv, two hours). From Silistra, two or three daily buses go to Varna, eight to Dobrich, four to Sofia, three to Shumen and one to Veliko Târnovo. From the **train station** (☎ 821 802) one daily train goes to Ruse and three to Samuil.

From Silistra port to Călăraşi (in Romania), a ferry operates every few hours (25/7 lv per car/passenger). Fares are payable in euros or leva. Public transport on the Romanian side is not reliable, however, so the border crossing at Ruse is probably easier.

DOBRICH ДОБРИЧ
☎ 058 / pop 113,800

A popular day trip for Black Sea tourists, Dobrich is not overwhelming but does have a long history of arts and crafts production, which is kept alive today in the shops of its ethnological complex. The town is quite old, having been settled originally in the 15th century. Most recently, Dobrich has made a name for itself due to the excellent agricultural products grown on the surrounding plains.

Information

The large central square, pl Svoboda, hosts the United Bulgarian Bank, the post office and telephone centre, plus restaurants and shops. For internet access, there's the **Top Gun internet café** (ul Nezavisimost; per hr 1 lv).

Sights
STARIYAT DOBRICH ETHNOLOGICAL MUSEUM COMPLEX

Some 37 shops, cafés, bars, restaurants and souvenir stalls co-inhabit this **complex** (☎ 29 068; ul Dr K Stoilov; admission free; ☺ 8am-6pm summer, 8.30am-6pm winter), set along cobblestone streets. You

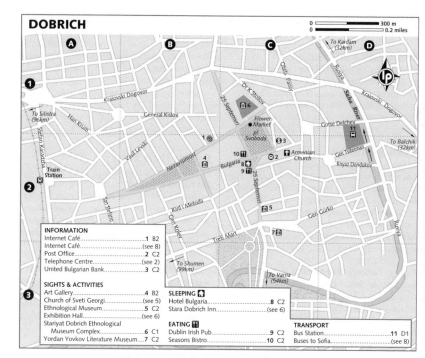

DOBRICH

can watch blacksmiths, potters, weavers and other artisans while they work, and sit out in the shady courtyard, lined with cafés. There's also a hotel (see right).

The complex is signposted at the southern entrance, behind a large modern construction. The **exhibition hall** (admission 1 lv) at the courtyard is best known for its antique jewellery. After watching the local artisans at work, feel free to shop, and so bring home some traditional Dobrich handicrafts.

ART GALLERY

The **Art Gallery** (☎ 602 215; www.dobrichgallery.org; ul Bulgaria 14; admission 0.50 lv, guided tour in English or German 1 lv; 9am-noon & 1.30-6pm Mon-Sat) houses more than 1700 artworks collected over a century, including many by the acknowledged master of modern Bulgarian painting, Vladimir Dimitrov.

YORDAN YOVKOV LITERATURE MUSEUM

This **museum** (☎ 624 308; ul Gen Gurko 4; admission 1 lv; 9am-6pm Mon-Fri, to 4pm Sat & Sun) features furniture, costumes, knick-knacks, books and photos relating to Bulgarian novelist Yordan

Yovkov. There's an informative leaflet available in English.

ETHNOLOGICAL MUSEUM

Inside the lovely courtyard of a Bulgarian National Revival–period home, this **museum** (ul 25 Septemvri; admission 2 lv; 8.30am-noon & 2-4.30pm Mon-Fri) exhibits traditional costumes and jewellery. It's adjacent to a park with a statue of Vasil Levski, in front of the **Church of Sveti Georgi** (admission free; 8am-6pm).

Sleeping

Stara Dobrich Inn (☎ 601 5904; Stariyat Dobrich Ethnological Museum Complex; s/d 50/68 lv) Right inside the traditional shopping complex, this rustic guesthouse offers clean, modern rooms with traditional furnishings. It's not well signposted, however: from the main square, turn right by the Rosexim sign, then turn left and go through the archway by the Western Union building. Walk through the museum complex and finally turn left.

Hotel Bulgaria (☎ /fax 625 444; pl Svoboda; s/d 70/100 lv; P □ ◙) This massive central hotel has large and comfortable, though old-fashioned rooms, each with a fan, TV and fridge. It's decent value and has a casino and fitness centre.

Eating

Cafés line ul 25 Septemvri, in the shady park to the south. There are excellent *mehanas* at the ethnological complex.

Seasons Bistro (ul Bulgaria; mains 5-7 lv) Near the Hotel Bulgaria, this is a popular spot for Bulgarian and European dishes.

Dublin Irish Pub (☎ 601 475; ul 25 Septemvri 19; mains 5-8 lv; ☼ 9am-11pm) This dependable quasi-Irish place on the square serves tasty pub grub and plenty of good beer. It's popular with locals.

Getting There & Away

From the **bus station** (☎ 690 120), on Dobrich's eastern side, buses and minibuses leave for Albena (4 lv, 45 minutes, every 30 minutes), Varna (4 lv, 40 minutes, every 15 minutes), Balchik (3.50 lv, 45 minutes, every 30 minutes) and Kavarna (4.50 lv, one hour). Two daily buses go to both Ruse (13 lv, three hours) and Silistra (6.50 lv, 1½ hours). All buses to Sofia (17 lv to 18 lv, seven to eight hours) leave from the Hotel Bulgaria car park, not from the bus station.

The **train station** (☎ 603 078), on the western edge of town, has regular trains westwards to Sofia (20.30 lv, 9½ hours) via Shumen (6.30 lv, three hours) and Gorna Oryakhovitsa (12 lv, six hours) for Veliko Târnovo. Trains also go east to Varna (4.10 lv, two hours). You can get a train to Kardam on the Romanian border, but you can't cross here. The station's Rila Bureau sells international tickets.

DIRECTORY

Directory

CONTENTS

ACCOMMODATION

Bulgaria offers pretty much every kind of accommodation option you can think of, from spartan mountain huts to the most opulent five-star hotels. Accommodation is most expensive in Sofia and other big cities, notably Plovdiv and Varna, although independent travellers will find prices at Black Sea resorts such as Albena, Sunny Beach (Slânchev Bryag) and Golden Sands (Zlatni Pyasâtsi) even more expensive in high season. Elsewhere, prices are still relatively cheap by Western European standards. If you're travelling independently around the country, one indispensable publication is the annual *Bulgaria Bed & Breakfasts*

Guidebook (17 lv) published by the **Bulgarian Association for Alternative Tourism** (☎ 02-980 7685; www.baatbg.org), which lists sustainable, family-run guesthouses all over Bulgaria. You can buy it at **Zig Zag Holidays** (Map p88; ☎ 02-980 5102; www.zigzagbg.com; bul Stamboliyski 20-V) in Sofia. It's also worth picking up the free **Authentic Bulgaria** (www.authenticbulgaria.org) guidebook, which has reviews of some of the best hotels and guesthouses in both the cities and remote villages.

Accommodation in this book has been divided into three price categories: budget, midrange and top end. In the budget category, double rooms cost up to 50 lv (or €25); in midrange they cost up to 100 lv (or €50); anything above that is regarded as top end. However, as accommodation in Sofia is priced so much higher than anywhere else, double rooms costing up to 200 lv (or €100) are placed in the midrange bracket for the capital, and anything over that is top end.

Budget accommodation is usually very simple, and includes private rooms, hostels and cheaper guesthouses, normally with shared bathroom facilities and no air-conditioning. Midrange options offer a much higher standard and will almost always include private bathrooms and extras such as fridges and TVs. Top-end accommodation is, naturally, the best available, or at least the most luxurious and dependable. This includes international chains as well as home-grown establishments, and most of these are very modern, with top-notch facilities; Sofia, in particular, has numerous top-end options to try out. Top-end hotels commonly offer discounted weekend prices (Friday to Sunday inclusive) and it may be worth asking for discounts for longer stays, too. Some hostels in Sofia may also be willing to offer discounted rates for long stays.

Note that hotels in seasonal spots, such as the Black Sea coast or skiing resorts, frequently close down outside the holiday seasons, or may operate on a much reduced basis, closing up part of the hotel and the restaurant or cutting back staff to a minimum. So if you're thinking of staying in, for example, Pamporovo in October or Nesebâr

---

PRACTICALITIES

▪ The metric system is used for weights and measures.

▪ Bulgaria runs on 220V, 50Hz AC and plugs are the standard round two-pin variety, sometimes called the 'europlug'.

▪ Videos work on the PAL system.

▪ If you're visiting Sofia, pick up the English-language *Sofia Echo*, published on Friday. Other English-language papers are the *Frontier Times*, published monthly in Veliko Târnovo (but available sporadically around the country) and the free monthly *Sunny Times*, available on the coast. *Vagabond* is a glossy, English-language lifestyle magazine, published monthly.

▪ If you get very bored, tune into the government-run TV channel (BNT) or one of two private ones (Nova Televisiya and BTV). Televisions in most – but certainly not all – hotel rooms can pick up a plethora of stations from around the region, so you can enjoy Romanian game shows, Greek movies and Turkish news programmes, as well as CNN, BBC, Euronews, Hallmark, MTV and German cable channels such as DW.

▪ In Sofia, tune into BG Radio (91.9FM), Radio Contact (106FM), Jazz FM (104FM), Retro Radio (98.3FM) and Classic FM (89.1FM). Darrik Radio, a nationwide network of stations that usually plays contemporary pop music, can be heard in Sofia (98.3FM), Varna (90.7FM), Plovdiv (94.6FM), Ruse (104FM) and Veliko Târnovo (88.9FM). Several international services can be found on the FM band in Sofia, including Voice of America (103.9FM), BBC (91FM), Deutsche Welle (95.7FM) and Radio France Internationale (103.6FM). If you understand Bulgarian, try the two national stations, Horizont (103FM) and Hristo Botev (92.8FM).

---

in February, you really should phone ahead to see what the current situation is.

Useful websites offering hotel booking facilities and discounts include www.bgglobe.net, www.hotelbg.com, www.hotelsbulgaria.com and, for the capital, www.sofiahotels.net.

Camping

Once a popular way to see the country on a tight budget, these days camping has lost its allure in Bulgaria. Camping grounds have struggled since losing government support and the industry, which once included over 100 locales nationwide (with half that number along the Black Sea coast), is in decline. Even privatised camping grounds tend to be run-down, so don't have high expectations.

Camping grounds in Bulgaria are rarely open between November and April, and some along the Black Sea coast operate only from June to early September. These tend to be very crowded in July and August: while camp sites will normally be available at this time, security, privacy and tranquillity are rarely guaranteed. In addition, camping grounds tend to be placed closer to noisy main roads (to attract passing customers) than to anywhere peaceful or picturesque such as a beach or lake, and are rarely convenient for anyone relying on public transport.

The cost of setting up a tent at a camping ground is about 8 lv to 10 lv per person per night, but tents are very rarely available for hire, so bring your own. Most camping grounds also rent out tiny bungalows for slightly more than the cost of camp sites, but these, too, are often far from inviting.

Camping in the wild (ie outside a camping ground) is technically prohibited but normally accepted if you're discreet and, most importantly, do not build wood fires (which attract attention and damage the environment).

Hostels

Backpacker hostels are a relatively recent phenomenon in Bulgaria. Sofia now boasts several excellent private establishments, and there is a handful of hostels around Varna and Plovdiv, but you'll find very few anywhere else in the country.

There are no hostels in Bulgaria affiliated with the Youth Hostels Association (YHA) or Hostelling International (HI), and only one or two hostels in Sofia will offer small discounts for holders of HI or International Student Identity Card (ISIC) cards. Other hostels around the country are more basic affairs, aimed at school groups, hikers and the like.

DIRECTORY

BOOK YOUR STAY ONLINE

For more accommodation reviews and recommendations by Lonely Planet authors, check out the online booking service at www.lonelyplanet.com/hotels. You'll find the true, insider lowdown on the best places to stay. Reviews are thorough and independent. Best of all, you can book online.

Hotels

Like anywhere else, the hotel scene in Bulgaria is varied: basically, you get what you pay for. While many of the older, formerly state-run hotels have now been privatised and renovated, those in less-visited locations are often shabby and run-down, with antiquated plumbing and old-fashioned attitudes to customer service.

Modern private hotels have sprung up everywhere and usually offer good value. Some hotels offer more expensive 'apartments'. These are usually double rooms that are more luxurious and feature more amenities. 'Suites' normally have either two double bedrooms or one bedroom and a lounge room, sometimes with an extra sofa-bed.

Hotels (but not private homes, mountain huts or hostels) are rated from one to five stars, but one- and two-star places are rarely proud of the fact so often don't advertise their rating. Some hotels do not offer single rooms or single rates in a double room. If this is the case, only the rates for doubles are listed in this book.

International chain hotels, such as Hilton, Sheraton and Radisson, now have a presence in Bulgaria and offer the usual high standards at the usual international rates.

Most smaller and more remote ski-resort hotels are closed in summer (from about mid-April to November), while many places along the Black Sea coast, especially the purpose-built resorts such as Albena, do not open between late October and early April. Hotels in cities such as Varna and Burgas will be less dependent on the weather for customers.

Whether breakfast is included depends on local competition. In some towns every hotel includes breakfast, while elsewhere it's optional, costing an extra 4 lv or 5 lv per person (or considerably more in a five-star hotel). Although it's convenient, breakfast in a local café will probably be tastier and cheaper.

Unless stated otherwise in this book, reserving a room in advance is not normally necessary, except if you're determined to stay at a particular place or are visiting at peak times (eg Nesebâr in August or Bansko at Christmas) or during a major festival. If you want to stay at one of the Black Sea coast's package resorts such as Sunny Beach (Slânchev Bryag) during the summer, it's advisable to book at least a few months ahead. You'll probably find it easier and cheaper to book a package deal in your home country.

Monasteries

About a dozen of the 160 monasteries around Bulgaria offer accommodation to anyone, of either sex, from pilgrims to foreign tourists. Some rooms are actually inside the monastery, such as at the Rila and Cherepish Monasteries, or at guesthouses within metres of the monastery gates, eg the Troyan, Dryanovo and Lopushanski Monasteries. Some only offer rooms on a sporadic basis and availability may be unreliable; contact the monasteries directly to see if they have room.

Mountain Huts

Anyone, especially those enjoying long-distance treks or shorter hikes, can stay at any *hizha* (mountain hut). Normally a *hizha* only offers basic, but clean and comfortable, dormitory beds with a shared bathroom, which cost from 10 lv to 35 lv per person per night. Most are open only from May to October, but those situated at or near major ski slopes are often also open in winter. In or around a town or village along a popular hiking/trekking route, you can also often find a *turisticheski dom* (tourist home; a fairly comfortable hotel with double rooms) or a *turisticheska spalnya* (tourist bedroom; a more basic, dorm-style hostel).

It's often not necessary to book these in advance, but beds at most of the 200 or more mountain huts, hotels and hostels can be reserved at the **Bulgarian Tourist Union** (BTC; Map p88; ☎ 02-980 1285; www.btsbg.org; bul Vasil Levski 75, Sofia). The office is tucked inside a photo shop in the underpass at the junction of bul Vasil Levski and ul General Gurko. The BTC office also sells some hiking maps and the *Hizhite v Bâlgariya* book (written in Cyrillic), which details the locations of, and amenities at, most places in the mountains. **Zig Zag Holidays** (Map p88; ☎ 02-980 5102; www.zigzagbg.com; bul Stamboliyski 20-V, Sofia) can also arrange accommodation in the mountains and villages.

BUYING PROPERTY IN BULGARIA

The Bulgarian property market is booming as never before: prices rose by as much as 27% in the second quarter of 2007 – the second-highest recorded rise anywhere in the world – and they show no sign of dipping. Prices are being pushed up by foreign investors; Brits especially have been flocking to the country in search of holiday homes, lured by low prices and the promise of long, hot summers by the sea, snowy winters in the expanding ski resorts and rustic country idylls. By Western standards, house prices are often amazingly cheap; it's still possible, for example, to pick up a run-down village house (with, ahem, lots of potential) for under €10,000. If you're looking to buy in hotspots such as Bansko or somewhere near the big Black Sea resorts, you can expect to pay from around €60,000-plus for a one-bedroom apartment in a luxury development, though prices vary considerably (and buying off-plan will be much cheaper).

This international interest has fuelled a building boom, with vast new holiday-home complexes appearing all along the coast and around the skiing centres in the mountains. Understandably, not everyone is happy with this situation, and environmentalists have campaigned vigorously against the seemingly unstoppable advance of the developers' bulldozers in pristine countryside areas. Locals, meanwhile, have been priced out of many areas where properties are increasingly being snapped up by foreigners and often used for only a few months a year. Money talks, however, and the building continues: marinas and golf-course complexes are among the latest wave of apartment construction while the ski resorts are expected to expand still further.

If you do decide to invest in a holiday home in Bulgaria, or even to move there permanently, remember that buying a property in a foreign country can be a complicated business. However, there are now countless estate agents specialising in all aspects of Bulgarian real estate, many of them based in the UK. Some of the more useful include www.bulgarianproperties.com, which has a huge number of houses, flats and studios for sale and up-to-date news on the property scene in Bulgaria, www.purelybulgaria.com, www.bulgarianventure.com and http://findbulgarianproperty .co.uk. For more localised offerings, www.blackseavillas.net, www.skipropertybg.com and www .bulgariandreams.com, a UK-based company, provide news and advice on buying property in various regions of the country. Those interested in northern Bulgarian properties should consult the experienced and straight-talking Englishman Steve Molyneux of **Molyneux Property Holdings** (www.buying-properties-in-bulgaria.co.uk) in Ruse. You will also find plenty of British estate agents' offices in Bulgaria, especially in Varna. For legal advice and information on mortgages, visit the UK-run **Bulgarian Home Loans** (www.bulgarianhomeloans.com).

There are also a number of informative books on the market: try *Buying a Property in Bulgaria* (2007) by Andy Anderson and Stephane Lambert or the similarly titled *Buying a Property in Bulgaria* (2005) by Jonathan White.

Private Rooms

As well as being a cheap accommodation option for foreign visitors, private rooms also offer a glimpse into real Bulgarian life. Standards vary, but usually these will be in nondescript apartment blocks with shared bathroom facilities. The hosts always seem to be elderly ladies, who are unlikely to speak English. Most are very welcoming and will provide breakfast and lengthy monologues in Bulgarian (whether you understand it or not), while others, of course, are in it purely for the money. If you don't mind sleeping in a room surrounded by kitschy knick-knacks and black-and-white photos of long-dead husbands in military uniform, it's a homely and evocative choice.

Rooms cost anywhere between 10 lv and 25 lv per person, but they're normally priced per number of beds, so people travelling alone sometimes have to pay for double rooms. Rooms in Sofia or Plovdiv will naturally be more expensive than those in small provincial towns and villages, while rooms in popular Black Sea coast towns such as Sozopol can cost up to 30 lv at the height of the summer season. These are often more comfortable, modernised places including private bathrooms but again, each place is different.

Stays in private rooms can often be arranged through an accommodation agency in a town centre, or at a bus or train station. Alternatively, you can wait to be approached in the street or keep an eye out for relevant signs in Bulgarian (see p309), English or German in shop windows or outside the actual home. The pensioners who hang around outside bus and train stations offering rooms in their homes are invariably living on very low incomes, so by paying them directly, without the commissions taken off by agencies, you will have the satisfaction of knowing that you're helping them get by and making a positive contribution to this form of sustainable tourism.

It's always important to find out where the rooms are before making a decision: in a village such as Melnik, all homes are central, but in a city such as Burgas the home may be in an outlying and dreary suburb.

ACTIVITIES

All kinds of outdoor activities are catered for in Bulgaria, with hiking, biking, mountaineering, rock-climbing, diving and skiing being just some of the sports and pastimes available. The country is being promoted as a growing ski destination, with new resorts being built in the Pirin mountains, while the country's unspoilt, mountainous terrain makes it ideal for trekking and hiking, with numerous well-marked trails and a system of mountain huts, or *hizhas,* for hikers to sleep in. Water sports are popular on the Black Sea coast, although these tend to be confined to the big package-holiday resorts. Windsurfing, paragliding, scuba diving and a host of other watery activities can be arranged during summer.

For more information and listings, see p75.

BUSINESS HOURS

Normally, government offices are open on weekdays (Monday to Friday) between 9am and 5pm, but they often close for around an hour between noon and 2pm. Private businesses more or less keep the same hours, but rarely have time for a leisurely lunch break. Most shops are open from about 9am to 7pm on weekdays, and from 9am to 1pm on weekends. Some operate shorter hours on Sunday (or close altogether) but shops in big cities such as Sofia and Plovdiv are often open later on weekends. Post offices are open weekdays from 8am to 6pm, and banks operate from 9am to 4pm weekdays. Some of the foreign exchange offices are open 24 hours but most operate between about 9am and 6pm, Monday to Saturday.

Restaurants generally open from 11am to 11pm. Frustratingly, many museums and tourist attractions, even those in major cities, close for one or two days a week, usually between Sunday and Tuesday (they often also close for lunch). Opening times do change regularly, so don't be surprised if a museum or art gallery is closed even though it should be open.

CHILDREN

Successful travel with young children requires planning and effort. Don't try to overdo things: even for adults, packing too much into the time available can cause problems. Make sure planned activities include the kids as well – balance the morning at a stuffy museum with an afternoon swim at the beach or a walk in the hills. And include children in the trip planning: if they've helped to work out where you'll be going, they'll be much more interested when they get there. For further general information and suggestions, try Lonely Planet's *Travel with Children* or get advice from other parents on the 'Kids to Go' branch of the Thorn Tree forum (www.lonelyplanet.com/thorntree).

Practicalities

Bulgaria is a safe and healthy country and medical facilities are generally pretty good. Most of the necessities for travelling with toddlers, such as nappies (diapers), baby food and fresh or powdered milk are readily available, and there are well-known international fast-food outlets all over the country.

The major international car rental firms can provide children's safety seats for a nominal extra cost, but it's essential to book these in advance. It's also worth noting that highchairs are almost unheard of in restaurants, public nappy-changing facilities are rare and childcare (baby-sitting) agencies are only common among the expatriate community in Sofia. However, some top-end hotels may offer this service, and the bigger hotels in the Black Sea resorts often have playgroups and kids' clubs. Breast-feeding in public is not usual and may attract stares. Cots are available only in the top-end, international chain hotels, though it's always worth asking at other modern hotels. Look out for other travellers with children and see if you can pick up some useful tips.

Sights & Activities

The most obvious attractions for young children are, of course, the long sandy beaches of the Black Sea, and the water parks, amusement rides and so on offered by the big resorts such as Golden Sands (Zlatni Pyasâtsi; p247), Sunny Beach (Slânchev Bryag; p235) and Albena (p249). Other activities such as parasailing and horse riding are often available. The kids might also like to visit some of the zoo parks (though the conditions are often poor and the animals look forlorn), see Bulgaria's rich wildlife in the nature parks and reserves around the country, or explore the dramatic fortresses and ruins that pepper the countryside. All towns and cities have parks with playground equipment. There are also many companies offering activities such as biking, hiking and horse riding trips that are suitable for older children (p75).

CLIMATE CHARTS

Bulgaria enjoys a temperate climate with hot, dry summers and cold, wet winters, often with heavy snow. Southern Bulgaria and the Black Sea coast record the highest temperatures, with Sandanski (p131) often named the sunniest and hottest town in the country; Smolyan (p158), the highest town in the country, is one of the coolest, as you'd expect. The Danube plain, meanwhile, is subject to the extremes of central Europe. Sofia's climate is generally favourable, with average daytime highs of around 28°C in July and August and 3°C from December to February. Rainfall is highest in the mountains and rural life is often disrupted in winter by huge snowfalls. See p16 for further details.

COURSES

There are a few language courses that are offered to foreigners, but make sure you book them before you arrive in Bulgaria.

Sofia University (Map p88; ☎ 02-971 7162; www.deo .uni-sofia.bg; bul Tsar Osvoboditel) offers Bulgarian language courses for foreigners, with one-to-one courses costing 220 lv for 20 hours' tuition. The university also runs classes in Bulgarian culture, dance and folklore: a two-week course costs 430 lv. Unfortunately, shorter courses are not available.

The **Sts Cyril & Methodius University of Veliko Târnovo** (☎ 062-20 070; www.uni-vt.bg) usually offers a one-month 'International Summer Seminar for Students in Bulgarian Language and Slavic Culture' every August. Contact the university for current programmes and costs.

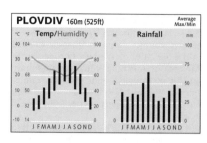

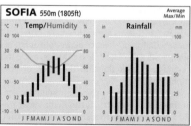

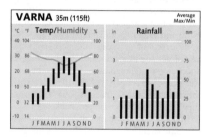

CUSTOMS

Whether you're inspected by customs officers depends on how you enter the country but bona fide tourists are generally left alone. If you're travelling between Bulgaria and another EU country, then normal EU rules on what you can import or export apply. You are allowed to bring into Bulgaria gifts up to the value of €175, plus up to 200 cigarettes, 50 cigars, 1L of spirits, 2L of wine and 50ml of perfume. If you enter or leave the country with more than 8000 lv on you (in any currency), you must declare it. Check with the customs service in your home country for advice on what you can import duty-free from Bulgaria.

For information about exporting unusual items (such as valuable archaeological artefacts) by air, contact the customs authorities at **Sofia airport** (☎ 02-717 051) or **Varna airport** (☎ 052-225 532).

DANGERS & ANNOYANCES

Bulgaria is a modern, peaceful and well-ordered country. If you can handle yourself in the big cities of Western Europe, North America or Australia, you'll certainly have little or no trouble dealing with the seamier sides of Bulgaria. You'll be fine if you look purposeful, keep alert and take the usual safety precautions.

Theft is not as much of a problem as it is in some countries, but obviously look after your belongings and watch out for pickpockets in busy markets and on crowded buses. Prime targets for thieves are parked cars, especially those with foreign licence plates and/or rental-agency stickers. Never leave things inside the car; always lock them in the boot, or take them with you.

Bulgarian drivers can be extremely reckless at times, and pedestrians should be very careful when crossing roads, especially in Sofia. Cars regularly park on pavements, blocking them for pedestrians. Inevitably, footpaths in towns throughout Bulgaria are often crumbling and under sporadic repair.

Beggars ply their trade around some churches and larger squares, but most are in real need and are very rarely aggressive or demanding. Be wary, however, of gangs of children who work the streets of big cities such as Sofia and Varna: they're often professional pickpockets.

Bulgaria has very harsh drug laws, being a common route for drugs (and arms) smuggled in from Turkey, Russia and Armenia and then across the continent. Don't attempt to buy, sell, transport or use drugs here unless you want an extended stay in Bulgaria's fearsome prisons.

Foreigners are sometimes set up for minor monetary rip-offs, but these are fairly obvious and easy to avoid: taxi drivers at airports, train stations and beach resorts normally overcharge outrageously, and moneychangers on the street sometimes offer ridiculously high exchange rates. (Changing money on the street is both illegal and unnecessary.)

Bulgaria is a major producer of tobacco, and smoking seems to be the national pastime. Cafés, bars and restaurants are often poorly ventilated, but this is less of a problem in summer when most patrons sit outside.

Construction work along the Black Sea shows no sign of slowing down and many places currently resemble vast, dusty building sites. New hotel and holiday-home developments are springing up at various locations – though the area around Sunny Beach (Slânchev Bryag) accounts for around a third of activity – and concrete and cranes dominate some existing resorts such as Sveti Vlas and parts of Pomorie. The ski resort of Bansko is also undergoing major building development. It's not easy to know when current work will be finished and where new projects are about to begin, but by law construction should not be taking place during the peak tourist seasons. For now, if you want to avoid the mess completely, you'll need to scout around for somewhere more to your liking; there are still quiet nooks to be found.

Mosquitoes can be an irritant in some areas during the summer, but sprays, creams and plug-in repellents can be bought cheaply at pharmacies and supermarkets.

Security

To keep money, passports etc safe from pickpockets, the best place is out of sight under your clothes. It's easy to make a cloth pouch that hangs around your neck or waist or is pinned under clothing. Alternatively, buy a money belt. Other methods include belts with concealed compartments and pouches worn around the leg. Try not to keep everything in one place; keep small change and a few banknotes in a shirt pocket to pay for bus tickets and small expenses without having to extract wads of cash from a secret hiding place. It may also help if you distribute valuables about your person and baggage, especially if you must carry all your belongings at once.

All important documents (eg passport data page and visa page, credit cards, travel insurance policy, air/bus/train tickets, driving licence) should be photocopied before you leave home. Leave one copy with someone at home and keep another with you, separate from the originals.

DISABLED TRAVELLERS

Unfortunately, Bulgaria is not an easy destination for disabled travellers. Uneven and broken footpaths make wheelchair mobility problematic, and ramps and special toilets for those in a wheelchair are few and far between, other than in a handful of top-end hotels in Sofia and other big cities. In accordance with EU guidelines, the Bulgarian government plans to upgrade wheelchair access in some existing buildings and make it compulsory for many new public structures, but this is still a long way from fruition. One Bulgarian organisation involved with disabled locals that is possibly worth contacting is the **Center for Independent Living in Sofia** (☎ 02-983 3117; www .cil-bg.org). You can also get advice and plan your trip with the help of the 'Travellers with Disabilities' branch of the Thorn Tree forum (www.lonelyplanet.com/thorntree).

DISCOUNT CARDS

The International Student Identification Card (ISIC) is available to full-time students of any age, and the International Youth Travel Card (IYTC) is available to anyone under 26 years of age. In Bulgaria, holders of either card can obtain discounts of 10% to 20% at museums, some major attractions, hotels and hostels and some medical and dental clinics, as well as at a few restaurants. Selected travel agencies also offer card holders discounts of up to 50% off domestic flights and 10% off train and bus tickets (depending on the agency and time of year). Cards may be purchased from branches of the **Usit Colours youth travel agency** (www .usitcolours.bg in Bulgarian), which should have lists (in Bulgarian only) of places that accept the card around the country. More general information about these cards is available on the website www.isic.org.

An International Teacher Identity Card (ITIC), identifying the holder as a teacher or professor, also offers similar discounts. More general information about this card is available on the website www.istc.org.

Many places in Bulgaria that should accept these cards don't advertise the fact, so it's always worth asking at the entrance (as long as you have the right card).

EMBASSIES & CONSULATES
Australia (Map p84; ☎ 02-946 1334; www.ausemb.gr; ul Trakia 37, Sofia)
Canada (Map p84; ☎ 02-969 9710; consular@canada -bg.org; ul Moskovska 9, Sofia)
France (Map p84; ☎ 02-965 1100; www.ambafrance-bg .org; ul Oborishte 27-29, Sofia)
Germany (Map p84; ☎ 02-918 380; www.sofia.diplo.de; ul Frederic Joliot-Curie 25, Sofia)
Greece Plovdiv (Map p140; ☎ 032-632 003; ul Preslav 10); Sofia (Map p88; ☎ 02-946 1027; http://info.greek embassy-sofia.org; ul San Stefano 33; ⊙ 9am-noon Mon-Fri)
Ireland (Map p88; ☎ 02-980 3425; info@embassyof ireland.bg; ul Bacho Kiro 26-28, Sofia)
Macedonia (Map p84; ☎ 02-870 5098; ul Frederic Joliot-Curie 17, Sofia; ⊙ 10am-1pm Mon-Fri)

Netherlands (Map p88; ☎ 02-816 0300; www.netherlandsembassy.bg; ul Oborishte 15, Sofia)
Romania (Map p84; ☎ 02-973 3081; ambsofro@vip .bg; bul Sitnyakovo 4, Sofia; ⊙ 3-5pm Tue, 10am-noon Wed & Thu)
Serbia (Map p84; ☎ 02-946 1633; www.emb-serbia.com; ul Veliko Târnovo 3, Sofia)
Turkey Burgas (Map p216; ☎ 056-844 2718; tcburkon@ bse.bg; bul Demokratsiya 38); Plovdiv (Map p140; ☎ 032-239 010; tcbk_filibe@plovdiv.ttm.bg; Filip Make-donski 10); Sofia (Map p88; ☎ 02-935 5500, 980 2270; turkel@techno-link.com; bul Vasil Levski 80)
UK (Map p88; ☎ 02-933 9222; www.british-embassy.bg; ul Moskovska 9, Sofia)
USA (Map p84; ☎ 02-937 5100; www.usembassy.bg; ul Kozyak 16, Sofia)

There is no New Zealand embassy in Bulgaria; in emergencies, citizens should contact the **New Zealand Mission to the EU** in Belgium (☎ 32 2 512 1040; nzemb.brussels@skynet.be; 7th fl, Square de Meeûs 1, Brussels).

FOOD
Eating out in Bulgaria is remarkably cheap, at least for Western travellers, and even if you're on a tight budget you'll have no problem eating well. In this book we've simply divided eating options into restaurants, where prices range from around 5 lv to 15 lv; cafés, where you're unlikely to spend more than 3 lv to 4 lv; and quick eats, which are the cheapest of all at around 2 lv to 3 lv. For more information on local cuisine and beverages, see p55.

GAY & LESBIAN TRAVELLERS
Homosexuality is legal in Bulgaria, and the age of consent is 16, the same as for heterosexuals. Although Bulgaria has not experienced the aggressive homophobia seen in some other Eastern European countries in recent years, it does remain a very conservative society. Same-sex couples should refrain from overt displays of affection and be discreet when booking into hotel rooms. A few gay clubs and bars can be found in Sofia and a couple of other major cities, although most attract a mixed crowd and there are no venues specifically aimed at lesbians. Attitudes are slowly changing, however. In 2006, Sofia hosted the first ever 'Mr Gay Balkans' competition, while Varna celebrated 'Gay Week' in September 2007.

The website www.gayguidebg.com is a comprehensive source of information, in English, on all aspects of gay (male) life in Bulgaria,

DIRECTORY

including details of gay-friendly bars, night-clubs and other businesses. Gay women can find some information at www.bg-lesbian.com. The major gay association is the **Bulgarian Gay Organization Gemini** (☎ 02-987 6872; www.bgogemini .org). Contact the group about current gay and gay-friendly bars and nightclubs in Sofia.

The *Spartacus International Gay Guide* by Bruno Gmünder is the best male-only inter-national directory of gay entertainment ven-ues in Europe. Lesbians should look out for *Damron's Women's Traveller* by Bob Damron. For the latest on the gay scene in Bulgaria, check out the 'Gay & Lesbian Travellers' branch of the Thorn Tree forum (www .lonelyplanet.com/thorntree).

HOLIDAYS

During official public holidays all government offices, banks, post offices and major busi-nesses will be closed. All hotels, restaurants, bars, national parks/reserves and museums stay open (unless the holiday coincides with a normal day off), as do most shops and petrol stations; border crossings and public transport continue to operate normally.

The official public holidays are:

New Year's Day (1 January) Banks and other offices often also close on New Year's Eve.

Liberation Day (3 March) Celebrates Bulgaria's inde-pendence after the Russo-Turkish War (1877–78); also known as National Day.

Easter (March/April) Orthodox Easter falls one week after Catholic/Protestant Easter.

St George's Day (6 May) Celebrates the start of the livestock breeding cycle.

Cyrillic Alphabet Day (24 May) Also known as Day of Bulgarian Culture.

Unification Day (6 September) Celebrates the final reunification of Bulgaria in 1885.

Bulgarian Independence Day (22 September) Celebrates official independence from Turkey in 1908.

National Revival Day (1 November) Celebrates the Bulgarian National Revival of the 19th century.

Christmas (25 and 26 December) During the communist era, Christmas Day was outlawed, so it was often celebrated on 26 December instead.

INSURANCE

A travel insurance policy to cover theft, loss and medical problems is a sensible idea. Some policies offer lower and higher medical-expense options. There is a wide variety of policies available, so check the small print.

Some policies specifically exclude 'danger-ous activities', which can include scuba diving,

motorcycling and even trekking. A locally acquired motorcycle licence is not valid under some policies.

You may prefer a policy that pays doctors or hospitals directly rather than you having to pay on the spot and claim later. If you have to claim later, make sure you keep all docu-mentation. Some policies ask you to call back (via reverse charges) to a centre in your home country where an immediate assessment of your problem can be made.

Check that the policy covers ambulances as well as an emergency flight home.

To buy an insurance policy online, visit www.lonelyplanet.com/bookings/insurance. For car insurance, see p302.

INTERNET ACCESS

Bulgaria is now well and truly 'connected', and even the smallest town has at least one internet centre. With about 150 internet service pro-viders throughout the country, competition is fierce and access is remarkably cheap, from as little as 0.80 lv per hour, although between 1 lv and 3 lv per hour is more common. Internet centres are usually open daily between about 10am and 9pm, sometimes later. Look for places with the word 'café' or 'centre' (often in English) rather than anywhere with the word 'games', because these latter places are usually cramped, smoky bunkers where teenage boys endlessly play violent and deafening compu-ter games. Bulgarian Telecommunications Company (BTC) centres offer the most reli-able and speedy connections, while the more modern, privately run internet cafés are usu-ally pretty good. However, in older places, es-pecially away from the big cities, connections tend to be painfully slow.

Most top-end hotels in cities such as Sofia, Varna and Plovdiv will provide modem con-nections for laptops in the room; elsewhere you may be able to plug into the regular phone socket, but this is by no means certain. Some internet centres may allow you to hook up your laptop, but don't count on it.

For internet resources, see p20.

LEGAL MATTERS

Bulgaria is a member state of the EU and more or less follows the same legal system as most of the rest of Europe. The days of blatant rip-ping off of foreign travellers are long gone; traffic police have to abide by a certain code of ethics, but residents do complain bitterly about corruption within some government departments, especially customs. If you do get into serious trouble with the police, it's best to contact your embassy (see p287).

MAPS

Good maps are easy to find in Bulgaria, but you might want to buy one or two before you come. For a useful overview of the region, buy Geocenter's *Eastern Europe* (1:2,000,000) map. The *Baedeker Bulgaria* (1:750,000) map and Bartholomew's *Bulgaria* (1:750,000) map will probably be available in your home country.

Proper road maps are essential if you're driving around Bulgaria. One of the best is the *Bulgaria Road Map* (1:500,000), published in English by Kartografia (with a red cover). Slightly better is *Bulgaria* (1:530,000), published in English by Datamap (with a blue cover). It's colourful, detailed and has several city maps on the other side. A smaller version (1:760,000), published in Cyrillic, has a red cover. These maps are readily available all over Bulgaria.

The maps in this guidebook will probably be more than sufficient for most visitors, but detailed maps (often in Cyrillic) are available in Bulgaria for most cities, towns and major attractions. Undoubtedly, the best publisher is Domino. It offers maps (usually with a red cover) of Bansko, Burgas, Blagoevgrad, Gabrovo, Haskovo, Kazanlâk, Koprivshtitsa, Melnik, Veliko Târnovo, Pleven, Plovdiv, Ruse, Sandanski, Smolyan, Sofia, Stara Zagora, Varna and Vidin. Most maps list street names in Cyrillic (which can be handy for linking maps with street signs), provide keys in Bulgarian and English and include other towns and places in the region. Another respected map publisher is Datamap, which produces an excellent country map as well as some city maps in English.

Also available in Bulgaria is a range of other maps for areas along the Black Sea coast and for hiking. If you are going to do some serious hiking, you will definitely need a detailed map. In Sofia, the best place to find these is **Zig Zag Holidays** (Map p88; ☎ 02-980 5102; www .zigzagbg.com; bul Stamboliyski 20-V), while elsewhere, local travel agencies or tourist information centres are your best bet. Other detailed and useful maps, which are not always easy to find, include *The Monasteries in Bulgaria,* published by Kartografia in Cyrillic, and *Wine Map Bulgaria,* published in English by Bars Agency.

MONEY

The local currency is the lev (plural: leva), comprised of 100 stotinki. It is almost always abbreviated to lv. The lev is a stable currency; see inside the front cover for the conversion rates of several major currencies at the time of research. For major purchases such as organised tours, airfares, car rental and midrange and top-end hotels, prices are almost always quoted by staff in euros, although payment is possible in leva too. (Bulgaria has no immediate plans to adopt the Euro as its national currency.) While some budget hotels and private rooms may quote their rates in euros, payments should be made in leva. The rates given in this book are in the currency stated by individual establishments; normally the leva price will simply be twice the given euro price (eg €10 = 20 lv), though some places may work out the precise exchange rate. All other transactions in Bulgaria are in leva and listed as such in this book.

See p17 for more information.

ATMs

ATMs that accept major credit cards (ie Cirrus, Maestro, JCB, Visa, MasterCard and American Express) are an increasingly common sight and can now be found in all sizable towns and cities. It's best to use credit cards as a backup for cash in case an ATM swallows your card (more likely if the card is issued outside Europe). Otherwise, bring two or three different cards. Also, before you leave home check with your bank about exchange rates (which, of course, usually work out in their favour) and commissions (which can be about 2%). The total amount you can withdraw depends on how much your bank will allow and on how much is in your account; the maximum allowed per day by most Bulgarian banks is usually 200 lv.

Black Market

With the currency stabilisation, no black market exists in Bulgaria. Foreigners may still be approached (especially in Sofia or Varna) and asked to change money, but this is illegal and there's a high chance you'll be given counterfeit leva, short-changed or robbed.

Cash

Bulgarian banknotes come in denominations of 2, 5, 10, 20 and 50 leva. Coins come in 1, 2, 5, 10, 20 and 50 stotinki and 1 lev. Prices for

DIRECTORY

smaller items are always quoted in leva or a fraction of a lev, eg on a bus ticket the fare will be listed as '0.50 lv' rather than '50 stotinki'.

When changing money, make sure that the foreign banknotes you have are not torn, marked or grubby, otherwise they may be refused or you may even be given a lower rate (without being told so in advance). Always make absolutely sure of the precise sum in leva you will receive before handing over any of your cash. Similarly, make sure that any leva given to you are not torn or marked. Foreigners may export and import up to 8000 lv (in any currency) without restrictions.

Credit Cards

Credit cards are still not as common or reliable in Bulgaria as in Western Europe, and their acceptance is decidedly uneven: you may be able to use your card for a 20 lv restaurant meal but have to hand over a wad of banknotes for a 200 lv hotel bill. However, American Express, Visa and MasterCard are gaining ground and can often be used at upmarket restaurants, souvenir shops, top-end hotels, car rental firms and travel agencies, but rarely anywhere else – despite signs indicating acceptance of credit cards. You cannot rely on using a credit card exclusively in Bulgaria; use it to get cash from banks and for major purchases only. Some places, particularly the more expensive hotels, will add a 5% surcharge to your bill if you use a credit card.

If no ATM is available, or you're worried about using one (in case it swallows your card), some larger branches of major banks will provide cash advances in leva over the counter; this service is also sometimes offered by foreign exchange offices. The fee is usually about 4% and you'll probably also be charged fees and commissions by your bank. The maximum withdrawal allowed for cash advances depends on what is determined by your bank.

International Transfers

Telegraphic transfers are not that expensive but they can be quite slow through a bank. Having money wired through American Express, MoneyGram or Western Union is fairly straightforward and faster than a bank (funds are sometimes available in less than one day). You should have the sender's full name, the exact amount and reference number and your passport; the money can be collected in euros or leva. The sender pays the fee, which can range from 5% to 15%.

Moneychangers

The currencies listed inside the front cover can be changed at any of the plethora of foreign exchange offices in every city and town and at major attractions. Most don't charge commission or fees, but some do – despite signs to the contrary on notice boards outside – so always check the final amount that you will be offered before handing over your cash.

The best currencies to take are euros, pounds sterling and US dollars. You may have trouble changing less familiar currencies, such as Australian or Canadian dollars, but you should be able to find somewhere in a city such as Sofia, Plovdiv or Varna that will accept most major international currencies.

Foreign exchange offices can generally be recognised by the huge 'exchange' signs, almost always written in English. Current rates are always displayed prominently, often on notice boards outside. These offices are normally open between about 9am and 6pm, Monday to Saturday, but offices in the centre of cities and larger towns are often open every day.

It's also easy to change cash at most of the larger banks found in cities and major towns; these include the United Bulgarian Bank, Unicredit Bulbank, Bulgarian Post Bank, Raffeisen Bank and Biochim Commercial Bank. The exchange rates listed on the electronic boards in bank windows may offer slightly higher rates than foreign exchange offices, but many banks charge commission. The other disadvantages with banks are that they're only open between 9am and 4pm from Monday to Friday, and queues can be long.

The lev is freely convertible, so there should be no problems changing excess leva back into sterling, dollars or other major foreign currencies. However, some readers have reported difficulties trying to change leva for local currency in other Eastern European countries.

Taxes

The value-added tax (VAT) of 20% is included in all prices quoted in Bulgaria, and is included in all prices listed in this guidebook. Some restaurants add service charges of 10%, and some top-end hotels list pre-VAT prices.

Tipping & Bargaining

Waiters normally round restaurant bills up to the nearest convenient figure and pocket the difference; the same applies to taxi drivers. In some restaurants an 8% to 10% service charge is already added, although this doesn't always stop the waiters from rounding up the bill again, or hovering expectantly for an extra tip. If it's not been added, and the service is good, add about 10%. Always leave the tip on the table (but make sure no beggars or street kids are within sight if you're sitting outside): it's socially unacceptable to give a tip to the waiter by hand.

Haggling is not customary in Bulgaria. An exception is at the seaside resorts where taxi drivers and landlords of private rooms habitually inflate prices for foreigners.

Travellers Cheques

Travellers cheques are not as easily convertible as cash, nor as convenient as credit cards, but they are a safe way of carrying money. The downside is that not all foreign exchange offices and banks will change travellers cheques, and those that do sometimes accept only American Express and Thomas Cook, with commission rates of 3% to 5%, so if you need to change travellers cheques, always look around for the best exchange rates. Some larger banks, such as the Unicredit Bulbank in Sofia, will change travellers cheques in US dollars into cash for a fee of about 2% to 3%.

Guaranteed personal cheques are another way of carrying money or obtaining cash. Eurocheques, available to European bank account holders, are guaranteed up to a certain limit. When cashing them, you'll be asked to show your Eurocheque card bearing your signature and registration number, and perhaps a passport or ID card. Many hotels and merchants in Bulgaria refuse to accept Eurocheques, however, because of the relatively large commissions involved.

PHOTOGRAPHY & VIDEO
Film & Equipment

Bulgaria is an extremely photogenic country, so bring (or buy along the way) plenty of film or a couple of memory cards if you're using a digital camera. Photographic and video film and equipment are available everywhere but, obviously, shops in the larger cities and towns have a wider selection, and everything for sale near tourist sites is overpriced. As an example of standard prices, a roll of 24- or 36-print film from a photographic shop in Sofia or Plovdiv costs about 5 lv to 8 lv. Developing costs are about 0.50 lv per print, more for larger prints or faster service. Slide film is not easy to find, so bring your own.

If you're using a digital camera, check that it has enough memory to store your snaps; two 128MB cards will probably be enough. Digital memory cards are widely available and prices vary. A 128MB card will cost roughly 20 lv to 30 lv. If you do run out of memory space your best bet is to burn your photos onto a CD-ROM. Increasing numbers of processing labs and some of the more modern internet cafés in the big cities now offer this service.

To download your pics at an internet café you'll need a USB cable and a card reader. Some places provide a USB cable on request, but be warned that many of the bigger chain cafés don't let you plug your gear into their computers, meaning that it's back to plan A – the CD-ROM.

Anyone serious about taking great snaps should pick up *Travel Photography*, published by Lonely Planet.

Restrictions

Taking pictures of anything in Bulgaria that might be considered of strategic importance, such as military camps and border crossings, is not advisable. These days officials are much less paranoid about photography than they used to be, but use common sense when it comes to this issue. It's best to ask permission before taking close-up photos of people.

POST

The standard cost of sending a postcard is 0.35 lv within Bulgaria, while a letter costs 0.55 lv. Postcards and letters weighing up to 20g cost 1 lv to elsewhere in Europe and 1.40 lv to the rest of the world.

To send a parcel from Bulgaria, you usually have to take it unwrapped to a main post office. Anything heavier than 2kg must often be taken to a special customs post office (ask at the post office for information).

SHOPPING

It's easy to spend lots of money on souvenirs but – not surprisingly – most of the stuff at popular tourist spots (such as resorts along the Black Sea coast) is tacky and overpriced. For more information about Bulgarian handicrafts such as woodcarving and weaving, see p53.

DIRECTORY

UNUSUAL SOUVENIRS

If you're looking for a souvenir of your time among the Bulgars and garish trinket boxes and amateur daubs of twee, timber-framed houses just won't do, there are plenty of more tasteful mementos for you to pick up. Hand-painted icons make a particularly evocative reminder of your stay; though often expensive, they do involve a huge amount of skill and time. How about a patterned *cherga*? These traditional, hand-woven rugs make a colourful addition to any room and, again, involve a great deal of work: even small rugs can take months to complete. Troyanska kapka pottery is common, but one of the more unusual products is a jug and set of shallow cups made specifically for serving and drinking the potent national spirit, *rakia* – it's sure to make a decorative conversation piece!

If you're here in March, see if you can find a *martenitza*. These little red-and-white woollen tassels, often in the form of a man and a woman, are worn by women and children on the breast or wrist (traditionally, men wear them tied round their left ankle or inside their left shoe) and tied to fruit trees at the first signs of spring, usually the first sighting of storks or migrating swallows.

Folding horn-handled knives, traditionally used by shepherds, are also good buys; get them straight from the blacksmith at Etâr (p187). Hand-knitted woollen socks from Bansko make useful and cosy mementos.

Foodstuffs worth bringing back include the widely used local seasoning Balkanska Sharena Sol (Balkan Mixed Salt), rose-petal jam, herbal tea bags and, of course, a good bottle of *rakia* or Bulgarian wine – try the 'national' red-grape variety, Rubin.

Some of the more attractive, and usable, mementos of your trip to Bulgaria may include pieces of Troyanska kapka pottery, decorated with the traditional *kapka* (droplet) design. Plates, bowls, cups, wine goblets and sugar bowls, among other things, are widely available. Most of these items are still made for everyday use, not just as tourist trinkets, so try looking in markets rather than pricier souvenir shops. Other worthwhile keepsakes include embroideries from Nesebâr, Varna and Sofia; paintings of traditional village life or landscapes from Varna, Nesebâr, Sofia and Plovdiv; woodcarvings from Tryavna; or carpets, rugs and bags from Koprivshtitsa, Chiprovtsi and Kotel. The National Fair and Exhibition of Arts & Crafts Complex (p191) in Oreshak is a marvellous place to spend up big on embroidery, pottery, ceramics, weaving, woodcarving and metalwork. The Etâr Ethnographic Village Museum (p187) near Gabrovo is a fantastic place to find traditional handmade crafts such as pottery, woodwork, metalwork and textiles.

As the regional centre for the Valley of Roses, Kazanlâk is the place to buy rose oil, perfume, shampoo, liqueur, tea bags and jam, though you can also pick these things up in Sofia and elsewhere. For antiques, head to the old towns in Veliko Târnovo and Plovdiv, but don't expect any bargains. The best range of other souvenirs such as books, CDs, textiles and jewellery is in Sofia.

Compact discs of foreign music are usually made outside Bulgaria and tend to be expensive, but CDs of Bulgarian music often cost only about 13 lv. Cassettes and CDs are available throughout the country, but the range is particularly extensive in Sofia and Plovdiv.

Note that counterfeit goods are common in Bulgaria, ranging from knock-off watches and fake perfumes sold at street stalls in places such as Nesebâr, Golden Sands (Zlatni Pyasâtsi) and Sunny Beach (Slânchev Bryag) to fake designer clothes and pirated software on sale in markets all over the country. Most of this is pretty obvious and priced accordingly, while some items can be quite expensive and may be designed to deceive. Be careful, too, when dealing with 'antiques', especially at street stalls in such places as Sofia. As always, use your common sense and make sure you know what you're buying; most of the time, those 'ancient coins' and Nazi knick-knacks are not the real thing.

SOLO TRAVELLERS

Solo travellers should face no specific problems in Bulgaria, other than the perennial annoyance of often having to pay for a double room in hotels, or facing the obvious disappointment of waiters in swankier restaurants when you ask for a 'table for one'. Private rooms and budget hotels are more likely to offer single prices, although it's always worth asking for discounts elsewhere, especially on weekends.

Macho culture prevails in Bulgaria, so women travelling alone may attract unwelcome attention, especially outside the big cities and resorts, where foreigners are more of a novelty, and in bars and clubs anywhere (see p295). Single men may be approached by pimps and prostitutes, some of whom can be aggressive in big cities such as Sofia and Varna.

Although solo independent travellers (other than business travellers) aren't that common a sight, numbers are increasing. Hostels in Sofia are the best places to meet like-minded fellow travellers, while renting rooms in private houses or sharing tables in busy restaurants are great ways to get to meet some of the locals on their home patch. Learning a few words of Bulgarian will help break the ice, too.

TELEPHONE
From Bulgaria it's easy to telephone anywhere in the world, via public telephone booths, telephone centres, private homes and hotels.

The two public telephone operators are Bulfon, with its orange booths, and the slightly more up-to-date Mobika, which has blue booths. Nearly all now only take phonecards, and some Mobika booths also accept Visa and MasterCard for long-distance calls (and have instructions in English). Cards for each system, ranging in price from 5 lv to 25 lv, can be bought at kiosks and in some shops.

Every big town throughout the country has a Bulgarian Telecommunications Company (BTC) centre, normally inside or very near to the main post office. BTC centres are normally open from at least 8am to 6pm daily, and often 24 hours a day in larger towns. Making a local or long-distance call at a BTC centre is simple: choose a booth (or take a token indicating which booth to use), call the number and pay the amount displayed on the counter above the telephone. BTC centres will normally have fax and internet facilities as well.

To ring Bulgaria from abroad, dial the international access code (which varies from country to country), add 359 (the country code for Bulgaria), the area code (minus the first zero) and then the number.

As the telecommunications systems in rural areas are being upgraded, some numbers will change, often with the addition of digits to the beginning of the number. If any numbers listed in this guidebook do

not work, check the telephone directory (mostly written in Bulgarian and English) or ring one of the inquiry numbers listed here. These numbers can be dialled toll-free anywhere within Bulgaria and there's a good chance one of the operators will speak English.

International directory inquiries (☎ 124)
International operator (☎ 0123)
National directory inquiries – businesses (☎ 144)
National directory inquiries – residential (☎ 145)
National operator (☎ 121)

Mobile Phones
Mobile (cell) phones have taken off in Bulgaria and are common pretty much everywhere in the country. Mobile telephone numbers have different codes (eg 087, 088 or 089) and are indicated by the abbreviations 'GSM' or 'mob'. Bulgaria has three mobile service providers – **Globul** (www.globul.bg), **M-Tel** (www.mtel.bg) and **Vivatel** (www.vivatel.bg) – who cover most of the country, but contact your own mobile phone company about whether you can use your own phone in Bulgaria.

TIME
Bulgaria is on Eastern European Time, ie GMT/UTC plus two hours, except during daylight saving, when clocks are put forward by one hour between the last Sunday in March and the last Sunday in October. There are no time zones within the country.

Bulgaria is one hour behind Serbia and Macedonia, and the same time as Romania, Greece and Turkey. Therefore, if it's noon in Sofia, it's 2am in Los Angeles, 5am in New York, 10am in London, 11am in Paris and 8pm in Sydney, not taking into account daylight saving (where applicable) in these countries. The 24-hour clock is commonly used throughout Bulgaria, and always utilised for bus and train timetables.

TOILETS
With the exception of a few Middle Eastern–style squat toilets near the Turkish border, almost all toilets in Bulgaria are of the sit-down European variety. All hotels provide toilet paper and soap, but these are rarely offered anywhere else. In the more basic hotels and private homes you may still come across old-fashioned toilets that have small bins beside them for used toilet paper (throwing paper

down the toilet may block the pipes), but fortunately these horrors are now becoming rare.

The standard of public toilets, especially at train and bus stations, is generally abominable and you'll be charged at least 0.30 lv per visit (more for a few squares of toilet paper). So if you can't get back to your hotel, visit a museum, classy bar, shopping mall or restaurant. Western fast-food franchises such as McDonald's always have clean toilets with toilet paper and often a queue to use these facilities. More acceptable, privately run toilets are available for about 0.40 lv in central Sofia and the Black Sea resorts.

TOURIST INFORMATION

Despite the large revenue generated by tourism, the increasing popularity of Bulgaria as a tourist destination, and constant pleas from travel agencies and tourist operators, Bulgaria still doesn't have a dedicated Ministry of Tourism. Tourism is the responsibility of the Ministry of Economy and Energy and gets a lower profile than it deserves.

Recently, however, tourist information offices have begun appearing in the big cities. In Sofia, the **National Tourist Information Centre** (Map p88; ☎ 987 9778; www.bulgariatravel .org; ul Sveta Sofia; ⊗ 9am-5pm Mon-Fri) is a brand-new tourist office offering free information, brochures and maps, while Burgas, Varna and Plovdiv also have new, helpful tourist centres. In an effort to boost regional tourism, the government has opened a number of autonomous local Tourist Information Centres (TICs) around the country. These TICs, however, are often little more than associations of travel agencies, rather than independent tourist offices dispensing free advice and useful maps. TICs of use to visitors are mentioned throughout this guidebook.

The former government-run tourism monopoly, Balkantourist, has been split up and privatised. The subsequent private agencies now operate under myriad different, though slightly ambiguous, names, such as Balkan Tours, Balkan Airtours and Balkan Holidays. These are essentially travel agencies and *not* tourist offices.

One of the more useful of the new private travel agencies is **Zig Zag Holidays** (Map p88; ☎ 02-980 5102; www.zigzagbg.com; bul Stamboliyski 20-V, Sofia), which can offer plenty of information to foreign travellers.

The **Bulgarian Association for Alternative Tourism** (Map p88; ☎ 02-980 7685; www.baatbg.org; bul Stamboliyski 20-V, Sofia), in the same building as Zig Zag, promotes sustainable alternative tourism across the country.

VISAS

Citizens of other EU member states and Australia, Canada, Israel, Japan, New Zealand and the USA can stay in Bulgaria visa-free for up to 90 days. Citizens of other countries should check the current requirements with their nearest Bulgarian embassy or consulate (see p287) before their departure. Visas cannot be obtained at border crossings.

Visa Extensions

At the time of writing, visitors wishing to extend their visit to Bulgaria beyond the 90-day limit have to apply for a residence permit at the **Immigration Office** (Map p88; ☎ 02-982 3764; bul Maria Luisa 48; ⊗ 9am-5pm Mon-Fri). This is likely to be a time-consuming, bureaucratic nightmare, and nobody here will speak anything but Bulgarian. It's probably far better to contact the Bulgarian Embassy in your own country for advice before you travel if you envisage being in the country for more than three months. The situation, especially for EU citizens, may well change over coming years.

VOLUNTEERING

If you're looking for a more satisfying holiday and you don't mind a bit of hard work, then there are a number of opportunities for volunteering in Bulgaria. Your first port of call should be **World Wide Opportunities on Organic Farms** (WWOOF; www.wwoofbulgaria.org), which now has a presence in Bulgaria and can direct you to current projects and openings for volunteers around the country. The **British Trust for Conservation Volunteers** (www.btcv.org) organises various working holidays in Bulgaria, with recent projects including helping to reintroduce vultures into the wild and building nesting sites for endangered birds.

St James Park (☎ 0884595174; www.stjamespark .biz) is a British-run venture in the village of Voditsa in northern Bulgaria. It's an 'alternative' campsite and organic farm that welcomes volunteers, either (through WWOOF) working 35 hours a week for board and lodging, or doing smaller, casual jobs for free meals. Contact them for exact dates and details.

Also worth checking out is the **Greenschool Village** (www.greenschool.cult.bg) in the eastern

Rodopi mountains. This educational project aims to re-create several old-style village houses, and provide local young people with the chance to learn traditional skills and crafts such as pottery and carpentry. It is hoped that this centre will also reinvigorate the local community and the local economy.

For invaluable information and inspiration to get you planning your perfect short or long-term volunteer experience anywhere in the world, visit www.lonelyplanet.com/volunteer.

WOMEN TRAVELLERS

In general, travelling around Bulgaria poses no particular difficulties for women. For the most part, sober men are polite and respectful, especially if you're clearly not interested in their advances, and women can usually meet and communicate with local men without their intentions necessarily being misconstrued. That doesn't mean, however, that women can go into a bar or nightclub unaccompanied and expect to be left alone. If you attract unwanted attention, saying *Omâzhena sâm* ('I am married') gives a pretty firm message; wearing a wedding ring might help, too.

Like most destinations in Eastern Europe, common sense is the best guide to dealing with possibly dangerous situations, such as hitchhiking, sharing hostel rooms and walking alone at night. For overnight train journeys, choose a sleeper compartment rather than a couchette. Young women in Sofia are comfortable wearing miniskirts and low-cut blouses, but more modest apparel is advisable if you're travelling outside the big cities or coastal resorts.

Feminine hygiene products such as tampons are widely available in supermarkets and pharmacies across the country.

Hear what female travellers are saying about Bulgaria on the 'Women Travellers' branch of the Thorn Tree forum (www.lonelyplanet.com/thorntree).

WORK

Since Bulgaria joined the EU in 2007, there are no longer any labour restrictions on citizens of other EU countries, but with high levels of domestic unemployment and some of the lowest wages in Europe, Bulgaria isn't going to be the most obvious destination for foreign jobseekers. There are rather more opportunities for entrepreneurs, though, and the government is keen for foreigners to establish businesses as long as most of the staff are Bulgarian. Most foreigners working in Bulgaria are specialists employed by multinational companies. These jobs are most often arranged before arriving in the country.

If you intend to seek employment in Bulgaria, you will need a work visa; contact your local Bulgarian embassy for details. If you do find a temporary job, the pay is likely to be very low. Do it for the experience, rather than the money, and you won't be disappointed. Teaching English is one way to make some extra cash, but the market is often saturated. A helpful website is run by the **Sofia Echo** (www.sofiaecho.com), Bulgaria's main English-language newspaper.

If you arrange a job before you arrive, your employer should plough through the frightening mass of paperwork from relevant government departments and pay the various fees. If you land a job *after* you arrive, or you're considering setting up a business in Bulgaria, contact some expats for current advice about the plethora of required forms and fees.

Work Your Way Around the World by Susan Griffith provides practical advice on a wide range of issues. Its publisher, Vacation Work, has many other useful titles, including *The Directory of Summer Jobs Abroad,* edited by David Woodworth. *Working Holidays* by Ben Jupp, published by the Central Bureau for Educational Visits and Exchanges in London, is another good source, as is *Now Hiring! Jobs in Eastern Europe* by Clarke Canfield.

Transport

CONTENTS

GETTING THERE & AWAY

ENTERING THE COUNTRY

Now that Bulgaria is inside the EU, citizens of other EU nations, at least, will face minimal border formalities. Officially, there is still a fairly vague bureaucratic requirement that foreigners register with the police within 48 hours of arrival, but nobody really bothers with this communist-era leftover any more. At hotels, hostels, camping grounds and, sometimes, private homes, staff normally take details from your passport, fill out the registration form (in Cyrillic) and give you a copy. Theoretically, you must then show these forms to immigration officials when you leave. However, you're unlikely to be asked to produce these forms when you leave, but keep hold of a couple, just in case.

Delays are common at border crossings, and customs officials are generally an unfriendly and suspicious lot; expect to be questioned on what business you have coming to Bulgaria and where you intend staying.

Passport

There are no restrictions on any foreign passport-holders entering Bulgaria, other than the length of time they are allowed to stay. See p294 for details of stamps and visas.

THINGS CHANGE...

The information in this chapter is particularly vulnerable to change. Check directly with the airline or a travel agent to make sure you understand how a fare (and ticket you may buy) works and be aware of the security requirements for international travel. Shop carefully. The details given in this chapter should be regarded as pointers and are not a substitute for your own careful, up-to-date research.

AIR
Airports & Airlines

The Bulgarian national carrier is **Bulgaria Air** (airline code FB; ☎ 02-937 3370; www.air.bg), operating out of Sofia airport. It has only been in existence since the end of 2002 and has an unblemished safety record. In 2007 it merged with Hemus Air.

The main international airport is **Sofia airport** (☎ 02-937 2211; www.sofia-airport.bg), though some airlines also fly to/from **Varna** (www.varna-airport.bg) and, in summer, to **Burgas** (www.bourgas-airport.com). Plovdiv airport is only used by occasional charter flights, for example bringing some package holidaymakers to the ski resorts.

AIRLINES FLYING TO/FROM BULGARIA

Major airlines flying to/from Bulgaria include the following. All offices are in Sofia.

Aeroflot (airline code SU; ☎ 943 4489; www.aeroflot.ru) Hub: Moscow airport.

Aerosvit (airline code AEW; ☎ 980 7880; www.aerosvit.com) Hub: Kiev airport.

Air France (airline code AF; ☎ 939 7010; www.airfrance.com) Hub: Paris airport.

Alitalia (airline code AZ; ☎ 981 6702; www.alitalia.it) Hub: Rome Fiumicino airport.

Austrian Airlines (airline code OS; ☎ 980 2323; www.aua.com) Hub: Vienna airport.

British Airways (airline code BA; ☎ 954 7000; www.britishairways.com) Hub: London Heathrow airport.

Czech Airlines (airline code OK; ☎ 981 5408; www.csa.cz) Hub: Prague airport.

easyJet (airline code EZY; www.easyjet.com) Hub: London Gatwick airport.

LOT Polish Airlines (airline code LO; ☎ 987 4562; www.lot.com) Hub: Warsaw airport.
Lufthansa Airlines (airline code LH; ☎ 930 4242; www.lufthansa.com) Hub: Frankfurt airport.
Malev-Hungarian Airlines (airline code MA; ☎ 981 5091; www.malev.hu) Hub: Budapest airport.
Olympic Airlines (airline code OA; ☎ 981 4545; www.olympicairlines.com) Hub: Athens airport.
Turkish Airlines (airline code TK; ☎ 988 3596; www.turkishairlines.com) Hub: Ankara airport.
Wizz Air (airline code WZZ; ☎ 960 3888; www.wizzair .com) Hub: Budapest airport.

Tickets

It pays to shop around for your air tickets, and though they're no substitute for the personal attention and advice you'll get from a travel agent, you're likely to find some of the better deals online, either through the websites of the airlines themselves, or through one of the growing number of dedicated internet flight shops. The following websites are worth a look:

Bargain Bucket (www.bargain-bucket.com) Useful links to many other online travel agencies.
Bulgaria Flights (www.bulgariaflights.com) Comprehensive dedicated site with cheap flights from many European cities to/from Sofia and Varna.
Cheap Flights (www.cheapflights.co.uk)
ebookers (www.ebookers.com)
Flights.com (www.flights.com, www.tiss.com)

Lonelyplanet.com (www.lonelyplanet.com/bookings) Book flights and rail passes through our recommended travel partners.
Travelocity (www.travelocity.com)

Full-time students and people under 26 years (under 30 in some countries) have access to better deals than other travellers. You have to show a document proving your date of birth, or a valid International Student Identity Card (ISIC), when buying your ticket and boarding the plane.

INTERCONTINENTAL (RTW) TICKETS

If you're flying to Bulgaria from the other side of the world, then round-the-world tickets may be very good value. The best places to look for these are **Star Alliance** (www.staralliance.com) and **One World** (www.oneworld.com). These airline alliances will offer a limited period, usually one year, to travel around the world, stopping off at destinations of your choosing.

Tailor-made round-the-world tickets can also be assembled by travel agents, and there are numerous online agencies that offer good deals; see the following sections for some ideas.

Australia

There are no airlines that offer direct flights to Bulgaria from Australia, so you'll have to

---

CLIMATE CHANGE & TRAVEL

Climate change is a serious threat to the ecosystems that humans rely upon, and air travel is the fastest-growing contributor to the problem. Lonely Planet regards travel, overall, as a global benefit, but believes we all have a responsibility to limit our personal impact on global warming.

Flying & Climate Change

Pretty much every form of motorised travel generates CO2 (the main cause of human-induced climate change) but planes are far and away the worst offenders, not just because of the sheer distances they allow us to travel, but because they release greenhouse gases high into the atmosphere. The statistics are frightening: two people taking a return flight between Europe and the US will contribute as much to climate change as an average household's gas and electricity consumption over a whole year.

Carbon Offset Schemes

Climatecare.org and other websites use 'carbon calculators' that allow travellers to offset the level of greenhouse gases they are responsible for with financial contributions to sustainable travel schemes that reduce global warming.

Lonely Planet, together with Rough Guides and other concerned partners in the travel industry, supports the carbon offset scheme run by www.climatecare.org. Lonely Planet offsets all of its staff and author travel.

For more information check out our website: lonelyplanet.com.

travel via one or more stopovers in Europe, such as London, Moscow or Frankfurt. Prices vary considerably, depending on the time of year you're travelling and the airline you choose to fly with.

STA Travel (☎ 134 782; www.statravel.com.au) offers cheap tickets, and has offices in all major cities and on many university campuses. **Flight Centre** (☎ 13 31 33; www.flightcentre.com.au) also has dozens of offices throughout Australia. **Student Flights** (☎ 1800 046 462; www.studentflights.com.au) is an excellent source for discounted flights, including round-the-world options.

Canada

Again, there are no direct flights between any Canadian airports and Bulgaria; instead you will need to fly to, say, London, Frankfurt or Rome, and pick up a connection there. **Travel CUTS** (☎ toll-free 1-866 246 9762; www.travelcuts.com) is Canada's national student travel agency and has offices in all major cities. Online, try **Travelocity** (☎ toll-free 877-282 2925; www.travelocity.ca).

Continental Europe

BALKANS

Bulgaria Air has five flights a week to Bucharest (one-way/return around €165/260). Olympic Airlines departs regularly from Athens and Bulgaria Air flies five times a week to the Greek capital. Bulgaria Air has one weekly flight to Tirana. Also, Turkish Airlines has regular flights to Sofia from Ankara and Istanbul, with prices from around €200 one way, and Bulgaria Air flies from Sofia to Istanbul.

FRANCE

Bulgaria Air and Air France both fly between Sofia and Paris daily. **Voyages Wasteels** (☎ 01-55 82 32 33; www.wasteels.fr) has 65 branches across France. For online flight deals, try the website www.opodo.fr.

GERMANY

There are more flights to Bulgaria from Germany than from any other European country. Bulgaria Air flies five times a week from Sofia to Berlin and daily to Frankfurt. Lufthansa Airlines flies daily from Frankfurt and Munich. Wizz Air flies twice weekly to Sofia from Dortmund.

STA Travel (☎ 069-743 032 92; www.statravel.de) has branches in major cities across the country. For online offers, visit www.opodo.de.

ELSEWHERE IN EUROPE

Numerous flights to Sofia are available from elsewhere in Europe. Prices vary widely, so shop around for the best deal. From Rome, Bulgaria Air flies five times a week. Alitalia also flies regularly from Milan and Rome. Both Austrian Airlines and Bulgaria Air connect Vienna with Sofia at least three times a week. Austrian Airlines also flies daily from Vienna to Varna and three times a week to Burgas.

Bulgaria Air runs daily flights between Sofia and Amsterdam; it also flies six times a week to Brussels, three times a week to Prague, three times a week to Zurich, six times a week to Madrid and three times a week to Barcelona. In summer it also operates weekly services to Malaga, Palma de Mallorca and Alicante.

Czech Airlines flies from Prague to Sofia five days a week. From Poland, LOT Polish Airlines departs daily from Warsaw, while Wizz Air flies from Katowice and Warsaw to Burgas; Wizz also flies from Budapest to both Varna and Burgas. Malev-Hungarian Airlines has regular flights to Sofia and Varna from Budapest. Both Aeroflot and Bulgaria Air travel regularly between Sofia and Moscow all year, and both fly at least once a week between Varna and Moscow. Aerosvit has a regular service to/from Kiev and Sofia.

Further afield, Bulgaria Air also flies to Larnaca and Paphos (in Cyprus), Beirut, Tripoli and Tel Aviv.

New Zealand

As with Australia, you'll need to fly via another European country to get to Bulgaria from New Zealand. **Flight Centre** (☎ toll-free 0800 243 544; www.flightcentre.co.nz) has branches throughout the country, and **STA Travel** (☎ toll-free 0800 474 400; www.statravel.co.nz) also has offices in the major cities.

UK

Both British Airways and Bulgaria Air fly daily between London and Sofia. Bulgaria Air is normally the cheaper of the two, with one-way/return flights costing around £120/165. Bulgaria Air also flies to Manchester three times weekly and connects London with Varna three times a week in summer. Budget airline Wizz Air flies three or four times a week between London Luton and Sofia, and in summer also flies to Burgas. Another budget carrier, easyJet, flies regularly between London Gatwick and Sofia.

STA Travel (☎ 0871 230 0040; www.statravel.co.uk) has offices across the UK. It sells tickets to all travellers, but caters especially to students and travellers under 26 years. **Student Flights** (☎ 0870 499 4004; www.studentflights.co.uk) and **Global Village Travel** (☎ 0844 844 2541; www.globalvillage -travel.com) are also worth a look. Online ticket agencies such as www.opodo.co.uk and www .expedia.co.uk often have competitive prices.

USA

There are no direct flights between Bulgaria and anywhere in the USA. You can take a British Airways flight to London, and another on to Sofia, or fly to any major European city, such as Rome, Frankfurt or Paris, and catch a regular flight to Sofia. Prices are subject to change, so check around for the best deals available at the time you wish to travel.

Discount travel agents in the USA and Canada are known as consolidators. San Francisco is the ticket-consolidator capital of America, though some good deals can also be found in most major cities. **Cheap Tickets Inc** (www.cheaptickets.com) is an air consolidator offering discounts of up to 25%. Also worth checking out is the **International Association of Air Travel Couriers** (IAATC; www.courier.org).

STA Travel (☎ toll-free 800-781 4040; www.statravel .com) has offices in most major cities. For online quotes, try **Airbrokers** (www.airbrokers.com).

LAND
Border Crossings

There are several crossings into Romania, but if you're driving, use the toll bridge at Ruse or a land border further east. For public transport, the quickest crossing is again at Ruse, but the crossing at Vidin is a more scenic place to enter Romania. You can also cross at Kardam–Negru Voda (accessible from Dobrich) and at Durankulak–Vama Veche (accessible from Varna), but there's no public transport to these points.

The only crossings into Greece are at Kulata–Promahonas and at Svilengrad–Ormenion.

The main border crossing into Turkey is Malko Târnovo–Derekoy. From Kapitan–Andreevo, near Svilengrad, travellers can cross the Turkish border to Edirne.

For Macedonia, the main crossings are between Gyueshevo (near Kyustendil) and Deve Bair (just east of Kriva Palanka); Zlatarevo (west of Kulata) and Delčevo; and Stanke Lisichkovo (near Blagoevgrad) and Novo Selo.

Travelling into Serbia, the main crossings link Kalotina (near Dragoman) and Dimitrovgrad; Vrâshka Chuka (near Vidin) and Zajc; and Strezimirovtsi (near Pernik) and Klisura. Be careful when travelling overland by train because crime is not uncommon on services within Serbia.

See p294 for details of stamps and visas.

Bus

Buses travel to Bulgaria from destinations all over Europe, offering a possibly 'greener' mode of transport than flying, although the sheer distances involved if you're coming from Western Europe can be daunting. From Sofia, buses run as far as Berlin (170 lv), Paris (190 lv), Rome (180 lv) and even London (260 lv). German cities have especially good bus connections with Sofia. International buses also leave from Plovdiv, Varna, Burgas and Haskovo. You will have to get off the bus at the border and walk through customs to present your passport. Long delays can be expected. When travelling out of Bulgaria by bus, the cost of entry visas for the countries concerned are not included in the prices of the bus tickets.

Car & Motorcycle

Driving is a great way of getting around, but do note that foreign cars are prime targets for thieves. It's probably better to hire a car inside the country (see p302).

Train

Bulgarian State Railways (BDZh; www.bdz-rila.com) operates all international train services.

Greece
BUS

The main departure/arrival points for buses to/from Greece are Sofia and Plovdiv. From Sofia, buses go to Athens (around 100 lv, 12 to 14 hours) and Thessaloniki (around 50 lv, eight to nine hours). Buses from Plovdiv also head to these cities; expect journey times of roughly 22 and 14 hours respectively, and prices of around 95 lv and 55 lv.

TRAIN

The *Trans-Balkan Express* (trains 460 and 461) runs between Bucharest in Romania and Thessaloniki in Greece, passing through Ruse, Pleven, Sofia, Blagoevgrad and Sandanski.

From Sofia, the journey time to Thessaloniki is roughly 15 hours.

The Sofia–Thessaloniki service (trains 361 and 362) links the two cities every day in summer (15 June to 30 September), taking about nine to 10 hours. Seats start at around 30 lv. Trains also travel between Svilengrad and Thessaloniki (nine to 10 hours).

Macedonia

Buses to Macedonia leave from Sofia, Blagoevgrad and Kyustendil. Buses from Sofia go to Skopje (24 lv, six hours) and Ohrid (40 lv, nine hours); buses from Kyustendil also go to Skopje (20 lv , five hours), while from Blagoevgrad, a daily service runs to Bitola (30 lv, around eight hours).

No trains travel directly between Bulgaria and Macedonia. The only way to Skopje by train from Sofia is to get a connection in Niš.

Bulgaria Air has three flights a week between Sofia and Skopje (one-way/return around €90/165).

Romania
BUS

There are four daily minibuses running between Ruse and Bucharest (one-way/return 20/30 lv).

CAR & MOTORCYCLE

Crossing the bridge from Giurgiu in Romania into Ruse will incur a toll of €6 per car and €2 per motorbike or bicycle. A compulsory €10 ecological tax is also levied by the Bulgarian authorities. You are not permitted to cross at Giurgiu without transport.

TRAIN

Most visitors travel to/from Romania by train and either start from or go through Ruse.

The *Bulgaria Express* runs between Sofia and Moscow, via Bucharest and Kiev, daily. The journey from Sofia to Bucharest takes around 12 hours.

Every day in summer, a train from Burgas and another from Varna connects with a train leaving Ruse for Bucharest (15 hours), which carries on towards Prague.

Also, every day in summer the *Sofia–Saratov* service travels to Bucharest. It departs from Sofia at 3.20pm and travels via Pleven, Gorna Oryakhovitsa and Ruse, before arriving at Bucharest about 13 hours later. It departs from Bucharest at 1.40pm.

Fares from Sofia to Bucharest are around 45 lv one way.

The *Trans-Balkan Express* (see Greece, p299) travels daily between Thessaloniki and Bucharest, with onward connections to Budapest, via Sandanski, Sofia, Pleven and Ruse.

The *Bosfor* (trains 498 and 499) links Istanbul with the Romanian capital, passing through Stara Zagora, Veliko Târnovo and Ruse. The train leaves Istanbul at 10pm, Stara Zagora at 7.40am and Ruse at 1.30pm, reaching Bucharest at 4.30pm.

Serbia

Buses to Serbia leave from Sofia. There are frequent services to/from Belgrade, which cost about 40 lv and take eight hours.

The *Balkan Express* (see Turkey, below) leaves Sofia and travels through Niš to Belgrade. It takes about nine hours from Sofia and a one-way ticket costs about 55 lv. The Sofia–Belgrade service (trains 292 and 293) also links the two capitals.

Bulgaria Air has a regular service between Sofia and Belgrade.

Turkey
BUS

Several companies operate bus services to/from Turkey, departing from Sofia (Istanbul 45 lv, 18 hours), Burgas (Istanbul 35 lv, seven hours) and Varna (Istanbul 40 lv, 10 hours). From Plovdiv and Haskovo, expect to pay around 25 lv for a bus to Istanbul, with journey times of around eight to 10 hours. See the relevant sections in the regional chapters for more details.

TRAIN

The daily *Bosfor* (trains 498 and 499) between Istanbul and Bucharest also crosses through Bulgaria year-round. It leaves Ruse for Istanbul passing through Gorna Oryakhovitsa and Stara Zagora (see www.bdz-rila.com for current times), and takes around 16 hours.

The *Balkan Express* (trains 490 and 491) travels daily between Istanbul and Belgrade, with onward connections to Zagreb and Venice, via Bulgaria. It passes through Plovdiv and Sofia. The journey from Sofia to Istanbul takes about 15 to 17 hours and costs roughly 50 lv.

RIVER & SEA

International sea travel to/from Bulgaria is limited to commercial cargo vessels. The

UKR Shipping Company (www.ukrferry.com) runs cargo ships between Varna and Ilyichevsk in Ukraine, and also accepts individual passengers. Check the website for current arrangements and prices. There are daily ferry services across the Danube to Romania from the ports of Vidin (p261) and Silistra (p277).

TOURS

Most tourists visit Bulgaria on package tours, the vast majority either based on the Black Sea coast or in the skiing resorts, while others come on tours specialising in bird-watching or hiking. For details about tour operators in Bulgaria, see p304.

One of the few foreign companies that offers organised sightseeing holidays to and around Bulgaria is the London-based **Exodus** (☎ 0845-863 9600; www.exodus.co.uk). Its nine-day 'Rodopi Mountains' tour costs around £600 per person, including flights from London. Check the website for exact prices, which vary through the year, and for other tours.

Balkan Holidays (www.balkanholidays.co.uk) is a leading specialist company offering package skiing and beach holidays in Bulgaria. A week in Golden Sands (Zlatni Pyasâtsi; p247) in July costs from around £300 per person, including the flight from London.

Inghams (☎ 020-8780 4433; www.inghams.co.uk) sells skiing breaks, offering a week in Bansko in January, including flights from the UK, from around £270 per person.

GETTING AROUND

Bulgaria is relatively easy to get around and a wide range of trains, buses and minibuses are available. To explore the country more fully, you might want to hire a car inside the country.

AIR

Bulgaria is reasonably compact, and bus and train services are reliable and cheap, but if an eight-hour bus journey from Sofia to the coast doesn't appeal, flying may be the answer.

Bulgaria Air (p296) operates the two domestic routes, flying between Sofia and Varna and Sofia and Burgas.

BICYCLE

Generally, cycling isn't the most practical (or safest) way of getting about in urban or built-up areas, and accidents involving cyclists are common on the busy roads of Sofia. Many roads are in poor condition, some major roads are always choked with traffic and bikes aren't allowed on highways. On the other hand, traffic is light along routes between villages and long-distance buses and trains will carry your bike for an extra 2 lv or so. Cycling is a more attractive option in the Black Sea resorts, where there will be plenty of places renting out bikes. Spare parts are available in cities and major towns, but it's better to bring your own. Mountain bikes are a more attractive option in the countryside, and are sporadically available for rent. There are several specific mountain-bike routes (see p80).

BUS

Buses link all cities and major towns and connect villages with the nearest transport hub. In some places, buses are run by the government. These buses are old, uncomfortable (when compared with city buses) and slow. Newer, quicker and more commodious private buses often operate in larger towns and cities, and normally cost little more than the fare on a ramshackle public bus.

There are also numerous private companies running services all across the country, the biggest of which are **Etap-Grup** (☎ 02-945 3939; www.etapgroup.com) and **Biomet** (☎ 02-963 1366; www.biomet-bg.com), which operate from Sofia and link up with most major towns and cities.

All timetables are listed (in Cyrillic) inside the bus stations and all buses have destination signs (in Cyrillic) in the front window.

For a public bus, you normally buy a ticket from the counter marked *kasa* (каса) inside the station. This way you're guaranteed a seat and you know the correct departure time and platform number. However, in some cases the cashier will tell you to buy a ticket on the bus.

Costs

Bus travel in Bulgaria is very cheap by Western standards, with a cross-country ticket from Sofia to Varna or Burgas costing around 20 lv to 25 lv, and a ticket from the capital to Sandanski in the far south just 8 lv.

Reservations

Tickets for public buses can rarely be booked in advance but seats on private buses can be reserved one or more days in advance. However, except for long-distance services at peak times, eg between Sofia and Varna in August, there's no need to book any bus more than a few hours ahead. In fact, if you arrive at the bus stop or station about 30 minutes before departure, you'll normally get a ticket for the bus you want.

CAR & MOTORCYCLE

Probably the best way to travel around Bulgaria – especially when visiting remote villages, monasteries and national parks – is to hire a car (or motorbike). However, there's no point hiring a car and then parking it for three days while you explore Plovdiv or Varna on foot, and it can be difficult driving around any city, particularly Sofia.

Automobile Associations

The **Union of Bulgarian Motorists** (Map p88; ☎ 02-935 7935; www.uab.org; pl Positano 3, Sofia) offers a 24-hour 'alarm centre for road assistance service' (☎ 02-980 3308) and has some helpful basic information on its website.

Bring Your Own Vehicle

If you do decide to drive your own car into Bulgaria, remember that car theft is very common and foreign cars especially are an immediate target. You will need all the original registration and ownership documents, or your vehicle may be impounded by the police. Before you can drive on motorways, you will need to purchase and display a 'vignette' in your vehicle. For a car, this costs €5/13 for one week/one month. Vignettes can be bought at border crossings when first entering the country, where they are priced in euros, or at post offices once inside Bulgaria, where you will have to pay in leva (one week/one month 10/25 lv). Foreign drivers must state which border crossing they plan to use when leaving.

Driving Licence

Drivers of private and rented cars (and motor-cycles) must carry registration papers. Your driving licence from home is valid in Bulgaria, so an international driving licence isn't necessary (but it may be useful if you're driving elsewhere in Eastern Europe).

Fuel

Petrol is available in unleaded super 95 and unleaded super 98, as well as diesel and LPG. Major brands such as Shell and OMV are often preferred by local drivers because

water has been known to make its way into other brands.

Petrol stations are found roughly every 15km to 20km along the highways, and are mostly open from 5am to 10pm. Some near Sofia and other big cities are open 24 hours.

Hire

To rent a car in Bulgaria you must be at least 21 years of age and have had a licence for at least one year. Rental outlets can be found all over Bulgaria, but the biggest choice is in Sofia. Prices start at around €30 per day, though international companies such as Avis and Hertz charge more. All major credit cards are normally accepted.

Some of the more reliable agencies that have offices in the capital and elsewhere:

Avis (☎ 02-945 9224; www.avis.bg)
Budget (☎ 02-937 3388; www.budget.bg)
Europcar (☎ 02-931 6000; www.europcar.bg)
Hertz (☎ 02-945 9217; office@hertz.autotechnica.bg)
Tany 97 (☎ 02-970 8500; www.tany97.bg)
Tourist Service (☎ 02-981 7253; www.tourist -service.com)

There are comparatively few places where you can rent a motorbike; one of the better places is **Motoroads** (off Map p84; ☎ 0885370298; www.moto roads.com; office 1, bl 279, Mladost 2, Sofia 1799) in Sofia. It offers a range of motorbikes, costing from €40 per day, plus a deposit of €300.

Insurance

Third-party 'liability insurance' is compulsory, and can be purchased at any Bulgarian border. Buying comprehensive insurance in your home country is a better idea (but make sure it's valid in Bulgaria). The Green (or Blue) Card – a routine extension of domestic motor insurance to cover most European countries – is valid in Bulgaria.

Road Conditions

Travelling around Bulgaria by private car or motorcycle is not as relaxing as it may be in Western Europe. Other than a few impressive highways, road conditions are generally taxing. Drivers must cope with potholes, roads under reconstruction, slow-moving vehicles, horses and carts and often erratic driving by other motorists.

You should never rely completely on road signs. They're often frustratingly ambiguous, or nonexistent, and most are written in

ROAD DISTANCES (KM)

	Blagoevgrad	Burgas	Dobrich	Gabrovo	Haskovo	Kulata	Kyustendil	Lovech	Pleven	Plovdiv	Ruse	Shumen	Silistra	Sliven	Smolyan	Sofia	Stara Zagora	Varna	Veliko Tărnovo	Vidin	Vratsa
Blagoevgrad	---																				
Burgas	464	---																			
Dobrich	613	185	---																		
Gabrovo	321	234	317	---																	
Haskovo	272	213	388	141	---																
Kulata	82	520	695	403	346	---															
Kyustendil	72	462	602	310	278	154	---														
Lovech	268	299	356	65	206	350	257	---													
Pleven	275	334	347	100	241	357	264	35	---												
Plovdiv	194	270	455	146	78	260	200	159	194	---											
Ruse	421	263	212	152	293	503	410	150	146	298	---										
Shumen	482	148	133	186	302	564	471	225	219	283	115	---									
Silistra	543	262	92	274	374	619	525	272	268	396	122	113	---								
Sliven	353	114	299	130	132	419	359	193	228	159	216	135	248	---							
Smolyan	244	357	541	241	141	207	302	261	296	102	393	356	474	232	---						
Sofia	101	385	512	220	234	183	90	167	174	156	320	381	443	279	258	---					
Stara Zagora	282	182	367	80	61	348	288	145	180	88	232	218	355	71	161	231	---				
Varna	571	134	51	274	371	652	559	313	304	398	203	90	143	248	477	469	316	---			
Veliko Tărnovo	342	224	271	46	187	424	331	85	120	192	106	140	228	110	287	241	126	228	---		
Vidin	300	538	558	308	433	382	289	243	208	355	356	429	478	429	457	199	388	515	328	---	
Vratsa	217	406	451	172	316	299	206	119	108	237	254	329	376	300	329	116	251	421	193	126	---

TRANSPORT

Cyrillic (except around major cities, along the Black Sea coast and at the borders). It is imperative that you buy an accurate map and be able to read Cyrillic.

Road Hazards

Vehicle security is a concern so take the usual precautions against car theft. If possible, use a guarded car park or hotel car park, or park under a street light. Never leave any valuables in the car.

And please take care as Bulgaria's roads are among the most dangerous in Europe; over 200 people lost their lives on the country's roads in the first few months of 2007 alone, and almost 2000 were injured. The worst time is the holiday season (July to September), with drink-driving, speeding and poor road conditions contributing to accidents. Sofia and roads along the Black Sea coast can be particularly nerve-wracking.

Road Rules

Although road signs are rare, the official speed limits for cars are 50km/h in built-up areas, 90km/h on main roads and 130km/h on motorways. Speed limits for motorcycles, trucks and buses are 50km/h in built-up areas and 80/100km/h on main roads/motorways. Traffic police have recently been given extra powers to flag down drivers for spot inspections, and fines have been increased. You can be fined up to 250 lv for speeding. Drivers and passengers in the front must wear seat belts, and motorcyclists must wear helmets. The blood-alcohol limit is 0.05% and traffic police are very unforgiving about drink-driving. Although the situation has improved over recent years, the Bulgarian traffic police have a reputation for corruption, and for being keen on stopping nice, expensive foreign cars. If you are fined, insist on receiving a proper receipt.

If you have an accident, you *must* wait with your vehicle and have someone call the local traffic police (see inside front cover).

HITCHING

Hitching is never entirely safe in any country in the world and we don't recommend it. Travellers who decide to hitch should understand that they are taking a small but potentially

TRANSPORT

serious risk. People who do choose to hitch will be safer if they travel in pairs and let someone know where they're planning to go.

Hitchhiking is officially illegal in Bulgaria, but people still do it, and hitching in rural Bulgaria may be preferable to being restricted by infrequent public transport (but travel will tend to be in fits and starts because many cars often only travel to the next village). The upsurge in crime over the last few years has dissuaded some Bulgarians from offering lifts to hitchhikers. Bulgaria's borders are not particularly 'user friendly', so hitching across them is not recommended.

LOCAL TRANSPORT
Minibus
Private and public minibuses ply routes between smaller villages, eg along the Black Sea coast and between urban centres and ski resorts in winter. Tickets for minibuses cost roughly the same as public buses but are usually bought from the driver (though always check this first at the counter inside the bus station). If you can choose between a public bus and minibus, take the latter because it's quicker, normally more comfortable and standing is rarely allowed. Destinations (in Cyrillic) and, often, departure times are indicated on the front window. Most minibuses leave from inside, or very close to, the major public bus station. In Sofia, minibuses called *marshroutki* run between the city centre and the suburbs, acting like shared taxis (see p107).

Public Transport
All cities and major towns have buses, but they tend to be overcrowded and uncomfortably hot in summer. New privately run minibuses operate in some cities, such as Sofia. The few places with useful bus and minibus routes are detailed in the relevant Getting Around sections throughout this book, but you're almost always better off using a taxi (see the next section). Bus tickets are regularly checked by conductors, especially in Sofia. Don't forget to buy an extra ticket for each piece of large luggage (ie suitcase or backpack). Major cities also have trams and trolleybuses (a cross between a tram and bus) and Sofia has a modern metro system.

Taxi
Taxis, which must be painted yellow and equipped with working meters, can be flagged down on most streets in every city and town throughout Bulgaria. They can be very cheap, but rates do vary enormously, so it pays to shop around before jumping in. Taxis can be chartered for longer trips at negotiable rates, which you can approximate by working out the distance and taxi rate per kilometre, plus waiting time.

All drivers must clearly display their rates on the taxi's windows. These rates are divided into three or four lines:

- The first line lists the rate per kilometre from 6am to 10pm (about 0.50 lv per kilometre is average), and the night-time rate (sometimes the same, but often about 10% more).
- The second lists, if applicable, the call-out fee of about 0.50 lv if you preorder a taxi (almost never necessary).
- The third (or second-last) lists the starting fee (0.30 lv to 0.50 lv).
- The fourth (last) lists the cost for waiting per minute (0.20 lv to 0.30 lv).

Some drivers try to overcharge unwary foreigners by claiming the meter 'doesn't work' (it must work by law) or offering a flat fare (which will always be at least double the proper metered fare). Dishonest drivers congregate outside airports, train and bus stations and city centres in Sofia, Plovdiv, Varna, Burgas and in the resorts along the Black Sea coast.

TOURS
As more and more independent foreign tourists 'discover' Bulgaria, new travel agencies have emerged to offer activity and special-interest tours. Some will just bus you off on the well-trodden paths to Rila Monastery and the like, and large groups are normally required, while others offer a more personal service. For some overseas-based companies that offer tours, see p301.

If you're pressed for time or find getting around a little difficult, an organised tour is worth considering. Even a one-day tour can be worthwhile, especially to remote monasteries and villages. Travel agencies and tourist offices that offer local tours are listed in the regional chapters of this book. Plenty of agencies at the Black Sea resorts of Albena, Sunny Beach (Slânchev Bryag) and Golden Sands (Zlatni Pyasâtsi) offer tours, but to avoid unnecessary expense, check out the local transport before booking a pricey 'excursion' to the nearest town.

Enterprising Bulgarian travel agencies that offer interesting tours around Bulgaria are surprisingly few and far between but you could try the following companies:

Motoroads (off Map p84; ☎ 0885370298; www.moto roads.com; office 1, bl 279, Mladost 2, Sofia 1799) Offers a wide choice of organised motorbike tours round the country.

Neophron (☎ 052-650 230, www.neophron.com; PO Box 492, Varna) Runs guided bird-watching trips on the coast and in the mountains, as well as other trips for those interested in botany or wild animals. It's run by professional ornithologists.

Odysseia-In Travel Agency (Map p88; ☎ 02-989 0538; www.odysseia-in.com; 1st fl, bul Stamboliyski 20-V, Sofia) Odysseia-In can book you on hiking, snow-shoeing, caving, bird-watching, botany or numerous other trips across the country. It can also book rooms in over 100 mountain huts, monasteries and village homes.

Zig Zag Holidays (Map p88; ☎ 02-980 5102; www.zigzagbg .com; bul Stamboliyski 20-V, Sofia) Offers environmentally sensitive tours and tailor-made outdoor activities, including hiking, climbing, caving and nature trips. Contact them for prices.

TRAIN

Bâlgarski Dârzhavni Zheleznitsi (БДЖ) – the **Bulgarian State Railways** (BDZh; ☎ 02-931 1111; www .bdz.bg) – boasts an impressive 4278km of tracks across the country, linking most sizable towns and cities, although some are on a spur track and only connected to a major railway line by infrequent services. Apart from on a couple of lines, including Sofia–Kyustendil and Sofia–Plovdiv, trains tend to be antiquated and shabby, and journey times are slow. Buses are normally quicker, more comfortable and more frequent, especially between cities and major towns, although on the plus side, you'll have more room in a train compartment, and the scenery is likely to be more rewarding.

Trains are classified as *ekspresen* (express), *bârz* (fast) or *pâtnicheski* (slow passenger). Unless you absolutely thrive on train travel, you want to visit a smaller village or you're travelling on a tight budget, use a fast or express train.

Two of the most spectacular train trips are along Iskâr Gorge, from Sofia to Mezdra, and on the narrow-gauge track between Septemvri and Bansko. Railway buffs often go on these trips for no other reason than the journey itself.

TRANSPORT

BULGARIAN RAILWAYS

Schematic Map of Railway Connections
— Express Train Lines
⊢–•–⊣ Fast Train Lines
⊦···⊦···⊦ Slow Passenger Train Lines

Train travel in Bulgaria is a normally safe and enjoyable experience, but there have been reports of robberies, pickpocketing and minor annoyances (such as drunkenness) on some cross-border routes, such as to/from Turkey or Serbia. If you are travelling late at night, sit with other passengers rather than in an empty compartment, and if you are making a long overnight trip across the border, try booking a bed in a couchette.

Classes

First-class compartments seat six people, eight are crammed into 2nd class, and the intercity express has individual seats in an open carriage. Sleepers and couchettes are available between Sofia and Burgas and Varna but must be booked in advance. Fares for 1st class are around 25% higher than for 2nd class. The carriages won't be any cleaner, but it's always worth paying the extra just to have a bit more space.

Costs

Although prices have risen in recent years, train travel within Bulgaria is still cheap by Western standards, with a cross-country trip between Sofia and Varna costing approximately 22 lv (2nd class). A 1st-class ticket on this route costs 27 lv, probably the most you'd ever pay for a seat on a domestic train service in Bulgaria. If you're travelling in a group (three or more people) you may get a slight discount.

Reservations

For frequent train services between the main cities there is rarely a problem if you simply turn up at the station and purchase a ticket for the next train (but be careful to allow at least 30 minutes to queue up). Advance tickets are

---

TICKETS

All tickets are printed in Cyrillic. Other than the place of departure and destination, tickets also contain other important details:

Клас – *klas* – '1' (1st class) or '2' (2nd class)

Категория – *kategoriya* – type of train, ie T (express), 255 (fast) or G (slow passenger)

Влак – *vlak* – train number

Час – *chas* – departure time

Дата – *data* – date of departure

Вагон – *vagon* – carriage number

Място – *myasto* – seat number

---

sometimes advisable on train services such as the intercity express to the Black Sea during a summer weekend. Advance tickets can be bought at specific counters within larger train stations and at Rila Bureaux in cities and major towns. Staff at Rila are normally far more helpful, knowledgeable and likely to speak English than anyone at a train station, so it's best to deal with Rila for advice, schedules and advance tickets.

Train Passes

BDZh is part of the InterRail system, and a one-country pass is available, but given the low cost of train travel in Bulgaria, this is unlikely to be cost-effective. These passes have to be bought outside the country. City Star rail passes are also valid in Bulgaria, for travel to various other European countries. Finally, Rail Plus cards offer 25% discounts on international routes for those under 26 (Rail Plus 26M) or over 60 (Rail Plus S). Cards cost 30 lv. For more details, visit www.bdz-rila.com.

Health

CONTENTS

Travel health depends on your predeparture preparations, your daily care while travelling and how you handle any medical problem that does develop. Bulgaria will not provide any major challenges to visitors' health.

BEFORE YOU GO

Prevention is the key to staying healthy while abroad. A little planning before departure, particularly for pre-existing illnesses or conditions, will save trouble later. Carry a spare pair of contact lenses and glasses, and take your optical prescription with you. Bring extra medications in their original, clearly labelled, containers. A signed and dated letter from your physician describing your medical conditions and medications, including generic names, is also a good idea. If carrying syringes or needles, be sure to have a physician's letter documenting their medical necessity.

INSURANCE

Citizens of other European Economic Area countries (EU countries plus Norway, Iceland and Liechtenstein) should pick up a European Health Insurance Card (EHIC) before they travel, which entitles you to the same immediate medical treatment available to Bulgarian nationals. However, you should also consider buying a policy that covers you for the worst possible scenario, such as an accident requiring an emergency flight home.

INTERNET RESOURCES

The World Health Organisation's publication *International Travel and Health* is revised annually and is available online at www.who .int/ith/. Other useful websites include:

www.ageconcern.org.uk Advice on travel for the elderly.
www.fitfortravel.scot.nhs.uk General travel advice for the layperson.
www.mariestopes.org.uk Providing information on women's health and contraception.
www.mdtravelhealth.com Travel health recommendations for every country; updated daily.

IN BULGARIA

AVAILABILITY OF HEALTH CARE

Every city and major town has a government hospital of an acceptable – albeit not excellent – standard, as well as more up-to-date private clinics. Smaller towns and villages may have a clinic, but for serious complaints you should travel to a larger town or ask your embassy /consulate to recommend a hospital, clinic, doctor or dentist. Dental clinics are easy to find in big cities and *apteka* (pharmacies) are common. Doctors at *bolnitsa* (government hospitals) are well trained and most speak English and/or German. However, equipment can be lacking and outdated. Staff at the more expensive *poliklinika* (private clinics), such as in Sofia (p85), are more likely to be fluent in English and German, and equipment is normally of a higher standard.

INFECTIOUS DISEASES
Tickborne Encephalitis

This is spread by tick bites. It is a serious infection of the brain and vaccination is advised for those in risk areas who are unable to avoid tick bites (such as campers, forestry workers and walkers). Two doses of vaccine will give a year's protection, three doses up to three years'.

Typhoid & Hepatitis A

These are spread through contaminated food (particularly shellfish) and water. Typhoid can cause septicaemia; Hepatitis A causes liver inflammation and jaundice. Neither is usually fatal but recovery can be prolonged. Hepatitis A and typhoid vaccines can be given as a single-dose vaccine, Hepatyrix or Viatim.

Rabies

This is a potential concern considering the number of stray dogs running around Bulgaria. If bitten, seek medical attention immediately (most main hospitals will have a rabies clinic), but don't panic; while rabies is transmitted via the animal's saliva, the rabies virus is present in saliva only during the final stages of the disease in the animal, often only in the last week of the dog's life. It is therefore a relatively rarely transmitted disease. Still, do not take any chances and seek medical attention. Any bite, scratch or even lick from an unknown animal should be cleaned immediately and thoroughly. Scrub with soap and running water, and then apply alcohol or iodine solution.

TRAVELLER'S DIARRHOEA

If you develop diarrhoea, be sure to drink plenty of fluids, preferably an oral rehydration solution (eg Dioralyte). A few loose stools don't require treatment, but if you start having more than four or five stools a day, you should start taking an antibiotic (usually a quinolone drug) and an antidiarrhoeal agent (such as loperamide). If diarrhoea is bloody, persists for more than 72 hours or is accompanied by fever, shaking, chills or severe abdominal pain, you should seek medical attention.

ENVIRONMENTAL HAZARDS
Air Pollution

Due to the large number of old, poorly maintained vehicles rattling around the roads in Bulgaria, the build up of traffic fumes can be unpleasant in Sofia and other big cities, and may affect those with respiratory problems. Thankfully, it's easy enough to escape the urban sprawl and get some fresh air in the country. Cigarette smoke, however, is harder to avoid. Bulgarians are notorious chainsmokers, and restaurants and bars can get particularly fuggy.

Hypothermia & Frostbite

Proper preparation will reduce the risk of getting hypothermia. Even on a hot day in the mountains, the weather can change rapidly, so carry waterproof garments and warm layers, and inform others of your route.

Acute hypothermia follows a sudden drop of temperature over a short time. Chronic hypothermia is caused by a gradual loss of temperature over hours.

Hypothermia starts with shivering, loss of judgment and clumsiness. Unless rewarming occurs, the sufferer deteriorates into apathy, confusion and coma. Prevent further heat loss by seeking shelter, warm dry clothing, hot sweet drinks and shared body warmth.

Frostbite is caused by freezing and subsequent damage to bodily extremities. It is dependent on wind-chill, temperature and length of exposure. Frostbite starts as frostnip (white, numb areas of skin) from which complete recovery is expected with rewarming. As frostbite develops, the skin blisters and then becomes black. Adequate clothing, staying dry, keeping well hydrated and ensuring adequate calorie intake best prevent frostbite. Treatment involves rapid rewarming.

Water

Tap water is generally considered safe to drink in all major towns and cities, although it might not taste particularly nice. Caution should be taken in smaller villages, and if staying at older or more remote hotels where the water pipes may be as old as the buildings themselves. The fountains in town parks and outside monasteries and churches provide an ideal source of drinkable water. *Cheshma* (water spouts), often found along main roads, also offer constant supplies of fresh, delicious and safe water.

If in doubt, purify water (with filters, iodine or chlorine) or boil it. At high altitude water boils at a lower temperature, so germs are less likely to be killed. Boil it for longer in these environments.

Easiest, and safest, of all, is to simply buy bottled water, which is inexpensive and sold everywhere. Fill the empty bottles up at public fountains to avoid unnecessary waste.

WOMEN'S HEALTH

Emotional stress, exhaustion and travelling through different time zones can all contribute to an upset in the menstrual pattern. If using oral contraceptives, remember some antibiotics, diarrhoea and vomiting can stop the pill from working and lead to the risk of pregnancy – remember to take condoms with you just in case. Time zones, gastrointestinal upsets and antibiotics do not affect injectable contraceptives. Travelling during pregnancy is usually possible, but always consult your doctor before planning your trip. The most risky times for travel are during the first 12 weeks of pregnancy and after 30 weeks.

Language

CONTENTS

THE BULGARIAN CYRILLIC ALPHABET

Cyrillic	Roman	Pronunciation
А а	a/uh	as in 'father'; as the 'a' in 'ago' in stressed syllables
Б б	b	as in 'boy'
В в	v	as in 'vice'
Г г	g	as in 'go'
Д д	d	as in 'door'
Е е	e	as in 'bet'
Ж ж	zh	as the 's' in 'pleasure'
З з	z	as in 'zoo'
И и	ee	as in 'feet'
Й й	y	as in 'yes'
К к	k	as in 'king'
Л л	l	as in 'let'
М м	m	as in 'met'
Н н	n	as in 'net'
О о	o	as in 'pot'
П п	p	as in 'pen'
Р р	r	like the trilled Scottish 'r'
С с	s	as in 'sit'
Т т	t	as in 'tip'
У у	oo	as in 'boot'
Ф ф	f	as in 'foot'
Х х	h	as breathy sound, as in 'hard'
Ц ц	ts	as in 'lets'
Ч ч	ch	as in 'chip'
Ш ш	sh	as in 'ship'
Щ щ	sht	as the '-shed' in 'pushed'
Ъ ъ	uh	a neutral vowel sound, roughly resembles the 'a' in 'ago'
Ю ю	yu	as the word 'you' but shorter
Я я	ya	as in 'yard' but shorter

Modern Bulgarian belongs to the group of South Slavonic languages. It's the descendant of the oldest Slavonic literary language, Old Bulgarian (also called Old Slavic or Old Church Slavonic). Originally formulated in connection with the missionary work of the Salonica brothers, Cyril (after whom the Cyrillic script he created is named) and Methodius, during the 9th century AD, Old Bulgarian flourished in the Bulgarian lands for several centuries, giving rise to an original literary and cultural tradition that continues to thrive.

Today Bulgarian is the native language of more than seven million speakers who make up the Slavonic ethnic majority of the Republic of Bulgaria. It is the second language of several linguistic minorities in the country, including speakers of Turkish, Romany, Armenian, Greek and Romanian. While Contemporary Standard Bulgarian is the official language of the Republic of Bulgaria, historical and social factors have given rise to regional varieties in neighbouring areas. In Bulgaria itself, a number of regional dialects are common, and Bulgarian is spoken by sizable groups in the former USSR, Canada, Argentina and in some other countries.

Bulgarian has affinities with all the other Slavonic languages, and is closely related to Russian. Unlike these languages, however, Modern Bulgarian has lost its grammatical case endings, making it a lot easier for English speakers to put together gramatically correct phrases.

Students in Bulgaria must learn at least one foreign language – either English, French, German or Russian – from an early age; many now opt for English. Older Bulgarians may speak Russian because it was a required school subject during the communist era, and a few others may also speak French or German. These days, young people, tourism workers and business people are more likely to speak English as a second language, although German is usually preferred in the Black Sea resorts.

LANGUAGE

It's essential to learn the Cyrillic alphabet, both the standard print (see p309) and written versions, because some letters are completely different and occasionally used interchangeably. You'll come across what might be called 'handwritten style' Cyrillic in printed form too, which can often cause confusion. In this popular style, the letter д ('d' sound) is represented by what looks like a small Latin 'g', the letter т ('t' sound) is represented by what looks like a small 'm' and the letter л ('l' sound) looks like an upside-down 'v'.

In this language guide we use the polite form unless otherwise indicated by the abbreviation 'inf' (informal) in brackets. If you'd like a more comprehensive language guide, get a copy of Lonely Planet's *Bulgarian Phrasebook*. Bilingual dictionaries in Bulgarian with English, German or French are also available from most bookshops throughout the country.

Bulgarians are generally friendly and very approachable. If you don't have the time to learn the intricacies of local etiquette and body language, rest assured that the use of the polite forms, accompanied by a friendly smile, will take you a long way in Bulgaria.

PRONUNCIATION

To a great extent Bulgarian spelling (unlike English) has an almost one-to-one letter-sound relationship. Most Bulgarian sounds occur in English as well – with a little practice you'll have no problem making yourself understood. The Bulgarian Cyrillic Alphabet chart on p309 shows the Roman letters we use to represent Cyrillic, and their approximate pronunciation.

ACCOMMODATION

Where's a/an ...?

Къде има ...?	kuh·*de ee*·ma ...
accommodation agency	
квартирно бюро	kvar·*teer*·no byoo·*ro*
camping ground	
къмпинг	*kuhm*·peeng
guesthouse	
пансион	pan·see·*on*
hotel	
хотел	ho·*tel*
private room	
частна квартира	*chast*·na kvar·*tee*·ra
youth hostel	
хостел	*hos*·tel

Do you have a ... room?

Има ли стая ...?	*ee*·ma lee *sta*·ya ...
single	
с едно единично легло	s ed·*no* e·dee·*neech*·no leg·*lo*
double	
с едно двойно легло	s ed·*no dvoy*·no leg·*lo*
twin	
с две легла	s dve leg·*la*

How much is it per ...?

Колко е на ...?	*kol*·ko e na ...
night	
вечер	*ve*·cher
person	
човек	cho·*vek*

Can I pay by ...?

Мога ли да платя с ...?	*mo*·guh lee da plat·*yuh* s ...
credit card	
кредитна карта	*kre*·deet·na *kar*·ta
travellers cheque	
пътнически чек	puht·*nee*·ches·kee chek

What's the address?

Какъв е адресът?
ka·*kuhv* e a·*dre*·suht

I'd like to book a room, please.

Искам да взема една стая, моля.
ees·kam da *vze*·muh ed·*na sta*·ya *mol*·yuh

I have a reservation.

Имам резервация.
ee·mam re·zer·*va*·tsee·ya

For (three) nights/weeks.

За (три) нощи/седмици.
za (tree) *nosh*·tee/*sed*·mee·tsee

From (2 July) to (6 July).

От (втори юли) до (шести юли).
ot (*vto*·ree *yoo*·lee) do (*shes*·tee *yoo*·lee)

May I see it?

Мога ли да я видя?
mo·guh lee da ya *veed*·yuh

I'll take it.

Ще я взема.
shte ya *vze*·muh

I'm leaving now.

Тръгвам сега.
truhg·vam se·*ga*

Is breakfast included?

Включена ли е закуската?
vklyoo·che·na lee e za·*koos*·ka·ta

Is there hot water all day?

Има ли топла вода през целия ден?
ee·ma lee *top*·la vo·*da* prez *tse*·lee·yuh den

There's no hot water.

Няма топла вода.
nya·ma *top*·la vo·*da*

Is the water drinkable?
Водата може ли да се пие?
vo·*da*·ta *mo*·zhe lee da se *pee*·e

Can I use the ...?
Мога ли да   *mo*·guh lee da
използвам ...?   eez·*polz*·vam ...
  internet
  Интернета   *een*·ter·ne·tuh
  kitchen
  кухнята   *kooh*·nya·ta
  laundry
  пералнята   pe·*ral*·nya·ta
  telephone
  телефона   te·le·*fo*·nuh

CONVERSATION & ESSENTIALS
Hello.
Здравейте. (pol)   zdra·*vey*·te
Hi.
Здравей. (inf)   zdra·*vey*
Good morning.
Добро утро.   dob·*ro oot*·ro
Good day/afternoon.
Добър ден.   *do*·buhr den
Good evening.
Добър вечер.   *do*·buhr *ve*·cher
Goodbye.
Довиждане.   do·*veezh*·da·ne
Bye.
Чао. (inf)   *cha*·o
See you later.
До скоро виждане.   do *sko*·ro *veezh*·da·ne
Good night.
Лека нощ.   *le*·ka nosht
Yes.
Да.   da
No.
Не.   ne
Please.
Моля.   *mol*·yuh
Thank you (very much).
(Много) Благодаря.   (*mno*·go) bla·go·dar·*yuh*
You're welcome.
Няма защо.   *nya*·ma zash·*to*
Sorry.
Съжалявам.   suh·zhal·*ya*·vam
Excuse me. (to get past)
Извинете.   eez·vee·*ne*·te
Excuse me. (to get attention, or before a request)
Моля.   *mol*·ya
How are you?
Как сте/си? (pol/inf) kak ste/see
Fine, thanks. And you?
Добре, благодаря.   dob·*re* bla·go·dar·*yuh*
А вие?   a *vee*·e

SIGNS	
Свободни Стаи	Rooms Available
Квартири	Quarters (rooms in private houses)
Отворено	Open
Затворено	Closed
Забранено	Prohibited
Полицейско Управление	Police Station
Тоалетни	Toilets/WC
Мъже (M)	Men
Жени (Ж)	Women

What's your name?
Как се казвате/? (pol) kak se *kaz*·va·te/*kaz*·vash
Как се казваш? (inf)   kak se *kaz*·va·te/*kaz*·vash
My name's ...
Казвам се ...   *kaz*·vam se ...
I'm pleased to meet you.
Приятно ми е да се   pree·*yat*·no mee e da se
запозна с вас.   za·poz·*na*·yuh s vas
Where are you from?
Откъде сте?   ot·kuh·*de* ste
I'm from ...
Аз съм от ...   az suhm ot ...
I (don't) like ...
(Не) Харесвам ...   (ne) ha·*res*·vam ...

Local Talk
Hey!   Хей!   hey
Great!   Супер!   *soo*·per
Sure.   Естествено.   es·*test*·ve·no
Maybe.   Може би.   *mo*·zhe bee
No way!   Няма начин!   *nya*·ma na·*cheen*
Just a minute. Един момент. e·*deen* mo·*ment*
Just joking. Шегувам се.   she·*goo*·vam se
It's OK.   Добре.   do·*bre*
No problem.   Няма проблем. *nya*·ma prob·*lem*

DIRECTIONS
Where can I find a/the ...?
Къде се намира ...?
kuh·*de* se na·*mee*·ra ...?
Where's a/the ...?
Къде има ...?
kuh·*de* ee·ma ...
How far is it?
На какво растояние е?
na kak·*vo* ras·to·*ya*·nee·e e
How do I get there?
Как да стигна дотам?
kak da *steeg*·nuh do·*tam*
Can you show me (on the map)?
Можете ли да ми покажете (на картата)?
mo·zhe·te lee da mee po·*ka*·zhe·te (na *kar*·ta·ta)

EMERGENCIES

Help!

Помощ! — po·mosht

There's been an accident.

Стана катастрофа. — sta·na ka·tas·tro·fa

I'm lost.

Загубих се. — za·goo·beeh se

Go away!

Махайте се! — ma·hai·te se

It's an emergency.

Случаят е спешен. — sloo·cha·yuht e spe·shen

Could you please help?

Моля ви за помощ. — mo·lyuh vee za po·mosht

Where are the toilets?

Къде са тоалетните? — kuh·de suh to·a·let·nee·te

Call ...!	Повикайте ...!	po·vee·kai·te ...
an ambulance	линейка	lee·ney·ka
a doctor	доктор	dok·tor
the police	полицията	po·lee·tsee·ya·ta!

It's ...	... е.	... e
close	Близо	blee·zo
far away	Далече	da·le·che
straight ahead	Направо	na·pra·vo

Turn ...		
Завийте ...	za·veey·te ...	
at the corner		
на ъгъла	na uh·guh·luh	
at the traffic lights		
при светофара	pree sve·to·fa·ruh	
left		
наляво	na·lya·vo	
right		
надясно	na·dyas·no	

on foot	пеша	pe·sha
north	север	se·ver
south	юг	yoog
east	изток	eez·tok
west	запад	za·pad

beach	плаж	plazh
bridge	мост	most
castle	замък	za·muhk
cathedral	катедрала	ka·te·dra·la
church	църква	tsuhr·kva
city centre	центърът на града	tsen·tuh·ruht na gra·duh
island	остров	os·trov
main square	централен площад	tsen·tra·len plosh·tad

monastery	манастир	ma·nas·teer
museum	музей	moo·zey
old city	старият град	sta·ree·yat grad
palace	дворец/палат	dvo·rets/pa·lat
riverbank	брега на реката	bre·ga na re·ka·ta
ruins	останки	o·stan·kee
square	площад	plosh·tad
tower	кула	ku·la

HEALTH

Where's the nearest ...?

Къде се намира най-близкият/най-близка ...? (m/f)

kuh·de se na·mee·ra nai·bleez·kee·yuht/nai·bleez·ka·ta ...

dentist

зъболекар (m) — zuh·bo·le·kar

doctor

лекар (m) — le·kar

hospital

болница (f) — bol·nee·tsa

pharmacy

аптека (f) — ap·te·ka

I'm sick.

Аз съм болен. (m) — az suhm bo·len

Аз съм болна. (f) — az suhm bol·na

It hurts here.

Боли ме тук. — bo·lee me took

I'm allergic to ...

Аз съм алергичен/алергична към ... (m/f)

az suhm a·ler·gee·chen/a·ler·geech·na kuhm ...

antibiotics

антибиотици — an·tee·bee·o·tee·tsee

bees

пчели — pche·lee

penicillin

пеницилин — pe·nee·tsee·leen

nuts

ядки — yad·kee

peanuts

фъстъци — fuh·stuh·tsee

seafood

морски продукти — mor·skee pro·dook·tee

antiseptic	антисептично	an·tee·sep·teech·no
asthma	астма	ast·ma
cold	простуда	pro·stoo·da
condoms	презерватив	pre·zer·va·teev
contraceptives	контрацептиви	kon·tra·tsep·tee·vee
diabetes	диабет	dee·a·bet
diarrhoea	разстройство	raz·stroys·tvo
fever	температура	tem·pe·ra·too·ra
headache	главоболие	gla·vo·bo·lee·e
nausea	гадене	ga·de·ne
pain	болка	bol·ka

LANGUAGE

painkillers	обезболяващи	o-bez-bol-*ya*-vash-tee
sore throat	възпалено гърло	vuhz-*pa*-le-no *guhr*-lo
sunblock cream	слънцезащитен крем	sluhn-tse-*zash*-tee-ten krem
tampons	тампон	tam-*pon*

LANGUAGE DIFFICULTIES

Do you speak (English)?
Говорите/Говориш ли (английски)? (pol/inf)
go-*vo*-ree-te/go-*vo*-reesh lee (an-*gleey*-skee)

Does anyone speak (English)?
Говори ли някой тук (английски)?
go-*vo*-ree lee *nya*-koy took (an-*gleey*-skee)

What's this called in Bulgarian?
Как се казва това на български?
kak se *kaz*-va to-*va* na *buhl*-gar-skee

I (don't) understand.
(Не) Разбирам.
(ne) raz-*bee*-ram

Could you please write it down?
Моля да напишете това.
mol-yuh da na-*pee*-she-te to-*va*

Can you show me (on the map)?
Можете ли да ми покажете (на картата)?
mo-zhe-te lee da mee po-*ka*-zhe-te (na *kar*-ta-ta)

NUMBERS

0	нула	*noo*-la
1	един (m)	e-*deen*
	една (f)	ed-*na*
	едно (n)	ed-*no*
2	два (m)/две (f&n)	dva/dve
3	три	tree
4	четири	*che*-tee-ree
5	пет	pet
6	шест	shest
7	седем	*se*-dem
8	осем	*o*-sem
9	девет	*de*-vet
10	десет	*de*-set
11	единайсет	e-dee-*nai*-set
12	дванайсет	dva-*nai*-set
13	тринайсет	tree-*nai*-set
14	четиринайсет	che-tee-ree-*nai*-set
15	петнайсет	pet-*nai*-set
16	шестнайсет	shest-*nai*-set
17	седемнайсет	se-dem-*nai*-set
18	осемнайсет	o-sem-*nai*-set
19	деветнайсет	de-vet-*nai*-set
20	двайсет	*dvai*-set
21	двайсет и (един/ една/едно) (m/f/n)	*dvai*-set ee e-*deen*/ ed-*na*/ed-*no*
22	двайсет и (два/ две) (m/f & n)	*dvai*-set ee (dva/ dve)

30	трийсет	*tree*-set
40	четирийсет	che-*tee*-ree-set
50	петдесет	pet-de-*set*
60	шестдесет	shest-de-*set*
70	седемдесет	se-dem-de-*set*
80	осемдесет	o-sem-de-*set*
90	деветдесет	de-vet-de-*set*
100	сто	sto
200	двеста	*dve*-sta
1000	хиляда	heel-*ya*-da
1,000,000	един милион	e-*deen* mee-lee-*yon*

PAPERWORK

name/surname
име/презиме
ee-me/*pre*-zee-me

nationality
националност
na-tsee-o-*nal*-nost

date of birth
дата на раждане
da-ta na *razh*-da-ne

place of birth
място на раждане
myas-to na *razh*-da-ne

sex
пол
pol

passport number
номер на паспорта
no-mer na pas-*por*-tuh

visa
виза
vee-za

driving licence
шофьорска книжка
sho-*fyor*-ska *kneezh*-ka

QUESTION WORDS

How?	Как?	kak
How many/ much?	Колко?	*kol*-ko
What?	Какво?	kak-*vo*
When?	Кога?	ko-*ga*
Where?	Къде?	kuh-*de*
Who?	Кой? (m sing)	koy
	Коя? (f sing)	ko-*ya*
	Кое? (n sing)	ko-*e*
	Кои? (pl)	ko-*ee*
Why?	Защо?	zash-*to*

SHOPPING & SERVICES

Where's a/the ...?
Къде има ...?
kuh-*de* ee-ma ...

ATM
банкомат
ban-ko-*mat*

bank
банка
ban-ka

department store
универсален магазин
oo-nee-ver-*sa*-len ma-ga-*zeen*

... embassy
посолството на ...
po-*solst* vo-to na ...

market
пазар
pa-*zar*

police
полиция   po·lee·tsee·ya
post office
поща   posh·ta
supermarket
супермаркет   soo·per·mar·ket
public toilet
обществена тоалетна   obsh·test·ve·na to·a·let·na
telephone centre
телефонна централа   te·le·fon·na tsen·tra·la
tourist information office
бюро за туристическа   byoo·ro za too·rees·tee·ches·ka
   информация   een·for·ma·tsee·ya

I'd like to buy (an adaptor plug).
Искам да си купя (адаптор).
ees·kam da see koop·yuh (a·dap·tor)
How much is it?
Колко струва?
kol·ko stroo·va
Can you write down the price?
Моля, напишете цената.
mol·yuh na·pee·she·te tse·na·ta
I'm just looking.
Само разгледам.
sa·mo raz·gle·dam
Can I look at it?
Мога ли да го видя?
mo·guh lee da go veed·yuh
Do you have any others?
Имате ли други от този вид?
ee·ma·te lee droo·gee ot to·zee veed
Can you lower the price?
Можете ли да свалите цената?
mo·zhe·te lee da sva·lee·te tse·na·ta
What times is the bank open?
Какво е работното време на банката?
kak·vo e ra·bot·no·to vre·me na ban·ka·ta
Where's the local internet café?
Къде се намира най-близкото Интернет-кафе?
kuh·de se na·mee·ra nai·bleez·ko·to een·ter·net·ka·fe
Please change it to the English-language setting.
Моля да смените настройката на английски език.
mol·yuh da sme·nee·te na·stroy·ka·ta na an·gleey·skee e·zeek

I'd like to ...
Искам да ...   ees·kam da ...
Where can I ...?
Къде мога да ...?   kuh·de mo·guh da ...
   check my email
   проверя своя е-мейл   pro·ver·yuh svo·yuh ee·meyl
   get internet access
   вляза в Интернета   vlya·zuh v een·ter·ne·tuh
change a travellers cheque
   осребря пътнически   o·sreb·ruh puht·nee·ches·kee
      чек   chek

change money
обменя пари   ob·men·yuh pa·ree

Do you accept ...?
Приемате ли ...?   pree·e·ma·te lee ...
   credit cards
   кредитни карти   kre·deet·nee kar·tee
   debit cards
   дебитни карти   de·beet·nee kar·tee
   travellers cheques
   пътнически чекове   puht·nee·ches·kee che·ko·ve

more   повече/още   po·ve·che/osh·te
less   по-малко   po·mal·ko
smaller   по-малък   po·ma·luhk
bigger   по-голям   po·go·lyam

TIME & DATES
What time is it?
   Колко е часът?   kol·ko e cha·suht
It's one o'clock.
   Часът е един.   cha·suht e e·deen
It's (two) o'clock.
   (Два) часа е.   (dva) cha·suh e
Quarter to (three).
   (Три) без петнайсет.   (tree) bez pet·nai·set
Twenty to (three).
   (Три) без двайсет.   (tree) bez dvai·set
At what time ...?
   В колко часа ...?   v kol·ko cha·suh ...

am   сутрин   soo·treen
pm   следобед   sle·do·bed
today   днес   dnes
tonight довечера   do·ve·che·ra

this ...   днес ...   dnes ...
tomorrow ...   утре ...   oo·tre ...
   morning   сутринта   soo·treen·ta
   afternoon   следобед   sle·do·bed
   evening   вечер   ve·cher

Monday   понеделник   po·ne·del·neek
Tuesday   вторник   vtor·neek
Wednesday сряда   srya·da
Thursday   четвъртък   chet·vuhr·tuhk
Friday   петък   pe·tuhk
Saturday   събота   suh·bo·ta
Sunday   неделя   ne·del·ya

January   януари   ya·noo·a·ree
February   февруари   fev·roo·a·ree
March   март   mart
April   април   ap·reel
May   май   mai

June	юни	*yoo*·nee
July	юли	*yoo*·lee
August	август	*av*·goost
September	септември	sep·*tem*·vree
October	октомври	ok·*tom*·vree
November	ноември	no·*em*·vree
December	декември	de·*kem*·vree

TRANSPORT
Public Transport
bus terminal
депо — de·*po*
(central) bus station
(централната) — (tsen·*tral*·na·ta)
автогара — av·to·*ga*·ra
left-luggage office
има гардероб — ee·ma gar·de·*rob*
luggage locker
има гардероб — ee·ma gar·de·*rob*
timetable
разписание — raz·pee·*sa*·nee·e

boat	кораб m	*ko*·rab
bus	автобус	av·to·*boos*
ferry	ферибот (m)	*fe*·ree·bot
minibus	маршрутка	marsh·*root*·ka
trolleybus	тролейбус	tro·*ley*·boos

How much is it?
Колко струва?
kol·ko *stroo*·va
How long does the trip take?
Колко трае пътуването?
kol·ko *tra*·ye puh·*too*·va·ne·to
What's the next station?
Коя е следващата спирка?
ko·*ya* e *sled*·vash·ta·ta *speer*·ka
Do I need to change?
Трябва ли да се прехвърля на друг влак?
tryab·va lee da se pre·*hvuhr*·lyuh na droog vlak
Which bus goes to (Pomorie)?
Кой е автобус за (Поморие)?
koy av·to·*boos* za (po·*mo*·ree·ye)
What time does it leave?
В колко часа тръгва?
v *kol*·ko cha·*suh* truhg·va
What time does it get to (Kyustendil)?
В колко часа пристига в (Кюстендил)?
v *kol*·ko cha·*suh* prees·*tee*·ga v (kyoo·sten·*deel*)
Please tell me when we get to (Plovdiv).
Кажете ми моля когато пристигнем в (Пловдив).
ka·*zhe*·te mee *mol*·yuh ko·*ga*·to prees·*teeg*·nem v (*plov*·deev)
Please stop here.
Моля, спрете тук.
mol·yuh *spre*·te took

When's the ...	Кога тръгва ...	ko·*ga* truhg·va ...
bus?	автобус?	av·to·*boos*
first	първият	*puhr*·vee·yuht
last	последният	po·*sled*·nee·yuht
next	следващият	*sled*·vash·tee·yuht

A ... ticket	Един ... билет	e·*deen* ... bee·*let*
(to Rila).	(за Рила).	(za *ree*·la)
1st-class	първокласен	*purh*·vo·kla·sen
2nd-class	второкласен	*vto*·ro·kla·sen
one-way	еднопосочен	ed·no·po·*so*·chen
return	двупосочен	dvoo·po·*so*·chen
student	студентски	stoo·*dent*·skee

Is this taxi available?
Такситo свободно ли е?
tak·*see*·to svo·*bod*·no lee e
Please take me to (this address).
Моля да ме закарате до (този адрес).
mol·yuh da me za·*ka*·ra·te do (*to*·zee ad·*res*)
Please put the meter on.
Моля да включите таксиметъра.
mol·yuh da *vklyoo*·chee·te tak·see·*me*·tuh·ra
How much is it to (the airport)?
Колко струва до (летището)?
kol·ko *stroo*·va do (le·*teesh*·te·to)

Private Transport
Except for **Стоп** (Stop), you'll hardly see any written road signs in Bulgaria – pictorial signs are used instead.

I'd like to hire a car/motorbike/bicycle.
Искам да взема под наем кола/мотопед/колело.
ees·kam da *vze*·muh pod *na*·em ko·*la*/mo·to·*ped*/ko·le·*lo*

How much for ... hire?		
Колко струва ...?	*kol*·ko *stroo*·va ...
daily		
на ден	na den
weekly		
на седмица	na *sed*·mee·tsa

Is this the road to (Blagoevgrad)?
Това ли е пътят за (Благоевград)?
to·*va* lee e *puht*·yuht za (bla·*go*·ev·grad)
Where's a petrol station?
Къде има бензиностанция?
kuh·*de* ee·ma ben·zee·no·*stan*·tsee·ya
Please fill it up.
Моля напълнете го до края.
mol·yuh na·puhl·*ne*·te go do *kra*·yuh
I'd like (25) litres.
Искам (двайсет и пет) литра.
ees·kam (*dvai*·set ee pet) *leet*·ra

Can I park here?
Мога ли да паркирам тук?
mo·guh lee da par·*kee*·ram took

How long can I park here?
Колко време мога да паркирам тук?
kol·ko *vre*·me *mo*·guh da par·*kee*·ram took

Do I have to pay?
Плаща ли се?
plash·ta lee se

diesel	дизел	*dee*·zel
leaded	оловен бензин	o·*lo*·ven ben·*zeen*
LPG	газ	gaz
regular	обикновен	o·beek·no·*ven*
	бензин	ben·*zeen*
unleaded	безоловен	bez·o·*lo*·ven

I need a mechanic.
Трябва ми монтьор.
tryab·va mee mon·*tyor*

I've had an accident.
Имах злополука.
ee·mah zlo·po·*loo*·ka

The car/motorbike has broken down (at ...).
Колата/Мотопедът претърпя авария (в ...).
ko·*la*·ta/mo·to·*ped*·uht pre·tuhr·*pya* a·*va*·ree·ya (v ...)

I've run out of petrol.
Нямам бензин.
nya·mam ben·*zeen*

I have a flat tyre.
Пукна ми се гумата.
pook·na mee se *goo*·ma·ta

Also available from Lonely Planet:
Bulgarian Phrasebook

TRAVEL WITH CHILDREN

Do you sell ...?
Продавате ли ...?
pro·*da*·va·te lee ...

  disposable nappies
  пелени за еднократна употреба
  pe·le·*nee* za ed·no·*krat*·ka *oo*·po·tre·ba

  painkillers for babies
  болкоуспокоутелни лекарства за бебета
  bol·ko·oos·po·ko·*ee*·tel·nee le·*kars*·tva za *be*·be·ta

  infant milk formula
  рецепта за приготвяне на храна за бебета
  re·*tsep*·ta za pri·*got*·vya·ne na hra·*na* za *be*·be·ta

Is there a ...?
Има ли ...?
ee·ma lee ...

I need a/an ...
Трябва ми ...
tryab·va mee ...

  baby seat (for the car)
  детска седалка (за кола)
  det·ska se·*dal*·ka (za ko·*la*)

  children's menu
  детско меню
  det·sko men·*yoo*

  (English-speaking) babysitter
  бавачка (говореща английски)
  ba·*vach*·ka (go·vo·resh·ta an·*gleey*·skee)

  booster seat
  детска седалка
  det·ska se·*dal*·ka

  highchair
  високо детско столче за хранене
  vee·*so*·ko *det*·sko *stol*·che za *hra*·ne·ne

  potty
  гърне
  guhr·*ne*

  pushchair/stroller
  детска количка
  det·ska ko·*leech*·ka

Are there any good places to take children around here?
Има ли в района добри места за разходка с деца?
ee·ma lee v ra·*yo*·nuh do·*bree* mes·*ta* za raz·*hod*·ka s de·*tsa*

Are children allowed?
Разрешено ли е за деца?
raz·re·*she*·no lee e za de·*tsa*

Where can I change a nappy?
Къде мога да сменя бебешките пелени?
kuh·*de* *mo*·guh da smen·*yuh* be·besh·kee·te pe·le·*nee*

LANGUAGE

Glossary

For food and drink terms see the Food & Drink chapter (p55). For general terms see the Language chapter (p309).

aleya – alley, lane
apteka – chemist or pharmacy
avtogara – bus station

Balkantourist – the former government-run tourism organisation
balneology – therapeutic bath of mineral waters, often enjoyed in a balneocentre
banya – bath; often signifies mineral baths in general
BDZh – abbreviation for the Bulgarian State Railways
besplaten – free (of charge)
bul – abbreviation of bulevard; main street or boulevard

chalga – upbeat Bulgarian folk-pop music, based on traditional melodies but played on modern instruments
charshiya – a street or area of traditional craft workshops
cherga – a traditional, colourful, hand-woven rug

dvorets – palace
dzhumaya – mosque

etazh – numbered floor (storey) of a building
ezero (m), **ezera** (f) – lake

fonokarta – phonecard for use in public telephones

gara – train station
gradina – garden; often referring to a public park

haidouks – Bulgarian rebels who fought against the Turks in the 18th and 19th centuries
hali – indoor market
hizha – hut; often refers to a mountain hut
house-museum – a home built in a style typical of the Bulgarian National Revival period and turned into a museum

iconostasis (s), **iconostases** (pl) – a screen, partition or door in an Eastern Orthodox church that separates the sanctuary from the nave; often richly decorated
iskhot – 'exit' (displayed on doors in public buildings)
iztok – east

kâshta – house
khan – king within a Bulgar tribe, or the subsequent Bulgarian empires; also known as a *tsar*

kilim – hand-woven woolen carpet, normally with colourful geometric patterns
kino – cinema
knyaz – prince
konak – police station built during Turkish rule
krepost – fortress
kurdjali – Turkish gangs that raided several Bulgarian towns during the 18th and 19th centuries
kvartiri – quarters/accommodation; often meaning private rooms for rent

lev (s), **leva** (pl) – monetary unit of Bulgaria; shortened to lv; equals 100 *stotinki*

malko – minor, small
manastir – monastery
mehana – tavern
more – sea
most – bridge

obshtina – municipality; also another word for town hall

pasha – high official during Turkish rule
peron – railway platform
peshtera – cave
pl – abbreviation of ploshtad: town or city square
planina – mountain
plazh – beach
Pomaks – literally 'helpers'; Slavs who converted to Islam during the era of Turkish rule

rakia – Bulgarian brandy, normally made from grapes, occasionally from plums or other fruit
reka – river

sever – north
spirka – bus stop/shelter
stotinka (s), **stotinki** (pl) – one-hundredth of a *lev*
sveti (m), **sveta** (f) – saint
svobodni stai – 'free rooms': advertised rooms for rent in private homes

toaletna – toilet
Troyanska kapka – 'Troyan droplet'; traditional glazed pottery with a distinctive 'drip' design
tsar – see *khan*
tsârkva – church
turisticheski dom – 'tourist home'; a fairly comfortable hotel with double rooms

GLOSSARY

GLOSSARY

turisticheska spalnya – 'tourist bedroom'; a more basic, dorm-style hostel

ul – abbreviation of ulitsa: street

varosha – centre of an old town
veliko – great, large

vhot – 'entrance' (displayed on doors in public buildings)

vilayet – a province of the Ottoman Turkish empire in the 19th century
vlak – train
vrâh – mountain peak

yug – south

zakuska – breakfast
zapad – west

The Authors

RICHARD WATKINS   Coordinating Author, Sofia, Black Sea Coast

Richard's first job after university was teaching conversational English to college students in Sofia. That was back in the summer of 1995, when Bulgaria seemed a much different, and much cheaper, place. Richard soon developed a real affection for this varied, rugged little country and its welcoming and unpretentious people. He has returned to Bulgaria several times since, discovering something new on each visit, and adding to his collection of Bulgarian movie posters and CDs. Richard has written about Bulgaria for other publications, including the previous edition of Lonely Planet's *Bulgaria*.

CHRISTOPHER DELISO   Central Bulgaria, Northern Bulgaria, Southern Bulgaria, Bulgarian Wine

It was while studying Byzantine Studies in Oxford a decade ago that the irresistible lure of eastern adventure drew Chris to the Balkans, where he's been more or less ever since, living in Greece, Turkey and Macedonia and writing about everything along the way. For him, experiencing the region's fascinatingly varied cultures and partaking in hearty bouts of eating and drinking are what make it all worthwhile. Bulgaria's tendency to manifest itself in unexpected acts of dynamism especially appeals to Chris; indeed, he's never been bored in this beautiful and spirited country.

LONELY PLANET AUTHORS

Why is our travel information the best in the world? It's simple: our authors are independent, dedicated travellers. They don't research using just the internet or phone, and they don't take freebies in exchange for positive coverage. They travel widely, to all the popular spots and off the beaten track. They personally visit thousands of hotels, restaurants, cafés, bars, galleries, palaces, museums and more – and they take pride in getting all the details right, and telling it how it is. Think you can do it? Find out how at lonelyplanet.com.

Behind the Scenes

THIS BOOK

This 3rd edition of *Bulgaria* was researched and written by Richard Watkins (coordinating author) and Christopher Deliso. The 1st edition was written by Paul Greenway, and the 2nd edition by Richard Watkins and Tom Masters. The Health chapter was adapted from material written by Dr Caroline Evans. This guidebook was commissioned in Lonely Planet's London office, and produced by the following:

Commissioning Editors Fayette Fox, Fiona Buchan
Coordinating Editor Ali Lemer
Coordinating Cartographer Owen Eszeki
Coordinating Layout Designer Katherine Marsh
Managing Editor Melanie Dankel
Managing Cartographers Mark Griffiths, Alison Lyall
Managing Layout Designers Adam McCrow, Celia Wood
Assisting Editors Michelle Bennett, Carly Hall, Helen Yeates
Assisting Cartographers Ross Butler, Mick Garrett, Indra Kilfoyle
Assisting Layout Designers Cara Smith
Cover Designer Pepi Bluck
Project Manager Rachel Imeson
Language Content Coordinator Quentin Frayne

Thanks to Imogen Bannister, Vicky Bull, David Burnett, Bruce Evans, Will Gourlay, Martin Heng, Laura Jane, Lisa Knights, Rebecca Lalor, Branislava Vladisavljevic

THANKS
RICHARD WATKINS

As always, a very big 'thank you' goes to Georgi Dimitrov and Lubomir Popiordanov at the Odysseia-In agency in Sofia for their welcome and for sharing their time and extensive knowledge of all things Bulgarian, and to the indefatigable Zig Zag girls downstairs, Milena Milanova, Rositsa Lozanova, Nevyana Teodosieva and Svidna Mihaylova, for all their help throughout my research. I'd also like to thank Margarita Borisova in Krapets for her advice and assistance, the staff at the tourist information centres in Burgas, Tsarevo and Sofia, the custodian at Kyustendil's History Museum who opened up especially for me, and the two chatty old ladies in Burgas who helped me practice my French over a pizza.

CHRISTOPHER DELISO

In researching this book I benefited tremendously from the experience, advice and, in some cases, hospitality of numerous kind people. They include: Ljubomir at Odysseia-In Travel (Sofia); Valery and Bogdan (Vidin); Mario the fireman (Vratsa); Angel (Belogradchik); Steve, Stojan and Boris Botsev (Ruse); Jerry and Mike Black (Srebârna); Toshe Hristov and the tourist information office staff (Veliko Târnovo); Dimitar, Petar, Neli,

---

THE LONELY PLANET STORY

Fresh from an epic journey across Europe, Asia and Australia in 1972, Tony and Maureen Wheeler sat at their kitchen table stapling together notes. The first Lonely Planet guidebook, *Across Asia on the Cheap*, was born.

Travellers snapped up the guides. Inspired by their success, the Wheelers began publishing books to Southeast Asia, India and beyond. Demand was prodigious, and the Wheelers expanded the business rapidly to keep up. Over the years, Lonely Planet extended its coverage to every country and into the virtual world via lonelyplanet.com and the Thorn Tree message board.

As Lonely Planet became a globally loved brand, Tony and Maureen received several offers for the company. But it wasn't until 2007 that they found a partner whom they trusted to remain true to the company's principles of travelling widely, treading lightly and giving sustainably. In October of that year, BBC Worldwide acquired a 75% share in the company, pledging to uphold Lonely Planet's commitment to independent travel, trustworthy advice and editorial independence.

Today, Lonely Planet has offices in Melbourne, London and Oakland, with over 500 staff members and 300 authors. Tony and Maureen are still actively involved with Lonely Planet. They're travelling more often than ever, and they're devoting their spare time to charitable projects. And the company is still driven by the philosophy of *Across Asia on the Cheap*: 'All you've got to do is decide to go and the hardest part is over. So go!'

SEND US YOUR FEEDBACK

We love to hear from travellers – your comments keep us on our toes and help make our books better. Our well-travelled team reads every word on what you loved or loathed about this book. Although we cannot reply individually to postal submissions, we always guarantee that your feedback goes straight to the appropriate authors, in time for the next edition. Each person who sends us information is thanked in the next edition – and the most useful submissions are rewarded with a free book.

To send us your updates – and find out about Lonely Planet events, newsletters and travel news – visit our award-winning website: **www.lonelyplanet.com/contact**.

Note: we may edit, reproduce and incorporate your comments in Lonely Planet products such as guidebooks, websites and digital products, so let us know if you don't want your comments reproduced or your name acknowledged. For a copy of our privacy policy visit www.lonelyplanet.com/privacy.

BEHIND THE SCENES

Natso, Franz and the gracious Dimitar and Rosalia Kirov (Plovdiv); Velika Kuchmova (Sliven); Hristina Dimitrova (Kotel); Irina Ilieva (Devin); Matilda at the tourist information centre (Smolyan); the tourist information centre staff (Koprivshtitsa); Elena, Stojko Stojkov (Blagoevgrad); Yane Kamenarov and Elena Georgieva-Kamenarova (Melnik); and Tanya Stancheva (Bansko).

OUR READERS

Many thanks to the travellers who used the last edition and wrote to us with helpful hints, useful advice and interesting anecdotes:

A Rony Abi-Aad, Mick Adams, Stephen Akehurst, Allard Alfrink, Blanca Alonso Alvarez, Trish Aspden **B** Skye Baloo, William Beach, Claire Bernier, Dagmar Biegon, Mogens Brock **C** Sara Caplain, Marta Catarino, Eun Ju Choi, Rebekah Cocoran, Shirly Cohen, Rebekah Corcoran, Eileen Cramer, Ruth Crocket **D** Margreet De Vries, Pierre Duffie-Parin **F** Bec Filby, Eve Fortescue-Beck **G** John Gallagher, Robert Gatterson, David Glass, Lilani Goonesena, Moshe Grimberg, Michael Grimes, Michael Groth, Otto Gutmensch **H** David Haines, Sonja Hanchar, Steve Harding, Chris Harris, Renee Heynen, Roy Hill, Gijs Hollestelle, Kate van Horck **I** Francesco Inglima **J** John Jackson, Karl Jørgensen **K** Rachel Kleinberg, Sonja Krause, Henrike Köhler **L** Ellie Lamb, Nurit Lev, Karen Lilling, Tikva Looijen, Pepe Lopez, Dennis Lozano **M** Michael Maerz, Diane Malone, Paolo Mari, Ian McCallum, Annemarie Mille, Peter Miller, Irina Mincheva, Bas Moekotte, Filipe Moetzler **N** Greg Nalencz, Rob Neff, Hannah Norris **P** Patrick Proche **R** Nicholas Radtke, Stefan Ratschan, Therisa Rogers **S** Nishma Shah, Momchil Shumackov, Sarah Slater, Wendy Smith, Pieter Soer, Detlef Spoetter, Arne Steen, Glenn Stewart, Ivan Stoyanov, Matt Sumpter, Andi Szavicsko **T** Mirjam Theelen, Jaume Tort, Robert Trachy, John Tredensco, Stoyan Tsolov **V** Flos Vingerhoets, **Y** Yunuz M Yunuz

ACKNOWLEDGMENTS

Many thanks to the following for the use of their content:

Globe on title page ©Mountain High Maps 1993 Digital Wisdom, Inc.

Index

INDEX

000 Map pages
000 Photograph pages